FROM THE OTHER SIDE OF THE CENTURY:
A NEW AMERICAN POETRY 1960 – 1990

From the Other Side of the Century:
A New American Poetry
1960 – 1990

□

Edited and with an Introduction by

Douglas Messerli

SUN &
MOON
CLASSICS
47

LOS ANGELES
SUN & MOON PRESS
1994

Sun & Moon Press
A Program of The Contemporary Arts Educational Project, Inc.
a nonprofit corporation
6026 Wilshire Boulevard, Los Angeles, California 90036

This edition first published in paperback in 1994 by Sun & Moon Press
10 9 8 7 6 5 4 3 2 1
FIRST EDITION
© Douglas Messerli, 1994
All rights reserved

This book was made possible, in part, through an operational grant from the
Andrew W. Mellon Foundation, and through contributions to
The Contemporary Arts Educational Project, Inc.,
a nonprofit corporation

Cover: Philip Guston, *Source*
Reprinted by permission of the Edward R. Broida Trust, New York
Design: Katie Messborn
Typography: Guy Bennett

LIBRARY OF CONGRESS CATALOGING IN PUBLICATION DATA
Messerli, Douglas, (1947)
ed. From the Other Side of the Century:
A New American Poetry 1960-1990
p. cm — (Sun & Moon Classics: 47)
ISBN: 1-55713-131-7
I. Title. II. Series.
811'.54—dc20

Printed in the United States of America on acid-free paper.

Forth" and "Saturday Night" are reprinted from *Sound As Thought: Poems 1982 – 1984* (Los Angeles: Sun & Moon Press, 1990), pp. 18, 133, ©1990 by Clark Coolidge. Reprinted by permission of Sun & Moon Press. "Glance in White Space" and "What Is Thought But Won't Hold Still" is reprinted from *Odes of Roba* (Great Barrington, Massachusetts, 1991), pp. 87, 88 – 89, ©1991 by Clark Coolidge. Reprinted by permission of The Figures.

LYN HEJINIAN. "A Mask of Anger" is reprinted from *A Mask of Motion* (Providence, RI: Burning Deck, 1977), unpaginated, ©1977 by Lyn Hejinian. Reprinted by permission of Lyn Hejinian. Selection from *My Life* (Los Angeles: Sun & Moon Press, 1987), pp. 47 – 49, ©1980, 1987 by Lyn Hejinian. Reprinted by permission of Sun & Moon Press. Selections from *The Guard* and *The Person* are reprinted from *The Cold of Poetry* (Los Angeles: Sun & Moon Press, 1994), pp. 11 – 14, 144 – 145, 159 – 160, 164 – 165, 176 – 177, ©1978, 1984, 1994 by Lyn Hejinian. Reprinted by permission of Sun & Moon Press. Selections reprinted from *The Cell* (Los Angeles: Sun & Moon Press, 1992), pp. 33, 57 – 58, 65, 140, ©1992 by Lyn Hejinian. Reprinted by permission of Sun & Moon Press. Selections reprinted from *Oxota: A Short Russian Novel* (Great Barrington, Massachusetts: The Figures, 1991), pp. 12, 19, 83, 86, 112 – 113, 159, 168, 170, 269, ©1991 by Lyn Hejinian. Reprinted by permission of The Figures.

ROBERT GRENIER. Selection reprinted from *Oakland* (Berkeley: Tuumba Press, 1980), unpaginated, ©1980 by Robert Grenier. Reprinted by permission of Tuumba Press. Selection reprinted from *Phantom Anthems* (Oakland: O Books, 1986), unpaginated. Reprinted by permission of O Books.

TED GREENWALD. "And, Hinges," "Privets Come into Season at High Tide," and "I Hear a Step" are reprinted from *Common Sense* (Kensington, California: L Publications, 1978), pp. 26 – 27, 33 – 34, 49 – 50, ©1978 by Ted Greenwald. Reprinted by permission of Ted Greenwald. "XIV" is reprinted from *Licorice Chronicles* (New York: The Kulchur Foundation, 1979), pp. 66 – 74, ©1979 by Ted Greenwald. Reprinted by permission of Ted Greenwald. Selection reprinted from *Word of Mouth* (Los Angeles: Sun & Moon Press, 1986), pp. 112 – 115, ©1986 by Ted Greenwald. Reprinted by permission of Sun & Moon Press.

NICK PIOMBINO. "My Lady Carries Stones," "[The simple poetry of sleep]," "The Pyramids," "[Any m meant they came to a destination]," and "Time Travel" are reprinted from *Poems* (Los Angeles: Sun & Moon Press, 1988), pp. 9, 10 – 12, 24, 45, 55 – 59, ©1988 by Nick Piombino. Reprinted by permission of Sun & Moon Press. "The Frozen Witness" is reprinted from an unpublished manuscript, ©1994 by Nick Piombino. Reprinted by permission of Nick Piombino.

RAY DI PALMA. "Sheaf Mark," is reprinted from *Roof* magazine, revised by the author, ©1994 by Ray DiPalma. Reprinted by permission of Ray DiPalma. "Fragment," "Poem [In danger of which]," Empire Smoke, Forgeries, Salient & The Ritz," "The Bed," "Hadrian's Lane," "The Table" and "When Torrid Rhymes Forehead" are reprinted from *Numbers and Tempers: Selected Early Poems 1966 – 1986* (Los Angeles: Sun & Moon Press, 1993), pp. 21, 23, 38 – 40, 62 – 67, 77 – 78, 81 – 82, 121 – 122, ©1993 by Ray DiPalma. Reprinted by permission of Sun & Moon Press. "Annotations Tropes and Lacunae of the Itoku Master" is reprinted from *Mock Fandango* (Los Angeles: Sun & Moon Press [20 Pages], 1991), unpaginated, ©1991 by Ray DiPalma. Reprinted by permission of Sun & Moon Press. "The Prerogative of Lieder" is reprinted from *Grand Street* magazine; "Motion of the Cypher" from *Motel* magazine, and "Poem for Claude" from *To* magazine. These poems are reprinted by permission of Ray DiPalma. "The Wrong Side of the Door" and "We Forego Mimicry" are reprinted from unpublished manuscripts, ©1994 by Ray DiPalma. Reprinted by permission of Ray DiPalma.

MICHAEL PALMER. "Dearest Reader," "Voice and Address," and "The Painted Cup" are reprinted from *First Figure* (Berkeley: North Point Press, 1984), pp. 3, 7 – 8, 40, ©1984 by Michael Palmer. Reprinted by permission of Michael Palmer. "Fifth Prose," "[mei-mei, here is the table]," "[You say / A miracle from Heaven]," "[Desire was a quotation from someone]," and "Sun" are reprinted from *Sun* (Berkeley: North Point Press, 1988), pp. 5 – 6, 11, 23, 37, 83 – 86, ©1988 by Michael Palmer. Reprinted by permission of Michael Palmer. "Eighth Sky," "Erolog (a reply)," and "Letter 5" from "Letters to Zanzotto" are reprinted from unpublished manuscripts, ©1994 by Michael Palmer. Reprinted by permission of Michael Palmer.

MICHAEL DAVIDSON. "The Feeling Type and His Friends" and "The Sensation Type and His Friends" are reprinted from *The Mutibilities & The Foul Papers* (Berkeley: Sand Dollar Books, 1976), pp. 61, 63, ©1976 by Michael Davidson. Reprinted by permission of Michael Davidson. "[Tonight is closer than we thought,]," and "[Concern for her scar made him think something like this:]" are reprinted from *The Prose of Fact* (Berkeley: The Figures, 1981), pp. 39, 65, ©1981 by Michael Davidson. Reprinted by permission of The Figures and Michael Davidson. "The Dream Dream," "The Landing of Rochambeau," and "Framing" are reprinted from *The Landing of Rochambeau* (Providence: Burning Deck, 1985), pp. 13 – 14, 24 – 27, 72 – 74, ©1985 by Michael Davidson. Reprinted by permission of Burning Deck. "Troth" and "Century of Hands" are reprinted from *Post Hoc* (Bolinas, California: Avenue B, 1990), pp. 50 – 51, 52 – 53, ©1990 by Michael Davidson. Reprinted by permission of Avenue B.

BERNADETTE MAYER. "The Aeschyleans," "The Port," "House Cap," "Boats," and "We've Solved the Problem" are reprinted from *Poetry* (New York: The Kulchur Foundation, 1976), pp. 25 – 26, 30, 31, 35 – 36, 58, ©1976 by Bernadette Mayer. Reprinted by permission of Bernadette Mayer. "The End of Human Reign on Bashan Hill," is reprinted from *The Golden Book of Words* (Lenox, Massachusetts: Angel Hair Books, 1978), unpaginated, ©1978 by Bernadette Mayer. Reprinted by permission of Bernadette Mayer. "Generic Elbows" is reprinted from *United Artists* magazine. Reprinted by permission of Bernadette Mayer. "The Garden," "Sonnet: Kamikaze," and "The Earthworkers' God Is Healed" are reprinted from *Mutual Aid* (New York: Mademoiselle de la Mole Press, 1985), ©1985 by Bernadette Mayer. Reprinted by permission of Bernadette Mayer.

JAMES SHERRY. "She'll Be Comin' Round" is reprinted from *Part Songs* (New York: Roof Books, 1978), unpaginated, ©1978 by James Sherry. Reprinted by permission of James Sherry. "Lepidoptery" is reprinted from *Roof* magazine, ©1978 by the Segue Foundation. Reprinted by permission of James Sherry. Selection reprinted from *In Case* (College Park, Maryland: Sun & Moon Press, 1981), pp. 5 – 10, ©1981 by James Sherry. Reprinted by permission of Sun & Moon Press. "Pay Cash Only," is reprinted from *The World I Like White Paint Considered* (Windsor, Vermont: Awede, 1986), unpaginated, ©1986 by James Sherry. Reprinted by permission of James Sherry. "Radiant," "Free Radicals," and "Hazardous Waste" are reprinted from *Our Nuclear Heritage* (Los Angeles: Sun & Moon Press, 1991), pp. 18 – 19, 20 – 23, 102 – 104, ©1991 by James Sherry. Reprinted by permission of Sun & Moon Press.

RON SILLIMAN. Selection reprinted from *Tjanting* (Great Barrington, Massachusetts: The Figures, 1981), pp. 11 – 20, ©1981 by Ron Silliman. Reprinted by permission of The Figures and Ron Silliman. Selection from "Hidden" is reprinted from *Demo to Ink* (Tucson: Chax Press, 1992), pp.123 – 131, ©1983, 1986, 1986, 1988, 1992 by Ron Silliman. Reprinted by permission of Chax Press and Ron Silliman.

RAE ARMANTROUT. "Generation" and "Winter" are reprinted from *Extremities* (Berkeley: The Figures, 1978), pp. 15, 28, ©1978 by Rae Armantrout. Reprinted by permission of The Figures. "Necromance," "The Garden," "Sense," "Getting Warm," and "Disown" are reprinted from *Necromance* (Los Angeles: Sun & Moon Press, 1991), pp. 7 – 8, 11, 24 – 25, 43, 47 – 49, ©1991 by Rae Armantrout.

1973, 1974, 1975, 1976, 1977, 1978 by Jerome Rothenberg. Reprinted by permission of New Directions. "The Structural Study of Myth," At The Castle," "Numerology," and "Aleph Poem" are reprinted from *Vienna Blood & Other Poems* (New York: New Directions, 1980), pp. 2, 3 – 4, 59, 60 – 61, ©1974, 1975, 1976, 1977, 1978, 1979, 1980 by Jerome Rothenberg. Reprinted by permission of New Directions. "That Dada Strain" is reprinted from *That Dada Strain* (New York: New Directions: 1983), p. 3, ©1979, 1980, 1981, 1982, 1983 by Jerome Rothenberg. Reprinted by permission of New Directions. "Dos Geshray (The Scream)" is reprinted from *Khurbn & Other Poems* (New York: New Directions, 1989), pp. 11 – 12, ©1983, 1984, 1985, 1986, 1987, 1988, 1989 by Jerome Rothenberg. Reprinted by permission of New Directions.

DAVID ANTIN. "real estate" is reprinted from *tuning* (New York: New Directions, 1984), pp. 53 – 79, ©1977, 1979, 1980, 1981, 1984 by David Antin. Reprinted by permission of New Directions.

AMIRI BARAKA. "A Contract" and "Wise 3" are reprinted from *The LeRoi Jones/Amiri Baraka Reader* (New York: Thunder Mouth's Press, 1991), pp. 51 – 52, 483, ©1960, 1961, 1963, 1964, 1965, 1966, 1967, 1968, 1969, 1970, 1971, 1975, 1979, 1980, 1984, 1985, 1987, 1989 by Amiri Baraka. Reprinted by permission of Amiri Baraka. "The Pause of Joe" is reprinted from *Sulfur* magazine, ©1988. Reprinted by permission of Amiri Baraka. "Alba" is reprinted from *Ribot* magazine, ©1993. Reprinted by permission of Amiri Baraka.

JOAN RETALLACK. "The Secret Life of Gilbert Bond," "Biographia Literaria," and "Woman Dragged by Welsh Corgis" is reprinted from *Circumstantial Evidence* (Washington, D.C.: S.O.S., 1985), pp. 43, 44, 46, ©1985 by Joan Retallack. Reprinted by permission of Joan Retallack. "Western Civ, 4 & 5" and "Not a Cage" are reprinted from *Aerial* magazine; "Japanese Presentation I & II" is reprinted from *O-blek*; and "Here's Looking at Your Francis Bacon" is reprinted from *6ix* magazine. These poems ©1994 by Joan Retallack. Reprinted by permission of Joan Retallack.

JOHN TAGGART. "Body and Soul: Poem for Two Readers," "Never Too Late," "Pen Vine and Scroll," and "Monk" are reprinted from *Loop* (Los Angeles: Sun & Moon Press, 1991), pp. 22 – 29, 103 – 106, 124, 178 – 180, ©1991 by John Taggart. Reprinted by permission of Sun & Moon Press. "Sainte-Chapelle" is reprinted from *Sulfur* magazine, ©1992, 1994 by John Taggart. Reprinted by permission of John Taggart.

NICOLE BROSSARD. "The Ordinary" from *Picture Theory* is reprinted from *Picture Theory*, translated from the French by Barbara Godard (Montreal: Guernica, 1991), pp. 13-37, ©1982, 1989 by Éditions de l'Hexagone and Nicole Brossard; translation ©1991 by Barbara Godard. Reprinted by permission of Guernica Editions and Nicole Brossard.

MAC WELLMAN. "Having Led a Charmed Life, He Had To Be Hanged Twice" is reprinted from *Satires* (St. Paul, Minnesota: New Rivers Press, 1985), pp 93 – 98, ©1985 by Mac Wellman. Reprinted by permission of New Rivers Press. "Mad Wolf in Lunar Web, Mad Brow on the Beach" is reprinted from *A Shelf in Woop's Clothing* (Los Angeles: Sun & Moon Press, 1990), pp. 31 – 35, ©1990 by Mac Wellman. Reprinted by permission of Sun & Moon Press. The selections from "Hollowness" and from "Terminal Hip" are reprinted from manuscript, ©1994 by Mac Welllman. These selections are reprinted by permission of Mac Wellman.

DOUGLAS MESSERLI. "This That & Then," "Actually Swallowed," "Angry with China," and "Harrowing" are reprinted from *Some Distance* (New York: Segue Books, 1982), pp. 18, 26, 27, 44, ©1982 by Douglas Messerli. Reprinted by permission of Douglas Messerli. "An Essay on Concrete" and "Going to Sea" are reprinted from *River to Rivet: A Manifesto* (Washington, D.C.: Sun & Moon Press, 1984), pp. 14, 19 – 20, ©1984 by Douglas Messerli. Reprinted by permission of Sun & Moon Press. "From Hear to Air," "Scared Cows," and "The Annunciation" are reprinted from *Maxims from My Mother's Milk/Hymns to Him: A Dialogue* (Los Angeles: Sun & Moon Press, 1988), pp. 19, 23 – 24, 46 – 47, ©1988 by Douglas Messerli. Reprinted by permission of Sun & Moon Press. The selection from *Along Without* is reprinted from *Along Without: A Fiction in Film for Poetry* (Los Angeles: Littoral Books, 1993), pp. 43 – 46, ©1993 by Douglas Messerli. Reprinted by permission of Littoral Books. The selection from *The Walls Come True* is reprinted from *The Walls Come True: An Opera for Spoken Voices* (Los Angeles: Littoral Books, 1994), ©1994 by Douglas Messerli. Reprinted by permission of Littoral Books. "Closure" is reprinted from manuscript, ©1994 by Douglas Messerli. Reprinted by permission of Douglas Messerli.

PETER INMAN. "Colloam" is reprinted from *Roof* magazine, ©1994 by Peter Inman. Reprinted by permission of Peter Inman. The selection from "Dust Bowl" is reprinted from *Think of One* (Elmwood, Connecticut: Potes & Poets Press, 1986), pp. 81 – 85, ©1986 by P. Inman. This work has been substantially revised by the author, ©1994 by Peter Inman. Reprinted by permission of Peter Inman. "Subtracted Words" "centered," and "XX" are reprinted from manuscript, ©1994 by Peter Inman. Reprinted by permission of Peter Inman.

STEVE MCCAFFERY. The selection from *Evoba* is reprinted from *Evoba* (Toronto: Coach House Press, 1987), pp. 46 – 52, ©1987 by Steve McCaffery. Reprinted by permission of Coach House Press. The selection from *Panopticon* is reprinted from *Panopticon* (Toronto: Blewointmentpress, 1984, unpaginated, ©1984 by Steve McCaffery. Reprinted by permission of Steve McCaffery. "Little Hans" is reprinted from *Theory of Sediment* (Vancouver: Talonbooks, 1991), pp. 88 – 90, ©1991 by Steve McCaffery. Reprinted by permission of Talonbooks.

NATHANIEL MACKEY. "Kiche Manitou," "Song of the Andoumboulou: 6," and "Song of the Andoumboulou: 7" are reprinted from *Eroding Witness* (Urbana: University of Illinois Press, 1984), pp. 6 – 9, 50 – 54, ©1985 by Nathaniel Mackey. Reprinted by permission of the University of Illinois Press. "Song of the Andoumboulou: 12," "Alphabet of Ahtt," and "Slipped Quadrant" are reprinted from *School of Udhra* (San Francisco: City Lights Books, 1993), pp. 9 – 10, 43 – 48, 86 – 87, ©1993 by Nathaniel Mackey. Reprinted by permission of City Lights Books.

LESLIE SCALAPINO. "Considering how exaggerated music is" is reprinted from *Considering how exaggerated music is* (San Francisco: North Point Press, 1982), pp. 119 – 138, ©1982 by Leslie Scalapino. Reprinted by permission of Leslie Scalapino. "Picasso and Anarchism" is reprinted from *How Phenomena Appear To Unfold* (Elmwood, Connecticut: Potes & Poets Press, 1990), pp. 99 – 100, ©1990 by Leslie Scalapino. Reprinted by permission of Potes & Poets Press. "Or / a play" is reprinted from *Crowd and not evening or light* (Oakland and Los Angeles: O Books/Sun & Moon Press, 1992), pp. 45 – 48, ©1992 by Leslie Scalapino. Reprinted by permission of O Books and Sun & Moon Press.

BRUCE ANDREWS. "[rich little circle south]" is reprinted from *Sonnets (Memento Mori)* (Berkeley: This, 1980), p. 22, ©1980 by Bruce Andrews. Reprinted by permission of This Press. "While," "Methodology," and "The Impatient Heart" are reprinted from *Wobbling* (New York: Roof Books, 1981), pp. 8, 45, 86, ©1981 by Bruce Andrews. Reprinted by permission of Roof Books. "West West" is reprinted from *Executive Summary* (Elmwood, Connecticut: Potes & Poets Press, 1991), pp. 40 – 45, ©1991 by Bruce Andrews. Reprinted by permission of Potes & Poets Press. "Gestalt Me Out!" is reprinted from *I Don't Have Any Paper So Shut Up (or, Social Romanticism)* (Los Angeles: Sun & Moon Press, 1992), pp. 96 – 98, ©1992 by Bruce Andrews. Reprinted by permission of Sun &

Moon Press. Sections 1, 2, 7, 9, and 31 from *Tizzy Boost* are reprinted from *Tizzy Boost* (Great Barrington, Massachusetts: The Figures, 1993), unpaginated, ©1993 by Bruce Andrews. Reprinted by permission of The Figures. "DDD" is reprinted from *Moebius* (Mentor, Ohio: Generator Press, 1993), pp. 8 – 9, ©1993 by Bruce Andrews. Reprinted by permission of Generator Press.

STEVE BENSON. "The Beaten Track" is reprinted from *As Is* (Berkeley, California: The Figures, 1978), p. 8, ©1978 by Steve Benson. Reprinted by permission of The Figures. "Beethoven's Sixth Symphony" and "Blue Book 18 Pages 1 – 4" are reprinted from *Blue Book* (Great Barrington, Massachusetts and New York: The Figures/Roof Books, 1988), pp. 154 – 157, 66 – 68, ©1988 by Steve Benson. Reprinted by permission of The Figures/Roof Books. The selection from *Reverse Order* is reprinted from *Reverse Order* (Elmwood, Connecticut: Potes & Poets Press, 1989), pp. 27-31, ©1989 by Steve Benson. Reprinted by permission of Potes & Poets Press.

ABIGAIL CHILD. "A Motive for Mayhem" is reprinted from *A Motive for Mayhem* (Elmwood, Connecticut: Potes & Poets Press, 1989), pp. 7 – 13, ©1989 by Abigail Child. Reprinted by permission of Potes & Poets Press. "Squeeze" and "Surplus" are from an unpublished manuscript, ©1994 by Abigail Child. Reprinted by permission of Abigail Child.

TINA DARRAGH. "'luteous' to 'lymph' for 'F'" and "'legion' to 'Lent' for 'R'" are reprinted from *on the corner to off the corner* (College Park, Maryland: Sun & Moon Press, 1981), pp. 10, 22, ©1981 by Tina Darragh. Reprinted by permission of Sun & Moon Press. "sis boom ba," "volcanic tuff," and "ludicrous stick" are reprinted from *Striking Resemblance* (Providence: Burning Deck, 1989), pp. 47, 48, ©1989 by Tina Darragh. Reprinted by permission of Burning Deck. "footnote at 'figure of speech,'" "a throwing out at \ of (com)pare / (dis)pair," "lattice at 'split,'" and "lattice at \ of (com)pare / dis(pair)" are reprinted from *a (gain)²st the odds* (Elmwood, Connecticut: Potes & Poets Press, 1989), unpaginated, ©1989 by Tina Darragh. Reprinted by permission of Potes & Poets Press.

FIONA TEMPLETON. "Act II" is reprinted from *You: the City* (New York: Roof Books, 1990), pp. 51 – 63, ©1990 by Fiona Templeton. Reprinted by permission of Roof Books.

CARLA HARRYMAN. "That Can Not Be Taken Away From It" is reprinted from *Animal Instincts* (Berkeley: This, 1989), pp. 58 – 61, ©1989 by Carla Harryman. Reprinted by permission of This. "Allegory," "Mothering (enigma)," "Matter," and "Magic (or Rousseau)" are reprinted from manuscript, ©1994 by Carla Harryman. Reprinted by permission of Carla Harryman.

TABLE OF CONTENTS

To the Reader   31

I

CHARLES REZNIKOFF
    Children   39
    from *By The Well of Living and Seeing*
        7   42
        12   44
        15   45
        18   46
    from *Jews in Babylonia*
        I   47
    Testimony: The United States (1901 – 1910)
      Recitative/The South
        8   49

LORINE NIEDECKER
    Will You Write Me a Christmas Poem?   51
    [You have power politics, Paul,]   53
    [I rose from marsh mud,]   53
    The Element Mother   54
    [If I were a bird]   55
    [Lights, lifts]   56
    [Cricket-song—]   56
    [Dusk]   56
    [River-marsh-drowse]   57
    War   57
    [The long/canoes)]   58
    [Through all this granite land]   58
    [And at the blue ice superior spot]   58
    [Schoolcraft left the Soo—canoes]   58
    [I married]   59
    Poems at the Porthole   60
    Paean to Place   61
    Fancy Another Day Gone   67

CARL RAKOSI
    Good Morning   73
    The Founding of New Hampshire   74
    Unswerving Marine   74
    Fluteplayers from Finmarken   75
    Origins   76

Paraguay   78
The January of a Gnat   79
Lord, What Is Man?   79
The Menage   80

LOUIS ZUKOFSKY
   "A" 15   84

GEORGE OPPEN
   Eclogue   100
   Resort   101
   Myself I Sing   101
   From a Photograph   102
   Dædalus: The Dirge   103
   Part of the Forest   103
   Survival: Infantry   104
   Power, the Enchanted World   105
   The Occurrences   107
   Animula   108
   from Some San Francisco Poems   109
   The Little Pin: Fragment   110
   Gold on Oak Leaves   112

CHARLES OLSON
   from *The Maximus Poems*
      Maximus Letter # whatever   113
      [I forced the calm grey waters, I wanted her] 114
      3rd letter of Georges, unwritten   115
      Monday, November 26th, 1962   116
      [he who walks with his house on]   117
      [she who met the serpent in the pond the adultress] 117
      [the woman who said she went out every Sunday] 118
      "at the boundary of the mighty world" H. (T) 620 foll. 119
      Maximus, to Gloucester, Letter 157   122
      ["home", to the shore]   125
      Cole's Island   126
      [afterwards, in between, and since]   128
      [Hector-body,]   129
      [the Mountain of no difference which I]   130
      Just as Morning Twilight and the Gulls,
          Gloucester, May 1966, The Full Flower Moon 132
      [The sea's / boiling the land's]   133
      December 18th   134
      [the left hand is the calyx of the Flower]   137
      [slownesses]   137
      [I live underneath]   138

ROBERT DUNCAN

    Roots and Branches   139
    A Dancing Concerning a Form of Women   139
    Structure of Rime XVIII   141
    A New Poem (for Jack Spicer)   142
    Bending the Bow   144
    Structure of Rime XXIII   145
    Chords / Passages 14   145
    My Mother Would be a Falconress   147
    Achilles' Song   149
    A Glimpse   152
    Passages 37   152
    Poems from the Margins of Thom Gunn's *Moly*
        PREFACE to the Suite   154
    A Little Language   156
    Letting the Beat Go   157
    The Presence of the Dance / The Resolution of the Music   158

ROBIN BLASER

    The Finder   163
    Suddenly,   164
    'The Universe Is Part of Ourselves'   165
    The Ruler   166
    Ah.   167
    Even on Sunday   168

JACK SPICER

    Lament for the Makers   172
    The Book of Galahad   172
    Thing Language   175
    Transformations   182
    from Love Poems
        6   184

ALLEN GINSBERG

    Galilee Shore   185
    Describe: The Rain on Dasaswamedh Ghat   186
    Last Night in Calcutta   187
    Why Is God Love, Jack?   188
    After Yeats   190
    Studying the Signs   190
    Wichita Vortex Sutra, Part I   191
    Easter Sunday   195

LARRY EIGNER

    If you weep, I think that   197
    back to it   198
    IT SOUNDED   199
    For Sleep   200
    Letter for Duncan   201
    live / ,bird which   202
    In Imitation   203
    [theatre "   charged with]   204
    [the figures, lines]   205
    [his life / the / open window]   206
    [a perfectly quiet car]   208
    E n v i r o n s   208
    [one died by this tremendous headache]   209
    [last year's pink]   210

GILBERT SORRENTINO

    Land of Cotton   212
    Magic Composer   213
    September in Kittery   213
    [Across this water sits a shore]   214
    [She was all in black. A statement]   215
    Zukofsky   215
    The Oranges Returned   216
    "Good Night!"   217
    Razzmatazz   217

JOHN WIENERS

    A Glimpse   219
    King Solomon's Magnetic Quiz   219
    Long Nook   220
    The Suck   221
    Acceptance   221
    To H.   222
    What Happened?   222
    Doll   224

ROBERT KELLY

    Injune   225
    Tune   234
    A Life of Intimate Fleeing   235
    Looking   236
    Recessional   237

RONALD JOHNSON
   from *Ark: The Foundations*
      Beam 30, *The Garden*   239
   from *Ark: The Spires*
      Ark 34, *Spire on the Death of L.Z.*   241
      Ark 44, *The Rod of Aaron*   244

ROSMARIE WALDROP
   from *The Reproduction of Profiles*
      Feverish Propositions   245
   Lawn of Excluded Middle   247

KENNETH IRBY
   January 1965, Looking On   256
   Sequence   257
   Heredom   260

CLARENCE MAJOR
   Swallow the Lake   266
   Beaulieu   267
   Balance and Beauty   268
   Lost in the Desert   268

SUSAN HOWE
   from *Secret History of the Dividing Line*
      [In its first dumb form]   275
      [Thorn, thistle, apron leaf]   276
      [Set out to learn what fear was]   276
      [I knew what war was]   277
   from *Pythagorean Silence*
      [He plodded way through drifts of i]   277
      1   278
      5   279
      9   280
      15   281
   from *Defenestration of Prague*
      Bride's Day   282
      Silence Wager Stories   287

FANNY HOWE
   [From a donkey, excuse me, one lesson is given]   297
   "seeking out His face in a cup"   298
   Scattered Light   301
   [Twill coat, rain-wet as a circular.]   303
   [Bruises in eastern winter sky.]   304

from "O'Clock"
    19:40   305
    15:34   305
    4:01   305
    3:22   306
What We Learned   306
First Chance Twice   307

BPNICHOL
Scraptures: 7th Sequence   308
Ferry Me Across   310
Some Nets   311
St. Anzas VI   313
St. Anzas IX   315
Monotones / XCV   319

AARON SHURIN
City of Men   320
Material's Daughter   324
Saturated   325
His Promise   325
Sailed   326
Blue Shade   327
Forward or Back   327

DENNIS PHILLIPS
from *Arena*
    2. Exile   329
from *Means*
    [The hounds are either the work of wind]   335
    [If twelve out of fourteen people.]   335
    [Having warned them and the pressure suggests.]   336
from *Twenty Questions*
    Five   337
from "Etudes"
    If It's Only Rhythm   338
    I Held the Vein, but Death   339
    On Entries Emptiness   339
    Which Sudden Crisis   340

CHRISTOPHER DEWDNEY
from *Spring Trances in the Control Emerald Night*
    Night   341
    Grid Erectile   345
from *Concordat Proviso Ascendant*

[She is liquid darkness occult with desire.] 347
[Distant apartment complexes moody empires
of light....] 348

2

BARBARA GUEST
Santa Fe Trail 353
Walking Buddha 354
A Way of Being 354
Red Lilies 357
Nebraska 358
Sassafras 359
Wild Gardens Overlooked by Night Lights 360
An Emphasis Falls on Reality 362
Heavy Violets 364
Words 364
Bleat 365
Geese Blood 366
Defensive Rapture 368
Otranto 370

JAMES SCHUYLER
Freely Espousing 375
Greetings from the Chateau 376
Royals 377
A Man in Blue 378
The Master of the Golden Glow 379
"Earth's Holocaust" 380
Spring 381
A Stone Knife 382
Grand Duo 383
Father or Son 385

FRANK O'HARA
Ode to Tanaquil Leclercq 386
You at the Pump 387
Mary Desti's Ass 388
Summer Breezes 390
Madrid 391
Poem [Lana Turner has collapsed!] 392
Captains Courageous 393
Rogers in Italy 394

JOHN ASHBERY
   "How Much Longer Will I Be Able to Inhabit
      the Divine Sepulcher..."   395
   Rain   398
   Rivers and Mountains   402
   These Lacustrine Cities   404
   Forties Flick   405
   The Other Tradition   406
   Houseboat Days   407
   Saying It to Keep It from Happening   408
   The Lament Upon the Waters   409
   Paradoxes and Oxymorons   410
   Morning Jitters   411
   Life As a Book That Has Been Put Down   412
   Hotel Lautréamont   413
   The Old Complex   415

JOSEPH CERAVOLO
   Spring of Work Storm   416
   Ho Ho Ho Caribou   416
   Spring in This World of Poor Mutts   420
   The Women   423
   Invisible Autumn   423
   Celebration   424
   Migratory Noon   424
   Stolen Away   425
   Conception   426
   Sunset   426

TED BERRIGAN
   from *The Sonnets*
      I   428
      III   428
      Real Life   429
      XXXIV   430
      XXXV   430
      LV   431
      LXX   431
      LXXVII   432
      LXXXVIII / A Final Sonnet   432

CHARLES NORTH
   Air and Angels   434
   From the French   435
   from Six Buildings
      Hospital   436

Concert Hall 436
Laundry 436
Leap Year 437
Sunrise with Sea Monster 437
Little Cape Cod Landscape 438
The Year of the Olive Oil 438
A Note to Tony Towle (AFTER WS) 440

RON PADGETT
Detach, Invading 441
Louisiana Perch 442
Tell Us, Josephine 442
Early Triangles 444
Lucky Strikes 445
Something or Other 446
Symbols of Transformation 446
First Drift 447

MICHAEL BROWNSTEIN
Stepping Out 449
War 450
The Glass Enclosure 451
Jet Set Melodrama 454
The Last Spell Cast 455
Paris Visitation 456
from *Oracle Night* 456

LEWIS WARSH
The Suicide Rates 460
Gout 468
The Static 469
Enmeshment 470

LORENZO THOMAS
Electricity of Blossoms 472
Clear Channel 473
Cameo in Sudden Light 474
Excitation 476

MARJORIE WELISH
Within This Book, Called Marguerite 481
Wild Sleeve 482
Blood or Color 483
Casting Sequences 484
Kiss Tomorrow Goodbye 485
Scalpel in Hand 486
If I Blindfold You 488

JOHN GODFREY
 Radiant Dog 491
 Unholy Spring 492
 Show Me a Rose 492
 Bath 493
 Reveille 494
 My Mother, Life 494
 In Front of a Large Number of People 495
 What Say 496
 What It Takes 497
 Air 497
 One or More Together 498

ALICE NOTLEY
 "Alice Ordered Me to Be Made" 500
 The White Peacock 503
 White Phosphorus 504

DIANE WARD
 Approximately 511
 Shakeout 512
 Tables in Pictures 513
 Absolution 514
 Limit 515
 Re-Verse 516
 Crossing 519

3

ROBERT CREELEY
 To And 523
 Song 523
 The Invitation 524
 The Turn 525
 The Language 526
 For W. C. W. 527
 The Window 528
 They 529
 The Hole 529
 "River Wandering Down. . ." 531
 Talking 532
 The House 533
 The Edge 534
 Fathers 535
 Memory Gardens 536
 Stairway to Heaven 537

The Company   538
Age   539
Body   541

HANNAH WEINER
from *Little Books/Indians*
    Little Books 137 / Silence / Mar 22 79   543
from *Spoke* / Aug 19   548
Remembered Sequel   551

DAVID BROMIGE
from Tight Corners   553
Log   555
The Point   555
The Logical Positivist   556
Choice   559
Eastward Ho! A Succession   561
The Edible World   562
Lines   564

CLARK COOLIDGE
The Tab   567
Leaving Rattle Bar   567
Manlius to Coeymans   569
Album — A Runthru   570
Some Glow on the Sill   571
This Garden Being: The Hanging of Books   572
Jerome in His Study   573
from *At Egypt*   576
Disturbing the Sallies Forth   580
Saturday Night   580
Glance in White Space   581
What Is Thought But Won't Hold Still   582

LYN HEJINIAN
A Mask of Anger   584
from *My Life*   585
from *The Guard*   586
from *The Person*   589
from *The Cell*   593
from *Oxota: A Short Russian Novel*   596

ROBERT GRENIER
from *Oakland*   603
from *Phantom Anthems*   616

TED GREENWALD

 And, Hinges   620

 Privets Come into Season at High Tide   621

 I Hear a Step   623

 from *Licorice Chronicles*

   XIV   624

 from *Word of Mouth*   632

NICK PIOMBINO

 My Lady Carries Stones   637

 [The simple poetry of sleep]   638

 The Pyramids   639

 [Any m meant they came to a destination.]   640

 Time Travel   640

 The Frozen Witness   643

RAY DI PALMA

 Sheaf Mark   644

 Fragment   644

 Poem [In danger of which]   645

 Empire Smoke, Forgeries, Salient & The Ritz   646

 The Bed   648

 Hadrian's Lane   652

 The Table   653

 Annotations Tropes and Lacunae of the Itoku Master   654

 When Torrid Rhymes with Forehead   658

 The Prerogative of Lieder   659

 Motion of the Cypher   660

 The Wrong Side of the Door   661

 We Forego Mimicry   662

 Poem for Claude   662

MICHAEL PALMER

 Dearest Reader   664

 Voice and Address   664

 The Painted Cup   666

 Fifth Prose   667

 [Mei–mei, here is the table]   668

 [You say / A miracle from Heaven]   669

 [Desire was a quotation from someone.]   669

 Sun   670

 Eighth Sky   673

 Erolog (a reply)   674

 From "Letters to Zanzotto"

   Letter 5   676

MICHAEL DAVIDSON
    The Feeling Type and His Friends   677
    The Sensation Type and His Friends   677
    [Tonight is closer than we thought...]   678
    [Concern for her scar made him think to
        think of something like this:]   678
    The Dream Dream   679
    The Landing of Rochambeau   681
    Framing   683
    Troth   685
    Century of Hands   687

BERNADETTE MAYER
    The Aeschyleans   689
    The Port   690
    House Cap   691
    Boats   692
    We've Solved the Problem   693
    The End of Human Reign on Bashan Hill   695
    Generic Elbows   696
    The Garden   699
    Sonnet: Kamikaze   701
    The Earthworkers' God Is Healed   701

JAMES SHERRY
    She'll Be Comin' 'Round   702
    Lepidoptery   703
    from *In Case*   704
    Pay Cash Only   707
    Radiant   708
    Free Radicals   709
    Hazardous Waste   711

RON SILLIMAN
    from *Tjanting*   713
    from Hidden   718

RAE ARMANTROUT
    Generation   722
    Winter   722
    Necromance   723
    The Garden   724
    Sense   725
    Getting Warm   726
    Disown   727
    Leaving   729
    Incidence   730

BOB PERELMAN
    China   732
    Seduced by Analogy   733
    The Broken Mirror   735
    Money   736
    The Marginalization of Poetry   739

BARRETT WATTEN
    from *Progress*   748

KIT ROBINSON
    Pontoon   759
    Tribute to Nervous   760
    On the Corner   762
    Severance   764
    from Up Early   767
    Nesting of Layer Protocols   768
    First Thing   769
    Nursery Rhyme   771

CHARLES BERNSTEIN
    "Take then, these..."   773
    Poem [here. Forget.]   773
    Loose Shoes   777
    Matters of Policy   779
    Gradation   789
    From Lines of Swinburne   790
    Dysraphism   791
    Of Time and the Line   798
    The Kiwi Bird in the Kiwi Tree   799
    Virtual Reality   800

ALAN DAVIES
    The Outer Layers of Nervousness   803
    from *Name*
        [The personality syndrome]   807
        [If the devices fail pens]   808
        [Thus far we have spoken]   808
        [I particularly want to keep]   809
        [The pictures of the maid]   809
        [The occlusion between this section]   810
        [Each one suggests]   810
    Thirty East Forty-Second Street   811
    The New Sentience   812

JEAN DAY
    "from momentary work, a wrench..."   814
    Moving Object   817

4

JOHN CAGE
    Lecture on Nothing   827

JACKSON MAC LOW
    7TH Light Poem: For John Cage — 17 June 1962   844
    1ST Dance—Making Things New—6 Febraury 1964   847
    27TH Dance—Walking—22 March 1964   848
    A Lack of Balance But Not Fatal   849
    Giant Otters   851
    from *Pieces o' Six*
        XVIII   852
        XXIV   855
    Almost Casanova Electricity {Forties 24}   858
    Giant Philosophical Otters   860

KENWARD ELMSLIE
    Marbled Chuckle in the Savannahs   862
    Fruit   862
    Island Celebration   863
    Duo-Tang   865
    Picnic   866
    Squatter in the Foreground   866
    One Night Stand   867
    Stage-Duo   868

JEROME ROTHENBERG
    Poland/1931 / "The Wedding"   870
    The Water of the Flowery Mill (II)   871
    Portrait of Myself with Arshile Gorky & Gertrude Stein   872
    The 12th Horse-Song of Frank Mitchell (Blue)   874
    Praises of the Bantu Kings (1-10)   876
    Realtheater Piece Two   878
    A Song of Quavering / "Exchanging Ribs"   879
    The Structural Study of Myth   882
    At the Castle   883
    Numerology   884
    Aleph Poem   886
    That Dada Strain   887
    Dos Geshray (The Scream)   887

DAVID ANTIN
    Real Estate   890

AMIRI BARAKA/LEROI JONES
    A Contract. (for the destruction and rebuilding of Paterson   917
    The Pause of Joe   918
    from *Why's/Wise*
        Wise 3   931
    Alba   932

JOAN RETALLACK
    The Secret Life of Gilbert Bond   933
    Biographia Literaria   934
    Woman Dragged by Welsh Corgis   935
    Western Civ, 4 & 5   936
    Not a Cage   939
    Japanese Presentation I & II   941
    Here's Looking at You Francis Bacon   943

JOHN TAGGART
    Body and Soul: Poem for Two Readers   946
    Never Too Late   954
    Pen Vine and Scroll   956
    Monk   957
    Sainte-Chapelle   958

NICOLE BROSSARD
    from *Picture Theory*
        The Ordinary   959

MAC WELLMAN
    Having Led a Charmed Life, He Had To Be Hanged Twice   972
    Mad Wolf in Lunar Web, Mad Crow on the Beach   977
    from Hollowness   980
    from Terminal Hip   982

DOUGLAS MESSERLI
    This That & Then   983
    Actually Swallowed   984
    Angry with China   985
    Harrowing   986
    An Essay on Concrete   986
    Going to Sea   987
    From Hear to Air   988
    Scared Cows   989

The Annunciation   990
from *Along Without: A Fiction in Film for Poetry*   991
from *The Walls Come True: An Opera for Spoken Voices*   994
Closure   996

PETER INMAN
Colloam   997
from Dust Bowl   998
Subtracted Words   1000
centered   1004
XX   1006

STEVE MCCAFFERY
from *Evoba*
     Can there be a collison between picture and application?   1008
from *Panopticon*   1012
Little Hans   1026

NATHANIEL MACKEY
Kiche Manitou   1028
Song of the Andoumboulou: 6   1031
Song of the Andoumboulou: 7   1032
Song of the Andoumboulou: 12   1036
Alphabet of Ahtt   1037
Slipped Quadrant   1041

LESLIE SCALAPINO
Considering how exaggerated music is   1044
Picasso and Anarchism   1049
Or / a play   1052

BRUCE ANDREWS
[rich little circle south]   1056
While   1057
Methodology   1058
The Impatient Heart   1058
West West   1059
Gestalt Me Out!   1062
from *Tizzy Boost*
     1.   1064
     2.   1065
     7.   1065
     9.   1066
     31.   1068
DDD   1069

STEVE BENSON

    The Beaten Track   1071

    Beethoven's Sixth Symphony   1072

    Blue Book 18 Pages 1 - 4   1075

    from *Reverse Order*   1077

ABIGAIL CHILD

    A Motive for Mayhem   1082

    Squeeze   1085

    Surplus   1086

TINA DARRAGH

    "luteous" to "lymph" for "F"   1088

    "legion" to "Lent" for "R"   1088

    sis boom ba   1089

    volcanic tuff   1090

    ludicrous stick   1091

    footnote at "figure of speech"   1092

    a throwing out at \ of (com)pare (dis)pair   1092

    lattice at "split"   1093

    lattice at \ of (com)pare (dis)pair   1093

FIONA TEMPLETON

    from *You: The City* / Act II - Crossing   1094

CARLA HARRYMAN

    That Can Not Be Taken Away From It   1107

    Allegory   1110

    Mothering (enigma)   1110

    Matter   1111

    Magic (or Rousseau)   1111

TO THE READER

In response to my first discussions of editing the volume in your hands, David Antin quipped, in 1984, "Anthologies are to poets what zoos are to animals." Ten years later, while I was completing this anthology, David Bromige observed that a major aspect of such books is the exclusion of people. Over the years I have worried that both poets are correct.

Certainly I knew some of the problems inherent in editing such a volume from the start. Anyone reading the history of modern poetry has had to recognize the dangers of poetry anthologies. From the battles of Pound, Williams and other modernists against the influence of Francis Palgrave's *A Little Golden Treasury of Poetry* to the frustrations of contemporary poets with the academized bastion of the *Norton Anthology of Modern Poetry*, anthologies have often been something poets have worked against rather than supported.

Accordingly, when, in 1985, I was asked by New Directions to edit an anthology of "Language" poetry—which interrupted my plans for this larger collection—it should have come as no surprise that not every poet would share my enthusiasm for the new project. The painful lessons I learned from that, however, helped me to rethink the role of anthologies in general, and to reexamine the approaches to editing one. Indeed, after *"Language" Poetries* appeared in 1987, I determined not to proceed with the larger anthology; and for three peaceful years I made no further forays into this thorny territory.

Since the late 1960s, however, dozens of poets, editors, and readers have talked of the need for such a work. The model for most of us has been Donald Allen's groundbreaking *The New American Poetry*, published in 1960, but no major volume has served our own generation—or even the earlier generation of poets such as Charles Reznikoff, Lorine Niedecker, Louis Zukofsky, George Oppen, and Carl Rakosi, whose major works appeared after the Allen collection. There have been well-meaning attempts, including a reedited version of the Allen anthology, *The Postmoderns*, Michael Lally's 1976 collection *None of the Above*, and Eliot Weinberger's recent *American Poetry Since 1950*. But these collections fail, from my point of view, for two reasons: they have not presented a significant enough selection of their poets to help readers contextualize the work, and their selections have too often been based on personal agendas rather than on broader aesthetic points of view. All anthologies are personal in the sense that they represent the values of their editors; but wasn't it possible, I wondered, to collect work that pointed at least to specific aesthetic choices—eclectic as those might be—and to represent those choices in writing sub-stantiative enough to provide the reader a prospect of each author's poetics?

In January of 1990 I determined to proceed with the anthology. We needed such an anthology—not only for use in college and university courses, but in order to reintroduce to younger generations a generous perspective of innovative American poetry and poetics. And nobody else, so it appeared, was going to edit such a book. I invited about 80 American and Canadian poets to join me in making a selection of their work.

In the meantime I made my own selections from each poet's work. As I received the poets' suggestions, I reread their work, attempting to discern the viewpoint from which, through that selection, they saw their own writing. In a large number of instances, the poets had chosen some of the same poems as I had; in other cases poets made choices which differed from mine in ways that were elucidating; and when we radically differed—and this occurred surprisingly seldom—we made com-promises. Often this process went back and forth several times, with the poet and editor suggesting alternatives. The result was fortuitous, for it helped me to avoid one of the pitfalls common to anthologies by directing my attention away from a fetishization of particular poems to a perception of the whole body of each poet's writing. In the years since 1984, I have read the published works of these and dozens of other North American poets several times. And, accordingly, my goal has always been (and is still) to lead the reader to each author's publications, not to contain him or her within the confines of this particular collation.

A good anthology can shed light not just on significant individual poets, but also on the relationships among poets. And with this in mind, I gathered Canadian and American poets writing from 1960 to the present, for the most part focusing on poets who previously had not been extensively anthologized and whose writing seemed to extend and challenge the tradition of innovative American poetry begin-ning with Emily Dickinson (who was first published just 100 years ago), Gertrude Stein, Ezra Pound, William Carlos Williams, H.D. and others. Taking my lead from Donald Allen, moreover, I felt that these poems could be grouped into smaller gath-erings which might help to illuminate some specific issues and concerns. The five gatherings of Allen's anthology—poets closely identified with the magazines *Origin* and *Black Mountain Review*, poets of the San Francisco Renaissance, The Beat Gen-eration, the New York Poets, and younger poets who "evolved their own original styles and new conceptions of poetry"—showed both the assets and liabilities of this approach. Indeed, as the so-called New York Poets and the "Language" writers of our own time have perceived, labeling can easily be used against individual poets working inside or outside such communities.

Accordingly, I have chosen four major gatherings, but have refrained from giving them titles. For the poets in each section are not necessarily connected to any one kind of writing or even to a particular poetic community or group. Moreover, most of the poets included in this anthology could just as easily be put in other sections than the ones in which I have placed them. For these gatherings do not fix a static terrain, but rather are editorial contexts into and out of which the poets can be seen to shift, move, and wander. Indeed, in a few cases I have placed poets in order to show up different aspects of their work and to point to the fluidity of the divisions.

Having said that, I still feel strongly that there are different focuses among these poets which do justify each gathering, and that these groupings, in turn, may help to reveal what I see as the major concerns of each poet's work; this may be of particular help in the classroom situation.

In the first gathering I have included poets who are concerned, on a very broad scale, with cultural issues and a complex of overlapping ideas about myth, politics, history, place, and religion. Beginning with poets who were at one time connected with the Objectivist "movement," these poets include writers Donald Allen associated with *Black Mountain* (Olson, Duncan, and Eigner), poets connected with the San Francisco Renaissance (Spicer and Blaser), and a Beat poet (Ginsberg). This gathering also helps to give a context to some of the "younger poets" of Allen's collection, such as Sorrentino and Wieners.

The second gathering of poets, while concerned with some of the same issues as the first gathering, nonetheless is more focused on issues of self, social group, urban and suburban landscape (as opposed to place), and visual art. Many of the poets in this grouping have directly worked with or written about art (Guest, O'Hara, Ashbery, North, Padgett, Schuyler, and Welish for example). That is, of course, a defining quality of what Allen called the New York Poets. But similar concerns can be recognized in the writings of poets not generally associated with the New York School (such as Thomas and Ward).

Indeed Ward and Guest, among others, could just as easily be located in the third gathering of poets, those whom I identify as placing an emphasis upon issues of language, reader, and writing communities. I have begun this gathering with Robert Creeley, whom Allen saw as tied to the Black Mountain poets, because I feel that, despite those alliances, Creeley's major concern is that of language and reader more than the thematic subjects of his poems, which often have to do with history and sexuality. His impact upon other poets in this section is strongly felt.

The final gathering is of poets who focus on issues of performance, voice, genre, dialogue, and personae. Some of these poets might as easily have been located elsewhere: Rothenberg in the first gathering, for example, Elmslie in the second, Mac Low in the first or third. But, in the end, each of these writers points toward a performative or theatrical relationship with poetry. Baraka, Mac Low, Elmslie, Wellman, Scalapino, Templeton, Harryman, and I also write plays. Cage, Mac Low, Antin, Rothenberg, McCaffery, Taggart, Retallack, Andrews, Benson, Templeton, and I have frequently performed our texts in ways that extend the format of a poetry reading. Baraka, Inman, Mackey, Child and Darragh all work closely with genres that explore sound/music/voice relationships.

Again I must reiterate, there is no poet included in this anthology who might not be thought of in another context, in another gathering. And all the poets included in this volume might be said to be concerned with most of the issues I have mentioned. Above all else, the poets in this volume are all extremely attentive to the ways in which language determines meaning and experience both for reader and author.

The final result of my selections is, as you may notice, too long in length. I had hoped to limit the number of pages of this anthology to about 500. That I ended with 1,100 pages is evidence of my commitment to the entire body of each poet's writing, and of unwillingness to exclude any more poets than I have. The most painful aspect of any such anthology, to my way of thinking, is having to choose from dozens of other poets, often of equal talent, whose work one finds significant. No doubt some poets were excluded because of my own failures as a reader; I am certain there will be authors whose work, when reread in one or two years, will seem of far greater interest than it did to me in 1993 or 1994. Similarly, poets of great talent whose writing has more to do with cultural, social, and political subjects than the more formally-conceived poems in this volume, must recognize the specific focus of this anthology. Younger poets must create their own anthologies, and their exclusion here has less to do with editorial selection than with the limits of production.

We need more anthologies, rather than a few. For anthologies, too often, are like zoos which capture and cage "types" of what they represent. The true reader must always enter the dark forests of libraries, must stalk down the barren plains of literary bookstore shelves to discover the living beast of poetry. My hope is that this tome serves not as a tomb, as memory of that beast, but as a travel guide to send readers scurrying in several directions.

Any such massive endeavor as this is the work of many. And this book could not have existed without the contributions of all the authors and the editors whose work is included within. In particular Charles Bernstein and Marjorie Perloff spent countless hours discussing the form and substance of this book and provided the encouragement necessary to keep me at work on it for over 10 years. Bruce Andrews, Lyn Hejinian, Ron Silliman, and James Sherry offered useful advice on all aspects of this volume. As students Joe Ross and Rod Smith helped to test out the effectiveness of some of my selections in the classroom.

The managing editor of Sun & Moon Press, Diana Daves, joyfully endured weeks of such detailed proofreading that her eyesight may never be the same; similarly, John McNally proofread much of this book, offering many editorial insights. Seldom has a typographer produced so many pages in such a short time with the keen attention to detail and design as Guy Bennett. And Reginald Jones sped our correspondence between authors, editors, and proofreaders across the country. Without these individuals this anthology would never have been completed.

Michael Anderson, Robert Bertholf, Peter Glassgold, Jerome Rothenberg, Paul Vangelisti, Jonathan Williams, and Bill Zavatsky contributed their editorial and bibliographical expertise.

Finally, Howard N. Fox, who has patiently subjected himself to more than 10 years of paeans, lectures, tirades, and lamentations on contemporary American poetry, should be blessed by the muses for his sustenance of the editor and project both.

Douglas Messerli

...from the other side of time, from a time
on the other side of yourself
—CHARLES OLSON

Across the Atlantic, I
inherit myself
semblance
of irish susans
dispersed
and narrowed to
home
—SUSAN HOWE

I am living out the logical conclusion of my books.
—JOHN WIENERS

Charles Reznikoff [1894 – 1976]

CHILDREN

1

Once, among the transports, was one with children—two freight
  cars full.
The young men sorting out the belongings of those taken to the
  gas chambers
had to undress the children—they were orphans—
and then take them to the "lazarette."
There the s.s. men shot them.

2

A large eight-wheeled car arrived at the hospital
where there were children;
in the two trailers—open trucks—were sick women and men
lying on the floor.
The Germans threw the children into the trucks
from the second floor and the balconies—
children from one-year-old to ten;
threw them upon the sick in the trucks.
Some of the children tried to hold on to the walls,
scratched at the walls with their nails;
but the shouting Germans
beat and pushed the children toward the windows.

3

The children arrived at the camp in buses,
guarded by gendarmes of the French Vichy government.
The buses stopped in the middle of the courtyard
and the children were quickly taken off
to make room for the buses following.
Frightened but quiet,
the children came down in groups of fifty or sixty to eighty;

the younger children holding on to older ones.
They were taken upstairs to empty halls—
without any furniture
and only dirty straw bags on the floor, full of bugs:
children as young as two, three, or four years of age,
all in torn clothes and dirty,
for they had already spent two or three weeks in other camps,
uncared for;
and were now on their way to a death camp in Poland.
Some had only one shoe.
Many had diarrhea
but they were not allowed in the courtyard
where the water-closets were;
and, although there were chamber pots in the corridor of each story,
these were too large for the small children.

The women in the camp who were also deportees
and about to be taken to other camps
were in tears:
they would get up before sunrise
and go into the halls where the children were—
in each a hundred to a hundred and twenty—
to mend the children's clothing;
but the women had no soap to clean the children,
no clean underwear to give them,
and only cold water with which to wash them.
When soup came for the children,
there were no spoons;
and it would be served in tins
but the tins were sometimes too hot for the children to hold.

After nine at night no one—except for three or four who had a
    permit—
was allowed to stay with the children.
Each room was then in darkness,
except for one bulb painted blue by blackout instructions.
The children would wake at night
calling for their mothers
and would then wake each other,
and sometimes all in the room would start crying out
and even wake the children in other rooms.

A visitor once stopped one of the children:
a boy of seven or eight, handsome, alert and gay.
He had only one shoe and the other foot was bare,
and his coat of good quality had no buttons.
The visitor asked him for his name
and then what his parents were doing;
and he said, "Father is working in the office
and Mother is playing the piano."
Then he asked the visitor if he would be joining his parents soon—
they always told the children they would be leaving soon to rejoin
     their parents—
and the visitor answered, "Certainly. In a day or two."
At that the child took out of his pocket
half an army biscuit he had been given in camp
and said, "I am keeping this half for Mother;"
and then the child who had been so gay
burst into tears.

4

Other children, also separated from their parents,
arrived in buses,
and were put down in the courtyard of the camp—
a courtyard surrounded by barbed wire
and guarded by gendarmes.
On the day of leaving for the death camp
they were awakened at five in the morning.
Irritable, half asleep, most of them refused to get up and go down to
     the courtyard.
Women—French volunteers, for they were still in France—
urged the children gently
to obey—they must!—and vacate the halls.
But many still would not leave the straw bags on which they slept
and then the gendarmes entered,
and took up the children in their arms;
the children screamed with fear,
struggled and tried to grasp each other.

5

Women guards at the women's section of the concentration camp
were putting little children into trucks
to be taken away to the gas chambers
and the children were screaming and crying, "Mamma, Mamma,"
even though the guards were trying to give them pieces of candy to
   quiet them.

(Holocaust, 1977)

from *BY THE WELL OF LIVING AND SEEING*

7

The highway I was walking on
went through a marsh. There were no houses:
nothing but the marsh.
No one else was walking on the highway
in the blazing sun.

I saw the dog a hundred feet away—
a burly fellow, half chow, I thought,
half German shepherd,
shaggy hair plastered with mud.
The dog saw me, too, and came running towards me.
I walked on, afraid the dog would bite.

I could hear the nails of his paws
clicking on the pavement.
But he passed me—never looked at me—
and ran along as I walked;
ten or twenty feet ahead,
ten or twenty feet behind.
I did not like his looks at all,
the heavy brow, the square jaws—
a shaggy dirty fellow.
The road was as lonely as ever:
marsh under the blazing sky
and the motorcars speeding past.

I could see the pavement of a street on the other side
and the bright blue sea. It would be cooler there,
and I might be rid of the dog.
The dog looked up, after a while,
saw me on the other side,
and came towards me, straight through the traffIc.
I stood stock-still,
waiting for the dog to be hit.
Sure enough, the second or third car struck him
and sent him sprawling on his back, squealing.
The brakes of the car screeched;
the dog leaped to his feet,
and was knocked down again,
and then came running towards me.

"You dope!" I said.
But I was touched at his devotion.
Now we went on side by side:
the dog close to me and I no longer afraid.
Now and then we came to a stairway
leading to the beach. Below, other dogs were running about on
     the sand
and the dog was eager to go down. But he stopped,
waiting for me at the head of each stairway,
and as I went on followed.
The street turned at last and we were back on the highway.

Now I was afraid to cross for fear the dog would be hit.
He stood beside me, looking up at me,
watching my hands and feet,
ready to spring forward.
At last there was a break in the traffIc—
only two cars coming. I could cross easily:
go part of the way, let the cars pass, and then cross over.
But I was afraid the dog would rush on
and be hit. "No," I said to him,
"no!"
And we walked along the edge of the highway without crossing.

As the dog ran on beside me, sturdy and true,
I thought of his lifted face,
the deep brown eyes watching mine;
yes, I should like to keep him.

Walking so together, we came to some houses.
These were at the sea—
cottages, refreshment stands, even a small merry-go-round.
I stopped at a stand.

"What should I get my dog to eat?" I asked the pleasant girl
behind the counter. She smiled at me,
and leaned over the counter to smile at the dog
as he stood beside me, wagging his tail.
"Hamburger," she said. "Dogs love it."
"All right."
"One or two?"
"Two."

She took the fresh cakes out of the icebox
and put them on a square of wax paper.
I walked to the corner of the stand. The dog followed
and I put the meat down.
The dog looked at it;
his tail drooped, his eyes were glazed with fear,
and he was off
as fast as he could go
bolting over the sand hills.

                              12

Four sailors on the bus, dressed in blue denim shirts,
ill-fitting jackets,
shoddy trousers that do not match the jackets:
one a Negro, another has some Negro blood,
the other two white—Spanish or Portuguese.
The mulatto or octaroon is the eldest—
a handsome fellow in the thirties.
The others chatter away, laugh and talk,
but he says little
although they keep looking at him to say something.
He speaks once, briefly, dryly—
and the three burst out laughing with delight.

One of the white men gives him a packet of photographs
to look at—snapshots;
and the other white man reaches for it.

The mulatto stops him with a gesture.
You would think the mulatto would slap his hand
or push him away
but he merely lifts his own hands
and keeps them lifted for a moment—
a moment in a dance.
Then when he has glanced through the pictures,
instead of giving them back or to his companion
who has snatched at them,
he offers them to a young woman seated nearby.

She is a stranger but her eyes
caught by the flicker of the photographs—
as anybody's would—
had strayed to them. And this time his gesture
has the grace of a man plucking a spray of flowers
from a bush he is passing
and giving them to the girl beside him.

15

Two men were seated near me in a bus:
well-dressed, well-fed; in the forties;
obviously respected members of their community;
talking together calmly,
the way men of good breeding and education talk,
and the speech may have been Greek or Italian.
I could not hear enough of it to decide.
Suddenly a woman seated directly behind them
began in a loud voice:
"Why don't you talk American?
You live here, don't you?
You make your living here!
Talk American!"

One of the men turned to glance at her
and then the two went on talking in Greek or Italian,
calmly, quietly
although every now and then the woman cried out,
"Talk American, why don't you?"

If these men were Jews, I thought,
how uneasy they would have become,
and their faces would show it.
One of them might even say to the woman—
if he knew enough English,
"This is a free country, isn't it?"
And there would be a noisy argument.
Or they might become silent.
The two men, however, continued to talk
as they had been doing
and neither turned to glance at the woman
or show by gesture or grimace
that they heard her.
Finally, she jumped up and sat down beside me.
"What do you think of these men?" she asked.
"Why don't they talk American?
They live here, don't they?
They make their money here!"

"You must not be so impatient," I said.
"English is not an easy language to learn.
Besides, if they don't learn it, their children will:
we have good schools, you know."
She looked at me suspiciously
and, when the bus stopped, hurried off—
fleeing our contamination.
One of the men then turned to me and said quietly
in the best of American with not a trace of a foreign accent:
"She's a little cracked, isn't she?"

18

I saw him walking along slowly at night
holding a tray of candy and chewing-gum:
a Jewish boy of fifteen or sixteen
with large black eyes and a gentle face.
He sidled into a saloon
and must have been ordered away
because he came out promptly
through the swinging doors.

I wondered what he was doing
far from a Jewish neighborhood.
(I knew the side streets
and the roughs standing about on the corners and stoops.)
What a prize this shambling boy with his tray!
I stepped up to warn him
against leaving the brightly-lit avenue.
He listened, eyed me steadily, and walked on calmly.
I looked at him in astonishment
and thought: has nothing frightened you?
Neither the capture of Jerusalem by the Babylonians, by the
    Romans, by the Crusaders?
No pogrom in Russia;
no Nazi death-camp in Germany?
How can you still go about so calmly?

(*Poems 1937 – 1975*, 1977)

from *JEWS IN BABYLONIA*

I

1

Plough, sow and reap,
thresh and winnow
in the season of the wind;
a woman is grinding wheat
or baking bread.
In the third watch of the night
the child sucks from the breast of its mother
and the woman talks with her husband.

Plough, sow and reap,
bind the sheaves, thresh and winnow;
shear the sheep,
wash the wool,
comb it and weave it.

Wheat and barley,
straw and stubble;
the cock crows, the horse neighs, and the ass brays;
an ox is grazing in a meadow or straying on the road
or rubbing itself against a wall
(a black ox for its hide,
a red one for its flesh,
and a white one for ploughing);

plough, sow, cut, bind, thresh, winnow, and set up a stack.

2

A cow to plough with
and an ass to drive;
a goat for milking
and an ewe for shearing.

A hen for laying eggs
and a date tree for its fruit;
a bed on which to sit
and a table at which to eat.

3

Plane the wood
into boards;
chisel the stones;
beat the wool and bleach it,
spin it and weave it.

A beast with its load
and a bit in its mouth
and a bell on its neck;
an ass with its bundle of wood
and a camel with a load of flax and an iron nose-ring
or a horse with bells between its eyes;
the horn gores,
the hoof kicks,
the teeth bite.

4

The bread has become moldy
and the dates blown down by the wind;
the iron has slipped from the helve.
The wool was to be dyed red
but the dyer dyed it black.

The dead woman has forgotten her comb
and tube of eye-paint;
the dead cobbler has forgotten his knife,
the dead butcher his chopper,
and the dead carpenter his adze.

A goat can be driven off with a shout.
But where is the man to shout?
The bricks pile up, the laths are trimmed,
and the beams are ready. Where is the builder?

To be buried in a linen shroud
or in a matting of reeds—
but where are the dead of the Flood
and where the dead of Nebuchadnezzar?

(*Poems 1937 – 1975*, 1977)

TESTIMONY:THE UNITED STATES (1901 – 1910) RECITATIVE/THE SOUTH

8

The boy, about eleven or twelve—
a bright boy—
had been working for him four or five years
at the house and in the store
and even acting as clerk.
But he caught him stealing—
just a petty theft—
and he stripped the boy naked
and whipped him for it about an hour

with a leather strap that had a knot at the end
until more than a hundred welts were raised on the boy's body
and the boy was blistered all over.
But still he whipped him
until the blisters burst
and kept on whipping him.

He was interrupted once
by a visitor
and then went back to whipping the boy,
although the boy kept begging him to stop,
until he was interrupted again—
by the boy's death.

> *(Testimony: The United States [1885–1915]*
> *Recitative/Volume II,* 1979)

Lorine Niedecker [1903 – 1970]

WILL YOU WRITE ME A CHRISTMAS POEM?

Will I!

The mad stimulus of Gay Gaunt Day
meet to put holly on a tree
and trim green bells
and trim green bells

Now candles come to faces.
You are wrong to-day
you are wrong to-day,
my dear. My dear—

One translucent morning
in the damp development of winter,
one fog to move a city backward—
Backward, backwards, backward!

You see the objects and the movable fingers,
Candy dripping from branches,
Horoscopes of summer
and you don't have Christmas ultimately—
Ultima Thule ultimately!

Spreads and whimpets
Good to the cherry drops,
Whom for a splendor
Whom for a splendor

I'm going off the paper I'm going off the pap-

Send two birds out
Send two birds out
And carol them in,
Cookies go round.

What a scandal is Christmas,
What a scandle Christmas is
a red stick-up
to a lily.

You flagellate my woes, you flagellate,
I interpret yours,
holly is a care divine
       holly is a care divine

and where are we all from here.
Drink for there is nothing else to do
but pray,
And where are we?

Throw out the ribbons
and tie your people in
All spans dissever
once the New Year opens
and snow derides
a doorway,
it spasms dissever

All spans dissever,
wherefore we, for instance, recuperate
no grief to modulate
no grief to modulate

The Christian cacophony
one word to another,
sound of gilt trailing the world
slippers to presume,
postludes, homiclea, sweet tenses
imbecile and corrupt,—
     failing the whirled, trailing the whirled

This great eventual heyday
to plenty the hour thereof,
fidelius.
Heyday! Hey-day! Hey-day!

I fade the color of my wine
that an afternoon might live
foiled with shine and brittle
I fade the color of my wine

Harmony in Egypt,
representative birthday.
Christ what a destiny
What a destiny's Christ's, Christ!

■

You have power politics, Paul,
You have "I'll call you, I'll call—"
which Indians did aptly
and more;—in the forest an Indian girl,
her washing spread out on a rock,
let a song fall.

You now see man hide behind
his ribs, loose grates, his kind
eye closed, the other one screwing
the savage sprays
of our steel woods' life-everlasting,
a filing refined.

But wait! In still wilder states
he'll be Needle That Clicks. Rays
will cause counters to sing
counter to sense
and man, the weapon, must obsolesce
as he radiates.

■

I rose from marsh mud,
algae, equisetum, willows,
sweet green, noisy
birds and frogs

to see her wed in the rich
rich silence of the church,
the little white slave-girl
in her diamond fronds.

In aisle and arch
the satin secret collects.
United for life to serve
silver. Possessed.

THE ELEMENT MOTHER

I *She's Dead*

The branches' snow is like the cotton fluff
she wore in her aching ears. In this deaf huff
after storm shall we speak of love?

As my absent father's distrait wife
she worked for us—knew us by sight.

We know her now by the way the snow
protects the plants before they go.

II *The Graves*

You were my mother, thorn apple bush,
armed against life's raw push.
But you my father catalpa tree
stood serene as now—he refused to see
that the other woman, the hummer he shaded
　　　　　　hotly cared
for his purse petals falling—
　　　　　　　　his mind in the air.

III *Kepler*

Comets you say shoot from nothing?
In heaven's name what other
than matter can be matter's mother.

■

If I were a bird

    I'd be a dainty contained cool
    Greek figurette
    on a morning shore—
    H.D.

    I'd flitter and feed and delouse myself
    close to Williams' house
    and his kind eyes

    I'd be a never-museumed tinted glass
    breakable from the shelves of Marianne Moore.

    On Stevens' fictive sibilant hibiscus flower
    I'd poise myself, a cuckoo, flamingo-pink.

    I'd plunge the depths with Zukofsky
    and all that means—stirred earth,
    cut sky, organ sounding, resounding
    anew, anew.

    I'd prick the sand in cunning, lean,
    Cummings irony, a little drunk dead sober.
    Man, that walk down the beach!

    I'd sit on a quiet fence
    and sing a quiet thing: sincere, sincere.
    And that would be Reznikoff.

■

Lights, lifts
parts nicely opposed
this white
        lice lithe
pink bird

■

Cricket-song—
what's in The Times—
    your name!
        Fame
here

on my doorstep
—an evening seedy
    quiet thing.
        It rings
a little.

■

Dusk

he's spearing from a boat—

How slippery is man
    in spring
        when the small fish
            spawn

■

River-marsh-drowse
and in flood
        moonlight
                gives sight
of no land

They fish, a man
takes his wife to town
with his rowboat's 10-horse
        ships his voice
to the herons

Sure they drink
—full foamy folk—
        till asleep
The place is asleep
on one leg in the weeds

WAR

The trees full of snipers, the new kind
        of bird
Men on the hunt for Russian furs
        for Ukrainian sausage
                and Chinese girls

They floated past a crescent moon
        to Sicily—
strings of diminished pearls
        in each pearl-parachute
                a tommy gun

The Russian—only a man from Georgia
        USSR
could dance like that
        My baby son?—in some
                secret zone

■

**(The long
canoes)**

'Birch Bark
and white Seder
for the ribs'

∎

Through all this granite land
the sign of the cross

Beauty: impurities in the rock

∎

And at the blue ice superior spot
priest-robed Marquette grazed
azoic rock, hornblende granite
basalt the common dark
in all the Earth

And his bones of such is coral
raised up out of his grave
were sunned and birch-bark-floated
to the straits

∎

Schoolcraft left the Soo—canoes
US pennants, masts, sails
chanting canoemen, barge
soldiers—for Minnesota

Their South Shore journey
as if Life's—
The Chocolate River
The Laughing Fish
and The River of the Dead

Passed peaks of volcanic thrust
Hornblende in massed granite
Wave-cut Cambrian rock
painted by soluble mineral oxides
wave-washed and the rains
did their work and a green
running as from copper

Sea-roaring caverns—
Chippewas threw deermeat
to the savage maws
'*Voyageurs* crossed themselves
tossed a twist of tobacco in'

∎

I married

in the world's black night
for warmth
     if not repose.
     At the close—
someone.

I hid with him
from the long range guns.
     We lay leg
     in the cupboard, head
in closet.

A slit of light
at no bird dawn—
     Untaught
     I thought
he drank

too much.
I say
     I married
     and lived unburied.
I thought—

POEMS AT THE PORTHOLE

Blue and white
china cups
glacier-adjacent

lost
in the foothills

□

The soil is poor
water scarce
    the people clothed
        in wind and cold—
Bolivia

□

Michelangelo

If matches had been my work
instead of marble poems
       —sulphur—
   I'd suffer
less

□

Wallace Stevens

What you say about the early
yellow springtime is also something
worth sticking to

□

The man of law
   on the uses
      of grief

The poet
on the law
of the oak leaf

□

Not all harsh sounds displease—
Yellowhead blackbirds cough
through reeds and fronds
as though pronged bronze

PAEAN TO PLACE

*And the place
was water*

Fish
fowl
flood
Water lily mud
My life

in the leaves and on water
My mother and I
born
in swale and swamp and sworn
to water

My father
thru marsh fog
sculled down
from high ground
saw her face

at the organ
bore the weight of lake water
and the cold—
he seined for carp to be sold
that their daughter

might go high
on land
    to learn
Saw his wife turn
deaf

and away
She
    who knew boats
    and ropes
no longer played

She helped him string out nets
for tarring
  And she could shoot
      He was cool
to the man

who stole his minnows
by night and next day offered
    to sell them back
        He brought in a sack
of dandelion greens

if no flood
No oranges—none at hand
    No marsh marigolds
        where the water rose
He kept us afloat

I mourn her not hearing canvasbacks
their blast-off rise
    from the water
        Not hearing sora
rail's sweet

spoon-tapped waterglass-
descending scale-
    tear-drop-tittle
        Did she giggle
as a girl?

His skiff skimmed
the coiled celery now gone
   from these streams
      due to carp
He knew duckweed

fall-migrates
toward Mud Lake bottom
   Knew what lay
      under leaf decay
and on pickerelweeds

before summer hum
To be counted on:
   new leaves
      new dead
leaves

He could not
—like water bugs—
   stride surface tension
      He netted
loneliness

As to his bright new car
my mother—her house
   next his—averred:
      A hummingbird
can't haul

Anchored here
in the rise and sink
   of life—
      middle years' nights
he sat

beside his shoes
rocking his chair
   Roped not 'looped
      in the loop
of her hair'

I grew in green
slide and slant
  of shore and shade
    Child-time—wade
thru weeds

Maples to swing from
Pewee-glissando
  sublime
    slime-
song
  ...
Grew riding the river
Books
  at home-pier
    Shelley could steer
as he read

I was the solitary plover
a pencil
  for a wing-bone
From the secret notes
I must tilt

upon the pressure
execute and adjust
  In us sea-air rhythm
'We live by the urgent wave
of the verse'

Seven-year molt
for the solitary bird
  and so young
Seven years the one
dress

for town once a week
One for home
  faded blue-striped
as she piped
her cry

Dancing grounds
my people had none
  woodcocks had—
  backland—
air around

Solemnities
such as what flower
  to take
  to grandfather's grave
unless

water lilies—
he who'd bowed his head
  to grass as he mowed
  Iris now grows
on fill

for the two
and for him
  where they lie
  How much less am I
in the dark than they?

Effort lay in us
before religions
  at pond bottom
    All things move toward
the light

except those
that freely work down
  to oceans' black depths
    In us an impulse tests
the unknown

River rising—flood
Now melt and leave home
  Return—broom wet
    naturally wet
Under

soak-heavy rug
water bugs hatched—
    no snake in the house
        Where were they?—
she

who knew how to clean up
after floods
    he who bailed boats, houses
        Water endows us
with buckled floors

You with sea water running
in your veins sit down in water
    Expect the long-stemmed blue
        speedwell to renew
itself

O my floating life
Do not save love
    for things
        Throw *things*
to the flood

ruined
by the flood
    Leave the new unbought—
        all one in the end—
water

I possessed
the high word:
        The boy my friend
                played his violin
in the great hall

On this stream
my moonnight memory
        washed of hardships
                maneuvers barges
thru the mouth

of the river
They fished in beauty
It was not always so
In Fishes
red Mars

rising
rides the sloughs and sluices
of my mind
with the persons
on the edge

FANCY ANOTHER DAY GONE

The glare from the brass horn makes sun-brown satin fit smoothly the girl by the window. Even the young man is straight and bright.

HE:
Please come. I want you to justify my landscape.
(*She looks out of the window and lights the late afternoon.*)

HE:
I love you magnificently. I've had every drop of
blood from the moonstone put into a venture for you.

SHE:
(*takes his hands*) It's a high hurt.

HE:
The plight of the individual is our happy finale.
(*Both absorbed by the glow move out.*)

GRANDMOTHER:
(*sidling the luminous flood*) She picks and promises and castillates the dew. And he's a tin whistle substitute, works for the wonder constructor who eats and then expectorates when he wants to build a lake where a hill is.
The family, entering, pales and points after tea-time.

MOTHER:
Studying? Why so stupid, son.

STUDY BOY:
(*in khaki*) They're putting us thru an elemental dog-trot in sargonic culture. We're now at the hammer and fan-wheel stage,—star-falling comes next.

MOTHER:
And this painting, daughter, that you hold so dear . .

FATHER:
A silk contortion heavily blotched toward the centre.

DAUGHTER:
He has issued also complaints in vast design.

BLUE TIE SON:
The very devil of a good thought.

GRANDMOTHER:
He ate a mushroom for breakfast. He can't be divine anymore.

MOTHER:
He wears that kind of practitioner's overcoat . .

BLUE TIE:
He repeatedly assumes his dais.

FATHER:
All the same, I'd write him and ask what his inventions are.

DAUGHTER:
He's done a great deal with words that look like pictures.

FATHER:
I don't suppose a father ever cocktailed his hopes to that.
(*chorus by two small children skipping in and out*): I don't suppose a man ever, no, I don't suppose a man ever.

MOTHER:
What unbooked revelry . .

GRANDMOTHER:
Today let us weep for tomorrow may be frought with foolishness.

MOTHER:
(*pauses in front of daughter before going off completely*) Darling, you've some bad laughter lines.

DAUGHTER:
But facts are a mass of coercives.
(*Children dance in to tea-table and away.*)

GRANDMOTHER:
Not a raisin goes to cookie in this house but what they know it.

STUDY BOY:
(*The room grows an even, late daylight—Study boy takes his books nearer the window.*)
This map has a cherry expedition punctured by toothpicks to rescind a felled hatred. Wind me a furlough. I'm bound to need air.

SLEEPY SON:
Feathering Heights—how they can dance up there.

BLUE TIE:
And let their seams out in the wind . . .

SLEEPY:
Sweet pillow, Madge. What exquisite tether and release. A little difficult, tho, to be a constant wind.

STUDY BOY:
Oh you don't use the right weapons.
(*small children and Grandmother sing out*):

>   "Rings on your fingers,
>   bells on your toes,"
>   Tether your feathers,
>   Tar all your foes . .

DAUGHTER:
Flightful conceit. . . .

GRANDMOTHER:
Somnambule enchants a wiry daisy, curvets and comes back.

STUDY BOY:
I prefer my women on paper.

BLUE TIE:
(*looking into cup*) Concatenations streaking a bird with a tail-light.

SLEEPY:
Hang your tea-cup relations.

BLUE TIE:
(*idling about the room, glances over father's shoulder at magazine*) Literate man would like to hear from readers interested in talking about things that count.

STUDY BOY:
What's a dismissed attavater?

BLUE TIE:
It means the ease comes out of the sound.

FATHER:
It's what is called imminent custody.
(*piano fortissimo from a nearby key*)

DAUGHTER:
Beethoven's ironworks. (*The room is a strong dusk and the window steel-blue*)
(*pianoworks*)

STUDY BOY:
Don't invert me. I wasn't so smelted in a long time.
(*Piano fades along with the family, the Octaves of Point Lessening.*) Tomes
at the window establish the smoke scene as the night of the mandolin query.

HE:
Vertebrate lives spread the hour. On the instable count no face line ever vented approach.

SHE:
Is the midnight capsule ready to gloat?

HE:
It's only lachrymose and octo-even by the enervator on the tombstone. Fentry the watchman restored his eyesight on that.

SHE:
These failings tie you up with home. For me it's just unknown distance.

HE:

My dear, I care a great deal for the pear-shaped of the lute species.

SHE:

It's hard to glutinize in leafless time.

HE:

Who has unsettled you about this matter?

SHE:

Oh—appetizers, upholders of the law . .

HE:

Drizzlers in the sink.

SHE:

My faint memory of viscera should be certainly viscarra. Let's rush the blood to some other point.

HE:

I suppose it's profound to guess whether . .

SHE:

(*plucks the mandolin*) Prayerful inebriate shelters his wings.

HE:

(*blows his cigarette smoke white in the dark*) I shall never be able to enlarge my scope as I wish.

SHE:

Have you been to the proper authorities?

HE:

Don't be nemeebic.

SHE:

I love you despite the coconut on your tie.

HE:

Would you be traditional in buttering your bread?

SHE:

Not if there were plums to placate the ardor.

HE:
Then what are we waiting for?

(*Grandmother candles her hopes to an empty room, has them blown by the wind at the window, trudges the length of the night.*)

(all selections reprinted from
From This Condensery: The Complete Writing of Lorine Niedecker, 1985)

Carl Rakosi [1903]

GOOD MORNING

A yellow feather
of a note,

delighted bounding
canary birdcry!

Up, my Norwich,
spit the bitter

gravel out,
throw out the little

ball in midair
grasp the cuttlebone

with male claws.
Come, my Coppy,

eat your seed.
The sun lights up

the lettuce leaf
between the bars!

(*Amulet*, 1967)

THE FOUNDING OF NEW HAMPSHIRE

A slender plank above a waterhole
planted on end to meet my wants,
I hear its whisper in the stock.
It does not sway a hair's breadth.

Another stake driven in and well shaved
points against the light from the layout.
The maple fits upon the joist like a flower,
                a picked beam,
a great wood to plane and saw.

I tell my wife the walls are up,
the strips nailed at snug right angles,
            the floors are oiled.
The Yankee poles are almost columns.

Braced against a gloomy magnitude,
I loiter civil on my soles and buffeted,
killing time in these traditions.

Are the woodsmells getting sweeter
or the broker working at my back
so that all the concord in the timber
can not warm this house?

                        (*Amulet*, 1967)

UNSWERVING MARINE

This is in the wind:
that an old seaman
                paces the planks again
as his weedy hull parts
                the saltseries inaudibly.
What ho! She carries full sails
and the chant of the grog-quaffers
                in an important manner.

But there is no port
and the wind is distracted
                    from her simple stern
like the mind.
Continuously the undefined plane
                              emerges
in the form of a ship,
her nose speeding in the brine–ellipsis,
routing the shads and alewives
                    from her shaping way.
And the wind
            and the mind sustain her
and there is really
                no step upon the gangway,
nothing but the salt deposits
                        of the open.

                    (*Amulet,* 1967)

FLUTEPLAYERS FROM FINMARKEN

How keen the nights
were, Svensen.
Not a star out,
not a beat of emotion
in the humming snowhull
(now and then an aweful swandive).

It seemed ordained then
that my feet slip on the seal bones
and my head come down suddenly
over a simple rock–cistvaen,
grief-stricken and archwise.
Thereon were stamped
the figures of the noble women
I had followed with my closed eyes
out to the central blubber
of the waters.

(There is not a pigeon
or a bee in sight.
My eyes are shut now
and my pulse dead as rock).

The Swedish mate says he recalls
this fungoid program
of the mind and matter
where the abstract signals
                   to the abstract
and the mind directs
                   a final white lens
on the spewing of the waterworm
and the wings of the midsea.

It was not clear what I was after
in this stunted flora
and husky worldcold
until the other flutes arrived....
four masters musing
from one polar qualm to another.

                 (*Amulet,* 1967)

ORIGINS

In the salt warp
was the plasma,
in the springhead
and the sulphurous water.

Jupiter the sire hawk
flew through Athens.
Then the Greeks sang
and the wings turned
through the light.

We sat upon a stone
with happy records,
shipping kelp and sulphur
through the islands.

Athens was a hawk.

And Corinth was once
a pedestal for wrestlers
in classical shorts.
What method in their manner!

Shall we say the gods
with lights behind us
have broken wind
in a changing system?

Yesterday behind the olive boughs
they seemed so lucid!

Send us again, O gods,
peppers and poppyseed,
porphyry and white cocks.

After a thousand years,
                              behold
the apple blossoms of the new world;
the early grapes;
the young man's cartograph
on which appears an arrow
pointed north to heaven.
There the gentle still idealize,
the heart is lighter,
and the Cross attends.

But we pass obscurely
from post to sleep,
opening the constructions
of the virtuous and loghouse
Puritans of Massachusetts.
They planted radishes
and hailed the Savior
spreading his alarming
feathers over the pickets.

A country house in April
after a thousand years:
poor headpiece,
you are unhappy.

Buy yourself some alcohol for winter
and a squirrel rifle
                   for Sunday morning.
You too will juggle
rabbits, eggs, bananas,
physical and resolute.

Tumblers in the nebula,
is not every man
his own host?

              (*Amulet*, 1967)

PARAGUAY

In the early hours
                 the lovebirds
colonized the palm.

We were looking for a totem.

In the east
where the sun deflects the falcons
from their sea positions
and the Indian smells
we found a frere
with no cathedral
but the daisies in May,
living on milk and wafers,
with the cross in one hand
and anatomy in the other.

              (*Amulet*, 1967)

THE JANUARY OF A GNAT

Snow panels, ice pipes, house the afternoon
whose poised arms lift prayer with the elm's antennae.
She has her wind of swift burrs, whose spiel is gruff,
scanning the white mind of the winter moon
with her blank miles. Her voice is lower
than the clovers or the bassviol of seastuff.

So void moons make a chaste anabasis
across the stalks of star and edelweiss
while Volga nixies and a Munich six
o'clock hear in the diaphane the rise
of one bassoon.
                   So the immense frosts fix
their vacant death, bugs spray the roots like lice.
High blizzards broom the cold for answer
to their ssh of vapors and their vowel ooo.

(*Amulet*, 1967)

LORD, WHAT IS MAN?

                   He looks into a glass
and sees a physical figure
                   looking back at him,
the two waiting immobile
                   for him to reappear
as the world knows him,
                   by name, by work, by habits,
in what particulars
                   he is significant,
and...why should it be embarrassing
                   to speak of this?
...in what endearing....
                   Is he honest?
and how he looks
                   when meditating......
all in a semblance characteristic
                   as his bones,

including that shade
                in the inwit of presence,
his secondary at the subliminal portal,
that stands for more
                potentiality than appears,
the quiet continent
                behind it feeling boundless
(the worse for him).

The final scene, the only scene,
                                inherent in the glass,
is that looker
                waiting for it to happen
and caught in the act.

(*The Collected Poems*, 1986)

THE MENAGE

Up stand
            six
yellow
            jonquils
in a
        glass/
the stems
                dark green,
paling
            as they descend
into the water/
                    seen through
a thicket
            of baby's breath, "a tall herb
bearing numerous small,
                        fragrant white flowers."
I have seen
                snow-drops larger.
I bent my face down.
                    To my delight
they were convoluted
                    like a rose.

They had no smell,
                    their white
the grain of Biblical dust,
                              which like the orchid itself
is as common as hayseed.
                         Their stems were thin and woody
but as tightly compacted
                         as a tree trunk,
greenish rubbings showing in spots
                                   through the brown;
wiry, forked twigs so close,
                             they made an impassable bush
which from a distance
                      looked like mist.
I could barely escape
                      from that wood of particulars...
the jonquils whose air within
                              was irradiated topaz,
silent as in an ear,
                     the stems leaning lightly
against the glass,
                   trisecting its inner circle
in the water,
              crossed like reverent hands
(ah, the imagination!
                      Benedicite.
Enter monks.
             Oops, sorry!
Trespassing
            on Japanese space.
Exit monks
           and all their lore
from grace).

I was moved by all this
                        and murmured
to my eyes, "Oh, Master!"
                          and became engrossed again
in that wood of particulars
                            until I found myself
out of character, singing
   "Tell me why you've settled here."

"Because my element is near."
and reflecting,
            "The eye of man cares. Yes!"

But a familiar voice
           broke into the wood,
a shade of mockery in it,
             and in her smile
a fore-knowledge
         of something playful,
something forbidden,
           something make-believe
something saucy,
         something delicious
about to pull me
       off guard:
"Do you want to be my Cupid-o?"

In fairness to her
         it must be said
that her freckles
        are always friendly
and that the anticipation
          of a prank
makes them radiate
        across her face
the way dandelions
        sprout in a field
after a summer shower.

"What makes you so fresh,
           my Wife of Bath?
What makes you so silly,
       o bright hen?"

"That's for you to find,
         old shoe, old shoe.
That's for you to find out
         if you can."

"Oh yeah!"

         (a mock chase and capture).
"Commit her

         into jonquil's custody.
She'll see a phallus

         in the pistil.
Let her work it off there."

But I was now myself

         under this stringent force
which ended,

         as real pastorals in time must,
in bed, with the great

         eye of man, rolling.

(*The Collected Poems,* 1986)

Louis Zukofsky [1904 – 1978]

"A" 15

An
  hinny
by
  stallion
out of
  she-ass

He neigh ha lie low h'who y'he gall mood
So roar cruel hire
Lo to achieve an eye leer rot off
Mass th'lo low o loam echo
How deal me many coeval yammer
Naked on face of white rock—sea.
Then I said: Liveforever my nest
Is arable hymn
Shore she root to water
Dew anew to branch.

Wind: Yahweh at Iyyob
Mien His roar 'Why yammer
Measly make short hates oh
By milling bleat doubt?
Eye sore gnaw key heaver haul its core
Weigh as I lug where hide any?
If you—had you towed beside the roots?
How goad Him—you'd do it by now—
My sum My made day a key to daw?
O Me not there allheal—a cave.

All mouth deny hot bough?
O Me you're raw—Heaven pinned Dawn stars
Brine I heard choir and weigh by care—
Why your ear would call by now Elohim:
Where was soak—bid lot tie in hum—

How would you have known to hum
How would you all oats rose snow lay
Assáy how'd a rock light rollick ore
Had the rush in you curb, ah bay,
Bay the shophar yammer *heigh horse*'

Wind: Yahweh at Iyyob 'Why yammer,'
Wind: Iyyob at Yahweh, 'Why yammer
How cold the mouth achieved echo.'
Wind: Yahweh at Iyyob 'Why yammer
Ha neigh now behēmoth and share I see see your make
Giddy pair—stones—whose rages go
Weigh raw all gay where how spill lay who'
Wind: Iyyob
'Rain without sun hated? *hurt no one*
In two we shadow, how hide any.'

The traffic below,
sound of it a wind
eleven stories
below: *The Parkway*
no parking there ever:
the deaths as
after it might be said
"ordered," the one
the two old
songsters would not
live to see—
the death of
the young man,
who had possibly
alleviated
the death of
the oldest
vagrantly back he
might have thought
from vying culturally
with the Russian
Puritan Bear—
to vagary of
Bear hug and King
Charles losing his head—
and the other

a decade younger
never international
emissary
at least not
for his President,
aged in a suburb
dying maundering
the language—
American—impatient now
sometimes extreme clarity—
to hurrȳ
his compost
to the hill
his grave—
(distance
    a gastank)

he would
miss
living thru the
assassination

were it forecast to him
the dying face
would look quizzical?

'In another week,
another month
another—
I shall be driven,
how shall
I look
at this sign
then—
how shall
I read
those letters
then—
that's a thing
to remember—
I should
like to remember

this—
how shall
I look
at it,
then'

Like, after all:
and as I know
failing eyes
imagine,
as shortly after
his mother died,
walking
with me
to my class
thru the swinging
red leather doors
of the Institute
he remarked on
a small square pane
of glass in each of them,
there to prevent
if students looked
those going out
and those going in
from swinging the doors
into so to speak
mutual faces,
when I pleaded blindness
'I've walked thru
some years now
and never till you
said saw these panes'
he consoled with
'mere chance
that I looked'

But the death—
years later
of the young man—
he did not live thru
(no *Drum Taps*
no *Memories*
as for Walt)

that the teacher
overhearing
a student
thought a stupid jest—
the class
shocked into a "holiday"

Flown back from Love Field, Dallas
love—so—divided—
the kittenish face
the paragon of fashion
widowed
with blood soaked stocking
beneath the wounded head
she held in her lap—
Até
crazier than ever
infatuation of history
steps on men's heads—
flown back from Love Field, Dallas
as in *Kings* 'dalas'
the poorest,
we had all,
the "English" teaching drudge
with a holiday on his hands
from "papers"
a time for
to atone for your souls
the nation
a world
mourned
three days in
dark and in
daylight
glued to
TV
grieved as a family
the Kennedys were a family—
Castro 'We should comprehend it
who repudiate assassination
a man is small
and relative in society
his death no joy'

not the joy of the Irish
a few weeks back
greeting their Parliament,
its actual house
the old Fitzgerald seat,
when the Boston Irish American President
on tour recalled
on his mother's side
his ancestral prototype who had left it
to write his own mother
from Paris
'that the seat of the Fitzgeralds
was not
conducive to serious thinking.'

Potentates (nominally)
dignitaries
cardinals
the military
mounted
and the horses
led the
tone

in politics
who's honest
true
to
death?
the off the cuff
opponent (Guildencrantz)
who'd stopped husking
for the nomination
until after the funeral
and after the funeral
forgot any day before
while conserving *Freedom*
nevermind *Liberty*—
honest—

the young dead's
great slip—
(pricing steel)

the twenty-third of April
only seven months laid (a
garland
for Shakespeare's birthday)
'My father always
told me
all business men
were sons-of-bitches.
I never
believed it
till now.'

or Vietnam's witch
despising
Buddhists'
human wicks
with sympathies
for Western
First Lady
widow to widow
(Queen Margaret and dying Edward's queen)
And see another as I see thee now
could mourning soften

Eloquence
words of
a senator's eulogy
da capo five times:
'In a moment it was no more.
And so she took a ring
from her finger and placed it
in his hands'
And he added the fifth time:
'and kissed him and closed
the lid of the coffin.'

'Bethink you
if Bach's feet deserved such bounty
what gift must the Prince have offered
to reward his hands'
Capella, *alpha* in Auriga, little first goat
early evening early autumn
driven before them—west—
fall stars of evening

of Vesper there
Vesper Olympus dig air
court orchestra of uniformed Haiduks
habit Bach himself wore
"concertmaster" of four string players
his income not generous
'Friedmann, shall we go
over to Dresden to hear pretty tunes'
Italy's arias Händel's successes

one hundred four pages
of Frescobaldi's *Musical Flowers*
to copy, paper the fringe benefit from the Duke,
or pupil Ziegler to remember
in playing a hymn
melody is not alone
speaking the words thru it
a rare banquet in cypress
orange almond and myrtle
fragrance to turn a winter's evening to summer

or the court company of comedians
whose dispersal synchronized with Bach's arrival
not 'useful to accept a post
poorer than the one he abandons'
finger exercises traceries little pieces of himself
played over, saying 'That's how it ought to go'
no searching over the keyboard better silent
if there's nothing, until parts
speak to their fellows, true counterpoint
variety free thru consistency
later Orpheuses, Arions

Weimar not a street perpetuates his name
where Lucas Cranach lived and some say
Bach in Herder's house
more certain he was arrested
for urging his own departure—
They perpetuate the young dead's name with place
statesman stumping *The Tabernacle,* Salt Lake City
quick with his story of the first step
of a journey of a thousand years
in behalf
of the Test Ban Treaty, all journeys must
begin with a first step

(not counting on 42 days
to the unexpected grave)
'not to our size, but to our spirit'

And 'because' *alive* 'he knew the midnight
as well as the high noon'
the travellers stood chilling
to a parade of the first step
of might be that Chinese sage a thousand
years out of counting
a little more than a half-moon, dusk
a burial
poet old enough
to write it old enough history
like the horse who took part in it
shying from it, balking
despite himself

The fetlocks ankles of a ballerina
'Black Jack' Sardar with black-
hilted sword black dangled in silver scabbard from
the saddle riderless rider
his life looked back
into silver stirrups and the
reversed boots in them.
Finally a valentine
before his death
had he asked for it
I should have inscribed to him,
After reading, a song
for his death
after I had read at Adams House

John to John-John to Johnson

so the nation grieved
each as for someone in his or her family
we want Kennedy—
and the stock market fell and rose
on the fourth day
holy holy tetraktys
of the Pythagorean eternal flowing creation
and again without the senses TV

went back to its commercials
boots reversed flapping backward
and in another month
brought back the Indian's summer
'I was dreaming a high hole in rock
from which flowed the Seine
because that was how it looked
and was showing my father
of whom I rarely dream back to
its source when the doorbell
rang (the letter carrier, shocked sleep)
but your sheepsilver was here
a chunk of a summer's
Muscovy glass from the new film
The Glass Mountain'
almost xmas—
and in less than another year
after 2000 years (a few less)
the dead's church
remembered not a moment too soon
to absolve the Jews of Yēshūa's (ah Jesu's)
cross—except for salvation

a smiling Gibbon's ground bass of a footnote
'spare them the pains of thinking'—
under the aspic of eternity
with the udder hand milking
the great Cow of Heaven—
Birjand, October five thousand nine hundred eleven
    (an anagram)
'hawking with the Amir (like old Briton)
a covey of see-see, the little partridge rose
with a whistle disappeared round a bend
the falconer leading held on gloved hand
by thong to a leg-ring the bright hawk
not hooded straining for release
which came shortly—rose
and brought the see-see to earth
the hawk poised on the quarry
claws gripped its neck
plucking the feathers: the falconer came up
took the neck of the living see-see
with the left hand and its legs in his right

and with one pull dismembered it
and gave the legs to the waiting hawk.'

He could not think another
thing that evening
simply a life
had stepped in in place of theory. Then love, young Isaac
burning for Rebecca, a comfort
not all and scorned in Augustine.

Eros agh nick hot hay mock on Eros us inked massy
  pipped eyes
now on th'heyday caught as thus mown

Dunk for the teeth that have rotted
(bread) soaked crust bare gums
glad car and cur bore the brunt of it
Woe woman woo woman
the fourth kingdom shall be as strong as iron
forasmuch as iron breaketh in pieces and
  subdueth all things
'perpetual violation of justice
.. maintained by .. political virtues
of prudence and courage ..
the rise of a city .. swellēd īnto .. empire ..
may deserve .. reflection of .. philosophic mind
.. decline of Rome .. the
effect of immoderate greatness.
Prosperity ripened .. decay;
the causes of destruction multiplied with
  the extent of conquest,
and as soon as time or accident had removed
the artificial supports, the stupendous fabric
yielded to the pressure of its own weight ..
instead of inquiring
why the Roman empire was destroyed ..
should rather be surprised
.. it had subsisted so long.
The victorious legions, who, in distant wars,
acquired the vices of strangers and mercenaries,
first oppressed the freedom of the republic, and
afterwards violated .. the purple ..
emperors, anxious for .. personal safety

and .. public peace .. reduced to the
expedient of corrupting the discipline
.. and the Roman world was overwhelmed by a
deluge of barbarians ..
vain emulation of luxury, not of merit ..
Extreme distress, which unites the virtue
of a free people, embitters .. factions ..
As the happiness of a *future* life
is the great object of religion
we may hear without surprise
or scandal
that .. at least the abuse of Christianity
had some influence on the decline
and fall of the Roman empire.
The clergy successfully
preached doctrines of patience and pusillanimity;
the active virtues of society were discouraged;
and the last remains of military
spirit were buried in the cloister:
a large portion of public and
private wealth .. consecrated .. charity and devotion;
and .. soldiers' pay .. lavished on useless
multitudes of both sexes who could only plead
the merits of abstinence and chastity ..
diverted from camps to synods ..
and the persecuted sects became
the secret enemies of their country ..
sacred indolence of monks was
devoutly embraced by a servile and effeminate age ..
Religious precepts are easily obeyed
which indulge and sanctify
the natural inclinations of their votaries ..
but the pure .. influence of Christianity
may be traced in its beneficial, though imperfect,
effects on the barbarian proselytes ..
This awful revolution may be
usefully applied to the instruction of the present
age .. The savage nations of the globe are the
common enemies of civilised society; and
we may inquire .. whether Europe is still
threatened with a repetition
of those calamities which formerly oppressed
the arms and institutions of Rome.

.. poor, voracious, and turbulent;
bold in arms and impatient
to ravish the fruits of industry .. The barbarian world
was agitated by the rapid impulse of war ..
the peace of Gaul or Italy was shaken
by the distant revolutions of China. ..
Cold, poverty, and a life of danger and fatigue
fortify the strength and courage of barbarians.
In every age .. oppressed
China, India and Persia,
who neglected, and still neglect
to counterbalance these natural powers
by the resources of military art ..
to command air and fire.
Mathematics, chemistry, mechanics,
architecture have been applied to the service of war;
and the adverse parties oppose to each other
the most elaborate modes of attack and defence.
Historians may indignantly observe
that the preparations of a siege
would found and maintain a flourishing colony;
yet we cannot be displeased that the
   subversion of a city
should be a work of cost and difficulty;
or that an industrious people
should be protected by those arts
which survive and supply the decay of military virtue.
Europe is secure from any future irruption
of barbarians; since before they can conquer,
they must cease to be barbarous. ..
Should these speculations be found doubtful
or fallacious, there still remains a more
humble source of comfort and hope. ..
no people, unless the face of nature
is changed, will relapse into their original barbarism.
The improvements of society
may be viewed under a threefold aspect.
   1. The poet or philosopher illustrates his age and
country by the efforts of a *single* mind;
but these superior powers of reason or fancy
are rare and spontaneous productions;
and the genius of Homer .. or Newton
would excite less admiration

if they could be created
by the will of .. a preceptor.
2. The benefits of law and policy of trade
and manufactures, of arts and sciences
are more solid and permanent;
and *many* individuals may be qualified,
by education and discipline,
to promote, in their respective stations,
the interest of the community.
But this general order is the effect of skill and labour;
and the complex machinery may be decayed by time,
or injured by violence.
3. Fortunately for mankind,
the more useful, or at least more necessary arts,
can be performed without superior talents
or national subordination;
without the powers of *one,*
or the union of the *many.*
Private genius and public industry may be extirpated ..
But the scythe, the invention
or emblem of Saturn,
still continued annually to mow
the harvests of Italy;
and the human feasts of the Laestrigons
have never been renewed
on the coast of Campania.'

No lady Rich is very poor
No, laid o rich is very poor

kneecheewoe—
marriageable
the first lady astronaut
returning to earth
bruised her nose.

The wives of the poets
flew higher.
And to show for it—
on the hill near town the little cemetery
that would be seen from the Erie?
—No eulogies, Louis,

no.
Perhaps to see where his friend's song
not too clear while one led his own
would *button into the*
rest of it
the life of the fugue of it
not come to talk
at the funeral.
The dog as the old friend lay dead
would not cross his threshold
he was not there anymore
his room not his room
what was there not
for the day to go into—
the estuary up the river—
later thruout the house he ruled
while the others were interring him
the friend left at home in it
hearing the other voice as *then*
'you have never
asked anyone anything'

and Nestor, 'Odysseus—where
did you get those horses
I have never set eyes on
horses like these'
and he who with his wife
deceived even pride as she suffered
'it is easy *for a god*
to bestow even better horses
than these'
.. bathed
and sat down to dine
ate thought
.. o poor .. away from all baths ..
Hecuba with bare breast
she once fed him
wailing,
and for still another—
Thetis
and the nymphs
Glaukë and Thaleia and Kumodokë
Nesaië and Speio, Thoë, Halië

Kumothoë and Actaië and Limnoreia
Melitë, Iaira, Amphitoë and Agauë
Doto and Proto, Pherousa and Dunamenë
Dexamenë and Amphinomë and Kallianeira
Doris and Panopë, Galateia
Nemertes and Apseudes and Kallianassa
Klumenë and Ianeira and Ianassa
Maira and Oreithuya and Amatheia
of the deepest bath

negritude no nearer or further
than the African violet
not deferred to
or if white, Job
white pods of *honesty*
satinflower

("*A*" *13 – 21*, 1969)

George Oppen [1908 – 1984]

ECLOGUE

The men talking
Near the room's center. They have said
More than they had intended.

Pinpointing in the uproar
Of the living room

An assault
On the quiet continent.

Beyond the window
Flesh and rock and hunger

Loose in the night sky
Hardened into soil

Tilting of itself to the sun once more, small
Vegetative leaves
And stems taking place

Outside—O small ones,
To be born!

(*The Materials,* 1962)

RESORT

There's a volcano snow-capped in the air some twenty miles
    from here
In clear lit air,
There is a tree in leaf here—

In dream an old man walking,
An old man's rounded head
Abruptly mine

Self-involved, strange, alien,
The familiar flesh
Walking. I saw his neck, his cheek

And called, called:
Called several times.

                (*The Materials*, 1962)

MYSELF I SING

Me! he says, hand on his chest.
Actually, his shirt.
                And there, perhaps,
The question.

Pioneers! But trailer people?
Wood box full of tools—
            The most
American. A sort of
Shrinking
        in themselves. A
Less than adult: old.

A pocket knife,
A tool—
        And I
Here talking to the man?
                The sky

That dawned along the road
And all I've been
Is not myself? I think myself
Is what I've seen and not myself

A man marooned
No longer looks for ships, imagines
Anything on the horizon. On the beach
The ocean ends in water. Finds a dune
And on the beach sits near it. Two.
He finds himself by two.

        Or more.
'Incapable of contact
Save in incidents'
             And yet at night
Their weight is part of mine.
For we are all housed now, all in our apartments,
The world untended to, unwatched.
And there is nothing left out there
As night falls, but the rocks

                (*The Materials*, 1962)

FROM A PHOTOGRAPH

Her arms around me—child—
Around my head, hugging with her whole arms,
Whole arms as if I were a loved and native rock,
The apple in her hand—her apple and her father, and my
  nose pressed
Hugely to the collar of her winter coat. There in the photo-
  graph

It is the child who is the branch
We fall from, where would be bramble,
Brush, bramble in the young Winter
With its blowing snow she must have thought
Was ours to give to her.

                (*The Materials*, 1962)

DAEDALUS: THE DIRGE

The boy accepted them;
His whole childhood in them, his difference
From the others. The wings
Gold,
Gold for credence,
Every feather of them. He believed more in the things
Than I, and less. Familiar as speech,
The family tongue. I remember
Now expedients, frauds, ridiculous
In the real withering sun blazing
Still. Who could have said
More, losing the boy anyway, anyway
In the bare field there old man, old potterer...

(*The Materials,* 1962)

PART OF THE FOREST

There are lovers who recall that
Moment of moonlight, lit
Instant—

But to be alone is to be lost
Altho the tree, the roots
Are there

It is an oak: the word
Terrifying spoken to the oak—

The young men therefore are determined to be men.
Beer bottle and a closed door
Makes them men.

Or car.—Approach
A town to be negotiated
By the big machine

Slow, for a young
Woman, kids
In hand. She is

A family. Isn't tenderness, God knows,
This long boned girl—it is a kind of war,
    A tower

In the suburb.

Then the road again. The car's
Companion.

(*The Materials*, 1962)

SURVIVAL: INFANTRY

And the world changed.
There had been trees and people,
Sidewalks and roads

There were fish in the sea.

Where did all the rocks come from?
And the smell of explosives
Iron standing in mud
We crawled everywhere on the ground without seeing the
    earth again

We were ashamed of our half life and our misery: we saw
    that everything had died.

And the letters came. People who addressed us thru our
    lives
They left us gasping. And in tears
In the same mud in the terrible ground

(*The Materials*, 1962)

POWER, THE ENCHANTED WORLD

1

Streets, in a poor district—

Crowded,
We mean the rooms

Crowded, they come to stand
In vacant streets

Streets vacant of power

Therefore the irrational roots

We are concerned with the given

2

...That come before the swallow dares...

The winds of March

Black winds, the gritty winds, mere squalls and rags

There is a force we disregarded and which disregarded us

I'd wanted friends
Who talked of a public justice

Very simple people
I forget what we said

3

Now we do most of the killing
Having found a logic

Which is control
Of the world, 'we'
And Russia

What does it mean to object
Since it will happen?
It is possible, therefore it will happen
And the dead, this time, dead

4

Power, which hides what it can

But within sight of the river

On a wall near a corner marked by the Marylyn Shoppe
And a branch bank

I saw scrawled in chalk the words, Put your hand on your
        heart

And elsewhere, in another hand,

Little Baby Ass

And it is those who find themselves in love with the world
Who suffer an anguish of mortality

5

Power ruptures at a thousand holes
Leaking the ancient air in,

The paraphernalia of a culture
On the gantries

And the grease of the engine itself
At the extremes of reality

Which was not what we wanted

The heart uselessly opens
To 3 words, which is too little

(*Of Being Numerous*, 1968)

THE OCCURRENCES

Limited air   drafts
In the treasure house moving and the movements of the living
Things fall   something balanced   Move
With all one's force
Into the commonplace that pierces or erodes

The mind's structure but nothing
Incredible happens
It will have happened to that other
The survivor   The survivor
To him it happened

Rooted in basalt
Night hums like the telephone dial tone blue gauze
Of the forge flames the pulse
Of infant
Sorrows at the crux

Of the timbers
When the middle Kingdom
Warred with beasts Middle Things the elves the

Magic people in their world
Among the plant roots   hopes
Which are the hopes
Of small self interest called

Superstition chitinous
Toys of the children wings
Of the wasp

(Seascape: Needle's Eye, 1972)

ANIMULA

animula blandula vagula

Chance and chance and thereby starlit
All that was to be thought
Yes
Comes down the road   Air of the waterfronts   black air

Over the iron bollard   the doors cracked

In the starlight things the things continue
Narrative   their long instruction and the tide running
Strong as a tug's wake   shorelights'

Fractured dances across rough water a music
Who would believe it
Not quite one's own
With one always   the black verse   the turn and the turn

At the lens' focus   the crystal pool   innavigable

Torrent torment Eden's
Flooded valley   dramas

Of dredged waters
A wind blowing out

And out to sea   the late the salt times cling

In panicked
Spirals at the hull's side sea's streaks floating
Curved on the sea little pleasant soul wandering

Frightened

The small mid-ocean
Moon lights the winches

(*Seascape: Needle's Eye,* 1972)

from SOME SAN FRANCISCO POEMS

6

Silver as
The needle's eye

Of the horizon in the noise
Of their entrance row on row the waves
Move landward   conviction's

Net of branches
In the horde of events the sacred swarm avalanche
Masked in the sunset

Needle after needle more numerous than planets

Or the liquid waves
In the tide rips

We believe   we believe

Beyond the cable car streets
And the picture window

Lives the glittering crumbling night
Of obstructions and the stark structures

That carry wires over the mountain
One writes in the presence of something
Moving close to fear
I dare pity no one
Let the rafters pity
The air in the room
Under the rafters
Pity
In the continual sound
Are chords
Not yet struck
Which will be struck
Nevertheless yes

8

THE TASTE

Old ships are preserved
For their queer silence of obedient seas
Their cutwaters floating in the still water
with their cozy black iron work
And Swedish seamen dead   the cabins
Hold the spaces of their deaths
And the hammered nails of necessity
Carried thru the oceans
Where the moon rises grandly
In the grandeur of cause
We have a taste for bedrock
Beneath this spectacle
To gawk at
Something is wrong with the antiques, a black fluid
Has covered them, a black splintering
Under the eyes of young wives
People talk wildly, we are beginning to talk wildly, the wind
At every summit
Our overcoats trip us
Running for the bus
Our arms stretched out
In a wind from what were sand dunes

(*Seascape: Needle's Eye,* 1972)

THE LITTLE PIN: FRAGMENT

> '*The journey fortunately* [*said the traveller*] *is
> truly immense*'

of this
all things
speak if they speak the estranged

unfamiliar sphere thin as air
of rescue   huge

pin-point

cold little pin unresting
small pin of the wind and the rayne

in the fields the pines the spruces the sea and
   the intricate

veins in the stones and the rock
of the mountains wandering

stars in the dark their one
moral in the breeze

of wherever it is history
goes the courses and breaking

High seas of history....Stagecraft
Statecraft the cast is absurd the seas
break on the beaches

of labor multitudinous
beach and the long cost

of dishonest
music

    Song?

astonishing

song?   the world
sometime be

world the wind
be wind o western
wind to speak

   of this

(*Collected Poems,* 1975)

GOLD ON OAK LEAVES

gold said her golden

young poem for she sleeps and impossible
truths move

brave   thru   the gold   the living
veins but for the gold

light I am lost

in the gold

light on this salt and sleepless

sea I haunt an old

ship   the sun

glints thru ragged
caulking I would go out
past the axioms

of wandering

timbers garboards keelson the keel   full

depth

of the ship in that
light into all

that never
knew me alone

in the sea fellow
me feminine

winds as you pass

(*Primitive*, 1978)

Charles Olson [1910 – 1970]

from THE MAXIMUS POEMS

Maximus Letter # whatever

chockablock   Once a man was traveling through the woods, and
he heard some distance off a sound of feet beat-
ing the ground. He went to find the people who
made the sound, and it was a full week before
he came to them. It was a man and his wife danc-
ing around a tree in the top of which was a rac-
coon. By their constant treading they had worn
a trench in the ground, and were in it up to their
waists. When the man asked them why they did it
they said they were hungry and they were trying
to dance the tree down to catch the raccoon.

Now the man told them there was a better way to
fell a tree, a new way, and he showed them how to
cut it down. In return for which he asked the skin
if they had the meat of the raccoon. So they tanned
it and off he went.

Another distance, in the path in the forest, he
met another man who was carrying his house on his
head. He was frightened at first but the man put
his house down and shook hands with him, and while
they had a smoke together, and talked, the man
noticed the raccoon skin and asked where he got
it. He told him, from the dancing man and his wife.

This was enough to get the other started. He offered
him anything for the skin and finally the house. Look-
ing it over our man was delighted to find it had so
many rooms and such good furniture. But he said I
never could carry it as you do. Yes, sd the man who
belonged somewhere else, just try it, and he found he
could, it was as light as a basket.

So he went off carrying his house until night when
he came to a hard-wood ridge near a good spring of
water and put it down. Inside was a wide bed covered
with a white bear-skin, and it was very soft, and he
was tired and he slept very well. In the morning, it
was even better. Hanging from the beams were deer-
meat, hams, duck, baskets of berries and maple sugar,
and as he reached out for them the rug itself melted
and it was white snow, and his arms turned into wings
and he flew up to the food and it was birch-boughs on
which it hung, and he was a partridge and it was spring.

[II.31]

■

I forced the calm grey waters, I wanted her
to come to the surface I had fought her,
long enough, below. I shaped her out of
the watery mass

and the dragger, cleaning its fish,
idled into
the scene, slipped across the empty water
where I had placed
the serpent, staring as hard as
I could (to make the snow
turn back to snow, the autos
to come to their
actual size, to stop
being smaller,
and far away. The sea does
contain the beauty I had looked at
until the sweat
stood out in my eyes. The wonder is
limitless, of my own term, the compound
to compound until the beast rises from the sea.

Maximus, March 1961 - 1
[II.32]

■

3rd letter of Georges, unwritten

/In this place is a poem which I have not been able
to write—or a story to be called the Eastern End of
Georges, about a captain I knew about, as of the days
when it was important to race to market—to the Boston
market, or directly in to Gloucester, when she had fresh
fish, and how this man had such careful charts of his
own of these very shallow waters along the way
to market if you were coming in from the Winter Cod
Grounds on the Eastern End—the point was to cut the
corner, if you were that good or that crazy, though he
was as good as they come, he even had the charts marked
in different colored pencils and could go over those
rips and shoals dug out in a storm, driving a full-
loaded vessel and down to her deck edge, across them
as a wagon might salt licks or unship her wheels and
ferry across—it is a vision or at least an experience
I make off as though I have had, to ride with a man
like that—even have the picture of him sitting on
his cabin floor following those charts like a race-
sheet while taking the calls down the stern passage-
way and if it sounds more like Henry Ware & Paul Cot-
ter in the Eyes of the Woods, it could be so, for I've
looked & looked for the verification, and the details
of sail at a time when there were no engines—and I
went to James Connolly expecting to be able to depend
upon him, but somehow he hasn't come across, or it's
all too prettied up, and it was either Bohlin or Syl-
vanus Smith or it may have been someone as late as
Marty Callaghan but the roar of this guy going through
the snow and bent to a north easter and not taking any
round about way off the shoals to the north but going
as he was up & down dale like a horseman out of some
English novel makes it with me, and I want that sense
here, of this fellow going home/

[II.107]

∎

Monday, November 26th, 1962

        and his nibs crawled up

        and sitting on Piper's Rocks

        with a crown on his head

        and looking at me with a silly grin

        on his face: I had left him out

        of my monuments around the town

[II.140]

■

I

       he who walks with his house on

       his head is heaven he

       who walks with his house

       on his head is heaven he who walks

       with his house on his head

[II.141]

■

II

       she who met the serpent in the pond the adulteress

       who met the serpent in the pond

       and was kissed

       by him was wrapped in his

       coils

       she had to die if she could not pass, by fucking,

       the poison

       on if her husband would not fuck with her

and die if by fucking she could not get rid of the

poison after

she had fucked with the king of the pool

[II.142]

III

the woman who said she went out every Sunday

and walked right through the rock of the mountain

and on the other side she said she was fucked

by the Mountain

all that, was her joy

every day of the week, and she was the happiest

of the tribe,

and that was her explanation, given by her, of why

and that was how it was she was

so happy

November 1962

[II.143]

■

"at the boundary of the mighty world" H. (T) 620 foll.

                              Now Called Gravel Hill—dogs eat
                                                        gravel

          Gravelly hill was 'the source and end (or boundary' of
          D'town on the way that leads from the town to Smallmans
          now Dwelling house, the Lower
          Road gravelly, how the hill was, not the modern usableness
          of any thing but leaving it as an adverb as though the Earth herself
          was active, she had her own characteristics, she could
          stick her head up out of the earth at a spot
          and say, to Athena I'm stuck here, all I can show
          is my head but please, do something about
          this person I am putting up out of the ground into your hands

                    Gravelly hill 'father' Pelops otherwise known as
          Mud Face founder of
          Dogtown. That sort of 'reason': leave things alone.
          As it is there isn't a single thing isn't an opportunity
          for some 'alert' person, including practically everybody
          by the 'greed', that, they are 'alive', therefore. Etc.
          That, in fact, there are 'conditions'. Gravelly Hill
          or any sort of situation for improvement, when
          the Earth was properly regarded as a 'garden
          tenement messuage orchard and if this is nostalgia
          let you take a breath of April showers
          let's us reason how is the dampness in your
          nasal passage—but I have had lunch
          in this 'pasture' (B. Ellery to
                    George Girdler Smith
                    'gentleman'
                    1799, for
                    £150)

          overlooking
          'the town'
          sitting there like
          the Memphite lord of
          all Creation

with my back—with Dogtown
over the Crown of
gravelly
hill

It is not bad
to be pissed off

where there is *any*
condition imposed, by whomever, no matter how close

any
quid pro quo
get out. Gravelly Hill says
leave me be, I am contingent, the end of the world
is the borders
of my being

I can even tell you
where I run out; and you can find
out. I lie here
so many feet up
from the end of an old creek
which used to run off
the Otter ponds. There is a bridge
of old heavy slab stones
still crossing the creek on
the 'Back Road' about three rods
from where I do end northerly, and from my Crown
you may observe, in fact Jeremiah Millett's
generous pasture
which, in fact, is the first 'house'
(of Dogtown) is a part of the slide of
my back, to the East: it isn't so decisive
how one thing does end
and another begin to be very obviously dull about it
I should like to take the time to be dull
there is obviously very much to be done and the fire depart-
    ment
rushed up here one day—they called it
Bull Field, in the newspaper—when just that
side of me I am talking about,

which belonged to Jeremiah Millett
and rises up rather sharply
—it became Mr Pulsifer's and then,
1799, the property of the town
of Gloucester—was burned off.
My point is, the end of myself,
happens, on the east side (Erechthonios)
to be the beginning of another set
of circumstance. The road,
which has gone around me, swings
just beyond where Jeremiah Millett had his house
and there's a big rock about ends my being,
properly, swings
to the northeast, and makes its way
generally staying northeast in direction
to Dogtown Square or the rear of
William Smallman's
house where rocks pile up
darkness,
in a cleft in the earth
made of a perfect pavement
            Dogtown Square
of rocks alone March, the holy month
            (the holy month,
       LXIII
of nothing but black granite turned
every piece,
downward,
to darkness,
to chill
and darkness. From which the height above it even
in such a fearful congery
with a dominant rock like a small mountain
above the Hellmouth the back of Smallmans is
that this source and end of the way from the town into
the woods is only—as I am the beginning, and Gaia's
child—*katavóthra*. Here you enter
darkness. Far away from me, to the northeast,
and higher than I, you enter
the Mount,
which looks merry,
and you go up into it

feels the very same as the corner
where the rocks all are
even smoking a cigarette on the mount
nothing around you, not even the sky
relieves the pressure of this declivity
which is so rich and packed.
It is Hell's mouth
where Dogtown ends
(on the lower
of the two roads into
the woods.
I am the beginning
on this side
nearest the town
and it—this paved hole in the earth
is the end (boundary
Disappear.

[II.160–162]

■

Maximus, to Gloucester, Letter 157

an old Indian chief as hant
sat on the rock between
Tarantino's and Mr
Randazza's and scared the piss out of
Mr Randazza so he ran back into
his house

The house I live in, and exactly on the back stairs,
is the sight

of the story
told me by

Mr Misuraca, that,
his mother, reports

that, the whole Fort Section, is
a breeding ground of the ghosts of,

dogs, and that, on those very steps, she saw,
as a girl, a fierce, blue, dog, come at her,

as she was going out, the door

      The Tarentines
      were the pests

        of the coast, a bunch of shore Indians
        who raided as far south

        as Gloucester, and were themselves conceivably
        parts among the Algonquin people

        of them there 1000 AD Wikings:
        as these Sicilians

        talk an Italian
        which is Punic. For the Tarantinos

        were Micmacs, first spotted off La Have,
        and had been dealing,

        before they got down here,
        as traders with fishermen

        since the beginning
        of the occupation of the coast

        from whom they got
        knives and kettles

        and coats and then sold them
        stolen corn, from peaceful

Indians or shamefully cowardly
Indians who put up with these

Tarentines, huddling in their
shabby huts begging the new-come white man to

help them up against this raiding bunch
of old tough remnants of the older

coast. Or they were dogs, the Tarentinos,
come in to feed on the after coast,

after the white man disease
—the yellowing disease,

the Indians themselves called
what no man yet has diagnosed,

except that Indians,
who had been hauled,

to London,
seem somewhere,

to have brought it
back. These Tarentines

were intrusions
on all the coast, east

of Penobscot Bay

[II.178]

■

"home", to the shore

bu-te pu-bu bu-nu-šu

bayt. "house,"

to the

shore

pa-ba pa-'i-to "Phaistos"

    pa, as in a for

      Apple

    tu tuppûh

and bird or ku is "town":

kr-ku (Her headland, over

the sea-shore

               Saturday March 14th 1964

[III.50]

COLE'S ISLAND

I met Death—he was a sportsman—on Cole's
Island. He was a property-owner. Or maybe
Cole's Island, was his. I don't know. The
point was I was there, walking, and—as it
often is, in the woods—a stranger, suddenly
showing up, makes the very thing you were do-
ing no longer the same. That is suddenly
what you thought, when you were alone, and
doing what you were doing, changes because someone else
shows up. He didn't bother me, or say anything. Which is
not surprising, a person might not, in the circumstances;
or at most a nod or something. Or they would. But they wouldn't,
or you wouldn't think to either, if it was Death. And
He certainly was, the moment I saw him. There wasn't any question
about that even though he may have looked like a sort of country
gentleman, going about his own land. Not quite. Not it being He.

A fowler, maybe—as though he was used to
hunting birds, and was out, this morning, keeping
his hand in, so to speak, moving around, noticing
what game were about. And how they seemed. And how the woods
were. As a matter of fact just before he had shown up,
so naturally, and as another person might walk
up on a scene of your own, I had noticed
a cock and hen pheasant cross easily the
road I was on and had tried, in fact,
to catch my son's attention quick enough for him
to see before they did walk off into the bayberry
or arbor vitae along the road.

                     My impression is we did—
that is, Death and myself, regard each other. And
there wasn't anything more than that, only that he had appeared,
and we did recognize each other—or I did, him, and he seemed
to have no question
about my presence there, even though I was uncomfortable.
   That is,
Cole's Island

is a queer isolated and gated place, and I was only there by will
to know more of the topography of it lying as it does out
over the Essex River. And as it now is, with no tenants that one can speak of,
it's more private than almost any place one might imagine.
And down in that part of it where I did meet him (about half way between the
two houses over the river and the carriage house
at the entrance) it was as quiet and as much a piece
of the earth as any place can be. But my difficulty,
when he did show up, was immediately at least that I was
an intruder, by being there at all
and yet, even if he seemed altogether
used to Cole's Island, and, like I say, as though he owned it,
even if I was sure he didn't, I noticed him, and he me, and he
went on without anything extraordinary at all.

Maybe he had gaiters on, or almost
a walking stick, in other words much more
habited than I,
who was in chinos actually and
only doing what I had set myself to do here
& in other places on Cape Ann.

    It was his eye perhaps which makes me
render him as Death? It isn't true, there wasn't anything
that different about his eye,
    it was not one thing more than that he was Death instantly
that he came into sight. Or that I was aware there was a person
here as well as myself. And son.

    We did exchange some glance. That is the fullest possible
account I can give, of the encounter.

                    Wednesday, September 9th, 1964

[III. 69-70]

My shore, my sounds, my earth,
afterwards, in between, and since
my place

[III.110]

∎

Hector-body,

my Cow to the left my Cow to the right:

                              Goddess-

shield Ajax

  or the Knossian

who is compared to Enyalios

    crossed in Helladic to

Troy

    now moves on east from

west of Albany

            got home again,

    Wednesday

January 20th

  1965

[III.71]

■

the Mountain of no difference which I

have climbed as other men and other men will

have no choice other than: there is no other

choice, you do have to listen to that Angel and

'write'down what he says (you don't your

other Angel does and you obey him

to the degree that it is almost impossible to

keep doing, that's for sure!

But,

does this Vision hold in faith

(as well as in credulity) and in my own experience crucially in
                                                [necessity,

in perfect measure of rhyme and Truth,

does it, in beauty too, take me

test, stiffly the modus

of this visione which

not as modulus, this

, that is, measurement

"throughout the system"

modulus precise finite segments

—"There are no infinitesimals"

all does rhyme   like is the measure of

   producing like, the Guardian

   does dictate correctly the message

    is a discrete & continuous conduction

     of the life from a sequence of events measurable

in time   none of this is contestable,

there is no measure without it or

with anything but this measure:

—it does, my Beloved's head grows to Heaven,

     does my Life grow

out of my "life" Likewise—likewise?

    is the Modus

absolute? [I say it,

as a Prayer

     Dixit,
     February 11th
     1966
      [Friday]

[III.124-125]

■

JUST AS MORNING TWILIGHT AND THE GULLS, GLOUCESTER, MAY 1966 THE FULL FLOWER MOON

Just as morning twilight and the gulls start talking the cinnamon moon

goes down over Stage Fort park one night short of full as I too

almost full also leave all those whom I have thought were

equally moving equally at least as much a part of this world and

its character as these rounds of planets—the sun, within

thirty-one further minutes will have started lighting up the East across

East Gloucester arm and, if I add this house or its place on the

Earth, three solid powers of being pass in property and

principle acausal also in this empirical world as I,

and as I still cannot believe my friends aren't too, no matter

that they choose or may, identity itself a recognition cognition

—that this moon in itself is cinnamon and bore

an image in my life as it now going on to China will

twelve hours from now bring tides again on this side, reverse

flow to the effect of its presence here 12 other

hours—I do not speak of solar proton ion force

effect on both their & my—these two friends, a man & woman

I have had reason to say were my only brother-sister, never having

but one, a brother who died at birth a year before myself was born—

that they or I were not effected too in birth and or conception or

in both by either ions stored in earth or thrown at her by

the sun at equinox, like-fluctuation to the moon's twy-

tidal affect. Go down, moon and teach me too to

swallow what by analogy and continuity I now, at 55 know is

as much condition as the purchase of my soul by love as they

May 3rd, 1966

[III.138]

■

The sea's

boiling   the land's

boiling   all the winds

of the earth are turning

the snow into sand—and

hiss, the land into

desert sands   the place

into hell.   snow wild

snow and hissing

waters

Monday January 8th
[1968]

[III.186]

■

December 18th
=============

And the rosy red is gone, the

2nd—3rd—story of

the Mansfield house, the darker

flower of the

street — oh Gloucester

has no longer a West

end. It is a

part of the

country now a mangled

mess of all parts swollen

& fallen

into

degradation, each bundle un-

bound and scattered

as so many

units of poor

sorts and strangulation   all hung up each one

like hanged

bodies

And suddenly even the sky itself, and the sea

is rummy too (nature is

effected by

men is no more

than man's

acquisition or improvement

of her—or at least his entrance

into her

picture. If he

becomes bad

husbandman she

goes away into

her unreflected

existence. And the pole

    (—the Poles, the Poles

    of Bond's Hill, of

    what was then

    'Town') are

        down too, like the bricks

        of

        what was Main

            street are now

        fake gasoline station

        and A & P supermarket

        construction

the fake

which covers the emptiness

is the loss

in the 2nd instance of the

distraction.   Gloucester too

        is out of her mind and

        is now indistinguishable from

        the USA.

            "We are not a narrow tribe of men...we are not a

        nation, so much as a world."

                        H. Melville

                        Redburn (1849)

[III.202–204]

                        ■

the left hand is the calyx of the Flower
can cup all things within itself, nothing else
there, itself, alone limb of being, acting
in the beneficent air, holding all tenderness
as though it were the soul itself, the Soul's
limb

Sun April 20th 'LXIX

[III.208]

■

slownesses
which are an
amount

way into the woods by
an original
topographical
road, and by an otter pond

to forecast a tied
ellipse in which a story
is told and the ends of the strings are
laid over and stand

as though the air
began again another
story by another man

Monday June 23rd

[after night of Sunday
to Monday early a.m.
& now Monday 8 plus
PM]

[III.210]

■

I live underneath
the light of day

   I am a stone,
or the ground beneath

My life is buried,
with all sorts of passages
both on the sides and on the face turned down
to the earth
or built out as long gifted generous northeastern Connecticut stone
                                        [walls are

through which 18th century roads still pass
as though they themselves were realms,

the stones they're made up of
are from the bottom such Ice-age megaliths

and the uplands the walls are the boundaries of
are defined with such non-niggardly definition

of the amount of distance between a road in & out
of the wood-lots or further passage-ways, further farms
are given

      that one suddenly is walking

in Tartarian-Erojan, Geaan-Ouranian
time and life love space
    time & exact
analogy   time & intellect   time & mind   time & time
spirit

     the initiation

   of another kind of nation

[III.228]

     (all selections reprinted from *The Maximus Poems*, 1983)

Robert Duncan [1919 – 1988]

ROOTS AND BRANCHES

Sail, Monarchs, rising and falling
orange merchants in spring's flowery markets!
messengers of March in warm currents of news floating,
    flitting into areas of aroma,
tracing out of air unseen roots and branches of sense
    I share in thought,
filaments woven and broken where the world might light
    casual certainties of me. There are

    echoes of what I am in what you perform
this morning. How you perfect my spirit!
    almost restore
an imaginary tree of the living in all its doctrines
    by fluttering about,
intent and easy as you are, the profusion of you!
awakening transports of an inner view of things.

(Roots and Branches, 1964)

A DANCING CONCERNING A FORM OF WOMEN

Poets
in a company
of four
arranged themselves for me

feet first
Coleridge and Creeley,
necks and
heads next,

bodily Emily
from where she'd hid
but gladly
dauncing,

and a bold Lady.
"Who are you?"
I said
"in the name of four

lines limnd
rightly
and Poetry?"
"You forgot,"

she replied and led me
backwards, "Creeley's
ma-
gic pot

and consequently that
my foot
in each verse
counts, my lament

livens the tune,
re-
arranges their feet and faces,
gives four walls to the room."

Now how good of my friend
to go
wholly
enthralld to Her

and yet to remember
cannily
while dancing
to reach round

forward to what
is behind and to find
through Coleridge's side
some likely

remembrance of me,
being there
where I werent,
and his

lifting the skirt of things this way
to show the Lady's knee and thigh
and then
recovering the Lady's thigh and knee.

"I," replied this Form of Women,
"showd him these things under
oath
and privately,

that now
he must make the most of
and needs show
to thee."

(*Roots and Branches*, 1964)

STRUCTURE OF RIME XVIII

Kundry was Wagner's creation. And they brought Tefnut back, from her wilderness, into their company, brought the wilderness into the heart of Egypt, drinking and dancing before her in masks of the dog and the mandrill. Have you not seen the Muse's face? her tawny eyes, her lips curld back from her flashing teeth? Have you not held Kundry's laugh at bay? Knowest thou pathos, the poet's art before time's abyss?

Wagner's head floating where ours was, flukes of chords going out from passion into leitmotif, gatherings of fervent listeners in the place where I was. To be at the end of things. To be in the beginning. Evening's *rot*. The morning's red. The red flowing out into the orchestral twilight. Passionate twinklings in women's hair.

At mid-century the bells ring where we are the numbers are. The years go on as once before. The seasonal heroes, the changing stanzas, the unfolding melodies, the fashioning of eternities.

Now, in the wind, sparrows ride the tossing branches of the pyracanthus. The burnd sea smokes into spray in the slanting light. Upward the birds from the bronze berries go.

Let this time have its canto.

(*Roots and Branches*, 1964)

A NEW POEM (for Jack Spicer)

You are right. What we call Poetry is the boat.
The first boat, the body—but it was a bed.
    The bed, but it was a car.
And the driver or sandman, the boatman,
    the familiar stranger, first lover,
is not with me.

            You are wrong.
What we call Poetry is the lake itself,
the bewildering circling water way—
having our power in what we know nothing of,
in this having neither father nor son,

our never having come into it,
our never having left it,
our misnaming it, our
giving it the lie so that it lies.

I would not be easy
calling the shadowy figure who refuses to guide the boat
but crosses and recrosses the heart ...

—He breaks a way among the lily pads.
He breaks away from the directions
    we cannot give—

I would not be easy calling him
    the Master of Truth,
but Master he is of turning right and wrong.

I cannot make light of it.
The boat has its own light.

The weight of the boat
is not in the boat. He will not
give me images but I must
give him images.
He will not give me his name
but I must give him...

name after name I give him.
But I will not name the grave easily,
the boat of bone
so light it turns as if earth
were wind and water.

Ka, I call him. The shadow
wavers and wears my own face.

Kaka, I call him. The
whole grey cerement replaces itself and shows
a hooded hole.

From what we call Poetry a cock crows
away off there at the break of something.

Lake of no shores I can name,
Body of no day or night I can account for,
snoring in the throws of sleep I came
sleepless to the joint of this poem,
as if there were a hinge in the ways.

Door opend or closed,
knuckled down where faces of a boat join,
Awake Asleep
from the hooded hold of the boat
join in. The farthest shore is so near
crows fly up and we know it is America.

No crow flies. It is not America.
From what we call Poetry
a bird I cannot name crows.

(*Roots and Branches*, 1964)

BENDING THE BOW

We've our business to attend Day's duties,
bend back the bow in dreams as we may
til the end rimes in the taut string
with the sending. Reveries are rivers and flow
where the cold light gleams reflecting the window upon the
    surface of the table,
the presst-glass creamer, the pewter sugar bowl, the litter
    of coffee cups and saucers,
carnations painted growing upon whose surfaces. The whole
composition of surfaces leads into the other
            current disturbing
what I would take hold of. I'd been

in the course of a letter—I am still
in the course of a letter—to a friend,
who comes close in to my thought so that
the day is hers. My hand writing here
there shakes in the currents of ... of air?
of an inner anticipation of ... ? reaching to touch
ghostly exhilarations in the thought of her.

        At the extremity of this
            design
"there is a connexion working in both directions, as in
        the bow and the lyre"—
only in that swift fulfillment of the wish
            that sleep
        can illustrate my hand
            sweeps the string.

You stand behind the where-I-am.
The deep tones and shadows I will call a woman.
The quick high notes ... You are a girl there too,
  having something of sister and of wife,
            inconsolate,
and I would play Orpheus for you again,

        recall the arrow or song
        to the trembling daylight
        from which it sprang.

                    (*Bending the Bow*, 1968)

STRUCTURE OF RIME XXIII

Only passages of a poetry, no more. No matter how many times the cards are handled and laid out to lay out their plan of the future—a fortune—only passages of what is happening. Passages of moonlight upon a floor.

Let me give you an illusion of grieving. In the room at the clean sweep of moonlight a young man stands looking down. An agony I have spoken of overtakes him, waves of loss and return.

But he would withdraw from the telling. We cannot tell whether rage (which rimes) or grief shakes him. Let me give you an illusion of not grieving.

(*Bending the Bow,* 1968)

CHORDS   PASSAGES 14

For the Thing we call Moon contains

   "many mountains, many cities, many houses"

And Nature, our Mother,

   hides us, even from ourselves, there;

   showing only in changes of the Moon • Time

"a serpent having heads growing from him

  • *a bull and a lion,*

     the face of a god-man in the middle,

 and he has also wings, and is calld

 ageless, Xronos, father of the ages,

    and Herakles";

is called Eros, Phanes, χρονος ευαμαρης θεος

having the seeds of all things in his body,

   Protogonos, Erikepaios, Dionysos •

These are the Names.   Wind Child, ὑπηνεμον

     of our Night Nature

in the Moon Egg: First-Born, Not-Yet-Born,

     Born-Where-We-Are • Golden Wings,

the unlookt for light in the *aither*

     gleaming amidst clouds.

What does it mean that the Tritopatores, *"doorkeepers and guardians of the winds"*, carry the human Psyche to Night's invisible palace,   to the Egg

    where Eros sleeps,

  the Protoegregorikos, the First Awakend? To *waken* Him

   they carried her into   his Sleep, the winds

disturbing the curtains at the window, moving

   the blind, the first   tap tap, the first count or

heart beat • the guardians of the winds (words)

   lifting her as the line lifts meaning and would

light the light,   the crack of dawn in the Egg

   Night's nature shelters before Time.

Before Time's altars, our Mother-Nature

   lighting the stars in order, setting

Her night-light   in the window the Egg will be.

The breath of the stars, moving before the stars,

breath of great Nature,   our own,   Logos,

that is all   milk and light •

These things reborn within Zeus,   happening anew.

"A dazzling light .. aither .. Eros .. Night"

where we are

The first being Fairyland,   the Shining Land.

(*Bending the Bow*, 1968)

MY MOTHER WOULD BE A FALCONRESS

My mother would be a falconress,
And I, her gay falcon treading her wrist,
would fly to bring back
from the blue of the sky to her, bleeding, a prize,
where I dream in my little hood with many bells
jangling when I'd turn my head.

My mother would be a falconress,
and she sends me as far as her will goes.
She lets me ride to the end of her curb
where I fall back in anguish.
I dread that she will cast me away,
for I fall, I mis-take, I fail in her mission.

She would bring down the little birds.
And I would bring down the little birds.
When will she let me bring down the little birds,
pierced from their flight with their necks broken,
the heads like flowers limp from the stem?

I tread my mother's wrist and would draw blood.
Behind the little hood my eyes are hooded.
I have gone back into my hooded silence,
talking to myself and dropping off to sleep.

For she has muffled my dreams in the hood she has made me,
sewn round with bells, jangling when I move.
She rides with her little falcon upon her wrist.
She uses a barb that brings me to cower.
She sends me abroad to try my wings
and I come back to her. I would bring down
the little birds to her
I may not tear into, I must bring back perfectly.

I tear at her wrist with my beak to draw blood,
and her eye holds me, anguisht, terrifying.
She draws a limit to my flight.
Never beyond my sight, she says.
She trains me to fetch and to limit myself in fetching.
She rewards me with meat for my dinner.
But I must never eat what she sends me to bring her.

Yet it would have been beautiful, if she would have carried me,
always, in a little hood with the bells ringing,
at her wrist, and her riding
to the great falcon hunt, and me
flying up to the curb of my heart from her heart
to bring down the skylark from the blue to her feet,
straining, and then released for the flight.

My mother would be a falconress,
and I her gerfalcon, raised at her will,
from her wrist sent flying, as if I were her own
pride, as if her pride
knew no limits, as if her mind
sought in me flight beyond the horizon.

Ah, but high, high in the air I flew.
And far, far beyond the curb of her will,
were the blue hills where the falcons nest.
And then I saw west to the dying sun—
it seemd my human soul went down in flames.

I tore at her wrist, at the hold she had for me,
until the blood ran hot and I heard her cry out,
far, far beyond the curb of her will •

to horizons of stars beyond the ringing hills of the world where
  the falcons nest
I saw, and I tore at her wrist with my savage beak.
I flew, as if sight flew from the anguish in her eye beyond her sight,
sent from my striking loose, from the cruel strike at her wrist,
striking out from the blood to be free of her.

My mother would be a falconress,
and even now, years after this,
when the wounds I left her had surely heald,
and the woman is dead,
her fierce eyes closed, and if her heart
were broken, it is stilld •

I would be a falcon and go free.
I tread her wrist and wear the hood,
talking to myself, and would draw blood.

(*Bending the Bow,* 1968)

ACHILLES' SONG

I do not know more than the Sea tells me,
told me long ago, or I overheard Her
  telling distant roar upon the sands,
waves of meaning in the cradle of whose
  sounding and resounding power I
slept.
        Manchild, She sang

—or was it a storm uplifting the night
  into a moving wall in which
I was carried as if a mothering nest had
  been made in dread?

the wave of a life darker than my
    life before me sped, and I,
larger than I was, grown dark as
    the shoreless depth,
arose from myself, shaking the last
    light of the sun
from me.

        Manchild, She said,

Come back to the shores of what you are.
Come back to the crumbling shores.

    All night
the mothering tides in which your
    life first formd in the brooding
light   have quencht the bloody
    splendors of the sun

and, under the triumphant processions
    of the moon,   lay down
thunder upon thunder of an old
    longing,   the beat

of whose repeated spell
    consumes you.

  ••

           Thetis, then,
  my mother, has promised me
the mirage of a boat, a vehicle
    of water within the water,
and my soul would return from
    the trials of its human state,
from the long siege, from the
    struggling companions upon the plain,
from the burning towers and deeds
    of honor and dishonor,
the deeper unsatisfied war beneath
    and behind the declared war,
and the rubble of beautiful, patiently
    workt moonstones, agates, jades, obsidians,

turnd and returnd in the wash of
   the tides, the gleaming waste,
   the pathetic wonder,

words turnd in the phrases of song
   before our song …or are they

beautiful, patiently workt remembrances of those
   long gone from me,
returnd anew, ghostly in the light
   of the moon, old faces?

For Thetis, my mother, has promised
   me a boat,
a lover, an up-lifter of my spirit
   into the rage of my first element
rising, a princedom
   in the unreal, a share in Death.

      *

Time, time. It's time,

The business of Troy has long been done.

  ••

Achilles in Leuke has come home.

And soon you too will be alone.

            —December 10, 1968

[NOTE: In our Anglo-American convention we would pronounce the diph-thong in *Leuke* to foreshadow the rime in the word you—but in my hearing of the line, remembering the voice of H.D.'s reading from her *Helen in Egypt,* the name *Leuke* came to me sounded as in the German convention to echo the diphthong in *Troy.*]

          (*Ground Work: Before the War,* 1984)

A GLIMPSE

Come, yellow broom
and lavender in bloom,
the path runs down to the shady stream,

and yet by your magic and the loud bees'
    hum,
    perfume of sage and lavender in bloom,

hot and dreaming in the morning sun,
I ever from where I am return,
as if from this boyhood privacy
my life burnd on in a smoke of me,

mixt with sage in the summer air
    and lavender,
and the stream from its shade
runs down to the bay and beyond to the sea.

(*Ground Work: Before the War*, 1984)

PASSAGES 37

O!

The constellation glitters.   Stars abound.
In every house   the night's aglow.   The window

    ...
Is Χαω *Cow*? !

    Compounded   Earth   Milk Maker
    the sweet myth mounting
        stems
        that from the understuff grow

in conversations with the light
    life's laboratories

Gap
first large language into leaf

    I

       ever

  green

      horn play

   my music

as it goes

     it comes to me.

   The tip

of the tongue

   before the mouth sings,

   in labor

  ..

the world cow's lips

    from which

—What an opening of the night it is!—

    this window

   her dewy calf

from his confinement

    the poem from the heart in labor

  springs.

      (*Ground Work: Before the War*, 1984)

POEMS FROM THE MARGINS OF THOM GUNN'S *MOLY*

PREFACE to the Suite

I

Childhood, boyhood, young manhood
ached at the heart with it, the unnameable,
the incompletion of desires, and at the margins
shook. O Wind, South Wind, dark
and laden with long awaited rains,
in me a likeness that is yours sings
—always sang—and now that manhood has grown full
and half a century of the seasons rehearsed,
again, again, adolescent to what new man,
you come in dreams and to the margins of my thought
stray.

O Need, beloved Adversary to Love's settlements,
Invader, the halcyon days are over.
A violent season tears the depth of the blue.
The kingfisher turns from his studies where
his nature grows disquiet in him, some
wildness of a winter is all his, and
looks out upon the alterd scene it belongs to,
hunting.

Today belongs to you, to the music
about to be heard, the distant luring call recalld,
the strain, the estrangement from all I knew,
another knowledge straining to be free.

O deepest Unrest, indelibly engraved in me,
the wilderness beyond the edge of town, the riverbottom road,
the lingering, the wandering, the going astray,
to find some wanton promise the derelict landscape most portrayd
                                                            [in me,

the fog's sad density of cold,
in me, the solitary and deserted paths,
in me, the marshy wastes, the levee road
where day after day as if driven by the wind
I impatient strode, day driven after day,

until the rush of impending weather was most me
in me, the dumb about-to-be, the country way
incapable of speech driven toward impending speech.

I was never there. He was never there.
In some clearing before I reacht it
or after I was gone, some *he*
had laid him down to sleep where Pan
under his winter sun had roused the wildness with his song,
and, long lingering,
the air was heavy with his absence there—
Lord of the Heat of Noon still palpable
where late shadows chill the dreaming land.

2

Ghosts and lovers of my sixteenth year, old themes
and changing keys of a persisting music,
here, the colors fade, I cannot recall the face, there,
some pattern revivifies the scheme. What
was the accurate contour of the fathering dream?

The year my father died died into me and dyed
anew the green of green, the gold gold shone from,
the blue that colors seas and skies to speak
of sadness innocence most knew, and into Man
a mystery to take the place of fatherhood he grew
in me, a ghostly bridegroom fathering his bride in me,
an emptiness in which an absence I call *You*
was present, a pride, a bright unanswering bliss,
consumed my heart. It was a fiery ghost,
a burning substitution darkening all the sexual ways,
striving in those urgencies to speak, to speak,
to heal unutterable injuries. It was a wounded mouth,
a stricken thing unable to release its word,
a panic spring no youthful coming could exhaust in me.

(*Ground Work: Before the War,* 1984)

A LITTLE LANGUAGE

I know a little language of my cat, though Dante says
that animals have no need of speech and Nature
abhors the superfluous. My cat is fluent. He
converses when he wants with me. To speak

is natural. And whales and wolves I've heard
in choral soundings of the sea and air
know harmony and have an eloquence that stirs
my mind and heart—they touch the soul. Here

Dante's religion that would set Man apart
damns the effluence of our life from us
to build therein its powerhouse.

It's in his animal communication Man is
    true, immediate, and
in immediacy, Man is all animal.

His senses quicken in the thick of the symphony,
    old circuits of animal rapture and alarm,
attentions and arousals in which an identity rearrives.
    He hears
particular voices among
    the concert,   the slightest
rustle in the undertones,
    rehearsing a nervous aptitude
yet to prove *his*. He sees the flick
    of significant red within the rushing mass
of ruddy wilderness and catches the glow
    of a green shirt
to delite him in a glowing field of green
    —it *speaks* to him—
and in the arc of the spectrum   color
    speaks to color.
The rainbow articulates
    a promise he remembers
he but imitates
    in noises that he makes,

this speech in every sense
    the world surrounding him.

He picks up on the fugitive tang of mace
  amidst the savory mass,
and taste in evolution is an everlasting key.
  There is a pun of scents in what makes sense.

  Myrrh it may have been,
the odor of the announcement that filld the house.

  He wakes from deepest sleep

upon a distant signal   and waits

  as if crouching, springs

  to life.

(*Ground Work: Before the War*, 1984)

LETTING THE BEAT GO

    Letting the beat go,
    the eagle, we know, does not
    soar to the stars, he rides
    the boundaries of the air—

    but let the "eagle"
    soar to the stars! there
    where he's "sent"! The stars
    are blazons then of a high glamor
        the mind beholds
    —less "real" for that?—
        a circling power.
    In holding so he flies, an idea
        increasing exaltation
    we know in the idea of it, a tower!

    O farflung valiant eagle
        venturing in immensities,
    wingd hunger   sent amongst starry
            powers,
    seraphic predator!

I'd hover here, a wheel of
   all the real life here below
   swept up—
   the glutted cities, choked streams,
   you think I do not know them all,
   the "facts" of this world, most
        in this mere sweeping-up?

They are the facts from which I fly

  aloft,

beyond our conversation, imperial,

insensate, "high",

  beyond this matter of our speech here,
  into this furthest reach, this

incidence of a rapacious

  silence,

gnostic invader of the "Sky"!

      (Ground Work: Before the War, 1984)

THE PRESENCE OF THE DANCE /
THE RESOLUTION OF THE MUSIC

  He had determined to dance the presence of the dance. He had been in fact determined to dance the presence of the dance, and, taking his stand then, in the determining, he found he took his stand in the presence of the dance.

  I am addressing a proposition of moving in a declaration independently of moving. He was about to be moving or he moves into being moving until an absolute stillness became possible. "Now" appeard to him in order to give him time to dance where he was moving. This lookt at first as if he could return to a place where he just now was. And he stood between simply standing and taking his stand. There was a weight awaiting something. "I can no longer stand it" came into it, and he came up to the edge of it: the dance ground was moving thruout toward and from an "it" he had now to confront.

Here he would have created the freedom not to have to confront "it", had the freedom of the dance not so entirely concernd him. I have fallen in love with the presence of the dance whom now I see then so that before me there will be as ever there is an other dancer. Where I am he calld "here", and where he is I will call "there". It became possible to change places.

At this stage he made a sign to read THE PRESENCE OF THE DANCE and, waking early in the morning before dawn, he wrote down instructions for the Imagination of the Dance.

"Everywhere thruout I alone will be there," he thought. "Everywhere there will be room meant for an other." This one each time will be calld first a thing happening in the dance, so that in the time of dancing there must be a company of dances to make a life. All in order to perform in its varieties the Presence of the Dance.

"We are entitled to dance *The Presence of the Dance*," he announced.

TWO

There are those in time moving in a great circle so that the figure of circling round comes into time. From time to time, even as the dancers pass around from dancer to dancer so that the circle is circling, lives pass so that the dancers are living. And sometimes, as I am moved now by the appearance of the living, Death appears to be dying in the Presence of the Dance.

This is to confess that all the time the Presence of the Dance has been present to me. I was calld into that presence. When I was a child, the world, the skies rolling with clouds, the whispering trees, the opening reaches of a country to be, would call me out of doors, to wandering in search of what was to be out there. Even as this morning calld me to write the Presence of the Dance and the Resolution of the Music for you, and I knew it was for you this very morning was calling me.

My Love, for a moment you present yourself or I present you, and this Presence, this Lord of Title, for he has title to me here, is the Night upon whose reaches this morning calld to me. Oberon, you said, you were to dance. Your role comes into the romance of a play the mind has been following. I said he was the Moon. But how entirely my thought ever circled you, taking the radiance of a dark Sun for kindling.

Did I want so to come into the question of an abyss of feeling? The whole company dancing I went round from dancer to dancer as if the Presence of the Dance were every where there beckoning, alluring. Each place a lure eluding me. Everywhere lingering, leaving me to wonder. Where I am. Left. Thruout now I am looking for you.

THREE

Glancing passes from eye to eye thruout the company. "As if an amusement had started up from where she had been sleeping. Merle Oberon turns round in the heart of the company where I cannot see him any longer I am entirely missing her in him." The moment calls for the presentation to be unbearably coy. It is when I can no longer follow the star flares.

FOUR

I am trying now to write of my calling, of order, of the order of dancers from left to right thruout the company. The members of the Dance in which I am writing. How lonely this remembering of the Dance is, this remembering of ever being calld. This memory of clouds advancing across the sky calling, this calling up of something startling in me, this about to be happening in the moving from left to right.

At the heart of morning, this memory of a darkness is kindling. Seeds of fire light flickering before the oncoming shadows his eyes his eyes bestow. Her his grey light eyes cast for me.
 Even as I am calld to dance, the fire of the dance devours me. Unknowing, the Prince of Darkness, my lover, has taken my heart away into knowing.

FIVE

In the longest night of the Year, awakening to where they are dancing a Midsummer's Night's dream out of time, a winter's tale or double take of lovers changing places with lovers in fidelity, a spectacle of powers to see by and the bewilderment of our poor hearts at the shortest end of our night watch. Let me be the Moon and stand in the shadow of that Wall I see or be it Well *over there* I saw in whose eyes again I will yet be beyond what I am. I would be the Moon crying. The tears of the Moon flow from me as if I were bereft of belonging, and so much a creature of the Night that my longing falls like a shadow before Day into the furnaces of the Sun. The flaring-up blinds me.

SO THAT THERE MIGHT BE A MUSIC

I

He is dancing in the change of humors the blackbird fairy prince of darkness clouded in a cloak of rumorous night he dwindles to the deep purple shadow under a leaf,

Marilyn, the shy girl laddy we were hiding from afraid to seek and now as in a spotlight of her drowning finding his own shining reveals herself anew to be our Merlin we knew long ago in our first reading the story we told.

•••

It is a question of his music. A questing of music for him. His muse. Meant for him.

The audience grows restive and they are disrobing. They want to be naked to hear what they are watching. This is the allure of music. They see him as Oberon, le Merle Noir. But he does not want there to be naked people there in the sound he has meant to be pure.

> O Love, how had we forgotten the
> Night Watch, the audience the Presence
> granted us, the Hearing we sought
> in the Courts of this Law.

2

"The title of the next piece is *The Presence of the Dance*."
"Again?"

"I love the feel of the house lights falling into darkness with only the hearth glow of the orchestra pit and the rise of the instruments tuning. The whole of the music could be in these tunings."
"Those are only noises and sounds, nasals and prenasal wheezings."
"Whistlings, whisperings, whiskings."
"Hush" — "Yes, hushing too.." *Coming to after listening.*

"I love the feel of a deep stillness in which there is no waiting to hear."
"O yes, dear, I am still here." — "My mind is wandering."
"Wait for me!" — "I am through out a waiting."
"Listenings, listings."

"What is happening is so truly naked and fully here it floods out taking over from our wanting what we were waiting for. It takes time from us." Keep time in the courses of dancing too.

3

"I thought of the theme as a tree, as the life of a tree flowing out season after season
into limbs rounding and a summer's foliage, into green growth anew and the deep
bare slumber of old age winter declares. The ring of dancers year upon year sur-
rounding the time of the thematic tree."

"I thought of the melody as the continuation of an Identity in a number of ways"
—*coming into the Presence of the Dance.*

"How does id sound now?"   —   "Again?"

"As I was coming along it was before me."

(*Ground Work: Before the War*, 1984)

Robin Blaser [1925]

THE FINDER

on the windows, the dirty film
in the sunlight   shaped by the shadows
of apple trees   dry winter branches

on English Bay   a ship appears,
its hiding over   two masts, a doubling
of the cross   two Christs

one matching the other   where
the world dies

the tabloids of fire, a Sunday supplement
to the San Francisco Examiner   out of place,
in this time   rises from the page

in a lightning storm   which holds
this man at the horizon in his apocalypse,
a war burning, if the heart scores

bodiless, a curious blood and reasons
in ourselves inheriting the intellect
from out there defined by a President

who is violence in this world,
a definition of this destiny we have
effected   all's well without

'your' intelligence where the world dies
I bend 'you' to my mouth
and suck 'your' breath away
only worlds caught

in the glinting lights of those
pieces of glass   found in the
forest   under a tree   crushed

and shining

for Louis Zukofsky

SUDDENLY,

I live in a room named East
on the map of the West   at the edge

near the door cedars and alders
mix and tower,
full of ravens   first thing each morning,
whose song is
          a sharpness

we quarrelled so
            over the genius
of the heart
          whose voice is capable

they come on horseback
in the middle of the night,
two of them,   with a horse for me,
and we ride,   bareback
clinging to the white manes
at the edge of the sea-splash,

burst open,

          to divine
the hidden and forgotten source,
who is transparent
where the moon drops out of the fog
to bathe,
but not to us

the retied heart
    where the wind glitters

for Ellen Tallman

(*Image-Nations 12 - 14, etc.,* 1975)

'THE UNIVERSE IS PART OF OURSELVES'

we have been everywhere, suddenly,
and twisted the clarities into bottles
and casements

it was the lintel concerned us
we walked through and wondered
above us

the larks of heaven perch and nothing

over the walls, the vision gossips
like rivers, and wishes, marvellous,
perishes

we have been everywhere, suddenly,
glorious texture   the chorus added
eagerness, swiftness

intellect whispers, meanders, softly
landed   remarkable ponds and
cattails

the ferns dream as they return
to green   the efformation, the
dis-creation, the kindness of fragments

the larks of heaven perch and nothing

for bpNichol

(*Pell Mell,* 1988)

THE RULER

alligator, hippopotamus, fox, rhinoceros
and frog
dog, bear, cat, mouse and badger
in rowing shells   frog and badger
with the megaphones   they're rowing to
a finish

it begins in the womb—with sound—in the tissue—speech
is later—the music of words

your eyes are wooden   where are the
deep pools   the moment of trees
and their suddenness among
thwarted winds around skyscrapers
and umbrellas

your eyes are like wood, yet she
talked to the images of kings and
queens, like everybody else, having
the power to be one

but that was because of cancer
and her eyes yellowed   she had
more life than I knew in her
rowing shell, gently, sweet river

and the images she spoke to were
not small and included the
little match girl frozen and
fiery outside the windows

she of such searching, who felled
the tree and planed the boards—'chuck   chuck
chuck   of the adze'

the ruler is a child's 25 centimetre
measure of the old foot—how tall are you?—
they are rowing in three dimensions,
never to get there

alligator, hippopotamus, fox, rhinoceros,
and frog
dog, bear, cat, mouse and badger,
in the shell of a boat, enchanted,
with honey wrapped up in the intelligence
between one boat and another

(*Pell Mell*, 1988)

AH.

under you, over you, on you,
about you, slaked in a desert, the
pools, the shadow of a face,
a perfect answer, it was not
myself I could not imagine, it
was the substance of no understanding,
leaning over the waterfront, going
out to sea, of honey and milk and
crackers

on the other hand, founded on
actual existence   the pool played
with its ripples widening to the edge,
growing the watercress, the
iced surface, the dinner table
sparkled with lamps, and the
silver moon waned into happy
nightingales and bright forests

(*Pell Mell*, 1988)

EVEN ON SUNDAY

I don't know anything about God but what the human record tells
me—in whatever languages I can muster—or by turning to
translators—or the centuries—of that blasphemy which defines god's
nature by our own hatred and prayers for vengeance and dominance—
that *he* (lower case and questionable pronoun) would destroy by a
hideous disease one lover of another   or by war, a nation for what
uprightness and economic hide-and-seek—and *he* (lower case and
questionable pronoun) is on the side of the always-ignorance of politics
in which we trust—the *polis* is at the "bottom of the sea," as Hannah
Arendt noticed—and *he* (lower case and interrogated pronoun) walks
among the manipulated incompetences of public thought

where I had hoped to find myself ordinary among others in the streets—
a "murmuring voice of societies"

and so one thinks them over—blasphemies all, against multiplicity,
which is all anyone knows about god—and one can only hate them
so much without becoming *halt and lame in their kingdom of single
mindedness*—their having taken a book to have been once and forever,
the language behind language that no one has ever spoken   god's
what-knot and *mystical rags* we call flags

as a friend said, "I'm going to become fundamentalist and call
everybody asshole"

and what would the gods be if I asked them—our nakedness didn't
quite fit—out, as it is, of nature—yet, there is a sentiment at *the
intersection between life and thought*—streaks of beyondness in that
careless relation

                    October came in August and petunias straggled,
sprawling white faces one at a time, lobelia browned and continued
blue   the neighbors cut down the sexual cottonwood which kept the
whole block from repainting door-steps for over a month—by the
fluffs of its happiness—

so we are in the midst of a *metaphysical washout*—take for example,
Verlaine and Rimbaud—as Hans Mayer says: *Being shut out of the
social order, they sought to heighten their condition by, say, publically embracing
in Brussels and thus providing the formula for a new 'condition humaine'*

that called out to be created—both failed—both remained in *outsiderdom*
—one continued to rhyme, the other gave up the whole damned
creation   behind this, an Enlightenment, which I'll return to
      and Sylvie asked,
"But what became of the Man?"
"Well, the Lion springed at him. But it came so slow, it were
three weeks in the air—"
"Did the Man wait for it all that time?" I asked
"Course he didn't!" Bruno replied, gliding head-first down the
stem of a fox-glove, for the story was evidently close to its end.
"He sold his house, and he packed up his things, while the Lion were coming.
And he went and lived in another town. So the Lion ate the wrong man."
      *This was evidently the Moral...*said Lewis Carroll

the moral is that something does devour the *existential given*—
Rimbaud, Mayer writes, *does not intertwine with visions of Sodom in order*
to provoke heaven's fire; it is simply the sole possibility of his own self-acceptance

being shut out of the social order   Rimbaud writes *de posséder la verité*
dans une âme et un corps, which Mayer interprets to say *being alive in*
the full sense of body and soul   the truth is being alive, until you break
on it

ah, Laius, when you ran off with the youth Chryssipus, the Sphinx
flew to a whistling stop in Thebes—and fire fell on Sodomites, on
each one of them, and, I'll be damned, almost everybody—tell me a
tale to explain sublime biology—then, tell me another to explain
sublime human nature—and murder, unmythologized, fell on 20th-
century outsiders   pollution of what in the momentary hangup of
the vast biology of things, desiring?   a covenant with whom?
    androsphinx, recumbent lion with the head of a man, answer me—
that is to say, each one of us

the sublime, dear everybody and everyday, is not so simply human—
overwhelms—*uncanny* is Hannah Arendt's word for the face of it—
dangerous—*severe, as a blow*—*mysterious*—on which the *existential*
given floats—the passions of

and Hans Mayer notes the tying and untying that confines things:
At the height of the Victorian era, the Bible is once again, as in Cromwell's
time,...the spiritual and social foundation of everyday life—O, the once-
again in which we trust—*Declaration is made in the Bible of what is*
proper for woman and what is not. The Bible depicts that which God punished

in Sodom. St. Paul only confirmed the curse   one's mind may have a
certain affinity with Christopher Marlowe's, if it is true, as his roommate
Thomas Kyd tells us, that he thought the apostle Paul a swindler—
who taught a curdled godhead and a curdling view of the *existential
given*—and the black milk of it is blasphemy, so to revile existence

in the midst of this, an Enlightenment which first and foremost posited
an *equality of men and women, including homosexuals*—religion and
sexuality go hand in hand in the apple-light

it was not to be merely law, like free speech, but a *mental practice*
     what developed, in the guise of a Darwinian terror advancing in
evolutionary form, was the lion body with a man's head, walking in
the garden, so that *the underlying principles of liberty and equality, not
even taking fraternity into account, inordinately encouraged combatting all
forms of outsiderdom in favor of what Ihab Hassan calls 'quantities of normed
phenomena'*—normed existence excludes the *existential given,* not being
alive in the full sense of body and soul—and *extends, not merely perverts*
that which calls itself normality into political form but Mayer asks, *what
is it then if the precipitating step outside, into the margins, is a condition of
birth, a result of one's sex, parentage, physical or spiritual makeup?   Then
one's existence itself becomes a breaking of boundaries*

we can thereby return to ourselves a *measure of freedom,* and take form—
the work of a lifetime—in this breaking of boundaries—
                                                              against,
as Mayer says, *a global disposition of thought toward annihilation, which
thinks to admit only majorities in the future and is determined to equate
minorities with 'worthless life'   Worthless are the Jews, there the blacks [and
aboriginals], somewhere else (and everywhere) the homosexuals, women of the
type of Judith and Delilah, not least the intellectuals keen on individuation....*

"They should all be gassed": the expression has crept into everyday language

*Woman is not equal to man. Man is a manly man, whatever is to be understood
by that: the feminine man stands out from the race and thereby becomes worthless
life. Shylock must be exterminated: the only final solutions are fire and gas*

extreme remedies—pharmakons—Mayer reminds us, have been
proposed: for example, Klaus Mann writing in 1949—remember
when that was!—*calls for...the concerted mass suicide of intellectuals: to
bring public opinion in the world, in the integrity and autonomy of which he
quite clearly still believed, to its right senses*

well, we know now that this would disappear with a headline in the
Entertainment pages, or it might make the Arts and Books section
along with obituaries and sportsmanship, in the *Globe & Mail*—and
intellectuals?—Mann had not noticed that point in the space of
intelligence where they join the system, higgledy-piggledy—I think
of that recent hustle in the United States, offering the end of history
like a dinky-toy, democracy, pinking, blueing, and off-whiting in plastic
—"My goodness!" everyone said, "They've discovered Hegel!" and *Time
Magazine* thought he was little known—and I said, "My goodness!
Francis Fukuyama, so we finally got here, there, anywhere"

so to be reminded once again of Puddin'head Wilson: *It was wonderful
to find America, but it would have been more wonderful to miss it*

this unified mankind—for that's who's there, quantity or lump, at the
end of a materialist's or an idealist's history—*conceived,* Mayer writes,
as a homogenized humanity. Woe to outsiders

so that was it, was it? an *Enlightenment that promised equality to men and
women, including homosexuals!*   an age in the hole, running three
centuries, surely allows one to say, "Listen, you assholes, a *metaphysical
washout* means you've lost your top soil"

and this system aims exactly—*at the heart of our social existence*   to
be an outsider *by virtue of our existence*—like statues come to life by
moonlight in the child's desiring mind—has the advantage of voices,
and their attentions, each to each, among quantified multitudes who
wander *the computations and rationalities that belong to no one*—also going,
going, gone into the *corpus Christianum* which its sadly separated body
and soul

among these voices, I think of Montaigne: *Embraces remembered (or still
vaguely hoped for) are 'our final accolades'*

in whose arms

even on Sunday

with considered use of
Hans Mayer's *Outsiders*
written for Gay Games III,
Vancouver, August 1990

(*The Holy Forest,* 1993)

Jack Spicer [1925 – 1965]

LAMENT FOR THE MAKERS

No call upon anyone but the timber drifting in the waves
Those blocks, those blobs of wood.
The sounds there, offshore, faint and short
They click or sound together—drift timber spending the night
   there floating just above this beach. Thump or sound
   together. The sound of driftwood the sound that is not
   really a sound at all.
At all
All of them
Cast
In the ghost of moonlight on them
On shore.

                                (Lament for the Makers, 1962)

THE BOOK OF GALAHAD

I

Backyards and barnlots
If he only could have stopped talking for a minute he could
   have understood the prairies of American
Whitman, I mean, not Galahad who were both born with the
   same message in their throats
Contemplating America from Long Island Sound or the Grail
   from purity is foolish, not in a bad sense but fool-ish as if
   words or poetry could save you.
The Indians who still walked around the Plains were dead and
   the Grail-searchers were dead and neither of them knew it.
Innocent in the wind, the sound of a real bird's voice
In-vented.

172

2

Galahad was invented by American spies. There is no reason to
   think he existed.
There are agents in the world to whom true and false are
   laughable. Galahad laughed
When he was born because his mother's womb had been so
   funny. He laughed at the feel of being a hero.
Pure. For as he laughed the flesh fell off him
And the Grail appeared before him like a flashlight.
Whatever was to be seen
Underneath.

3

"We're off the see the Wizard, the wonderful Wizard of Oz,"
Damned Austrailians marching into Greece on a fool's errand.
The cup said "Drink me" so we drank
Shrinking or rising in size depending how the bullets hit us
Galahad had a clearer vision. Was an ss officer in that war or a
   nervous officer (Albanian, say), trying to outline the cup
   through his glasses.
The Grail lives and hovers
Like bees
Around the camp and their love, their corpses. Honey-makers
Damned Austrailians marching into Greece on a fool's errand.

4

To drink that hard liquor from the cold bitter cup.
I'll tell you the story. Galahad, bastard son of Elaine
Was the only one allowed to find it. Found it in such a way that
   the dead stayed dead, the waste land stayed a waste land.
   There were no shoots from the briers or elm trees.
I'll teach you to love the Ranger Command
To hold a six-shooter and never to run
The brier and elm, not being human endure
The long walk down somebody's half-dream. Terrible.

5

Transformation then. Becoming not a fool of the grail like the
　　others were but an arrow, ground-fog that rose up and
　　down marshes, loosing whatever soul he had in the shadows
Tears of ivy. The whole lost land coming out to meet this
　　soldier
Sole dier in a land of those who had to stay alive,
Cheat of dream
Monster
Casually, ghostlessly
Leaving the story
And the land was the same
The story the same
No hand
Creeping out of the shadows.

6

The Grail was merely a cannibal pot
Where some were served and some were not
This Galahad thinks.

The Grail was mainly the upper air
Where men don't fuck and women don't stare
This Galahad thinks.

The Grail's alive as a starling at dawn
That shatters the earth with her noisy song
This Galahad thinks.

But the Grail is there. Like a red balloon
It carries him with it up past the moon
Poor Galahad thinks.

Blood in the stars and food on the ground
The only connection that ever was found
Is what rich Galahad thinks.

7

The Grail is as common as rats or seaweed
Not lost but misplaced.
Someone searching for a letter that he knows is around the
    house
And finding it, no better for the letter.
The grail-country damp now from a heavy rain
And growing pumpkins or artichokes or cabbage or whatever
    they used to grow before they started worrying about the
    weather. Man
Has finally no place to go but upward: Galahad's
Testament.

                    End of Book of Galahad

                                    (*The Holy Grail*, 1964)

                    THING LANGUAGE

    This ocean, humiliating in its disguises
    Tougher than anything.
    No one listens to poetry. The ocean
    Does not mean to be listened to. A drop
    Or crash of water. It means
    Nothing.
    It
    Is bread and butter
    Pepper and salt. The death
    That young men hope for. Aimlessly
    It pounds the shore. White and aimless signals. No
    One listens to poetry.

                          □

SPORTING LIFE

The trouble with comparing a poet with a radio is that radios
    don't develop scar-tissue. The tubes burn out, or with a
    transistor, which most souls are, the battery or diagram
    burns out replaceable or not replaceable, but not like that
    punchdrunk fighter in the bar. The poet
Takes too many messages. The right to the ear that floored him
    in New Jersey. The right to say that he stood six rounds with
    a champion.
Then they sell beer or go on sporting commissions, or, if the
    scar tissue is too heavy, demonstrate in a bar where the
    invisible champions might not have hit him. Too many of
    them.
The poet is a radio. The poet is a liar. The poet is a
    counterpunching radio.
And those messages (God would not damn them) do not even
    know they are champions.

□

I hear a banging on the door of the night
Buzz, buzz; buzz, buzz; buzz, buzz
If you open the door does it let in light?
Buzz, buzz, buzz, buzz; buzz, buzzz.

If the day appears like a yellow raft
Meow, meow; meow, meoww
Is it really on top of a yellow giraffe
Meow, meow, meow, meow. Meow, meow

If the door caves in as the darkness slides
Knocking and knocking; knock, knock, knock
What can tell the light of whatever's inside?
Knocking and knocking; knock, knock, knock

Or the light and the darkness dance in your eye
Shadows falling one by one
Pigs, and eels, and open sky
Dancers falling one by one
Dancers shrieking one by one.

□

Baseball Predictions, April 1, 1964

National League   American League

1. Philadelphia   1. President DeGaulle
2. Los Angeles   will be assassinated
3. Houston   by a Communist named
4. San Francisco   John Foster Oswald before
5. Milwaukee   the Yankees clinch
6. St. Louis   the pennant.
7. Cincinnati
8. Pittsburgh
9. Chicago
10. New York

□

The log in the fire
Asks a lot
When it is lighted
Or knot

Timber comes
From seas mainly
Sometimes burns green
-Ly

When it is lighted
The knot
Burns like a joke
With the color of smoke

Save us, with birthdays, whatever is in the fire or not in the
                                                    [fire,
   immortal
We cannot be
A chimney tree
Or give grace to what's mere-
Ly fatal.

☐

Finally the messages penetrate
There is a corpse of an image—they penetrate
The corpse of a radio. Cocteau used a car radio on account of
    NO SPEED LIMIT. In any case the messages penetrate the
    radio and render it (and the radio) ultimately useless.
Prayer
Is exactly that
The kneeling radio down to the tomb of some saint
Uselessness sung and danced (the radio dead but alive it can
    connect things
Into sound. Their prayer
Its only connection.

☐

Heros eat soup like anyone else. Sometimes the kitchen is so far
    away
That there is no soup. No kitchen. An open space of ground
    recovered by
The sky.
Heros eat soup like anyone else. False ground.

Soup
Of the evening
Beautifull soup.
And the sky stays there not an image
But the heros
Like the image of an image
(What is made of soup from)
Zooms.

☐

Smoke signals
Like in the Eskimo villages on the coast where the earthquake
  hit
Bang, snap, crack. They will never know what hit them
On the coast of Alaska. They expect everybody to be insane.
This is a poem about the death of John F. Kennedy.

□

A redwood forest is not invisible at night. The blackness covers it but it covers the blackness.

If they had turned Jeffers into a parking lot death would have been eliminated and birth also. The lights shine 24 hours a day on a parking lot.

True conversation is the effort of the artist and the private man to keep things true. Trees and the cliffs in Big Sur breathe in the dark. Jeffers knew the pain of their breath and the pain was the death of a first-born baby breathing.

Death is not final. Only parking lots.

□

The whorship of beauty
Of beautiful things take a long time getting used to.
There is no past in beauty. The car going at 97.5 miles an hour.
  The time changes
As you cross each border.
Daffodils, ceremonies of spring, sprang, sprung
And it is August
Another century.
Take each past, combine it with its present. Death
Is a tooth among
Strangers.

□

It comes May and the summers renew themselves
(39 of them) Baseball seasons
Utter logic
Where a man is faced with a high curve.
No telling what happened in this game. Except one didn't strike
     out. One feels they fielded it badly at second base.
Oceans of wildflowers. Utter logic of the form and color.

                              □

       Thanatos, the death-plant in the skull
       Grows wings and grows enormous.
       The herb of the whole system.
       Systematically blotting out the anise weed and the trap-door
             spider of the vacant lot.
       Worse than static or crabgrass.
       Thanatos, bone at the bottom, Saint
       Francis, that botanist in Santa Rosa
       (Bless me now, for I am a plant and an animal)
       Called him Brother Death.

                              □

1st SF Home Rainout Since. Bounce Tabby-Cat Giants.
     Newspapers
Left in my house.
My house is Aquarius. I don't believe
The water-bearer
Has equal weight on his shoulders.
The lines never do.
We give equal
Space to everything in our lives. Eich-
Mann proved that false in killing like you raise wildflowers.
     Witlessly
I
Can-
not
accord
sympathy

to
those
who
do
not
recognize
The human crisis.

□

The country is not very well defined.
Whether they are bat-people or real people. The sea-
Coast of Bohemia. The in-
Visible world.
A man counts his fingers in these situations. Whether there are
    five or ten of them or udders as we might go sea-bathing in
    dream.
But dream is not enough. We waking hear the call of the
In-
Visible world
Not seen. Hinted at only. By some vorpals, some sea-lions,
    some scraggs.
Almost too big to get used to, its dimensions amaze us, who are
    blind to Whatever
Is rising and falling with us.

□

I squint my eyes to cry
(No tears, a barren salt-mine) and then take two sniffles
    through my nose
This means emotion. Chaplinesque
As the fellow says.
We pantomime every action of our bodies
Do not wait
On one sad hill
For one sad turn. I've had it
Principly because you're young.

□

The metallurgical analysis of the stone that was my heart shows
   an alarming percentage of silicon.
Silicon, as George would be the first to tell you, is not a metal.
   It is present in glass, glue and since glue is made from horses
   —living substance.
I love you. But as the iron clangs, the glass, the glue, the living
   substance (which, God knows, has been to as many glue
   factories as it can remember) muffles what the rest of the
   heart says.
I see you cowering in the corner and the metal in my heart
   bangs. Too personal
The glass and glue in my heart reply. And they are living
   substance.
You cannot bake glass in a pie or fry glue in an omelette
"If I speak in the tongue of men and angels..."
The sounding brass of my heart says
"Love."

                                          (*Language,* 1965)

TRANSFORMATIONS

Transformations 1

They say "he need (present) enemy (plural)"
I am not them. This is the first transformation.
They say "we need (present) no enemy (singular)" No enemy in
   the universe is theirs worth having. We is an intimate
   pronoun which shifts its context almost as the I blinks at it.
   Those
Swans we saw in the garden coming out of the water we hated
   them. "Out of place," you said in passing. Those swans and
   I (a blink in context), all out of place we hated you.
He need (present) enemy (plural) and now it is the swans and
   me against you
Everything out of place
(And now another blink of moment) the last swan back in
   place. We
Hated them.

Transformations II

"In Scarlet Town where I was born
There was a fair maid dwelling."
We make up a different language for poetry
And for the heart—ungrammatical.
It is not that the name of the town changes
(Scarlet becomes Charlotte or even in Gold City I once heard a
   good Western singer make it Tonapah. We don't have
   towns here)
(That sort of thing would please the Jungian astronauts)
But that the syntax changes. This is older than towns.
Troy was a baby when Greek sentence structure emerged. This
   was the real Trojan Horse.
The order changes. The Trojans
Having no idea of true or false syntax and having no recorded
 language
Never knew what him them.

Transformations III

This is the melancholy Dane
That built all the houses that lived in the lane
Across from the house that Jack built.
This is the maiden all forlorn, a
   crumpled cow with a crumpled horn
Who lived in the house that Jack built.
This is the crab-god shiny and bright
   who sunned by day and wrote by night
   And lived in the house that Jack built.
This is the end of it, very dear friend, this
   is the end of us.

(*Language*, 1965)

from LOVE POEMS

6

Sable arrested a fine comb.
It is not for the ears. Hearing
Merely prevents progress. Take a step back and view the
  sentence.
Sable arrested a fine comb. On the road to Big Sur (1945) the
  fuses blew every time we braked. Lights out, every kind of
  action. A deer
Hit us once (1945) and walked sulkily into the bushes as we
  braked into silence.
No big white, lightless automobiles for him. If he's hit, let them
  show him.
Sable arrested a last stop . . . I think it was in Watsonville
  (1945 sable arrested fine comb a)
Past danger into the fog we
Used the last fuse.

(*Language,* 1965)

Allen Ginsberg [1926]

GALILEE SHORE

With the blue-dark dome old-starred at night, green boat-lights purring over
    water,
a faraway necklace of cliff-top Syrian electrics,
bells ashore, music from a juke-box trumpeted,
shadow of death against my left breast prest
—cigarette, match-flare, skull wetting its lips—

Fisherman-nets over wood walls, light wind in dead willow branch
on a grassy bank—the saxophone relaxed and brutal, silver horns echo—
Was there a man named Solomon? Peter walked here? Christ on this sweet
    water?
Blessings on thee Peacemaker!
                    English spoken
on the street bearded Jews' sandals & Arab white head cloth—
the silence between Hebrew and Arabic—
the thrill of the first Hashish in a holy land—
Over hill down the valley in a blue bus, past Cana no weddings—
I have no name I wander in a nameless countryside—
young boys all at the movies seeing a great Western—
art gallery closed, pipe razor & tobacco on the floor.

To touch the beard of Martin Buber
to watch a skull faced Gershom Scholem lace his shoes
to pronounce Capernaum's name & see stone doors of a tomb
to be meek, alone, beside a big dark lake at night—
to pass thru Nazareth dusty afternoon, and smell the urine down near Mary's
    well
to watch the orange moon peep over Syria, weird promise—
to wait beside Galilee—night with Orion, lightning, negro voices, Burger's
    Disease, a glass of lemon tea—feel my left hand on my shaved chin—
all you have to do is suffer the metaphysical pain of dying.
Art is just a shadow, like cows or tea—

keep the future open, make no dates it's all here
with moonrise and soft music on phonograph memory—
Just think how amazing! someone getting up and walking on the water.

Tiberias, October 1961

(*Planet News*, 1968)

DESCRIBE: THE RAIN ON DASASWAMEDH GHAT

Kali Ma tottering up steps to shelter tin roof, feeling her way to curb, around
    bicycle & leper seated on her way—to piss on a broom
left by the Stone Cutters who last night were shaking the street with Boom!
    of Stone blocks unloaded from truck
Forcing the blindman in his gray rags to retreat from his spot in the middle
    of the road where he sleeps & shakes under his blanket
Jai Ram all night telling his beads or sex on a burlap carpet
Past which cows donkeys dogs camels elephants marriage processions drum-
    mers tourists lepers and bathing devotees
step to the whine of serpent-pipes & roar of car motors around his black
    ears—
Today on a balcony in shorts leaning on iron rail I watched the leper who
    sat hidden behind a bicycle
emerge dragging his buttocks on the gray rainy ground by the glove-bandaged
    stumps of hands,
one foot chopped off below knee, round stump-knob wrapped with black
    rubber
pushing a tin can shiny size of his head with left hand (from which only a
    thumb emerged from leprous swathings)
beside him, lifting it with both ragbound palms down the curb into the
    puddled road,
balancing his body down next to the can & crawling forward on his behind
trailing a heavy rag for seat, and leaving a path thru the street wavering
like the Snail's slime track—imprint of his crawl on the muddy asphalt
    market entrance—stopping
to drag his can along stubbornly konking on the paved surface near the water
    pump—
Where a turban'd workman stared at him moving along—his back humped
    with rags—
and inquired why didn't he put his can to wash in the pump altarplace—and
    why go that way when free rice

Came from the alley back there by the river—As the leper looked up &
    rested, conversing curiously, can by his side approaching a puddle.
Kali had pissed standing up & then felt her way back to the Shop Steps on
    thin brown legs
her hands in the air—feeling with feet for her rag pile on the stone steps'
    wetness—
as a cow busied its mouth chewing her rags left wet on the ground for five
    minutes digesting
Till the comb-&-hair-oil-booth keeper woke & chased her away with a stick
Because a dog barked at a madman with dirty wild black hair who rag round
    his midriff & water pot in hand
Stopped in midstreet turned round & gazed up at the balconies, windows,
    shops and city stagery filled with glum activity
Shrugged & said *Jai Shankar!* to the imaginary audience of Me's,
While a white robed Baul Singer carrying his one stringed dried pumpkin
    Guitar
Sat down near the cigarette stand and surveyed his new scene, just arrived
    in the Holy City of Benares.

Benares, February 1963

(Planet News, 1968)

LAST NIGHT IN CALCUTTA

Still night. The old clock Ticks,
half past two. A ringing of crickets
awake in the ceiling. The gate is locked
on the street outside—sleepers, mustaches,
nakedness, but no desire. A few mosquitoes
waken the itch, the fan turns slowly—
a car thunders along the black asphalt,
a bull snorts, something is expected—
Time sits solid in the four yellow walls.
No one is here, emptiness filled with train
whistles & dog barks, answered a block away.
Pushkin sits on the bookself, Shakespeare's
complete works as well as Blake's unread—
O Spirit of Poetry, no use calling on you
babbling in this emptiness furnished with beds
under the bright oval mirror—perfect

night for sleepers to dissolve in tranquil
blackness, and rest there eight hours
—Waking to stained fingers, bitter mouth
and lung gripped by cigarette hunger,
what to do with this big toe, this arm
this eye in the starving skeleton-filled
sore horse tramcar-heated Calcutta in
Eternity—sweating and teeth rotted away—
Rilke at least could dream about lovers,
the old breast excitement and trembling belly,
is that it? And the vast starry space—
If the brain changes matter breathes
fearfully back on man—But now
the great crash of buildings and planets
breaks thru the walls of language and drowns
me under its Ganges heaviness forever.
No escape but thru Bangkok and New York death.
Skin is sufficient to be skin, that's all
it ever could be, tho screams of pain in the kidney
make it sick of itself, a wavy dream
dying to finish its all too famous misery
—Leave immortality for another to suffer like a fool,
not get stuck in the corner of the universe
sticking morphine in the arm and eating meat.

May 22, 1963

(*Planet News*, 1968)

WHY IS GOD LOVE, JACK?

Because I lay my
   head on pillows,
Because I weep in the
   tombed studio
Because my heart
   sinks below my navel
because I have an
   old airy belly
filled with soft
   sighing, and

remembered breast
  sobs—or
a hand's touch makes
  tender—
Because I get scared—
Because I raise my
  voice singing to
    my beloved self—
Because I do love thee
  my darling, my
  other, my living
    bride
my friend, my old lord
  of soft tender eyes—
Because I am in the
  Power of life & can
  do no more than
  submit to the feeling
  that I am the One
    Lost
Seeking still seeking the
  thrill—delicious
  bliss in the
    heart abdomen loins
    & thighs
Not refusing this
  38 yr. 145 lb. head
  arms & feet of meat
Nor one single Whitmanic
  toenail contemn
nor hair prophetic banish
  to remorseless Hell,
Because wrapped with machinery
I confess my ashamed desire.
                    New York, 1963

                (*Planet News*, 1968)

AFTER YEATS

Now incense fills the air
and delight follows delight,
quiet supper in the carpet room,
music twangling from the Orient to my ear,
old friends at rest on bright mattresses,
old paintings on the walls, old poetry
thought anew, laughing at a mystic toy
statue painted gold, tea on the white table.

New York, April 26, 1964

(*Planet News*, 1968)

STUDYING THE SIGNS

After Reading Briggflatts

White light's wet glaze on asphalt city floor,
the *Guinness Time* house clock hangs sky misty,
yellow *Cathay* food lamps blink, rain falls
on rose neon *Swiss Watch* under Regent archway,
Sun Alliance and London Insurance Group stands
granite—"Everybody gets torn down". . .as a high
black taxi with orange doorlight passes around
iron railing blazoned with red sigma *Underground*—
Ah where the cars glide slowly around Eros
shooting down on one who stands in Empire's Hub
under his shining silver breast, look at Man's
sleepy face under half-spread metal wings—
Swan & Edgar's battlement walls the moving Circus,
princely high windows barred (shadow bank
interior office stairway marble) behind castiron
green balconies emblemed with single swans afloat
like white teacups what—*Boots'* blue sign lit up
over an enamel weight-machine's mirror clockface
at door betwixt plateglass *Revlon* & slimming biscuit
plaques and that alchemical blood-crimson pharmacy
bottle perched on street display. *A Severed Head*

"relished uproariously" above the masq'd *Criterion*
marquee, with Thespis and Ceres plaster Graces lifting
white arms in the shelled niches above a fire gong
on the wooden-pillared facade whose mansard gables
lean in blue-black sky drizzle, thin flagpole.
Like the prow of a Queen Mary the curved building
sign *Players* package, blue capped center
Navvy encircled by his life-belt a sweet bearded
profile against 19th century sea waves—
last a giant red delicious *Coca-Cola* signature
covers half the building back to gold *Cathay*.
Cars stop three abreast for the light, race forward,
turtleneck youths jump the fence toward *Boots*,
the night-gang in Mod slacks and ties sip
coffee at the *Snac-A-Matic* corner opendoor,
a boy leaned under *Cartoon Cinema* lifts hand
puffs white smoke and waits agaze—a wakened
pigeon flutters down from streetlamp to the fountain,
primly walks and pecks the empty pave—now deep
blue planet-light dawns in Piccadilly's low sky.

June 12, 1965

(*Planet News*, 1968)

WICHITA VORTEX SUTRA, PART I

Turn Right Next Corner
  The Biggest Little Town in Kansas
    Macpherson
Red sun setting flat plains west streaked
     with gauzy veils, chimney mist spread
   around christmas-tree-bulbed refineries—aluminum
    white tanks squat beneath
  winking signal towers' bright plane-lights,
     orange gas flares
  beneath pillows of smoke, flames in machinery—
    transparent towers at dusk

In advance of the Cold Wave
   Snow is spreading eastward to
      the Great Lakes
  News Broadcast & old clarinets
   Watertower dome Lighted on the flat plain
     car radio speeding acrost railroad tracks—

Kansas! Kansas! Shuddering at last!
    PERSON appearing in Kansas!
  angry telephone calls to the University
  Police dumbfounded leaning on
      their radiocar hoods
  While Poets chant to Allah in the roadhouse Showboat!
Blue eyed children dance and hold thy Hand O aged Walt
  who came from Lawrence to Topeka to envision
     Iron interlaced upon the city plain—
  Telegraph wires strung from city to city O Melville!
    Television brightening thy *rills of Kansas lone*
I come,
    lone man from the void, riding a bus
    hypnotized by red tail lights on the straight
       space road ahead—
  & the Methodist minister with cracked eyes
      leaning over the table
    quoting Kierkegaard "death of God"
      a million dollars
  in the bank owns all West Wichita
       come to Nothing!
    Prajnaparamita Sutra over coffee—Vortex
of telephone radio aircraft assembly frame ammunition
petroleum nightclub Newspaper streets illuminated by Bright
      EMPTINESS—

Thy sins are forgiven, Wichita!
    Thy lonesomeness annulled, O Kansas dear!
     as the western Twang prophesied
  thru banjo, when lone cowboy walked the railroad track
    past an empty station toward the sun
    sinking giant-bulbed orange down the box canyon—
  Music strung over his back
    and empty handed singing on this planet earth
      I'm a lonely Dog, O Mother!
Come, Nebraska, sing & dance with me—

Come lovers of Lincoln and Omaha,
            hear my soft voice at last
As Babes need the chemical touch of flesh in pink infancy
      lest they die Idiot returning to Inhuman—
                              Nothing—
So, tender lipt adolescent girl, pale youth,
                        give me back my soft kiss
      Hold me in your innocent arms,
                  accept my tears as yours to harvest
                  equal   in nature to the Wheat
            that made your bodies' muscular bones
                  broad shouldered, boy bicept—
            from leaning on cows & drinking Milk
                        in Midwest Solitude—
No more fear of tenderness, much delight in weeping, ecstasy
      in singing, laughter rises that confounds
            staring Idiot mayors
                  and stony politicians eyeing
                  Thy breast,
                        O Man of America, be born!
Truth breaks through!
            How big is the prick of the President?
            How big is Cardinal Vietnam?
      How little the prince of the FBI, unmarried all these years!
            How big are all the Public Figures?
      What kind of flesh hangs, hidden behind their Images?

                              Approaching Salina,
Prehistoric excavation, *Apache Uprising*
                        in the drive-in theater
      Shelling Bombing Range   mapped in the distance,
      Crime Prevention Show, sponsor Wrigley's Spearmint
      Dinosaur Sinclair advertisement, glowing green—
South 9th Street lined with poplar & elm branch
            spread over evening's tiny headlights—
      Salina Highschool's brick darkens Gothic
                  over a night-lit door—
      What wreaths of naked bodies, thighs and faces,
                  small hairy bun'd vaginas,
                  silver cocks, armpits and breasts
            moistened by tears
                        for 20 years, for 40 years?
Peking Radio surveyed by Luden's Coughdrops

Attacks on the Russians & Japanese,
Big Dipper leaning above the Nebraska border,
                         handle down to the blackened plains,
      telephone-pole ghosts crossed
                         by roadside, dim headlights—
dark night, & giant T-bone steaks,
      and in *The Village Voice*
      New Frontier Productions present
            Camp Comedy: *Fairies I Have Met.*
Blue highway lamps strung along the horizon east at Hebron
            Homestead National Monument near Beatrice—

Language, language
         black Earth-circle in the rear window,
                      no cars for miles along highway
            beacon lights on oceanic plain
      language, language
                  over Big Blue River
            chanting *La illaha el (lill) Allah hu*
            revolving my head to my heart like my mother
            chin abreast at Allah
                  Eyes closed, blackness
vaster than midnight prairies,
            Nebraskas of solitary Allah,
                  Joy, I am I
            the lone One singing to myself
                         God come true—
                  Thrills of fear.
                  nearer than the vein in my neck—?
What if I opened my soul to sing to my absolute self
      Singing as the car crash chomped thru blood & muscle
                               tendon skull?
      What if I sang, and loosed the chords of fear brow?
         What exquisite noise wd
                         shiver my car companions?
         I am the Universe tonite
                  riding in all my Power riding
chauffeured thru my self by a long haired saint with eyeglasses
What if I sang till Students knew I was free
      of Vietnam, trousers, free of my own meat,
      free to die in my thoughtful shivering Throne?
            freer than Nebraska, freer than America—
               May I disappear

in magic Joy-smoke! Pouf! reddish Vapor,
Faustus vanishes weeping & laughing
under stars on Highway 77 between Beatrice & Lincoln—
"Better not to move but let things be" Reverend Preacher?
We've all already disappeared!

Space highway open, entering Lincoln's ear
ground to a stop Tracks Warning
Pioneer Boulevard—
William Jennings Bryan sang
Thou shalt not crucify mankind upon a cross of Gold!
O Baby Doe! Gold's
Department Store hulks o'er 10th Street now
—an unregenerate old fop who didn't want to be a monkey
now's the Highest Perfect Wisdom dust
and Lindsay's cry
survives compassionate in the Highschool Anthology—
a giant dormitory brilliant on the evening plain
drifts with his memories—
There's a nice white door over there
for me O dear!   on Zero Street.
February 15, 1966

(*Planet News*, 1968)

EASTER SUNDAY

Slope woods' snows melt
Streams gush, ducks stand one foot
beak eye buried in backfeathers,
Jerusalem pillars' gold sunlight
yellow in window-shine, bright
rays spikey-white flashed in mud,
coo coo ripples thru maple branch,
horse limps head down, pale grass shoots
green winter's brown vegetable
hair—washed by transparent trickling
ice water freshets
earth's rusty slough bathed clean,
streams ripple leaf-bottomed

channels sounded vocal, white light
afternoon sky end—

Goat bells move, black kids bounce,
butting mother's hairy side & tender tit
one maa'ing child hangs under Bessie's udder
ducks waggle yellow beaks, new grass flooded,
tiger cat maeows on barn straw,
herb patch by stone wall's a shiny marsh,
dimpling snow water glimmers, birds whistle
from icecrystal beds under bare bushes,
breeze blows rooster crow thru chill light
extended from the piney horizon.

1969

(*The Fall of America, Poems of These States,* 1973)

Larry Eigner [1927]

IF YOU WEEP, I THINK THAT

If you weep, I think that
others might cry
though it is no matter   The rain
is more fruitful
   to the earth breaking
heavy with birds
and leaves we could
not hold   I
      you push
           and the fog
shadowing tides

          filling the
             island, farther
out dampering it down
until the wet congeals
everywhere in the great
arches
           for which our sight even
becomes too thin, weed
sand and stone, and the tolerant subdued cats
     the sea,   the sun

         arching   beyond
everything there is
   here and the birds' scream

hunger or puff
to the silencing light

    and the eyes open
    again, at the
    blind rain

in fear and removal

you cough   and it is
not the same

(*On My Eyes*, 1960)

BACK TO IT

The good things go by so softly
Themselves it is our strengths
that run wild

The good and the strong,   dissipant,
        an ob- jective joy
                                sky
is empty   there are clouds
there must be sound
there

        the horizons are nothing

                                the rain sometimes is not
                                negligible

            out on the sky
                    the other direction
        growing until it is nothing

there are mirages and numberless deserts

            inside the other house

lines, broken curbs

                        travel and distance
proportion themselves

        we must be animate,   and walk

turn, abruptly

the lines are irregular

(*On My Eyes*, 1960)

IT SOUNDED

and tangled dry—

      like fire
   at the start of the day
     the engines
        control
but the wind in the twigs
or thistles,   stalk

    the birds are violent
    the spring

they function by shouting

suddenly

all day

the houses stand some paint in
glass the dusty sun

with the fresh air

and the man who fixes the roof

top and

the transformer below

nothing except the wires
and the trees

and the boys climbing
             the shed
         (to leap
      and break

         (*On My Eyes*, 1960)

FOR SLEEP

I depend on the stars
and the places of night

That is what it is

intent space, and
the speed which is light, growing
past any shape

the half-door or the door
slightly open

   this is what happens when I move
   (or I see motion,   all of it

       I'm in it

   the world depopulated
   those configurations of spirits

   scattered and gone

   so to disappear

   the side of this road

                nothing

      I want room

         (*On My Eyes*, 1960)

LETTER FOR DUNCAN

just because I forget
to perch different ways
                    the fish
            go monotonous

                the
            sudden hulks of the tress
                in a glorious summer
you don't realize
        how mature you get
                at 21

        but you look back

            wherever a summer
                continue 70 seasons

                this one
                    has been so various

                    was the spring hot?

every habit

    to read

nothing you've done you have

        older

                the fish
            can't bother screaming

            flap by hook

        the working pain

                    jaws by trying a head   bodies

        you'll always go to sleep
            more times than you'll wake

                    (*Another Time in Fragments,* 1967)

LIVE / , BIRD WHICH

live
, bird which
sings
      above
and underneath

  or two birds, may
          all

     go subtly

       we are

        in the air

   feet

          on the ground

      the air goes
      thin then
      budding relieve
      the branches like
      fresh children

        leaves
      die, fitful
        mass of voices, curled, in
          continuous air

(*Another Time in Fragments*, 1967)

IN IMITATION

(a shot of Rbt Creeley)

What has that face got to do with that
poetry? In

    order to have one you need the other, yes

        the sky
    would do as well   I know
Questions are funny, a flower

    of life then   Let's
  go on   What are the leaves
      in back   What's
    the sky doing in your head? The

    photos of some of your
"predecessors" What

  has your voice to do with
the thoughts which at least pass
in my own life, its

    hurry
        While the churches
are open as the earth   There are statues

    in all the museums and
around them and now in the park and

      even in the wilds
      again

    and paintings of stars, nights,
in walls
      opposite mirrors

(Another Time in Fragments, 1967)

■

theatre   "   charged with
shapes   mountains that loom
    names

    tined   lump surfs   ace
    black
            red
        the blinding
        from inside   clog

    Is it at night   the smooth

        you call for material
    which might be abundant

                    armor for ships

                            hedge
        plunge down   rails of

                        cut sleepers

            waters aloud

        now farms most of the time

                pause anywhere

        remember the lines continue

    I will be a bee above

            the local

            I will

        if the trees were higher
            under the white,   or the moon

the sky thrown wide

arms

climbing positions

or through branches

that is a hill   july leaves

the western grade

where they grew pigs

riddled as a fence
in delve on suns

and there the generals
of arms
like birds
with captions

there are different speeds

the path

changes
scale

(*Things Stirring Together or Far Away,* 1974)

■

the figures,   lines

the hidden
roots and rivers
of the under

turn up

beyond cables

and offices

cutting the air, stream
thin   space

the sides shown

the ghostly tongues
of water   finer edged

than the mud flats
                        flowering
                            into your streets

                        palpable

times, the snarl
oneness, legumes
of ripped loam, swirling,

proliferant planes, impressions,

headlong to zero

a light mouth
an open bay

(*The World and Its Streets, Places,* 1977)

■

his life
the
open window

where the clock sounds fade

what is it?
branches out there

can you
  stop
  the war

        crickets   stars

      no birds   the more air
        sing   in the leaves

  Get up and
  speak

    something   whatever it is

                wilds   around

      now   now

        children are within you
          guts are outside

          red sky
        meant wind

      as is a hole to
          turn out of this

          year on year
            the grass

                wave after wave
                  the snow

        there are no wormy

            men

      (*The World and Its Streets, Places,* 1977)

                ■

a perfectly quiet car
   how easily pushed it
self a boat   the invisible
    effort   completion of
     the movement here, some factory
   product, as of all these years
    hot day waters the street
           the slant paint rides
      turn and go back
       the way they came

        the horn blowing once

     beyond the confused mass
   of the real sea, the bay, in resistance
   to the moon, the air

   that light bulk
       continues the years

         the solid in my childish mind

   that boy at the wheel was
    a proper choice, the others
    went back and forth, too, he
     said something

    (*Flat and Round,* 1969; 1980)

ENVIRON S

Many shapes of wings
on the sky and the table;
and large men carefully at dusk
lengthened by lights   watering their lawns

turn, paterfamilias

  and the sweet hay as I go
  from one foot to the other

more so than I might
mingled with barber's tonic
from the morning's shops
  of papers and bright rag
      as if we could
        take time out for life

  and the afternoon's seas, like yards

At some smell of smoke
I found a spray behind me
and the two on my right gone
  tending the grass, all night
everyone beautifully
  (by themselves   the same thing

time   for the surroundings

      against the strip of hill
  ending low, a space
  on the side, hut for clouds

        (*Waters / Places / A Time*, 1983)

■

one died by this tremendous headache
drowning in laughter
the tv was a gas
some kind of vacation in the wards
      then many went down and voted

        the whole year round
      stars frosty or something
          wonderful view
          at the edge of your seat

      the moon off
          polluted waters
                degrees merge

        miles
         clear sunday

     the one-round fight
   everybody watched
   they had expectations
     chew it , it
         can drop

       tomorrow morning

romance of the moon

     across curtain, strings
               plaster different from panes
   an even coat of paint

         (*Waters / Places / A Time,* 1983)

                    ■

     last year's pink
   poison   a notice
       the wind howled
   yesterday , blew up the tide
       beyond the sky-line from tress
     through branches   even more
                   the days before

           out of
     the bark clear half
     the garage trellis
       two arms of the vine
     tack   crossed way over

       the bare
     sun filling the air
   the roof melting snowcap
       down water   past
     summer, with the rays
         some angle eventually

            slips through
      the flow

            the inferred motion
              from the continuous, your eyes

            followed, or being
                dance

            the remainder was good

            the two windows shook

      and an outer stream on the
        house drainpipe

            covering a side

            those folds
        leak point of the exit

            (*Waters / Places / A Time*, 1983)

Gilbert Sorrentino [1929]

LAND OF COTTON

One remembers hysterical laughter
a summer night, when no one was happy.

Sam, come from the town, come the fire
consumes you, the trees are ablaze, the church
the money
is burning, any old photo

will prove it so.

The guernseys, the holsteins,
brahma bulls screaming in terror!

(Cold, ice cold sauternes
through all the whisky
fog, the dawn near.

   Sam, the town is burning,
your Byronic scarf
will not save you. Here, *phlox* is not
the decorative flower,

come from the town Sam, you are
burning. I call you Sam to
come, gazing at the photo where you stand

while all around you rages.

              (*Corrosive Sublimate,* 1971)

MAGIC COMPOSER

Who knows what the moonlight means?
Shake shake sonora!

Gripped in the leafy leaves
or tendrils green and tender
certain creatures of the glens and glades.

Shake shake!

A pinch of tergamoom, one teaspoon
bajji, add plenty water. And a rock
on the lid.

A glass of beer? A glass of beer
oh magic in the loony light. Note how
the color glows amber, copper. A new penny

helps settle the sediment.

Fame is the spur, oh! Soft waters.
How hold anything anywhere for long
and long. In the moonbeams
tears of acid. A good old wagon

but he done broke down. Shake it.

(*Sun & Moon* magazine, 1976)

SEPTEMBER IN KITTERY

Those were the lobsters
many poets write of, compare
to us and our lives: blindly
crawling, dark in the dark.

Whereas I write: vanilla, then
lavender, then—anything.

What is there to compare
with what? Here is sun the snow
is melting. Here a crow
of memory. Old Valentines.

    Priests who were afraid and
    those who drank too much.

Bad wine, blended whisky, the special
on beer. A white sail
on the Sound off Connecticut, breathless!
Ask the maniac, Artaud.

                  (*White Sail*, 1977)

■

Across this water sits a shore
patched together out of dim and smudgy colors.
It brings to mind a cartoon oddly porous.
Static on a worn-out sponge. Yet a core
of translucent light seems to spring
from the center of what looks a town or market
and drenches the lime-green haze of the park
I put there. One seesaw, one fountain, and one swing.

    Mothers and children in blue
    filled with good humor, china blue
    eyes and the rest, plus the sky is blue.

You can see I'm trying to get there
seriously. When I get there
I'll be young again. I forgot orange. There.

              (*The Orangery*, 1978)

■

She was all in black. A statement
to take its place in "The History of Ideas."

We know black here in America.
Why, it's a scream.

Stick a point of orange in it
just for fun. Just to see what comes of it.

　　After which: Prove that the light
　　of bowling alleys is romantic.
　　Is the very gravy of romance.
　　"The crème!" yells a voice.

　　Then, years later, drones the comic,
　　I recall standing on a corner
　　in the Bronx waiting for a bus.
　　Yes, yes. Waiting for a bus.

　　　　　　(*The Orangery*, 1978)

ZUKOFSKY

　　　Who
　　　was that who
　　　saw
　　　his father
　　　in
　　　his shorts,
　　　mother laughing?

　　　Who
　　　decided on
　　　the
　　　pattern?
　　　Of
　　　oranges?
　　　On white.

Who was that?
Who
saw his father?
In his shorts!
Mother
laughing.
Who?

Who
decided?
On the
pattern of
oranges
on
white.

(*The Orangery*, 1978)

THE ORANGES RETURNED

In a disingenuous letter
sent from a quiet snowy place
an old friend asks why I returned
   a gift of oranges.

I am too old to answer such questions.
Even the words sat numb. His was always
a brilliant mind yet he asks about
   his gift of oranges.

I put him in a poem once. God knows
he's had his slow shock in the mirror.
Perhaps it was that grey head sent
   the gift of oranges.

It is a maniac time, friends cast about
to touch. To reawaken. Meaningless gifts.

(*The Orangery*, 1978)

"GOOD NIGHT!"

She was blushing in the misty green of August
and I tell you that's a lapidary recollection
although the pitch and cadence of her voice is lost.
A lot of Christmas trees have occurred since then
and ice-skaters by the thousands dead and buried.
There shone softly a bathing suit of pastel stripes
and her thighs "kissed" so that young orthodontists
leaned and leaned smiling on her doorbell.
There is a use in shoveling through these eggshells
orange peels greasy paper bags and stinking bones
from which are stitched together songs to stun the
     drunkards.
One sees by the stars and the date on the paper
that the old year is as usual vanishing.
The dim and unintelligible smile in the department
     store
a vague and cryptic memorandum. "Get ornaments and
     tinsel."
"Have loving cup engraved." It falters in men's
     haberdashery
and the heat is too oppressive to be borne.

(*Selected Poems 1958 – 1980*, 1981)

RAZZMATAZZ

Young and willing to learn (but what?) he was the boy
With the sweaty face the boy of the *Daily News*
The boy of bananas peanut butter and lemon–lime
Who read Ching Chow waiting for the punch line
Who watched the sun more often than not a bursting rose
Swathe the odd haze and clumps of the far-off shore.

Who watched the sun more often than not a bursting rose?
"Things" were in Greek, as: the unmixed wine; thalassa!
Tears dropping into head cheese and boiled spare ribs
Lacked that notorious piquancy of the delicious tragic.
There was something to be concocted of all this trash
(But what?) if he could but avoid the stable clerkships.

The boy of bananas peanut better and lemon-lime
Decided on certain girls beautiful in starched blouses
And imagined their confessions in the dirty dark.
And everyone grew older to A String of Pearls.
Smoke rings slid soft and creamy into creamy haze
He reached that shore and found it was only Staten Island.

Ching Chow, waiting for the punch line, grinned
And read a book without a title on a unicycle.
The jokes were mixed into the wild perfume of wives
And honeymoons and girls a country fair of lusts.
All this in the days when nuns were nuns and ageless
Yet somehow almost all the fathers abruptly disappeared.

With the sweaty face the boy of the *Daily News*
Was not real, spoke no Italian, never dined
And was in actuality Kayo or in all events his derby.
Old women with that little mick under their oxters
Crossed themselves as frozen trolleys passed Our Lady
Of Popeyes chipped plaster and a spooky babe in arms.

The odd haze and clumps of the far-off shore
My God! were buildings fallen into disrepair
And complete with rats slaving to keep their teeth short.
Quite wonderful how it all was simply there
Just there and devoid of any meaning or portent.
In the mirror he honked a saxophone and conjured thighs.

Young and willing to learn (but what?) he was the boy
Who found that those fabled dreams were fabled
In that their meaning was their own blurred being
Who suddenly found his alien body to be the material
From which could be made a gent or even life. Life?
Young and willing to learn oh certainly. But what?

(*Selected Poems 1958 – 1980*, 1981)

John Wieners [1934]

A GLIMPSE

There is a knot in the middle of my head
that will never be untied.
                           Two monkeys sit there
one on the right turned towards me, the
                               other crouched and turned

        away. They
have red hair and do not play
               with their chains. But sit on a ledge
above Venice? Anyway a city with canals
                  painted by Breughel, I see
them in a mirror when I look for my own face.

              (unpublished manuscript, dated 1959)

KING SOLOMON'S MAGNETIC QUIZ

And when I went to the woods
           I heard the whispering of lovers
               ages ago. Was it
lights or my eyes playing tricks on me? The trees were
forms, was rain dropping on the ground like feet,
     fog and my own game at hand.
            On my back I saw

the stars creeping up the hill and thought of sex in the dark,
catching him surprised coming around some corner, cradling
  his cock in his hands. Hard it was

on me to lay there
with only the ground under me. Bits of it stuck
to my coat.   Let it go
I think; Rise up from this waste. There is no lover
in the dark. No nightmare stallion

turning into a tree to see
you; are alone. I rose and went out
by the street bush I came in.

(for RC

(unpublished manuscript, dated 1959)

LONG NOOK

There she took her lover to sea
and laid herself in the sand.
Go up and undress in the dark.

He is fast, was down the dune
with silk around his waist.
Her scarf was small.

She opened her clothes to the moon.
Her underarms were shaved.
The wind was a wall between them.

Waves break over the tide,
hands tied to her side with silk,
their mind was lost in the night.

The green light at Provincetown
became an emerald on the beach,
and like stars fell on Alabama.

(*Ace of Pentacles*, 1964)

THE SUCK

This morning
last evening, yes
terday afternoon

in the hall
your voice, full
of complement

turns to strike
someone you do not

know as a wife or brother,

shaking, trembling
in your arms
sweating like seventeen

again under young middle-aged

bellies in the summer

(*Nerves*, 1970)

ACCEPTANCE

Should I wear a shadowed eye,
grow moustaches
delineate my chin

accept spit as offering,
attach a silver earring
grease my hair

give orders to legions
of lovers to maintain manhood
scimitars away as souvenirs?

Sooush, beloved! here is my tongue.

(*Nerves*, 1970)

TO H.

I like Sunday evenings after you're here.
I use your perfume to pretend you're near
in the night. My eyes are bright, why
can't I have a man of my own?

Your wife's necklace's around my neck
and even though I do shave I pretend
I'm a woman for you
you make love to me like a man.

Even though I hear you say why man
he doesn't even have any teeth
when I take out my plate
I make it up to you in other ways.

I will write this poem.

(*Selected Poems*, 1972)

WHAT HAPPENED?

Better than a closet martinet.
            Better than a locket
                in a lozenge.
            At the market, try and top it
                            in the Ritz.

Better than a marmoset
                at the Grossets,
            better than a mussel
                in your pockets.
                    Better than a faucet
                        for your locker,
                            better not
                        clock it.
            Better than a sachet
                in your cloche,

better than a hatchet
in Massachusetts,
Ponkapog.
Pudget
Sound
lost and found.

Better than an aspirin—
aperitif does it.
Better not ask
how you caught it
what has happened to me?

Better not lack it—
or packet in at the Rickenbackers.
Better tack it back
in a basket
for Davy Crockett

Better not stack it.
Better stash it
on the moon.

Oh Pomagranate
ah Pawtucket.

Oh Winsocki or
Narragansett.

Better not claque it. Better cash it in
at Hackensack.
Better not lock it
up again.

(*Cultural Affairs in Boston: Poetry &
Prose 1956 – 1985*, 1988)

DOLL

How many loves had I
in young boy's bed,
at Humarock, or Provincetown's
Cape Cod, under sweating summer sun,

after Land's End, before their interruption.
How many loves had I?

in discourse by firelight, after highballs
to records of Marlene Dietrich and Cole Porter,
how many loves had I?

in Swampscott flat, or Beacon Hill house,
Beacon Street garage or Fiedler overpass,
how many loves had I?

How many loves, in Annandale
before payment or threat, in the Public Gardens
or Fifth Avenue park, how many loves—

None, none, none at all.

(*Cultural Affairs in Boston: Poetry &*
Prose 1956 – 1985, 1988)

Robert Kelly [1935]

INJUNE

In June was a jar had
honey in it. Honey in its
head. Had.

The beacons came to play on
it. Publican weather.

I tell you the history of a
conspicuous jar, one long

derangement

like a song through a door

a door ajar.

Door had.
Hardly opened.
When.

The honey in the jar would be a
history of our tribe, until
a young man got the honey
in his head.

The beacon was a star
beckoned. Crystals
in the old sleepy forest.

What do we know.

First gist of honey:
June was the way in.

Cancer (sign)
Life in its shell.

We know
the glib
of mountaineers,
got goitre
but not
when they lived by the shore
so
man must be littoral.
(a parenthesis)

June was this jar
or how life began.

Breakfast was clotted milk
because the stars.

As we ate
the bread was baking in the earth.
The hearth was never far.

Fire was never hard.
We cared.
This was the way in,
cool look of a June morning
I remember in July.

Milk & honey.
The jar was heaven,
broke & poured down.
Man's life is spilled milk.

A boy saving rain.

The stars were jars, were doors
& we kept looking back,

angel at the fiery gate,
boy, delivery boy, looking
down at the smashed quart.

This angel is this boy.

The doors are open all night long,
that's where the cool wind comes
that blows the honey into our heads,
is sleep.

Crust of vision on the new-woke eyes.
Sleep in my eyes.

What happened to the head,
the head's on straight, the Lion
we see in the stars
reminds us of our own,

the girl was lovely but inexperienced,
slipped,
they both got honey in the head.

But hers was heavier
& remembered earth
& all the caves
filled up with jewels, & gold
ran down into the ground to hide,
to be
the secret content of her
honey thought,
her heavy head
thinking grapes on to the vine
(wild
 taste of the bitten apple!)

She slipped. His lion
slipped out, his lighter head
sticky with honey
stuck to the sky.

It was June. We were born.

The gate her kindly inefficiency,
his eager lion
running
to bask in her.

Now all this is legend
(not myth, not a miss
to make up an earlier mile)
& the jar
is the milecastles on Hadrian's wall.
Is the grass I havent planted
the broken lawn & the promises
that ooze like honey
from the hive of whys,
  six-sided chambers
filled with infant questions
  growing to serve
by endless labor
    the search of the hive:

Once this queen was woman,
    was the sun
& all their humming was for her
& what she turned them towards,
  rational answers
to the needs of every day,
  how a man can live
without breaking the jar
    & still
walk back between the stars
perfect as they are, & long-lived.

□

A chapter of precisions.

needed to go further:

The primal component of legend is
   fact.

The primal component of myth is
   desire.

The fact of desire is
how we got this way.

Meaning is the end of any process.
  It draws. Drags.

We can enrich the process.

Smelt. Refine. Decline. Consume.

The gold
hides in the ground

the way tomorrow's weather
hides in the air,

the way what I will finally know
hides in me now.

        □

Injune is a verb, the way a word
  makes flesh, is begotten not
  created.

Injune is our coming to this place.

On the Mayflower
we came to June.

The gates of Cancer
aim us at the moon.

We act as if we came here to injune.

      (Injune yourself!
      it's wetter than you think.

      The Queens of Oil
      are melancholy,

      the Kings of Honey
      have captured them,

      shot into their hives
      a curious message

      shaped like themselves.
      Their joys arrive

      & set fire to the ocean.
      The prince of fire

is the last to come.)

□

June is the name of our commitment.
The sun stands still
to watch us tumble,
fumble, crawl over ourselves,
hit the light, thumb
in my mouth, tasting

an inconceivable yesterday.

(End of this chapter of precisions)

□

Honey lasts forever.
Men can eat honey,
    Pelagius said,
& know themselves slowly,
meeting each act or not-act
as the bee meets the flower,
capable by her nature
of choosing the right one.

The sin would not be doing this.
Doubting the act,
  doubting your digestion.

The magical bees of the island of Britain
sang in his head

where all the honey went
the sea god his father sent

to nourish the chance
of human possibility.

All we can do
(as things stand,
  as the bees decide)
is know what we do.

Tastes like honey.

In June the bees are busy at the linden
& all of this
is only a few feet away,
I speak of an actual tree
rarer than remorse.

□

(A Narrative):

An angel came to me today & told me that my vaunted dislike of narrative reveals an
unwillingness on my part to be accountable for anyone's acts, including my own. I
contended that narrative in fact implies a guilt-greediness, a false insistence on se-
lection. Let the selection be natural (I punned), let what happened reveal itself more
fully, truly, in what–happens–next. If that were true (he smiled), I would need only
one pair of wings. You are clearly in the grip of a comfortable belief in causality, &
excuse yourself from natural act. Though the corn ripens in its own seasons, you
can *go with it* while it grows. That makes all the difference in the world.

Look (I said), I hate the theatre, I want *now* to turn into
then in such a subtle, self-motivated way it feels like *now* all the time, only this one
present moment, where I am responsible for what I do now. That's why I've been
quoting Pelagius, & now that other Irishman who said History was a nightmare
from which he strove to awaken. I'm glad you spoke of ripening, because that is
what I want, to let the moment ripen, to be a *momentum*. I do not want to turn back
before.

The angel smiled again at me (as one smiles kindly at a deft
prevarication) & said: That sounds nice. But these three pairs of wings I wear are to
hide & reveal, to propel my intelligence through the enigma of time, perhaps to deny
it at last, since the Work or Arcanum of angels is the End of Time. You are striving
to assert what some would call an angelic intelligence, total in each motion. In call-
ing it that, you confuse the end of time with the beginning of time. You are just
another lover of time, stalling, slurping up the honey, warring & creating & theolo-
gizing to keep the sun still on the mountain. You trust causality implicitly because
you are begotten, not created. Angels are created beings, & all their science is will.
Even now you have forgotten your own intention in these pages: to discover some-
thing in form or in music, & already you're making me speak prose. Learn narrative,
& be kind to it, so you can learn the operation of will in time, & what kinds of
creatures have will, or whether will is your tricky name for what everything in the
world keeps on doing. How can you know your will until you've seen & seen re-
corded everything you've ever "done," everything that has ever happened in your
sensorium? You think you're quoting Pelagius, but it is I who brought you to con-
sider him, first of the self-styled Christians to make it plain that we are accountable
for each act, every act & every abstention—*& are responsible for nothing beyond that.*

I was getting angry then, though I was being convinced.

There's a war going on (I said), there is violence & stupidity and self-destruction;
the planets run & recur in their cycles, & every jolt they give us spills over into war

& cruelty. The sons of God, who honor god in flesh & openness, are everywhere slain & imprisoned. It is not just now—it is at every stage of human history, the greed & cruelty that enslave & destroy. How do we even have a right to talk, walk on our feet, stand on a continent where Cortez did what he did, where anger & fear & hatred & suspicion & murder are the natural condition? Where the books of the Aztecs were burnt & black men were sold & young men today are made slaves of war? It was never different. In Pelagius' time the slaves were sold & citizens enslaved, rulers flayed alive. His God dies on the cross. What is the sense of narrative? What can it tell us? We do not love, we do not live in honor. If there are causes, we have never deciphered them. If there is a cure, it has been hidden from the beginning of time. Why do men take pleasure in killing & destroying? What is that pleasure? Is *history* the name of it? Did anything else *ever* happen? The animal delights in his *here-&-now*, & poets now have tried to recover that again, declare it, a plenary experience, the moment filled. Our cortical memories, that are supposed to be stocked with situational devices, to warn or protect us, are they anything but treasure houses of barbarous images, records of torture & dismay? If that is the world's will, I turn against it, "turn my body from the sun" in search of the exact moment.

The angel seemed to pause; at first I thought he was stuck for any kind of answer. Then I knew he was waiting for my anger to simmer down. This time he did not smile. These facts & stories in your mind are accurate, he said, but where in them do you see anything but what a man did to something, or to another man? The tale of human ugliness has only one meaning—men did these things, & only one hope— men could *choose* not to do them. It seems, as you suggest, a vain hope, or an unlikely one. Cancer is the sign of incarnation, the souls coming down to choose human bodies to work out their meanings, their "salvation." Capricorn is the gate of return, the way out, at least of this human condition. In between stretch the deserts of horror you've spoken of (clumsily—you could do it better if you knew more of the history you disdain). What men could *Will* is a joke, an unreal thing. Human will is what men have always done, mechanically, unconsciously; will is the vector a mathematician could *infer* from their behavior. But that behavior can be changed by conscious awareness. It takes a million years, but it took many millions for you to become the super-killers you are now.

Or you are a jar into which all the honey of time has been poured. When time ends, the jar will break & there will be left only the honey you've gathered or restored. Do you understand? I dont think you do. But stay with it, tell the story of all past time, make all the things & songs & environments you can. Remember your intention as you began to work these pages out. Bring them a new thing.

(*The Alchemist to Mercury*, 1981)

TUNE

(listening to Benjamin Boretz play)

A sheep was. And a purse dangled from his arm. A sporran jogged between his lies.
From out this pouch a cloth uncluttered, spills a spent candle and a saved penny—
these to the grass. And around what let fall he graze. The relation is simple, a recip-
rocal. A window lets light in. The other side of the equation is the sheep. Say a
sheep. Say a sheep at Stonehenge. Say a single limiter of a square wave. Say a jagged
amazur, a smooth alcalde, a black pot full of juice. Say a barbarophone and a literal
linguist meet at the club. Say one is a sheep what do you say. Say to a shorn sheep
what the wind shames to? A sworn sheep in a true time, by counsel led and his brief
pleading, let me speak your cause, remented animal, who from the dip think deeply
and the poor night foretell, joseph on joseph, fat counsellors and lean pharaoh.
Fadeout is funk no more. I span and you delve, so I win and you more-than-kiss my
wed feet. I am a pale bride and I clutter your home with my compunctions, nightly
conceive, a bleak bird hops in and I proffer. My feet to your case. My fact to your
face. Kiss me. The seat is wet from all his lies. A sheep is. Simply a sheep is, that's
how it goes, is, a sheep is. The might of the silliest animal means us. Plafond. The
funds of the nephew (deepest form nephew) hunger in Unc's bank. She woke "hump-
ing the bed" from a hope of other she heard singing the whiles. Have a try, deceit of
musical. Heart? Have a cart. Might? I was the sheep, my full wool wet I run run
between your legs you know it well. I run through you in this way, by hope incarnate
dewsome in your interface. Let me be your piece of cloth. A piece of cloth. Clad and
clutter, bleed and better, "difference between listening and really hearing," mouth-
open one drowses—this reception is musical, is it? We had a band to the opening,
lots of leap and a hallful later. A tight swaddling sort of sound would calm a little
lamb. But a tight sort, a probing sort of impertinent closeness, is it? Say a sheep
under Stonehenge. Is this the sun you meant to mime so long ago, its animal rising
and sullen song where your eyes are on it, are lifting up with it and perception is a
take-off, holding pattern and arrival all jinxed into one? Might? I revise the animal.
How do you listen? I hear with my hands.

(Under Words, 1983*)*

A LIFE OF INTIMATE FLEEING

Under the cypresses the air is still
the long meditations of the mosses
have gotten nowhere. Tangled in themselves
they forgot what they were thinking.
"No, we were just thinking. There is
no object, only subject, so we are
as the poem is, a nest of brackets
enclosing"

        brackets, does memory
have a *core?*

And under the cypress on drier ground
one takes off clothes,
takes and takes
and there is only clothes
one by one cast into the vanilla-scented
    gearwork, branches
of these infinitely slow machines.

From image to image
we flee by night.
It is a passion
of running.
We who live in gardens
have no point
but the next flower.
Why is it winter?
Make things and touch people—
is there another law?

    2

From room to room
immensity.

An hour, by touch.
Excitement by shape
promises a kind

of knowing that is new.
And then another street.

And always the same Law.

The law a boat
the beast a passenger
we steer.

Since going is the loveliest,

and when it runs
splay-silked against the uddery wind
it also like water quivers
among the tall grasses as
if this kind of water can stand up
and shape the wind that stirs it

                    3

a nest of brackets
enclosing sky

fork of the great tree.

                    (*Under Words*, 1983)

LOOKING

Once when I read the funnies
I took my little magnifying glass
and looked too close.

Forms became colors and colors
were just arrays of dots
and between the dots I saw the rough bleak
storyless legend of the pulp paper
empty as the winter moon

and dreaded it.
I had looked right through,
when I wanted a universe
that sustains
looker and looking and the seen
forever, detail after detail
never ending. And all I had found
was between. But between
had its own song:
Find it in the space between—

it is just as empty as it seems
but this blankness is your mother.

(*Under Words*, 1983)

RECESSIONAL

Spyan ras gzigs la na mo

Into the underneath—

the used teabag
is drying among ashes,
stained delicate mauve—
hibiscus flowers in it
and the gamboge of chamomile.
Meanwhile she reads Proust.

The places lust conducts me to,
a cup, a fallen petal
from a ruined anemone,
sly fiftiesish jazz ooping along
in or as grey daylight.
How much meat there is on the bone!

Not much in this culture
left for me. I will arise
and go into the future,
to the country I take it

joggers are also trotting to
beyond quiche and croissants,
beyond the poignant resurrections
each commodity promises and fails.

I see a rough grey gravel hill there
I am suddenly determined to climb
and set a pebble down to praise
all those who came before me
knowing no more than I do of the way.

(*Not This Island Music,* 1987)

Ronald Johnson [1935]

BEAM 30, *The Garden*   for Patricia Anderson

"To do as Adam did"
through the twilight's fluoride glare Mercury in perihilion
(rotating exactly three times
while circling the sun twice)
to Pluto foot tilt up the slide at either plane
and build a Garden of the brain.

Internetted eternities, interspersed
with cypresses
ply ringed air about the many spectacled apples there.
Flamestitch niches orb in swivel orb, The Muses thrush at center
turning. *Phospheros arborescens* they sing
sense's

struck crystal clarities
to knock the knees
(or scarlet hollyhock, against a near blue sky).
No end of fountains lost among the shrubberies full eye may bare.
Fixed stars
with fireflies jam the lilac.

The Lord is a delicate hammerer.
Gold hive upon gray matter
He taps synapse ("carrying to") ("carrying away")
an immense bronze pinecone moon-knit at the end of a vista
of sunny *jets d'eau*, silver poplars. All
shivered in a pool.

Literally, a flowing: form-take-hand
-with-form
(That Which Fasteneth Us)
pillar to pillar the great dance arch itself through all that
is or was or will be, ¾ time. This will be a glade
at the head of one stream

and a resonant gnomon before it will stretch regions of signaling
gnat–like resiliencies in the atmosphere
of where we are—
or were.
Or will be, when the mingled frame of mind
of man is celebration.

Gates, which separate the wings
of tiered ilex, open
in caverns of atoms passing from one into another's zenith
of periodic movement, vast helicoidal shift:
a vaulting of arteries
beating their heads against the dark.

This is the body of light.

Vertically in a chromatic spread chord
—Elysian elision—
J'avais bâti, dans un rêve, un palais, un château ou des
grottes
along the lines of sight.
Dear Garden:

This is the way the world begins, the word begins.
Through here,
where grow the galax and aster together,
I have planted Shadow illuminating The Field of Glittering
Opposites
ange arc–en–ciel

flocons de neige
I have attempted a temple as if hierarchies of music
beating against time gone adagio, that is the Secret Pool we return
to. And not to stone
but to the world behind its human
mirror.

This is the way the word begins, the world begins,
wrestling the old ineffable to Bosch's amazing white giraffe
—or St. Rousseau

intent a symmetry of whisker.
Love itself is a kind of *mirage* nesting it all
together. Around a center

no one can see the end of, at the Well of The Bottomless,
I have placed parallels of bright guardians
"along with the trill
of the Nightingale,
and the call of the European quail"
as in The Pastoral

(Signed) *THE GARDENER*

P.S.

"I have refracted it with Prismes, and reflected with it Bodies which in Day-light
were of other colours; I have intercepted it with the coloured film of Air interceding
two compressed plates of glass; transmitted it through coloured Mediums, and
through Mediums irradiated with other sorts of Rays, and diversly terminated it:
and yet could never produce any new colour out of it. But the most surprising, and
wonderful composition was that

of *Whiteness*."

(*Ark: The Foundations: 1 – 33,* 1980)

ARK 34, *Spire on the Death of L.Z.*

is this happening,
a quick as a squirrel's tail
spright of deer
but burnished as a
grackle
foci
evenly distributed as nesting sights
or silvery layers of film
over rotifers
trapeze
of paraphrase

in a sphere clumped
pool all a mareshiver
of lights
executed in pure
katydid
half Mozart
fits and starts, half stars
both
holywork of oracular oak
thought through
dust's
simplest
scherzo scarecrow
tactics an acorn might
knuckle under
paradise
and pairs of eyes
past
all believing

an edifice
of matched snailshell
faced to watch
Bach
in cherubim cliffed hayseed, rayed
cloud in plaster
forever
or near it
as consonance gets without
clef
to unraveled blizzard
huzzah cooperating with treble instances
such as orioles
between tulip trees
seizing the summerier dissonances
of worm
bees purring a
cappella
in utter emerald cornfield
till the cows come
purple home
this is paradise
this is

happening
on the surface of a bubble
time and again
fire sculpt of notwithstanding
dark
the whole parted world
in choir

when the wind's bright horses
hooves break earth in thunder
that,
that is paradise
Lord Hades, whom we all will meet
crackling up
like a wall of prairie fire
in a somersault silver
to climb blank air
around us
to say then head wedded nail and hammer to the
work of vision
of the word
at hand
that is paradise,
this is called spine of white cypress
roughly cylindrical
based
on the principle
of the intervals between cuckoos
and molecules, and molecules
reechoing:
these are the carpets of
protoplast, this
the hall of crystcycling waltz
down carbon atom
this, red clay
grassland
where the cloud steeds clatter out wide stars
this is

(*Ark 50: Spires: 34 – 50*, 1984)

ARK 44, *The Rod of Aaron*

rose might of the winds
blind fold
shadow forth stilt thyrsus thus
who once have sung
snug in the oblong
soon life bright spent

Planted at stake
Old Sarpint
himself, bent at the outfoot
everyday Arbor Vitae:
turf fit to burst
shall see us off.
Holy Ghost
praise be, knocking bedrock
like the screen door
in a dust storm,
pitched Lord knows how
all of a piece
peculiar grace

that yet
brancht forth.

(*Ark 50: Spires: 34 – 50*, 1984)

Rosmarie Waldrop [1935]

from THE REPRODUCTION OF PROFILES

FEVERISH PROPOSITIONS

You told me, if something is not used it is meaningless, and took my temperature which I had thought to save for a more difficult day. In the mirror, every night, the same face, a bit more threadbare, a dress worn too long. The moon was out in the cold, along with the restless, dissatisfied wind that seemed to change the location of the sycamores. I expected reproaches because I had mentioned the word love, but you only accused me of stealing your pencil, and sadness disappeared with sense. You made a ceremony out of holding your head in your hands because, you said, it could not be contained in itself.

□

If we could just go on walking through these woods and let the pine branches brush our faces, living would still make beads of sweat on your forehead, but you wouldn't have to worry about what you call my exhibitionism. All you liked about trees was the way the light came through the leaves in sheets of precise, parallel rays, like slant rain. This may be an incomplete explanation of our relation, but we've always feared the dark inside the body. You agree there could be no seduction if the structures of propositions did not stand in a physical relation, so that we could get from one to the other. Even so, not every moment of happiness is to hang one's clothes on.

□

I might have known you wouldn't talk to me. But to claim you just didn't want to disguise your thoughts! We've walked along this road before, I said, though perhaps in heavier coats not designed to reveal the form of the body. Later, the moon came out and threw the shadows of branches across the street where they remained, broken. Feverishly you examined the tacit conventions on which conversation depends. I sighed as one does at night, looking down into the river. I wondered if by throwing myself in I could penetrate to the essence of its character, or should I wait for you to stab me as you had practiced in your dream? You said this question, like most philosophical problems, arose from failing to understand the tale of the two youths, two horses, and two lilies. You could prove to me that the deepest rivers are, in fact, no rivers at all.

□

From this observation we turned to consider passion. Looking at the glints of light on the water, you tried to make me tell you not to risk the excitement—to recommend cold baths. The lack of certainty, of direction, of duration, was its own argument, unlike going into a bar to get drunk and getting drunk. Your face was alternately hot and cold, as if translating one language into another—gusts from the storm in your heart, the pink ribbon in your pocket. Its actual color turned out to be unimportant, but its presence disclosed something essential about membranes. You said there was still time, you could still break it off, go abroad, make a movie. I said (politely, I thought) this wouldn't help you. You'd have to kill yourself.

□

Tearing your shirt open, you drew my attention to three dogs in a knot. This served to show how something general can be recorded in unpedigreed notation. I pointed to a bench by a willow, from which we could see the gas tanks across the river, because I thought a bench was a simple possibility: one could sit on it. The black hulks of the tanks began to sharpen in the cold dawn light, though when you leaned against the railing I could smell your hair, which ended in a clean round line on your neck, as was the fashion that year. I had always resented how nimble your neck became whenever you met a woman, regardless of rain falling outside or other calamities. Now, at least, you hunched your shoulders against the shadow of doubt.

□

This time of day, hesitation can mean tottering on the edge, just before the water breaks into the steep rush and spray of the fall. What could I do but turn with the current and get choked by my inner speed? You tried to breathe against the acceleration, waiting for the air to consent. All the while, we behaved as if this search for a pace were useful, like reaching for a plank or wearing rain coats. I was afraid we would die before we could make a statement, but you said that language presupposed meaning, which would be swallowed by the roar of the waterfall.

Toward morning, walking along the river, you tossed simple objects into the air which was indifferent around us, though it moved off a little, and again as you put your hand back in your pocket to test the degree of hardness. Everything else remained the same. This is why, you said, there was no fiction.

(*The Reproduction of Profiles*, 1987)

LAWN OF EXCLUDED MIDDLE

I

When I say I believe that women have a soul and that its substance contains two carbon rings the picture in the foreground makes it difficult to find its application back where the corridors get lost in ritual sacrifice and hidden bleeding. But the four points of the compass are equal on the lawn of the excluded middle where full maturity of meaning takes time the way you eat a fish, morsel by morsel, off the bone. Something that can be held in the mouth, deeply, like darkness by someone blind or the empty space I place at the center of each poem to allow penetration.

2

I'm looking out the window at other windows. Though the pane masquerades as transparent I know it is impenetrable just as too great a show of frankness gives you a mere paper draft on revelations. As if words were passports, or arrows that point to the application we might make of them without considering the difference of biography and life. Still, depth of field allows the mind to drift beyond its negative pole to sun catching on a maple leaf already red in August, already thinner, more translucent, preparing to strip off all that separates it from its smooth skeleton. Beautiful, flamboyant phrase that trails off without predicate, intending disappearance by approaching it, a toss in the air.

3

I put a ruler in my handbag, having heard men talk about their sex. Now we have correct measurements and a stickiness between collar and neck. It is one thing to insert yourself into a mirror, but quite another to get your image out again and have your errors pass for objectivity. Vitreous. As in humor. A change in perspective is caused by the ciliary muscle, but need not be conciliatory. Still, the eye is a camera, room for everything that is to enter, like the cylinder called the satisfaction of hollow space. Only language grows such grass-green grass.

4

Even if a woman sits at a loom, it does not mean she must weave a cosmogony or clothes to cover the emptiness underneath. It might just be a piece of cloth which, like any center of attention, absorbs the available light the way a waterfall can form a curtain of solid noise through which only time can pass. She has been taught to imagine other things, but does not explain, disdaining defense while her consciousness streams down the rapids. The light converges on what might be the hollow of desire or the incomplete self, or just lint in her pocket. Her hour will also come with the breaking of water.

5

Because I refuse to accept the opposition of night and day I must pit other, subtler periodicities against the emptiness of being an adult. Their traces inside my body attempt precariously, like any sign, to produce understanding, but though nothing may come of that, the grass is growing. Can words play my parts and also find their own way to the house next door as rays converge and solve their differences? Or do notes follow because drawn to a conclusion? If we don't signal our love, reason will eat our heart out before it can admit its form of mere intention, and we won't know what has departed.

6

All roads lead, but how does a sentence do it? Nothing seems hidden, but it goes by so fast when I should like to see it laid open to view whether the engine resembles combustion so that form becomes its own explanation. We've been taught to apply solar principles, but must find on our own where to look for Rome the way words rally to the blanks between them and thus augment the volume of their resonance.

7

It's a tall order that expects pain to crystallize into beauty. And we must close our eyes to conceive of heaven. The inside of the lid is fertile in images unprovoked by experience, or perhaps its pressure on the eyeball equals prayer in the same way that inference is a transition toward assertion, even observing rites of dawn against a dark and empty background. I have read that female prisoners to be hanged must wear rubber pants and a dress sewn shut around the knees because uterus and ovaries spill with the shock down the shaft.

8

The meaning of certainty is getting burned. Though truth will still escape us, we must put our hands on bodies. Staying safe is a different death, the instruments of defense eating inward without evening out the score. As the desire to explore my body's labyrinth did, leading straight to the center of nothing. From which projected my daily world of representation with bright fictional fireworks. Had I over-invested in spectacle? In mere fluctuations of light which, like a bird's wingbeat, must with time slow to the point of vanishing? What about buying bread or singing in the dark? Even if the ground for our assumptions is the umber of burnt childhood we're driven toward the sun as if logic had no other exit.

9

Though the way I see you depends on I don't know how many codes I have absorbed unawares, like germs or radiation, I am certain the conflicting possibilities of logic and chemistry have contaminated the space between us. Emptiness is imperative for feeling to take on substance, for its vibrations to grow tangible, a faintly trembling beam that supports the whole edifice. Caught between the thickness of desire and chill clarity, depth dissolved its contours with intemperate movements inside the body where much can be gathered. Can I not say a cry, a laugh are full of meaning, a denseness for which I have no words which would not channel its force into shallower waters, mere echo of oracles?

10

My anxiety made you wary. As if I tried to draw you into a new kind of sexuality, a flutter of inner emptiness implying hunger to frame the momentary flight of birds with emotional reference and heat. Any initiation anticipates absolute abandon with the body misunderstood as solid, whereas images dissolve their objects. Even with deep water ahead, even though the shores of syllogism may be flooded, we must not turn around. Behind us, incursions into our own field of vision, a mirror to lose our body out of the corner of an eye. It may look like a sentence we understand, yet quenches no thirst, no matter how hard we stroke it. But anxiety is a password which does not require a special tone of voice. Rather than to immersion in mysteries I was only leading you to common ground.

11

Whenever you're surprised that I should speak your language I am suddenly wearing too many necklaces and breasts, even though feeling does not produce what is felt, and the object of observation is something else again. Not modulating keys, not the splash that makes us take to another element, just my body alarmingly tangible, like furniture that exceeds its function, a shape I cannot get around. The way one suddenly knows the boulder in the road for a boulder, immovable, as if not always there, unmodified by inner hollows or the stray weeds and their dusty green, a solid obstacle with only trompe-l'oeil exits toward the subtler body of light accumulating in the distance.

12

I worried about the gap between expression and intent, afraid the world might see a fluorescent advertisement where I meant to show a face. Sincerity is no help once we admit to the lies we tell on nocturnal occasions, even in the solitude of our own heart, wishcraft slanting the naked figure from need to seduce to fear of possession. Far better to cultivate the gap itself with its high grass for privacy and reference gone astray. Never mind that it is not philosophy, but raw electrons jumping from orbit to orbit to ready the pit for the orchestra, scrap meanings amplifying the succession of green perspectives, moist fissures, spasms on the lips.

13

Words too can be wrung from us like a cry from that space which doesn't seem to be the body nor a metaphor curving into perspective. Rather the thickness silence gains when pressed. The ghosts of grammar veer toward shape while my hopes still lie embedded in a quiet myopia from which they don't want to arise. The mistake is to look for explanations where we should just watch the slow fuse burning. Nerve of confession. What we let go we let go.

14

Because we use the negative as if no explanation were needed the void we cater to is, like anorexia, a ferment of hallucinations. Here, the bird's body equals the rhythm of wingbeats which, frantic, disturb their own lack of origin, fear of falling, indigenous grey. Static electricity. Strobe map. Gap gardening. The sun feeds on its dark core for a set of glistening blood, in a space we can't fathom except as pollution colors it.

15

The word "not" seems like a poor expedient to designate all that escapes my under-standing like the extra space between us when I press my body against yours, per-haps the distance of desire, which we carry like a skyline and which never allows us to be where we are, as if past and future had their place whereas the present dips and disappears under your feet, so suddenly your stomach is squeezed up into your throat as the plane crashes. This is why some try to stretch their shadow across the gap as future fame while the rest of us take up residence in the falling away of land, even though our nature is closer to water.

16

The affirmation of the double negative tempts us to invent a myth of meaning where the light loops its wavelength through dark hollows into unheard-of Americas, or a double-tongued flute speeds decimals over the whole acoustic range of the land-scape till it exhausts itself with excess of effect brought home. Can I walk in your sleep, in order to defer obedience and assent to my own waking? Or will the weight of error pull me down below the symmetries of the round world? Touching bottom means the water's over your head. And you can't annul a shake of that by shaking it again.

17

In Providence, you can encounter extinct species, an equestrian statue, say, left hoof raised in progress toward the memory of tourists. Caught in its career of immobility, but with surface intact, waiting to prove that it can resist the attack of eyes even though dampened by real weather, even though historical atmosphere is mixed with exhaust like etymology with the use of a word or bone with sentence structure. No wonder we tend to stay indoors.

18

A window can draw you into the distance within proximity all the way to where it vanishes with the point. This is not a hocuspocus which can be performed only by kinship terms. The glass seems to secure perspectives that can shoulder the cold stare of so many third persons while our image is resolved in favor of inaccessible riverbeds. Alternating small and large measures, the dust on the pane is part of the attraction, a way of allowing the environment in. So would a stone's throw, substi-tuting the high frequencies of shattering for the play of reflections.

19

We know that swallows are drawn to window panes, etching swift lurching streaks across and sometimes crashing. I picked up the body as if easing the vast sky through a narrow pulse toppling over itself. Caught between simulacrum and paradox, the hard air. Even if a body could survive entering its own image, the mirror is left empty, no fault in the glass breaking the evenness of light.

20

What's left over if I subtract the fact that my leg goes up from the fact that I raise it? A link to free will or never trying, as only our body knows to disobey an even trade to the sound of a fiddle. Something tells me not to ask this question and accept the movement. The speed of desire like a hot wind sweeping the grass or flash of water under the bridge. For doing itself seems not to have any volume: an extensionless point, the point of a needle out to draw blood regardless.

21

This is not thinking, you said, more what colors it, like a smell entering our breath even to the seat of faith under the left nipple. Like the children I could have borne shaping my body toward submission and subterfuge. It is possible, I admitted, to do physics in inches as well as in centimeters, but a concept is more than a convenience. It takes us through earnest doorways to always the same kind of example. No chance of denser vegetation, of the cool shadow of firs extending this line of reasoning into the dark.

22

My love was deep and therefore lasted only the space of one second, unable to expand in more than one dimension at a time. The same way deeper meaning may constrict a sentence right out of the language into an uneasiness with lakes and ponds. In language nothing is hidden or our own, its light indifferent to holes in the present or postulates beginning with ourselves. Still, you may travel alone and yet be accompanied by my good wishes.

23

Look in thy heart and write, you quoted. As if we could derive the object from desire, or proper breathing from the structure of transitivity. It's true, the brain is desperate for an available emptiness to house its clutter, as a tone can only grow from a space of silence, lifted by inaudible echoes as birds are by the air inside their bones. So we reach down, although it cannot save us, to the hollows inside the body, to extend them into so many journeys into the world, so many words shelling the echo of absence onto the dry land.

24

In the way well-being contains the possibility of pain a young boy may show the meekness we associate with girls, or an excess of sperm, on occasion, come close to spirituality. But a name is an itch to let the picture take root inside its contour though sentences keep shifting like sand, and a red patch may be there or not. All heights are fearful. We must cast arbitrary nets over the unknown, knot the earth's rim to the sky with a rope of orisons. For safety. For once human always an acrobat.

25

Meaning is like going up to someone I would be with, though often the distance doesn't seem to lessen no matter how straight my course. Busy moving ahead, I can't also observe myself moving, let alone assess the speed of full steam minus fiction and sidetracked in metric crevices. It's hard to identify with the image of an arrow even if it points only to the application we make of it. But then, meandering does not guarantee thought either though it simulates its course toward wider angles, which make us later than we are, our fingers the space of already rust from the key. Even the weight of things can no longer measure our calculations. Conquered by our own scope we offer no resistance to the blue transparency, the startling down-pour of sun.

26

I wanted to settle down on a surface, a map perhaps, where my near-sightedness might help me see the facts. But grammar is deep. Even though it only describes, it submerges the mind in a maelstrom without discernable bottom, the dimensions of possibles swirling over the fixed edge of nothingness. Like looking into blue eyes all the way through to the blue sky without even a cloudbank or flock of birds to cling to. What are we searching behind the words as if a body of information could not also bruise? It is the skeleton that holds on longest to its native land.

27

For a red curve to be a smile it needs a face around it, company of its kind to capture our attention by the between, the bait of difference and constant of desire. Then color sweeping over cheeks is both expansion of internal transport and an airing of emotion. Understanding, too, enters more easily through a gap between than where a line is closed upon itself. This is why comparisons, for all their limping, go farther even than the distance of beauty, rose or fingered dawn, or of remembering contracts signed in blood.

28

Electric seasons. Night has become as improbable as a sea forever at high tide. The sheer excess of light makes for a lack of depth, denying our fall from grace, the way a membrane is all surface. Or the way we, clamoring for sense, exclude so many unions of words from the sphere of language. As if one could fall off the edge of the earth. Why do we fear the dark as unavoidable defeat when it alone is constant, and we'd starve if it stopped watering the lawn of dreams.

29

You were determined to get rid of your soul by expressing it completely, rubbing the silver off the mirror in hope of a new innocence of body on the other side of knowing. A limpid zone which would not wholly depend on our grammar in the way the sea draws its color from the sky. Noon light, harsh, without shadow. Each gesture intending only its involvement with gravity, a pure figure of reach, as the hyperbola is for its asymptotes or circles widening on the water for the stone that broke the surface. But the emigration is rallied, reflections regather across the ripples. Everything in our universe curves back to the apple.

30

The capacity to move my hand from left to right arises on a margin of indecision and doubt winding into vertiginous inner stairwells, but only when adjacent shadows have cooled the long summer sun toward a more introverted, solitary quality of light for the benefit of eyes tensing to see the dark before concepts. This is an attempt to make up for inner emptiness in the way that Fred Astaire and Ginger Rogers dance with more desperate brio to add to a third dimension to their characters. Nevertheless the capacity does not explain how the meaning of individual words can make a tent over a whole argument. It is not a feeling, but a circular movement to represent the transfer of visibility toward dream without abrogating the claims of body.

31

As if I had to navigate both forward and backward, part of me turned away from where I'm going, taking the distance of long corridors to allow for delay and trouble, for keeping in the dark while being led on. In this way Chinese characters seem to offer their secret without revealing it, invitation to enter a labyrinth which, like that of the heart, may not have a center. It is replaced by being lost which I don't like to dwell on because the search for motivation can only drive us downward toward potential that is frightening in proportion to its depth and sluicegates to disappearance. It is much better, I have been advised, just to drift with the stream. The ink washes into a deeper language, and in the end the water runs clear.

(*Lawn of Excluded Middle*, 1993)

Kenneth Irby [1936]

JANUARY 1965, LOOKING ON

Moss in the gratings
of a sewer vent

And past me have gone
a lady cop in a yellow slicker
ticketing in the rain
and those who have come in and out
after books

There is no image the flesh
does not take in, sink, the hook, there is
a weight beyond me all afternoon, into the drizzle
uncertainties of
how to look

A man comes in selling ballpoint pens
"I won't be back to bother you for a long time, not till April—
I'll let you have all three for 75¢—they all write"

And in the dust on the floor of that used-book store?
So seared, the scars he must have had so long
any look back at him
is not even felt?

Moss
on the sewer plates

And on Clement Street
leads straight to the Pacific
men dead on their feet
come—back? home? down hard—
to die. The clod prim slickered copess

And there is no footprint

no print in the moss
the wet, sopped weeks of rain
does not take out of men, bodies
the bodies sopped
staining the filthy concrete

The rancors of texts and elucidations

And the quiet light down on the dust, in the windows, in this store

My God, my hands stuffed in my dirty pockets

11 Jan 65

(*Relation*, 1970)

SEQUENCE

So we wait on the verge of—
                    the want to move on again
The pressure that becomes unbearable to stay in one place any
                              longer

American history is the only history

Local history is the only history

            it is the
                         body
        answers

                              □

P. came in this morning and told me
his wife had been raped Friday night—coming home
drunk from a party they waited over an hour for a bus
and arguing he got mad and walked home by himself—she tried
the people at the party and called a cab, and waiting
3 guys hit her—

                         "after 2 days of eating ourselves

apart over that, we decided to move—to Albuquerque,
Tucson, the sw somewhere like that"

And in the lunchcounter later, drinking coffee,
he talked about George Catlin—*everytime I go east
I feel I'm going against an enormous tide*

□

I'd said when I came to San Francisco, the only way to go east
after you've come this full tilt west to the ocean
is north and then east again—the great
clockwise undercurrents of the continent

But we'll go the south route next month
to Albuquerque to pick up my books that are stored there
and they'll probably go with us

□

That is, what makes us move?
                         This thing
for them—
             they'd been talking about leaving for months,
moving to a new apartment soon, anyway—

this rape

They tend no cattle in the sunned pastures
of these streets, not even a car
what grass flesh milk dessert sustains
past the regurgitation of oneself, and eaten all again?

it is the pressure cooker's lid blown off
of the lady who lived behind us in Fort Scott
her face and arms burned into scars

what dispossesses us
what we do not have to take
      sitting down,
                    but move—

□

All day has been the necessary tedium
      to come to this quiet—
left alone as Mary's gone to pick up Michael
      and lost in Melville lost into *Clarel*—
put again by your phonecall
      upon the turn we move upon, where
pivot us, old throaty night quiet songs
      before we leave, tell us
where we've lived, here, sweaty
      drawers left, garbage sacks thrown out the window—

Mary come home asks me to take the garbage out
and in the yard the amaryllis' smell is thick, their pink—
so soft they turn in the dark yard the stamens clink
    filter butts in the grass thrown out of the upstairs window
        roll cold against my feet

The important question of our movement
is how different it is to go this in & out I have tonight
and you to move that move to come to Albuquerque

—to come to this quiet

even Michael's shouts and machinegun rasps
do not disturb, garbage sacks or clock ticks

is from or to that same movement you move on now? all
lost shit necessary first to rest at all? what done
to come to whatever ease, lasts now, while it is, endless—last
fall in isolation on 48th Avenue, wandering Golden Gate Park
where groundhogs came and went and doberman bitches
to greet me, what pain of loving a friend I could not touch,
slow turn up and down night mattresses without, as rose and fell
the geraniums' saturation glow, the fog that came and left

we move, to lose the pain? I moved
to this yard, it took months, it's taken
months to reach this ease tonight—

the difference of the distance of the travel, the length of the steps,
      long time—

and then we wait on the verge of—?

as I wait on any step at all out there in the yard
for the chink, the clink, in the amaryllis, to open
or to begin to bore into—

as you endure the lapsed long pain of *where?*
and a weekend of rape and after eaten into and out again

to face any new place
and rechallenge the power of your roots
       to sink into

Let it come, let it come
the age of our desire

I have endured so long
I have forgotten everything

                                23-24 Aug 65

                    (*Relation,* 1970)

HEREDOM

☐

lobe of opalescent glass
    broken in the irreplaceable lampshade

out of the shoulder, the corridor
    down the street the kids from junior high
        come by in t-shirts for the warmth of February
                                    pigeons overhead
    stamp and cry in their sleep

gathered, the branch of acacia
    fused through the green swirled
        Egyptian thorn milk waters
raised, itself, of the lost and gathered body of mastery

or all the highschool years again, unslept, reviewing the annual faces over and over
    till they run green in the movies after the eyes are closed
        and still as distant as they were in person

            the society of ordinary
        highschool days, never left, will it?

        against the society of the widow's son, those
          who on the elephant's back
            be freed?

the generation of mourning doves' cries
    is from twilight in the mind
               releasing and attracting us

☐

parsley
       pubic hair above the bread
          body torn to pieces and thrown at the audience

    or where the sun is gone
      or where we watch the empty place we were

claimed by the garden
    work to right again
        to grab the rock hair green
          up out of the dirt

grabbing against and to be in those rites
    whose body in the bed, whose car lights down the street
        through the monk's cloth curtains
          or by the corridor of the shoulder

        every bundle of the exultant stride of walking home

☐

in the life of the laundry   the hand goes down
                                    into the patch

        upside down the parsley hangs

and very very young the mothers are
one child already 3 or 4
the one her mother calls "hey asshole"

we want to watch where each master *was*
the shape of the space left
just a curl of smoke behind
Aaron's cigarette in front of the brazen serpent, or some dope, or the cold in
on the breath

in the same room

□

[for Mary Josephine Buffington Newman, 20 Jul 1884 – 20 Feb 1977]

in the well between our houses
where the houses have gone to stare
away from all their inhabitants

three violinists play your procession away
under the pear tree, under the liriodendron
under the ghost of the pear tree

the well of roses, the well of iris
in back, in the alley
down the ravine the waters carry away

•

call of the Frisco diesel in the middle of the night

answering cry in the pigeons' sleep

waking not in a sweat but the smell of the sweat of waking

so far the call

□

even so the wavering fires

now just ordinary flameshaped lightbulbs set in a
triangle, purposefully crude and bare

but as a child it was the unexperienced richness
that made wonder

in the palm of the youngest entered initiate
without asking in the dark pupils watching, unseen

Light can be ordinary even when revealed and still by the spoken word
astound the body least of all attended
out on the playground

I dropped the bag of groceries I didn't even mean to bring
I shit my pants *after* coming down from under the pine trees

from the old authoritarian high degrees of Europe
one aging man left to confer

the camps, unattended, meant Westward

kept going on the decks, dark adepts at the flames

□

children of excitement
purses of the abandonment—not *yours* but *you*

the Prince of the Captivity with a defective brain
chased down the street by his father
oblivio-naked to the usedto judgement of the kids looking on

the jewel hangs from a rattle string
broken rattle rayed with stars coming out from behind the occultation

and bars, like candy, out of prison

sperm
might as well have been hyacinth jizz or dandelion
fuming on the palm

the man that might have been
master still and covered, to rise again

□

early Summer in SE Kansas
>the 2d weekend in April, Good Friday, 85°

>>broiled in bourbon before the Council of the Emperors of the East & West, hickory smoked
>>>in almonds, and the redbuds in glory, call

>and in the temple to be the temple substitute after the temple destroyed
>and until

>not of Jerusalem yet of a secrecy within, of Jerusalem
>>such election, which takes that history as its own
>>>as ordinary and electable, rare, attended, as each tulip
>>>>each hyacinth passed, to each grape hyacinth, kinless, except

is still just beginning Spring

>>>and in the temple, under the immense weight of tulips
>>>the lights are extinguished
>>>>and the halls for the space of 3 days
>>>>>wait dark in the heart, cool

□

from The Camp the cries of burnt Templars
>rise into a canopy of transparent tintinnabulating leaves
>>over the tents of the *tengu* and outward
>>>over the nonagon of the body, over the levees of patrol

you've probably caught sight of The Camp at times
>>coming unexpectedly into a clearing and looking up
>>the quick flags
>>>>thinking a fairy ring of mushrooms
>>>>or Kim's Red Bull on a Green Field

but it does not remain to the eyes
>or even, since there may be no other name, at all
and yet returns

it might have been having word of an old highschool friend
>living in New Orleans now, grown large as his father
>that I circled Louisiana last night, marking only

a couple of tents, or banners, or worn places in front of the grass
      named by the friends I knew were there

it is said as the troops move about The Camp and take up their positions with their speeches taped
                                      to their spear shafts

     that the seven is empty

          so there is a space to look out on
                from the beasts and the heart of the ark between the palms
           and into from the tents

          where the shade and choir of torment
            make an alleyway of repose to walk in
              from the work done, in the pause, on
                to the anticipation of the ball lying just out of hiding around the bend
            and the shot clear to
                    but not to any hole in the hand or the eye, waiting

The Camp if it is a camp rotates slowly on an axis
    not the Grand Commander or the Mill of the Heavens or the Transparency of the Tree or all
                              the Years of Reunion Rituals
that are the pole of the body

□

across the street, in the next block North and East, next door to Howell's old place
                        next door to Jents' old place

    a new van, chocolate brown and cream, parked in front, everybody out looking at looking at

      the Prince of the Captivity ran just there

  Princess now, raced past me as I came back from Whiteside's last Thursday afternoon
      her mother just after her, calling

                so the word is passed on
           and equally not known
     till how much later, the thrill of recognizing can still be known

the iris guard young flesh, probably

                              [Feb – May, 1977
                              Fort Scott, Kansas]

                              (*Orexis*, 1981)

Clarence Major [1936]

SWALLOW THE LAKE

Gave me things I
could not use. Then. Now.
Rain night bursting upon & into. I
shine updown into Lake Michigan

like the glow from the cold lights of the Loop.
Walks. Deaths. Births.
Streets. Things I could not give back. Nor
use. Or night or day or night or

loneliness. Other ways   feelings I could not
put into words   into themselves into people.
Blank monkeys of the hierarchy. More deaths—
stupidity & death turning them on

into the beat of my droopy heart   my middle
passage blues my corroding hate my release
while I come to become neon iron eyes stainless lungs
blond zincgripped steel I
come up abstract

not able to take their bricks. Tar. Nor their flesh.
I ran: stung. Loop fumes hung
                              in my smoky lungs.

ideas I could not break nor form. Gave me
things I
see break & run down the crawling down the
game.

Illusion illusion, and you
would swear before screaming somehow
choked voices in me.

The crawling thing in the blood, the
huge immune loneliness. One becomes immune
to the bricks the feelings. One becomes
death.
One becomes each one and every person I
become. I could not
I COULD NOT
I could not whistle and walk in storms
along Lake Michigan's shore. Concrete walks.
I could not swallow the lake

(*Swallow the Lake*, 1970)

BEAULIEU

Red mullet, rosy in its sleep
profile, red mullet on a white plate.
Straight ahead!
Blue table cloth as frame.
Mullus barbatus does not smile up
from its dead trilia beidha eye.
Olive oil glows on its scales.
Red mullet, red mullet
olive oil is not its blood.

Before *you* eat the red mullet,
embrace at the table : especially
if you are not a mullidae expert.
The goatfish will kick.
Pray to the Red Sea and
the Suez Canal. Become skilled
at fishing, and fishing
around the bones. Do not tickle
its erectile barbels. It will
not laugh at itself.
Scrape the slime from your body.
Have a loved one drag a rake
along your thighs. Clip
the matted hair. Clean under
your finger nails.

(*Inside Diameter: The France Poems*, 1985)

BALANCE AND BEAUTY

We go over to see the head of a woman,
even more: night and Mandolin.
One has to be right
handed to get into the microcosm.
We slip in the back
door: both working from the other
side of our brains. At Port Lympia
nobody notices how skillful
I am in cracking crab shells
with my right: easy as a bird's head.
Don't anticipate.
Up here, slightly above the skyline
nothing invades our rests
in shaded cavities of this hillside.
This is no picnic at Saint Philippe.
The head of the woman remains
an unrealized objective.
In the village of Helene
they ask why am I so sure
about this left-handed business.
I show them a map of my nervous system.
They say this proves nothing.

(*Inside Diameter: The France Poems*, 1985)

LOST IN THE DESERT

I

The sun,
    in her memory,
           held itself high
above its bed,
    the mountains—to the South.
Human bone, beaded dolls, chunks
         of turquoise,
were the relics of her cove.

The "Coral direction" pleased her,
            looking down that range
to the sound of tesese (once she
                tapped the taut skin
    herself and heard the power of
                    sound
lift up from the orifice).

Her throat dried faster than the pit
  of a clay oven when
              the match is
  struck to paper
          beneath the wood.
In silence, she turned
            her small emery wheel.
In silence, in silence.
The sun
        disappeared
behind the range like a prairie wolf
entering
        a path through desert rock.

She was out
           here now (in the music).
Her heart was a terrified cactus wren
        gripped
in a dirty fist.
           Unseen Hands was not there
to protect her
    from the Mystery—
          and its danger:
he's a gray fox—
          they're in a desert
and she's a desert rat.

          In the mirror
she sees the beginning
        of the full moon
and more: herself as windstorm,
          as summer flood,
          as migrating coyote,
          as spotted skunk
            on the run;

as sheepherder
                    rounding up strays,
                              cutting cattle
for the Nastacio family ...
            It was the summer her brother taught
her to fly
            like a bat
(instead of eating
                    the mutton, she fed it
to the wild dogs) and like the other
      things
that came while she slept.

            "You look like you
just saw a ghost!"
            Somebody in the desert
was frying pork chops.
            She could smell
the smoke, blue as leaves—at dusk.

He spread the blanket
                  and made the fire;
she concentrated
                  on radio static
inside her chest. Once in a while
in it she heard muskrats
                  and wolves sniffing
the air in the cliffs
            above Zuni
where the clans
            had their summer
                        feasts and dances.

The sun,
            in her memory,
was going to be her moonlight
                        all this night long!

II

It gets very cold   here
                in the valley
below Sacred Mountain ...
        Her father proposed
to sell her to a richer family

        ... so she could eat.
"I told him I didn't want to eat."
        So she eats with her fingers,
chili stew ...
The cold made the hunger worse.
        She stood between two
bee-hive shaped ovens
                        in the yard.

In protest her mother
        refused to pack her clothes
so the father had
        to do it himself.
"My grandma told him the BIA
        was against selling children."
Zuni law wasn't
                he said,
against selling.
        She put on her buckskin,
                        moccasins,
ready to go.

The shouting?
        She ran, stumbled—
fell into the catfish-river
        got rear-ended up
the stream, grunting like a Coronado
                        pig,
broken like a Coronado horse,
        the dyes washing
off her skin
        as though she were an olla jar
painted with mudfrogs
                not so carefully
and with the wrong stuff.

III

Stiff, by the light of kerosene,
                on an orange crate,
by a clay pot
        with mudfrogs and delicate
                                plants,
also this—turned the wrong way—
                    this arrangement
by the bed … She saw
                    a young man looking
        down
up-
        on her, waking.
He said, "Unseen Hands
                    placed food before you.
Eat."

        Up, back against wall,
the platter of catfish
                    on her knees,
still her hunger didn't reach   out
                to it. Of more interest
was the lighted side
        of the wide face
                            above her.
"Who are you?"
                He made his sign,
his fingers, little hapas
        with the corpse-demon heads
you expect.

IV

About the desert,
                    she whispered
like a Ramah Mormon peeking
                        into folded hands.
        Not from the terrace
of an old house, not by a fire-
                            place
while using frybread

as a spoon in stew
or a wrapping for the catfish,
    her father ...
about this desert—the opposite
    of "my people lost in the lake"—
she whispered in a clearing
halfway between Saint John's
    and Surprise Valley,
as though she actually stood
  at a juncture between
the Colorado River and
    the Zuni River north
      of Hunt,
smelling brush burning but
    with no sight
of Sacred Lake. Nothing about this
     desert
reminded her of tomatoes melons
    and peppers.
She whispered with awe
feeling herself sinking in sand,
  as in
water, dying, consumed ...
    Thought about guilt,
poverty—
  of the ancient ones, all those
hundreds, hundreds of measured time,
      coming
down from The mesa
    (for no clear reason,
as they had gone up for none).
  If the infants became too
troublesome, why
    wouldn't the ancient ones
       drop
them in a lake? ("In our belief
 these children who *fell*
in the lake
  became the first kachinas.")
They live down at
    the bottom, and come
up at night and dance:
  in the plaza.

Not always friendly, these—
    You could be left
a bleeding victim of one's rage!

Which way, this Sacred Lake?
At Dowa Yallane it was never mentioned.
Nothing about it and nothing
      about the desert either ...

but it goes on: memory, sound
  all of it, the scrapings
on wood, the turnings, Moonlight?
Sun!
The help of Unseen Hands,
      seeing a way through
windstorms, all of it!

Out here, one needed to learn
      to be as untrusting
as the coyotes. Yes,
    moving the way they move;
        carefully.

(*Some Observations of a Stranger
at Zuni in the Latter Part of the
Century*, 1989)

Susan Howe [1937]

from SECRET HISTORY OF THE DIVIDING LINE

In its first dumb form

language was gesture

technique of travelling over sea ice
silent

before great landscapes and glittering processions

vastness of a great white looney north

of our forebeing.

Died of what?
Probably Death.

I know all that
I was only thinking—

quintessential clarity of inarticulation

family and familiar friends of family

pacing the floes nervously

climbing little ridges

the journey first
before all change in future

westward and still westward
matches coughing like live things.

■

Thorn, thistle, apron leaf

throughout each scene
man covers his body

calling "I have heard"

to a cadaverous throng
of revelers

who pose and gesture
acting out roles.

It is an dream
Enchantment

the animals speak

impaled again
in a netting of fences.

■

Set out to learn what fear was

little footsteps of a child
direction she had taken

under a bush crying bitterly

or nearly perishing with cold

marks and signs
I followed the track

hunted couple where they sheltered
running beside the chariots

no pocket compass or notched tree.

■

I knew what war was

Nelson wore a wig
and after a battle handed it to his valet
to have the bullets combed out.

Parents swept by
sheltering them I gave them my bed

watched their ardor from a hostile border
dreamed peals and clarions of stars.

Noontide in my mother's garden
saw clearly on the far horizon

lurid light of conflagration

lunacy leapt to the tongue of my brain

entering the city I sang for the beseiging forces
sang to the ear of remote wheels

"Oh King thou art betrayed."

I learned things
fighting off various wolves that hung around the door

gleam of a lance or helmet, heredity always smouldering.

(*Secret History of the Dividing Line*, 1978)

from PYTHAGOREAN SILENCE

He plodded away through drifts of i

ce

away into inapprehensible Peace

A portable altar strapped on his back

pure and severe

A portable altar strapped on his back

pure and severe

In the forest of Germany he will feed

on aromatic grass and browse in leaves

■

I

age of earth and us all chattering

a sentence   or character
suddenly

steps out to seek for truth   fails
falls

into a stream of ink   Sequence
trails off

must go on

waving fables and faces   War
doings of the war

manoeuvering between points
between

any two points   which is
what we want   (issues at stake)

bearings and so

holes in a cloud   are minutes passing
which is

which
view   odds of images swept rag-tag

silver and grey
epitomes

seconds   forgeries engender
(are blue)   or blacker
flocks of words flying together   tense
as an order

cast off to crows

                          5

I thought I did not live in night

for the future   I used to say
lighting the light

farewell to star   and star
As if light spreading

from some sounding center   might
measure even how

familiar
in the forest   losing the trees

Shadows   only shadows
met my gaze   Mediator

I lay down and conceived   Love
(my dear Imaginary) Maze-believer

I remember   you were called
sure-footed

and yet off the path   (Where
are you) warmed and warming   Body

turned and turning   Soul
identical soul   abandoned

to Sleep   (where
are you crying)

crying for a mother's help   (fell

forests or plant forests)   Dreams
wheel their pale course

We write in sand
three thousand proverbs and songs

bottom is there   but depth
conceals it   Dreams wander

through the body of a parent
Rub hands together   stressing how

we are made of earth   inevitable
our death   Wisdom

a sorry thing   dream in a Dream
remembering a dream

mimic presentation stained with mortality

                    9

Rapt away to darkness   at home in
Perilous

Helios flees secretly across a lost
country   Zodiacal sign

Sun
— this is a circle and serpent in

circle —
fit for green fable   Firmament

and it was so

Visionary events stretching back to
Eden   Thraldom

seeds to be sorted   Where
have I been I say to myself   Mother

winding as she does around the axis
How far

back through Memory   does memory

extend   a gap
in knowledge   before all people

tell
historical past   the historical

truth
a Parlance   spoken by strangers

to interpreters
Sneaping wind   a winter setting

salty sea thudding
salty sea thudding

national anthem of my love Lucifer

might so black the centuries cannot
see

15

Perspectives enter

and disappear
The perpetual dead embark   Hoop

of horizon
negation pursuit and illusion

fourscore and fade

a moving doom of brood
(ideas gems games dodges

scaffolding)

Long pythagorean lustrum

nothing new can come into being
Change

and juxtaposition
(heavenly systems move monotonous

motion)
Green grows the morning

in a first college of Something
austere music

ideal republic
Language ripples our lips

Sparrows peck at the gravel
(caged words

setting them free)
Sing the golden verses of Pythagoras

(were they ever really written)
Sweet notes

deaf sea
Outside at the back of the sky

biography blows away

(*Pythagorean Silence,* 1982)

from DEFENESTRATION OF PRAGUE

BRIDE'S DAY

asleap
  sleap
      am welcome drifting
                    Mystery
      all the mysteries   Oh
  welcome Fierce

Carved out of cloudy Row wet
my Seagray
Distant sorcerers draw violent gestures
Unquiet sacrificer
Pool of Forgetfulness
headlong maiden
apple in hand
yellow in trees to skyBow

□

Shall obediently approach Love

Where

Lines blown to the north wind

Tenting

Seagray stone mirror and master

Eros

Dim artificer enchantment proud

Father

Countless secrets hissing together

Seemseem

□

Night pastures knell number Watch

hours out
Wanderer

Figures for sake her

2

atwake of ancient proverb

Prospectives divide

Wheat on the dust of open

Millennium

smile statue into my facesStone

□

Straw dress
straw mask

hike woman
horn and heel

O syllable
O footfall

hand before face
Messenger

Drowned ship
Bright city

fragmentary half—
remembered beauty

Drift and fling
of time

Sun lighting future
to flame

Old man
white hair streaming

weary of victims
flare wings flapping

Self and Anti-self
chemical wedding

Visionary soul
remembering Rebellion

willow willow willow
sleuth women telling

Haste who are youngest
alone and alone

□

Lost intellectual structures

records of the Conquerors

Into grit glooming

Thrown something

Indignant barbarity

animal kingdom of necessity

restoration of Order

collective north night of a murder

Obsessional snatched away

nameless and a changeling

scornbite stray

□

Hound memory lie down

hare and the moon

Hurl shivering sacrifice
hearth to break in pieces

Finn like fire
Finn in magic mantle

Shouts of the blue men

weary of war

Elopement forays wooing and voyages

no written traces

Souls sighing thrash branches
Threshold of sleep

Scatter and ravening

Fairs held on hilltops
(mummer and strawboy)

Pastoral freedom of hills

Walk three time sunwise round the fire
Ensure a year

Vague Gods

Bed of the down of birds
My hair streams out as wind water

woods

□

Inward memory

Mystery passing myth sanctuary

Secret isle and mortal father
Shelf half of my face

Eden or ebb of the sea

(*Defenestration of Prague*, 1983)

SILENCE WAGER STORIES

When I come to view

about steadfastness

Espousal is as ever

Evil never unravels

Memory was and will be

yet mercy flows

Mercies to me and mine

Night rainy my family

in private and family

☐

I know I know short conviction

have losses then let me see why

To what distance and by what path

I thought you would come away

1

Battered out of Isaiah

Prophets stand gazing

Formed from earth

In sure and certain

What can be thought

Who go down to hell alive

is the theme of this work

I walk its broad shield

Every sign by itself

havoc brood from afar

Letting the slip out

Glorious in faithfulness

Reason never thought saw

2

You already have brine

Reason swept all away

Disciples are fishermen

Go to them for direction

Gospel of law Gospel of shadow

in the vale of behavior

who is the transgressor

Far thought for thought

nearer one to the other

I know and do not know

Non attachment dwell on nothing

Peace be in this house

Only his name and truth

3

Having a great way to go

it struck at my life

how you conformed to dust

I have taken the library

Volumes might be written

ambiguous signs by name

Near nightfall it touches it

Nothing can forbear it

So fierce and so flaring

Sometimes by the seaside

all echoes link as air

Not I cannot tell what

so wanton and so all about

4

Fields have vanished

The Mower his hopes

Bow broke time loose

none but my shadow

she to have lived on

with the wood-siege

nesting in this poem

Departed from the body

at home of the story

I'm free and I'm famished

And so to the Irish

Patrol sentinel ensign

Please feel my arms open

5

The issue of legitimation

Identity of the subject

Circumcision of a heart

driven outside its secret

Elysian solitary imagination

by doubt but not by sight

Fear that forever forever

perfect Charity casts out

The Canticle is an allegory

unchangeable but changeable

Fluttering robes of Covetous

He is incomprehensible he

makes darkness his covert

6

Ages pre-supposed ages

the darkness of life

out of necessity night

being a defense by day

the cause and way to it

From same to the same

These joining together

and having allegiance

Words are an illusion

are vibrations of air

Fabricating senselessness

He has shattered gates

thrown open to himself

7

Though lost I love

Love unburied lies

No echo newlyfledge

Thought but thought

the moving cause

the execution of it

Only for theft's sake

even though even

perturb the peace

But for the hate of it

questionless limit

unassuaged newlyfledge

A counter-Covenant

8

Mysterious as night itself

All negligently scenery

if Nothing could be seen

Sacraments are mysterious

Ambiguous in literal meaning

the Pentateuch the Angels John

all men form a silent man

who wrote the author down

Sackcloth itself is humility

a word prerogatives array

Language a wood for thought

over the pantomime of thought

Words words night unto night

9

Drift of human mortality

what is the drift of words

Pure thoughts are coupled

Turn your face to what told me

love grazed here at least

mutinous predominant unapparent

What is unseen is eternal

Judgments are a great deep

Confession comes to nought

half to be taken half left

From communion of wrongdoing

doubleness among the nouns

I feed and feed upon names

10

Claim foreign order

dismantling mortal

Begotten possibility

plummet fetter seem

So coldly systems break

Fraught advantaging

Two tell againstself

Theme theme heart fury

all in mutiny

Troubleless or sadder

Estranged of all strange

Let my soul quell

Give my soul ease

11

Antic prelate treason

I put on haircloth

Clear unutterable

Secret but tell

What diadem bright

Theme theme heart fury

Winged knowledge hush

Billeted near presage

such themes do quell

Claim foreign order

Plummet fetter seem

wild as loveDeath

Two tell against self

12

Strange fear of sleep

am bafflement gone

Bat winged dim dawn

herthe midmost wide

I did this and I

But forever you say

Bafflement nether elegy

herthe otherwise I

Irreconcilable theme

keep silent then

Strange always strange

Estrange that I desire

Keep cover come cover

13

Lies are stirring storms

I listen spheres from far

Whereunder shoreward away

you walked here Protector

unassuaged asunder thought

you walked here Overshadow

I listen spheres of stars

I draw you close ever so

Communion come down and down

Quiet place to stop here

Who knows ever no one knows

to know unlove no forgive

———————

Half thought thought otherwise

loveless and sleepless the sea

Where you are where I would be

half thought thought otherwise

Loveless and sleepless the sea

(*The Nonconformist's Memorial*, 1993)

Fanny Howe [1940]

From a donkey, excuse me, one lesson is given
in pity. There is little so deserving
of charity as that beast and its weather.
Like the beatitude of sleeping kindness
is a habit can't be kicked, since 'say goodbye
to what's troubling you'advice doesn't work,
is a donkey's crucifix in fur.

Such a miraculous mark
is pure as a character defect, permanent
where it loiters on a farm, and nostrils
of its weathers drip and the stench of dung surrounds
the pumpkin's tomato.
That's being responsible.

The other way to learn about pity is out
on the wide-hot streets
of a city instructing in the love of angries, the first
ones empty of sleep, but objects of pity.
Alert, suspicious, they hit the nail on the head,
often a person's. Of course nothing can break it.
Even laughing.

You can't escape here or there. Back on the farm
the object of your pity returns
in aother form thru very untidy routes,
to the place which contains all the reasons for
righteous wrath. This one never finds them often,
or leaves as a mass of fringes and fingers.

Whose hatred of cruelty can tell the truth
which will kill its pity's object?
Thirty nine ways of knowing your own murder
all punctures and pulsing,

can't animate contempt.
Slept kindness doesn't 'ask for it' but lolls
like a donkey, smelling of weather and grace,

and is put to good use

(Poem from a Single Pallet, 1980)

"seeking out His face in a cup"

Her future, all in her, presented an avenue of gloom, as if to say Go on, do what you can! All the lights in the crematorium were for her too bright, too hot. It was the usual pale light of autumn that improved her hours on earth. I moved the shadows, when I lifted the latch, dragged the gate into the sun, and locked it with a gold key.

The length of the shadows was about six inches, which made the time close after noon. The shade lines lay like pipes, facing the water. I sat down and opened my brown bag. First I spread the paper napkin on my knees but it started to fly away. The top of the water rippled simultaneously.

It's crucial, I realized, in designing cemeteries, to keep the mathematics of shadows in mind. No one's going to fork out thousands of dollars for a vault that is shady all day. I pinned down the four corners of my napkin with each part of my sandwich so I couldn't eat.

She could tell her hands apart, with her eyes shut, even if they were rearranged. The position, though, of people she knew was random, if not the statues they had built around her. She was born adoring and indifferent. She had, then, everything to lose, being rich in the ability to be happy.

He had brutally judged her, but she absolved him again and again, since the passion he had aroused in her was what provided her with steam for her flight. She could have consulted old texts in the library and found out the identity of the sin from which she sped, except there would be no mention of her, or him.

Papa's illness was a kind of contemporary furniture, a complete immersion in presence. He only knew that a female fiction moved about the ward; the links were missing. He saw shadows—he who worried about his work as if he had to save mankind!

At Cottage House, by the Charlie River, he dashed off a batch of letters daily. Out of the unwritten book of his imagination, and ink, a correspondence was created that many compared to perfume on the wing of an Olympian breeze. No vice was liked by him, but grace, youth, symmetry, and honesty. His favorite smile he dubbed "cynical."

I watched a sable stroke wobble on the pavement, a shadow of smoke really, from the dreariest chimneystack on earth. A marble angel had a smutty face due to the outpouring from that same vent. The predominant emotion of my heart was the dread associated with burning. I might have stood on a chessboard waiting for some hand to raise me. My petitions were swallowed with each gulp of air.

It was a nosegay in a little straw basket—oil-stained pansies among fresh jonquils— which I once stood holding; and, later, a vignette of fresh wild blackberries shaking inside green leaves. But what am I to do with the citadel of time which stands between that she and the cemetery? I will, I know, rebuke the virgin who rejects the seeds as they are shaken from the ripe stem. My childish game of shake-the-pod-and-free-the-seed will, instead, occupy my hours. The world rolls around and around, and each day I take a walk with the weight of a man's spirit which pines for worldly success, but crying out, I must help others!

That day I wore a white dress trimmed with black dogs. Long sprays of hawthorne ushered me into the shade, and in the back garden bleeding-heart was enameled against the wall. A clash of bells summoned others to church, but I paced the edge of the carport with my basket. Papa looked up like Ezekiel staring into the oven of the sun. The muslin curtains were webbed in flames. The first to love is the first to lose it. With a slight bend of the head and a serious smile, he pocketed his property and returned me to the punishment of a false forgiveness.

At every next morning, I heard birds respond to the singing trolley and my illness made me sick; it made me.

One night near the apartment a shot split the air and signals boomed from north to south. The hunched figure of a shabby private stood by the table sipping a cordial. It was the purple zone, time for evening prayers where those who say them say them, the war was ended and the witty sally between the men quickly turned into whispers. I went to my room, a narrow chamber with pale blue walls, and pulled down my woolen stockings, which itched. I hated the shush of the sick room, so like sex and guilt.

I've never had luck in spooky houses. Under a slab in one of the passages a skeleton was half-modernized. In the primitive kitchen were a tureen of cold potatoes turning blue, a teapot, a dirty rag, a scrub brush, a tin of stale pecan sandies, and more.

She was tempted to climb out the window, but there might be apparitions flourishing around the garden walls. Leaping dogs.

In her cotton nightie scattered with silk violets, she tilted into the hall instead, and, mute, listened. He was sitting on a stool near the passage and in that smoky room they hit out and didn't care whom they touched. Hilarity kept the truce of G-d away, and lovingkindness. He never flapped his wings, that one, but soared. She had told a horrid fib when she was just a daughter then. And her eyes of innocent light didn't account for any of it.

If she should grow up clever, he might like her better than her low-class mother; but she felt that cunning put bad blood in her veins, while she hid among dusty draperies and watched his progress. White fire sometimes blazed on the tips of her fingers— rhinestone stars sewed into her little costume gloves—and she sucked a finger until the cloth was drenched. She walked around in somebody d—d's old shoes. The white vote of uniformed salutes was raised above her head; she cowered, deliberately stupidly.

When she faked being a dog, it was always with her head down, her tongue hanging out, bruised and beaten from floggings. She climbed the padded stairs on all fours, panting. Explain why he distressed me so. Can anything cauterize these fears till they grown numb as air?

Her winter window was like a scarlet box; the crimson curtains flushed and flickered and outside twilight was striped with the roots of bare trees; they were up drinking the sky. Don't worry about me, she would say without sincerity, I love a red window. There was suspicion in his face, but I had to ponder over its meaning. Why did I lie that day? An embarrassment so profound I pitied myself? But that's a sin. He wanted me to.

Always in cloister, park, or garden, the world seemed without photographs or newspapers, and the key put into her hand was the key to the canceled truth. Go. She should have been slapped or hanged for what she did; instead she was sold.

Now she heard a soft plash in the stillness and saw a monkish bird taking a bath in a puddle. In the pond the water was slow and tepid and some orange leaves were strewn across its surface. Nothing more could sink which hadn't already.

If she could scale Heaven to wear the consort-crown of a visionary, perhaps that would justify the droop of her head. She sat in a valley of rocks. When she stood up, as always she sought a gap in the crumbling walls. The yard gates were covered now with shade, and they creaked open, a heavy rusty iron. She would have preferred to exit through a tunnel of stones. But the greyest hours of autumn fail toward a kind of household light.

(*The Lives of a Spirit*, 1987)

SCATTERED LIGHT

Some patios won't allow the shadow of a maid
It's where I want to go with my tray
See heat unbearably white
Each book must fall, a scholar's mind
Like a shoal of mackerel
Will go through the roof. Now sleep
Is the container of all hope
Where underlover sends signals
To hang up the calendar
Face to the wall and to hell with the soup

□

Cool air drowns in a sigh
I need as much space between my enemies
As inside my cell
Breathing unwillingly you can honestly say
Some actions give no more away
Than the boss who dubs himself
While unclean rubbings
Over the fire of the flesh
Make defects of male and female, the drops fall
And further some perfection after all

□

Like a ballerina in a thirty pound costume
Some gardens are little Edens. Adam and Eve
Hover at the evening gate, a couple
In the green and shine; she
Shadowless turns twice
And each one spills
Weighted drops of light
On the ground coloring and killing
These places and provisions
From the windshield to the river

□

It was a night be left alone
To dig out fifteen pounds of pumpkin guts
Stick in a candle and water the curtains
I phoned a friend with What do you want
Money and luck they said
When I asked the angel in the bottle
She fluttered and cried
I want to die!
Sex, too, squeezes out a lot of pleasure
Till nothing is left but the neck

☐

Far from early grass a peach of a light
Braves the morning chill
Close to space probes and telescopes
In a lowly bed
My dreams are servants wreathed in sleep
Its body inverted flannel in a mount of rubble
Leopards, men and colorful birds
Come rearing over a mountain
And race into that head's habitat, at
The wall of the moon inside, and as black

☐

When needs are like ground ignored
A cumulus cloud
Becomes the image of a ladder
Whose architect speaks geometry
We can understand. It's a mess
But puts hope in shape for
The freedom of an even lesser form
Oh Heaven...There's a curtain between
Probable and actual
A curtain of blinding realism

☐

On black stones they mine
Dots of gold with their happy rakes
The alcoholics in the hotel
Are happy too, everyone
Looks ready to be right if I'm not wrong
The sun is the only money and goal
Where decks stop short and turn back
Around 14-karat rings which scrub
On the ones whom nobody cares to know
Except those who have lists of interests

□

Son the One who was also called Sun
I crave your heat but fear the burning
Domesticate your fire and send sufficiency
Zero has gathered into a hole
By the road where living gives
An atavistic echo, the bank's
A thief. And I am without
Retinue. The feel of accidie
Is a collar, metal and economic,
When the world takes up no space but I

(*The Vineyard*, 1988)

■

Twill coat, rain-wet as a circular.
The devil circled the perfect garden.
Red as roses. A tower torn up by the stones.
Gargoyles dreamed they were clay.

He surveyed the prison.
"The prison is the measure of the person."

Wind propelled the dust motes down
And paper fell so far, it severed grass.
De-regulated angels

Left their waste in pigeon-pots.

Those who fit in, complained of the fit.
Those who didn't, complained of neglect.

Photographers turned
To their colored images—

All the black around them gay.

Why put a woman in the picture anyway?
"To give the man a story."

(*The Quietist*, 1992)

■

Bruises in eastern winter sky.

Emotional circus. Aridity ending.

Nut-brown walkway. Beam on a high wire.

Delicate ankles, abbey bells.

Father. Fanfare. Whirls of silver

At stick's end. The devil takes form as a pigeon.

As a face in a window, living dolls—severed

Possibilities in each one.

The elephant goes down on its knees

Like the body of work moving through history.

(*The Quietist*, 1992)

from "O'CLOCK"

19:40

Set golden butter out in a dish
Beside a mill, a stream and a tree.
Say: Oh my love, loved by me,
Give me your heart, your soul, your body.
Then see.

15:34

You float inside your water
glass among inverted tree
lines, gold & thin as wands

Your time is really fluid—
or painted in fluid—
your limbs tiny and breaking

Green leaves are like pages, waterized.

I can drink the image up,
or wait for you to do it.
Whoever acts, divides.

4:01

The edge of the dome is slipping
like a fool's pudding
under silver. I'm awake, aggressively begging:

Give me a penitent hairstyle
and a cell—not a hospital—
to contemplate my errors in

And no answers, please, to my crazy questions!

3:22

Speaking of slap-wings
of washing being shook
out to yesterday, my home
is that mound that moved, melting.

Shine from the snowgoose
now gone to sterling or worse:
to worthless winters in a warm climate.

("O'Clock," 1994)

WHAT WE LEARNED

Unavoidable violence
left the people silent

This is how we knew it
from the kind we had constructed

as a battle—and how
we talked about it! Hard mystery

is rarely turned into a story—
no strategy. Sheep honk & cows shoot moos

into the air—some emergency
in gun-running country—

one cow has given birth to three

When I get to choose
between following the lives of the beasts or the men

I still choose the latter, it makes no sense

(*manuscript*)

FIRST CHANCE TWICE

Pain—I'm pro it
if it abolishes systems

where the person has to be
productive for the physician

Take old age—
I can go mad
at last—smoke—drink—
get stoned—meditate—

as long as I keep my ankles
up from the chill—

take walks—smell
the sea & rub garlic

on the soles of my feet

It will be my first chance to be

as wild as the weeds of the field
since I was a child

(*manuscript*)

bpNichol [1944 – 1988]

SCRAPTURES: 7TH SEQUENCE

1

green yellow dog up. i have not. i am. green red cat down. i is not. i is.
over under upside up is. i's is not is i's.

iffen ever never youd deside size seize says theodore
(green yellow glum) i'd marry you. truth heart hard confusions confess
all never neither tithe or whether with her lovers lever leaving her alone.

no no.

chest paws and chin.

no.

2

insect. incest. c'est in. infant. in fonts. onts. onts. ptonts. pontoons. la
lune. la lun.

la lun en juin est?

c'est la lune from votre fenêtre. vos. vouloir. i wish. i wish. i
may. i might. june night

and the lovers

loafers, low firs, old frrrs, la lovers, la lrrrs.

3

liturgical turge dirge dinta krak kree fintab latlina santa danka schoen
fane sa paws claws le foret. my love coo lamna mandreen sont vallejo.

oh valleys and hills lie open ingkra sintle

list la list cistern turning down.

je ne sais pas madam. je ne sais pas mademoiselle.
je ne sais pas l'amour mirroring mes yeux meilleur my urging for you.

4

an infinite statement. a finite statement. a statement of infancy. a fine line
state line. a finger of stalemate. a feeling a saint meant ointment.

tremble.

a region religion
reigns in. a returning. turning return the lovers. the retrospect of
relationships always returning. the burning of the urge. the surge forward
in animal being inside us. the catatosis van del reeba rebus suburbs of our
imagination. last church of the lurching word worked weird in our heads.

5

great small lovers move home. red the church caught up relishes dog.
lovers sainthood loses oversur. oh i growing hopeless lies in ruin. u in i
hope beet root.

6

halo. hello. i cover red my sentiment. blankets return the running ships
back. clock. tock tock tick tock.

so he loves her. the red dog green home. geth ponts returns a
meister shaft. statements each one and any you rather the could've
repent—alright?il n'est pas sont école la plume plum or apples in
imagining je ne désirez pause. je ne sais pas. je ne sais. je pas.

7

il y a la lever la lune. l'amour est le ridicule of a life sont partir dans
moors. le velschtang est huos le jardin d'amour, un chanson populaire in
the revolution.

mon amour est un
chérie, a cherry, a cheery rose with shy petals to sly on. saint reat will
teach me songs to woo her.

8

au revoir. le reveille sounds up the coach. les pieds de la chevalier voleur
sont ma mère en la nuance de ma votoveto.
                              oh maman. oh papan pa pan pa pa pan pa
pan pan. le choux dériver la now du chien from dog. le chat cat is back
who has forgotten his name.

1967

(*gIFTS: The Martyrology Book(s) 7 &...,* 1990)

FERRY ME ACROSS

all these journeys
all these bodies of water, air,
between this world
& some other
named or unnamed

all these readings of the current
waves   sines
                ⎧ embarkment
final dis ⎨
                ⎩ charge
on some other shore

all this striking of
cymbals/drumming/ringing
invisible bell
weather
wake of consciousness
how there can be only one true sign for God
H or El or
how the two together form a Hell
unspoken

because to speak the true name
presumes the power to invoke
not yours, outside the i
worlds we pass between

uncalm

prehending

Victoria to Vancouver
June 1, 1988
Assumptions

(*gIFTS: The Martyrology Book(s) 7 &..., 1990*)

SOME NETS
for Paul Dutton

I

three days after (*) *the lightning hit it* / or the beat, (*) check this, I can play around it, with it, there / *what's left of* (*) *the barn* (*) *still smoulders in the sun* / unresolved (*) notes or chords, should've been of wood, (*) paper, burning / *sending clouds of smoke across* (*) *the highway* / dislocating / *darkness* / son / *i awoke into* / nets / *hearing the voices from the Fire Hall across the lake* (*) / i remember this, angry, i thot it was a party, felt foolish / *seeing the flickering lights above the trees* / start looking for ways out, of this diction / *knowing* (*) *something was happening* / is happening, not in the way you intended, the way (*) that's always intended, you don't intend that / *unable to* (*) *determine* (*) *till the next day* / that tone, as tho the unravelling of this one event made the whole complex that is the world make sense, that (*) misuse of meta-phor / *it was the barn's burning had awakened me* / it was the barn (*) burning, not the world

(*) *and poetry is like this too* (*) / or can be, shouldn't be, contains those smug assur-ances that the whole thing is (*) containable / *voices that disturb your sleep* / "only great events can create a great literature" / *lines* (*) *you write down* / the daily life, what we call the "mundane" / *unable to determine till the next day* / or longer (*) even, centuries, millennia / *the true* (*) *nature of what has awakened you* / that long-ing, all these years, for this, freedom to be, simple / or (*) *those other lines* / the ones you meant to write, celebrating (*) the ordinary effort of being, shorn of the old idealization of heroism and suffering, an (*) imagination of (*) peace to inform those desires for it / *that smoulder within you* / desire to be written / *three days or more* / searching for (*) the tone / *and even tho you write them down* (*) / (*) the lines i mean, prayers / *there is a darkness there* / literal, as tho the words on the page were not the words inside your brain (*) the moment that you went to write them, no / *at the core* / some other phrase or sentence / *some source that is not yet tapped or* / not yet believed or / *fully listened to* / beyond the rhetoric of intent / *far below the visible surface* / right at the surface of this page / (*) *burning* (*) / these words are, worlds are, lives, (*) are

2

things remarked on, (yes) not remarked on, (no) connections / *the night the man drowned in the canal* / another, (yes) nameless body / *in front of our room on Reguliersgracht* / "ours, " (no) transitory reference, (yes) Paul & me, using the room for sleeping mostly / *hand reaching up from the water* / (no) i didn't "see" it (no) / *not reaching us as we slept on, oblivious,* (yes) / the "news" was out there, what the newspapers thrive on, our bodies (yes) / *tho the crowds gathered,* (yes) *the police came,* / reporters, things you read about / *the boats dragged the water searching for him* / looking for signs on the surface (yes) / *we dreamt of nothing* (no) *or* / dreamt the fragments thru which our daily lives continue (yes) / *so many things we could recall none of them* (no) / intrusion of the discursive voice (yes) / *troubled all night by something we could not reach,* / could not understand / *someone calling to us,* (no) *or worse* / naming / *the absolute silence into which a plea for help can fall* (yes) (yes)

murmurings, indistinct voices &/or musics / *& the next day, the Hotelkeeper brought us breakfast,* / it was like that / *asked how we'd slept, we answered "fine, "* / a description / *not really thinking, assuming the usual exchange of vagaries,* / the empty words, the empty place, signs as signals of another order / *until he told us of the man who'd drowned* / just that / *underneath our window,* (yes) *& put the breakfast tray down*

3

at night, (at night) *looking out from the Lido* (at night) / hotel on the corner, (at night) river taxis tied to the docks below us (at night) / *the lights of Venice in the distance* (at night) / shining (at night) / *names,* (at night) *that they do invoke* (at night) / even a stranger's (at night) / *&* (at night) *in invoking* (at night) *evoke, call forth* / things that linger at the edge of perception / *into the bright sunlight sparkles off the water's choppy surface* / yes (at night)

being carried up the canal by water ferry (the next day) / retracing the route we had taken (the next day) / *past the stone fences in the fenced-in gardens* (the next day) / details of your life forgotten as rapidly as they occur (the next day) / *the decaying foundations & steps* (the next day) / flashbacks that lead nowhere (the next day) / *narrow landings into narrower courtyards* (the next day) / seeking for connections where none may exist (the next day) / *the boats plying their trade* (the next day) / working (the next day) / *gondoliers & all that quote romantic unquote garbage* (the next day) / thru & past you (the next day) / *adrift off the prow* (the next day) / detritus of thot forms (the next day) / *pressing towards Piazza le Roma* (the next day) / back sore from too much luggage (the next day) / *the train station beyond* (the next day) / not sure where we were going (the next day) / *naming* (the next day) / in a strange language (the next day) / *& on* (the next day) / yes (the next day)

Rice Lake/Amsterdam/Venice/Toronto
July 17, 1985, thru March 1988
Assumptions

(*gIFTS: The Martyrology Book(s) 7 &...*, 1990)

ST. ANZAS VI

three that end the same way
or did once, before revision hey?!
i saw the whole thing all over again
differently—the clouds, the gate—patterns,
rhythms   against which st.
anzas   or out of which the core
us looks for answers among the shifting
illusions
illuminations
illustrations any language allows.
alaws. rules by which the light flows thru
into this dim
ensions where the tongue's tension
                                        be   holds it

or din
savage nary
crisp as in broken
ten latterly
none

simple as the
is is
flat & in the difference
dawn or any garden
just so if waiting apoplectic
pollenized

nothing's as simple as it seems,
as dense. the st. icks,
the st. ones, break the bones of
naming. the nouns
hurt you, hem you in
you look for clearings in the throat, to dance—
phlegmenco

diff rich
ridden roared
assumptive alliteration. quantum mince
leaden roads along above which
on the other overcast
flat latitudes among the glistening
seven to simple longings as attitudes
sordid dreaming
essential inference & then
lovely   lovely   lovely

flour essence. light from which the flower grows,
fills the head. ai of faith, slothfulness,
ah the daze
which is de a z of being,
or the slo thfulness ought to be shared,
to search for radical marks, question?
's definition, surely, nothing sure there
or sure is there
there for sure
there

clung

segmented

if of shift
of life

reasonable rack

dissent

light made lighter without the i

(*gIFTS: The Martyrology Book(s) 7 &...*, 1990)

ST. ANZAS IX

the basis then, of belief: base 10? base alphabet? base
emotions, f stops, g spots—what? the 10
commandments. why'd He write 'em down, eH? & why
He, She say. Honour Thy Father, Thy Mother, Who say?
Oral sex. A tradition. The burning bush. The talking bush.
We're all bush league here, we say. B girls. G men. X & Y & then
the human race begins again.

grazi. the origin or night fever, split—the
rush of antiquarian grapes. punch. prego.

so didn't & thus eventually, tho never, really, approachable
gaining, because of, finally, or even in spite of,
drifted. that. no no no no. that.

seated in this stanza, Hotel Goya...possoa averray il conto?
count 1 to 7. begin again. account in the language & the base
chosen. move from stanza to stanza in a life. the basis?
for belief. l'acenseur non funzione. that one feels faith.
and if believing is believing? use the stairs then—
st. airs & st. ares—st. able in her vanishing...elevate her.
premier piano, row housing. a tone row or
lac thereof, the skill. are these hands his own?
turn this page? your'n. imagination
of a future place & time, turning, over. an act of
faith. stupidity. trust. the keys. turned over to you.
rooms such thots occupy. this room with you.
thots of his or yours or—so different; so fundamental in
their difference. this voice in
its time machine. not a voice; only words. "only, " he says

and his heart aches. "that don't change the facts. " never.
the less the facts keep changing. fax them to you
a page at a time. all this line and feeling transformed,
scatter of electrons, reformed. wired. y erred. Who?

possibilities. of. how? the new. space and
nothing to reason over but. this and, after all that
dozen matter.

open. latter to letter &. open. reason red option begins bleak.
open. systematic. open
God is? was? what? poets as receivers? as fax machines?
passing it all on to you
"a page at a time, " and
who's interested? no thanx. all that noise &
interference scrambling the message. godlo
vesyou. "here comes another one!" but
who do we send them to when
there are no home addresses?
how does we address you? sender? return to sender? Who
're we talking to? for? from?
dom dei dame dom? he wonders who i is. i
wonders who he is. She?
"who is this anyway?" nothing but heavy breathing on
the cosmic phone. tapping the stars from the galaxy edge.
"anybody here?" you're only encouraging them
when you don't hang up. when you don't break
the connection. "you're only encouraging them. " break
(he makes a note) the (another one) connection.
dance tunes. dei tyde
& time wait for no man
ma'am. mad? (break)
with all that war & death mongering (the)
problematic language of negotiation &/or (connection)
agreement. hang up or get hung up.
flip the hinge up. open

patterns. elegaic composed separated caesura.
the grew lay weathered sigh. first and
abandoned the this alas! it. and by now
the and, the may,
he there hold eftsoons, he the and the,
the he and

the the merrily,
below,
below.

five a though rhymes on rary rondeau.
four refrain except are, the idiom page.
and repeated for as rondolet four.
six as the shown, the a.

sigh.
say cred.
"cred. "
i–ble. bi–ble. two bulls in a field. bib loss.
all this spittle, this drool lord.
loord.
away from the true path.
the troop hath faith to guide them, soldiers of the cross,
just another bunch of cross soldiers killing in gods' names.
"Nay, ms, that's not the way 'tis. " say who?
"Say Cred. " you?
2nd person. tracking of such otherness.
Blessed Oliver Plunkett,
his head still here to guide us. ahead of himself,
like some cautionary tale.
make yourself clear.
how else can these words address you?

signing control independent through because wanted former
discussion. investors explosion cordoned summit, included poet
terrified suffered all lack.
plays.
country knows.
ultimatum as
dignity, impediments, analyzed accept particularly personal.
child thousands. imports another fish. responsibilities.
economist mothers and
249, 000 traditional, smoked and nearly majority
shell.

composed, harvested battlecries, chalk redoubts. pain,
bounty, syllabics, a and final hero repetition quartered.
relentless slice, a tiresome fleck and moaning, wearing
the setting steel, the quarrelsome wreckage, the
ladder continous moving.

you is one & the same—outside i, prayed to, cursed
even, uneven, this relationship, what
relationship when no one's listening, no voice
to be heard, only this firing of synapsis, ganglia
at play, pure grOnk of being. he say, "i say, "
but you don't hear him speaking.

"I Battlewolf I
Sing Sing Sing Sing Sing Sing
I Armed Blood's We
A Stirring The Lusty The Blade Hand
At And Blood
I In
In On Brynnich's Carcasses The For Hosts
To For Battlefield's Shield-Carrying Court's Beware

"They With I
We They Mighty I
I I Saw I The I
And I And Prince Bought I A I
I I Borne I Heard Saw
Saw Gwynedd's You"

it is that way, the say of praise, prayer, one to
an other, taken on what base? eight? ten?
belief? a counting. double entry of address.
addressing who cannot be named or placed.
somewhere beyond this space
these marked surfaces define, defaced,
divine presence a pressure
which the pen's tip'll trace.
y. o. u. you.
ewe.
the lamb's blood we are washed in.
washes through us too.

(gIFTS: The Martyrology Book(s) 7 &..., 1990)

MONOTONES

XCV

out of your head the sky is taken
pieces of the moon

ride your horse too close to the earth
end up in the zoo
mind

    time over time
falling into a sea

a ghost of forms
shifting as the table moves
around you

      hands linked

sinking into the hush of voices
my head falls apart in my fingers

                        eyes' light
such tongues explode
ears fear to fold them
false prose

pores open skin's delight
coming into focus thru the room's constraint
define your motion

shrieking

crazy

    "like a loon" are

      (*gIFTS: The Martyrology Books(s) 7 &...*, 1990)

Aaron Shurin [1947]

CITY OF MEN

I heard my name, the day rose and disappear over the beach. the day on each breath tasted my food, that night roll slowly cover in the cool, his face around my breast. the day inhaling grow pale and disappear, water on his way, up the shores hissing. under the night stillness inclined my morning beach, undressing my friend of liquid, my most same. at evening while whispering from the bed by me, his way was accomplished. his full perfect arm a health of ripe waters. the day received moon laughing, love lay me that night

□

love growth, manly types have been young men, my year my nights, comrades. projecting tongues clear my world; I feed, tell all the secret, offering delicious profit away from the clank. respond myself for all the need secluded, from standards to pleasures rejoices. escaped here; paths clear to speak: I can spot men and exhibit as I dare

□

fair warning. further affections perhaps destructive. expect your long room in the open air. on your kiss permit be carried into sleep, caught me that I have written this, go your hand on your way upon my hip, that hit I hinted at, perhaps more trial. put your lips back, new husband, who would sign himself a candidate for my affections? in hand one thing will be all, suspicious, destructive, give up all else, exhausting your conformity, troubling your hand from my shoulders. I gawk unborn with you on a hill; upon mine, lips, I permit your throbs; beneath your clothing I have escaped from me. which way? many times reading it not understand. some trial for I emerge uncertain, theory around would have to be abandoned. feel me go forth. touching is wood, is rock, is air sea island roof enough

□

diligently sought it many year at random, among animals, lapping apples and lemons, pairing fitful grossest nature and what goes with them. yearning for any and attracting whoever you are. swimmer naked in the bath from head to foot and what it arouses, trembling curve and the clinch of hips, the mouth makes me fainting from exultation and relief, embrace in the night the cling of any man drunk eyes, the storm that loves me, by the pliant loins a moment emerging stars. blending each body from the gnaw, wet overture anticipating the perfect face, for myself from you two hawks in the air, waves of nearness, floating the divine list to possess a lawless sea. I yield to the vessel, sliding fingers and thrusting hands, warp and woof, victory and relief, close pressure makes excess divine. pushes anticipating the strain exhaust each other; side by side on the coverlet lying and floating. from that, myself, without which...

□

I have lived orgies and will one day make pageants. bright windows with continual feast: those eyes' swift flash as I pass. O I make rows of you, streets of you, processions, spectacles...

□

boys up and down the road, priests of ourselves, wrenching and owning the other. fingers stretching elbows, alarming the air, making no law less than loving, ease on down fearless power

□

the arm, the arm, sleepless...underneath what you say my measureless name...walks within him at night wandering with other men...ocean of hand in hand...tenderest pictures hang in my woods...another curved shoulder...

□

acrid river drain itself, blowing suppleness and strength from judges. milk commands mystery, moisture of the right man delights the earth, shame knows how to shoot for own sake. nothing lacking in gushing showers, warm-blooded rivers wrestle suns. deposit within me the pent-up winds of myself, crops from the birth of deliciousness, plant of you to awake at the touch of a man. greater heroes sleep in sex, wrap a thousand years in slow rude muscle of themselves, accumulated purities deposit gods on earth. onward pour the stuff; distill from the fruit of the fruit meaning's delicacies...

□

growing up above the tomb there, pink-tinged heart ascend the atmosphere; rise with it breast in your sweet way. behind the mask of materials take control of all, emerge under you roots of sound and odor, scented show folded in shifting forms. spring unbare this serve me lovers, conveyed essential shape inhale the bloom. burn and sting will not be freeze, reverberations give tone to delicate blood. exhilarating immortal death, inseparably grow and dissipate, last beyond all in comrades body

□

sighs in night in rage not subtle, dismiss chattering words to savage wrists. willful broken oath, nourishment of beating and pounding, defiances thrown in the wilds of hungry pantings. dissatisfied dreams of every day show dead words, limbs and senses thrown from heaving skies. not savage but cries and laughter, pulse of stystole/diastole sounded in air

□

a certain number standing alone, me twined around. it hung down and glistens there, unbending. wide flat companion of lusty oak makes me a little moss, stood for my sight and I grew wonder. lover in the dark brought to live green

□

produce boys! greed eats me, wholesome bunch saturate my palms. mounting my friend, waist hanging over my shoulder, dripping spiral, the hot hand that flushes. encircling red animal, purple lurking thumb, paternity of liquid will be torment and tide. odor of lips glued together; curves, brothers, that feelers may be trembling sweats; visions lie willing and naked under the ripening sun. whitened with the souse of primitive men, sleep together with crushed mint and sap, climbers after body blow husks from indecent eyes, find themselves breasts and bellies up and down the night. hairy murmurs and firm legs match the man to mountain, climbing my man I light the hillside. toss him, plucked from chastity, to saturate the sea; all men carry men, lurking. tight pause and edge to pressure, roaming hand-whirl, I glow spontaneous, know what he is dreaming. the same content, airs intimate that fill my place with him, smell of wild relief, welcome falling...

☐

two simple men modeled under full sail, splendor of one neck envelops the other... spread around me, crowd of glory, I saw the pass and kissed him

☐

appearances, after all, may be only speculations; identities are of the real. hold me by the hand, that is subtle air, impalpable, curiously words hold untellable. reason confound us, sense surround us, he travels to me and these are the shining things I perceive. I walk in the fable of a man, charged with points of view, skies of colors, densities, and something yet to be known...

☐

full of you and become you. any number could be me. read these and become a comrade. with you I am one

(*A's Dream*, 1989)

MATERIAL'S DAUGHTER

I wandered away from my early childhood, framed by her massive hair. Officials rob and flog them; martyrs my guiding stars. I had had nothing, had had had nothing to eat; a comrade assured me he wasn't hungry. His intensity walked up the stairs, but beautiful things are necessities. Given work I marveled about the ecstasy music could create in me; I talked on, lanky daily struggle, customers of the grocery in discussions with an agitator and a nurse. Radiant voice contracted the first time into weeks of disclosure, anticipation and escape. Living things began to cry. I picked him up cooing. Think back; if you spill a drop nights pay the price. The operation did not take place.

But there was no other yard, fields, hills, purgatory. Cleaning gruff boots, scrubbing burnt almonds, so violently the room in a heap was put to bed and petted. Our lives were busy in foreign languages, beg from me public stories about scandal, toilers articulate a mysterious young woman on a truck. Led away whispered "the island of splendid bearing," flowers bumped into trees on the natural sidewalks. I read, I flung my arm, I too would go, I went in search, it was flaming, I hung on his lips, I was the speaker. Some pawnshop would find that evening revealed on the vanishing step, waving and snatched away from a very clear idea of material's daughter.

Economic categories picked up an entirely new type; perhaps on Monday a perfunctory letter shook an old woman free. Public opinion sat dumbfounded on many faces. He had immediately opened into unconsciousness but would answer no questions, a cry trying to open his mouth nearly broke the bullet. I found an article, the avenger, began pouring to beat back his thrusts, purity should hear and carried on a ferocious campaign to action. If only they knew she was being made to suffer for me. I knocked and informed me for a long time, startled by my looks. Nature could not extract that swelling in the throat. I gave an assumed name but wouldn't deny my identity—no no no, the yellowed paper was a strong young tree, I gulped coal and raised the hall to ferment.

In the afternoon I was told to wait; time settled into a small room; little objects passed into my mouth, childhood, schooldays, teacher, tender. Out of the window nothing had been broken—just flattened a bit. Human things reached motives in her estimation. I chose to walk, so many crimes fascinated me.

(A's Dream, 1989)

SATURATED

Up the ravine the sun was choking with dust. Emotion on the windows from the sideways heat, breathless their heads hang—they've stooped—and went in through the low doorway. On this dark corner table two glasses. His bold cheeks, his full lips— the ox. He was looking beneath the sunlight; every object was almost cool in the stream. Into his hands his pockets threw their coins.

I found a few words about each; nickname, unmarried, career, places in a mist of obscurity. In our part of the country, no one knew anyone, visited anyone, had money, noticed much. There were puzzling forces, inactive, having iron control. I have met no one else.

He played with his moods like a toy, climbed out of his skin. His gaze softened his lips into flourishes. He grew embarrassed and burst into laughter. All their eyes uncovered his face; far away began to fly into the room.

Like a trembling finger, the path lay across the field. At low tide I saw long wings oblivious of us. Everyone opened, as if silence was his…

Talking loudly—splutter up in the air and wave—they kept on repeating, "Come on, come on!"; his face was transfigured across the counter, summoned over to happiness.

I went out; the film of heat hung black over the blue sky. The grass had left behind no wind, against the windowpane wet hair was dancing. New faces had collected in the room. The sky was walking.

(A's Dream, 1989)

HIS PROMISE

Yesterday, I have always seen him. I followed him into Paris: here was the entrance. In the light—and hearing—luxury descended over soothing waves, the boulevard with the sign of fraternal beatitude.

If I give their eyes then I have never seen eyes. Seated, we ate/drank the hours. Impalpable useless smoked slowly soul, and familiarity shown, say, in a homesick pact. I lifted my glass and of its creation: perfectability! His aroma explained progress up to the present moment.

I share a reputation admitted beloved brothers, possession in every corner persuade the devil his brimming pleasures. On this subject I have met with the most invisible companions. We bow to each other like memory, to wipe out old grudges.

At last, shivering, sung by poets and philosophers, it said to me, "I want to take you away." Famous remembrance, "to compensate for your loss I shall come seeking you." Flattery and adoration know all this intoxication, flowers warm as he rose me with a smile...

To thank him I left him, little by little crept back to bed. On my knees at the feet of that vast assembly I murmured my prayers: his promise. Half asleep with indifference I seemed to remember waiting for him before...

(*Into Distances*, 1993)

SAILED

Under a sky, in a garden, there are serious women and beautiful men, were talking. "You are much more beautiful," they implore, and can't help their red cheeks from flaming. "You are terrifying, too," and speak in the same voice.

He is already far away, is going to other trees on the horizon, disappear behind that cloud and drew around him closer a sleeping voice, lowered to a rolling feeling. In the dark she is sleeping, stroking on forever, buried in her hair this garden while the eyes of stupefaction widened, and the light curls lighting up this boy in the clouds would find him in some thick aureole covering her back and waking somewhere else...

I walk straight ahead, pays attention without always seeing, playing music the way I'd like to live. His lamentations would bring the cymbals together. I wanted to find out where they were enjoying themselves, followed them at a distance to where the beautiful nights dance like bears. I've remembered a cup of brandy, and went to sleep turned toward their faces, the stars.

From the air there was his eye in his forehead, the sun had a brother. One of them said, "Yesterday moves so slowly." One of them said, "Seemed to linger with pleasure in the great hollow sky." One of them said, "Each setting out in solemnity from a beautiful night like this..."

(*Into Distances*, 1993)

BLUE SHADE

She leaned in a small fist on the cushions, buds in her pajamas. "Make me a story about a tower room and fresh air."

There was a girl fluttering her fingers. She sent down for her peach-colored suitcase, the high clouds of the balconies. A whisper smiled his smile, smoothing the long waves of her name.

The hand of her opened slowly, hummed down and swelled a waltz over the carpet. A lazy push opened the door and started to slip in; the girl watched the shadow sprayed on the wall.

She's been here for days, wordless and plump. It went slowly. Syllables flicked at it and went away.

(Into Distances, 1993)

FORWARD OR BACK

Its eyes falling back against the interior of their cylinders, opened—thus laying—both their embarrassments, his dress, his extremity. A fabulous reconstitution of fear—she lit a cigarette—does something to a person's identity—hands trembled—into the head as a spoon of thought of the night —velvet piss—of one city for me while I'm coming to seek the world.

Into the testimony of the two—of the other—from the waist with the back eye in a dark place—contraction—full of permission to touch itself upon your rumpled chest of hair, a sediment.

He get crime. Drags upward while the thin flesh—it means fury—it is in her—inhaling among the debris pushed into the pillow. A different rage: the egg portion of night. His partners pound the horizontal muscles of a man's beloved.

The estrangement is on the neck of the creature, husked. I'm coming to know a detachment with one hand—sitting between twilights—by the girl I am I may be those circular years—the face of uncertainty from which love and fear are shining—it loves one of them—muted, holding her hands through the target, in the toilets without aim, kneeling between tongues.

The waters make you immortal. The song—its other name—is "Eyes Wide Open." There is no direct way. Distinction radiating.

She has the face of the subject, the feeling of removal, orifices of someone else, and is collecting the rest of destiny. Have been born by degrees to the narrative who was leaning forward.

We have a restless place awaiting you—this particular night with a knowledge mixed eye to eye—they come eternally into it alone—rummaging through photographs who had been spared a face but twined with ivy. I saw her pouring down the steps—dropping the cloak of his neck—shoulders sideways like a cat—kissed upon their knees my health and put it in words, throne for the deed.

I want a thing in the world full of minor objects thicker than contemplation. Thick ones with their sweet collected creation. He went a long way beyond what they are to himself. Sitting there shaking at opposite ends with connections.

(Into Distances, 1993)

Dennis Phillips [1951]

from ARENA

2. Exile

But perfectly random and coastal.

A convention that forgot you.
People, whose names would be dropped.

Would it be an offense to approach them?
They sit there, each one, thinking things.
Eyes so focused. Mouths tight.

Your means of travel extraordinary,
private, even secret.

Or just physically, the restaurant dark,
large windows, south-facing,
overlooking a huge crescent bay; tables
full of families.

□

Where *any* phrase might come from.
Goddess slept on middle C.

Or a witness in olive drab.

Convocation of members, filial,
although outside the cars pass oblivious.

It would be so bright where they'd send us.

It was she (not it) who didn't come or if she did
it was a careful secret that only she could reveal and only
she controlled and if that's not abandonment then
maybe she *was* there and what I wore, just by accident,
was the uniform of the place so that no one would ask questions.

It was only my time.

☐

When suddenly you slice open a belly
or cut off a hand.

☐

A small discretion
an accent (target)

accepted compression

We counted laps and reports
trusts and comments,
fearful predators and benign ones.

Perfectly random and coastal.

And you sank into a noon
of expectation and history.

Not an annotated history or a homeland
of your displaced hero.

Time then acquaintance.

The dance more appealing without sound.

☐

Light embedded in the devil's name.

A family gathers on hot nights
under a full moon.

If you were alone.

Light, generated not reflected.
Like heat, or lightning.

You hear voices. No weather to propose.
A fire in the distance.

□

Who gets to carbon first.

Footsteps filtered through parchment.

Conflict of possession.

A convention that forgets you.

□

And we who assemble. Packed goods carried in.
On shining trays. That oil is pressed
and used, drilled and pumped.

Or arteries which once did not know
and now know, or their brains
or their research.

This would be towns. Congregation.
Human intercourse but first
a person or family then
a bend of river or fertile plain.

And we who gather together.

That far away there'd be a farm. That many farms
and villages and towns and coitus and train tracks,
highways, jetways, shipping lanes, language.

Or a laboratory.
That once none of these now all of these.

Gathered together with faces.
Esteemed colleagues.
Many dozens. Silent spines.

And time, a factor. Time and acquaintance?
Or only time. Then acquaintance. Then
acquaintance and other factors.
History and culture.

A chart.

□

A captor who disappears
who reappears, who's beyond harm.

And morning because even dewyness can't yield directories,
no neighbors no signposts in other words even if I escaped.

His shudder, my fear, random and coastal, a prelude

□

But I *fell* asleep and the tunes
were comforting, sappy, despicable.

Or imagined how it would be without a brain stem.

So I fell asleep, dreamed of the O.E.D.

Those captives are shades not marbles.
Or in dreams they persuade you.

Only the difference encouraging.
The dance more appealing without sound.

In this neighborhood cars run static, alone.

"It's because your writing is 'crafty'"

Then they defoliate. Their greatest joy
until blocks and blocks are bare.

The foreground is shadowed by glimpses
populated by things that have been taken.

Phantom sensations. Lost contact.

The background here.

                              □

Or just this day. Where data.

Or he chose the long route because it followed the sea.
Perfectly random and coastal.
It must not be broken off: the ideas, the voices
that repeat as impression. Your moves. Then boredom.

Resolves into a fantasy of travel; of sojourn
in austere hotels, at the headwaters of historic rivers.
Not about popular culture and not not about it.

And counted how many would attend and how many wouldn't.
Saw the small cards and felt sorrow then elation.
Divided time into pitiful increments
where before the week was whole. The day
a tiny chip, adrift.

□

The mysterious date an entry
(who gets to carbon first)

sharp voices from muffled rooms
or do the walls cause it?

Only a rhythm. Not the voices but between them.
Phantom sensations. Lost contact.

Then your name. In other mouths.
Are they heat or light?
And when you don't hear them?

Your hero against burlap. Soundless, preserved.

And when they do? Tap out the meter.

These are three dimensions.
Different histories.

□

Thunder or aircraft.

This all toward clarity
modest, retaining mystery.

Or: tasks to consume time
when time wants to be prolonged.

The mystery must never be in the line.
It is winter. It is 1729.

(*Arena*, 1991)

from MEANS

The hounds are either the work of wind
or at a certain hour eveything will frantically move.
Dark and feral.

Every label a sound.

There's no need to replicate nature
and yet realism.

Seeing in a terminus the creation of danger
nor movement, nor sound, nor nature.

Having come upon a difficult manifesto.
Light will echo too rapidly.

If slowness is a virtue.

Posit a single concept with conviction and then repudiate it.

In the woods without light.

World without end.

■

If twelve out of fourteen people.

Or elegance: Angle of incidence, angle of reflection.

Then the sound that enters your room at night.

This would also be a "philosophical investigation."

Hoping for example to find a methodology
compliant enough to include everything.

Assuming that there could be a ghost.

Or any walking at night.

■

Having warned them and the pressure that suggests.
Attractive, though, a wanderer slated to begin the talks.
In this constant battle of matching refuge.

While cruising from village to village in the central region
they often stopped at a quaint inn or tavern
asking the proprietor for supper and directions.

It was destined to be a period of dislocation and anxiety.
Time allotted in a more ideal setting seemed possible even now.
Yet it was a great distance to consider, an inconvenience too.

Here the idea of continuity carried over into all that they did.
Only a table-serving for twelve (notice the even number)
threatened their seemingly perfect impression.

Nor with signs nor words but rather tone. And yet the temptation
can be so great.

The artists had perfected a mere studied, self-concious pose,
and yet they were not ready to oblige the request for modesty.

Flags had been set out at pre-arranged posts and the engendered
feelings of predictability gave a sense of combat despite what lay
ahead.

Nothing could be predicted they knew and hence the meaning
of any caution.

(*Means*, 1991)

from TWENTY QUESTIONS

FIVE

There is a temper of atmosphere which prevents rain.

The fear of random gunshots kept them indoors.

His only consolation was that he knew she would think of him sometime during the day.

To arrive on time is only a shame in certain countries.

They could agree on movies but realized this was nothing.

Preferably during sex.

The substance so wished for which falls, runs, or exudes.

There were the few concerns they took with them into the new decade although some argued that the decade wouldn't begin for a year.

Such celebrations were common only in the most violent societies such as the United States and El Salvador and Lebanon.

The inexorable passage of time.

The recent orgy of biographical readings served to set his mind at ease—some of the other geniuses.

It would be simpler just to say that nothing had happened.

In projecting the response to new forms the oddest alliances were considered.

Or after sex then.

A drought could last a whole decade taking deceptive forms such as deluge or ozone depletion.

Back east it snowed severely.

Some event which he knew to have been traumatic was beyond his ability to remember.

The ritual then, in and of itself.

Held as sacred the first phial of liquid was sand in her dream of drawers.

Just think of the potential.

(20 Questions, 1992)

from "ETUDES"

IF IT'S ONLY RHYTHM

Because a thermal motif heard
in the hands of the bedouin child
you cannot allow to guide you.

Sure, we've waited a decade
or a millennium to find a system of letters.

This is a study where only air is solved.

The metals which cover other metals
or ceramics which cushion high voltage
or how can you just lie there and listen
because the whole coast is lit?

Your face which burned so many eyelids.

If it's only rhythm then what's the dew point?
As if following a procedure.
A point of fire on every peak.

I HELD THE VEIN, BUT DEATH

They had a verb.
Nor a disjuncture or harmony:
it's how to garner attention
when the elders sleep at the ceremony.

I'm proud to walk
the bricks her beauty are new and beige
there is a flooring called terrazzo
and this excites in me a memory
of an old land in a new dimension.
I'm lost and deceived.
They awaken.

No form of assistance will ring better.
You are a witness: This is acute activity
and activity cannot be replaced with sentiment.

ON ENTRIES EMPTINESS

Cut the pear or I cut the pear.
Syntax at the beginning is not it at the end.
She wouldn't say she was spoiled, but her behavior.

As at other times a scene
rendered from a dream
or a distant memory recurs:
The low, bleached coastal town,
the labyrinthine train tunnels,
a kind of herd but voices.
Syntax or division, coupled, measured, opened.
It is stored as sugar or fat or protein
and as a residue. The sweet moments
under the shade of passing jet wings
and running by the map they impose.

WHICH SUDDEN CRISIS

Attempted to clear vacate but couldn't.
Attempted to reduce pressure but shallow.
A feeling of "Deja Vu."
Silence you enjoy while others.
This box or cradle.

Nothing happened they continued to breathe.
The pockets forced a chain of associations
a "blustery winter's day" was conjured.
And who has the audacity to ask about subject.

They had whistled and I had rehearsed.

Mail came and everything in the house was sorted.
Why you might have remembered me
in the middle of your involving dream.

His last sensation rising.

("Etudes," 1994)

Christopher Dewdney [1951]

from SPRING TRANCES IN THE CONTROL EMERALD NIGHT

August a haze amniotic our dream aether and lens of distance. Tree sentinels in calmness and grace with vicious night flowering in the inky strata of sexual vision. The awesome rumbling of far storms. Limestone corridors within stone libraries dreaming the grey rainless days of hot August. The forest proceeds before us in an opulent Fragonard brain–coral, spotted with sun. Water droplets posing relationships to dawn as *dimly the calculations of an abacus in the gravitational field of the moon.* Fall the colour of light these leaves absorbed in the summer spectrum each has witnessed.

o

Dolomite temple walls rise from an Ordovician lily pond, trickling water leaving limestreaks out of pale green copper tubing. Luna moths cluster in the rectangle of the lily pond, fading into the dream's edge.

Here at the panavistic surface our voices dissolve, some hand or shadow moving through the words.

o

Certain people seem to stand behind one.

□

This is of two worlds—the one diurnal men know and that other world where lunar mottled eels stir like dreams in shallow forest water. Allowing both these mechanisms to continue operating, we slowly remove and replace theiyr parts with corresponding and interlocking nothings. The glass machinery is equally filled with allusion to our aestive carnality, an infinite part of the pattern which regenerates itself with its own repetitive logic.

Terrasic afternoons in early October.

Each huge spring bud a transparent chrysalis pregnant with moth wings unfolding into bats. (Every nuance & cartesian plotted in radar-tunnels.) The secrecy of your voice behind me in a crowd, remoras vacuous and cold that lurk in the eddies of your passing.

The air is water.

The skin, neither moist nor dry, is a permeable membrane of cells dividing the summer landscape into pink and blue. Spring aches in the heart and stomach, the surfacing of women in moist soil and moonlight.

□

There is a daerkness outside of those confined to light.

We are strangers here (nocturnal) in the fiction of (absolute) our own hearts.

The source a distant thunder in August the cumuloid and fetal pink intrusions of stone within sky.

Rumblings from the earth.

Land breaking like ice into light.

A familiar woman gazes at a glacial lake. Her vision grows flowers on plants. And on the musicians, their divine arguments.

o

Events accumulate through time—a cephalopod washes up on a grey Silurian beach, no plants, little oxygen. And on the sandbanks of Greenway park, pebbles of edible beige limestone, frosted with ossicles. The sand granular orange from ant excavations sliding, drying in the sun.

o

Purple and lime the Brazilian nights as jewelled insects bead the lights. The glistening highlight continuous through all living creatures. August refracted through the etched crystal of erosion. While April possesses certain cold grey days of which limestone caverns religious hold captive the slow organic branchings of the glass machinery. An intrusion of love solidifies to be eroded later into a curious stone tree. The leaves blow in some hollow interglacial autumn to the Scarborough bluffs.

The light in these afternoons is the reverse of morning and are there those who can truly tell dawn from dusk.

There is a path for you here if you see it.

□

Form of the graceful white elms that flowered all of beneath into above & translated it perfectly. Night elm corridors—a green instrument panel bobbing phosphorescent in the manifold. The valley filled with a slow motion wind of haze & golden the sun in clear warm water.

Paris was there before the name. Kitchener is a thousand miles northwest of Paris, London is two thousand miles south of Ingersoll. Hungry Hollow's epicentre is near Rochester, New York. Asphalt oozes out of the ground near Leamington.

The forest is filled with eyes, clear unblinking surprises—intelligence formulates its own disguises.

o

Delight tantric & warm the microclimatic inclusion of our created bodies, currency the wind begins to give to oceans of leaves. Our white palms pressed together, the hands the wind parted. There is a home in Northern Ontario. Summer wasteland, June, limestone village park into country & the moon arena. At Bayfield the White Sands testing blue sky with the clarity of aerospace suspends a distant speck of jet with no contrail, no clouds, no earth. One soon loses the sensation of falling. The wisdom of her lineaments curl & vanish into the landscape. Tall elms, bilateral clouds of English coal and limestone smoke in 1908. Corridors of gigantic elms, Egyptian in the motionless stadium heat of August. Moss and rain on limestone with milk snakes & milk sliding couples.

o

It all happens quite rapidly.

The land is honeycombed with entrances to caverns.

A theatre of bark. A large room in an ancient museum whose walls are wallpapered in a stage rendition (unusual depth & clarity) of a forest. The forest is naked.

The pad of feet on packed soil, her flesh on humus & nipples erect stuck bits of leaf to. Her squatting all night after a rain having a large toadstool emerge up into her vagina. Pale orange toadstool of immense budding right up into her cunt, her molluscan pool.

o

Small humid cumulus alternately daerken white rooms as they pass through the sulphur-water clarity and support of summer sky. Salamanders' viscous throats pulsating beneath rocks as the secret harmony of all life unfolds itself in silence and without witness. Space solidifies into limestone each time the sum perceptual memory of a life-unit becomes trapped in the sediments. The dim pop of a weather Zonde clicks in the high thin air of the ionosphere.

o

There is peace at this point. The dry whispering celluloid hills of grass. The insects gather at night lights in their teak and obsidian regalia of summer foliage— this meaning not camouflage but magnification.

o

Pit vipers.

The two pilots sweat with incredible tension and the precision of theiyr task. Infra-red snakes sway at night in the desert, the air inebriates the eyes never quite open enough for the detail.

And touching you were that my fingers water dispersing porous into the foliage of your nervous system.

(*Spring Trances in the Control Emerald Night*, 1982)

GRID ERECTILE

Because of its erotic & cool underparts & the sunset emblazoned on its
  membranous back. Its electric litheness.
Because it is a living precipitate of twilight.
Because it is large & soft with external gills.
Because it is tropical and changes colours.
Because the pattern on its back is a thin point.
Because they are so numerous and docile.
Because it whispers through foliage. An animate mobile
  tendril of chlorophyll.
Because it is like an adder, spawning mythology.
Because it is beautiful like a sleek girl with a choker.
For the milk sliding couples beaded with honey.
Because it is large and primitive & therefore closer to the dinosaurs.
Because they are the only lizards we have.
Because they fly around mercury vapour lamps at night &
  alight on suburban screens with their exotic & large bodies.
Because of their silent glittering black flight.
Because of a summer evening in 1954. It opened its wings &
  I received its revelation.
Because of summer nights behind the mosque.
Because it signals the height of summer.
Because of its mathematical precision at the infinite disposal of
  curiosity. Because its markings are the summation of military
  heraldry, the olive green of the English military.
Because it is a tropical species here in Southwestern Ontario.
Because they are nocturnal, tropical thin points of extreme beauty.
  Sculptural perfection in living and dense wood.
Because their chrysalis resembles a vase. Their humming flight &
  the insoluble intricacy of their June camouflage.
Because of the size & gothic modelling of their pincers, their
  chestnut brown elytra.
Because it is so tiny. (Weighs as much as a dime.)
Because it is pale underneath. Tawny above.
Because it is the eyes of night.
Because it is even larger, like a fox bat.
Because it is our largest and only cat.
Because they are capricious night gliders.
Because it is a predator.
Because of its inky fur. Tunnels twisting around roots.
Because it is a southern species migrating northwards.

Evidence for an inter-glacial warming trend.
Because of their glowing eyes in the driveway at night.
   Their rasping marsupial cries.
Because of the caves.
Because of its unearthly face.
Because it is all of night.
Because it is a falcon.
Because it is sub-tropical.
Because it is a stilted & accurate blue mist.
Because it is the north, unwarranted in an ox-bow pond.
Because it is a tropical species slowly migrating north,
   starting at Pt. Pelee.
Because it is a sub-tropical iridescent metal.
Because it is the arctic migrating at the centre of blizzards.
Because they are astonishing aerialists.
Because the vacuum of space is so near.
Because of a dream.
Because they draw out the soul.
Anticipation. Electric gradients. The irresistible approach of the arc
   hammer. Excitation in the ion shadows.
Because they come after you & seem to float in dreams,
   the bend sinister.
Because of the storm.
Because of an erotic insularity in the moist almost tropical wind.
Because they illuminate everything in a grey powdery light
   and turn the outside into a surreal theatre of marvellous intent.
   The warmth allows the spectators to remove their clothes.
Lunacy & a saturnalian trance of corporeal clarity.
Because they are tropical.
Because they are both out of place & welcome.
Because they witnessed extinct races of fabulous creatures.
Because it is carnivorous & wet.
Because it is a carnivorous morning jewel in the sphagnum.
Because they are full lips & vulvas & are all of summer.
Because they are a tropical species here in Southwestern Ontario.
Because it has huge leaves and is tropical with cerise jurassic fruit.
Because it is fragrant and tropical.
Because its fruits are pungent.
Because the flowers are huge. Night glowing & perfumed.
Because of the pools.
Because their smooth mahogany pebbles are enclosed in
   vegetable geodes.
Because of Fovea Centralis.

Because they flowered all of beneath into above and translated it perfectly.
Because it is a living fossil.
Because of the colour & smoothness of its bark, the silence & level loam
floor of the beech forest.
Because of the fragrance of its gum.
Because of the wooden petals of their flowers.
Because of the waterfalls & the morning glen.
Because it is the memory capital of Canada.
Because I perceived an order there.
Because the concretions are there.
Because of mid-summer nights, memory steeped in fireflies.
Because it overlooks Lake Huron.
Because the cedar pools are nearby.
For it was once submerged.
Because it is a huge invisible river.
Because of the collections in grey powdery light of Toronto winter afternoons
spent in the Devonian era.
Because it is semi-tropical & on the same latitude as California.
Because it is a beautiful & glorious natural shrine of limestone.
Because it is awesome.
Because chronology was commenced there.
Because of the black river formation. Last hold-out of the White Elm.
Because of the beech forest & what came after.
Because I got to know Lake Erie & glacial clay there.
Because I grew up beside them & they taught me everything I know.
Because it is a huge & silent underwater predator.
Because it is huge and primitive.
Because it cruises, hovering, long snouted crocodilian.
Because it is primitive.

(*The Cenozoic Asylum*, 1982)

from CONCORDAT PROVISO ASCENDANT

She is liquid darkness occult with desire.

An abandoned airplane hangar, scattered curls of corrugated steel littering the
floor punctate with sun discs. The naked air electric anticipation we unite glistening
in the radance of giant atmospheric machines rising above the horizon. The sky
filled with sound furious insistent joy as she cries, aching chorus of electrolumines-
cent orgasm. Heat-bleached August fields. Sunburned foliage in the shallow ravine.

Cool green lawns under moist tree caverns. Earthen paths packed & powdered. Lambton forest a cool sensual intuition. Limestone trestles under the railway bridge. Night perfume of the magnolia blossoms. Cicadas shimmering in the late summer trees. Storm flooded city streets. Aromatic twigs. Her incendiary hands. September heatwave, a single katydid rasping in the night tree. Humid wind & magnified leaf shadows a restless cinema under the backyard floodlight. Wild grapes purple on the vine. Particulate smoky blue haze of hot October afternoons. Indian summer in the Berkshires. Manhattan. Wild rhododendrons in the Hudson valley.

By becoming myself I have become someone else. My adoration the natural fulfillment of her sacral narcissism. She is eros displayed. Lank salient grace of her thighs as she consumes me. There is a forest with ferns primaeval down there. She drew a shade of stratus. Chunks of stone erode into Mayan friezes. Gold scarabs at Clark point. She won't stop until you've come unnaturally again and again. Creek newts frankly relaxed in the sandy aquarium delta foliage. An otter near the forks of the Ervin and Grand. Cedar roots dowsing Silurian strata. Prodigious acrobatics of the mud swallows. She is here now. Her face a dark lantern blossoming in the twilight. Every path the most expedient solution of opposite destinations. She lies down amongst the ferns. Manitoulin cecropias. A flute lost in the sound of the rapids. Scarab grubs harboured in the scrub oaks. We merge in the windy forest, in the rushing neo–silence of a hot August wind, in the mute aqueous clamour of leaves under the wild hush of the canopy. Our clothes sullen layers of skin. Our giant bodies a glistening electric surface continuous with the forest. Close upon us now this afternoon an atmosphere of flesh. The smell of rain in the wind. August enthralled in the cool depths of the lake. Mudpuppy. Hellbender. September heatwave stone temple haze along the beach distant signal fires glimmering orange. Her water broke the slow fall of evening leaves, waves of silver green the boughs above human creatures coupling wondrous beneath. Chlorophyll mist. The sky ringing with our music.

■

Distant apartment complexes moody empires of light, subdued orange constellations in the hazy twilight. The revelation of the rainy day. Late night resurrection of a forgotten love, a vanished civilization, where the waning moon is the accusational eye of a discarded lover. Velvet metaphysics in the dusty light on the trunks of the norway spruce, cicada husks at their bases. Windbreak colonnade. Love's absence is still love, the heart a celestial wound. August a certain Aegean light through us all. The beach a commotion of light and waves, cries of gulls and children blending in the wind. Honeysuckle vines redolent with evening, a dusky corona of ruby throats. Surprising articulation of children's backs, an advanced hominid wisdom. Wild cherry gum on raw copper. The dull gleam of tin roofs. Field of hydroelectric power flickering in the continuous darkness at the bottom of the lake.

She is delightfully augmented. In the distance vandals break windows in a deserted factory, disembodied locus of fear. Meander. She walks almost laboriously around her endowments, a libidinous & circuitous grace. She is crippled with sex, ripe fruit on a slender bough. Resume the broken discourse of the gods. A quick vertigo of lust. The milky way wheeling on a hub of antimatter through abandoned zodiacs in the mysterious depths of an intergalactic summer night. A continuous indoor atmosphere which extends uniformly & infinitely in all directions.

(*Concordat Proviso Ascendant*, 1991)

I am / really here and not in a novel
—FRANK O'HARA

The skin is broken
—JOHN ASHBERY

I enclose my equal flesh,
—DIANE WARD

It's 2 A.M. at Anne & Lewis's which is where it's at
—TED BERRIGAN
AND DICK GALLUP

Barbara Guest [1920]

SANTA FE TRAIL

I go separately
The sweet knees of oxen have pressed a path for me
ghosts with ingots have burned their bare hands
it is the dungaree darkness with China stitched
where the westerly winds
and the traveler's checks
the evensong of salesmen
the glistening paraphernalia of twin suitcases
where no one speaks English.
I go separately
It is the wind, the rubber wind
when we brush our teeth in the way station
a climate to beard. What forks these roads?
Who clammers o'er the twain?
What murmurs and rustles in the distance
in the white branches where the light is whipped
piercing at the crossing as into the dunes we simmer
and toss ourselves awhile the motor pants like a forest
where owls from their bandaged eyes send messages
to the Indian couple. Peaks have you heard?
I go separately
We have reached the arithmetics, are partially quenched
while it growls and hints in the lost trapper's voice
She is coming toward us like a session of pines
in the wild wooden air where rabbits are frozen,
O mother of lakes and glaciers, save us gamblers
whose wagon is perilously rapt.

(*Poems*, 1962)

WALKING BUDDHA

Should I forget your scales
in confirmation of your knighthood

    or voice what is petal-soft
    in the cracked eye-lift?

Not circular or fleeting
but *swinging*

    pushed forward by your idiom
    like a giantess opening a window sash

you refuse to remark
the offering below your building

    you refuse to go downstairs
    your gait is forward
    we must go around you

Brilliant decision!

    a frangipane rewards you
    with color streak

in the wet season

    the coloring protects

better than ghee, better than opium

A metal eye that cannot open
stretched as far as elephant, yet firm
in its enclosure

    Diadem head!

The masons have finished their research

not a cubic inch more

There is:

The arm whose elongation

the open hand

the chest measurements

        Rough cement ruled

an original *Art Brut*

unrailed staircase

a smash knee surface

conceal the bronze asperity

        essential of being classical
        in a violent world before the decline

under slip-shoe palm

                        (*The Blue Stairs*, 1968)

A WAY OF BEING

There we go in cars, did you guess we wore sandals?
Carrying the till, memorizing its numbers,
apt at the essential such as rearranging
languages. They occur from route to route
like savages who wear shells.

"I cannot place him." Yet I do.
He must ascend indefinitely as airs
he must regard his image as plastic,
adhering to the easeful carpet that needs
footprints and cares for them.
as is their wont in houses, the ones we pass by.

Such a day/or such a night
reeling from cabin to cabin
looking at the cakewalk or merely dancing.
These adventures in broad/or slim
lamplight,

　　　　　Yet the cars
do not cheat, even their colors perform in storm.
We never feel the scratch, they do.
When lightning strikes it's safer to ride
on rubber going down a mountain,
safer than trees, or sand, more preventive
to be hid in a cloud we sing, remembering

The old manse and robins. One tear,
a salty one knowing we have escaped
the charm of being native. Even as your glance
through the windshield tells me you've seen
another mishap of nature

　　　　　　you would willingly forget,
prefer to be like him near the hearth
where woodsmoke makes a screen of numbers and signs
where the bedstead it's not so foreign as this lake.

　　　　　The plateau, excursionist,
is ahead. After that twenty volumes
of farmland. Then I must guide us
to the wood garage someone has whitened
where the light enters through one window
like a novel. You must peer at it
without weakening, without feeling
hero, or heroine,

　　　　　Understanding the distances
between characters, their wakeful
or sleep searchingness, as far from the twilight ring
the slow sunset, the quick dark.

　　　　　　　(*The Blue Stairs*, 1968)

RED LILIES

Someone has remembered to dry the dishes;
they have taken the accident out of the stove.
Afterward lilies for supper; there
the lines in front of the window
are rubbed on the table of stone

The paper flies up
then down as the wind
repeats. repeats its birdsong.

Those arms under the pillow
the burrowing arms they cleave
at night as the tug kneads water
calling themselves branches

The tree is you
the blanket is what warms it
snow erupts from thistle
to toe; the snow pours out of you.

A cold hand on the dishes
placing a saucer inside
her who undressed for supper
gliding that hair to the snow

The pilot light
went out on the stove

The paper folded like a napkin
other wings flew into the stone.

(*Moscow Mansions*, 1973)

NEBRASKA

Climate succumbing continously as water gathered
into foam or Nebraska elevated by ships
withholds what is glorious in its climb like
a waiter balancing a waterglass while the tray
slips that was necklace in the arch of bridge
now the island settles linear its paragraph of tree
vibrates the natural cymbal with its other tongue
strikes an attitude we have drawn there on the limb
when icicle against the sail will darken the wind
eftsooning it and the ways lap with spices as
buoyancy once the galloping area where grain
is rinsed and care requires we choose our walk

And the swift nodding becomes delicate
smoke is also a flow the pastoral calm where
each leaf has a shadow fortuitous as word
with its pine and cone its seedling a curl
like smoke with the ashy retrograding slopes
at the station up or down and musically
a notation as when smoke enters sky

The swift nodding becomes delicate
'lifelike' is pastoral an ambrosia where calm
produces a leaf with a shadow fortuitous as word
with its pine and cone its seedling we saw
yesterday with the natural flow in our hand
thought of as sunlight and wisely found rocks
sand that were orisons there a city in
our minds we called silence and bird droppings
where the staircase ended that was only roof

Hallucinated as Nebraska the swift blue
appears formerly hid when approached now it
chides with a tone the prow striking a grim
atmosphere appealing and intimate as if a verse
were to water somewhere and hues emerge
and distance erased a swan concluding bridge
the sky with her neck possibly brightening
the machinery as a leaf arches through its yellow
syllables so Nebraska's throat

(Moscow Mansions, 1973)

SASSAFRAS

[for H. B.]

Today a field of pumpkins
yes.
       Also the sea imagining granaries
the slight narrow fish tangled in its weed.
Pretending.

Imaginary objects
      and what isn't
there's Sleughfoot on the rug
attacking his quarry
as if it were alabaster and not a door
      a cat!

      Which isn't as imaginative
as your kicking in the glass door of
Metropolitan Telephone and Co.

      Or rain fancying windows.
You said,
      Ellington travels so much in his music
everyone bumps into him.

      Considering the wind
on the plains out middle west;
the strict mountains whose claim
(in our time) never varies. Can
we say they have imagination? We know
they are far out; the plain was an introduction.

      There is conjecture.
Fog on the mallows. Bloom of mallow
in the fog. Now you cannot see it,
      was it 'invention'

      Or sassafras
a tonic,
      whose bark
a digestive

or to be taken
when wild red harshnesses
range the system
            causative
of sillabubs; they make
for disorder
            they lend themselves
to the imagination
            like Nereids

You are absolutely crazy
racing past their scream

(*Moscow Mansions*, 1973)

WILD GARDENS OVERLOOKED BY NIGHT LIGHTS

Wild gardens overlooked by night lights. Parking
lot trucks overlooked by night lights. Buildings
with their escapes overlooked by lights

They urge me to seek here on the heights
amid the electrical lighting that self who exists,
who witnesses light and fears its expunging,

I take from my wall the landscape with its water
of blue color, its gentle expression of rose,
pink, the sunset reaches outward in strokes as the west wind
rises, the sun sinks and color flees into the delicate
skies it inherited,
I place there a scene from "The Tale of the Genji."

An episode where Genji recognizes his son.
Each turns his face away from so much emotion,
so that the picture is one of profiles floating
elsewhere from their permanence,

a line of green displaces these relatives,
black also intervenes at correct distances,
the shapes of the hair are black.

Black describes the feeling,
is recognized as remorse, sadness,
black is a headdress while lines slant swiftly,
the space is slanted vertically with its graduating
need for movement,

Thus the grip of realism has found
a picture chosen to cover the space
occupied by another picture
establishing a flexibility so we are not immobile
like a car that spends its night
outside a window, but mobile like a spirit.

I float over this dwelling, and when I choose
enter it. I have an ethnological interest
in this building, because I inhabit it
and upon me has been bestowed the decision of changing
an abstract picture of light into a ghost-like story
of a prince whose principality I now share,
into whose confidence I have wandered.

Screens were selected to prevent this intrusion
of exacting light and add a chiaroscuro,
so that Genji may turn his face from his son,
from recognition which here is painful,
and he allows himself to be positioned on a screen,
this prince as noble as ever,
songs from the haunted distance
presenting themselves in silks.

The light of fiction and light of surface
sink into vision whose illumination
exacts its shades,

The Genji when they arose
strolled outside reality
their screen dismantled,
upon that modern wondering space
flash lights from the wild gardens.

(*Fair Realism*, 1989)

AN EMPHASIS FALLS ON REALITY

Cloud fields change into furniture
furniture metamorphizes into fields
an emphasis falls on reality.

"It snowed toward morning," a barcarole
the words stretched severely

silhouettes they arrived in trenchant cut
the face of lilies....

I was envious of fair realism.

I desired sunrise to revise itself
as apparition, majestic in evocativeness,
two fountains traced nearby on a lawn....

you recall treatments
of 'being' and 'nothingness'
illuminations apt
to appear from variable directions—
they are orderly as motors
floating on the waterway,

so silence is pictorial
when silence is real.

The wall is more real than shadow
or that letter composed of calligraphy
each vowel replaces a wall

a costume taken from space
donated by walls....

These metaphors may be apprehended after
they have brought their dogs and cats
born on roads near willows,

willows are not real trees
they entangle us in looseness,
the natural world spins in green.

A column chosen from distance
mounts into the sky while the font
is classical,

they will destroy the disturbed font
as it enters modernity and is rare....

The necessary idealizing of you reality
is part of the search, the journey
where two figures embrace

This house was drawn for them
it looks like a real house
perhaps they will move in today

into ephemeral dusk and
move out of that into night
selective night with trees,

The darkened copies of all trees.

(*Fair Realism*, 1989)

HEAVY VIOLETS

Heavy violets there is no way
if the door clicks the cushion
makes murmur noise and the woman
on the sofa turns half in half out
a tooth slipping from velvet.

The world makes this division
copies by words each with a leaf
attached to images it makes of this
half in air and half out
like haloes or wrists

That separate while they spin
airs or shadows if you wish,
once or twice half in half out
a real twirl jostles there
lips creased with violets you wish.

(*Fair Realism*, 1989)

WORDS

The simple contact with a wooden spoon and the word
recovered itself, began to spread as grass, forced
as it lay sprawling to consider the monument where
patience looked at grief, where warfare ceased
eyes curled outside themes to search the paper
now gleaming and potent, wise and resilient, word
entered its continent eager to find another as
capable as a thorn. The nearest possession would
house them both, they being then two might glide
into this house and presently create a rather larger
mansion filled with spoons and condiments, gracious
as a newly laid table where related objects might gather
to enjoy the interplay of gravity upon facetious hints,
the chocolate dish presuming an endowment, the ladle
of galactic rhythm primed as a relish dish, curved

knives, finger bowls, morsel carriages words might
choose and savor before swallowing so much was the
sumptuousness and substance of a rented house where words
placed dressing gowns as rosemary entered their scent
percipient as elder branches in the night where words
gathered, warped, then straightened, marking new wands.

(*Fair Realism*, 1989)

BLEAT

drawn on the burden of light
the pottery throw
in bleat turning

ballast makes fingers twitch
shutters close
"going to pour"

wet to root and pavement
tent sagging like an oyster

"the city has another soul"

gnat passes someone swallows
"another soul"

figurines

"the city also"
stole the bench and echoes

blight and shuttered bleat
soul chews a wilted corner

(*Fair Realism*, 1989)

GEESE BLOOD

height of trees

the papered chamber—

a breathy click—low volumed—

the stalking men—

outer motions

leading to holes—unstable lacing—

an elevation—

controlled surface—

seizures—the fallow lining—

a bird interrupts—

groping for layers—

lip fold—

loosed on the hillside—   dun panorama

continues a secondary

reliance on ledge—the nearest forest—reversed

kilometres—a brusque rim—the outer motion—

as figurative—

extension of features—

leading to holes—an elevated fissure;

these intervals control—

in bold gaps—marked by flaking—The empty lining—

The bird in fallow sky—the motion

exits into forest shelter—

the lighter than expected—height of trees—

aware the figure

now withdrawn in commotive patterns—agitates

low volume—men stalking—the open visor—

ruffled leaves

held with cotton—gloves—in pursuit of sunlight—

the raw bloom—polarized—

tunneling.

the ace spring—   an inch into—

mosaic.

eye bell—

a mirror dice—   an opening.

sand bowls in—

cotton gloves—

two hunting knives—

the dried-up glint—

spirit guide—

under three arches—green hand.   sunken bowls.

'red geese blood'.

(*Defensive Rapture*, 1993)

DEFENSIVE RAPTURE

Width of a cube spans defensive rapture
cube from blocks of liquid theme
phantom of lily stark
in running rooms.

adoration of hut performs a clear function
illusive column extending dust
protective screen the red
objects pavilion.

deep layered in tradition moonlight
folkloric pleads the rakish
sooted idiom
supernatural diadem.

stilled grain of equinox
turbulence the domicile
host robed arm white
crackled motives.

sensitive timbre with complex
astral sign open tent hermetic
toss of sand swan reeds
torrents of uneveness.

surround a lusted fabric
hut sequence modal shy
as verdigris hallow force
massive intimacy.

slant fuse the wived
mosaic a chamber astrakhan
amorous welding
the sober descant.

turns in the mind bathes
the rapture bone a guardian
ploy indolent lighted
strew of doubt.

commends internal habitude
bush the roof
day stare gliding
double measures.

qualms the weights of night
medusæ raft clothed sky
radiant strike the oars
skim cirrus.

evolve a fable husk
aged silkiness the roan
planet mowed like ears
beaded grip.

suppose the hooded grass
numb moat alum trench a solemn
glaze the sexual estuary
floats an edge.

(*Defensive Rapture,* 1993)

OTRANTO

At sunset from the top of the stair watching

the castle mallets wrenched from their socket

fell from ambush into flame flew into hiding;

above the stoneware a latch like muscle hid

the green; he stood waist high under the rapt

ceiling and hanged the sparrow; where the kitchen

had been a mirror of eggs served in a tumbler he

saw the ring when a lancet pierced and threw it.

In a basket and lowered it where sails enter

the harbor over a parchment like dominoes;

the petrel–like eyelash.

To the sun and its rites were pulled the dried

banners; they flew past the ruins the tower

and window where ivory guided the mist on his back;

he rubbed his eyes and counted them kneeling

wrinkled as grass.

A ghost in their nostrils put a heel at their

forehead; they only the moon as it

fasted.

ii

If the ship meant anything if he heard a world

view in the midst of his rhythm or the spell

lustrous like hair on his arm; that groaned as

it struck near the tumble down or

combing hair; words burnt as they quickened.

The bitter they share crept into forage and

muster is in their skin; the grey

worked like a vise they brushed this

to turn arrows; they shut off the vast

cellar and the turret leaped to a pattern;

the mosaic blended was untouched.

iii

The frankish hills and hummocks metered

the greed over sun and cloud; voluptuous

in the straits turbanned held scarves to the

water each sail embroidered;

who washed in their music a lattice.

A major or borrowed sky this aspect provides

the lily stalk inside the frame; a gesture the lily

pointing north as if the wrench from sky decides

cold rain or change of tide; the lily

she chooses.

iv

Waking in must the high pierced window dew on

the furnaced bar the poaching hour the cup

takes smoke from the tower; they drink

in the smoke the print cradled; cut in dark.

The siege made cloth a transfer

learned from invaders who craved it;

spindle thieves.

She sang high notes and pebbles went into her

work where it changed into marks; in that room

the armor-like wrens:

rites turned with thread a dower

begs lapis; eglantine on a spoon; the castle

breeds tallow.

V

A change of tide might delay the run

they watched as if by simple water

read magisterially whatever the book decided;

night outside covered with filmic screen

ghosts they store; then bring an experimental

wheel out of hiding.

Even the Nile wind; fortune cards

jugglers a remedy from old clothes;

to appease the fable—pearls

rolling in straw.

The way a cowslip bends

they remember or Troilus as he stared;

they agree on brighter covers; looser

shifts fluent tower to tower.

More ephemeral than roundness or

the grown pear tree connected

with vision a rose briar.

vi

There was only a rugged footpath

above the indifferent straits and a shelf where the

castle lay perhaps it was sphered like Otranto;

there the traveller stood naked and talked

aloud or found a lily and thought a sword;

or dragged a carcass upon blunt stone like a

corded animal. In weeds in spiritual

seclusion a felt hand lifted.

(*Defensive Rapture*, 1993)

James Schuyler [1923 – 1991]

FREELY ESPOUSING

a commingling sky

       a semi-tropic night
       that cast the blackest shadow
       of the easily torn, untrembling banana leaf

or Quebec! what a horrible city
so Steubenville is better?
         the sinking sensation
when someone drowns thinking, "This can't be happening to me!"
the profit of excavating the battlefield where Hannibal whomped the
                     Romans
the sinuous beauty of words like allergy
the tonic resonance of
pill when used as in
"she is a pill"
on the other hand I am not going to espouse any short stories in
              which lawn mowers clack.
No, it is absolutely forbidden
for words to echo the act described; or try to. Except very directly
as in
bong. And tickle. Oh it is inescapable kiss.
Marriages of the atmosphere
are worth celebrating
         where Tudor City
catches the sky or the glass side
of a building lit up at night in fog
"What is that gold-green tetrahedron down the river?"
"You are experiencing a new sensation."

     if the touch-me-nots
     are not in bloom
     neither are the chrysanthemums

the bales of pink cotton candy
in the slanting light
        are ornamental cherry trees.
        The greens around them, and
        the browns, the grays, are the park.

It's. Hmm. No.
        Their scallop shell of quiet
        is the S.S. *United States.*
        It is not so quiet and they
        are a medium-size couple who
        when they fold each other up
        well, thrill. That's their story.

               (*Freely Espousing,* 1969)

GREETINGS FROM THE CHATEAU

for David Noakes

Why did Massenet compose *Thaïs?*
Why was there spiteful silence in the prune orchard?
He rests his arms on the pond balustrade.
He has bread in his hands.
Pianos sing in the palace,
the Empress bathes, the Emperor
climbs short flights of library steps
to take down a world's smallest atlas.

Alas. It is very hot and the carp
flew off into the wood, Rosa's bull
boarded up in the Square. "Dinner.
Champagne at five. My letters answered.
Remember to mend the tape recorder."

In the palace, the double-bodied sphinxes
stare at the geometry of the gardens
delighting another dusk, and the canal to the sky.

               (*Freely Espousing,* 1969)

ROYALS

Called dog men,
they go out and have encounters.
Their blue eyes pick up and discharge
the green of their jackets, or ties.
Men with clear-green eyes unnerve angels.

Or perhaps they are unnerving as angels.
It is certain they are not angels.
They may be of another order,
between us and heaven like the atmosphere
between us and the sky, appointed
to clarify deathbed facts.
Unable to talk with us,
they know about us and argue about the facts
and the motives we may not know ourselves.
Their arguing might be clarifying
to those who know them whom they do not know
as they know us who do not know them.
We see them of course,
talk with them and even touch them,
are struck by their glances.
We show them our secret, however ill-kept.
They tell us nothing about themselves.
They seem to tell everything,
what they are is obvious when we see them.
We accept as facts our conjectures about them
we were not aware we had made.
They help make real our conjectures.

They live in rooms around town
and perhaps are what we become for a part of life
without knowing afterward.
This is no stranger than their rooms,
the inside of a cloud of red dust (it is, however, a room),
a room grown with lichens with a moon in it,
or wherever we pass them, or a roof.

(*Freely Espousing*, 1969)

A MAN IN BLUE

Under the French horns of a November afternoon
a man in blue is raking leaves
with a wide wooden rake (whose teeth are pegs
or rather, dowels). Next door
boys play soccer: "You got to start
over!" sort of. A round attic window
in a radiant gray house waits like a kettledrum.
"You got to start..." The Brahmsian day
lapses from waltz to march. The grass,
rough-cropped as Bruno Walter's hair,
is stretched, strewn and humped beneath a sycamore
wide and high as an idea of heaven
in which Brahms turns his face like a bearded thumb
and says, "There is something I must tell you!"
to Bruno Walter. "In the first movement
of my Second, think of it as a family
planning where to go next summer
in terms of other summers. A material ecstasy,
subdued, recollective." Bruno Walter
in a funny jacket with a turned-up collar
says, "Let me sing it for you."
He waves his hands and through the vocalese-shaped spaces
of naked elms he draws a copper beech
ignited with a few late leaves. He bluely glazes
a rhododendron "a sea of leaves" against gold grass.
There is a snapping from the brightwork
of parked and rolling cars.
There almost has to be a heaven! so there could be
a place for Bruno Walter
who never needed the cry of a baton.
Immortality—
in a small, dusty, rather gritty, somewhat scratchy
Magnavox from which a forte
drops like a used Brillo Pad?
Frayed. But it's hard to think of the sky as a thick glass floor
with thick-soled Viennese boots tromping about on it.
It's a whole lot harder thinking of Brahms
in something soft, white and flowing.
"Life," he cries (here, in the last movement),
"is something more than beer and skittles!"

"And the something more
is a whole lot better than beer and skittles,"
says Bruno Walter,
darkly, under the sod. I don't suppose it seems so dark
to a root. Who are these men in evening coats?
What are these thumps?
Where is Brahms?
And Bruno Walter?
Ensconced in resonant plump easy chairs
covered with scuffed brown leather
in a pungent autumn that blends leaf smoke
(sycamore, tobacco, other),
their nobility wound in a finale
like this calico cat
asleep, curled up in a breadbasket,
on a sideboard where the sun falls.

(*Freely Espousing*, 1969)

THE MASTER OF THE GOLDEN GLOW

An irregular rattle (shutters) and
a ferule tapped
on a blackboard—or where you come from
do they say chalkboard?—anyway it's not any sort of pointer
it's a sash facing west
wood and glass drummed on by autumn tatters.
Say, who are you
anyway? "I think we may have met before.
God knows I've heard enough about you."
That largest maple—
half its leaves an undreamt of butter:
it only safflower oil
were the color of its name
the way olive oil is. "Why,
don't you *like* butter?"
The doctor's youngest son
paddles the canoe while he (the doctor) casts
for mud-flavored carp in the long brackish pond:
Agawam, meaning lake. Lake Pond,

Pond Lake, Lake Lake, Pond Pond,
its short waves jumping up and down
in one place with surplus energy to spend.
Somewhere, out of the wind,
the wind collects a ripe debris.
"I'll tell you who I am: someone
you never met
though on a train you studied a boil on my neck
or bumped into me
leaving a late late party
                            'Sorry'
or saw throwing bones in the ocean
for an inexhaustible retriever."
The wind drops. The sky darkens
to an unfathomable gray
and through hardware cloth one
leaf is seen to fall
describing the helixes of conch-shell cores
gathered in summer, thrown out in autumn.
More litter, less clutter.

(*Freely Espousing,* 1969)

"EARTH'S HOLOCAUST"

It's time again.
Tear up the violets
and plant something more difficult to grow.
Everything a little cleaner, a little more ugly:
cast cement tubs of malevolent ageratums,
and: "Your grandmother baked
and froze that pie. We saved it
for a special occasion." Codicils
don't add up to much when there's nothing to leave:
a bedroom, stretching from Portland
to Richmond stunningly furnished in
French-motel provincial. On the brighter side
plastic seaweed has proved
an unqualified success. As have ready-glued scrapbooks
which if out of style

still epitomize. In this one
is your first matchbook cover,
an advertisement with a misprint,
a pair of bronze baby shoes,
a tinted enlargement of a tintype.
Twins on the upswing: there are more people.
A regular Shriners' parade of funerals.
But there are not less people.
There are more people
of all sorts, conditions and flavors.
Getting to shake each
by the hand takes time.
Not more though
than abstracting the grain of dust
from each raindrop. Starfish
have no sense of time, at all.

(*Freely Espousing,* 1969)

SPRING

    snow thick and wet, porous
    as foam rubber yet
    crystals, an early Easter sugar.
    Twigs
    aflush.
    A crocus
    startled or stunned
    (or so it looks: crocus
    thoughts are few) reclines
    on wet crumble
    a puddle of leas. It
    isn't winter and it isn't spring
    yes it is the sun
    sets where it should and
    the east
    glows
    rose. No.
    Willow.

(*The Crystal Lithium,* 1972)

A STONE KNIFE

December 26, 1969

Dear Kenward,
                    What a pearl
of a letter knife. It's just
the thing I needed, something
to rest my eyes on, and always
wanted, which is to say
it's that of which I
felt the lack but
didn't know of, of no
real use and yet
essential as a button
box, or maps, green
morning skies, islands and
canals in oatmeal, the steam
off oyster stew. Brown
agate, veined as a woods
by smoke that has to it
the watery twist of eel grass
in a quick, rust-discolored
cove. Undulating lines of
northern evening—a Munch
without the angst—a
hint of almost amber:
to the nose, a resinous
thought, to the eye, a
lacquered needle green
where no green is, a
present after-image.
Sleek as an ax, bare
and elegant as a tarn,
manly as a lingam,
November weather petrified,
it is just the thing
to do what with? To
open letters? No, it
is just the thing, an
object, dark, fierce
and beautiful in which
the surprise is that

the surprise, once
past, is always there:
which to enjoy is
not to consume. The un-
recapturable returns
in a brown world
made out of wood,
snow streaked, storm epi-
center still in stone.

(*The Crystal Lithium*, 1972)

GRAND DUO

An improvisation for Arthur Gold and Robert Fizdale

the Seine
    "transcend, be real"
        she vanished
    "like a light"

                        *

Timeless, tireless, sketched, soft

                cleft mountains
                clothed in wolves and conifers
                breathe on clockwork towns
a river enters
petrified sponge
            perilously water falls
            under weeping skies
            rift by a kiss

                    *

Rain lashed the windows of a careening train.
    Tunnels,
boulders, crevasses. Vapors and clouds parted on
    blue.

*

Art is formality, courtesy, passion, control, practice,
   rehearsing the unrehearsed
            art is no is
                melodiously
                repeated endlessly
                varies naturally

Sweet basic monotone
                heavens of gray
                melt away
green on the blue land   all things awash in jewel and
   beverage colors

*

Your fingers on keys
sentiments drawn unanxiously
by hyper-accuracy
            Austria! lederhosen, spas and beer
            cookies and the dragon of Klagenfurt
   Music! Schubert! Song!
         a bird declining the verb to be
Florence teaching a child to sing
            nightingale
in German so around sung silence
            nightingales in silence sing

*

Schubert put his spectacle on
He wrote, *Grand Duo*. Probably,
a four-hand version of a lost symphony. Anyone
may hear it only if you play it.
                Life
            methodical
            unquenchable
(meadows dress themselves in green and daisies
kine fodder. A smiling boy points out the
   way to town)
            in rainbows
         after rain, in rain, letters, a recipe

Summers in town are unnatural.
So is the beach. The sun
flushes the cheek of a peach.
            A gesture in the air
        unhectoring as a smile
                "be quick   prolong"
Rapt in a hoked-up coda dream
tumultuous applause of piano history
        the first forte was played on an instrument
built out of wood that marched back from Dunsinane

            Schubert

Franz Schubert

                            (*The Home Book*, 1977)

FATHER OR SON

Detected little things: a peach pit basket watch chain charm, an ivory cross wound
with ivory ivy, a natural cross. The Tatoosh Mountains, opaque crater lakes, a
knickerbockered boy who drowned smiles for a seeming ever on ice skates on ice-
skate-scratched ice, an enlarged scratched snapshot. Taken, taken. Mad charges
corrupt to madness their sane nurses. Virginia creeper, Loose Tooth tanned black
snake skins, shot crows for crow wings for a black servant's hat, lapped hot milk,
slung mud in a Bible reader's crotch: "You oughtn't read the Bible nekkid!" Family
opals, selfishness changed hands. Tatoosh Mountains, opaque crater lakes, find me
the fish skeleton enclosed in a fish skeleton (fish ate fish) he had.

                            (*The Home Book*, 1977)

Frank O'Hara [1926 – 1966]

ODE TO TANAQUIL LECLERCQ

Smiling through my own memories of painful excitement your wide eyes
stare
    and narrow like a lost forest of childhood stolen from gypsies
two eyes that are the sunset of
                      two knees
                          two wrists
                              two minds
and the extended philosophical column, when they conducted the dialogues
        in distant Athens, rests on your two ribbon-wrapped hearts, white
    credibly agile
            flashing
                scimitars of a city-state

where in the innocence of my watching had those ribbons become entangled
      dragging me upward into lilac-colored ozone where I gasped
          and you continued to smile as you dropped the bloody scarf of my life
                    from way up there, my neck hurt

      you were always changing into something else
      and always will be
      always plumage, perfection's broken heart, wings

      and wide eyes in which everything you do
      repeats yourself simultaneously and simply
                as a window "gives" on something

it seems sometimes as if you were only breathing
    and everything happened around you
because when you disappeared in the wings nothing was there
      but the motion of some extraordinary happening I hadn't understood
the superb arc of a question, of a decision about death

because you are beautiful you are hunted
   and with the courage of a vase
      you refuse to become a deer or tree
   and the world holds its breath
      to see if you are there, and safe

         are you?

(*The Collected Poems*, 1972)

YOU AT THE PUMP

(*History of North and South*)

   A bouquet of zephyr-flowers hitched to a hitching
post in far off Roanoke

   a child watches the hitch tense

   here an Indian
   there a bag of marbles
   here a strange sunrise
   there suffused with odors
   and behind the restored door
   a change of clothing
   fresh as baking bread
   the child sits quietly
   with his nose stuck in a
   rose in the village square
   where the dust is

   and a tall man comes along and spreads water everywhere
for the flowers to drink and enjoy us

   it is a small mystery of America

   how northerly the wind
   sweeping into the square
   what icicle of color
   reaches the bag

of young sensibility
and makes him think
I love you, Pocahontas
where his feet are

(*Love Poems* [Tentative Title], 1965)

MARY DESTI'S ASS

In Bayreuth once
we were very good friends of the Wagners
and I stepped in once
for Isadora so perfectly
she would never allow me to dance again
that's the way it was in Bayreuth

the way it was in Hackensack
was different
there one never did anything
and everyone hated you anyway
it was fun, it was clear
you knew where you stood

in Boston you were never really standing
I was usually lying
it was amusing to be lying all
the time for everybody
it was like exercise

it means something to exercise
in Norfolk Virginia
it means you've been to bed with a Nigra
well it is exercise
the only difference is it's better than Boston

I was walking along the street
of Cincinnati
and I met Kenneth Koch's mother
fresh from the Istanbul Hilton
she liked me and I liked her
we both liked Istanbul

then in Waukegan I met a furniture manufacturer
and it wiped out all dreams of pleasantness from my mind
it was like being pushed down hard
on a chair
it was like something horrible you hadn't expected
which is the most horrible thing

and in Singapore I got a dreadful
disease it was amusing to have bumps
except they went into my veins
and rose to the surface like Vesuvius
getting cured was like learning to smoke

yet I always loved Baltimore
the porches which hurt your ass
no, they were the steps
well you have a wet ass anyway
if they'd only stop scrubbing

and Frisco where I saw
Toumanova "the baby ballerina" except
she looked like a cow
I didn't know the history of the ballet yet
not that that taught me much

now if you feel like you want to deal with
Tokyo
you've really got something to handle
it's like Times Square at midnight
you don't know where you're going
but you know

and then in Harbin I knew
how to behave it was glorious that
was love sneaking up on me through the snow
and I felt it was because of all
the postcards and the smiles and kisses and the grunts
that was love but I kept on traveling

(*Lunch Poems*, 1964)

SUMMER BREEZES

(F. Y.(M.)M.B.I.)

An element of mischief contributed
                                        to the float
                                        in the lake
                    the pool stood on its ear, dripping aqua
                                                    irritating eyes
they swam all day in the torrid cool
                    and at night they sunned each other
it was idyllic
                there was a lot of space between them
                                                it was not a grave
then Uncle Ned came and ruined everything
Lois said she was pregnant
the gardener said he was guilty
Lois said he wasn't
            what an eruption!
                                        (everyone knew it was Cherry
                                        he played basketball winters)
            mother flew in from Des Moines
                                        with her dog
the whole damn vacation was really ruined!
                                        it wasn't so much
what happened as having all those people around, I thought

                    yet when Lois got fired I was sorry
                    I was very fond of Cherry

                    (AND OTHER BREEZES)
which made me think a lot
                    (that *Gone With the Wind* must be right) and
I looked and looked, but there was nobody for me to do anything with
what a summer!
                    so I lay on the float on my belly and thought of
Indians (Eastern and Western, but mostly Western—Apache and Iroquois,
that is)
            Zanzibar   shishkebab   South Seas   sharks
ridingboots   lotusleaves   whippings   lipstick   unicorns
        panthers (preferably black panthers, no, preferably blonde panthers)
tigersandleopardstoo   champagneandothermoviedrinks   blood
pearls   snow   windycrevasses   a gigantic tornado followed

immediately by the eruption of the biggest volcano in the world and
the crash of an oversized comet!

and that summer my swimming improved
a lot

(*The Collected Poems*, 1972)

MADRID

Spain! much more beautiful than Egypt!
better than France and Alsace and Livorno! or Théophile Gautier!
nothing but rummies in Nice

and junkies in Tunis
but everything convulses under the silver tent of Spain
the dark

the dry

the shark-bite sand-colored mouth
of Europa, the raped and swarthy goddess of speed! o Spain
to be in your arms again

and the dung-bright olives
bluely smiling at the quivering angulas

smudge
against the wall of mind

where the silver turns
against the railroad tracks

and breath goes down
and down and down

into the cool moonlight
where the hotel room is on wheels
and there all buttocks are black and blue

dun
is the color of the streets and sacks of beer
where dopes lead horses with a knight on each

do you care if the rotunda is sparrowy
caught behind the arras of distaste and sorrow

did you
wait, wait very long
or was it simply dark and you standing there

I saw the end of a very long tale
being delivered in the Rastro on Sunday morning
and you were crying, and I was crying right away too

the Retiro confided in us
all those betrayals
                    we never meant but had to do, the leaves
            the foolish boats like High School
                        before the Alhambra
                before the echo of your voice
I have done other things but never against you

            now I am going home
            I am watering the park for La Violetera
            I am cherishing the black and white of your love

                            (*The Collected Poems*, 1972)

POEM

            Lana Turner has collapsed!
            I was trotting along and suddenly
            it started raining and snowing
            and you said it was hailing
            but hailing hits you on the head
            hard so it was really snowing and
            raining and I was in such a hurry
            to meet you but the traffic
            was acting exactly like the sky
            and suddenly I see a headline
            LANA TURNER HAS COLLAPSED!
            there is no snow in Hollywood
            there is no rain in California
            I have been to lots of parties
            and acted perfectly disgraceful
            but I never actually collapsed
            oh Lana Turner we love you get up

                            (*Lunch Poems*, 1964)

CAPTAINS COURAGEOUS

"He fell off a barn on his head
and he played with rag dolls for 30 years"

        do you really think they fish in heaven"

hey! my heart! I find it a great comfort to read this cable
     made of paper and rolled like a cigarette
but the walk took a long time
                rude snow fell and Lavoris-colored rain
    I was bored on board a ship at sea and walk

"passing a barn there was a thump
but the dazzling end came full of papers flushed with hash and pot"

               a step at a time and flopped"

I neglected worldliness
              it did not make me a pure extirpated brother
I wonder what the geography is I hope the fish don't cry
    I remember the Green Banks your invisible hat the Flying Swan
    I remember you
          that Rudyard Kipling knew what he was walking about

             there was a dinge
             holed up in the
             hold thought death
             was near Cape Hook

Now I am entirely enclosed within this pine tree
and no magical spirit sweeps forward into the latterly
      the trident shook deservedly I must obey his art is of such
        when you have remembered

batfowling I saw thine eye and cheek proclaim a matter which is not
        what anything's about and
         yet crown face head imagination our shoulders are reveries
       of afternoons in Pied Ninny

I like to pull horsehairs out of lapels of jackets
the easy emptiness of Ella Cinders
                              "as rootedly as I"
and the cannon usurps the sidewalk during a heated argument
      so that the end will not justify a benevolent need, so tall

                    (*The Collected Poems,* 1972)

ROGERS IN ITALY

Warm plantains and chilled light radishes
of morning, the Wildean dawn comprehensive and
chilling, instantly finishing a sentence before
the sentence has begun. So clear and astute,
the day under the catbird has already done with
all my meanings that I got up to see, cares
only for the trees and grass, even the house
shivers and moans in the early light.
                              All
those insomniac decisions are gone because
the day is already over, so I go in to sleep.
Not without feeling betrayed and hating it.

I wake up at 10:30 and the telegrams start
arriving and the phones start ringing, for
though here in the villa I have only one room
I have several phones. And a dictograph.
One would imagine that Giulia had gone insane
but never mind that. The day is over, there
is no more insanity.
                  When I think of that
bastard swimming that dreary creek in his
irregular fashion, at least I assume so since
he walks that way, it makes my blood boil.
The last a metaphor for breakfast, which I
soon valiantly consume.
                        And now at last I am
alone again and night, at last, has come.
I shall find again those solutions which the
day has took, and make my history into a hat.

                    (*The Collected Poems,* 1972)

John Ashbery [1927]

"HOW MUCH LONGER WILL I BE ABLE TO INHABIT THE DIVINE SEPULCHER..."

How much longer will I be able to inhabit the divine sepulcher
Of life, my great love? Do dolphins plunge bottomward
To find the light? Or is it rock
That is searched? Unrelentingly? Huh. And if some day

Men with orange shovels come to break open the rock
Which encases me, what about the light that comes in then?
What about the smell of the light?
What about the moss?

In pilgrim times he wounded me
Since then I only lie
My bed of light is a furnace choking me
with hell (and sometimes I hear salt water dripping).

I mean it—because I'm one of the few
To have held my breath under the house. I'll trade
One red sucker for two blue ones. I'm
Named Tom. The

Light bounces off mossy rocks down to me
In this glen (the neat villa! which
When he'd had he would not had he of
And jests under the smarting of privet

Which on hot spring nights perfumes the empty rooms
With the smell of sperm flushed down toilets
On hot summer afternoons within sight of the sea.
If you knew why then professor) reads

To his friends: Drink to me only with
And the reader is carried away
By a great shadow under the sea.
Behind the steering wheel

The boy took out his own forehead.
His girlfriend's head was a green bag
Of narcissus stems. "OK you win
But meet me anyway at Cohen's Drug Store

In 22 minutes." What a marvel is ancient man!
Under the tulip roots he has figured out a way to be a religious animal
And would be a mathematician. But where in unsuitable heaven
Can he get the heat that will make him grow?

For he needs something or will forever remain a dwarf,
Though a perfect one, and possessing a normal-sized brain
But he has got to be released by giants from things.
And as the plant grows older it realizes it will never be a tree,

Will probably always be haunted by a bee
And cultivates stupid impressions
So as not to become part of the dirt. The dirt
Is mounting like a sea. And we say goodbye

Shaking hands in front of the crashing of the waves
That give our words lonesomeness, and make these flabby hands seem
            ours—
Hands that are always writing things
On mirrors for people to see later—

Do you want them to water
Plant, tear listlessly among the exchangeable ivy—
Carrying food to mouth, touching genitals—
But no doubt you have understood

It all now and I am a fool. It remains
For me to get better, and to understand you so
Like a chair-sized man. Boots
Were heard on the floor above. In the garden the sunlight was still purple

But what buzzed in it had changed slightly
But not forever... but casting its shadow
On sticks, and looking around for an opening in the air, was quite as if it
      had never refused to exist differently. Guys
In the yard handled the belt he had made

Stars
Painted the garage roof crimson and black
He is not a man
Who can read these signs... his bones were stays...

And even refused to live
In a world and refunded the hiss
Of all that exists terribly near us
Like you, my love, and light.

For what is obedience but the air around us
To the house? For which the federal men came
In a minute after the sidewalk
Had taken you home? ("Latin... blossom...")

After which you led me to water
And bade me drink, which I did, owing to your kindness.
You would not let me out for two days and three nights,
Bringing me books bound in wild thyme and scented wild grasses

As if reading had any interest for me, you...
Now you are laughing.
Darkness interrupts my story.
Turn on the light.

Meanwhile what am I going to do?
I am growing up again, in school, the crisis will be very soon.
And you twist the darkness in your fingers, you
Who are slightly older...

Who are you, anyway?
And it is the color of sand,
The darkness, as it sifts through your hand
Because what does anything mean,

The ivy and the sand? That boat
Pulled up on the shore? Am I wonder,
Strategically, and in the light
Of the long sepulcher that hid death and hides me?

(*The Tennis Court Oath*, 1962)

RAIN

I.

The spoon of your head
crossed by livid stems

The chestnuts' large clovers wiped

You see only the white page its faint frame of red
You hear the viola's death sound
A woman sits in black and white tile

Why, you are pale

Light sucks up what I did
In the room two months ago
Spray of darkness across the back,
Tree flowers...

Taxis took us far apart
And will...
over the shuddering page of a sea
The sofa

Hay
blown in the window
The boards dark as night sea
Pot of flowers fixed in the wind

Last year... the gray snow falling
The building... pictures
His eye into the forest

And people alright
Those stiff lead rods
Silver in the afternoon light
Near where it stops
Where they drink tea from a glass smaller than a thimble
Head of shade

And many stiff little weeds that grew

beside the kidney-shaped lake
A wooden cage painted green
   sand

       And the green streets though parallel run
         far from each other

Cupped under the small lead surface of that cloud you see you are
going to die
Burnt by the powder of that view
      The day of the week will not save you

Mixture of air and wind
Sand then mud
A flower, lost in someone's back yard.

       II.

    The first coffee of the morning
    Soon the stars.

     and broken feldspar black
     squares against the light
    message—a handwriting
     Dip pen in solution

    They would be playing now
      The sky
  Flowers sucked in—stone rhinunculus
     amaryllis—red
   Freesia and existence

The letter arrives—seeing the stamp
    The van
  New York under the umbrella

    A photograph of what

     Fumes
   Features in the lake
    The light
   The shadow of a hand
    soft on the lock

staring wax
scraped with a pin, reflection of the face
The time
principal thing
Train
Hand holding watch
silver vase
against the plaid
Comfort me
The hedge coming up to meet me that way in the dried red sun
The meadows down I mean
At night
Curious—I'd seen this tall girl

I urge the deep prune of the mirror
That stick she carries
The book—a trap

The facts have hinged on my reply

calm
Hat against the sky
Eyes of forest

memory of cars
You buried in the hot avenue: and to all of them, you cannot be and are,
naming me.

III.

The missing letter—the crumb of confidence
His love boiling up to me
Forever will I be the only
In sofa I know
The darkness on his back
Fleeing to darkness of my side

It is the time
We do not live in but on
And this young man
like a soldier

Into the dust
    Words drip from the wound
Spring mounts in me
        of dandelion—lots of it
And the little one
    the hooded lost one
        near the pillow

    A fine young man

       IV.

The storm coming—
        Not to have ever been exactly on this street with cats
Because the houses were vanishing behind a cloud
    The plants on the rugs look nice
        Yet I have never been here before

       Glass

    regime

Which is in the tepee of the great city
I build to you every moment
Ice lily of the sewers
In a thousand thoughts
Mindful in a thousand dresser drawers you pull out
Mufti of the gray crocus silent on the wood diamond floor
Or if I asked you for a game with rods and balls
You stood up with me to play

But fatal laxity undoes
The stiff, dark and busy streets
Through which any help must roll.
The third of runners who are upon are past you
The opal snows the moppet
You behind me in the van
The flat sea rushing away

      (*The Tennis Court Oath*, 1962)

RIVERS AND MOUNTAINS

On the secret map the assassins
Cloistered, the Moon River was marked
Near the eighteen peaks and the city
Of humiliation and defeat—wan ending
Of the trail among dry, papery leaves
Gray-brown quills like thoughts
In the melodious but vast mass of today's
Writing through fields and swamps
Marked, on the map, with little bunches of weeds.
Certainly squirrels lived in the woods
But devastation and dull sleep still
Hung over the land, quelled
The rioters turned out of sleep in the peace of prisons
Singing on marble factory walls
Deaf consolation of minor tunes that pack
The air with heavy invisible rods
Pent in some sand valley from
Which only quiet walking ever instructs.
The bird flew over and
Sat—there was nothing else to do.
Do not mistake its silence for pride or strength
Or the waterfall for a harbor
Full of light boats that is there
Performing for thousands of people
In clothes some with places to go
Or games. Sometimes over the pillar
Of square stones its impact
Makes a light print.

So going around cities
To get to other places you found
It all on paper but the land
Was made of paper processed
To look like ferns, mud or other
Whose sea unrolled its magic
Distances and then rolled them up
Its secret was only a pocket
After all but some corners are darker
Than these moonless nights spent as on a raft
In the seclusion of a melody heard

As though through trees
And you can never ignite their touch
Long but there were homes
Flung far out near the asperities
Of a sharp, rocky pinnacle
And other collective places
Shadows of vineyards whose wine
Tasted of the forest floor
Fisheries and oyster beds
Tides under the pole
Seminaries of instruction, public
Places for electric light
And the major tax assessment area
Wrinkled on the plan
Of election to public office
Sixty-two years old bath and breakfast
The formal traffic, shadows
To make it not worth joining
After the ox had pulled away the cart.

Your plan was to separate the enemy into two groups
With the razor-edged mountains between.
It worked well on paper
But their camp had grown
To be the mountains and the map
Carefully peeled away and not torn
Was the light, a tender but tough bark
On everything. Fortunately the war was solved
In another way by isolating the two sections
Of the enemy's navy so that the mainland
Warded away the big floating ships.
Light bounced off the ends
Of the small gray waves to tell
Them in the observatory
About the great drama that was being won
To turn off the machinery
And quietly move among the rustic landscape
Scooping snow off the mountains rinsing
The coarser ones that love had
Slowly risen in the night to overflow
Wetting pillow and petal
Determined to place the letter
On the unassassinated president's desk

So that a stamp could reproduce all this
In detail, down to the last autumn leaf
And the affliction of June ride
Slowly out into the sun-blackened landscape.

(*Rivers and Mountains*, 1966)

THESE LACUSTRINE CITIES

These lacustrine cities grew out of loathing
Into something forgetful, although angry with history.
They are the product of an idea: that man is horrible,
   for instance,
Though this is only one example.

They emerged until a tower
Controlled the sky, and with artifice dipped back
Into the past for swans and tapering branches,
Burning, until all that hate was transformed into useless love.

Then you are left with an idea of yourself
And the feeling of ascending emptiness of the afternoon
Which must be charged to the embarrassment of others
Who fly by you like beacons.

The night is a sentinel.
Much of your time has been occupied by creative games
Until now, but we have all-inclusive plans for you.
We had thought, for instance, of sending you to the middle
   of the desert,

To a violent sea, or of having the closeness of the others be air
To you, pressing you back into a startled dream
As sea-breezes greet a child's face.
But the past is already here, and you are nursing some private project.

The worst is not over, yet I know
You will be happy here. Because of the logic
Of your situation, which is something no climate can outsmart.
Tender and insouciant by turns, you see

You have built a mountain of something,
Thoughtfully pouring all your energy into this single monument,
Whose wind is desire starching a petal,
whose disappointment broke into a rainbow of tears.

(*Rivers and Mountains*, 1966)

FORTIES FLICK

The shadow of the Venetian blind on the painted wall,
Shadows of the snake-plant and cacti, the plaster animals,
Focus the tragic melancholy of the bright stare
Into nowhere, a hole like the black holes in space.
In bra and panties she sidles to the window:
Zip! Up with the blind. A fragile street scene offers itself,
With wafer-thin pedestrians who know where they are going.
The blind comes down slowly, the slats are slowly tilted up.

Why must it always end this way?
A dais with woman reading, with the ruckus of her hair
And all that is unsaid about her pulling us back to her, with her
Into the silence that night alone can't explain.
Silence of the library, of the telephone with its pad,
But we didn't have to reinvent these either:
They had gone away into the plot of a story,
The "art" part—knowing what important details to leave out
And the way character is developed. Things too real
To be of much concern, hence artificial, yet now all over the page,
The indoors with the outside becoming part of you
As you find you had never left off laughing at death,
The background, dark vine at the edge of the porch.

(*Self-Portrait in a Convex Mirror*, 1975)

THE OTHER TRADITION

They all came, some wore sentiments
Emblazoned on T-shirts, proclaiming the lateness
Of the hour, and indeed the sun slanted its rays
Through branches of Norfolk Island pine as though
Politely clearing its throat, and all ideas settled
In a fuzz of dust under trees when it's drizzling:
The endless games of Scrabble, the boosters,
The celebrated omelette au Cantal, and through it
The roar of time plunging unchecked through the sluices
Of the days, dragging every sexual moment of it
Past the lenses: the end of something.
Only then did you glance up from your book,
Unable to comprehend what had been taking place, or
Say what you had been reading. More chairs
Were brought, and lamps were lit, but it tells
Nothing of how all this proceeded to materialize
Before you and the people waiting outside and in the next
Street, repeating its name over and over, until silence
Moved halfway up the darkened trunks,
And the meeting was called to order.
                                        I still remember
How they found you, after a dream, in your thimble hat,
Studious as a butterfuly in a parking lot.
The road home was nicer then. Dispersing, each of the
Troubadours had something to say about how charity
Had run its race and won, leaving you the ex-president
Of the event, and how, though many of those present
Had wished something to come of it, if only a distant
Wisp of smoke, yet none was so deceived as to hanker
After that cool non-being of just a few minutes before,
Now that the idea of a forest had clamped itself
Over the minutiae of the scene. You found this
Charming, but turned your face fully toward night,
Speaking into it like a megaphone, not hearing
Or caring, although these still live and are generous
And all ways contained, allowed to come and go
Indefinitely in and out of the stockade
They have so much trouble remembering, when your forgetting
Rescues them at last, as a star absorbs the night.

(*Houseboat Days*, 1977)

HOUSEBOAT DAYS

"The skin is broken. The hotel breakfast china
Poking ahead to the last week in August, not really
Very much at all, found the land where you began..."
The hills smouldered up blue that day, again
You walk five feet along the shore, and you duck
As a common heresy sweeps over. We can botanize
About this for centuries, and the little dazey
Blooms again in the cities. The mind
Is so hospitable, taking in everything
Like boarders, and you don't see until
It's all over how little there was to learn
Once the stench of knowledge has dissipated, and the trouvailles
Of every one of the senses fallen back. Really, he
Said, that insincerity of reasoning on behalf of one's
Sincere convictions, true or false in themselves
As the case may be, to which, if we are unwise enough
To argue at all with each other, we must be tempted
At times—do you see where it leads? To pain,
And the triumph over pain, still hidden
In these low-lying hills which rob us
Of all privacy, as though one were always about to meet
One's double through the chain of cigar smoke
And then it...happens, like an explosion in the brain,
Only it's a catastrophe on another planet to which
One has been invited, and as surely cannot refuse:
Pain in the cistern, in the gutters, and if we merely
Wait awhile, that denial, as though a universe of pain
Had been created just so as to deny its own existence.
But I don't set much stock in things
Beyond the weather and the certainties of living and dying:
The rest is optional. To praise this, blame that,
Leads one subtly away from the beginning, where
We must stay, in motion. To flash light
Into the house within, its many chambers,
Its memories and associations, upon its inscribed
And pictured walls, argues enough that life is various.
Life is beautiful. He who reads that
As in the window of some distant, speeding train
Knows what he wants, and what will befall.

Pinpricks of rain fall again.
And from across the quite wide median with its
Little white flowers, a reply is broadcast:
"Dissolve parliament. Hold new elections."
It would be deplorable if the rain also washed away
This profile at the window that moves, and moves on,
Knowing that it moves, and knows nothing else. It is the light
At the end of the tunnel as it might be seen
By him looking out somberly at the shower,
The picture of hope a dying man might turn away from,
Realizing that hope is something else, something concrete
You can't have. So, winding past certain pillars
Until you get to evening's malachite one, it becomes a vast dream
Of having that can topple governments, level towns and cities
With the pressure of sleep building up behind it.
The surge creates its own edge
And you must proceed this way: mornings of assent,
Indifferent noons leading to the ripple of the question
Of late afternoon projected into evening.
Arabesques and runnels are the result
Over the public address system, on the seismograph at Berkeley.
A little simple arithmetic tells you that to be with you
In this passage, this movement, is what the instance costs:
A sail out of some afternoon, beyond amazement, astonished,
Apparently not tampered with. As the rain gathers and protects
Its own darkness, the place in the slipcover is noticed
For the first and last time, fading like the spine
Of an adventure novel behind glass, behind the teacups.

(*Houseboat Days*, 1977)

SAYING IT TO KEEP IT FROM HAPPENING

Some depature from the norm
Will occur as time grows more open about it.
The consensus gradually changed; nobody
Lies about it any more. Rust dark pouring
Over the body, changing it without decay—
People with too many things on their minds, but we live
In the interstices, between a vacant stare and the ceiling,

Our lives remind us. Finally this is consciousness
And the other livers of it get off at the same stop.
How careless. Yet in the end each of us
Is seen to have traveled the same distance—it's time
That counts, and how deeply you have invested in it,
Crossing the street of an event, as though coming out of it were
The same as making it happen. You're not sorry,
Of course, especially if this was the way it had to happen,
Yet would like an exacter share, something about time
That only a clock can tell you: how it feels, not what it means.
It is a long field, and we know only the far end of it,
Not the part we presumably had to go through to get there.
If it isn't enough, take the idea
Inherent in the day, armloads of wheat and flowers
Lying around flat on handtrucks, if maybe it means more
In pertaining to you, yet what is is what happens in the end
As though you cared. The event combined with
Beams leading up to it for the look of force adapted to the wiser
Usages of age, but it's both there
And not there, like washing or sawdust in the sunlight,
At the back of the mind, where we live now.

(Houseboat Days, 1977)

THE LAMENT UPON THE WATERS

For the disciple nothing had changed. The mood was still
Gray tolerance, as the road marched along
Singing its little song of despair. Once, a cry
Started up out of the hills. That old, puzzling persuasion

Again. Sex was part of this,
And the shock of day turning into night.
Though we always found something delicate (too delicate
For some tastes, perhaps) to touch, to desire.

And we made much of this sort of materiality
That clogged the weight of starlight, made it seem
Fibrous, yet there was a chance in this
To see the present as it never had existed,

Clear and shapeless, in an atmosphere like cut glass.
At Latour-Maubourg you said this was a good thing, and on the steps
Of Métro Jasmin the couriers nodded to us correctly, and the
Pact was sealed in the sky. But now moments surround us

Like a crowd, some inquisitive faces, some hostile ones,
Some enigmatic or turned away to an anterior form of time
Given once and for all. The jetstream inscribes a final flourish
That melts as it stays. The problem isn't how to proceed

But is one of being: whether this ever was, and whose
It shall be. To be starting out, just one step
Off the sidewalk, and as such pulled back into the glittering
Snowstorm of stinging tentacles of how that would be worked out

If we ever work it out. And the voice came back at him
Across the water, rubbing it the wrong way: "Thou
Canst but undo the wrong thou hast done." The sackbuts
Embellish it, and we are never any closer to the collision

Of the waters, the peace of light drowning light,
Grabbing it, holding it up streaming. It is all one. It lies
All around, its new message, guilt, the admission
Of guilt, your new act. Time buys

The receiver, the onlooker of the earlier system, but cannot
Buy back the rest. It is night that fell
At the edge of your footsteps as the music stopped.
And we heard the bells for the first time. It is your chapter, I said.

(*Houseboat Days*, 1977)

PARADOXES AND OXYMORONS

This poem is concerned with language on a very plain level.
Look at it talking to you. You look out a window
Or pretend to fidget. You have it but you don't have it.
You miss it, it misses you. You miss each other.

The poem is sad because it wants to be yours, and cannot be.
What's a plain level? It is that and other things,
Bringing a system of them into play. Play?
Well, actually, yes, but I consider play to be

A deeper outside thing, a dreamed role-pattern,
As in the division of grace these long August days
Without proof. Open-ended. And before you know it
It gets lost in the steam and chatter of typewriters.

It has been played once more. I think you exist only
To tease me into doing it, on your level, and then you aren't there
Or have adopted a different attitude. And the poem
Has set me softly down beside you. The poem is you.

(*Shadow Train*, 1981)

MORNING JITTERS

And the storm reestablished itself
As a hole in the sheet of time
And of the weariness of the world,
And all the old work that remains to be done on its surface.
Came morning and the husband was back on the shore
To ask another favor of the fish,
Leviathan now, patience wearing thin. Whose answer
Bubbled out of the waves' crenellations:

"*Too late!* Yet if you analyze
The abstract good fortune that has brought you
To this floor, you must also unpluck the bees
Immured in the hive of your mind and bring the nuisance
And the glory into sharper focus. Why,
Others too will have implored before forgetting
To remove a stick of night from the scrub-forest
That keeps us wondering about ourselves
Until luck or nepotism has run its course! Only I say,
Your uniqueness isn't that unique
And doors must close in the shaved head
Before they can spring ajar. Take this.

Its promise equals power." To be shaken thus
Vehemently back into one's trance doesn't promise
Any petitioner much, even the servile ones. But night in its singleness
Of motive rewards all equally for what cannot
Appear disinterested survival tactics from the vantage
Point of some rival planet. Things go on being the same,
As darkness and ships ruffle the sky.

(*April Galleons*, 1987)

LIFE AS A BOOK THAT HAS BEEN PUT DOWN

We have erased each letter
And the statement still remains vaguely,
Like an inscription over the door of a bank
With hard-to-figure-out Roman numerals
That say perhaps too much, in their way.

Weren't we being surrealists? And why
Did strangers at the bar analyze your hair
And fingernails, as though the body
Wouldn't seek and find that most comfortable position,
And your head, that strange thing,
Become more problematic each time the door was shut?

We have talked to each other,
Taken each thing only just so far,
But in the right order, so it is music,
Or something close to music, telling from afar.
We have only some knowledge,
And more than the required ambition
To shape it into a fruit made of cloud
That will protect us until it goes away.

But the juice thereof is bitter,
We have not such in our gardens,
And you should go up into knowledge
With this careless sarcasm and be told there
For once, it is not here.
Only the smoke stays,

And silence, and old age
That we have come to construe as a landscape
Somehow, and the peace that breaks all records,
And singing in the land, delight
That will be and does not know us.

(*April Galleons*, 1987)

HOTEL LAUTRÉAMONT

1/

Research has shown that ballads were produced by all of society
working as a team. They didn't just happen. There was no guesswork.
The people, then, knew what they wanted and how to get it.
We see the results in works as diverse as "Windsor Forest" and "The Wife of
   Usher's Well."

Working as a team, they didn't just happen. There was no guesswork.
The horns of elfland swing past, and in a few seconds
We see the results in works as diverse as "Windsor Forest" and "The Wife of
   Usher's Well,"
or, on a more modern note, in the finale of the Sibelius violin concerto.

The horns of elfland swing past, and in a few seconds
The world, as we know it, sinks into dementia, proving narrative passé,
or in the finale of the Sibelius violin concerto.
Not to worry, many hands are making work light again.

The world, as we know it, sinks into dementia, proving narrative passé.
In any case the ruling was long overdue.
Not to worry, many hands are making work light again,
so we stay indoors. The quest was only another adventure.

2/

In any case, the ruling was long overdue.
The people are beside themselves with rapture
so we stay indoors. The quest was only another adventure
and the solution problematic, at any rate far off in the future.

The people are beside themselves with rapture
yet no one thinks to question the source of so much collective euphoria,
and the solution: problematic, at any rate far off in the future.
The saxophone wails, the martini glass is drained.

Yet no one thinks to question the source of so much collective euphoria.
In troubled times one looked to the shaman or priest for comfort and counsel.
The saxophone wails, the martini glass is drained,
And night like black swansdown settles on the city.

In troubled times one looked to the shaman or priest for comfort and counsel
Now, only the willing are fated to receive death as a reward,
and night like black swansdown settles on the city.
If we tried to leave, would being naked help us?

3/

Now, only the willing are fated to receive death as a reward.
Children twist hula-hoops, imagining a door to the outside.
If we tried to leave, would being naked help us?
And what of older, lighter concerns? What of the river?

Children twist hula-hoops, imagining a door to the outside,
when all we think of is how much we can carry with us.
And what of older, lighter concerns? What of the river?
All the behemoths have filed through the maze of time.

When all we think of is how much we can carry with us
Small wonder that those at home sit, nervous, by the unlit grate.
All the behemoths have filed through the maze of time.
It remains for us to come to terms with *our* commonalty.

Small wonder that those at home sit nervous by the unlit grate.
It was their choice, after all, that spurred us to feats of the imagination.
It remains for us to come to terms with our commonalty
And in so doing deprive time of further hostages.

4/

It was their choice, after all, that spurred us to feats of the imagination.
Now, silently as one mounts a stair we emerge into the open
and in so doing deprive time of further hostages,
to end the standoff that history long ago began.

Now, silently as one mounts a stair we emerge into the open
but it is shrouded, veiled: we must have made some ghastly error.
To end the standoff that history long ago began
Must we thrust ever onward, into perversity?

But it is shrouded, veiled: we must have made some ghastly error.
You mop your forehead with a rose, recommending its thorns.
Must we thrust ever onward, into perversity?
Only night knows for sure; the secret is safe with her.

You mop your forehead with a rose, recommending its thorns.
Research has shown that ballads were produced by all of society;
Only night knows for sure. The secret is safe with her:
the people, then, knew what they wanted and how to get it.

(*Hotel Lautréamont*, 1992)

THE OLD COMPLEX

As structures go, it wasn't such a bad one,
and it filled the space before the eye
with loving, sinister patches. A modest
eyesore. It reduced them to a sort of paste
wherein each finds his account, goes off
to live among the shore's bashed-in hulks.

Of course you have to actually take the medicine.
For it to work, I mean. Spending much time upstairs
now, I can regulate the solitude,
the rugged blade of anger, note
the occasional black steed. Evening warbles away.

You are free to go now, to go free.
Still, it would help if you'd stay one more day.
I press her hand, strange thing.

(*Hotel Lautréamont*, 1992)

Joseph Ceravolo [1934 – 1988]

SPRING OF WORK STORM

Down near   "The river
barges"   I looked around me
Where could I wait?

My friend was always
human   I threw myself
beside; I turned the
new head

I took his paw   It
was tender   And kissed
its texture   Like a
bee

Stars were darker
I felt the oil
in the sand

(Wild Flowers Out of Gas, 1967)

HO HO HO CARIBOU

for Rosemary

I
Leaped at the caribou.
My son looked at the caribou.
The kangaroo leaped on the
fruit tree. I am a white
man and my children
are hungry

which is like paradise.
The doll is sleeping.
It lay down to creep into
the plate.
It was clean and flying.

II
Where you….the axes
are. Why is this home so
hard. So much
like the sent over the
courses below the home
having a porch.

Felt it on my gate in the place
where caribous jumped
over. Where geese sons
and pouches of daughters look at
me and say "I'm hungry
daddy."

III
Not alone in the
gastrous desert. We are looking
at the caribous out in the water
swimming around. We
want to go in the ocean
along the dunes.
Where do we like?
   Like little lice in the sand
we look into a fruit expanse.
Oh the sky is so cold.
We run into the water.
Lice in heaven.

IV
My heel. Ten o'clock the class.
Underwater fish
brush by us. Oh leg
not reaching!

The show is stopping
at the sky to drive in the
truck. Tell us where to
stop and eat. And
drink which comes to us out
in the sand is
                at a star.
My pants are damp.
Is tonight treating us
but not reaching through the window.

V

Where is that bug going?
Why are your hips
rounded as the sand?
What is jewelry?

Baby sleeps. Sleeping on
the cliff is dangerous.
The television of all voice is
way far behind.
Do we flow nothing?
Where did you follow that bug
to?
   See quick....is flying.

VI

Caribou, what have I
done? See how her
heart moves like a little
bug......under my thumb.
Throw me deeply.
I am the floes.
Ho ho ho caribou,
light brown and wetness
caribou. I stink and
I know it.
"Screw you!....you're right."

VII
Every one has seen us out
with the caribou but
no one has seen us out in
the car. You passed
beyond us.
We saw your knees
but the other night we
couldn't call you.
You were more far than a
widow feeling you.
Nothing has been terrible.
We are the people who have
been running with
animals.
More than when we run?

VIII
Tell us where o eat to stop and eat.
The diner is never gonna come.
The forest things are passing.
I did drink my milk
like a mother of wolves.
Wolves on the desert
of ice cold love, of
fireproof breasts and the breast
I took like snow.
Following me
I love you
and I fall beyond
and I eat you like a
bow and arrow withering in the
     desert.

IX
No one should be mean.
Making affection and all the green
winters wide awake.
Blubber is desert. Out on
the firm lake, o firm
and aboriginal kiss.

To dance, to hunt, to sing,
no one should be mean.
Not needing these things.

   X

Like a flower, little light, you open
and we make believe
we die. We die all around
you like a snake in a
well and we come up out
of the warm well and
are born again out of dry
mammas, nourishing mammas, always
holding you as I
love you and am
revived inside you, but
die in you and am
never born again in
the same place; never
stop!

(*Spring in This World of Poor Mutts,* 1968)

SPRING IN THIS WORLD OF POOR MUTTS

I kiss your lips
on a grain: the forest,

the fifth, how many do
you want on here?
This is the same you
I kiss, you hear
me, you help:

I'm thirty years old.
I want to think in summer now.
Here it goes, here it's summer

(A disintegrated robot)
over us.
We are mortal. We ride
the merry-go-round. A drummer like
this is together.
Let's go feel the water.
  Here it goes!

Again and it's morning "boom"
   autumn
"boom" autumn
and the corn is sleeping.
It is sleeping and sweating
and draws the beautiful
soft green sky.

Walk home with the
animal on my shoulder
in the river, the river gets
deeper , the Esso gets
deeper; morning,
  morning,
   cigarette,
family and animal
and parents along the river.
Oh imagination. That's how I need you.

A flying duck or an antler refrains.
The small deer at the
animal farm walks up
to us.

A waterbug comes into
the bathroom.
The north sky is all frozen over
like a river.
Like a pimple a waterbug
comes into us
and our lives are full
of rivers. Heavy waterbug!

This is the robot and he
continues across the street.
Looking at a bird
his penis is hanging down;
a wind for
its emotions.
    I don't want to sleep.
The cold around my arms.
Like an iron lung.
As sleep comes closer to the robot's
emotion. Iron.

Spring. Spring. Spring......
        Spring!
Spring down! come down!
There it goes! there it goes!
Arm belly strike.
Press friend push.
Teeth cruel arrow. I cannot
do without,
without do I cannot, Spring.

Chrome gladly press.
Between me, my wings. Listen as
the fireflies organize.
O save me, this Spring, please!
Before I hurt her
        I hurt her only life
        too much
and it carries in this
iron bug crawling all around.
        Is this Spring?
and it carries me,
iron bug, through the Spring.

(*Spring in This World of Poor Mutts*, 1968)

THE WOMEN

They have the corner
half seated on their thighs,
and long braids tied like drainpipes.
Their hair is a drainpipe
closed from rain.
In the corner of their eyes
is a building of grass.
Their smile cracks
plaster of paris streets.
When they look down
their eyes are orange slices.
They sell little peaches
with brown small rotten dots.

(*Transmigration Solo,* 1979)

INVISIBLE AUTUMN

The blade days——
like Summer rush

Apollo leans.
The way the sun comes up,
the sun leans.
The sun leans less than
in the north, but one lean
is as good as another.
Now it's autumn, but
you would never know.

The blade days
like Summer, rush

(*Transmigration Solo,* 1979)

CELEBRATION

The music is played. Play
the music
    O washable towns
Open wall   the wall
studio of moons,
Sell my bananas, I
mean buy my stones
of yellow obscure, of no
similarity. There are walls.
Something the same from nowhere rides.
  Get off! there
are many fenders that
sound like some green place
without all this gravity.
The soft wind tonight——
comes through trees
and river.
The town is people,
the people talk about town
about everything that isn't
town, that ends in people
and drizzle, that think
about a bottle and corn,
and some light on them
from the sweet sixteen party

(*Transmigration Solo,* 1979)

MIGRATORY NOON

Cold and the cranes.
Cranes in the
    wind
like cellophane tape
on a school book.
The wind bangs
the car, but I sing out loud,

help, help
as sky gets white
  and whiter and whiter and whiter.
Where are you
  in the reincarnate
      blossoms of the cold?

(*Transmigration Solo,* 1979)

STOLEN AWAY

How do people feel
      in this cold
  in this win... win....windy nest
  in the gloss like a
          cold nest
      in the tendon of life.

  The benches   feel
  like green alligators,
  crocodiles in the snow

I get
  a warm mouth
  on the hair
Someone has kissed me.
That boy and girl
fight and kiss in the car.
      A deep sound comes from it.
The birds fly down
  one by one, drop by drop.

(*Transmigration Solo,* 1979)

CONCEPTION

The pains flip me around
and one rain is enough to fill my bladder.

The chair, the knife,
the nipples of this volcano
one kisses to be living.

The guns shoot a lonely
    runaway slave.
The daffodils
    bleed into summer.

The knife, the napkin,
but still the footsteps
of an angel overhead
haunts every blink
my eyes make.

(*Millenium Dust*, 1982)

SUNSET

Why do I follow you

through these woods?

Now I've found

that grey and yellow bird

dying in my hand.
What do I do with it?
A song of the night

wakes me

and in my hand lies you

in the matter of all fear.

A song of the people,
of forbidden lies,
of surrounding night and legs
and emptiness.
A call in the night!
O beggars, O masters,
Why leave? We are only beggars
as we pull ourselves up
in the erotic stratifications
before the sunset of your blush.

(*O–Blēk* magazine, 1989)

Ted Berrigan [1934 – 1983]

from THE SONNETS

I

His piercing pince-nez. Some dim frieze
Hands point to a dim frieze, in the dark night.
In the book of his music the corners have straightened:
Which owe their presence to our sleeping hands.
The ox-blood from the hands which play
For fire for warmth for hands for growth
Is there room in the room that you room in?
Upon his structured tomb:
Still they mean something. For the dance
And the architecture.
Weave among incidents
May be portentous to him
We are the sleeping fragments of his sky,
Wind giving presence to fragments.

III

Stronger than alcohol, more great than song,
deep in whose reeds great elephants decay;
I, an island, sail, and my shores toss
on a fragrant evening, fraught with sadness
bristling hate.
It's true, I weep too much. Dawns break
slow kisses on the eyelids of the sea,
what other men sometimes have thought they've seen.
And since then I've been bathing in the poem
lifting her shadowy flowers up for me,
and hurled by hurricanes to a birdless place
the waving flags, nor pass by prison ships
O let me burst, and I be lost at sea!
and fall on my knees then, womanly.

REAL LIFE

1. *The fool*

He eats of the fruits of the great Speckle
Bird, pissing in the grass! Is it possible
He is incomplete, bringing you Ginger Ale
Of the interminably frolicsome gushing summer showers?
You were a Campfire Girl,
Only a part-time mother and father; I
Was large, stern, acrid, and undissuadable!
Ah, Bernie, we wear complete
The indexed Webster Unabridged Dictionary.
And lunch is not lacking, ants and clover
On the grass. To think of you alone
Suffering the poem of these states!
Oh Lord, it is bosky, giggling happy here,
And you, and me, the juice, at last extinct!

2. *the fiend*

Red-faced and romping in the wind
I too am reading the technical journals, but
Keeping Christmas-safe each city block
With tail-pin. My angels are losing patience,
Never win. Except at night. Then
I would like a silken thread
Tied round the solid blooming winter.
Trees stand stark-naked guarding bridal paths;
The cooling wind keeps blowing, and
There is a faint chance in geometic boxes!
It doesn't matter, though, to show he is
Your champion. Days are nursed on science fiction
And you tremble at the books upon the earth
As my strength and I walk out and look for you.

XXXIV

Times flies by like a great whale
And I find my hand grows stale at the throttle
Of my many faceted and fake appearance
Who bucks and spouts by detour under the sheets
Hollow portals of solid appearance
Movies are poems, a holy bible, the great mother to us
People go by in the fragrant day
Accelerate softly my blood
But blood is still blood and tall as a mountain blood
Behind me green rubber grows, feet walk
In wet water, and dusty heads grow wide
Padré, Father, or fat old man, as you will,
I am afraid to succeed, afraid to fail
Tell me now, again, who I am

XXXV

You can make this swooped transition on your lips
Go to the sea, the lake, the tree
And the dog days come
Your head spins when the old bull rushes
Back in the airy daylight, he was not a midget
And preferred to be known as a stunt-man.
His stand-in was named Herman, but came rarely.
Why do you begin to yawn so soon, who seemed
so hard, feather-bitten   back in the airy daylight
Put away your hair. The black heart beside the 15 pieces
    of glass
Spins when the old bull rushes. The words say
    I LOVE YOU
Go to the sea, the lake, the tree
Glistering, bristling, cozzening whatever disguises

LV

"Grace to be born
and live as variously
as possible"
—Frank O'Hara

Grace to be born and live as variously as possible
White boats   green banks   black dust   atremble
Massive as Anne's thighs upon the page
I rage in a blue shirt at a brown desk in a
Bright room sustained by a bellyful of pills
"The Poems" is not a dream   for all things come to them
Gratuitously   In quick New York we imagine the blue
    Charles
Patsy awakens in heat and ready to squabble
No Poems she demands in a blanket command   belly
To hot belly we have laid   serenely white
Only my sweating pores are true in the empty night
Baffling combustions are everywhere! we hunger and
    taste
And go to the movies   then run home drenched in flame
To the grace of the make-believe bed

LXX

after Arthur Rimbaud

Sweeter than sour apples flesh to boys
The brine of brackish water pierced my hulk
Cleansing me of rot-gut wine and puke
Sweeping away my anchor in its swell
And since then I've been bathing in the poem
Of the star-steeped milky flowing mystic sea
Devouring great sweeps of azure green and
Watching flotsam, dead men, float by me
Where, dyeing all the blue, the maddened flames
And stately rhythms of the sun, stronger

Than alcohol, more great than song,
Fermented the bright red bitterness of love
I've seen skies split with light, and night,
And surfs, currents, waterspouts; I know
What evening means, and doves, and I have seen
What other men sometimes have thought they've seen

LXXVII

"DEAR CHRIS

it is 3:17 a.m. in New York city, yes, it is
1962, it is the year of parrot fever. In
Brandenburg, and by the granite gates, the
old come-all-ye's streel into the streets. Yes, it is now,
the season of delight. I am writing to you to say that
I have gone mad. Now I am sowing the seeds which shall,
when ripe, master the day, and
portion out the night. Be watching for me when blood
flows down the streets. Pineapples are a sign
that I am coming. My darling, it is nearly time. Dress
the snowman in the Easter sonnet we made for him
when scissors were in style. For now, goodbye, and
all my love,
        The Snake."

LXXXVIII

A FINAL SONNET

for Chris

How strange to be gone in a minute!   A man
Signs a shovel and so he digs   Everything
Turns into writing a name for a day
                              Someone
is having a birthday and someone is getting

married and someone is telling a joke   my dream
a white tree   I dream of the code of the west
But this rough magic I here abjure   and
When I have required some heavenly music   which even
    now
I do   to work mine end upon *their* senses
That this aery charm is for   I'll break
My staff   bury it certain fathoms in the earth
And deeper than did every plummet sound
I'll drown my book.
It is 5:15 a.m.   Dear Chris, hello.

(*The Sonnets,* 1964; 1982)

Charles North [1941]

AIR AND ANGELS

Sine qua non of bed wetting
Sire of too-close recall, conquering mastiff

The one that got away, of obloquy,
Compressor of doubt into a herd of gold

Genius of the herdsman, sex of the idiot,
Rheingold of disaster, litigant of hardened arteries

Spearhead of the most devastating alliances
The widow of despair (widow's peak of kindness)

And cleanliness, that hair trigger
Speech, once it is judged halcyon, hair space

The covenant kindles, slice of life
In the homophonous descent towards cover,

That flaws the vandal and brings the liaison to grief
By tilting the atoms of its attachment,

There, among the revivalism finery, beyond the fertile
Awe that makes an axiom of opacity, and beyond

Distraction peals in the lymph of gazes, glazed
Gender pudding that gavels the fall-out, as

In Buck Rogers; Rhenish; Hebrew euphony that
Startles; Chartism of Icarus, toward that copper reticle

Trifling with hate, havoc's cognate, to certainty,
Junta that films its dog days, bright tiger eye

(*Elizabethan & Nova Scotian Music,* 1974)

FROM THE FRENCH

The color of coral and of your lips
Tilts the car of night and its silent axles.
The door is fragrant, the alcove large and dark.
And there among the flowers, in the dark,
I find for your fabulous hair a silent bed.

I will show you, meanwhile, the countries of snow
Where the amorous star devours and dazzles.
And where a false calm aspires to defraud
You of your gifts, the night will deafen it
In notes of your extravagant praise.

Yet to be with you while wanting you in the night
I allow you some space in which to move.
If you should appear as a blue flower
On the drape of the moon the sky will receive you,
Permitting space and voice to go without reference.

(*Six Buildings,* 1977)

from SIX BUILDINGS

HOSPITAL

Large, low, whirring block of perfectly white, perfectly flat marble, on chrome legs which creak up and down to let persons in and out. The landscaping consists of a hollow tree trunk filled with sweet colored water and transparent urns containing beautiful but deadly looking anemones or very large dahlias. Ideally the portions surrounding the hospital, as reflected in the eye, should not be red but should reflect the presence of past weeping replaced by resignation and near despair, contrasting sharply with the bright salmon of the vestigial lid.

CONCERT HALL

A stucco or fieldstone "former stable" whose ceiling is nowhere and whose fireplace is everywhere. This is really a practice stage for the performances which take place indelibly in waking life—the difference being that pretenses are left in a large chest beside the brass door decorated with windows from the quiet lineup of the composers. Musicians and singers enter and exit along filaments like those inside light bulbs, with the particles made visible by passing through charged air and acoustical tile. If a clarinet is too confining, a French horn can be the mold; but in this case the outer facing should be coated in a fine rosewood with a vague smell of lanolin, black with reddish lights and ultraviolet highlights impervious to intellect and housing the sun during the blackest of the 24 hours.

LAUNDRY

A perfectible sky. But the perfection must be in infinitesimal doses like life on a wandering asteroid or sprinkler system, and uniform tonic swirling the air. What dominates is thus the exact tone and consistency of what was already there. The appearance of a single star, e.g., north, must not overpopulate the effect of dispelling individual differences, white on white, or definiteness (which is paper-thin anyway), and the perfection is that it is total, wrung like wet clothes into a white-hot vat covering the waste: like a sled on skis. Perfection doesn't rule out the star; but it makes it apologetic, or sheepish, as a solar system, detached, would first appear to swing randomly on its hinges, then fold presumably and smell like any other prerogative of the constabulary mind. Or like almonds, not roasted, not up, forming a tree in the limelight like the pink apparition of milk, whichever way you look.

(Six Buildings, 1977)

LEAP YEAR

In the language of the spirit
one of the waist-high metal ashtrays is on fire!
Ah, in the lounge of the spirit.
I'm always on the verge of waking

up in it, as that roof is clearly
melting into the sky,
the sky in the shoestore,
as if hills were boats and the way out
were to paint everything turquoise
the night crowded by stars,
people drinking everything in sight,
a bus taking air from one city river
to another, charmed in the glow
of not knowing the ending.

(*Leap Year: Poems 1968-1978*, 1978)

SUNRISE WITH SEA MONSTER

Well, we either do it or we don't, as the pigeon said to
     the loaf of bread
doubling as the sky, that is, unaffectedly rocky and clay
     gray, the color of rocks
bordering but not reflecting oceans and in particular the
     one that finds its way here
every so often, though not right now; a function of light
     and surface qualities
such as polish, facet, regularity of design,
implied or announced mineral content, the ability to stand
     still in a storm,
and those qualities that enter surface and suffuse it, or
     melt suddenly
into the next door apartment building, swept down into the
     back garden tow,
like transitions whether in writing or in music that aren't
     really transitional

so that cadence is a matter, ordinarily, of being stunned
   rather than construed,
but no diminishment, as in "fancy" and "open fifths" and
   "environmental sweepstakes"

                  (*The Year of the Olive Oil,* 1989)

LITTLE CAPE COD LANDSCAPE

for Darragh Park

The garbage is bagged, deposited in the dump, and several
months later produces its interest, roses.

Late last night some people walking near the harbor were
half-bagged and wanted to walk all the way out on the
slippery jetty. Their roses were all talk, but they man-
aged to accomplish their goal in spite of their questionable
condition. Sleep roses, roses of the derailed train, rose
roses and more roses.

                  (*The Year of the Olive Oil,* 1989)

THE YEAR OF THE OLIVE OIL

for Yuki Hartman

I sing the olive oil, I who lately sang
The clarinets in their sturdy packing case, the failure
Of the economy to be both seasonal and self-sufficient,
Packed off like cargo ships into the dim asperities of twilight.
Spread on Italian bread it became the summer sky—
And sometimes (brittle as failure) as musical as crystal.
One bottle contained all the arts. Another stimulated conversation
Which was itself the first pressing.
Darker pressings for the night
And each dawn had its geographical nuances, French and Spanish

Greek and Syrian, as on overcast days there were lumps
Of tough, overworked dough, gray and suffocating, with just a trace of gloss.
Then success was measured in thinness like an expensive watch;
Failures were as muddy as colors mixed by an infant.
Even virtual sewing machine oil, rancid with use, had a place
Beside winters when spears of sunlight, like armed tears,
Fenced in flame-blue iris and more ingenious pupil.
There were kingdoms advertising their future connections
(In crystal palaces with silver flags, cork-like minarets)
Fields of long, slender wheat coated with spring rain:
Sharing with the Jams the flow of shade
And with the Glues and Ointments a calculator-like display
Of the forces of temperature and pressure, as on August days in city
    office buildings.
One type was restricted to the human body, as its perfection and condiment.
Before this, there would have been no adhesive
For the world scrape, no solution (admittedly fugitive).
Music caught in the throat like peanut butter
And chords were torn apart, something like peaceful war-resisters
Until there was little sense of connection.
People read and wrote in fits, misunderstanding the true nature of the
    medium.
Then or soon after the intellect was felt to be
A part of life's suspension, and barbers never had to oil
Their scissors. If there was an occasional
Domestic squabble, it ran to gentle advice.
It is clear that vegetables, as in Andrew Marvell, were the chief
Image and model of human desire; and like water off a duck's back
—Pressed to golden brown, with pale gold juices intact and *no* fat—
Slid the momentary chagrins and anxieties, the bankruptcies
Spiritual and otherwise—otherwise irremediable; except for
Long slow decanting like passages of pure virgin time.
They had, as far as I can see, no word for friction.
It looked like a partial though real changeover to ball-bearings
on the part of even the most adamant faculties of mind and body,
Writer's cement block and fractious self-interest group (the quiet ferment
Made clear by the necessity to be glass-clad, stoppered)
Enabling human achievement to flourish like a gold breeze,
Circular and reforming in the glow and liquid fragment.

(*The Year of the Olive Oil,* 1989)

A NOTE TO TONY TOWLE (AFTER WS)

One must have breakfasted often on automobile primer
not to sense an occasional darkening in the weather joining art and life;
and have read *Paradise Lost* aloud many times in a Yiddish accent

not to wake up and feel the morning air as a collaborator
thrown from some bluer and more intelligent planet
where life, despite the future's escalating ambitions, has ramified

in every direction except UP; and have been asleep a long time
in the air bonded to night not to feel the force of the present
shimmering in the downtown buildings, like European walled cities

whose walls have all but disappeared via benign invasion
and touristic drift; even the World Trade Center
for all the enigmas concerning *who* is trading *what* to *whom*

and while deracination is fast qualifying as essence
rather than attribute, towards the brush with open sea.

                    (*The Year of the Olive Oil,* 1989)

Ron Padgett [1942]

DETACH, INVADING

Oh humming all and
Then a something from above came rooting
And tooting onto the sprayers
Profaning in the console morning
Of the pointing afternoon
Back to dawn by police word to sprinkle it
Over the lotions that ever change
On locks
Of German, room and perforate
To sprinkle I say
On the grinding slot of rye
And the bandage that falls down
On the slots as they exude their gas
And the rabbit lingers that pushes it

To blot the lumber
Like a gradually hard mode
All bring and forehead in the starry grab
That pulverizes
And its slivers
Off bending down the thrown gulp
In funny threes
So the old fat flies toward the brain
And a dent on brilliance

The large pig at which the intense cones beat
Wishes O you and O me
O cough release! a rosy bar
Whose mist rarifies even the strokers
Where to go
Strapping, apricot

(*Great Balls of Fire*, 1969)

LOUISIANA PERCH

Certain words disappear from a language:
their meanings become attenuated
grow antique, insanely remote or small,
vanish.
          Or become something else:
transport. Mac
the truck driver falls for a waitress
      where the water flows. The

great words are those without meaning:
  from a their or
  Or the for a the
  The those

The rest are fragile, transitory
    like the waitress, a

beautiful slender young girl!
I love her! Want to
marry her! Have hamburgers!
Have hamburgers! Have hamburgers!

(*Toujours l'amour,* 1976)

TELL US, JOSEPHINE

The blue and white tie arrived at the man's neck through
    merchandising:
He walked up to a store window, reached in his pocket
    and, inside, completed the transaction.
Now, as he walks away, he exercises his body. It improves
    his health.
The blue and white stripes of the tie improve his
    appearance.
It improves his gray shirt, a palm tree improves a desolate
    landscape,
A desolate landscape improves empty space

And his spirits are improved, if cheefulness is an improvement.
The eyes of his face now seem meaningful and happy to be so,
The smile that rides below the eyes reflects the moonlight
That glances off the roaring and shimmering dress of sequins,
Maroon sharks that flow down the body of the girl from Martinique,
The girl who smokes a cigarette, darkly, in his mind,
As he walks into the darkened room and waits for his
    eyes to catch up with his past.

Dark red, almost black, the long sharp fingernails click
    against the varnish smoke floats in waves on
And a lime grows cold against a cube
Of ice that couldn't remain solid. Cooler,
The air along the floor flows along legs of table and lady
Who shifts slowly in her chair to keep the blood evenly
    distributed—
She does not like her legs buzzing unpleasantly.
They rest here, then there, their surfaces smooth against
    the black silk
That sheathes her body. It is so dark in there!
And so quiet, only skin on silk, click of nails, tiny sequins
    crashing like tiny cymbals for which we get tiny ears,
    and gentle zephyrs
In curls of smoke lifted from her lungs.
I don't think she has any thoughts!
I don't thi... the man in the blue and white tie appears
    in the doorway.
She moves her hand. The room bursts into flame.
Both die in the holocaust. Statues are erected in their honor.
Leaves fall down from trees. The sap rises. The sun rises.
Prices go up and people sit under the ground.
The ground rises. It has wings. It is an airplane.
After a while it levels off over the clouds, cruising at an
    altitude of 56,000 feet and a speed of 300 miles per
    hour.
You are alone on the plane: there is not even the pilot!
You have stolen the airplane, with no one to drive it, and
    now you must suffer the consequences.
But the first consequence is your pleasure at being alone
    up so high all silver and blue
Over pink and gray cloud patches that blur to orange wisps
    over there
And down to a rather artificial-looking purple beyond that.

Could that be real, so purple?
Your attention is drawn to that cloud, how could it be so purple?
And then your spirit is drawn down to it, utterly riveted
    to that flowing shape, the intensity is aural, it is
    awful—O let me go, cloud!
And poof it parts gracefully and evaporates...
Behind it the man and the girl from Martinique are parting and
    evaporating
And as they do your ignorance parts and evaporates and
    you remember: you are a pilot

(Toujours l'amour, 1976)

EARLY TRIANGLES

Can you feel the swell—
or is there one?—
of something vast & wonderful
coming over America?
Or is that just the glow
of lights from Montpelier?
I stood out in the woods
and spoke to the trees with their leaves,
and they answered back. They said,
"Jerome, Jerome,
return to your village."
I did so, and began
to lick postage stamps.
Red ones and green ones, some
with pink and yellow,
delicate triangles in the afternoon.

(Triangles in the Afternoon, 1979)

LUCKY STRIKES

Turn me every which way, three-cornered God,
and batter the corncobs with your fury,
that I might be everywhere I am
and those who do not understand this
fall into the fold of the paper they are written on,
others written on the wind, seraphic
creatures! tilted sideways
so as to enter your heart the easier
once you have opened it up to them,
and like metrical perfection that disappears
in its very perfectness,
your heart will be of wind,
your head up in the clouds,
where the hard candy of all nations
floats in colored wrappers the sun hits.

Unfortunately, most of the people
have alarm clocks that run down the road
as fast as they can, from sheer fright.
Eventually, over the blue hills, you'll
hear a distant ringing, a feeble, final ding
that causes all the Bodhisattvas in heaven
to rise in their yellow robes
and cry Hurrah to the ever-expanding soda crackers,
next to the tomato soup
that steams tranquilly in the breakfast nook
where a rainbow woman, striped pretty colors,
radiates across the toy kitchen.
Yes, it was only a play house,
it was only a play
written for the toys that had come
all the way from Bethlehem,
camels and all.

(*Triangles in the Afternoon,* 1979)

SOMETHING OR OTHER

The open-mouthed quail
while the closed-mouth stomp
along a runway of Declarations of Independence
and you burst into flight

and burst into song.
Oh, this person is going to die.

There is a separation
between life and death
where flowers grow

and that is where I want to go
this weekend,

to forget about my assignments
and my horn-rimmed glasses which fall repeatedly to the floor.
O give me the ambiguity of a table
resurrected from the tree
sawn down by a lantern-jawed fellow
named John, John Something or Other.

(*Tulsa Kid*, 1979)

SYMBOLS OF TRANSFORMATION

The yellows and creams
blaze a little brighter
when you get older;
the blue-grey of the office furniture
doesn't look so bad.
The details are different
because you are Grandma Moses:
the cows come right up
into your face and moo,
sunlight pours out of a large hole
and the trees are toothpicks

and it's okay like this, it's
a little
like staring at yourself
in a funhouse mirror: your body
has melted into your shoes
and your neck extends into a curve in time-space
and the flashbulb pops,
the graduates heave a sigh of relief
and their mortarboards
into the back seat.
Driving home, you watched
the streelights flash on the seat covers
and when you pulled into the driveway
it wasn't mom and dad who got out of the car,
but two large goats
who hobbled into the house ahead of you.

(*Tulsa Kid,* 1979)

FIRST DRIFT

The writing of poems
and the living of life
seem to require
paying hard attention
to any and everything,
and experiencing
a kind of mental orgasm.
Yikes! Do I
mean that?
Unfortunately, I'm afraid
I did, dipped to scoop
an idea from the roadside,
the mental roadside that runs
alongside the mental highway
that leads to a mental hospital.
I have never been a patient
in a mental hospital, because
I think it would be an extremely bad place to be.
So I stay out.

And stay home.
And go down the street,
looking intently at everything.
Sometimes the people in the street
laugh and turn into sheet music
torn from the sky and left to flutter down
into the metaphor that hides behind the deity,
and will not show itself,
like a basement beneath the ocean,
with a tree that grew through a sheet of glass
on which your face was painted,
like a clown's, in the early morning
when it was just starting to rain
and the animals are moving, and the tents
are rippling in the breeze, and inside Glenda
the chimpanzee is completing a quadruple somersault
from shining bar to shining bar.

(*The Big Something*, 1990)

Michael Brownstein [1943]

STEPPING OUT

A tile is loose for splendid feet
Of cognition running with arms outspread.
An airman who treasures the small silver wings pinned
At his shoulder by a functionary so he can take off
Without necessarily a clear conscious, but an ordered
One, a vertible flying bridge.

If the tile is loose, throw it away

Suddenly Syria: midday: telegrams call
In the upper air, as a muezzin drones from a mosque
Or that muezzin drones from that mosque
Just to the left, and your forget your bags,
Transfixed.

       Transfixed and
Gone, like an artichoke Louisiana has peeled.
She has eaten. She gathers the great purple folds
Of her mammy dress together and with a purposeful sigh,
Strides off. "Not enough commas in this poem," she mutters.
That may be true, there aren't many pauses in the poem
Of life, but just like her to say so, she
                being illiterate mammy.
And bearing her simple grudge she gains upon the distance.

If the tile is truly loose, drop it in your pocket

Or paste it back in its pattern
On the floor of the mosque. Quick, before
The murderous Arabs see you. They see you: it is too late?

The cool delicious floor your feet touch
Stepping out of the midday heat (midday again?)
With the rest of your body, not at all a coming-out party,
But a soothing and honest rest on the actual precious stones.

(*Highway to the Sky*, 1969)

WAR

You can't spend all day staring into the sea, however
As if it were your favorite book
Until an especially coddled page detaches itself
From the light, floating toward you through the grove
At the edge of which Hernando stands with the battalion
Bent to the amplification of his will, louder
And louder as it hums among the spindles
Of the fruit and garden trees. You *can*
Spend the day clearing out the porch and
Cease staring into that sea because it is
An unenlightening sea, furtively complex like an icy bath
With the washrag saleman's daughter. Laughter.
Wind ruffling the skirts of the citrus trees.
Soldiers are whining to seal off this port.
                    Oppose these soldiers.
Ignore them if they take your picture off
the wall...They take your picture from the wall
And walk through. You however are eating a pear
And don't need to see them down the rest
Of the hall to the door, out into the street
And crabbing, disappear into a fault. A busy town goes up.
You are not a traffic signal. But as it changes
A cop revolves, seriously intent on detaining you.
He doesn't care about the traffic, adding up behind you
Like a stifled thought, because he is whispering
Softly near your ear. The sun sinks along
His nightstick, all things relaxing into silence
Except for that stifled thought.

(*Highway to the Sky*, 1969)

THE GLASS ENCLOSURE

Glassine envelopes trampoline the pigmeat into a final awakening.
It is the greater awakening. It is bleeding, bubbling and runny and
                                        it's funny that way.
The plastic knife acts extra-friendly today.
The matching plastic spoon and fork look on.
The paper plate pronounces a complete cellophane word.
The little girl treads water at the surface of a public moat
Its spidery fretwork of styrofoam roots supporting a bed
Of swirling metal apples whose hot white crust rides free.
And from the great unknown above her an ancient pie crust
Encloses a squirt of apple juice that hops and skips
Up the lovely burnished golden legs & down the silver-alloy arms
Of that greater fraction of young people
Required to strip themselves of their spirit and flee.
Their denouement comes at the moment of interment.

□

They cried like abandoned babies, who did not want to have to go
                                        through with this:
It is a black lump of coal in the throat
It is a miner's lamp of circumspection
It is the succulent baby checkerboard we pour milk on,
Milk as rich as eggs whose yolks of promise ride the air:
A stringy richness wrapping up the heart lies striken there.
Its apoplectic textures weave a smack.
…While deep underground the railroadmen we love so, wearing their
distinctive hats like inverted maple syrup buckets and biting into huge
lunchbuckets, are gone from us forever.
The trains themselves don't anymore seem to work at all either,
Or if they do it's only up and down that they work, these trains—
Up and down from the eggs to the mines.

□

And the filling station too is filling up;
The glassine dogs play hurriedly with their envelopes,
Afraid the noise their shapes call forth
Will crack the dogs their noses bring, like a familiar glass person
Whose blithe, living spirit intersects its mechanical amble

And fills your smoky questioning hole with soda water:
The man who slew the dragon is selling used cars on the corner.

But that only happens later, after you've contemplated
The glass enclosure in your maturity, and come to the following
Tentative set of conclusions:
1.—That the wigs turning discreetly in their shop window are
                                    turning for you,
Turning and turning on their trim white plastic heads.
2.—That the glass envelope briskly rubbed back and forth aborigine-style
Will set the palm of your hand on fire.
3.—That the clumsy message in the child's hot brain was freeze-dried
By the sets of ambidextrous parasols that rows of parents wield,
Who sweetly but firmly move forward to shield their children from
                        the rays that beat down and bounce up,
Discharging twinkling sunlight into the lamps of the afternoon…
The one random child whose freedom was made the exception to
                                    this rule
Set fire to the hand that fed him and is now but rarely seen,
An errant satellite consuming itself in the heavens above the glass.
You look up at dusk and see a tiny speck of smack
Relaying satellite-type information to his earth and fantasizing the rest.
4.—That in the best of all possible worlds every neighborhood would
have several restaurants like this one, each sunk in its own tradition, a
little island of simple ethnicity carefully preserving its methods and
standards amid its metropolitan reduction to eccentricity.
5.—That your two coaxial eyeballs search feverishly for a pair of breasts
to alight upon, a hand to hold.
6.—That a serenely academic pair of breasts now wears eyeglasses
To better verify the torrent of deeply-felt emotions
Their quivering nipples must sacrifice to a briskly changing scene:
First it is a mechanical millionaire, then a truckload of oppressed
                        migrant workers, then a busy city street.
Now it is a teetering office tower filling up with workers
From the street. They are white-collar workers who eye the giant
                                    breast uncomfortably,
And their collars, though lately daringly and even arrogantly
Stained with fiery tabasco sauce, still retain
Their essential ancient stiffness and secret pain—
It is much too tight, the veins on the neck protrude, the forehead's
                        red and bulging, but very few complain.
The toasters heat up in the morning, the washer-dryers whir at night.
…And this a good dozen years after incoherent long-haired cartoon

characters invaded the confines of the Institute and ran screaming and
leering down its antiseptic white halls, disrupting the pools of typists at
their task by spraying them with chemicals that ran their stockings and
turned their brisk, prim statutory activities into a comic opera night-
mare!
No wonder these ruthless noisy little ruffians were reviled and shat
                                    upon!
Yes, the collar is too tight but the majority cannot complain
Since if they did, their open necks would in short order
Burn closed forever in a sort of coppery-red tropical lunceon meat
Located bleeding quietly and compulsively in the mud beneath the
                                    stairs:
At least, "The Face in the Carpet" says such a grisly fate is theirs.

                                    □

And believe it or not, this queer myth still persists in minds and hearts today.
To me, it is a sub-picturesque or post-picturesque way of delaying their
                                    departure
Until a combination Metaphysical Interior-and-Small Arms Factory can be
                                    erected on the site
To house and occupy the horde of red-blooded workers inside the great glass
                                    interior
That owes its existence to one architect's monumental homesickness:
He is wasting away his epic lung capacity on tiny numbered cubicles,
Lost like a broken toaster in the Valley of the Furniture Movers.
He contemplates with proud disdain the infinite functional anaconda of
                                    garbage and noise that encircles him.
He disquiets the glass enclosure by abandoning his blueprint and embracing
                                    messy self-disclosure instead.
Low rumbles are heard in the distance, seismic tremors, and for the first time
Dust settles on the massive octagonal panes.
Two or three of the limitless glass molecules are cracked.

                                    (*Strange Days Ahead*, 1975)

JET SET MELODRAMA

"Give us your very best table," I swaggered, taking the head waiter aside and slipping him a huge wad of play money.... "But of course, sir," the bald little man purred as he pocketed the cash and steered us to the most outstanding table in the whole place. A truly amazing table it was, complete with swimming pool, two-car garage, spiritual advisor, and a landscaped garden which dwarfed even Versailles because of a bonus: the garden sloped down to a rocky massive seacoast that swayed gently in refreshing shoreline breezes wafted across the table to us by matched pairs of eunuch Nubian servants bending their palm fans with sultry efficiency in the really knock-out evening light spilling across our plates from the depths of the deep blue sea....

"Jesus, this is really something, isn't it?" Mary Lou breathed as she hung at my side, dropping narcotic mints into the mouths of the intelligent super-graceful house-broken wildcats that roamed across the tablecloth. Their rhinestone-studded collars...strings of Christmas lights along their tails...their claws and nipples click-ing against the china...their eyes doing a dance of fire for the foggy, debauched rednecks nodding out around gleaming knives and forks. "I don't know," I answered, "I'm not even sure I understand what's happening." At that moment the waiter reappeared and began to unfold a heavy, complicated menu with suggestions that ran on for sixty pages, moaning softly as he whispered to us, "You have your choice! Anything you want."

"Fuck it!" I squeaked, upsetting the table which slid with a low reverberating roar into the garden below, "all I wanted was a little peace of mind!"

"Yeah, right," Mary Lou chorused as we swept out the door into the nowhere moonlight of our humble paisan heritage.... "No, Mary Lou, you should stay," I insisted, trying to avoid her shocked, hurt eyes as I pushed her back toward the door, the tears streaming down her face and hands. "I'll go get a cheeseburger or some-thing, I don't really care, but you should stay here, it would be a crime to waste all this luxury on the heartless neurotic wallflowers who are devouring it now. This place, there's no other way to describe it—it cries out like a wine bottle for the wholesome, beautiful girl who will close her mouth around its neck: heart, body, and soul."

(*Brainstorms*, 1971)

THE LAST SPELL CAST

The last spell cast came late one afternoon in a brown study. I was studying myself and suddenly separated in two. One of me ran along the four walls with a stick, playing the grooves in the boards of the walls like a xylophone while I sat at the kitchen table and watched. I even ate a meal, it was blue food garnished by hard yellow scallops of butter that broke open with a fork to reveal mini-small photographs of my friends. These pictures were head shots taken by I don't know who I don't know how many years ago. My friends look different today than they look in those photos, I know that much. Inside the blue food is a paste made from the houses of the past. Blue food cracks open to show me the houses, corners and streets where tiny particulate memories were formed of all the roads I've taken since. There is a blue streetlight at the top of a hill. Children roll elegant narrow wheels down the hill with long sticks, which they also switch into their opposite hand to rub against the rungs of the cast-iron fences as they run. This makes a peculiar sonorous clicking sound, like a mallet run quickly across the wooden keys of a xylophone. Behind the cast-iron fences and well-kept lawns are middle classs two and three story houses, out of every single one of which I emerge onto the patio, attracted by the sound of the sticks in the fences. I am distracted and restless, I am supposed to be studying but I cannot study. Tomorrow morning the test everyone is waiting for will come, to see if I will pass. If I pass my future is secure, if not I must scramble and scurry for the rest of my life just to get by. I know this perfectly well yet I exhaust myself running and running at a fixed hypnotic gait around and around the room. I watch myself as I run, making the sound of children and iron fences, humming and even wailing outlandishly to myself until the whole room quivers with a dangerous kind of freedom, and even though I long to tear myself away from this scene and go on eating I cannot, and even though I should close my eyes and go lie down on the bed I cannot. While I'm running I watch myself trying to eat and I also see the photographs of faces and the houses and corners and streets, and I hear a sound I can't identify always to my right side, a progression of grand booming sounds like the ribs of the earth being tickled, being struck one after the other, by a long stick in the hand of a stranger. And if I keep running and if I keep talking and if I keep eating...and if not, I'm the witness,the manufacturer as well as the witness of the last spell cast. Though nothing reverses this universe the way it reverses forever if I stop and run the other way. Then I am not simply running, I am running back, and the last spell cast twists inside out and starts over.

(*When Nobody's Looking,* 1981)

PARIS VISITATION

I can hear the voice of Boris Vian, which is something because of course I never heard or met Vian and my French is not very good and I read only one of his books not all the way through, but it's not even his voice as much as it is Boris Vian in a nightclub in St. Germain des Pres in springtime during the day, he knows the proprietor, the door is open to the sidewalk and the warm sun pours through the open doorway but no further, and from in back as I pause on the sidewalk and lean into the doorway I can hear Vian talking, I see cigarette smoke and two or three men in shirtsleeves, I hear coughing and laughing and one chair leg scraping, coffee is being made and liquor being drunk, it is three-thirty, Boris Vian is talking to the proprietor about nothing, he's not talking a mile a minute about be bop jazz and he's not talking a mile a minute about phraseology or his girl friend or his trumpet, he's not making up funny desperate American characters in a spectacular flat American small town nowhereland somewhere inside his head, he's not quick punning while he's drinking and smoking, quick punning short gasps about the people he knows, the people they all know, the delicious barbs strike home, delicious quick gasps of laughter, clattering of dishes, hacking rapidly at the smoky air surrounding him as he leans into a crisp vivid memory of a woman he once made love to and will never make love to again, a woman who's now a tight red jersey moving along the wall, a turn of the face, hair swinging, she's gone, Vian's coughing, he's bent over now and coughing but still not far enough gone not to notice the lovely sweet freshness of the springtime air this day in 1951, this brief moment in 1951, when I stop alongside the windows and almost weep as I hear clearly through the open doorway that voice I never could have heard, as I look through the doorway and see arms and scarves and faces, short high movements so quickly gone, through the dark and the noise and smoke, way back in there.

(When Nobody's Looking, 1981)

from ORACLE NIGHT

Oracle night
the porch is frozen
inside the house, warmth and light
helical burrows made by ancestors
when this same design is found elsewhere
it is less than a semblance
like circus animals after their exercise

my evenings have calm nothingness of languor
with a stiletto in my gizzard some fine afternoon
since the truth-functions can be ordered in series
by clever analogies
for example, the tusks of extinct mammoths
echo among the flying saucers
that go the wrong way
in parts of Nebraska and Wyoming
they gyrate in a counterclockwise spiral
next to falling into the canal
which would be of no use
since I can swim—
then I changed the way I saw you
I looked inside you and found
irregular features: bright, mobile, but elusive
black rocks, and then far off, capped with clouds
melting blue of the sky
vertiginous shadows
split into blue chasms
sparkling with a pure snow
that delighted my childhood
rushing ahead of the train that ran beside it
in some silvery rendition of dispersed radiation
with the beautiful eyes of a goat
a divination ceremony in the middle of the street
composed of raw apples anf fried potatoes
rubbing medicine into your weapons
other nipples, little finger
top of chest, front of throat
big finger, spear finger
little bone back, big bone joint
right ear, right eye, nose and mouth
when with a thousand kisses wandering over
your hand, your foot, your very look's a cunt
in the crisis of its power
intersected with small canals or ditches
to attenuate and keep up the ethereal part of you
viewed in retrospect
as a swooping swallow
hollow flank like a whippet's
a reddish scrap of cloth
your delicate hands, never washed
a proud mouth full of tiny fissures

a beautiful set of teeth and ageless eyes
and a blue arrow that runs down the center of your chin
under the cold eye of science
the leaf-crunching days of the dinosaurs
like hot corn in a popper
sperms had taken over the world
to cover the bare earth until one day
there were over six thousand species
of black, grumbling bees
that became strangely altered
flying little except when feeding
when a thin, descending wail could be heard
their song a dream of perpetual navigation
for this was a slack time
slow continental upthrust
green lines which surrounded the world
the seashore cliffs had vanished
the air now, hot blooded
high speed mechanics
and bison appeared
and resistant tooth-enamel
for the planet was a grassland
apes were to become men
as impressive as the dim-brained dinousaurs
but with more reproductive mechanisms
and would ride the wind for miles
soaring restlessly for untold hours
coming down less and less frequently to rest
a remarkable instance of helical flight
the balls hit water and floated around
meaning the people then refused old age
and were always young
a more versatile human species
captivated by classy superstitions
footprints, ashes, bits of wood
the mammary of an oak
if it relates to the future
deciphered by the lines on your face
seated in the nook of your cave
first to think around corners
keeping all swirls inside you
bird of magic, four-spoked wheel
big bronze kettledrum by the door

and height and depth, and east and west
fixed by the mouth at five places
where the end of the tongue meets the throat
between the lips at the head of the tongue
on the back third of a divided tongue
the wheel turns forward and back
the tongue low and flat
notes sadder than words
dividing into male and female
impossible to tell one from the other
two stones building two houses
three stones building six houses
six stones building seven hundred and twenty houses
everything pulled apart
flooding my mouth
when eyes changed their tint like peaches
water pouring out from between them
darkened rooms, gambling and indolence
rather rude young creatures
glittering in diamonds
were to dominate the earth
thin chests bedizened with loud cravats
between two doors
their end lodged in their beginning
for it is said
the creatures ran and they returned
transparent and milky as moonstones
equipped with floating laboratories
and the sound of pursuing feet
floating down into the dark
with those bulging pop eyes trained on us
as we hiked along the corkscrew of the moment
a land of hollow reeds and bubbling marshes
between the heel and the hand
where I took your body as my home
letting everyone see what I had done
I built a chair and sat down
putting a floor under it
and rode inside
like a ghost

(*Oracle Night*, 1982)

Lewis Warsh [1944]

THE SUICIDE RATES

for Liam O'Gallagher

I

The bell was not a jar, when
I woke that night I was listening to the rain.
The wing of the gull was not hidden beneath the glass.

Lights, as they go on, watch
the shadows melt backwards
and the ladder cross the shade.
Like a drop parting with the brick, watch
this silence go unending.

The houses we occupy
are empty in our trust.

The bell was not made to be rung
as an alarm. Small hotels and places
we can no longer assume vacant.

Small eyes blush at the windowsill
a geranium bends its wings into the crease, the
lights are the flashlights
finding the trail, breaking the line

We can no longer assume
that the forest was only memory
        The branches were like lead cables.

Hands   palms down
personal ashes dead now
a calm fire in calm wood
encircles, I see a bluff

I see a corner of the mouth
a light breaking the line

Here
      I see a gambling room and the men
      stacking cards, I see

a bluff on their faces
the streaks of light go
the hint of light wavering

I see the child who is the hip breathing
and the bottom rise from under, undersea

The calm stack he took one number from his sleeve

2

How many ways to die for a window

It is dead night, far from home,
I sit back, dazed,
for a moment we affect the equality of places
of other nights, eyes, and a casual stare, a price.

A longing that is not mutual
passes as a swan passes
other swans, a passing

The hunting lodge door fell open
the door of a gambling hall
was open, a jack-knife
(he swam away)
the blade became a buckle, in
his belt there were twenty odd revolvers
how many ways to die was left unmentioned

We did not speak
though my gesture made one/fifth
upon the bar
          reveal itself

The child was not hard
he lived as long as a room is born
the left hand was not the first to go
it was the other, covering the deck

The doorman opened his door and a mouse
leaped out

3

The photographs that are dead before
the other photographs of his hands
were made public

Sperm or juice
and I am going to sleep tonight, early,
tilting the cup towards the blue uniformed stranger

Opening doors   feeling the board rock
as you dive

4

How long must we wait before these
numbers proportionally swell?
In a ratio at every fourth step
we take our chances.

A board rocks, a child refuses
to dive and dies

Lost in mid-afternoon
lost and the sun, pages
of sweat mount on my face

This grave is stone
the occupants of this room
turn obediently
Their backs are like lead
or so I would have it

A light does not turn with them.
An address book changes hands, how
many directions do we walk, walk
on our hands, on the joints
between our fingers, exploding
like underground mines miles away.

How many lines form at your door, are
they queues of longing, symbols
of that mid-afternoon
lost in sunlight, sweat,
crawling back across the sudden fine tear?

The job was not a bridge-builder.
It was to tabulate
the frenzy of the wall
to whichyou clung. Losing
sleep over the memories
you forget.

5

Rain cannot
keep falling, it
releases
a tension.
        The bare back and arms of a cloud
moves at my side. I lie, I
listen the sudden darkness of vehicles
down below. Sterility combs the helm.

My boat I will refunish
for a casino on the sea.
All the gamblers in their tight black dress.

All the small children taunting numerals
on my thigh. If there was not this fear
that the darkness throws overboard.

Lie awake, my own bare arm re
                        flexes.
They're gone tonight into the glamorous black beyond.

The gambling hall is closed,
a narrow line, a light, seems to move beneath the door.

In the realm of valises
I am all at once a passage
of tourists returning home for the weekend via my hands.
Of tourists replete with all their divine insights.

I lean, I lie awake, the
minute scratches em-bed your moving face.
At my elbow, a caution, a tension of springs.
The mattress   locked wire
makes sound the rain makes
I listen   I lose myself
I lose my hands
they are bound with the tossing
your plane is tossing in a clear blue sky,
it alights

6

Now I see photographs of the wild
and open vehicles of our time.
Too many means which transport the wavering eye.

A calm fire, fear enrages us, engraved
and partially naked, too many leaves release us.
Rain climbs down our skulls, the
pins of our forearms arc
                        in readiness, they
re-burst. These goods

we do not appraise. They
surround us with prices, the
numbers are on their tags. I seal
myself in.

Behind me a large window
and a party for small poems.
Small and gentle truces, watch
these keys clip wildly
hear them strike in the spirit
they unwillingly entice.

At most, the leaves do not
beg here to be swept.
From all sides, all lines
desert us and desire us.
From all windows this window
seems almost glamorous
to be alone. Write

these poems here
for the sake of writing,
at most it will make for us
an accumulative gesture,
a book for sonnetforms
and a grammar that leaves the ground.
                Last night, in
a doorway on 53rd street, for
a moment I was holding
your cane, your homberg.
I was trying to explain myself,
a mania for my hands!

Last night on 53rd the
leaves did not
release, they
balanced. No
mention of your place
now, your presence
amid these poems, I
am writing to get
over, to turn
over

7

Almost blind light
and the hourly violence
of paino-keys
                thru whose wall this music comes

The victrola plays on, the
needle goes no farther than the surface
and breaks the thread

I sigh and see
my breath readily contagious

Almost blind
like light, yet
luminous, a rough shedding
shone on her ankle, countless
scratches on her fingers, her
fingertips a claw:
that is the wound, that
is defeat. I brush
the back of her elbows
with my shoes, like
a lost detail
or the crows lost out at sea
or the crows amid other birds
pitting their wings on the insides of our voices
I see and seem to understand real stone.
It is comfort to brace
ones body on the real.
It is not enough
to keep this night from dying.

I see a bluff. I concede
all the dangers
and the comparable Autumn lights.
Somewhere the flash of a star
bleeds over his body.
A network of relative expressions
rapidly changes, changing face.

8

My own arm, my eyes.
The brick he lifts, was
it a mason
down below? In
the streets
we are given and we
accept, green
objects.

My eyes repeat that
the figures are
not discerned. They
are portions of the fire:
lost waking, blue moon rising.

Products of the calm.
A photograph that was his wrist
and the sleeve, the weightless flesh.

Quiet gambles it away.

9

Like small foreign villages whose gates have been
destroyed by bonfires
so the cities nearest my hands
are destroyed by the rust and the rustling of cool ashes.

Cool gray enters my throat.
It is painful to be foreign from you now,
to hear from others that your letters
spill like numbers
between the cracks of the avenues of the villages
that are not burning, that
have been spared

Huge windows corrupt me.
Between each ripple
the sun admits
duplicity. A
different face,
a room in which I lie and listen,
clawing for the grate
from which the gas breathes
in my hands.
          It
hangs in space
above me
The loins hang

10

Small oaths snap like twigs
beneath our feet. Smaller
things impersonate
us, now that you are gone
a century of unappraised items
goes released. The leaves
were not real gold,
they made replicas to establish
the dead end of the season.

Firm branches dip
against the blue arms
of the laborer, blue
lips from the cold
firm branches knead his flesh.
The leaves that the child touched
were almost real sounds.
Counting the attempts that the sun makes as it emerges,
counting the chimneys and the smoke about to rise.
A dim light leads the way.
Thru a crowd of countless deaths your face emerges
a map
moving and charting the rain across this glass

Firm branches dip the blue, blue lips from the cold

(*The Suicide Rates*, 1967)

GOUT

He changes into a bird, and that's
the only difference. Rain
on the improved sidewalk seems
inspired after so much heat.
Look at the objects
that have already wilted and died.
Someone is losing hair trying
to penetrate the meaning of death—rather

language which postpones dying
is inventing a drug to keep us alive.
Being similar never made his body more true. Bills
for electricity and answering
service are burning inside the hearth.
My dream, to have a hearth and
set an example for fading
youth. The conspicuous peacock
neither turns nor changes,
yet suddenly loses its feathers, buckles
in the dust and dies. The
meaning is as fantastic as any truth. Language
invents a painkilling drug for restoring youth—an
occasion inviting feelings which
jolt and never subside. I mean
he is dying again, slowly, as he gains time.

(*Moving Through Air,* 1968)

THE STATIC

for Jonathan Cott

We pick off dots like runners, between
two clouds, and possess
in moments, when language fails, the view
of ourselves lit by turn-of-the-century
bulbs, which suddenly go out
in the middle of night. I need them
most then, I need
the cruelty which settles in their
mist. A candle melts and
fingers of the lake slowly abound.
I need that request of light
about me always, for stalking
myself blindly as a stranger in the night.
When language fails, as pretense,
do we refuse this arc forward, again, and
who needs us to determine the haste?
I think about the future. We quarrel.

Gaiety settles in wards, and cruelty
the fingers of the lake, slowly abound.
The static between strangers continues
in the bar. And afterwards
as we part our collars to the skin, the
naked dots like runners will possess us
immediately, and the change from
one century to another will take place.

(*Moving Through Air,* 1968)

ENMESHMENT

I listened to the voices that shattered
my heart, strange prerequisite, followed
by silence (I was an unrequited lover
again), my being contained an ampersand
dividing me from others & me from myself,
& the others (like plants desirous of light
& water) reflected through other eyes the casualness
of what I said, I could be aggressive, I could
be a "type" of person, I could even live a lie,
one imagines a bowl of light & a volatile bottle
which we could use to dynamite the walls of a public
bulding, I could harbor resentment till it flew
over my head like a dagger & passed through the heart
of an innocent bystander, one might look dumbstruck
in comparison to others from whom knowledge was a cherished
companion, my dependencies demand compensation
(an eye that opens like a shutter), I had what
you might call a "breakthru" but which for me
was "normal love," I wore the straight-jacket
of love's decline like the door of a locked room
with two people cowering behind it, I read how
achievement had nothing to do with the possession
of property, I had lunch with Peggy
but I couldn't eat (when it came
time to order all I could say was "I'll take
the same"), there was no distinction or space but
there was room for improvement, I saw myself as a special

plant or flower (a wild bleeding heart or black-eyed
susan) but I forgot about immunity & the right
to remain silent, I thought of affection as a way of expressing
something to someone you loved
(in the simplest sense, like brushing the hair
out of a person's eyes), I grew accustomed
to cold spaces, unmade beds, dishes in the sink
the laundry piled up on the bathroom floor, a couch
with no legs, I saw anger as a way of slipping
down a well with no sides, I limited myself
to what was most fortuitous (a rock or shell
washed up on the shore), I climbed tenement steps
to find an island with a broad vista
& discovered a window with a transparent curtain & a bamboo shade
I denied love's passsage into memory, & all the digressions
blue earrings, a furrowed brow, two shadows on the page.

(1984)

Lorenzo Thomas [1944]

ELECTRICITY OF BLOSSOMS

for Janet

Plentiful light

Their voices glow in mirror language
A high tension key winding
Brightness called "sky"
These things are atmospheric

Another electricity blossoms
The formal illusionist's hoop

Wireless

  Outside of the daylight
Inisde,
 If one could be
 Outside of the light

  The light would appear
From within

Faith

I said, "Little brown electric flower/woman"

Convention

Lady your smile
A shock to my eyes

   An oriel in a tree

Your concern is the tree

  Your frown leaves

Plentiful light

Feelings are almost arabic in this poem

Levitation

My idea blossoms & varies like Light
Embracing light in the glass of a mirror.
A Woman. Illusion of someone
Desiring magic tuxedos of mirrors

People who grow closer to surfacing

See stepping out of TG&Y or LEONARD'S
Closer to escaping into day
       trams

           (*Chances Are Few*, 1979)

CLEAR CHANNEL

Ha ha. You searching
For money
Find affection.
An object found

Touched by that one's hand

Kirlian fetish

This is supposed to go on
Without interruption
Until something surprising
emerges or surfaces and

Contemplates the reversal:

For an instnat
Teardrops and raindrops
Ascend like fountains,

Then back to gravity cliches

It's all your fault, Edgerton!

(*Chances Are Few*, 1979)

CAMEO IN SUDDEN LIGHT

How possibly could I
Fall in love with you
From looking at the back of your
Head
The care of studious hands
Shadowed curls
One broken sequin
Glittering and hiding
On gray carpeted step
Rustle of an intruding word
In a sea of paper, full of words
Fading and slowly writhing
Like traders of fable
In a haunted green quadrant
Carefully natural and tended
Tourista allure
a 2-foot stack of powdering disasters,
Yellowing pathos, wrinkled household
Hints
Frayed recipes and task force reports
Of one dowdy crisis after another
Discovered the deed
Costing into the thousands
As the shy light of a lost sequin
Blurts into fuchsia anxiety
No, I don't want you to see me

We are stealing avalanches of light
We
These several things
Seeking glimmers of focus

Each in our part of the room
Hiding and shining
Kuji Kiri the Ninja technique
Of performing hypnotic hand movements
Sha   the 5th center of power
Opening the Eight Psychic Channels
Begins at the base of the balls
Flows to the solar plexus
Tu Mo the base of the spine
Jen Mo at home in your brain
The body is one ocean
After another, secret and blue
Holding treasures when you have mastered
This motion

Much is promised
Power
Is useful only when
She hides her face
within the shadow of a jeweled hand
When she beckons
A mystic light in Bermudian waters
A potted tree that forces you
To cross gleaming lobbies
To prove that the blossoms are silk
And abject poverty and ingenuity
And love of beauty
Will steer our troubled course
As long as there are sad-faced maidens
Bending and shaping flowers in Taiwan
We are bright and alive in our security
Gasping as if rocketing upward
Out of travel brochure blue
Is not of the much that is promised

Amusing wall shadows are included
Attract popular and becoming friends!

High side those who once snubbed you!
Strange and colorful phonecalls
Will come to you from unpronounceable places!
But power is one thing you won't get
How could I
Possibly
Go on this way
Without you
At least sending some
Some discreetly placed
Signal
Seal it
With the voice of a seashell
The whorl of a conch
Or gleam of ancilla
Salvager,
for god's sake
turn around

Houston, Texas
1988

(*Long News in the Short Century* magazine, 1992)

EXCITATION

O wondrous thing it is
Oh what a wondrous thing it is
We often thought, to live
Through the senses
When they quicken and stir at even

One
Assays kaleidoscopes of failing light
Another
Revels in the moist kiss of the night
Approaching

soon though chased,
The kiss, by the dry scentlessness of central heat
So Prussian, so precise

When nature struggles against artifice
In a madly sensuous pas de deux
Lovely as the chevrons of late traffic
Dancing across high ceilings, cooling walls
Fleeting to sight yet permanent
In the mind's storage place of kinetics
To be unrapped some day when words fail
And, like any forgotten bundle in a warehouse
Puzzling because no one remembers what they were
What use they serve
Where did this stuff come from!
Or even how the hell it got here
Such simple-minded mysteries can make your day

ALL OF THIS IS A CERTIFIED EXCERPT FROM A DREAM.
THERE WERE SPIRITS
HOVERING OVER OR AS IN THE OLD LANGUAGE'S SIGNS
"UP ABOVE MY HEAD"
A SPECIAL SORT OF MUSIC IN THE AIR...SOMETHING
THAT WAKES YOU UP
JUST LIKE SUNLIGHT
LIKE A PHONECALL AT DAWN
15 MINUTES BEFORE THE ALARM GOES OFF
A ROUGH AND ROLLING MUSIC
LIKE THE 1940S BLUES
WHISKEY & WOMEN AND ALL THE OTHER JIVE
THE JIVERS KNEW
ALL THE SINGERS OF SENSE WHO HAD NO SENSE
OR ELSE THEY WOULDN'T HAVE BEEN SINGING
"WELL, YOU KNOW...."

The permutations,   or
                just   listening
        Roscoe Gordon
                        Peppermint
        "I Been Booted"

                         or is it "...just got
        FAT GIRL BOOGIE
                              & sordid ordered trash
                 The permutated sounds
                 of a special estranged English
            And who in hell
                         and this is it, if nowhere else
    will ever ever understand
    That all of these cats
                         were Charles Brown
                 yes, even
                 Nat "King" Cole
             urbane and suave
                              his pictures in the best of JET
    In those pulp days, pulp times
    A hundred years past slavery still
    The same old shuffle
                    In Alabama, where the redneck fans
          attacked poor Nat on stage   just like Roland Hayes
             knocked him down, down to the ground
             sd, "Nigger!"

        Such raw country voices, the Ku Klux Klan meets Rhythm & Blues

    IT SOUNDS LIKE THIS: Byebye, bye
                                Baby
                                     byebye
                         Oh what a wondrous thing
                             I think it is
                         But goddam baby
                                     baptist to the heart
                 I'm getting tithed of you, momma
                             But I love, Lord knows
                         most as much as I loves
                                     myself

        AND LOST LOTS OF FOOLS
        MOANING & GOING ON   (in the background)

    Certainly, this should awaken the mind
    And the senses should shut down in shame

But it is such a lovely clear break in the day
Only a fool who would remain a fool
Would have the nerve to shoo this shoofly away

"Anytime you bother me, Bubba..."
But, momma,
You
Can bother the heck
Out of me!

                        If you were me
                    Or anywhere
                                by me
                    Or near,
                Baby baby baby
                What a scene this cd be here
                        Oh baby baby baby
                    And lots of lost fools
                    Moaning & going on   (way in the background y'know)
                    Just like church   way back
                                in the wildwood
                            just like in the arbor
                                somewhere just outside
                And lost fools
                        just like church   way back
                                in the wildwood
                moaning & going on
                            like in de brush arbor
                                somewhere just outside
                    up   down
                    back of town

So much to say, we negroes here
O yes, we've had some fun
Have sang the blues and did what had to be done
We often thought, to live
O what a wondrous thing
Fleeting to sight yet permanent
To sit despised on the outskirts of your town
Black fat deprived & jap-eyed

Yes, we sing. "Bbaby baby baby, why you?"
When nature struggles against artifice
To be unwrapped some day when bullshit fails
And, like any forgotten bundle in a warehouse
Lovely as the chevrons of late traffic
      So Prussian, so precise
      Like a phonecall at dawn from your baby
      Moaning & going on...
      Such simple-minded mysteries can make your day

      The jivers knew
      All all of these acts
      Were Charles Brown's
      A rough and rolling music
      Just like sunlight
      Just like Church
      Fleeting to sight yet permanent
      To be unwarpped someday
      When words fail
      What use they serve
      Or else they wouldn't have been
      Singing

                Houston, Texas

(*Long News in the Short Century* magazine, 1991)

Marjorie Welish [1944]

WITHIN THIS BOOK, CALLED MARGUERITE

The sky is overcast and behind it an infinite regress
of vision is pulling nearer (and yet beneath)
in bashful ruts. I wonder if the mind will ever stop pursuing
rival minds or at least rival murmuring. It is a long sky
that convenes this endlessness.

                  Persons cunningly blent
to suggest a consensus—this is what is meant by serious
    entertainment
of opposing and hastening points of view, each of whose
sense of history is mutually exclusive.

                  Deck chairs
are making a return. I remember when stacking and ganging
chairs were innovative and David Rowland won an industrial award
for the campanile of steel chairs climbing to the sky.

                  As time separates us
from the evaporating architectonics to sweeten mythopoetic
substances, you start to count heroically
hurled down upon a profile of an as yet
unrevealed know-how.

                  You are unaccompanied
like the great unaccompanied counting
for solo violin that has arisen from the other side
of the mind and hand, the dark, tangled side of the hand,
with its great length of stay.

            (*The Windows Flew Open*, 1991)

WILD SLEEVE

Falling from a sleeve,

the meanders in Figure One, and wildness
anterior to pattern
in lines that swim with every response.
The audience finds them beautiful.

"White lines meander wildly over a black ground,"
the question is...and a hand
churns across the vulnerability at home.

White lines swimming away...,
but then isn't that dismissing them too early?
How erasures crush and how a shadow leaves for what is not
even a dawn. What is holding this drama together?
The least swimming casts notions
prophetically into ordinariness
though ordinariness seems least possible.

White, wild emergencies want our path, or rather the entire sky
folds in the hand like a trick. Neither you nor I
admire the maneuver drawn from the sleeve
of the guileless: "Wings of swans that wounded us"
because they were beautiful and because they were a trick.

And here are emergencies that streak
across a dark sheet of paper, quick and inventive, anatomically
    correct:
Isn't that too early?
The summer is crushing and impossible.
It is impossible to draw these innumerable responses, the white flowers
that trick and suffocate us. Drowning in flowers,
we leave fascination to the fascinated.
"Because of their beauty they wound us."

In the history of pattern, antecedent wallpaper
is murderous, quick, and only later, a bower welcoming
    sedated peonies
which sends the possibility of a perfect
abridgment of wildness; and so we leave. A belated thank you
for inviting us to your home.

In Figure Two
an abetting landscape of a mind's voluntary betrayal
of its own xenophobia shows itself
when the host adopts the manners and customs of the stranger
who is his guest. The exit surrounding his mind
unfolds symmetrically planted apology and lupine,
growing among the verticals that float the hand.

(*The Windows Flew Open*, 1991)

BLOOD OR COLOR

Across a room,
a handshake in a late, large design
has caught the overflow of the heart, the human figure as a source.
"Have you sent me my bouquet of gladiolus?" the poet asks.
"No, I haven't," I say, "but I have emphasized it."

Across a room, a writer queries,
"Have you reached my claim check and my watercolors,
    have you introduced a bouquet of gladiolus?"
"No," I say, compressed in ambiguous space,
"but I have brought you your bouquet of gladiators."

"No," I say,
"but as in the arena of this room,
interrogation is impaled on intimacy: gladiators burst
and metamorphose into the womanly bright remains of our city."

This pediment forfeits nothing; these gladiolus are inextinguishable.
The most brilliant blue eyes obtained by natural means
flare as if in a greeting, herd or flock.
A herd or flock is numerically great.
Is this my gift: the human figure pierced and confessed?
But the sky had altered:

Pierced and splashed, and driven
like the arena of command
drives the volume, line and light
of rooms we enter,

here is a man, some victory;
some victory, though not all of it,
some victory with outstretched arm
like Alexander,
the marble face
with hurtful tools at the deepest level.
"They are afraid of you.
That's why they are so obsequious."

(*The Windows Flew Open*, 1991)

CASTING SEQUENCES

A page dramatically estranged, nor lacking
                                      bombardment out of sync
with the event that
                      annihilated into sudden pianissimo
a few songs.
                Where death is naked to the waist
in radiance,
                and sudden extension
piloted across a vocal line
                          finds an event,
the page lies still, a chaotic catchall of springtime.

Alphabetizing the cards
                        slavishly
the person comes first,
                    in cold blood
and spelled out...
                "pale and enfeebled by the remoteness"
of actuality.
                Of actual number, pale
and spelled in cold,
                a person is impeturbably
alphabetizing cards
                torn from himself,
casting from himself riddle and raven,
                          riddle and reticule.

Mildew
        "of adjacent realities"
and recurrent themes
            and recursive themes,
assisting the physics of a sinking fastball or aerodynamic
stall—speculative,
              half-visible—and all talking at once,
the only such televised
              obliquities in which
the elite and public are exactly coincident
                  and lifted up.
To get livelier,
           to accelerate the unridable lift,
the only such televised praxis, half-visible
                breaking pitches
wince—
      and they all remark on it,
              they all recur
in the slower moving air.

            (*Casting Sequences,* 1993)

KISS TOMORROW GOODBYE

I

Among us are those who apply
dysfunctional tactics to convened ordinariness
of setting, as in certain booby-trapped stories.

For similar reasons,
a narrative complete with lunch menu and
   stereoscopic thugs...,
complete with cigarette yet for all that a narrative clad in
   itself...,
or a ventriloquist and dummy, minus the ventriloquist...,
all threaten the logical unit.

Complete with cigarette
yet disturbing the infinitesimal trash, the depiction,

this ventriloquist set a bowler-hatted dummy
on one knee, served up a twin
on the other.

                 Thus translated,
and torn limb from limb, "naively,"
the rivers ran
and Osiris spread showering selves, showering down
existence after death.

2

Death served up a twin
the rivers ran
limb from limb
trash the depiction
minus the depiction
as in certain booby-trapped stories
for similiar reasons
narrative clad in itself
on one knee
on the other
convened ordinariness
complete with cigarette.

                (*Casting Sequences*, 1993)

SCALPEL IN HAND

I

Let us effect a moratorium on things.

Let us say
an object is not an image, aerodynamically speaking.

Let us say
"Speak, or be silent."

Let us legislate
"the sound elements in a spoken language."

For argument's sake,
let us say the craze for black
may be dazed with shape, size, and color of commodity.

For argument's sake,
the flutter of nearby bleeding does not render a charcoal
    lemon tragic,
although tragedy eclipsed by subject matter
may be eligible for illustration by Grandville;
"an object is not an image."
Say the subtly bled shape does not induce suffering in
    lemons, however
blackened, however centrally massed the putative anguish.
Let us legislate anguish,
let us say "anguish" in unison very loud.
In a spoken language, syllables are extinguished
once gathered by the silhouette dissembling death.

2

In the center, rays from the sun and much still life
denied body, denied pantomime
and yet much language whenever and wherever

land radii. Abstract and sanitary bodilessness.
If no evidence, if no physionomic
ignition, then just what does the author mean?

In conversation with the author, find
a charcoal axis drawn *soto voce,* denied body,
denied yet blurting out whatever unjustly perishable

sacrifice or contingency,
much ostension of cipher
and rays of the sun.

3

An object is not an image,
aerodynamically speaking.
Verblessness in space
reserving passive
rather than active tawdriness
of those sparse
accoutrements in free fall.
In this falling through painted
representation, object and image:
snails versus "snails'
genitals in the form of stars,"
depending on how we construe
the symbolic
vanishing magnitude.
In vanishing magnitude,
the symbolic.
Depending on our construal,
stars in exhaustion
and genitals suspended on a string.
Ephemera, illustrate this.
Free fall, illustrate this,
scalpel in hand,
in an acutely skeptical reading
of the snail incised with dotted
passivity in tawdriness,
the object obsolescent, abject or gone.
When is an object not an object?

(*Casting Sequences*, 1993)

IF I BLINDFOLD YOU

Remnants of counterclockwise.
Remnants of inclement tardiness.

Elephants are equidistant,
are irreversible.

If I blindfold you and take you into the kitchen...
Navigational path

past and present
hyacinth

following a given brawl downstream,
narrating an episode of patrimony.

□

Remnants of tardiness, very sweet.
And soft are remnants of tardiness.

Through the mountain pass came the outermost species,
elephants empowering Hannibal, astride the mountain pass.

If I blindfold you and take you into your kitchen...
While in your familiar kitchen, you could be blind and not
  know it.

Throw one's weight into the scale
of a) associative b) not associative temperatures, be they in
  words, images or diagrams,

following a given brawl downstream,
following it upstream to patrimony.

Impenetrable to others,
those cubical forms in coral.

Because we must add
a chastening bruise

to stark abstemiousness of order, of orders
we assume for a moment the necessity of it

semiparalyzed
or gathered via Ionian shyness

to fall across the porch of incorrigible states
and upon the sentence set within

a song or hymn in praise of gladness:
"Let us wipe away any incapacity in our mark!"

□

Wishing to make metaphysical plaster
Wishing to be a matrix.

To this we must add a chastening bruise
It has come to our attention…a chastening thought

assuming the designation "pain"
to refer to certain prolific

fissures commencing in the present, in presences
of mental states, stageworthy

once paralyzed rather than thought through thoroughly.
Since not given to thought, paralysis prompts our plan

of nonidentical yet necessarily correlated colonnades—
our thickened entities, as with a sentence, our sentence
  in antis

or anthem that wipes away any servility
in the epistemic realm.

(*Casting Sequences*, 1993)

John Godfrey [1945]

RADIANT DOG

Radiant dog on doublecross, and I,
by night, a raven fly. My fear
is that eternity has an alm
that is ordinary to ten thousand
and worn from my strings, my console
of limbs, and I a missing part.
It is the world that's new, not I,
and submarines can shoot the land
from the wheelbarrow of sickly pastorals.
Give me the swamp any day! or the huts
that pave the slave to freedom.
From a small cloud in my ears
the song has leapt the valley
curtained with snow, and for ascendant
harmony the gambler thumbs his cards.
Of all the queens one is a witch
whose curse is that she's held.
The horses roll the stone and trot
after their maturity sweepstakes.
This time the homeliest won't ride
my bet into hasty subtract glue.
The pieces fly and here I lie,
triangle of head and gut and thigh.
Put me on my mount, Tomahawk, and
past the river our cortege will dust
the heavy fur, and peasants' prayers
will touch the smell of holy cadaver.
I will have sun and manly rage,
and Mike Atlas will trim me up
to rip the bier from my brother's
hearse, and avenge me for my loss.
The gallows hurt! and for my scheme
I hang on the bridge's span
where my mother will trust my lips
with tears, the ones I send her now.

(*Dabble: Poems 1966 – 1980*, 1982)

UNHOLY SPRING

Insomniac trees rattle silken little
tongues, emphasis all day-bleached
and charm accompanies vigilance
past fenced park gates for
a circular stoll among *el pueblo bajo*
Your shirt, amigo, should be salmon
and your mustache nurse birdlings
but I am sure you are fruitful
in some other meagre way you daily forget
Balm is the blue sleeve returned
to the sky, and brown people
baring their arms, such candy!
And so much impatience, beneath
char tones of premature boughs
as the spirit climbs, fingers
threatened by boots, and desperate
I walk brittle grass well armed
unweighed by hopeful goblets
My profile conveyed in dust afresh
concedes nothing, as it and light enmesh

(*Dabble: Poems 1966 – 1980*, 1982)

SHOW ME A ROSE

Somewhere does the sky bend into itself
become an integral piece of finity, where
my head regains its shape after whitewater nights

I needs must have a rose, the sick man's reward
I needs, I wants, I never knows, does I?
And roses glow as from pooled forces

and skitter the top card across fish-stained table
You call. You pass. You flush. Allover
comes the dew behind all that rain, blood

invades dessert on the terrace, showing through
clothes, such ladylike things are inspired in me
as ever showered upon membrane cell froth

Think alkaline, speak in tongues from languid attitude
Appear at the end of the crimson serenade

(*Dabble: Poems 1966 – 1980*, 1982)

BATH

The fountain to which we
retire to mix our blood

I knock on her door twice
with elongated tongue

Ultimate more than vivacious
she radiates sparks from her scalp

Fingertips long as candles melt
in all of her flaming crannies

O pine-drop of mine you foresaw
the river coiling around

the streets unto mutation
They dissolve her face in plash

They chase live coals back
to the oyster bed from the sky

11–18–82

(*manuscript*)

REVEILLE

Under mercury light the little pup strives. A sinister shadow ducks under the curb—
I must describe it all over again, it confuses acquiescence into fertility. How it speeds
up the sky and prolongs the night. It is false. It is brilliance in miniature and alludes
to her face.

Miles of cruciform sidewalk. Enticed by magazines that are really radios, odd couples
nag each other as one strays to a window and one to a cellar. They are expansive
because they are small. A tall boy is the man, a short woman is the girl, alarm and its
buffer. Both need more than enthusiasm. How mental is your queen when distur-
bance is the rule! A thousand such couples wave in inert profusion at one figure
across the street. I imagine their kiss, I project passion into strange fittings to make
it confess a hymn that is my song after all.

I simmer in the half-light of a stoop, raising beers under a pompadour on the first
brisk night, pressure more potent than any barometer can read. To see your hand to
the tramp of feet is a way to measure strangers. To feel your hair on my finger
accidentally is common sense, a way of leading you to me as the watch moves. We
return to our bed through the bakery smells of daybreak, sky palling, empty of jets.
The schedule is suspended, then resumes like gray dead hands in the east, and I
want you never to die.

(Where the Weather Suits My Clothes, 1984)

MY MOTHER, LIFE

She came as a falling star to the lakes. She the lithesome virgin not to be turned into
a tree, she who would never dress like a penguin. An original want-not, she believed
in philosophy, but she called it faith. And so her talk entered my lungs and came out
as a call to the unnumerable vessels that are the wives of time.

Then there is the long span of silence. Every totem to acceptance she wore as an
accessory. While the tropic darkened palm wore its microbe haunt she carried a
burdened prose that was barely written, never spoken. She could look and look, and
never imagine the stimulation of the lake when she saw the ocean there, so
unneighboring. The circle of lake and the core of ocean depicted themselves after
every rain, in sunlit rainbow. She had found a complex image that added up. So she
rested, and from her rest I derived my strength.

Consider open accidents of flesh, consider perfection of fur in a cat, consider the curatorial mode of an almost wholly passed age, consider the feeling that has a character it emanates from. The fruit is no more costly than its retrieval, the light it gets is subject to cultivation, the dark it needs is infallibly measured, and then there is cool.

(Where the Weather Suits My Clothes, 1984)

IN FRONT OF A LARGE NUMBER OF PEOPLE

Up my backside a core of charcoal does its slither. I have completed my feast and broke all the glasses. Asteroids of smell crash fearlessly around me, it brings out the soldier in my evil turned-away back.

Despite all my efforts life is if anything bigger than ever. At every stage of its termination. Identify the flower inside the flower using what little knowledge I have of women. To think I have become a naturalist!

I didn't say I would, I said I wish I could sing to you. But mercy isn't my song, nor is it in the birds' employ when they wet their eggs. My address is the month. Out of all the lines at least two are parallel after all so they tend to fix me. My calls have graduated from prayers so that the continuum begins to emerge from the downtown background. My eyes are just as heavy as the light. It is not impossible to accept your fingers across my cheek.

It must be ecstasy to die in action. To think children are afforded this privilege. The sky suddenly comes up real close and your body is on its own in the middle of the whole world. Deboned legs of such a drug are roasting in a room next to the one I am in. Hunters are waiting to be paid. Without the moon things go better. All the heroes come out of the firmament smelling blood.

(Midnight on Your Left, 1988)

WHAT SAY

The NEWS peels off my arms and legs in a wind that doesn't quite hurt. The bubbling sound is my eighth sense which ferments in the yellow spectrum of light. The powers that would have me rubbed-out are just not that kind of powers. I might have been born to swim, undisturbed by frigid stuff, and the hardening of food. What propels me comes strafing down out of great altitudes, clean like many mean things. Considering all of this brings everyone to mind and here I am nearly naked. To soothe myself I imagine a voice that can truly say "I am the River."

Just to walk down that street meant paying out some of your nerve to appear bold going through a hoop made up of your own fingers. I open my arms and run towards the northwest side of the triangle, where a field drops abruptly away from the sidewalk. I reply to the mutterings I hear from below with mutterings of my own. I can understand why you believe anything that enables you to see is magic. You are descended from so many creatures that hid nothing at night.

But I, three bags in hand, and you wouldn't believe who else is around. The rain dropping out of the twilight is the best fruit up and down the avenue. I ruminate that he who has two lives is hard to fit. Then my higher self puts my head down and gets the stuff home dry. I only shake hands with the guy who shakes hands in the jungle, follows the mud path through the bush. The taste of emergency in the mouth that makes it so rewarding when I slow down, slow down, slow down....

And it was haste that brought us together. It was something in our lives that snapped shut like a mouth fishing in the dark. And now it is so hard to remember and to be real at the same time. We meet in streetlight that could be called the color comedy. A lacquered sea that runs against me anyway, so why not?

Headlights proceed what I do. I want something new all the time whatever I do. You take without keeping whatever I do. Action lubricates whatever I do. I water the pillows. I sound cruel. It's a scandal.

(Midnight on Your Left, 1988)

WHAT IT TAKES

Send me jewels from starboard
See to the pendants for my ears
I am dazed by the round thing
I stand on, I walk near
the curb with my eyes
on the white line
where sexy legs cross
O public direction service
of my home avenue!
I sing louder than you
to be heard on a balcony
by a lady of smog

Vultures know I am not dead to rights
I dress as an officer at night
I wear the gray city perfume
that is as garlic to a martyr's sniff
while in vain punks kiss at my heels

What is the difference
between morning and sleep?
Wasteful morning, irresolutely tender
I can ignore the sun
but I remember the night

(*Midnight on Your Left*, 1988)

AIR

Light I don't have slanting through broken walls
My money, it's still mine, dance with me?
Stopping in the fog the wrong address
will kill you every time
I was lost after 399 days
I was around the flames because I was cold
I was around the flames

Your portrait counted in the lottery
The ashes went on the growth
The wind didn't hurt awhile
It's hard to believe but my arms are empty
What did I pay you afterall?
The marks where the bark split on trees
The familiar tone speaking to me
I allow it mockery
It allows me love

Come, come let me now
The apostrophe of dead
is called a voice
Talk of sad rinds on the shoreline
and of hair in cement

(*Midnight on Your Left*, 1988)

ONE OR MORE TOGETHER

She's my lover
Yeah, I cover
her back

I see her
when she's here
I believe

My tongue learns
to suffer
precision

She's asleep
This arm keeps
her close

The other's
the arm that
would smother

I'm so strong
it sings songs
and does not

(*Midnight on Your Left*, 1988)

Alice Notley [1945]

"ALICE ORDERED ME TO BE MADE"

intricate ship

Thing well
in my heart

"Alice ordered me to be made"

Waltz to Repel Invaders

machinery was in use by carving jade

bolts of silk instead of memory

at first they made only small,
ritual chopsticks

old rags to supplement advice

the heartlands and the furniture

the mist tiny human
bloodties study the first
porcelain

throughout the rose
to prominence

       lilaceous bus of the Missouri
or an injury, lights and darks reversed
tend to attract affection, the
shaft of a column constricted part-
tooth to caress in love
a body useful in combination

how could you? and durability
of its figure or timbre or
profane the pardon with
cosmetics over rocks out-
guessing outside the rings,
an act of shocking outskirts

Sound of a word tic waters.
Of certain fabrics surface so
formed, fine hair, downy, any
of several American
gooseflesh. A plain de-
tached window openings.
And saved to be sewn to-
gether. And West Africa
And black. horse. Angle
round

     and tell me the
twist amorphous
flesh or dust to muscle, I
mean if the leaves plant
the Trojan War does the
key wide true does the
pretender smell God?

               Yes.
As the twig is bent
I nestle
to retrace the radiant
puddle of all remarks. Ravish
raw hay thaw the theater
               Preposition
He was presumptuous enough to call
the president by his first name:
lost leaves. I had an impulse to
strike all vaccinations
but I leak too many burning
stars
of human affection

as warriors take position
thousands of them
as leaves and flowers appear in their season
hearts burning to break them
singers without memory
curved sea wandering the wild
hearts
where silver is first begotten
a thing shameful but bringing joy to the enemy
me.
Colorful utter foolishness and utter sense
supposedly work well miracles together.
A miracle: not that the crown jewels
are forbidding, but that per-
sonally who stars

I wicked as a lens or wine or legendary queen

shimmering lets fall a light
tear. Did this every happen?
She who is only a little thing
first. The shining wine and
pleasuring the heart. Divine
salt to lighten the ship, sacro-
sanct, we are all held in a
single honor, light as the
strip. But around my own
shelter and beside my black ship
I think.

   Well.

        A libation to
the divine Dawn, the
lovely-haired flashes, the
inward heart, circle and
spear; the stars have
gone far on their course

        sounds rose
        Dawn rose
        the wearisome goddess
        incessant rose

difficultly wrought iron
storm of
dust rose
the fire's rush

Single one sheer. Bless
darkness and brazen slumber.

 The sea stood apart
rejoicing

 she bewitched her
shining eyes. Shamefastness
and lovely with a veil: pattern–
pierced zone

tears like a dark running

sheer is the heart

my love loves me

Near my father dying in hospital
April 1975

(*Alice Ordered Me to Be Made*, 1975)

THE WHITE PEACOCK

Worthy of a lover have I loved
Childhood, girlhood, river
Glad Ghosts. Have I told you how good
In goodness is something? A flower
Painter chiefly known for peonies
Lies in ascertaining
Where the concealed words are. "He

Was the Pole who'd been faithful all his life
   to one woman:
Any fragile blond with a morbid expression."
Growing as the sun has mounted
Stand on these open Pansies
Kangaroo, The Woman Who Rode Away
In a recognizable chair, with anything—
Life makes them do it to it—
To compare it with, my friend
Which reasons like a mollusk.

(*A Diamond Necklace*, 1977)

WHITE PHOSPHORUS

"Whose heart" "might be lost?" "Whose mask is this?" "Who has a mask,
& a heart?" "Has your money" "been published, been shown?" "Who can &
can't breathe?" "Who went" "to Vietnam?" ("We know who died *there*")
"This was then" "Is now." "Whose heart?" "All our heart" "the national
heart" "Whose mask?" "has its own heart?" "A mother's" "mask"
"Whose money" "do we mean?" "A woman's money" "Woman's money" "Who

went" "to Vietnam" "& just died of it?" "A son" "Evolved"
"a man" "evolved" "a woman" "into America" "into the" "just before now"
"It was just before now..." "When men made the forms" "& women made the
Air" ("& now no one does that, & who can breathe now?") "Who cares, in the
Air?" ("All *our* poems, women's were there," "there, too invisible" "and
now" "become male" "acceptable") "Accepted." "And they're welcoming us"

"among" "their forms" "among their forms only" ("what forms might we
have made?" "which ones did" "we make?") "Whose heart is lost?" "oh not
mine, & not my darling's" "Or only our whole heart?" "not mine, & not my
warrior's" ("has your money" "been accepted?") "And this is what happened,"
"he went to a war" "old style, he went" "to that war" "No one cared"
"that he went there" "as no one cared" "what was lost" "with our air"

"no magnanimity" "to an enemy" "no feeling for what" "is invisible" "for
magnanimity" "for what's lost" "to air, in air" "As if nothing
replaced chivalry, not something" "invisible" "but nothing." "No one
cared" "what was lost" "with our air" ("All the forms were already"

"men") ("politics, a man" "philosophy, a man; a building a" "painting a"
poem, a man" "science, a man") ("Now, we can all" "be men") "This

is what happened." "She is a mother." "This is what happened."
"or she could be a lover" "or a sister" "This happened" "Find green air
green breath" "Later, he tries to become" ("did he become") "air,
air, as again" "This is what happened. And she's trying" "to breathe"
("the mother") "And she's trying to wash" "to wash off" "America"
"from herself" "but what" "is a mother" "now?" "In America,

everyone is else" ("else" "aside" "aside from their" "whole heart
has crumbled") ("take your own small heart, own heart & go")
("& breathe" "try to breathe") "Who is she? and who" "is he?"
"Whose mask is this?" "Whose heart might be lost to the" "bigger heart"
("not his nor hers but") "whole country of heart" "might be lost"
"to the bigger heart" "biggest heart" "heart of the universe" "heart that

might not give it back" ("we maimed" "another, a native land, we"
"helped maim another") "Please" "give it back" "Give us our heart,
whose" "heart might be lost."

□

"Air" "What that's real" "happens in air?" ("She wasn't pure dream")
"Air full of us, full" "of live soul, live" "of the dead & the
living" "Thinking & talk" "Play, dream & merging" ("She's active,
& working") "What's real" "is war" "they say" "some say" "some say,
war is" "the only" "reality" "The warriors mistake war for" "reality,
the reality" "Because they pierce" "the centers" "the physical centers"
"of each other" "Addicted to this?" "Addicted" "& our govenment
of men" "organizes" "this addiction" "in the guise of, protecting us all"
"All of us part of it" "part of" "this addiction" "protector, protected"

"And when he came back" "from Nam" "at first" "he wanted" "to go back"
"back there, was it where" "he belonged now? war?" "He wanted"
"to go back" "into the bush" "'where I belonged'" "And then later"
"that's exactly" "where he was, in his head" "years later, he was back there"
"in his head" "where everything" "everything" "had happened." "He had
a family" "but he'd" "fought families" "He had a family" "he'd been
made to" "fight families" "How can we" "compete" "with that?" "Pierced
their physical" "centers" "pierced" "Is that" "the only" "reality?"
"How can we compete with" "that?" "How can we" "have him" "back?"

"Can't he come back?" "Fifteen years later" "Can't he come back?"
"Years after" "he'd left" "Vietnam" "Can't ever come back" "Can't ever"
"His soul" "soul" "He couldn't believe" "that had been he?" "he
couldn't have" "lived through that," "done that, in Nam?" "And in his
soul" "he hadn't done that" "no" "And in his soul" "he hadn't"
"And his memory self" "went back there, went back" "constantly in dreams"
"How can we" "compete with" "that?" "They finger our souls"
"for their addictions" "we let them, we comply" "After 15" "years,"
"he said he'd been used" "We were talking, talking, in green & blue air"

"He was very" "nearly back" "nearly back" "We were (four of us)" "sitting
on grass" "This moment will last" "last forever" "lying down" "I was
lying" "beneath" "tall trees" ("like Nam, he'd said," "without elephant
grass") ("he said it was where he" "needed to be" "Outside, in the
trees" "behind the rehab") "we & he" "very nearly home." "But
he was dying, already" "dying" "nearly home" "dying of dying of" "what"
"will answer the call of" "I think it is something like, gravity"
"will die, of the Furies" "but will die" "of a pull" "from the center"
"of the earth" "& from the sky" "Or will die" ("most honorably") "of

something like power" "Power, become his, & so powerful" "Something
I've felt before" "flooding & pulling" "Can't you feel it? I've felt it"
"He's dying" "of his power" "Go" "He came home & died" "Go" "Power
of, power of" "forgiving" "forgiving himself for so much" "It took too
much power & he died" "He died of that, power of that."

□

"Who is the one who's" "behind the mask?" "mother," "first one"
"Who is that nature of ours?" "What have we done" "Bring her home" "she
should be freed" "by us" "bring her home" "He is covered in white,
fresh flowers" "at home" "He's innocent, now" "& now, we won't"
"let *her* come home," "let someone be her" "won't let one be that"
("who is she") "first mother, & only" "& one who lives" "a spreading
life, not a" "job, not" "doing what no one needs" "doing it for
the unseen," "Who is she?" "& Not just music (& not" "just poetry")
"Afraid" "of a mother" "afraid" "afraid of what has no currency"
"The last of what" "has no currency."

"It takes so long to free him" "no light loves are left" "freeing a
soldier from guilt" ("frees himself") "But she can't be free, exactly"
"No place for a mother no" "place for a full-time" "person is left"
"*Everyone's* just like a soldier" "everyone fights, everyone works"

"For the army of money we guess" "Slave to a faceless" "our country is
unthinking soldier" "money the" "uniform government texture of air,
army of money" "Everyone says it, don't they" "& So" "& so there's no pity"
"& only, mathematics" "a mother's no currency" "grief is what filters"
"filtering out my light loves" "my tolerance for" "Money is numbers
dead bodies are numbers" "dead veterans are numbers like

hours we've worked" "country of numbers" "mother of numbers"
"your child will be numbers" "mother of numbers" "your lover is
numbers, walking the numbers" "to numbers of hours worked, for salary
of numbers" "working for" "Father of numbers." "& She"
"Mother Nature" "Without Father Nature" "Father Nature mostly dead"
"thousands of years" "Mother Nature will become" "Mother of Numbers:" "Says I
sent you my" "sent you" "my self" "I sent you my self" "you said,
'there's no self'" "my love & you called me too selfless" "I
sent you my self & you asked for a form you could recognize" "a
dollar a number—or painting or book" "by a man-like

woman" ("as good as a man") "But my one
my soldier is dead, my" "one who was numbered" "I sent you my self
was it he" "he was part" "The body-counts" "remember" "remember them"
"they" "wouldn't let him" "they wouldn't count" "ones he killed not
in uniform" "& you, you don't count the" "ones not in uniform" "the
child the mother" "& you don't count me" "what I do; for I" "send you
my self" "all I have" "I will" "put on this mask" "put back on my mask"
"Streaked with dirt" "I have made my own mask" "faint pieces of money"
"faint numbers & words" "And I have a mask" "to wear" "for you"
"I wear this mask, but"

"leaks" "skin of the planet" "leaks" "leaks" "white phosphorus"

□

"Flowery mantle." "Homeric sacrifice?" "noise of darkness" "fear of
darkness" "now mantle of innocence" "King of his death now" "Home"
"I've come home" "He said, 'I've come home'" "They were sacrificed for
nothing, for distant" "instants of thought" "All for your thinking"
"He said, 'I've come home; I've finally come home' then he died" "flowers"
"Magnolias & lilies" "innocent now" "I've come home. Who's there?
at home? all the dead?" "To come home from the war" "years after" "To die" "To"

wear mantle light honey" "mantle dead white" "in sunlight, in late"
"Homeric?" "he said it was hideous" "all of it" "hideous" "every

instant in Nam" "theatre of worsts" "now mantle of
white" "phosphorus & lilies?" "trees now lean down" "over our faces"
"Tell details of battle?" "As" "in an epic?" "As" "in lies?"
"We don't want that now" "We want only our mother of
dirt" "our mantle of white" "want each other of soul; and"

"we want" "our mother of spirit" ("rich sweet in dirt") "we want"
"our father" "of leaves" "We want our fate fragmented to air for
our children to breathe;" "light on water for widows to think near"
"moonlight on water to ease you" "we want no poet, we want our
homes in the earth" "that's all we can have" "want no place in
history or poetry" "want our wanderings our sorrows, after the war,
not remembered," "we want not

to pain her" "we want our love mingled" "with yours" "no place in
history" "only in love" "remove us from history," "All of us sacri-
ficed" "all for a thought" "They played with our souls." "Used our
souls to fight, be their willfullness" "willfulness" "we were made their
willfulness," "nothing but that—" "And you too, you yielded, one
way or another" "to their will." "They" "who are
the subject" "of all history" "& of poems" "as if"

"we have ever, in all ways" "yielded to them" "by speaking of" "always
speaking of" "Kings" "presidents" "the Great men" "their mistresses"
"Generals" "Communist Kings" "Leaders" "Warriors" "West Point of Greeks"
"West Point of Greeks against" "West Point of Trojans" "Isn't it more
beautiful, under the Earth?" "Or to be sunlight, not history?"
"Now I can love, & only" "now" "Remove us from history but
not from your air" "History is willfulness" "is" "precious parts"

"History's for those" "who ask not" "to be forgiven"
"We ask to be forgiven" "& loved" "No, we ask" "to be absolved"
"And to be" "elemental" "ask leaves & wind"
"Ask leaves bending down towards our faces" "Ask light & dirt" "we ask"
"our children" "we ask our wives" "Ask that they live" "We ask
to be" "with the ones that we killed" "To history" "saying nothing"
"being that" ("nothing") "& to history" "having been" "nothing."

□

"In this moment" "before" "anyone, ever" "died" "before we were born?"
"in this moment forever before" "before we went to a war"
"Before we died" "In this moment, now" "In this moment before, it is

not before" "In this very moment" "where is it" "where we
haven't died" "or died inside" "In this moment we haven't" "in this
moment, no one" "in this moment, no one has ever, died" ("But I have
been born") "in this moment" "where, where is it" "in moment" "who's here"
"Catch it catch it" "moment where we are" "merely as it is autonomous,"

"autonomous moment" "Without a war" "without a guilt,"
"Can we exist" "Outside of what was?" "in the air of our thoughtless,
female, moment" "the air of our moment" "not grievous not iron"
"moment, not air" "but air of our moment" ("woman-made?") "faithful,
faithful & boundless" "reticent & light" "fond, & kindly" "not reticent
but shiny," "morning-starry, not bloody" "not bloody, in the morning"
"in the star" "it is a star" "it is autonomous" "star & it's mild" "Is
it a little" "of us" "from before" "we were born?" ("that was

never") ("I know") "It is now" "autonomous" "moment of white,"
"white flowers, stars & white flowers," "not before we were born, in
this moment our childhood" "have we our childhood" "in
this moment he has his childhood, I think, it is center of"
"moment, of childhood" "center of, moment" "wings of his pigeons" "white
& grey wings" "moment a feathery" "center of senses" "center of
sensation, is this moment" "Center, as sensation falls away"
"He has his love" "this moment" "forever" "center of brown eyes"

"seen through his eyes" "Only through" "the eyes" "the real eyes"
"of the dead" "this moment" "through his eyes" "as child, as
childhood" "Only through" "the personality" "can this be" "of the
dead" "the lovely person" "holding" "this moment" "this moment in
place" "this moment forever" "center of sensation" "Soldiers,
we are center" "of the morning" "we are moment" "we are dearest"
"we are heart" "Soldiers," "we are pleasing" "we are center"
"we are moment" "are not soldiers" "never soldiers" "never were."

□

"Mask now" "is complies" "complies" "with the forms (too much of everything,
everywhere") "All of this is" "the mask" "my mother's mask" "& mine"
"wronglike forms, too many of" "Complying, to live here" "always, more
complying" "Too many things" "machines" "too many" "too many clothes"
"cheap roses" "kleenexes" "membranous" "bags, of plastic" "Too many
ideas" "vocabularies no color" "too many paintings" "too many songs"
"too many Tarot decks" "& poems" "& books" "Too many" "things to eat"
"too many" "machines" "magic machines" "too much magic" "much too much of it"

"Stupor" "distress" "& abandoning of others" "too much news" "news"
"everything" "made the same" "too many names" "too much knowledge"

("knowledge, so endless" "is nothing") "A war" "more news, more
to know about, to know" "Excuse for anger" "indignation" "you can still
keep your money" "know the terms of news" "terms" "& Not be nature"
"don't be nature" "mute" "not knowing the" "terms" "Know what news knows"
"What words know" "Do words know?" "No they don't, only flesh knows only
soul knows" "in the words" "A mask is rigid" "on warm flesh on
dreaming mind" "on fleshly mind" "rigid" "But my brother now is
nature, pure nature" "however that be" "Or I have dreamed so" "Owl,
not an albatross" "He's an owl," "not an albatross" "I have twice"
"dreamed that Al" "is an owl" "intricate with" "feathers" "texture of

thousands of feathers" ("I've seen" "an owl" "only in" "a museum") "Owl,
I didn't know him, I searched" "the owl's face for its" "identity"
("Al died later" "that day") "grey owl great grey owl" "wisdom, & war"
"Master of nights (Al's terrible" "nightmares") "He rose up, finally
as an owl" "Is he owl?" "Where is owl now" "I've never seen one" "I
later" "dreamed after" "I'd realized" "Owl was Al" "that he was a" "snowy owl"
"white, with black spots" "A man said," "he's not an albatross"
"Owl, not an albatross" "Al" "whom I have seen" "also seen in a
small" "waking vision" "standing, in his living room" "wearing
a white mantle, flower mantle a" "mantle" "of fresh, white flowers"

"petals, like feathers" "white petals" "white feathers" "a cloak
of nature of" "purity" "of purification" "wilder, milder, he is
nature" "he is better mind" "My brother" "is owl" "Athena-like" "wise"
"I know things only" "this way" "My brother" "is Owl."

                                                        (*Homer's Art,* 1990)

Diane Ward [1956]

APPROXIMATELY

meaning a context or vision to confer with this which could be a book.
meaning what I just said confers with this but a licking sound.
Amplified and forming an idea far from original.
A distance which becomes whimsical tension.
For instance, then an origin, an image a fantasy becomes ironic; at home.
Flat as you once thought a centering unlike mysteries in your imagining
an animal.
Difference in eye levels.
Difference in relation and system.
Elevating a problem in placement or face and in which direction.
A metal square gradually marked.
A metal square which is confrontational engaging.
Off into intensity which is hard to concentrate.
Two of the spaces of words with their own containment each
of eighty directions.
Two aesthetics granting activity value without practical functions.
Following the implied direction of possessions, environment is a room
more specific a person.
You said something visual versus a thought you were attacking.
You said change/cigarettes versus intimate intricate and which is more
interesting.
Later a time motions are visual or visualizations which translate objects
into words.
A mass of timid outlines to each rigid color.
A mass of smiles destroys a given warmth.
Without only a loneliness to cherish.
More specific a conversation hopefully beginning now.
More specific the toxic and poison contributed to a phrase now dated and
like a date benign.
Respectable ideas are random, laying low or following up so forget what I
just said or I think.
Impossible only an advancing of thoughts their elements and results.
No worth for what they're saying or value exists for this.
It's fine that it brings tears to your eyes or doesn't.

It's probably fine that what moves you is below you or not above you.
Formulas to constrict imagination to a mind what it's saying thinking and
what you want its direction.
For this there's an age to define as urgent as people.
For this habit a catchy title like *musings handfuls*.
More points exist around which become you than are not.
Ends based on emotional gusts; the hands are yours that wish to hold.
Ends as a pivotal screen viewing concealed metaphors for beauty.
What the question value in days formulated frequent written
words weeks.
I don't know an arching sounding around us.
I don't know where movements standing pointing as vacuum.
Where the word which wasn't interesting belongs as redefinition.
Where speed replaces the idea and becomes it.
Internal is categorically beautiful bombing as we expected them
whose sentences erupt up and fall.
Headlong, concrete piece by concrete piece a sight or irrational pleasure.
Heading away to detail and immediacy.
Another form is untouchable and moves a cage into softness.
A wooden syntax of shadow forms a pillar of its own.
A highly syntax confusing both image and word and detail and notation.
A shape which is rounded off so that corners fall away.
Blank and another ordering attention paying off.
Blank intensity stares.

(*Never Without One*, 1984)

SHAKEOUT

some without remote interview
capabilities, say yes.
Lovers are reminded with-
out discipline, clash.
Stutter, grab, allow me
to include you in
my frenetic vision.
Titles for pensivity,
postures repetitive
reveries indicators.
Hang your head and flow

in inaccurate linear
directions to there
& there & here, closely.
Messing around with
a fractionally mental whiz
past so undertake great
crashing final fun.
My presence strains will
endure even this,
formal countenance.
All I remain is precedence
great jovial shuffle.
A monument enhancing
benefits deterioration.
A curving insistence
places you as if
in traffic, that
mind of its own.

(*Never Without One*, 1984)

TABLES IN PICTURES

for Phyllis Rosenzweig

Starting at the center
out, edges contain nothing.
Nothing falls out
of radiating compositions.
"I like wine" the green
bottle's glow. Emerald
green, money-color. Real ink
won't rub off.
Four tiny pinpoints (FLASH)
the redundant effect of
ill-defined light source—
out of sight. Your gaze
goes down darkly, a hand
holds the opposite's
wrist just above the wrist

watch. There's no longer
a Victorian bust. Nor a way
women hunker down to
get things done. There's
a table. An object
holding conflicting associations:
(birth/death) operate write confer and
eat. (birth/death) solitude company.
Manners, dressing, work. There there
each time. At the table and/or
across the room.
What will be in and be in focus.

(*Relation*, 1989)

ABSOLUTION

My arms are given
clean away, heaven forgiven.

I live in arms, touched
by sentence, treble up, sentence.

Reaching out across the states,
statements, clear mess of states.

If my fingers were longer, if central,
south, north, if we.

Set free a fortune by taking up
arms, each man must, each woman...

Purge us of touch, including you,
the weight of emotion above.

I see my feet: footsteps; arms:
touched by delivery, destination.

I suppose I love that too, and you
in a formal setting, deep-heating.

And where, apart from us, motioning
away from us, gesture, come here.

It's gone. They were my arms–
reach within my arms-length.

It's not an airplane, not a part
of me. The motion, not the ocean, comprehended.

This is absolutely untrue. Within
my arms I have. I don't have you.

(*Relation*, 1989)

LIMIT

at the end of delight, one
who or that which revolves

more than chests have
to heave "...where gold,

dirt, and blood flow
together"! : margins

the family, not personal
fallibility leads

to instrumentality
in self-restraint

the scale of dignity
has no tears, and yet

I have no elevated
language for the moving

staircase, its components
denying *to begin* and *to end*

relentless and no language
for my body that jerks short

every floor submits ardently
physicality is me

(*Relation*, 1989)

RE-VERSE

(May – September 1991)

    sensing the next
    latitude grown heavy
    through heavy metals
    fuschia sunsets
    extremities to the elegy

    indifference to difference
    bent on flowing toward
    as an indescribable other
    digital interloper
    the blue hour's
    birth of commerce

□

    its surface passes
    indentation corresponds
    to the background
    the head-like in our town
    deviate and focus

given it's market-driven
within ditties
protruberance heightens the jinx
chairman : doorman(person)
curl up! we'll change the nets
the vertebral column it takes
to act back

□

the profile confirms your face
in skeptical spaces
create a California
no succor toward below
suction off

a half face of 3 seconds
assenting hierarchy
shut down in slender town
bedlam communities
the incentive to

□

broad pink hairy hands
hold the waxy face
the cloth away
from the neck

accelerate to penciled stops
cry out specific sites
sleep in altogether primer
the commotion's distance in me

□

survive as if in two
as windows in the desert
air waves
water from the moldy jar
sidelong and living

melt away to a singular fence
no uprights, apertures, no placement
I, willing to oscillate
arid and unlike the body's
loamier life

□

one bell left in the phone
my own atmosphere
is more like a cylinder
shoulders flow up in turn
we don't meet community hours
we know you're keeping track

noxious clouds on the horizon
same blue gray everyday
now war *is* like tv:

inversion presses down
the hills' perspective disappears
until you forget they were
what was ever there

(*Imaginary Movie*, 1992)

CROSSING

thought bounded
rigid edges glued
this voice calls

Imagine doom partitioned off from this discharge, peripheral
object slides away off taunting the fringe. Never secured as
never named. A view fixed in your reflection can't contain you.
The farthest figure possesses no shoes but walks anyway, walking
through the room, sliding along the chair, falling in
conversation with your reflection. And touches you in all
tenderness, serious. Prices get fixed, you remain. Adamant in
all the confident extremity. Pay yourself strict lip service.
Disadvantages are sealed to your lips. A release rimming like
epoxy around the brink of judgment. In articulation, desire
commands utterance, words crawl to the surface. You're going to
be a wheel someday, ringing the world in all its lace-like
response as it floats thoughtless checking out the view, you.
What you've created is strictly limit. You've contained the
upper hand right up to the center, the ultimate tip.

□

indicate hands
grown slow in sound
crush itself

Speed marked by duration, bodies crammed narrow into the night.
Individual gestures so tight, left-handed forefinger raised
painfully toward the upper lip, name delivered up and gone. I
must have said this before: face-to-face germination, deliver me
from penmanship, many many opportunities. Dense deceleration, a
gesture beyond vision long long delayed. Blaring in tedious
silence, a flawless rift in the sound, sleep without beat,
reverberation felt inland and crammed into consciousness to
denote sensible damage and solid desire. Any failure now has the
tenor of natural selection. Any lucid selection now is pulped
into crowded process. We wished we weren't real and tried for
consummation. Failure's pristine echoes of continuity. Fate has
it our fingers are intact, an arhythmic crack.

(Abacus magazine, 1990)

Escaping on a word, for air....
—CLARK COOLIDGE

My name, my name / is hers....
—MICHAEL DAVIDSON

*The mountains have climbed / for a little
recreation behind hermeneutics,*
—DOUGLAS MESSERLI

Just south of the meaning is the / interpretation.
—NICK PIOMBINO

Robert Creeley [1926]

TO AND

To and
back and forth,
direction
is a third

or simple fourth
of the intention
like it
goes and goes.

No
more snow this
winter?
No more snow.

Then what replaces
all the faces,
wasted,
wasted.

(*For Love*, 1962)

SONG

What I took in my hand
grew in weight. You must
understand it
was not obscene.

Night comes. We sleep.
Then if you know what

say it.
Don't pretend.

Guises are
what enemies wear. You
and I live
in a prayer.

Helpless. Helpless,
should I speak.
Would you.
What do you think of me.

No woman ever was,
was wiser
than you. None is
more true.

But fate, love, fate
scares me. What
I took in my hand
grows in weight.

(*For Love*, 1962)

THE INVITATION

If it ever is
as it will be,
then enough is
enough. They

think in clusters
round the interminable
subject all but
lost to my mind.

Well, here I am,
they say, together.
Or here you are,
them, and it.

Let's build a house of
human pieces, arms
and hair, not telling
any one. Shout

from the feet, face
facts as accumulations,
we can
do it.

Or and, and as
it's done, what flesh
can do, home again
we'll say,

we'll fall down streets
rolling,
balls
of clear substance.

(*Words*, 1967)

THE TURN

Each way the turn
twists, to be apprehended:
now she is
there, now she

is not, goes, but
did she, having gone,
went before
the eye saw

nothing. The tree
cannot walk, all its
going must
be violence. They listen

to the saw cut, the
roots scream. And in eating

even a stalk of celery
there will be pathetic screaming.

But what we want
is not what we get.
What we saw, we think
we will see again?

We will not. Moving,
we will
move, and then
stop.

(*Words*, 1967)

THE LANGUAGE

Locate *I*
love you some-
where in

teeth and
eyes, bite
it but

take care not
to hurt, you
want so

much so
little. Words
say everything.

I
love you
again,

then what
is emptiness
for. To

fill, fill.
I heard words
and words full

of holes
aching. Speech
is a mouth.

(*Words*, 1967)

FOR W.C.W.

The rhyme is after
all the repeated
insistence.

There, you say, and
there, and there,
and *and* becomes

just so. And
what one wants is
what one wants,

yet complexly
as you
say.

Let's
let it go.
I want—

Then there is—
and,
I want.

(*Words*, 1967)

THE WINDOW

Position is where you
put it, where it is,
did you, for example, that

large tank there, silvered,
with the white church along-
side, lift

all that, to what
purpose? How
heavy the slow

world is with
everything put
in place. Some

man walks by, a
car beside him on
the dropped

road, a leaf of
yellow color is
going to

fall. It
all drops into
place. My

face is heavy
with the sight. I can
feel my eye breaking.

(*Words*, 1967)

THEY

I wondered what had
happened to the chords.
There was a music,

they were following
a pattern. It was
an intention perhaps.

No field
but they walk
in it. No place

without them, any
discretion is useless.
They want a time, they

have a time, each
one in his place, an
endless arrival.

(*Words*, 1967)

THE HOLE

There is
a silence
to fill. A
foot, a fit,

fall,
filled. If
you are
not careful all

the water spills.
One day
at the lake I took

off my bathing
suit

in the water,
peed
with pleasure, all
out, all

the water. Wipe
yourself, into
the tight
ass paper is pushed. Fatty

Arbuckle, the one
hero of the school,
took a coke bottle,
pushed it up his girl.

But I
wouldn't dare,
later,
felt there,

opened
myself.
Broken glass,
broken silence,

filled with screaming,
on the bed
she didn't want
it, but said, after,

the only time
it felt right. Was
I to force
her. Mother,

sister, once
seen, had breasts.
My father
I can't remember

but a man
in some building,
we were all swimming,
took out his

to piss, it
was large. He was
the teacher.
Everywhere

there is pleasure,
deep,
with hands
and feet.

I want
to, now I
can't wait any
longer. Talk

to me, fill
emptiness with
you, empty
hole.

(*Words*, 1967)

"RIVER WANDERING DOWN..."

River wandering down
below in the widening green
fields between the hills—
and the sea and the town.

Time settled, or waiting,
or about to be. People,
the old couple, the two babies,
beside me—the so-called

aeroplane. Now
be born,
be born.

(*Hello,* 1978)

TALKING

Faded back last night
into older dreams, some

boyhood lost innocences.
The streets have become inaccessible

and when I think of people,
I am somehow not one of them.

Talking to the doctor-
novelist, he read me a poem

of a man's horror, in Vietnam,
child and wife lost to him—

his own son sat across from me,
about eight, thin, intent—

and myself was like a huge,
fading balloon, that could hear

but not be heard, though we
talked and became clear friends.

I wanted to tell him I was
an honest, caring man. I wanted

the world to be more simple,
for all of us. His wife said,

driving back, that my hotel's bar
was a swinging place in the '50s.

It was a dark, fading night.
She spoke quickly, obliquely,

along for the ride, sitting
in the front seat beside him.

I could have disappeared, gone
away, seen them fading too,

war and peace, death,
life, still no one.

(*Hello*, 1978)

THE HOUSE

Mas-Soñer
Restaurat—Any—
1920...Old
slope of roof,

gutted windows,
doors, the walls,
with crumbling stucco
shows the mortar

and stones
underneath. Sit
on stone wall adjacent
topped with brick,

ground roundabout's weeds,
red dirt, bare rock.
Then look east
down through valley—

fruit trees in their rows,
the careful fields,
the tops of the other
farmhouses below—

then the city, in haze,
the sea. Look
back in time
if you can—

think of the
myriad people
contained in this instant
in mind. But the well

top's gone, and debris
litters entrance.
Yet no sadness,
no fears

life's gone out.
Could put it all right,
given time,
and need, and money,

make this place sing,
the rooms open
and warm, and spring
come in at the windows

with the breeze—
the white blossom
of apple
still make this song.

(*Later*, 1979)

THE EDGE

Long over whatever edge,
backward a false distance,
here and now, sentiment—

to begin again, forfeit
in whatever sense an end,
to give up thought of it—

hanging on to the weather's edge,
hope, a sufficiency, thinking
of love's accident, this

long way come with no purpose,
face again, changing,
these hands, feet, beyond me,

coming home, an intersection,
crossing of one and many,
having all, having nothing—

Feeling thought, heart, head
generalities, all abstract—
no place for me or mine—

I take the world and lose it,
miss it, misplace it,
put it back or try to, can't

find it, fool it, even feel it.
The snow from a high sky,
grey, floats down to me softly.

This must be the edge
of being before the thought of it
blurs it, can only try to recall it.

(*Mirrors*, 1983)

FATHERS

Scattered, aslant
faded faces a column
a rise of the packed
peculiar place to a
modest height makes
a view of common lots
in winter then, a ground
of battered snow crusted

at the edges under
it all, there under
my fathers their
faded women, friends,
the family all echoed,
names trees more tangible
physical place more tangible
the air of this place the road
going past to Watertown
or down to my mother's
grave, my father's grave, not
now this resonance of
each other one was his, his
survival only, his curious
reticence, his dead state,
his emptiness, his acerbic
edge cuts the hands to
hold him, hold on, wants
the ground, *wants* this frozen ground.

(*Memory Gardens*, 1986)

MEMORY GARDENS

Had gone up to
down or across dis-
placed eagerly
unwitting hoped for

mother's place in time
for supper just
to say anything
to her again one

simple clarity her
unstuck glued
deadness emptied
into vagueness hair

remembered wisp that
smile like half
her eyes brown eyes
her thinning arms

could lift her
in my arms so
hold to her so
take her in my arms.

(*Memory Gardens*, 1986)

STAIRWAY TO HEAVEN

Point of hill
we'd come to, small
rise there, the friends
now separate, cars
back of us by
lane, the stones,
Bowditch, etc., location,
Tulip Path, hard
to find on the
shaft, that insistent
rise to heaven
goes down and down,
with names like floors,
ledges of these echoes,
Charlotte, Sarah,
Thomas, Annie
and all, as with
wave of hand I'd
wanted them one
way or other to
come, go with them.

(*Windows*, 1988)

THE COMPANY

for the Signet Society, April 11, 1985

Backward—as if retentive.
"The child is father to the man"
or some such echo of device,
a parallel of use and circumstance.

Scale become implication.
Place, postcard determinant—
only because someone sent it.
Relations—best if convenient.

"Out of all this emptiness
something must come…" Concomitant
with the insistent banality, small, still
face in mirror looks simply vacant.

Hence blather, disjunct, incessant
indecision, moving along on
road to next town where what waited
was great expectations again, empty plate.

So there they were, expectably ambivalent,
given the Second World War
"to one who has been long in city pent,"
trying to make sense of it.

We—*morituri*—blasted from classic
humanistic *noblesse oblige*, all the garbage
of either so-called side, hung on
to what we thought we had, an existential

raison d'être like a pea
some faded princess tries to sleep on,
and when that was expectably soon gone,
we left. We walked away.

Recorders ages hence will look for us
not only in books, one hopes, nor only under rocks
but in some common places of feeling,
small enough—but isn't the human

just that echoing, resonant edge
of what it knows it knows,
takes heart in remembering
only the good times, yet

can't forget whatever it was,
comes here again, fearing this
is the last day, this is the last,
the last, the last.

(*Windows*, 1988)

AGE

Most explicit—
the sense of trap

as a narrowing
cone one's got

stuck into and
any movement

forward simply
wedges one more—

but where
or quite when,

even with whom,
since now there is no one

quite with you— Quite? Quiet?
English expression: *Quait?*

Language of singular
impedance? A dance? An

involuntary gesture to
others *not* there? What's

wrong here? How
reach out to the

other side all
others live on as

now you see the
two doctors, behind

you, in mind's eye,
probe into your anus,

or ass, or bottom,
behind you, the roto–

rooter-like device
sees all up, concludes

"like a worn–out inner tube,"
"old," prose prolapsed, person's

problems won't do, must
cut into, cut out…

The world is a round but
diminishing ball, a spherical

ice cube, a dusty
joke, a fading,

faint echo of its
former self but remembers,

sometimes, its past, sees
friends, places, reflections,

talks to itself in a fond,
judgemental murmur,

alone at last.
I stood so close

to you I could have
reached out and

touched you just
as you turned

over and began to
snore not unattractively,

no, never less than
attractively, my love,

my love—but in this
curiously glowing dark, this

finite emptiness, *you, you, you*
are crucial, hear the

whimpering back of
the talk, the approaching

fears when I may
cease to be me, all

lost or rather lumped
here in a retrograded,

dislocating, imploding
self, a uselessness

talks, even if finally to no one,
talks and talks.

(*Windows*, 1988)

BODY

Slope of it,
hope of it—
echoes faded,
what waited

up late inside
old desires

saw through
the screwed importunities.

This regret?
Nothing's left.
Skin's old,
story's told—

but still touch,
selfed body,
wants other,
another mother

to him, her
insistent "sin"
he lets in
to hold him.

Selfish bastard,
headless catastrophe.
Sans tits, cunt,
wholly blunt—

fucked it up,
roof top, loving cup,
sweatered room,
old love's tune.

Age dies old,
both men and women cold,
hold at last no one,
die alone.

Body lasts forever,
pointless conduit,
floods in its fever,
so issues others parturient.

Through legs wide,
from common hole site,
aching information's dumb tide
rides to the far side.

(*Selected Poems*, 1991)

Hannah Weiner [1928]

from LITTLE BOOKS / INDIANS

LITTLE BOOKS 137   SILENCE   MAR 22 79

HENRY THE GRANDFATHER
BOYS WE LEAVE
I DONST BELIEVE
HIM SOON
I have a terrible
time struggling
with it
MARY CROW DOG HITS HARD
SITS US IN SILENCE SISTER

I spoken to Mary
on the phone
and written it is
Hannah its very hard
FORGIVEN
to live with Indians

I said written it is
boys are we scolded
this is his book
and it has pictures
in it
I wants to hear it
in my silence
stupid
    CHILDISH

Hannahs Ive
written it in
boys we love
sequence next
boys we are hard
it is written it in
last line next page

Hannahs we may
meet in May
sentence
ins silence
play it hard
thas enough

ENOUGH
Hannah it is
written it in
already it is
the boys know
that we
    AGAIN
I said scolded
JIMMIE

STOP THINKING OF IT
Hannah its the
sound first
its original
WE KNOW IT
before it happens
   3 YEARS MOST
stupid
HANNAH THATS CLEAR

Hannahs we must
learn it forever
it is written its
and we hides
    itself
Hannahs I have
learned too much
already
    HINT

I donst think it
really funny
that he
    FORGETS
Hannah skips poem
Hannahs handle

me directly
that means aloud
nos it doesnt
Hannahs it must
learn something else

He is writing
it is in ENGLISH
Grandson is listening
to it
describe your scene
WITH THE BOYS
I SAID LEARN
we are speaking
of knowledge of course

HANNAH ITS SIMPLE
theres big trouble
in South Dakota
and we are forbidden
to enter here
unless he asks
me directly
THATS WHY We DELAY

Hannah its a
horrible sentence
not another year
in jail
we pray hard
Mary does
WE WINS

Son is speaking
to us in our
silence dear
stupid
ands we listen
Hannahs youre
VERY HUNGRY

Grandson is just
SILENCE

a little   like us
ANDS MEANS
we walk together
because of the
DONT SPEAK

POWER IS HIDDEN
SOMETIMES
thats his own theory
BECAUSE IT HURTS
ands in silence
TRUNGPA

We learn
Hannah its obvious
isnt it
DONST SPEAK
its our knowledge
correctly spelled
Hannah Im frightened of it
Hannah it is our
knowledge we
hold it in our silence

GRANDSON IS VERY HARD ON US AGAIN
and we learn
SKIP 2 PAGES

Hannah that means we hold
our knowledge in common

thats Jimmie
he is very hard
Son
     SEQUENCE
is playing very
hard on us
MAKE IT OBVIOUS
and it hurts
Trungpa says

Hannah we cant
HEAVY PAGE

survive without
our secret
knowledge
Hannah handles
it in her silence
SO DOES GRANDSON
forget the rest
THAS A HINT
GURUS SPEAK
LAST PAGE PLEASE

thats how the son
teaches us
NEXT PAGE PLEASE

TOOTS STOP WRITING IT IN

end of sentence
THIS BOOK IT IS
   ENDED
AND SPOKEN TO IT
  SIGNED

SECOND POEM FOLLOWS THIS

SKIP TWO PAGES

HANNAHS HE SITS STILL THERE
THAT ENDS THIS POEM STUPID
AND CLOSED
SIGNED BOOK
SPEAKS TO MARY
SECOND POEM FOLLOWS

SILENT TEACHER

(*Little Books/Indians*, 1980)

from SPOKE Aug 19

SEEN WORDS

We Went Westward   o social telepathy at the
                                                    1 0 CLOCK
in the afternoon Brown cramped style university swimming

pool   o construction feeling campus   o second sentence   I

was remembered as I opened this book   sent   hieroglyphics

werent so easy to read either or supposed either or limit

sundance Aug 15 was closed date closing at the scene   I

was swimming in it at the pool
                              AND SEE WORDS
over the hill oh sometime myname I was delivered from it

eventually so I went broke and sick at the hospital re$_{co_{r_d}}$
                CONSTRUCTION

I was darling it hurts to read
                the words in the
                              inset

o silent being   o prose continue   I was a trouble shooter

backwards anyway so I didnt miss my Wednesday afternoon nap

but lay down in the grass my aunt has a different philosophy

myname several people think we're about the weigh in scale

is absolutely comfort white pants perfect and   and dont hold
                                          dont scream
                                    before September
yourself together attheend

for a blue pad and ink   I slimy fingers erased myname

I have a big letter A
WONDERFUL MOTHER
inside the house

with absolutely every thing to calm me down except parlor

sunshine which she craves also in a little ol swimming

pool porch it has to

WEDNESDAY

be set in the backyard or swim set easily in the scratch

pen   I think I was turned also the CONTINUE o so broke

impolited page into the center fold in the swimming pool

slowly infield   Tues is important next week   because

I may leave early   and I gets hot in the swimming pool
     in September
over the Wed night   sis if its hard put the right arm

human condition down for the swimming instructor says stay

calm writing about circle the beach yard and so to read

the book on the right shoulder grass   sis I think we

complained GIVING HINTS about douse the shoulder from

cramps   so the next page is next andclimb
and the resting hole
indeed

the sweater blue is horrible   I wear them long underwear

over the girl underside over the reverse situation on the

underside complex SATURDAY

it was having right shoulder hurts a little fun   when I dont

write alway GLASSES in the fun sun   sis its sorry which is
                                  about Tuesday swimming
the bottle for the name WHO IS IN IT little letters

                                    sincere   ly
                                     yours

myname   who was in the dream last person
             night as cold some people
             study letter writing oh miss I the egg

                  S BE LET T
               O H   E R

oh so to be a letter writer   oh to be glasses instead   oh

to be name impersonal   I should be letter writer   I should

ohs simple as   I should be shename   myname dont hesitate please

            LAST NAME

oh to be in the left hand paragraph   sunges stinks the words

are everlasting   turn the page myname   I was to be simple

writer   I was a coffee conscious   I would drink   I was in

interrupted coffee the drink cup
                         FINISH THURSDAY youre wrong

                          dont substitute your sentences
avoid the pink sweater plural as possible attheend andclear the end

and so the pages finishes andcomplete   MOTHER'S SENTENCE

                                  SILENT TEACHER

                        (*Spoke*, 1984)

REMEMBERED SEQUEL

Clairvoyantly Written   SILENT TEACHER

put in something else like page bonded to a neutrality my brother
arrange quit he was forbidden ordinarily he was quit ordinary like
some quit on the page forgot hannah put me on the page where
I began like book notwithstanding the brother he stood elegantly
someone gladly someone should once twice omitted because he
complete was afraid sentence completed in hungry write another
page complete like brother   symmetry has been condoned before
simple and twice   he complicated some pages like concluded sis
he's a stranger almost

paragraph begins I was almost forgotten reminded myself someplace
recommended his struggle   sis he was twice eliminated from say
writing concluded put it in writing some concludes you were brother
omitted like I was glad two pages eliminated because completed
accordance over controlled without simple sacrifice to make happy
estranger   enjoyment oversized and obedient like him

mother begins a new sacrifice say paragraph complete with omit
sequence and some tough undeniably attractive finish the sentence
an appetite to fight with two said hannah it finishes name publishes without
eliminating subject about brother he said omit providence because next line
please say omitted because you were company forcefully to come to the
conclusion that I was happy the unwavering fondness of make it clear the sea
was the structure complete ended like sentence provided

hannah he struggles without confidence in his upbringing explain
because I was older more confident and glad explain confidence
tighter someplace like say school brother concludes somewhat
confident over his application sis conclude with a page just say
concluded scream at without sentence concluded he was sacrificed
name marries safely important to perform one piano immediately
piano   complete one sentence but scrambled by hand james concludes it was
a tendency to strike put in brother starved   complications
when he was forty weight overloaded like complete sentence like
book aggravated by complete insistence   and complete some tendency
to combine structure overlook clear sentence begins with some
instructions that I received some clear some obvious that when he
took me someplace start a sentence overlooked by otherwise only a
moth prevent   sacrifice continue can perceive continue

james concludes I was forgotten by jokes under surveillance but I
was enjoyed sentence included subject overlooked integrated besides
with some who were close to me by complicated interference twice
recorded and publish forget the irreconcilable and make clear the
imaginable same paragraph some elegant Indians were also with me

sis is said Indians brother ignored and was almost please say Indians were
political and clear like one two concluded included some practical advantage
over say sentence complete advertise white make clear it not too many ways to
hear yourself included alone make sacrifice make clear Indians without
independence struggle to overcome political advantages like white people
have even in their homes   submit this paragraph

james concludes that I was political obvious when political communist clear
almost and divided between anarchists and make comment you were at school
when you became obvious and got fired
for association in the fifties when it was hard to belong communist you were
not committed yourself but you fought like them sis you lost your job and
returned to your home said twenty skip page and paragraph political enough
listen unconsolably to the constant irremovable content let it go and para-
graph ended politics   and make clear

(*Raddle Moon* magazine, 1990)

David Bromige [1933]

from TIGHT CORNERS

He thought it humanity's lot for ever to be persuading a huge rock up a mountainside, & at the top it would roll back down the same side, unaided. Those who would disagree with him were at liberty to remark the beauty of the Alpine meadows, the whiteness of the Eidelweiss, & the unearthly peace of the pauses in this process, but not to deny they had rocks in their heads.

If the workers were alienated, their so-called betters were doubly so. The society in its deadly way dragged on & on & nothing could redeem it short of a spiritual revolution to put men & women in touch with their immediate needs, so that what came to hand would show one where one's head was at. Her guru, whose ruminations these sentences derive from, had performed one final miracle before dying, 30 years ago: he'd willed that no decay should disturb his well-loved form. Now she found herself in Tibet, cutting her guru's hair & fingernails.

An angel stood before him in a vision & told him to catch the next number 67 bus. An inner voice announced it was time to plant the lettuce. On the bus he found a penny. This meant he was going to get money. In the penny a man's face appeared. He was going to be president. It was time to get off. A sound too high for human hearing assured him no birds would be flying today. A flock of birds flew past. This meant war, R,A,W, means war.

The unconscious is a station on the Metro. No trains ever stop there. That's why the platform is so crowded. Whenever he alighted there, he found it all attention. Something obscure was always vanishing, into the tunnel or out of it.

All the most brilliant periods of history flashed before his eyes as the sun glinted up off the sea. He was blinded momentarily & alone with some red & green dots & patches. But something that drummed in his ears reassured him. That was the ocean of his dreams.

Beauty is truth, they say. The boys sauntered up the driveway, & as they went they used their sticks to lop the blossoms off the irises lining it. They were talking about something else.

As it fell out, he fell out of the train he chanced to have caught, & by sheer good fortune landed in a passing river. He was fished out by a couple of picturesque game-keepers who, unable to believe what their luck had brought them, realized he meant nothing to them & left him for dead on the bank. Here an occasional heiress revived him on a mere whim, not knowing what to make of him. Already his will was to make the truth of his life the purely arbitrary.

But expressiveness is a myth: it is only the convention of expressiveness. How cold the real thing can sound.

The streets intersected at right angles. You might say they met. He did one time go through a wall, but that was to avoid the traffic cop. And on each corner, he saw a small semi-circle that meant 90 degrees. When it snows this is no longer visible. Then the man could have traced his steps.

Rosemary is an insidious herb. Its results are quite as predictable as those of alcohol. The twiggy stuff is crumbled between the fingers & it doesn't matter whose, death ensues. There was also the fear of others bumping into him. Now they would put their foot into the rosemary bush.

Higher intelligences are sending messages not to be thoroughly deciphered until the cataclysmic event they would save us from shall occur. They live at the center of the galaxy while human life is on the edge. Lower intelligences too are active, & their messages are looking for some center.

It was in Leo & she was a Leo. It was hot. These men were drawn to her by the power of that conjunction. Would she give them away in September? They were getting to be an irritant. She remembered to hunt for her medication. No-one here-abouts dispensed it. She couldn't dispense with it. Now she was getting warm. It was under the almanac.

(*Tight Corners & What's Around Them*, 1974)

LOG

Fire's here, that won't be forgotten.
Nor will light, & ways to shade it.
The fire too has a stony hearth
to keep it in its place, and keep us safe.
Chairs will not & nor will tables
fade from the mind, walls & roof make shelter
because of cold & wind.
Dispose them in what attitudes one will

if belief seduces you to show the way—
else nothing can appear
in this place that's not this house
where the intermittent ground-beat
of those flames & what they feed on
sounds like wind against an obstacle.

(*Desire*, 1988)

THE POINT

The point is not the point—
the hand that indicates,
attended to, is meaningless,
too familiar to engage—

the barn that's indicated
burns but what of that?
We know wood catches fire.
It's just sensational.

Someone is pointing at the flames—
attention has been caught,
desire ignites—we see ourselves
as someone points them out.

(*Desire*, 1988)

THE LOGICAL POSITIVIST

Has painted his hands blue
to disturb assumptions perhaps
but more credibly, to pass muster
at the costume St. Valentine's party

he attends clad in the same drab
we identify him by in the Philosophy
Dept.'s corridors, & is about to dance
all night with your date, an enthusiast

naive, who finds herself fascinated
by his brusque request for sex & the lake
(after all, mainly ornamental) to stay
calm. Much later, weeping, this beauty

will return to you insisting
she was too young to know
a heel when she held one in her own
pulsing embrace, & that flowers

(for isn't she a dilly) don't open
overnight, an obvious contradiction
given the condition of her corsage.
Either way, reject her or accept her

pathos, he wins. Except
your fantasies can't matter
to him, & so he hasn't
triumphed over you, rendered

ridiculous now in yellow (not
your most flattering color), the necessary
outfit if you want to go as a jingle
(her idea) from an old toothpaste ad.

(She wore yellow too, a knock-out
with eyes of cornflower blue & skin
so fair of hue the feelings
register immediately as the heart

sends blood wherever ordered to.)
Say he undressed her, he undressed
anybody. Told her she didn't exist
per se so she took her costume off.

We sat on the stairs to the cellar,
I didn't know what to do. Later,
(years go by), he was recalled
as a bitter twist in speaking,

a mordant humorist, one of your
pas sourir bespectacled
numbers—he enjoyed a drink
one heard: feel that slide down!

"The basic condition of our ideation
comes to this: universal facticity
vs. hierarchy, but if the latter,
by whom declared?" So at last

we come to *you*, not that I
think it essential to proclaim
the presence of a person in a construct
someone had to make; no, nor conceal.

What they think of me
stays a problem in identity.
The occasion of their fancies
salutes them, but not I.

We laugh at free will trapped
in a mechanical model, unable
to prevent ourselves. Meanwhile,
she marries a third fellow,

has five children, lives in a converted
windmill, & you . . .
were always too young for what occurred,
that's why this burrow was provided

to drag yourself & its remains
into, rare subterranean
ruminant disguised as a suburban
unit in the Year (& what isn't)

of the Irresistible Force.
People pay for answers not questions
around here. This is, it has no, end,
high spirits. Indicating that praxis

wherefrom we abstain: the creation
of just life, for considering the
relation between style & the unfamiliar,
those who have nothing to say

are those who count eventually.
This is the party, no more speechifying,
come as you are, representing
more than you ever dreamed

of witnessing under the Japanese
lanterns to disgraceful strains
the dancers whirl to, upended on the water's
surface, whose depth's not yet decided, never was.

At midnight, out of it
emerges this furious
creature of unfashionable drama
crying "Glorious excess,

uncalled-for arrangements!
It's going to be all right!
It hurts so good! God bless!"
Language lets the ripples lap the edge

then recoil: or recoils;
all instances are final, none
evades decisiveness nor breaks
its circuitry; what else is death to do?

(*Desire*, 1988)

CHOICE

The Way of Geometry

And there are three ways
through the marshes

The Way of Sainthood

Impossible to know
which of the three men
on the deck at sunset

There is the gaze off into the distance
but that is a pose

There are the "marshes"
a regional matter

or a reasonable affair
or as in selecting one
from a basket of gourds

She sang in the bath

Then there is the silver pipe
with a guard or filter on top

The sum of the hypotenuse
The song of the river-horse

Of the three figures, one is
dapper, and faces us

"We waited nine months"
as in "common" or "lot"

His shadow cast against the door
The door somewhat ajar
and the sense of being trapped

A bad time to sneeze
or the seals to go
in the transmission

Who held the camera
or the protractor
She must have been very beautiful

when there were four ways

and he played the piano so thrillingly
This is about setting-out

the deck of cards, the hands and faces
and how it seems night
the light artificial

and something unnamed
though known

as another way, those trees
spindly and profuse
with blue among them

And the triangle
a diamond in the lake

Blue and black at each apex

yet merely dark
at one, the one
beneath the shoe

red to begin with, redder
in that sun

(*The Harbormaster of Hong Kong*, 1993)

EASTWARD HO! A SUCCESSION

This he said to american poetry.

Ad hominem, ad lectorem?

It is alleged he slept in school
and was kept in afterwards.

They shot the mother but the kittens lived.

Word, word, were one by one.

He said he only meant the phrases
to take the place of those unable to attend.

Shot the mother but the kitchen lived.

A picture of a man with eyes shut
reading what appear to be proofs.

Gnashing his teeth. Correct that.

The old man proved his earlier ideas
must be invalid, it was said

by his contradictory behavior.
The man whose cat

curls purring in his lap.
The dictionary upon his table, shut.

The man with a face in his hat.

(*The Harbormaster of Hong Kong*, 1993)

THE EDIBLE WORLD

I

Tourists
Wonder

their ideas
Idea

The huts, streets,
struts

hats, tattoos
like little socks

and stop a little
longer

Wistful
Grateful
to be not one of those

Hemmed, jammed

yet enabled
these ruins
kept up

the bells,
the flowers

the rats

The tourist's ponder
before the next

Cyclopean I
adorns the neck
stuck out for the instance

2

That is the cardinal points
That the disposition of stars
That these systems of high pressure

accommodate

That one can be bent
into the straight

People catlike at the beach
register the next

The eased body
is its mind eased

Glancing up
off the cars
delivering and returning

the goods
destination
generated

Child in the wave
Watched by the parent

That nothing will occur
that hasn't yet

let go the string
when the balloon floats up

(*The Harbormaster of Hong Kong*, 1993)

LINES

repressive desublimation

_____

a child is being eaten

        dark night of the soul

        _____

        currently unemployable

as slight as possible

_____

how much greater then the chance
it will sound authentic

        in a tone of sincerity

        _____

        believed it myself at the time

i sound like you

_____

that's what you think

my forehead's wrinkled my eyes all squinted up

---

poetry is supposed to supply us with a picture

i won't bore you with quotation

---

well what will you use instead

division of labor

---

i write it
i admire it

in the event of a crash

---

you are free to move about the cabin

you're so alienated you don't even know it

---

of course i took it as a compliment

not every trembling hand can make us squeak

———————————————————————

my god wallace your breasts are like mice

save time

————————

kill it

something of the misanthrope

——————————————————

thinks too well of people

to be human is to be a conversation

——————————————————————

i'm doin okay

unemployed and feel useless

——————————————————

but helping keep wages down

(*The Harbormaster of Hong Kong*, 1993, revised)

Clark Coolidge [1939]

THE TAB

mica flask moves layout hasty
bunkum geode olive loin candle
mines repeating sky hot dregs, in cast
lank oiler blocks, hats sink
wig pyrite & hasty troll by the rim

myhrr louvres coinage hovers
the mast glitter planting new bulgers tolling
stained-glass hole of suds, repeater
shaking in salt, mud domes falling
trellis concretion, one green mote

the gas farm on Blue Ledge
pine mist into "darlings" chasten
elevator lap rest to the lead block
chain arrival starting, a silver flight
hunks sharpen up, in the fold of coin

spines bee air tower in azure launch
on streaming hair, slid rock
tipped grind to shelve-cirrus shake-up
pale take-off
shale widens, baking

(*Flag Flutter & U.S. Electric*, 1966)

LEAVING RATTLE BAR

what buck last cattle lap form pits
righting whelm   left lung   gallery imbroglio
to wrist hip bone fin   tiler weeps

swollen   peddle codder   cart weigher
soap long & told   crenulate   enjoin
in rattler   cheese spikes   of nature
cone ladder   rifts   specks

    late rifles   tours
castle grant rack slip   rock main
garnering   kites laugh   flik elderberry
in canyon   remove   the chart a fat
harm   & way in a armor   stapler

    short will chars
bunker am maid   limn file so close
a pack part a mitter   relock
unplate   the globes iron chalk
blend too   so writhe eights   fish
fish had tree threes   clouts
un or louds   blanks   was
material

     maybe lights
go   sable organous cape
trail rip
     siren orange   some
pelt garden snowball lesson
misery turns   buckle   hinges
lob back   correct that   sturb
clay bunker

     lab style scotch timing leader
guides
    so pelt than harm   specks
       sea glancer

owls
  tight

        (*Space*, 1970)

MANLIUS TO COEYMANS

But could it come up into a limestone to correct, teeth
would be slim by comparison. Have to go under the waterfall
for health and a mouth to pour. White powder pile could be
of snow or rock in flake. Seeds that hold all lime in ledge
to grasp.

Step over on that rock while I picture the edge.
Click of brachiopods, passing on by. Tin can candle in
a pottery hole. Asleep in a slot of two feet, pressing.
An angle that's a cleft that's a move, sky slice opening.
Two hands, two feet, a face. You tell me.

Piling up a ladder to down the scree. Meeting a ledge at
the grass. Dipping metal in water, dumb tone. Rain is ice
to a rock.

Nobody's pine. It sounded odd, that it couldn't be seen.
Not a fit time, glancing the rock for. Position, grain
revision.

A copper center to a grey old hill. Dome airs its load.
Viability placenta. Stairs to the Inn via Nose. Come to.
Lime cave rich in ribs. Nodes of excorial abutment.
And you freeze. Then you twirl your knees. Whole mine
in pockets.

The car to a limestone. Pinning eats in cracks. Tub
lined in dripstone. String them to see it. Climb the ladder
to ring your gong. Assent to a flash, and the smoke that
mutes it. Jams it goes. Type up the shells that complete it.
Enter a stone for some air.

And I've sighted the rock I've seen to its remaining.
Active verb, stone, sense against. A pond in a tree.

(*Own Face*, 1978)

ALBUM—A RUNTHRU

I look in that one kind of dwindled. And in this,
look up, a truncheon in my fist, tin pot
on my head, the war. My father, I'm looking at, is my
age then and thin, his pants streak to the ground,
shadows of rosevines His father sits beneath
a cat. Here the shadow has more flavor than my
trains, elbow on livingroom floor, bangs that
curl, opera broadcast, The Surreptitious Adventures of
Nightstick. I lie in the wind of the sun and hear
toots and smell aluminium smoke. The tiny oval
of my mother's youth in back and the rest is dark.
Sundays, the floor was black. At the beach, here
I'm a nest of seaweed, an earlier portrait of
surrealists I saw later, a stem of grey what
rises from my scalp. My hair is peaked in brine.
And this here hat, dark green fedora over same green
corduroy suit for a trip to the nation's capitol,
how far askance I've been since and never another
hat. Chromium rods, the hand in the guide's pocket
seems far removed. Blurry shoes on sandstone steps,
double and over exposed. Then in this one the SECRET
points to my head, shaved, and emblem, OPEN, striped
in "pirate" T-shirt and HERE IT IS. My elbow bent,
upright this time, behind a pole. I had yet to
enter at this snap the cavern beneath my sneakers.
To the right my soles protrude from beneath a boulder,
for I had trapped my mother and she asked Why.
Taken. Given. Flashlight brighter than my face,
another grotto, where the ball of twine, indirection,
gave out but we never got very far in, Connecticut.
I swim out of another cave in a further frame, cramped
gaze of sunlit days, apparel forgot. Later I reel
in a yell as my cousin takes a bite from my shank
beneath ranchhouse breezy curtains of Marion. On a trudge up
from the gasoline rockpit in the gaze of Judy Lamb,
she carries my pack, my jeans rolled as I step on
a pipe, Estwing in hand and svelte as only youthful can.
Most of those rocks remain and she married a so-so
clarinetist. My greygreen zipper jacket leans against
a concrete teepee, my father looking bullchested stands

before. Perhaps we had just argued. Central Park cement
steps of pigeons, the snow removed. Overexposed
whiteshirt at the drums, stick fingers ride cymbal
at the camera raised, livingroom Brenton with orange
& black "sea" wallpaper and orange&black tubs. I wore
a wristwatch then and never again, drumtime hitching
me past it. I graduate from highschool in white dinner
jacket and diploma and frown, too many hot shadows
back of the garage. Must roll up the bedroll with
skinny arms and lam for the caves. Dave & A. Bell by
the Ford Country Squire first time allowed alone to tool.
Bleak grass scapes of Knox farm. Rope down a crack,
mosquitoes and Koolade, sun dapple leaf moss sandwiches, ache.
Then in this group more drums on the roof, the gravel
and the flat, a cover attempt for no album even thought.
I tap and step in the dim known street. Lean on a
chimney to inhabit the sky, deep with drops. Here
I'm pressed on a wall of Tennessee limes, stones-throw
from mouth of the underground we camped in. Too many
thoughts, elide. Then lie on a beach in a doughnut
pattern shirt with a stick, a pipe?, in my mouth as my
cousin grins shiny beyond. Truro, also waiting for the
caves. With the poets then I'm fat and the driveway is
dark, the clapboards all white in a day of all talk.
This then all ends in color, my red bandana and shirt out
on Devil's Pulpit, open hand addressed to the grey
where Hawthorne and Melville now view of a highschool.
While the water still spills, and the cat squints at leaves
blown, my father wears Brahms, families lean in on one
for a group shot, and the rock remains shattered in a star.

(*Own Face*, 1978)

SOME GLOW ON THE SILL

The bottle contained a little amber and a little
alcoholic water in whatever relations, itself
very small nearly hand-sized. Lynchburg
to me means a place of some cave. Then a man
pressed flat between sandy ledges. Edges

only where there will be no snow. How is it
that it's early but never too late for a drink.
A man turns his pocket inside out, flap flat
on the surface begins to seep through. A little
lumpy mostly with keys and some coins.
No one has the time in all the buildings
of this city at once, for once. Only the few
feathers dry of Tennessee. Keep the inside
wet but the outside dry and you flow.

(*Own Face*, 1978)

THIS GARDEN BEING: THE HANGING OF BOOKS

I live between. I stalk space of these authors shunt
phrasing to a definition drops about trees.
But it is not their leaves. It is narrow
this shuttle amidst bows. Not much room in lots of pencil.
The knowledge is a temperature to be finished. And
the flare held to is a floor. Simple spellings amounting
stumps. Liars of Dynamism that smell out their slots in rates.
I guess it's known that Bob Watson scored the millionth run
in baseball history. Baudelaire opened his chocolate in
lavender pretense, as I revealed my garnets on a velvet floor.
The world chugs alarming 'tween thicks and thins, a
Rimbaud to stop it. The thighs of a wet mattress,
a million volts. At arm's length Chirico's farms, the boiling
sodium moles of a magnetic censorship. Tanguy in his liner
that would squeak dream peripherals. Vision is a monkey,
fiddling with a strap. And the ounces taken from gelatin
will starmap the block. I am caught, how will the walls slide,
to take up with pluck domain in this Magnetic Cheat.
Poe would deliver in a massing hover the crawls from the stares,
in a drift slipping the word from its droit. The mot juste
is not a puncture-sealer. Laughter is acidity of goal.
The rusty turns of a bird are the absent pipings of my nose,
a breaking back snide of sod brilliance. I examine faces
and I say to myself, Face off! The Imbrication of Chosens
in all this leash of bushes, yes, the rain will solve your tiles.
Here the broken snores of whole radiator zero. As you might

say to me, or a man decked out to the nines in Alexandrines
(Valéry), it will take a geologically absent mind for him
to be finally fallen. The snore in the snow is a zero.
Let's listen at the zinc door to the white chat. Rebaggage
the sore of the roseate tons, revelation here no more than
a long black veil. I have picked at the hill of crusts
to reveal no less than a fine crystal drainage for the system of
a city. And that letter hasted from pipe to tube is a soap.
Stop farming. Be a pillar to this nation's shade. All this
and in strains of magic I pace between. No more pressive alive
than the spines of trees. That here will be born
the preparative leaner.

(*Solution Passage*, 1986)

JEROME IN HIS STUDY

I

He wants to wonder not look so
he points to the skull which has rolled
lost its socket, jaw gone and there's a brass
spout-neck pot hung from a chain in an alcove
where drink should come but it's tipped too forward
a bit in a hover, a gold offering plate just below
what's that white stripe just next prayer shawl
straight out down with blacked snooze edge or toilet
roll too long let out modern paint straight edge wipe
or adhesive tape ripped free leaves a swath of light?
Bordering that is a door edge its various darks,
such rules, such flint absence of palaver
the leather tomes piled out to float over
a possible foolish doorway drop, stand aside,
and the retort bulb of ink hugged farther back
shelf lip to corner samovar could never warm to cover.
It's not a coven it's a cell and all the adding up
of storages there forces there to be a knowledge there
if one could longly hold one's head the right in air
in crimson tapped or portal mapped the blue range
with lusted tree in winds of the antabuse sea.
It's an oil in the oil of coming to be, the

coiled off wisdom in a strapped book delicate
of its own ledge angled and blackness stored
which also stores the pen the discus hat the
skull its position in hoardy rhymes of the word
the turn to the why is it always righthand
casement of the sun on a town of porters idling and
cows of the stalwart darkest jade-green bush, thread of onyx
the stork sack of salt thongs behind him in a drop
to the fire wall of keenest pipe soot, bridled
to a shell, no haze, in fact a thought so clear
the jesus is crossed out tiny from shade of its tendril niche
and the bird invisible in its radio cage next space
nothing soars for the moment nothing is strained
to the thought pounced to brightest bolt of jet
the murmurs flee here the finger to the bone
of the word no nearer known is the point to a
task so barely opened the lips lock in purse
no further adept, no one's liquor in the world
tracing of the looks back to angle's end
in point blank he shows
in step left
the ceiling lengths burn

2

What does he have knowlege of
and what does he permit it of
the lowering of a hurl oh so object
of the word place to be where things are placed
the gone by spirit to be held
down by one finger point at a time
the world outside was all furled in a heave
the balance all heaven to the fundament pendulum
all standards erased in the circling race but here
in lacquer glass lead and bone cell of dispute
over pages that flutter over pages locked shut
to the quill stuck in darkness of a pile you could hum
here is the height of the Semblance of Death
elbows bent at border of night's sure table
Reasoning, a knocking at your river
a border uncomposed of all you call up
to a point of bare tapping to know

to near be to fear
so to hold
the finger graze down

3

I shout but he is throatless
the outlines of thing-bearing light the threat
to braise the tone over
the exact and pinch
all the ache of itch at inch in thrall to
anglest throng, in alcove in miter in tong
the code of cold coals clad in ace
of reach thought quickest spall
until they hum
away stall and light
in the portal toward night
so reasonable an oil
his church is too loose
his temple fingers fight

4

What do I know such an ordinal brightness
it lasted the ages, a candle rest till now
                showed day
sort of rings set of things
but muted as a pewter were snuffed
so we see as if through
a numbering in ices glassed without heat
of kneeling on an elbow by drift skull cold
it seems perfect beyond reason
without squadron or banner of sanctity spoiled
but he is there
so near to calling where
his prayer cogged to lodge
all thing to lodge him

after Joos van Cleve the Elder
1521

(*Solution Passage*, 1986)

from AT EGYPT

IX

Morning muezzin in orange and a mosquito
rooster donkey tree toad and chainsaw snore
the dart of a needle through felt trauma
they mass and band, collide in screens for light
unlung the tongue in far head, wiping the mist from the whisper

Only the spoken
Words follow

But it is in the flying up again
in the seeing back where the rock heads
splitting soft to the forces that take time
running into siftage of some edge, a table say
or soda hoard no matter its age, a sty
uncleared in whatever tongue, washed in time and huge
as any language mass

I see it stretched dry down to a Utah brown
the heaven's floor more sinister from a silver cylinder
into the far on the tones of dry river bleaks and squints
they all retreat into source cake Sahara, where nothing
ends they steal chickens, it's made of leavings

Plain isn't it? that I seize and clap from the bends
the air capsizes and tea spills on the dust prints of a floor vast
or is it actually soft, all this distance, these tabled plans?
here you can see down all the roads back from, a lashed dragging
to the sides, as in all wrong ways, you must wait till the driver slows
stops this whistling stall and turns to us

From what is a flight to start?

(*At Egypt*, 1988)

XI

On the edge of the house, the desert on the edge of the stamp
on the pitch of a resonance, nothing there will
be free, not even if you
reached the sea, then he laughed at me
a stretch
a panel, a woolen tip
and it busted, it *was* rested
then he placed me in his mouth, then I went with him

There are always nods by the light wood, by the hard sea
grandstand and wholly stolen, black and fully numbered
working a pack of tan dogs by the sacred baboon
and it rested (desert must be a strong verb)

Suddenly loose and in another direction
   (inspection is another)
a block of which ignore
   (suspicion) and it just turned off
it's a proximity turn-off
barking out as in
another direction, clearing section
tan the dogs that attack the white one

But somehow he gets out and is
hanging pins in a coffee cup at window service
the one
having the switch to suddenly ignore them
a white one, turned off
at the brass tent rest house
where numbers whirl out in a barking direction

This is what we're lured to hunch and come witness:
tomb and temple pigments, certain primaries
talking about: lapis blue, turquoise blue slab
Nile green, almost plasticene tone
ochre red, pink red
gold yellow, black
lamp black? white
gypsum?

They put the stones down in
the margin, top of each morning
to the nothing pyramid tip it's
the blankets come back from the absence

But the place where it all came back from wheels away
headed then handed down about the airport darts
and listened to the opening reports, the selvage lists
Carter's second quartet, monkeys who live in aborigine pacification
a sand tong triangular ridge, block of soap in a waiting adit
all of which would be the time he achieved, the garnet center of
                                                    [the dome
for his rill-washed troubles, far from any man-hewn tip
do we treat each other of the center? better a
rock's leather and dynamite under a moon

And one last walk
in the space that simply
maybe they had played the trouble from it?
blocks
that are just about, an hour and back, breast-pocket height

                    What is the Death Name?

He is the one who lights in two
lands more than the sun
he is the one who wheels from
the hell of a pyramid up

                    Where is the order to pass?

He is the one silent that the moment is gone
he is the one of no hands
the one in the presence of like books
the one to whom the hidden matters in a line of sand

                    What is the order of
                    This is the world?

He is the one who walks toward later
and slowly talking, he is the one to be talking about it
the one to whom this book is silent
the one one with all doubt, without land

What sort
Lock
At the sill of number?

The picture of a death from a long way off
the one who had chanced to be spinning missing
the one whistled down in a blood-driven dent
flight is all headed in the one direction

Which hewn name
At which
Death is shown?

That who shall be able to hear this shall say
how like toward it is, how like later
how like heavily and moving slowly
how in the smaller and the talking about it
who like finally, like in silence a book

This only
spoken words follow
like hooks in the pigment
books in the presence
an entanglement weightiness

The which was his head
Fluid red to the following

That the book fell from
past
half way to the start or the end

(*At Egypt*, 1988)

DISTURBING THE SALLIES FORTH

What has been brought to a finish
I do not want to see, face.
Watch the earth as a heavening ball
wound in hand to press the land,
be stumped. The works are alive.
And say, Drop your plans in waves of
thought wider than rift at the edge
of widening pact. Haul on reason
and snap. When did the change turn up
that makers found their materials
twins to matters? When did
we enter? Caught now awake
simultaneous inside and out there, nevermore
the need for such a travel, poised at the point
of a work in light lines of blood.
World, worlds, the shout vision of just another
ball wavers in the void of edged weights.
Nights the battery juice peers over the coiled prow.
I have an answer collection, patent leaning.
I lean a ledge on which apples are painted.
I jingle all histories in my anchor pocket
and stand by a window of birds erased by trunks.
Happiness calls from the cold mines beneath my sanity.
And wonder is a twine of wands lodged
to spine of nothing I know at least to hold.

(*Sound as Thought*, 1990)

SATURDAY NIGHT

It goes away from you suddenly, doesn't it surely first?
in the chair the pipe drawings flood your envelope
the wills delve and at elbows terminate
I couldn't spell and still
it spins the pole and shall

Loose apple tendencies, wended as wasitcoat
the we rhyme, and the you set, the plotted me
I act felt, structure structure, but what does it matter
the man on the sly, the pearly fist, plods waiting accident
nothing but facts stop

The illusion is the daylight, whatever stripe, no movies
don't sling you into a chair with a cup or is it?
a placid dominance, of three ring roundings, of partial
the name is a scar or the fret of sentence melodic
you come home, I'll jail

Remembrance of spotted things, or sported hands
on the covering links, on the wholly able zoo, the treat
all things their endings and sling style its seat
three hands a wall block, wrist songs a slice
the clogged shines that we meet

I have the dealing, a naming, I have a ceiling I'm falling
the tone nodes are surely, have merely, did miss me
you in a scowl, and they, a scrappier they, a thong
these slab rates string us, out of brace, out in skinny power
beyond the doubleness is rising that the nothing waits

(*Sound as Thought*, 1990)

GLANCE IN WHITE SPACE

No detail here, nothing but you. Unbroken gaze,
whole of the body, words cast away. It is level with
meaning, this white horizon. And when the air comes
together we bend.

Little strokes. The air has parted many. That the
perking lights all are you. And the time is a favor
presented to no one. Previously, whole.

Gone out like a wish, forgotten spoken. Dividing line
each touch. Novels could be ignored, or spent
in this chamber.

Little more than you telling me, with a brightness here
or now. Beneath skin, where the flesh begins.
Our clothing an imitation, a skin to remove.

Blush of red soak on the glass, into itself.
On the morning the unknown colors start, and the ones
we know imprisoned change.

Enclosing wind, air in lace chains. Torn flowers,
bronzed hedgerows, the moon as cut a sign.
The you I will be before you.

(*Odes of Roba*, 1991)

WHAT IS THOUGHT BUT WON'T HOLD STILL

for Bernadette

But what is more thought than a dark over the sun?
You could not move from it till it moves, it
a dissembler of cracking movies, humour as fist
of god, damages as thought damages? going
it's going, and the mind as if in fall keep up?

Thought a questioning of the inner linings left
on boiling hold, on meeting tuesdays, nothing left from
accumulant sundays, the rod in the tomb, and the hum
in the friar's cell as he plants his gaze at the zoom
of our lord, thought goes away, as tongue and as if
the sun burned it, and so passed on

For how many has Name been first thought?
Me not, but ope instead for open, rooms
to be thought and thought on then and the subsequent
thoughts made rhyme of beads as seldom poem,
seldom being Thought for alone, illumined in bare stone
a brain painted in multiplication of cells

But having thought all of life then what do you think?
That building is moving away? That sun and its humours
rend us from our lofts in sundering rails of next
the sky will illumine the remains of a plan? a total
left to fizzle and pile up footfalls at rock base
in ruins, where the lozenge of every which thought
curls and darts up as stirring decimals in the dark?

I have the thought I have eloped from chambers
of intellectual mood, instead want to press finger
into something just hard enough, just weaned enough
from word to weave a further style of sight and
heard as if the heel struck the resonant note of
cell held for lone me, in brightness, in temporary and
shifted over from spark of the nothing that you see

(*Odes of Roba*, 1991)

Lyn Hejinian [1941]

A MASK OF ANGER

he said I should try something harder
a mask of rage

says of snakes
says of broken glass
says of aged foundations
unconsolable wildness,
an imagination uncomforted,
says without comfort

where are the gods who support the event

crashed into the circle

took the blue out of the sky

walled the warbler; turned the walker

wrong and wrong

there's no song but what's said
felt it
and no thought but what's bitten

(*A Mask of Motion*, 1977)

from MY LIFE

It was only a
coincidence

The tree rows in orchards are capable of patterns. What were Cæsar's battles but Cæsar's prose. A name trimmed with colored ribbons. We "took" a trip as if that were part of the baggage we carried. In other words, we "took our time." The experience of a great passion, a great love, would remove me, elevate me, enable me at last to be both special and ignorant of the other people around me, so that I could be free at last from the necessity of appealing to them, responding to them. That is, to be nearly useless but at rest. There were cut flowers in vases and some arrangements of artificial flowers and ceramic bouquets, but in those days they did not keep any living houseplants. The old fragmentary texts, early Egyptian and Persian writings, say, or the works of Sappho, were intriguing and lovely, a mystery adhering to the lost lines. At the time, the perpetual Latin of love kept things hidden. It was not his fate to be as famous as Segovia. Nonetheless, I wrote my name in every one of his books. Language is the history that gave me shape and hypochondria. And followed it with a date, as if by my name I took the book and by the date, historically, I contextualized its contents, affixed to them a reading. And memory a wall. My grandmother had been a great beauty and she always won at cards. As for we who "love to be astonished," the ear is less active than the eye. The artichoke has done its best, armored, with scales, barbed, and hiding in its interior the soft hairs so aptly called the choke. I suppose I had always hoped that, through an act of will and the effort of practice, I might be someone else, might alter my personality and even my appearance, that I might in fact create myself, but instead I found myself trapped in the very character which made such a thought possible and such a wish mine. Any work dealing with questions of possibility must lead to new work. In between pieces, they shuffled their feet. The white legs of the pear trees, protected from the sun. Imagine, please: morbid myopia. The puppy is perplexed by the lizard which moves but has no smell. We were like plump birds along the shore, unable to run from the water. Could there be swans in the swamp. Of course, one continues to write, and thus to "be a writer," because one has not yet written that "ultimate" work. Exercise will do it. I insert a description: of agonizing spring morning freshness, when through the open window a smell of cold dust and buds of broken early grass, of schoolbooks and rotting apples, trails the distant sound of an airplane and a flock of crows. I thought that for a woman health and comfort must come after love. Any photographer will tell you the same. So I wouldn't wear boots in the snow, nor socks in the cold. Shufflers scuff. That sense of responsibility was merely the context of the search for a lover, or, rather, for a love. Let someone from the other lane in. Each boat leaned toward us as it turned and we, pretending to know more than we did, identified each class as it was blown by. Politics get wider as one gets older. I was learning a certain geometry of purely decorative shapes. One could base a model for form on a crystal or the lungs. She showed the left profile, the good one. What she felt, she had heard as a girl. The point of the foghorns is that you can't see them, need to hear them. More by hive than by heart the mathematics of droves makes it noticeable. It was May, 1958 and reading was antianonymous. She disapproved of background music.

(*My Life*, 1980, 1987)

from THE GUARD

I

Can one take captives by writing—
"Humans repeat themselves."
The full moon falls on the first. I
"whatever interrupts." Weather and air
drawn to us. The open mouths of people
are yellow & red—of pupils.
Cannot be taught and therefore cannot be.
As a political leading article would offer
to its illustrator. But they don't invent
they trace. You match your chair.

Such hopes are set, aroused
against interruption. Thus—
in securing sleep against interpretation.
Anyone who could believe can reveal
it can conceal. A drive of remarks

and short rejoinders. The seance
or session. The concentric lapping.
If the world is round & the gates are gone....
The landscape is a moment of time

that has gotten in position.
Why not arrive until dawn. Cannot be taught
and therefore cannot be
what human cunning can conceal.
Every stop is unstationlike, flutters
the standard for staring through windows

through walls. It was of saving children
in the path of a runaway bus.
The heavy tenable euphoria.
Resemblance of luggage, and how raw.
How far the length of time it takes.
Repetition in copying
seems to mean to say "I, too"

I advise you. My familiar home is thickset.
In leaves to live in the machine.
The chronic idea turns up
a sunny day as an arresting abstract.
Which follows a dialogue made up.
Who believe they are warm if called Romantics.

It takes hollow red & yellow factories.
The tongue a total clearance
adopting habits. The fear of death
is a misprint. Memory a mouth.
On my fist my fingers and they trace.
Introspection, cancellation, the concentric
session. Water stills the stalk

between drawing and doodling. The tree
stands up aching in the sun.
The car drives past, whose we'll never know.
A jet is the vanishing point
the contrail reaches. As optics, red
dots, probity is waiting to hear the spit
of stately rhyme blowing in geometry.
Tossed off, serene, Chinese

windmills turn horizontally. The caves cooperate
with factories. Deep
in their mountains they move
spread on lattice, pitched for days
as still as the print on the wall.
The sky was packed

which by appearing endless seems inevitable.
The flag droops straight down. The horse
in dry sand walks with a chirping noise
from friction of the particles

and counterarguments like pack ice
puff in the waves there, blowing fountains
of pearl. The ground.

Painting cannot take captives.
I remember much the same about all my interests
repetitious circular interests, of which a roving
and impressionable mind like that of an hysteric
seeks disclosure. Of science
for its practitioners. Of stacked convexities.
The two notes to the motor

in March the object of the dark
restricted dirt, not deception nor transparency.
He sits to piano, it's an attack
on the sound of lips. Who seem
to be in a cage of parakeets
turning clothes, following a dialogue

made up of science for its practitioners.
The silence fills. Scenes thread bridges.
Such air always flies
to the heart and liver, faces nature
with its changing pan, floating boats on the bay
far from authority, sent truly
speaking in little weights
without knowing French and don't pronounce.

The rubber dawn and its expense.
The silence of the sensible horizon is intelligibly
awkward. The skin containing character.
Some things slip through the mesh
and others go rotten. Nothing
distresses me exactly.
I sleep with self-styled procrastination.
Whose next day I don't know personally.

from THE PERSON

THE PERSON

a.

The solitude flared out
Ears—almost every person has some
The stain of urgent wordiness on idea life
In the rain is the let & flow
The positions of the head are finite
More obstacle than the rain is the hour in the air
The air woolly as one wakens, the light oppressive rather than expansive
But that's not fair! I complained, the room merely tinted with spatiality
My intuition tells me that light is discontinuous
There are only brief, unrelated lights
Day and night—they lie within these

I hear the sounds of the many stones outside pronoun
Household substantives (long life, hyperspace, domestic genders, our
    predictability, our trajectory, and so on) in the talk about talk—
    it wounds the feelings
A tide denied to the little pond, even a tiny one
What I learn is the link of weeds as I like it
There are lifespan and detection
Their object a dead weight, then empathy drops
Pathos and limp clustering

The internal objects stand
Publishing—is that public or maternal activity?
A person puts meals in its head
Then craving for information might mimic craving for noise
The season is drawn and they follow the captivity
Here I depict a trunk of a tree as a funnel and a day is disgorged
Divides on solicitude
A concentric scrape and it's converted
And I digress on destination

b.

Don't be afraid—predicaments make a person apparent
Matter what

THE PERSON

I want things to be real; of course!
The self is a lobe or palm
Scrupulously to think of the hand
        so well-buttoned
Perceiver dispatched to the motions
        of the moment
A, C, K, and so on
There is a record of them somewhere
There is an anxiety to make one

The bulk—sparks and jets drop off the bulk
The hands remember them in their locations
I've forgotten
A certain kind of prior life, say a happy one—it has
        a pungent bulk, resembling light
Death is a blanching

But I exaggerate
The great sequences of incompleteness flutter
Many standards in nature crimp
Ego, Body, Position
I went to see
I rode a kind of engine of gender, a motive for bonding

Things see their argument go to and fro before my eyes
It takes science, patience
A refusal to recede
Do you remember your hand years ago? or
        was it all anticipation to have flaked and vegetated
Perhaps time snaps
The patter of the hand
The snapping meant for recovery
There's no lack of rhythm for getting around to
        accumulate, with fingers and a capacity and
        possible use as a cover

THE PERSON

I envy those deeper in mineral
The peach brass that rings
Its ice, its chance

The chalcedony that pours
The waters come in order, scoop
This can only be understood
Not new but they are original
They are sunk in a particle
The lozenge has both slosh and radius
            to which it has been fixed

Opaque cloud on opaque flow, each sounding
            a separate, a polar note
Immersion
We are using the distance between us
            for magnification
Forward now! Accidentally!
Everyone naturally inclines to rhythm
The billows are pocked, their air bubbles turn walled
            up in the ocean
We have expressive eyes and this is one
            of their expressions
The ocean operates
The impression instantly increases, even
            the words are resumed
I will show you that the sole solidity bobs between
            the least parts
The two places, the two times, the two methods (of
            inquiry and memory), the two experiences (of
            disillusionment and perception)

The ocean is an outer self, displaying conversions and suctions
The light exaggerates
Inquiry has slash
And cook, too
But is it aggressive to be old
Is it pitiless, incited

The ocean implodes from the mouth
Or something—you can feel
            with astonishment the urge to observe silence

THE PERSON

If you want to see my handwriting—here it is
In the person (of a possible amputation)
affirming and feeling—the cross-draft
Yes, the coldness of the palpable

How long before we get there? it realized
Enthusiastic things—edges
Time is surrounding everything
in its voluminous halts

and generating—the anxiety
of funniness, of big trees
who take the landscape up
with the monotony of lightning when it divides

on solitude

THE PERSON

There is no time
for rewriting
My thoughts
are in my neck
Self-consciousness
is discontinuous
The very word "diary"
embarrasses me

There are schools of autobiography
far removed—into them
too socialism hums
as mercury, spilled, splits
and is solid
The head is a case with genitals
I laugh because things fit
This is the solace of fatalism
I distinguish it
from non-literary reality

Anything that decomposes
rather than a person
into temporal rather than spatial parts
must be a person's life
The rubbing of the grains of light
Here the vanishing point is on every word
The sun on the water that forms rings
and they implode
Streets stirring the desire
to abandon territory
The sky displaying love of the continuous

In my neck, there's only time
a bigness of the city that is
I don't possess space—that's clear enough
Feelings sink to the surface
Kindness and worry, haste and interpretation
Here I translate my thought
into language—to double fate

But fate imposes its very interesting exercise: select
You yourself could generate the aesthetic heat
of globes and stops, of shore and drone
This makes for altruism—
the generosity of the poem
If you know what to want you will be free

from THE CELL

In the dark sky there
    are constellations, all of them
    erotic and they break open
    the streets
The streets exceed the house
On occasion the body exceeds
    the self
Everyday someone replaces someone and
    someone's mother is sad so
    as to exceed
The bed is a popular
    enclosure from which to depart

Outside the stars are stunning
   —touching
It is a question of
   scale
It is erotic when parts
   exceed their scale

November 15, 1986

If reality is simply that
   which is accessible to reason
   when it folds over and
   it sticks up
Then sexuality is very optimistic—
   a very optimistic interest
It is a cyclops with
   a sharp eye for the
   apparent position and the actual
   position
And a working eye
Until we have a whole
   landscape of undivided situations
Although beauty is divided somewhat
   freely
The boundaries between me and
   the rosey cobblestones and leaves
   are nowhere parallel
But slide who are insatiable,
   genuine, solemn, looming
The ghost is only the
   poor attempt of nature to
   present herself as me in
   the language of inquiry
The naked breasts we call
   night and day or me
   and not-me
Inseparable from exposure, inspiration is
   what the ghost contained or
   could supply
Qualified praises—flesh rises to
an emotion

The reasonable outlook, knowledge
It is based on acknowledgement
   in the end
Provocations
Justice, joy—if a cyclops
   perhaps squinting and springing coincidentally
   upright until partially blinded
Of anything that is, there
   might be more

January 16, 1987

Avarice culminated in explanation...the
   plug
It's hospitable...so, material
In my feeling propaganda, I was...
It's optimistic to xerox...pounce...
   ornithologize...where poetry does not
   resist alone in books...
Or coin: a circle and
   lid...means the trajectory
The trajectory is eager for
   more reality and more recognition
Strutting with explanation...with characteristic
   restlessness
I could not remain long
   from home...for sight and
   cell

January 27 & 28, 1987

This is the female opinion
   in several inseparable places and
   I will keep my confession,
   my syntax
It's my position
Syntax is a measure, and
   on it are increments of
   pleasure

Wherein is what they register
And wide
Why to know about poetics
What to know about consonants
My containment
A moment of lumber in
    the building of a society
    for members
But it isn't space that's
    subdivided into units of a
    situation when one says legs
They might place one or
    take the place in an
    emotion
But the perambulation is coherent
    —though coherence doesn't go (being
    lovelike) without saying
This specific crisis in consciousness
Sex is the pleasure of
    inexactitude

April 28, 1988

(*The Cell*, 1992)

from *OXOTA: A SHORT RUSSIAN NOVEL*

Chapter Two

No form at all—it's impossible to imagine its being
    seen from above
Nor sense of time because work is only done
    discontinuously
I had no sense of making an impression
The blue shadows of footprints and a diffuse pink or
    green light between them on the saturated park
    were soaking the snow
A reflection of the violent word MIR painted green was
    mirrored warped on a stretch of deserted ice

All my memories then as Leningrad lay like the shallow
    sheets of water banked by rubble and melting snow
    which covered the field in a northern housing
    district of the city across which we were often
    walking toward the housing blocks in winter, its
    surface wildly broken by the light
Something impossible to freeze, or the very lack of
    thing
Dusk as it continued to be
In the evenings particularly we made notes and took
    dictation in anticipation of writing a short Russian
    novel, something neither invented nor constructed but
    moving through that time as I experienced it unable to
    take part personally in the hunting
Taking patience and suddenness—even sleeping in
    preparedness, in sadness
No paper for books
I had lost all sense of forming expressions
No paper at all in the south, and the butcher stuffs pieces of
    greasy black beef into the women's purses
Other links exist, on other levels, between our affairs

Chapter Nine

There is room in Pushkin's small house at Pavlovsk and
    it's the same yellow
Somewhat sentimental or really so after the palace
Sentimental asides
The locking of asides
Snow was falling in the yard around a hard currency
    hospital of the same color
The rubles too as thick as snowflakes
And here at my window, said Arkadii Trofimovich, is my
    west
But where was Pushkin's bed
He can't decide what he decides
Two anti-Semites thundering about "north guys" and
    "blue eyes" and "black guys"
They were drumming on Parshchikov's side
His face was pale, the skin thin and dry, his eyes full

but of what he couldn't say, asleep and awake,
    awful nights
More idiots! said the colonel, almost catching the
    intonation of the cab driver
Pushkin remains himself, but what self has he to remain

Chapter Seventy-Two: Nature

The frost falls from a tree
We have a state of nature
Maybe I need the tree—it will acknowledge and thereby
    authorize me
Nature as describer—with the Russian names for things
Nature, which I regard across the table of which it's the
    proprietor
It is the third (inhuman) person
Waning interest, sugar rationing, a thumb before the moon
    without hyprocrisy
The natural part of that thought is from a dream
I in my progress passing this
A hunger is in its artlessness
Nature results in the lack of privacy (personality) that would
    go with it
It pursues the impersonal narrative—here, our endless it
So I was feeling an inferior weariness, an inability to
    acknowledge anything
It was snowing, and the snow was rippled by the people
    walking in it while at the same time the people were
    reflected in it

Chapter Seventy-Five: Passion

Passion is the alienation that love provides
Drifting winter tinted where we lifted, plowed
Jealousy is a flake of a different passion
It was hungry to be plunging in disruption
The wobble and mattering of the sensing muscles which combine
People are not joined in passion but divulged

They diverge—but that sight was unseen
But all this is muffled in banalities, I said
It is not passion to nod in
It is passion for no one to listen
One with closed eyes and the other one's opened
The snowfall offered all the colors of apple
There was passion in its thud and exhilaration
Patience itself pushes over—given a body for what

Chapter One Hundred

Outside the mouth all is gray and green
But there's village and the dry violence there
Each morning one weakens and some moths issue like dogs
Thus the orange bus came pissing into the snow bank
The novel is without additional resemblance
And yet—things must put me in order

Song in Order

Bed whose tongue was burned
is turned by name excited
Let's begin to everything
To snow

It's cold whose snow was turned—
Recklessness makes difference
But difference is slow and deaf
to stone

Life whose state was learned
is made by name desired
The city would state anything
as home

We slow to stone in name
But we love without completion
Life is complete at any turn
to know

Rice and such erudition
Persons feed themselves in the small sense known
As I said to Arkadii, that one's your novel—you should call
    it *War and Space*
Each to protect an interest
A Pushkin
A bucket
Fine green sand
We are all incredibly lazy

Chapter 144: Description

My description gives my face in space, my story changes it
All narration is set with change
Atheism now is an adequate description, as free as air, as
    independent as fire
But in an era without religion, you can't tell an infidel from
    a buffalo
Maybe my face was set with fate
But my narration was embraced by particular rubble
Some broken concrete, a length of pipe, a poster proclaiming
    memory defaced
The grannies gathered close to see the excitement
They stared at my coat
You have gone to the incredible lengths of material prosperity
    and far from having disappeared you have turned up
    awaiting the 100th bus
But what's funny will turn out sad if you stand in front of it
    long enough
So it's essential to know how to sleep and at what time
The grime's scraping on reason reflected the face
    self-consciously
They waited and the drama sank in later

Chapter 152

The cold low, the white in a light, the yellow in sight
It is the amazing enormous apparatus
It is fascinating to be afraid and not to possess it
Details of tender response to a violence not seen
I mean I have my experience but do I give it
It requires a high level of consciousness along with the loss of self
The authority of waking is lost
I sympathize by talking and taking in sleep
I cannot synchronize waking scale—if a person lives self-
    consciously it must be in a distant land—but the clock of
    observation sits on the kitchen table
And that is the scarab, Arkadii says, pointing at the small green
    TV
It is scale and ballad
And a painting is an eye-socket—or, no, a novel is
I've never dreamed of Leningrad, I said
I can't because it has no screen

Chapter 154

The tint in the weather and yet another tint
They are exhaustive
Hints
But the hunt is intelligible
There is stagnant humidity and ozone
Animosity and lack of remorse that provoke at the same time a
    love intrigue
Perhaps we are reaching the end of the era of the three great
    determinisms
The end of the eros of a terminus
Here the poetic method requires an exercise of free will
Love provokes the exercise of frost
But we can't keep on always curled in the same way
We must curl in reverse
We must curl in cruelty
We must eat

Chapter 250

Self-consciousness is in a metaphor
Sleeps are links in its chain of necessities
Can we climb it to reach
A complex system of shackle and rustle, sill and canal
All muttered in amber
But then one wakes first
Folds then unfolded
The first breath of a day to which we've returned, oval and oval

    Song in Oval

        Know, whose pace is pages
        how to know is oval
        cared for, clouded

        How to know is place
        elided, sound the slow
        removal, rounded

It was cold in the novel
I climbed off the sofa in old difference
A science in silence at a scene in mutability
There's perpetuity but it's divided
A time was in my head, the water braided
I sat with the coffee and waited

        (*Oxota*, 1991)

Robert Grenier [1941]

EYES

open the door Oakland

FRESH AIR

rusty clothesline

two clothespins

no diapers

RHYMING

dry

green eyes

WHAAT

someone walking

A ROUND

the block

CLASSIC HEDGES

after brain sleeps

BRUSHED

teeth and

my gums

MOONLIGHT

turns it dock

LIVE OAKS

shadow one

with the leaves

FOR AMY

hot day

returning rollerskater

WHERE ARE

the vehicle

HOUSES SEEKING

housefronts

long ago

s'allright Fred

s'ok Harry

SUNSHINE LINE

shadow substance one

as is in the wind

stricken stick in the ground

clothes on the wind

THERE WASN'T A SOUL PLAYING BASKETBALL

naturally it was too hot

but on another day the same source

laughing & arguing sweaty bodies

POUNDING ON THE FRONT DOOR UPSTAIRS

heinous traffic busses

rush & roar of cars

URNS

ugly really

GUMS

delight you gums

SWIMMING THE CRAWL FORWARD HEAD DOWN

stopping stroking backward

flipping backward over

into the backstroke gulping fresh air

B BOOM

boom boom boom

boom boom boom boom

WHERE'S AMY

it's after four

SIX DARK HOUSES

must there be if the
streetlight out

porch lights too
houses are

three on two sides
flat on four sides

OBLONG

tasks are equal

a house will be thought sold

or a neighbor will be truthful

random vines

really vines or are vines

one Mercedes two Mercedes

BAKING SODA BOXES

maroon baking soda bathrobes

delayed in stores as fast food space

LOOTING

train whistles

moving a

shipment through town

silver dollar federal

THING

any sum or

number some

or none

I piss on such the like

IT'S ITS

handmade

vary

THREE

AWNING

legged dog

yawing & yep

yawing & yamming

KNOCK WOULD EXPLAIN NOTHING

crossing to the window to look nothing

the bus pulled out from under the tree

from PHANTOM ANTHEMS

EASTER ROSES

for Ken Irby

so I experienced

sneezing as a

ecstatic

contorting

of the

soul

attempting to

from

its shape

through pain &

ecstasy into an

resplendant

being

stretching

upward

out

of

itself

ROSE

not by

'today' but

by

recurrent light

its course

of blossoming

is not effected

by the sun at all?

'powers of

darkness' at large?

it 'unfolds'

'unfolding'

flowering

of powers of

darkness at large?

I 'see' at 'dawn'?

EARS IN MOONLIGHT

   for Lyn Hejinian

hear the wind out both directions

together with thinking making more & one

withal leaves & blue sky culture heaving

without thinking making more than one

NUT

day dawns doesn't it you rhythm fiend

THIS YEAR

it's really more

a chorus of

blossoms spilling o'er

up from the top

pray for my heart

periodontics

as a waterfall

of chewing yellow gums

'regardful of masses'

red roses red

roses 'pressed into

service' up and

up & at 'Easter'

each which the eyes behold

with the beauty of day this

River of Roses coming

down from the ground

ROSE APPELLATE PROJECT (ENTWURF)

   for Kathleen Frumkin

yellow rose into the composite fathom of the dark day ah

train whistle breaking prolonged still extant under the walnut tree sky

three 'wardens' Chumash moving 'all such birdlike creatures' show as flying

sunlight tissue 'foot' from forms live on so shapes can do

hand writes as a motion of timeless vast phenomena scoring

wall viz. 'miracle muscle' living distinction credence insect

presence style ye gods eyeballs-eyesight differentiation stance belief

spelling light for hymn to day recast around loved sound phantom

petal vocable apparent rose stride forward bulky from the tomb

Ted Greenwald [1942]

AND, HINGES

Fog hanged over the park, the night cold, and, clean
against the tree you leaned in the sunlight, breathing
he spinned the car out on fine gravel near the gate
she laughing at the tree   standing straggly   over the fence.

And, the drain clogs, when I shower, with my hair,
queasily, paper rolling out of your handbag, glinting sequins,
and, she stood, laughing   over her shoulder   by the spinning
    wheels
"how do you get to the station, from here?"

Skin   smelling clean, after the shower, and, dark
merrily, tempting   me to talk to you, and, asking if you've seen,
and, turning to her friend, tall, and, skinny next to her,
"Taking the first   turning you come to   in the book, and curve

round it."   Warm moisture rising, I rise sluggishly,
the latest news from Paris, tho I've never been there, calm
"he never could control the damn thing, and, thinks he's Fangio."
She knew better than to laugh, but she did   anyway   , laughing

hide behind a tree, and, light bark late, keeping the neighbors late,
and, you ask me "have you seen the latest news from Paris?"
Out back someone   mugging laughter   , and, he thought over the
    problem
to bust her gut.   "Did you see that turning   the horse   made
    dog?"

Hours arranged handily on the wrist, I scrutinize them,
and, and tell you "I've never been there myself, have you?"
How to get back on the road, and, keeping his hands intact.
"Absolutely splendor, the light on   shimmering her hand."

Hourly,and, after dinner they scrutinize me.   "How we love,"
and, you answer, "yes, dozens of times."   I look at my watch
He's such a bore.   Always running around fast over the place."
She knew better than to know   know better than his local hands,
    placed

filling mail order slips, out, sleeping afterward   in the down,
and, you shiver, and, laugh, "it's really terrible what's happening!"
how it sounds in reverse.   Scared, and, the hairs turning prematurely
gray, respectably, over the nearest sand mound in the pile

pillow I puff up with my hand   before the light   goes out
"oh yes, I agree, would you care to join me for lunch,"
spun gravel rising under the wheels, and, him sitting.   The clay
    lump
she picked up some too, running it thru   her veiled fingers

in the fireplace.   And, you say "you are thirsty," and, I believe,
and, you take my hand, handily switching your pursing lips
to the other side clinging higher under the screech, and, wheel.
And, she looked at him, blinking owlly back tears.   And, they

came anyway, you, and, "I am thirsty too, for more dinner wine"
"not having any money, but wanting to speak to you so much."
"Who?   Who?   Does he think he is?   Anyway?"
She knew there was nothing to do but curve out the light ground

under her, and, several more candles to warm the room.   To the other
side of your mouth.   "That's okay, I love lunch in the park, anyhow."
His phantom figure stalking shadow after shadow after dark.
And, cry til a little pool formed, and, she rose to go home.

                    (*Common Sense*, 1978)

PRIVETS COME INTO SEASON AT HIGH TIDE

Privets come into season at high tide.
The night on the Great Neck side
near Steppingstone the bargeman walks
over the water the refrigerator opened the mailman fell out.

Opening the closet the grocery boy fell out
banging his head on the floor his knee.
The snow bushes 40 years preparing dinner,
or the laugh on the rug, gold threads weaving in
& out over the bodies on the floor.
First sack, the corrugated box lit up
under the lawn lamp the rippled footsteps
running from the scene of the hiding, tumbled out on-
to the floor. "What are you doing in there?"
"I am searching. It is good to be free again."

The first race we took a beating
lurching free from the vain control of sense.
As your hair goes so
goes the subtle undercurrents passing thru the foot in-
to the chin, & up. Even if you ground
yourself with the closet door the tension
is mixed, the filth of corners have no effect
& proselytic airs the room have no effect.
The hum. The prop limbs stacked in the corner
penetrate handle & space between finger-
tip plastered the original conviction.

Dialogue:
white hair melting in the warm air
rising from the radiator in the corner, the whiteness.
The hand. The space between fingers.
Walking slowly on the rocks.

Character:
nubile
syrup the syrup
marrow from the lips of well
the spray, the seaweed, her grass side,
sweating with a light touch on the neck,
walking the ghastly hours deliveries are made;
dotted hours, & the rabid denture chewing the long gloss.

Her maple thigh—mole...cheek—
the chattering of teeth on the ground,
count out plums & grapes
leading the eyelid bay & stars. The line.
The whim drawing the danger thru the dust out of the corner.
The underbrush kelp. Transforming the hedge circuits.

(*Common Sense*, 1978)

I HEAR A STEP

1

I hear a step. A step.
The piping on the side of the couch
patterns of roses & the wispy stem of
rolled cloth dangling from the lip.
The first time it was hard coping with your breasts
magnolias cutting patterns from the clouds.
My feet crunch pinecones.
You were beneath me on the couch, the cushion,
the floor. I don't remember. Still.
You flung sounds at me. The silence.
Snow covered the ground between the barn & farmhouse.
A fleck of snow buried itself in the rooster's skull.
The skin was cold. The heat off for the evening.
You draped your mouth with feathers & flowers.
The muffled kiss.
Snow on your neck, the collar of your coat grazing your cheeks.
I am used to the grain now. It tastes circuitous.

2 CAPSULE

I swallowed early this morning the highway burning my foot.
The gingerbread on the edge of the roof.
Twin peaks rise to the lightning, explode,
a web of vine leaves exhausting the vane's tip
sink in a swell of dust. Still.

The distance between your fingers, & the water when you swallow,
bloats my eyes—waiting for the puffing of rug,
piled muffins, one-by-one in your mouth—
the campfire relieving the shadow of the dawn on the road.
A sleepy fox crosses the zig-zag of the road resting
between segments. I am hungry
& eat leaves along the edge of the straight shoulder.

3 BREAKOUT

The distance. A black car pulls to the side of the road.
The Cow got out piling the raincoat collar at the neck.
"Will he be ready? We have a long trip ahead."

The narrow granite wall explodes clearing the smoke.
He steps out onto your foot the floor of the road the sinking gravel.

"Ready?" He nodded. The distance disappeared in
the car moving down the road tiptoeing round the curve.

(*Common Sense*, 1978)

from LICORICE CHRONICLES

XIV

coordinating cities gulls still gull, and, arms binged with wine, as wine

pin roars in galeforce over lines,

horizon on gum letting loose a brack

of crickets by the door

near lowering eyes of a schooled quench

begging for a glass of water, and I sit watching

a jar of water with grass

in it watching amoebas swimming around and, I conclude

everything far as jar or jars is concerned is

plain dough   starting to be known   by a bad smell

heading bearing out conclusion   air as seams

that where there's smoke there's   and, whichever way you burn

one, both, or one foot is still

flat on the ground

and, sunrising further in the east   whereever that is, each day

leading to conclusions :

I watch a brief rumple on my arms called "luck"

and listen to the sound of ants crawling around in the ivy,

cooling down several frazzled josssticks

I found moving under my nose. and, dry moss's crumbling at the base

of the wall of my room, and, a.m. turns p.m. turns a.m., levying etc

again lining mindwharf with vinyl stew.

you shout "bonvoyage," "good luck" to me,

drolly throw a couple of streamers, fling confetti,

and, turn your back on the water. I wish you "good luck, too."

and the notorious Hedge ends for the day, say...

there's a cold wind   "here's chilled wine"

blowing over catskills, means cold wind

blows under alps or andes or himalayas or rockies, blowing

in dream between my heart

and, a journey rises to my eyes in pastels

somewhere never quite white or black, but dark,

nevertheless, as clouds ledge burst down on paper ledge

for a second, then pass,

rain thru snow,

leak into street. I sit on the border with a mountain sliding into my lap

passing for pins and needles ?

watching various prongs of lightning silently lip a cloud

and, watching rain watch me

and watching a drop give me

kiss of death...WATCH IT...rain's letting up till full fur

white-on-white (tear) turns clear-on-clear

wincing more hills (as evidence)

row of slow regard

out of pouring lines

bearing size out, somewhere missing the point,

reeks of meshes :

some yellow confetti's in my ear.

wall disappears under ivy.

ivy disappears under wind.

there's haut tree smells geschicte "of thee" :

cock your ear. shake out lemon drops.

hear?

can you hear revels burgeon?

can you hear?

silence?

well.....

          does New York, say, bring sense of Paris in spring?

          does Paris bring, say, sense of New York in spring?

          or sense, say, of Paris

          in and out of season?

          or say, no spring, say,

          no seasons competing with airtight nodes

          where synthetic fabric seals in

          timechanges as shoes pinch :

          arch revealing

          either silence or strangeness of mind : say silence,

          where dreams levee and "questions mean naught"

          watching past peel back in slow motions,

          plasmic emphasis of same sounds

leeching still wind : pulse...and, abrupt blue

pendant staggering across a throaty sky,

eye following with

pouring old blood

over your face :

taking a late walk,

turn, say, for the worse,

around block,

past lemon trees

past apple and cherry trees

past arbors

with fig trees on each side

in central park...?...

revolving odd turn of mind

in backward glance, squinch eye

with "huh"

an owl.

owl's are thought wise.

they have talons.

talons help them catch rats.

they eat rats.

who? owls or talons?

owls do.

BEWARE.

do not be an owl.

do not, moreover, be a rat.

all men are rats.

rats have four legs.

men have two legs. they are half rats.

who?

men.

men are friends.

they help each other learn.

they love learning for its own sake.

it pays to learn for its own sake.

it does not pay to be an owl.

it pays to be half rat. rats are waxy.

watch the sky burgundy.

it will leap into your soul like a hot roll in gravy.

it tastes sparkling. like owl soup.

soon there's nothing left.

nothing.

let's sit down to another new meal.

let us break bread together.

it pays to learn love for its own sake.

nothing.

watch it, tho. you can get drunk on nothing.

next morning just add water. you're drunk again.

on nothing.

nothing is nourishing.

what is happening?

nothing's happening.

nothing?

nothing.

happening?

happening? nothing's happening.

can't you smell it,
stretch your head out a little.

soon your head is an odd nose.

now…smell.

mmmmmmmmmmmmmmmmmmmmmmmmmmmmmmmmmmmmm

O! O! America.

O! America.

O! America. America. etc.

turn your brown nose upwind.

that's what's happening!

swooping "cree"

kissing airturn

phrase turning, suddenly, in swoop

over sea ledge :

one shall tout noblesse oblige. one shall change with changing times.

one shall prove ordinary mating.

one shall change to remain the same :

one shall remain airtight.

one shall prove very fat and wise.

one shall prove very sleek, too.

one shall wane and wax.

one will prove one shell. eating out one's own one heart. one.

lie down. curl up.

let butterflies flutter out your ear.

listen...

"you'll live a long and furry life"

fleshgold dawn of mon

tauk silvering a sheet of cloud

slatewalk for eye

and, eye for sun

threading horizon, then, rising loom...

and down burns

threads, synthetic stroke

under much bringing to life   "than eye can see"

colors, out of breath jarring me breathless, and, leaving

hum stickling book of routines unread...weaving changes into blood,

sleeves inflow to total plasm, without sense of roast duck

but weighing intangible oranges,

turning goose cooking cooked goose

smothered in brine, with water chestnuts and lemons.

APR 1966

(*Licorice Chronicles*, 1979)

from WORD OF MOUTH

Open mouth open through

And through   Make body

And odious window   With

Mind projected into   Turn

Out the lights   Lets watch

Latch onto for all purposes

Suppose as motion what-

Ever seems to even take

Odd possession of the cease-

Less session obliterating

A literature of season

Apertures without question

Snore   Dotting   Glance a

Last little back   Familiar

Cough   Interesting leg

Over right arm   Sit

Like that for awhile   Gaze

Slightly off on center

Fill with refrigerator

Idiocy   Dial mercy

Recline through an in-

Clination to carry a

Slope further than or-

Iginally thought indigo

Whole year focus on

Pull down chiaroscuro

Shades   See an immense

Range of angel things

In hinge black and

White   Avoid any heights

Step on scale   Weigh

Self   Subtract other

Blubber famously into

Tape   Ape a kind of

Surrounding prosperous

Phosphorous posterity

Walker passers   Wire

Desire to be alone to

A system of interest

Plus interlocking loans

To be paid no matter

What is any principle

Prepare steak in it

Remind to eat   To con-

Summate a summer

Summation   Hum under-

Standably a complete

Range of standing standards

Arrange to meet some-

Where   Subtle to catch

Talk shows where going

Habits   Obits to a com-

Plex of mornings   Neither

Pleasant nor interesting

Pressure building   Grow

Sure, make sure   Plant

Comma tend   Come out

Of it out of a coma   Cut

Interstate intestines in

Half   Follow shit up

System of departures   Sta-

Tionary writing on sta-

Tions in life   Statutes to

Live and work by   Ties

That bind to   Ions to re-

Lease indicators of ease

But dot dot dot

A way of plotting

rigid

other functions

movement table

trace back

(*Word of Mouth*, 1986)

Nick Piombino [1942]

MY LADY CARRIES STONES

to me. Somewhere they are building
I go for a walk
and all eyes are closed
buzzing around my head
where the box containing old things
mixed with twigs and leaves
catches the bus to the beach alright.
They were speaking soft
to be accepted as they are
itch and scratch
and the dizzy blessing
pays his money quickly
such as gadgets and miniature
long dresses and sticks
yellow petals and completely
half here. They listen
for a check. Wet on the rocks.
Enters the church worried
gets into his car and hurries
like tall stones. My bandages
snap and bite me. Can you borrow
remain here with me? Summer
is transferred to another department
in the 15th Century. Lying there

(*Poems*, 1988)

■

The simple poetry of sleep
Enclosed in the hand held absence
Of narrative time
Who would dare
To call it a mistake
If the words were not forthcoming
All the evidence of life was there anyway
Slightly askew diagrammatic evocation of a galaxy
Something felt like it wanted to come into existence
And then chose to wait and let it happen
Compelled to listen for the presence of mystery
What was satisfied caused to descend polyphonically
Abetted by the implication of vocable sound
Heard between random intervals of meaning
Voices rising in chromatic insignificant phrases
Against the lapping of specific waves
Minute portions brush granite aural forms
Density glitters between vibrant afterimages
In a world of green vegetation and brown arid hills
Very close to the sea
The obscure aberrations of flora and fauna
Astonished the oceanographers
The infinite variety of evolving forms
The immensely long natural tracks between wooded hills
The mere suggestion of lunar ridges and shadows
Added a strangely silent atmosphere to the now faded photographs
Of this non-event in space and time
Which existed only in its virtual state
These were actual pockets of reality
Embedded in a completely hypothetical situation
Of which all the emblems, significations, symbols and signs
Were utterly verbal in form
The horizon—its mask, its secret periphery
At the closest zone of its solitude
Pressing its ultimate, final realization
In a position contrary to its margin
The poem is intrinsic to the machine
The notes have a duration which corresponds
To the illuminated objects bright as they are
Over aeons become their signs
And when the distances contract at their maximum velocity
Time is almost completely under the influence
Of all those forces which are precursors to events

The oldest trees and the youngest stars
Have been talking a long time
The unwinking hills, the apostrophes of small paths
Slowly take their places on the constellations of language
The commentaries spoken in computerized tongues
The soft technology improvised within the logarithmic system
Of substitutions and exchanges
Of concepts and energy

(Poems, 1988)

THE PYRAMIDS

Write the poem

before the pleasure's

lost. Make it yours.

There are disturbances.

Mother holds a scarf

to her face, "Father

I sang so beautifully

tonight. Paste my words

to your lips…"

(Poems, 1988)

■

Any m meant they came to a destination. Tracing their way
on a map of words: meant, say, diagram, variation. It names
either isolation. This camp on a south, that on a fifth,
variation of design indicates a segment. Caught parallel words
attract artifacts by naming. This word in a sentence is named
violet. This, however, is merely the name of the word, not
the word. Dealt a deuce, in the story it is secondary,
therefore lies in the background with an infinity of possible
future consequences. Just south of the meaning is the
interpretation. That they are nameable, distinguishable as the
words assigned to hieroglyphically signify the words ascribed
to their writer who associates them to past references. These
are black on a canvas. The stream of associations cast away.
Past pines, past trains. Certainty. As in a story, cast away in
the typing, the memory of uses for the appointment book.
The things hold sway, they are so large, gleaming.

(*Poems*, 1988)

TIME TRAVEL

All about. All about all with a word seeming across the world
to an other. It a time, ventures forth, teeming a way and over
the place, bending fast and ending forward. That the place
who signals a last, pleading away to feel this way to take, and
outward, nearing the f which is fortunate, skipping a side to
make it tip, about to either when then never has to of wake
and clear, approach it, sifting, never a way but now a play, to
brush to light, alight, so fear remarks turning a core near the
back, darker there, tipped forward, surround, urgent, near to,
lifting a stationary object, from one perspective to another,
measuring the latitude, lending credence to their stare,
wondering, wandering. To place above, had a chance but
where (who), unless biding the time breaks fast into motto,
stay there: a hint, to lend, unending mystery of creation, but
butter suffices, a gun dismisses and the mention, edging into
a furor but lost, abounds, treats masses and a salute. Hey,
hey, butter them up or gun them down, the lessee the least
structured element in a shrewd dialogue of awakening which
is translated unevenly later, but wait: then a tup, a type, not
naughty but also not brave, existing for the absolute just
about. Shift.

Leave it alone. The strip a smooth shadow backing
slowly into purple dawn, permit the ambassador the unearthly
fee of remembering the beginning which is simply complex.
Pleading, bleeding, not the inside thoughts but considerations
bound to move inside the forgotten evidence, moving not an
inch but a millionth of a space, because this accurate scrap
has all the knowledge needed to act and something else was
stopping the word-character from slipping into its usual role of
deriving the differences between the x'es. That is, if the
actual person is hidden more than twice within not the lies
and the misfortunes of error and intentional deviance, but the
mere hint of a subject which by now any of the purported
members could be accused of. You could say this is an exact
copy but this is not accurate in that there is no defining
circuitry to determine the routes back to the center, regarding
the changes of light, habitude and gleaning all that could be
gathered from those that had observed the situation as closely
as possible and this was difficult to do without generating
immense amounts of unnecessary embarrassment, but the
image (and this is partly a fantasy) is an image that actually
defied understanding completely. Although this kind of
defining process seems useless in this context, the narrow
turn of feeling that was defined there would seem illustration
enough of an inner decision which had been insufficiently
wrought. This is not a way of pardoning the error, but it is a
way of questioning the intent in persecuting the attacker,
which, in its guise of deft translator, is a burden which could
indeed have been dispensed with. Such are the arguments of
a verbal pivot, which, in its very function, deserves some
notice. Not to passion, but to turn, not to turn on but to
passage, founding a territory which has boundaries parallel to
a transitive function. And on.

Circling a device immobilizes it, catching the fragrance
signifies the unnerving tendency to doubt, of which the
underlying function is ambiguous. Take the breath. Should
voice confound the nearness of wish, they protrude by edging
noiselessly towards the border whispering their opinions to
each other on the far side of the desk, having the sun treat
this photograph to a variety of reflections. A pause. Wherein
the saturated emotions invite inquiry, bending the average
conversation into an attitude of mercy and grandiose
overtones. The choice of word silences the moment which,
in this imprecise way covers the alternate significance which
ranges from the mere implication to the full transmission of

choral amplitude. Set out on this voyage to gain witness to
this particularity of which not the gradual return is the most
difficult, but the ageless hesitation to reveal its own intent,
hiding it (coveting it) and revealing it constantly, in an
oscillating movement, characteristic of a slow funnelling sonic
configuration, braced by a far earlier wall of pronouncements.
One at a time, urging a cleansing, washing away, rocking a
quietude, first held, wanting an estimate, felt last, praising a
gathering whirl of meanings, brushed back and gently
caressing (of course, and framing) the face.

Far from an utterance of explanation, the first growl
widens into a yawn, settling the head on a large rock, reading
the clouds. Moon, in all of its emissions, swept backwards,
clouds with their calm, icy detachment spelling a dissatisfied
halo. This nurse, who houses the barely born, dresses herself
quickly setting out to the sentence's name. Heed this, they
say searingly and the television clicks on, the tape player
whirring, each letter caught off guard and split from its
anchor, she poured out her solitude into an iron counter,
scratching and biting the meanings from their origins,
listening, a gathering listening having preceded this for
centuries, for aeons. Festooned and congratulated, the
heaving groans and shattering applause touch off a fuse
which, over this unthinkable stretch of time, has moved
slightly from its original position. Farther and farther, blessing
and playing, in all the puzzles and tests, the information
straying and combining and changing, they tack it to a wall,
facing a telescope towards one plane and a microscope
towards the other. Yet nearer still the breath imposes its
attributes, its sticky and throaty vowels leaking and cracking
the surface, while below the image is partly clearing and
partly fading, an indecipherable system of signs disclosing the
most apparent symbolism and method.

A sound disturbs, reminds, not the end but a trail,
hesitating before an unjust juror, the complainant voices a
fact. This clasps a sentence, begs it to succeed, armoring
intent with confidence, teetering on the edge of
apprehension. And again, not the noise, not the indifference,
not the teaching or the inadequate notation, but the ceaseless
voice of sputtering, the yielding, unending voice of caution.
Who obeys. Long the, while the, participate relax, veering

away from atomic discussions, the lingering melody touching
here then there among their attentive minds, a cynical voice
adds, is necessary, with irony hidden inside this phrase,
reminding us now that too much clarity narrows speech,
silent speech, deflecting and inflecting insurmountable doubt.
Alerting them, at last, lulled to the last syllable of accorded
reason, soundlessly and songlessly asleep.

(*Poems*, 1988)

THE FROZEN WITNESS

Some moments stolen by a slave...
A way of sifting, a kind of secret stuffing
Comes to reunite the lost and found.

What is invisible is most conceivable,
A missing object unconsciously engulfed,
An inanimate combining that measures emptiness.

And out of nothing, something comes,
A clanging memory, a wrenching glance,
Illicit and unfounded gasps,

Gaps of silence widened to a world.
Such probabilities attend to sense
The way the eye invades a room,

The way the slightest attention to a doubt
Will fix forever a foggy afternoon
On a quiet street in a nameless part of town,

The way the unknown finally begets the known.
And, if so, what's worth retaining
Of what remains, in spite of constant turning

(manuscript)

Ray DiPalma [1943]

SHEAF MARK

A spontaneous momentum
imposed on character
reflective part by part

Wit tack and hitch

Rocks ripen

Lair focus and bricked-up logic

What's behind the greener level

Brass

Tone gnaws the grey wick

Gauge the yawning mool
No pretending the far thought
or ponder's briar and cobble

A nostalgia for barbarism
setting forth the grievance

(*Roof* magazine, 1979)

FRAGMENT

sooner or later the sun cracks rebecca
sooner or later the sun hits
and not much is left of her
and cabbage the dog

misery is singing its pennies on the horizon
and rebecca of the sleek mechanics kisses
her knuckles

sick rebecca
of the tick and lop
inches through the dry foliage
cashes in her stockings

1001 sharks the sun
re–b re–b re–b
hawks and sharp stones

(*Numbers and Tempers*, 1993)

POEM

In danger of which
all other things are
part matter part remark

Good morning
and afternoon floundering
in its own extravagance

In danger of ending
and none too soon to light
the modest impression we have of light

No candle no wick no taper
torch or rotting log
we can forgive the head its buryings

The clasp of resources
to the ebbing image
this too is still an elevation

Mood needs a sampler now and again
now and again
blue sitting forgiving the dark

victims especially

(*Numbers and Tempers*, 1993)

EMPIRE SMOKE, FORGERIES,
SALIENT & THE RITZ

China island dream
   dragging blot centuries
suddenly smoke
   boxes rather close
Virginia determination
   echo drowned luncheon
dyspeptic lodgings cigarette
   electricity put into words
and always in silence
   taken color
reminiscent climax for evil
   sanctuary driven
common flames louder glance
   temperate dancing
books claret shake pose boots
   hire steps bird angle
wagon pity

   matters eight occasion
unequal glorious coin line
   set matters loan pier
sterling abbey post amber
   merit thread
doorway grace lemon cull
   conditions back shop duke from kicking
green stifle measures vein lob
   bas-relief cork tomb cardinal
about sunset air
   sixteen figs and two small loaves
dense finches
   rattling craters
broad bracelets of blue beads
   envy of the rain
storm bay
   anchors famine rocks coral proper lagoon

cogent arrow
  porous strata accurate mill roots
great certain registers genius
  blister hill pry speech
cosmic matrix
  a tribal fold in the other
court marine wafer flame
  savant beat
skids plateau
  wide timid basking
husks sham cries arc lane
  image gable as attitude
gates limbo
  does he epitome sort fumes
gusts ranger moment pole
  bulk mere field zones
cave droll

  flint pylons
daylight board
  alcohol sand current
shepherd garden deuce
  in beg whisper mount
just dull wedge lord
  buoyant neon
chronic kindle motif
  stippled vizier tambourine
vicar bone vents torpor
  gazette canal
rain crow walking the load
  ticket lips
turf lace
  buckle chin
pressure mole
  shed berry

pairings fever junction
  warp shoot
tropical vapor pulse
  cool blown dark hovel
chant rind
  grey beams dome chimes
mandolin corners

half bronze clear shore
coup manor check
    festival inches
palms and pastels
    brass vials and sector
aureole gate
    bubble wire
atmosphere dart
    sly garlic and caporal
after soft sketches

(*Numbers and Tempers*, 1993)

THE BED

Dark o'clock
Be solid maybe inside
But adequately
Dead one by the sequence

And tumble
Light
Presses daylight
Brick to waver brick

To build or boundary
You'd think
Come closer
And the voices

All so flat
Half-fallen off
Hunting the careless
In the parade

How can white be
The moon looks down
And turns
Thin and bitter

So I'll go back
We'll reach
Every back and mirror
Turning dangerous

Between the nostrils
Earning a little borrowed air
Right right proportions
Crabbing and opaque between yawns

A first coat a
Second coat or
Are you hearing things
Perfect decoys

Like the tug of yellow
Like neighboring thumb and finger
Yours and hers
Mine and yours or not yours and hers

Delicate and unperturbed
A slithering irridescence
That would be inscrutable
Were it not fact

Wan clever minutely natural
Nearly perfect
Gone to seed like columbine
Nearly perfect

As when all the lights
Go out you can walk backwards
With perfect impunity
And say so

How clever to be invisible
A length of iron pipe in your pocket
Your voice a shadow
Behind your teeth

An inheritor
Pumping the space with decimals
Approach the cultivating claw
Brother

Where four billion years
Of nature two million dollars
One million miles and thirteen
Hours inspire chat

There there now the coincidences
Back to back the convincing quirks
Make for the calmly circumspect
A perfect garden in which to dance

Moves winding meticulous
As buds twist a branch
Light dismantling a wave
Memory copying touch

A surge and violent hush
Composed aurora but can't trust
The wind now though it's a great response
I prefer to the ripeness of words

Passing through a perfect frame
Of backlit steam reds greens blues
Pausing just long enough
To take the measure

The lines the four corners
Embody memory large and impersonal
No better to say
The stiff angles of deflection

No better
To say no better to say
Comes and goes but just so far
Purpling as it happens

Amicably solemn
The remote terrors of proportion
Confide the raw
Dreaming the intricate

Unaccompanied
The word of a stranger
Nostrums and random exceptions
Inclination or opinion

The fastidious analogue
The ballad and the prejudice
Intense solitude
Wilderness to wilderness

The coin or the kindness
A high tambourine
Shrugged shoulders
Spectacle volunteer

Peculiar to certain orders
Like the assassin
Broken imperfectly on a conviction
But enthralled by a mere prospect

Dependable phantoms
The song after the music
Not the chase but
The paint drying

Grammar is black
Syntax is starch
Hello Reverend X
Hello Reverend Y

A thin black line
The collar of the coat turned up
Evertheless I liked the way mere touch
Could make the beads spin

Make me feel tribal
In my secure sense of objectivity
Like a great ritual vessel
Lost but floating free

Stock water disguise functions
You pay for the freedom
To come with me
Water and brain chemistry

Wine brandy apples rosin
Cork paper toys perfumes
Oil pitch tar oak pewter
Linen silk lace salt gin

Good loam soil weighs
Eighty pounds a cubic foot
Clay carries a strong negative electric
Charge so things cling to it

(*Numbers and Tempers*, 1993)

HADRIAN'S LANE

What fills the whisper and
all want fragments why along to check
the short page what your convictions
this is shudder and this antenna mail

Not from here like a lot of wax lost wax
in fact misplaced the emptying the song
finishers indexing the aces ring phone
and circulate here and there a wave or

Something much harder for sleep like dance
rendering the up trace or cross cowers
for a bow makes for silence the big
polar wag the shift heads to roam

The volume cores the abject delirium of
capital the compressors fill from middle out
with a weird blue light too much focus on
the night too few stars a big chunk of it

How inert the dutiful to stare right into
how inflected as it were to bend or shape
from a straight to a narrow this is the way
from however to how best you hound the path

Remote air logic to take the measure
from ether logic to casual fulcrum block
can it go up and out into that remoteness
strain to the then and then and then softer flight

Well it seems there's a drubbed restraint
makes for the go road and empty bit of hum
nice target maybe or perspective's arena
squared in the calm wake of looksee

And then has a gander for totals
sprints the high street and makes for the fog
number shadow clue and mark it from rut to rut
frost heaves apprehend then the gallery of trees

Appetites tug at the argument and mood freight
a brain nab for smooth talk addlers of give go
all so much carbon the think's gummed
coordinated like currents but breaks the ankle

Obdurate wince to scuff the instanter
the junk prick cracking the ellipse
so now it's how you say an oval and hung
in a corrosive pose you get at it prying

(*Numbers and Tempers*, 1993)

THE TABLE

Not wide but a wing
Balancing a sphere
Dissolving in a reward
Of fog—conversation's
Beard of light

Interest reaches
And there are large white plates
Indicators
Wintering
Tall glasses and a bowl of salt

Cold but agreeable
The place for it
The abstract agriculture of stones
The extended hand and
Bent neck of the earnest pilgrim

Just a hand around the curve
Once enough
And to believe
An accident
In the dark

(*Numbers and Tempers*, 1993)

ANNOTATIONS TROPES AND LACUNAE
OF THE ITOKU MASTER

The Japanese paragraph
with the silver light

The hair pulled back
at the nape of the neck

into a four inch [*plait*]
[*search for accurate Chinese term*]

Incandescent aquamarine
a lion kite tracing the tide-line

(It's a *queue* from the Latin *cauda*)
Perfect fragments hexahedrons and dodecahedrons

But no long answers
and a choice of glass beads

Ashamed to yawn
a secret garden in which to do so

A reflector a recorder [*not a scribe*]
walking slowly through the apparition

Burnt lavender and alfalfa
many chimneys then the dunes

A circle of leaves to push against
the phrase [*quavers*] [*circles taken*]

In the dance it's permissible
for this to show

[*What should the face wear*]
[*Where should the face be*]

Black and white brought to sepia
Reflection mindful of the reverse

The passage of 300 years
Short step short step and stride

What would you have
What would you take

The answer is impossible to lift
[*The mountain has outgrown its name*]

No need to ask again
Would you have another description of a surface

Fired clay or the paper coat
[*The pilgrim wears*]

This frozen cup
for every moment used

A bowl with a double bezel
[*To remind the mouth of speech*]

Noises that begin in the night
Single syllables and continued radicals

[*Out of the leaf and branch*]
[*Fingers to the hands*] answered in the roots

Groans in the affirmative
the inner phrase

In one breath [*A motionless thickness*]
the stone quill

maneuvers of the moon
[*river rites of the barge men*]

guides of sleep and dreams initiative
a handful of sphagnum [*summer heat*]

[*ropes*] [*marsh fog*] [*fires on the shore*]
[*miners and farmers*] a soaking rain

scrub pines at the water's edge
a spider's thread drops from the morning star

sneers of dialect [*overheard*] amid the clatter
of pots and bowls and rising steam

strange fish and marking the days
on the fingers of one hand

launched along this rind
[*exile*] monks hauling a huge bell

[*worked from panels and ladders*]
[*a gong timed with the breeze*]

a black hand repainted red
to ornament a wooden bowl meant for fruit

I watched [*I did not see*]
[*a stone perch halfway up the cliffs*]

the player stops his piece before
the final two notes and begins again

a stone-fall [*an earthquake in the north-west*]
[*the labor of claws*] a colonnade of timbered arches

persuasive shadows and the bodies that rely
upon their confines and [*exclusions*]

frame of bones [*bone*] [*its grain*]
diplomats [*bird chasers*] from the provinces

fill the arcades with the weight of chatter
[*the exhausted echo*] bobbing and shuffling

through the reeds at the pond's edge
the moon extends its light across

the unplanned examination [*prunings*]
[*the map a landscape painted*] no more

idle and unsmiling an episode's remove from
a sudden [*whiteness*] roots in the boundary

the arrival on foot marked by green [*banners*]
and a [*pageant*] of circling dogs

assertions and disputations where the periphery
begins [*crude ornamentals*] inverted straw figures

an ark filled with raw fish at the entrance
of every hut [*illusion into fable*]

rumors that a small group of warriors
had died in their sleep after their ascent

to the shrine a cone of [*salt*] at the foot
of each body

no solace in plots of supersition
[*anonymous*] [*staunchings*]

(*Mock Fandango*, 1991)

WHEN TORRID RHYMES WITH FOREHEAD

The beautiful solution
Is the rotate and build-up
A hurricane beat just to stay alive
That part of the action
That goes through the window
Arms crossed over the eyes
Crisscross salt with the big music
And no one knows the stranger's face
A nice hat though and a surge
In the car
        Here's where
When the tough get going
The weird get wired
Saxophones rough with the dervish loons
And oracle sports short-cut
The harmonies and technicians
Only put electricity in the cardboard
But meeting the expectations
Of humor's restraint
Is a proton event not
Eternity's gas leak
        The fat name
Returned in the lion's mouth
Hero foam and
Hot legs sharp shirts coats off
And it looks like it
Won't have to rain for a while
And there'll be a whole lot of music
Before anyone gets knocked down
Tim Tom Jocko Bill Ted Larry Fred Mike
Al Burt John Dale Chuck George Mel Joe
We're all watching the ghosts
Back in the long long ago

(*Numbers and Tempers*, 1993)

THE PREROGATIVE OF LIEDER

Here comes the question
The weather the sun and its shadow
The unauthorized itch that was scratched
Here comes the question

Intuition devotion before or after
An answer a question an answer
Surely far below but on high
Dramatic steams cast in the sulks

Means more clouds
Space interviews the rhyme
And the entire weight decides not
With a shall instead of a will

Momentarily a cormorant is the distance
Knotted no lurking in quietude
The floral pot-shaped voice is autumn
Papered over with a spectacle of grieving wit

The customary harping immersed in a story
Truthful to remembering the asking where
And telling backwards from the poured hymn
Propped along the winter and profane

(*Grand Street* magazine, 1992)

MOTION OF THE CYPHER

Accepting
the seduction
fosters
the once organized
imperfect
outside
that was the model
of center.

Not focus
but the turned-to
culled from
the eliminated
and balanced
a pejorgraph
of choice and
limn.

The sprawl
before
and the sprawl
after balanced
outside
of language
and inside
the pattern.

To be taken so
in the hush
of impulse
and worth how
is it done
to be done
to the order
and its shiver.

(*Motel* magazine, 1991)

THE WRONG SIDE OF THE DOOR

Supplementary to the account
Are a series of tangled memories
And observations at random
Written in a logbook bound in burlap

After the first day
We crossed a series of interlocking rectangles
Whose perimeters were planted with palm trees
As though it were an act of generosity

No thought was given to the distance
We had come—remaining outside of responsibility
On the second day we neglected to make
A statement of position and description of place

On the third day we encountered
A wave-line etched with salt in a granite wall
We considered a name for this mark
But moved north when the rains came

Crossing the calamities of 75,000 years of top soil
All that could be said was
"I think I agree with you" and despite a
Lack of precision a certain brilliance was the result

We began to merge with the unimportant and superfluous
Aspects of our going—the submission to detail and the mention
Of secondary regrets—all that mattered was the order
And ceremony mediated by and from the immediate mind

(manuscript, 1992)

WE FOREGO MIMICRY

Thrift alone for meaning ceases
As this then starts from the middle out
The primitive halcyon required

Unpeopled knowledge waiting for creatures
Erect reactions
In a comic mode outside the cave
Is architecture

Not the mountain but the thrown shaft
The describer to the real
Transfixing the included reflection
That's at last made to count

The foreignness of the syllable
And the visible
Watched in prolonged alleviation
Of ever-changing epigram

(manuscript, 1993)

POEM FOR CLAUDE

The sterile line glows
A serpent of pallid lightning

To achieve a filament of white granite
And red marl

In the absence
An erasure

A pleat in the vague scald
Restores the dome
With irreparable logic
And smothers it
In anticipation of vindictive clarity

The mute word read
Watched like an indecipherable crime

Toneless scraping around the silhouette
The flint quill swollen with ink

Migratory burlesques
Patched to the wings

Triangulation
Of the blind scruple

Predatory margins and
The aloof tilt of uncial ground smooth

(*To* magazine, 1993)

Michael Palmer [1943]

DEAREST READER

He painted the mountain over and over again
from his place in the cave, agape
at the light, its absence, the mantled
skull with blue-tinted hollows, wren-
like bird plucking berries from the fire
her hair alight and so on
lemon grass in cafe in clear glass.
Dearest reader there were trees
formed of wire, broad entryways
beneath balconies beneath spires
youthful head come to rest in meadow
beside bend in gravel road, still
body of milky liquid
her hair alight and so on
successive halls, flowered carpets and doors
or the photograph of nothing but pigeons
and grackles by the shadow of a fountain.

(First Figure, 1984)

VOICE AND ADDRESS

You are the owner of one complete thought

Its sons and daughters
march toward the capital

There are growing apprehensions to the south

It is ringed about
by enclaves of those who have escaped

You would like to live somewhere else

away from the exaggerated music
in a new, exaggerated shirt

a place where colored stones have no value

This hill is temporary
but convenient for lunch

Does she mean that the afternoon should pass

in such a manner
not exactly rapidly

and with a studied inattention

He has lost his new car
of which you were, once,

a willing prisoner

a blister in your palm
identical with the sky's bowl

reflected in the empty sentence

whose glare we have completely shed
ignoring its freshness

The message has been sent

across the lesser fractures in the glass
where the listeners are expendable

The heart is thus flexible

now straight now slightly bent
and yesterday was the day for watching it

from the shadow of its curious house

Your photo has appeared
an island of calm

in a sea of priapic doubt

You are the keeper of one secret thought
the rose and its thorn no longer stand for

You would like to live somewhere

but this is not permitted
You may not even think of it

lest the thinking appear as words

and the words as things
arriving in competing waves

from the ruins of that place

(*First Figure*, 1984)

THE PAINTED CUP

This was not experience
but life itself and the hills
not visible an iron
table set among the blues. Un-
acknowledged years will have passed
across their faces, so the long-billed
ibis, cautiously
to take bread at your hand
like the infant named
for the one who laughs and,
laughing, fills the painted cup
with coarse salt. The angled
areas between them then, cast
in a range of hues
that to speech are as distant,
or dissonant, matter.

(*First Figure*, 1984)

FIFTH PROSE

Because I'm writing about the snow not the sentence
Because there is a card—a visitor's card—and on that card
    there are words of ours arranged in a row

and on those words we have written house, we have written
    leave this house, we
have written be this house, the spiral of a house, channels
    through this house

and we have written The Provinces and The Reversal and
    something called the Human Poems
though we live in a valley on the Hill of Ghosts

Still for many days the rain will continue to fall
A voice will say Father I am burning

Father I've removed a stone from a wall, erased a picture from
    that wall,
a picture of ships—cloud ships—pressing toward the sea

words only
taken limb by limb apart

Because we are not alive not alone
but ordinary extracts from the tablets

Hassan the Arab and his wife
who did vaulting and balancing

Coleman and Burgess, and Adele Newsome
pitched among the spectators one night

Lizzie Keys
and Fred who fell from the trapeze

into the sawdust
and wasn't hurt at all

and Jacob Hall the rope-dancer
Little Sandy and Sam Sault

Because there is a literal shore, a letter that's blood-red
Because in this dialect the eyes are crossed or quartz

seeing swimmer and seeing rock
statue then shadow

and here in the lake
first a razor then a fact

(Sun, 1988)

■

Mei-mei, here is the table
Who knows the word for it

Sikhs today are dancing in the streets,
some say a dance of death

Bernadette has written *Utopia*

A quadrate sun is entering

and Sappho tells Alcaeus
You are a scratch on a vase

Perfect things here and there,
small marks in stolen house

eyes rolled back inside,
vein, milk and rust

chin's hardness
"forehead filled with dust"

(Sun, 1988)

■

You say
A miracle from Heaven

You say
I'm fine I'm fine I'm really going blind

Gay as a skylark today
You say

I haven't an ache or a pain
in me in my body inside

I'm fine I'm fine I'm really going blind
It's a joy to be alive

I had a vistor tonight
with suit and beard and Malacca cane

climbed through my window
and entered me

Is this such a bad thing
Is this a thing at all

Each evening there's a poppy in my brain
which closes before dawn

Whatever happened then will not happen again
Please move my arm

(*Sun*, 1988)

■

Desire was a quotation from someone.

Someone says, This This. Someone says, Is.

The tribe confronts a landscape of ice.

He says, I will see you in the parallel life.

She says, A miser has died from the cold; he spoke all his sentences
and meant no harm.

My voice is clipped, yours a pattern of dots.

Three unmailed have preceded this, a kind of illness.

Now I give you these lines without any marks, not even a breeze

dumb words mangled by use

like reciting a lesson or the Lord's Prayer.

How lovely the unspeakable must be. You have only to say it and it
tells a story.

A few dead and a few missing

and the tribe to show you its tongue. It has only one.

                                        (*Sun*, 1988)

SUN

Write this. We have burned all their villages

Write this. We have burned all the villages and the people in them

Write this. We have adopted their customs and their manner of dress

Write this. A word may be shaped like a bed, a basket of tears or an X

In the notebooks it says, It is the time of mutations, laughter at jokes,
secrets beyond the boundaries of speech

I now turn to my use of suffixes and punctuation, closing Mr. Circle with a single stroke, tearing the canvas from its wall, joined to her, experiencing the same thoughts at the same moment, inscribing them on a loquat leaf

Write this. We have begun to have bodies, a now here and a now gone, a past long ago and one still to come

Let go of me for I have died and am in a novel and was a lyric poet, certainly, who attracted crowds to mountaintops. For a nickel I will appear from this box. For a dollar I will have text with you and answer three questions

First question. We entered the forest, followed its winding paths, and emerged blind

Second question. My townhouse, of the Jugendstil, lies by Darmstadt

Third question. He knows he will wake from this dream, conducted in the mother-tongue

Third question. He knows his breathing organs are manipulated by God, so that he is compelled to scream

Third question. I will converse with no one on those days of the week which end in y

Write this. This is pleasure and pain and there are marks and signs. A word may be shaped like a fig or a pig, an effigy or an egg
but
there is only time for fasting and desire, device and design, there is only time to swerve without limbs, organs or face into a
scientific
silence, pinhole of light

Say this. I was born on an island among the dead. I learned language
on this island but did not speak on this island. I am writing to you
from this island. I am writing to the dancers from this island. The
writers do not dance on this island

Say this. There is a sentence in my mouth, there is a chariot in my
mouth. There is a ladder. There is a lamp whose light fills empty
space and a space which swallows light

A word is beside itself. Here the poem is called What Speaking Means
to Say
        though I have no memory of my name

Here the poem is called Theory of the Real, its name is Let's Call This,
and its name is called A Wooden Stick. It goes yes-yes, no-no. It goes
one and one

I have been writing a book, not in my native language, about violins
and smoke, lines and dots, free to speak and become the things we
speak, pages which sit up, look around and row resolutely toward
the setting sun

Pages torn from their spines and added to the pyre, so that they will
resemble thought

Pages which accept no ink

Pages we've never seen—first called Narrow Street, then Half a Fragment,
Plain of Jars or Plain of Reeds, taking each syllable in her mouth, shifting
position and passing it to him

Let me say this. Neak Luong is a blur. It is Tuesday in the hardwood forest. I
am a visitor here, with a notebook

The notebook lists My New Words and Flag above White. It claims
to have no inside
        only characters like A-against-Herself, B, C, L, and
N, Sam, Hans Magnus, T. Sphere, all speaking in the dark with their
hands

    G for Gramsci or Goebbels, blue hills, cities, cities with hills,
modern and at the edge of time

                F for alphabet, Z for A, an H in
an arbor, shadow, silent wreckage, W or M among stars

What last. Lapwing. Tesseract. X perhaps for X. The villages are known as
These Letters—humid, sunless. The writing occurs on their walls

                        (*Sun*, 1988)

EIGHTH SKY

It is scribbled along the body
Impossible even to say a word

An alphabet has been stored beneath the ground
It is a practice alphabet, work of the hand

Yet not, not marks inside a box
For example, this is a mirror box

Spinoza designed such a box
and called it the Eighth Sky

called it the Nevercadabra House
as a joke

Yet not, not so much a joke
not Notes for Electronic Harp

on a day free of sounds
(but I meant to write "clouds")

At night these same boulevards fill with snow
Lancers and dancers pass a poisoned syringe,

as you wrote, writing of death in the snow,
Patroclus and a Pharaoh on Rue Ravignan

It is scribbled across each body
Impossible even to name a word

Look, you would say, how the sky falls
at first gently, then not at all

Two chemicals within the firefly are the cause
Twin ships, twin nemeses

preparing to metamorphose
into an alphabet in stone

St.-Benoît-sur-Loire
to Max Jacob

(manuscript)

EROLOG

(a reply)

Asked, Don't you dream, do you ever
or once, did you once—the white

(he)—the white
rain, railings, head-high, erased, no

shadow. And our menhirs, watch-
towers, carbon shores, our almosts—

of speaking, or speaking-seeing, her
lifting, the alphabets and nets.

And the body—listen—and the
body—who's to say—tossed up

in storm the night before.
Or the gnomon or the hourglass or a comb

drawn slowly through the hair
again and again, the droplets of sweat

intermingling, each one a lens, each a question
visible along the surface of the skin.

But did you ever—do you—did you once—
or then—did you then—nights

(he)—nights
had their sentries and gates,

passages where—decibels—maybe folds where—
and I'm speaking from memory here,

memory could not interfere.
So if the fingers, lunate,

could remember the hand
could account for it

could summon the wrist,
fashion gestures and figures.

And if the hallways and stairs,
the slow flares as they settled

to perplex geometry,
angels invisible at the parapets

and the bent, lettristic acrobats
now deaf, held still and

fearing themselves. And you think
you are making a picture

uttering a sound
saying a thing

and you pretend to wrest the helix from its sleep,
to free its threads

amidst the rubble of the square,
whoever was awake and waiting there.

We pointed toward space
as it is before day.

(manuscript)

from "LETTERS TO ZANZOTTO"

LETTER 5

Desired, the snow falls upward,
the perfect future, a text
of wheels. You were born here
between noise and anti-noise
in first bits of film,

silvers of image, the *of*
and its parts—particle
as wave—the perfect
future's steps, its thousand lakes
bells, remarks, lunations and dismays

Days were called the speed book
then the scream book, rail
book then the book of rust, perfect-
bound, perfect shadow of a clock
the photophilographer assembles in negative,

negative sun or negative shade,
negative dust pulled from the ground
and the images negated in ornate frames,
firebricks, funnels and trucks,
figment and testament as one

(manuscript)

Michael Davidson [1944]

THE FEELING TYPE AND HIS FRIENDS

He cannot imagine a doorknob,
it comes off in his hands,
the golden doors designed to provoke
an end to writing
stand unopened, semiotics
rallies behind the market,
all approaches are green and yellow
hitchhiking over the Sierras
yet he has lost all feeling
and the beautiful cortege
will remember him in Reno,
flags bristling against the desert
while he reads the marks
in the pavement
and the sounds they make
are the voices of his friends
playing chess in the dark

(*The Mutibilities*, 1976)

THE SENSATION TYPE AND HIS FRIENDS

A button,
a basket of buttons, a cheese
a fat mama and bacon, a race
in the mountains, a glass
of young women;
he tries to forget everything,
along the way he picks up travellers
in specific directions,
they fill in the spaces

with what they've seen, a garden
a stench of butter, a reeking
of stairways, old gaffers
hugging their treasures under the docks,
America bereft of depth
into you go I, He, We, It, She and Them
go touch what you asked us to give you,
a big bent fender,
a big rear ender.

(*The Mutabilities*, 1976)

■

Tonight is closer than we thought (he meant to writer "colder" but moved closer to the heater instead). The words on the way sounded like "bright star" and "hieroglyph" and "centaur" for the persistence of darkness surrounding brilliant outlines. Traversals of the room, of the lower heavens, of the traversals themselves in which wronged words fuse. He moved closer to the heater instead. It got hotter, and the words melted slightly into "heavens" and "aprons" and "arbors" for the continuity of darkness, spacing and pairing. The light so given to the room that the heavens are here, wearing their dark capes and bearing our outlines. We see through them as they shape and wrap these sensible things in aether and distance ("either endistanced" he heard) or a horse from a rider. I am the centaur at the edge of hemispheres. He wrote, simply, "spheres" and they melted.

(*The Prose of Fact*, 1981)

■

> "*The Professor said he was curious to see how the story would proceed, now we had the frame.*"
>
> —H.D.

Concern for her scar made him think to think something like this:
She could read scare as something that had entered them.
The voice scored what he wrote as having heard.
The ear loves to be wrong about the head.
The heather they saw in the park while running, the color that stayed
There.

A purple or violet reminder, a violent remains.
Out of empty cards some game could be made out of hearts.
He conceived out of what she left: she left.
In her little house, the many chambers, the little figures encased.
Sometimes he loved to be wrong about the head, sometimes he was hot.
If it doesn't hurt, a scar is visible pain, a word for it.
The heart, made of its little men and women, its little glissandi.
If out of something that had entered them nothing remained
That was something, that was a frame.
We are in March, Pisces, but I don't think I thought that,
He remembered instead.

(*The Prose of Fact*, 1981)

THE DREAM DREAM

I am in the book
(or "book")
I see my name
answering back

I am in a building
with stalls
I fall asleep
in the book

each stall sells
a different cure
the doors are locked
which is a cure

I am in "her" house
but these are "my" friends
the ramps and stairs
are steep

he offers to open the doors
for a price
I am outraged
I am eighteeen

and riding a plane
made of glass
the books rise
to the ceiling

there is (are)
a man (men)
chasing me
with pincers

I am twenty-one
and riding a plane
and someone named "me"
gives me

my name, my name
is hers
she is twenty-one
or eighteen

depending on the boat
(or book)
or the name for you
that is very small

and hard to spell
or why I need
to read it
I am late for the boat

but it will wait
it is not a boat
but a wake.

(*The Landing of Rochambeau*, 1985)

THE LANDING OF ROCHAMBEAU

The Captain calls his crew to the deck
we are landing, he says
he doesn't know what to say next
so he adds, be back by noon me hearties
they don't believe him
this is not *Kidnapped*
and he would never use the word "hearties"
besides it is 1780, the harbor
is filled sails
and the postmark covers some of them.

The Captain has gone below to pack
I have never landed before, he thinks,
what do I wear?
so he stands looking into the mirror
am I Rochambeau
or is this the name of my ship
or have we arrived at last in the Port
of Rochambeau where we will strike a deal
with natives, then he remembers
it is 1780, the water is jade green.

The Captain is astonished to learn
that the Colonies have defeated the British
because of a "Stamp Tax," we have landed
too late, he mourns and looks out the window
to his right (our left), tall masts jut
into the Fragonard sky
against which USA 10¢ is branded forever,
he approves of the lettering and decides
not to go ashore after all
but writes a postcard home:

We have landed, the Captain writes
but not very well: it is 1780 and they are rowing
out to meet us: it is impossible to tell
whether we are rowing or they are rowing
or who they might be; many sails fill
the harbor and the postmark is rolling towards us
from Brooklyn on the left (my right),

please advise: this is history and I am
caught in it without a thing to wear
if only my name were Napoleon.

As it is, my life takes up
only seven lines in *The Reader's Encyclopedia*
where it is clear that Washington and I
defeated Cornwallis at Yorktown
and with the French Fleet (which must explain
those sails!) forces "his" capitulation,
the entry leaves "his" a bit vague
in order to make the landing of Rochambeau
a surprise for both sides
including the reader's
who notices the pink sky of Watteau.

I am the Captain of this letter which begins
Dear Home, how I miss the Lisbon Earthquake
the Jansenist purges and leeks with egg,
remember Rochambeau in a foreign port
who must be content with corn and the inflated rhetoric
in pamphlets; I look up, he looks up
we regard him pausing mid-history
for a figure of speech like the ones he used to use
when writing Mme R. in Potsdam
like you are the author of my heart.

But it is 1780 and the Captain never writes postcards,
after all, he is a man of action
and he knows his fleet, the harbor
in which his ships lie at anchor,
he knows the sky, so common to USA
and the water, emerald blue
I'll go ashore, he says, throwing down his pen
and have a drink avec mon equipage
dans les petites boites du port
I know at last what to wear.

For I am Jean Baptiste Donatien de Vimeur
le Comte de Rochambeau and I have landed,
the water is blood red with history
and we are in its claws (he likes
the figure and writes it in his journal

then strides up to the deck
where the weather is clear)
"Lower the boats" he cries to a sailor,
"I will go ashore to The Bronx
where my name will be streets and parks."

But there is no sailor to hear him,
the deck is empty and the postmark
covers most of the fleet,
it has turned cold since Rochambeau landed
and when the French learn of what USA 10¢ means
they will cut off his title, Le Comte
no longer, only a name
in a time on a stamp on a card
for a reader who turns away from 1780
and remembers the water, white as their eyes.

(*The Landing of Rochambeau*, 1985)

FRAMING

> *He openeth our eyes to see the frames of*
> *our enemyes*
> —BISHOP WATSON

We live down here
between the noise
and the words for noise
they begin at night

as the sound of a saw
cutting into wood
and become the dream
of a man opening his eyes

if we need air
it is not for lack of space
or door
but for the density

of persons clamoring for attention,
a child, for example, drowns
in the swimming pool
built that he might be eternal

we stretch the image
beyond music
and when dancing
we leave a portion of emptiness

for the birds that represent us,
in this way
we are protected from distance
that encroaches

all too willingly
there will be no dancing
although a foot raised in the night
might signify a gay mood

when the plane carries someone
you have forgotten how to love
you can still see the silver
and create a story around it

the persistence of its lyrics
stays in the water
long after you have swum past
and that place has closed over

we hear ourselves breathing
that gives texture to silence
and the insomniac has something to do
while waiting for light

if we are tired
there is a list of diversions
if we are not tired
there is a list of diversions

to descend into water
or cook in the northern manner
using tomatoes and ginger
this is an entrance

a marinade using mint and cumin
lemon and cloves
this provides nuance
where the seasons melt one

to the next: emphasis
enters in the form of children
selling cookies
we live over here

between the broker
and the authority on growth
the breeze picks up in the afternoon
and by evening we dream of sleep.

(*The Landing of Rochambeau*, 1985)

TROTH

It's not much of a choice
cut off his head with a really big sword
return next year
and he cuts off yours

forests intervene
trails lead into other trails
green stands for everything
the trail isn't

home with its turrets of gold
flags bent in the wind
recedes behind a stencil of hills
why

repeat the instructions
to the letter
to the letter
is it

a. for what the old woodman wants
b. before c
in a sequence demanding
a cup

and what's inscribed
around its rim
he's been expecting you
and you

know his bony finger
pointing towards a spire
is all there is
of this forest

but signs are intentions
and you follow
besides she's bound
to be attractive

and it's a year later
this is the test:
to be true
not to the tale

as it becomes you
but to the choice
of losing your head
for its telling, troth

takes you to Trotsky
in a book without ideas
they deal with him from a distance
so it is written

(*Post Hoc*, 1990)

CENTURY OF HANDS

The libido portion goes haywire
I fly off in several directions
and occur to myself
at the same time

in a number of colors
alors, I am a liquid substance
and receive letters from the sun
tiens, I believe a rock

is an intelligent machine
with designs on my inside
first the spleen
like a red tongue, then the liver

known as the bad aubergine
no one must know this
I whisper in a bent-over posture
to my mirror

and when they turn off the water
and lock all the doors
it is my books they refuse me
my map my gun

who is it has made my tongue so treacherous
that the most seductive caller
is told I am an aging widower
who has moved out of town

who plants these deceptive fungi
next to the fence
that I may be tested again and again
in the crucible of taxonomies

may he be prevented from witnessing
my Nova, light pouring
out of the sky, may he
become doxa, the speech

of clerks and shopkeepers
that we become the words
for lathe and forge
pounded out of capital

I exit history through the rear
the only orifice left unguarded
what was intended for me
is a bomb in a bouquet

and I am its sender, either way
I return
as the one who opens the box
and checks the numbers

filthy messenger
of that effulgence destined only for me
I make the words
dance, I make the silence

(*Post Hoc*, 1990)

Bernadette Mayer [1945]

THE AESCHYLEANS

These berries, with their choices, come to earth
To scatter and confuse the sainted warriors,
A part of crime's return to grace
And the innocence of criminals which
Enervates us like the coarser forms
Of truculence. Rude labors are ordinary and still.

They speed the haphazard. Slow manners still
Desires long buried in the earth
Among the exigencies of place and concurrent forms
Which once frightened even staid warriors.
I have caught a desire for silent markets which
May transfix the movements of warriors. To grace

These corridors with flowers is a chance for grace
As if ancient events were surfeited and still.
These are the plays, the act's discovered ways which
While on earth, will show what the earth
May return to—the severed heads of warriors
No longer dancing with the chance of reeds. The forms

Of edges bring us to such forms,
As homage makes its stonier pledge to grace
Belonging in retribution to the warriors
Whose hearts dispell in plays what is still
And what is closed, close to the attitude of earth.
The arbiter of innocence is a stone which

Is turbulent, and a memory which
No desire affirms, an old resort to forms,
Which forms the quieter winds of earth
And stirs the edges, silent pools, to grace.
The harbored art of influence is still
And silence, buried among the warriors

And the sound of warriors.
The flowers of illusions are the seeds which
Controlling lightning from below, still
The first desire for an assault which forms,
Informing turbulence with a sudden ancient grace.
The canons are unearthed, but this is not the earth.

The earth is a place for warriors
And for the grace of winds, a steady grace which
When it forms, forms only what is still.

(*Poetry*, 1976)

THE PORT

We told them the myths about others

Sitting around the old and stately ship

And the ship's table, which had been shipped

From some faraway port.

The steward came to call for the mail

Hoping for a word from a nearby port

But, like the wine we had drunk too soon,

Our hearts were with the ship

Where after all our table had been set.

Part of our attention was placed

On the storm which flailed us about as if rain

Could outweigh the presence of others

And the old devotion of the captain's address.

The captain preferred ancient modes of opening

To those that were short

And had intercepted the steward's letter

In the course of his own first address,

Abbreviated with praise for the ship's company.

He accused us of being old and drunk

And of growing mustaches which caught

In the salt of the sea we were sailing

If only we could leave the port.

(*Poetry*, 1976)

HOUSE CAP

this is made
when opened.
            exclusively
only an obtuse point.
and trimmings.
            you must do it
when opened.

of net, and formed
is left of sufficient
the strings.
            and two wide.
round at the
nails long
the remainder in small plaits.
over the front
is left of sufficient
            , which

is left of sufficient
blonde and a bow
      length to form
the strings.

is neat and nails
      the point of the
      insertion work
a square of seven nails
hollowed out
you then
whipped and gathered
      of the insertion
you then a simple flower
or lace
double front border addition.
seven nails
of the insertion.

(*Poetry*, 1976)

BOATS

On sunnier days a new coat of arms made the ocean high
 on the edge of the land a manifestation to axes and cones
here at the door, after floating what a relief then
    it is a feast to us downstairs the matter of the bottle
  when you go over the sea here is the part which turns
in the wake of the reservoir first our belief in altitude
    in terms overlooking us

        we were on to you we walked by
 we tumbled before the steeple finding
    some see the east differently from the comfort of travels
supposed it was the solstice courses taken over the safe flood
   in ox-hide and oaken titles to arise by land
borne by comparison and services and use

the north transept
as the blind bewail the southern side is a new residence
we our table and sea-coats beside us sing
with subject files we erect a statue turning toward the west
coming forward in the shadows
about face as the mail is to come only such boats & sea-chairs
& ovens inexorable boats on the sea
you should never begin to race
in paint so red and bark as a mason in the current of events
down the line in place in advance as a stone
downstairs a dry permission to build respects interring
the city walls

the boats rise as high as a stone
oars are floating you should never come and work
so readily in confusion never come here stitched in sides
edging over stages spoken like a tiger repeatedly
some feasts edge into questioning

of traveling of seeing lights
in the hall the place is still airs within the tapestries
end and are offered end and are placed
to finally part before such a building
by night I respect the address and reflect
and spring arriving at letters
then spend the final revolution
in old red paint on the mantle

(*Poetry*, 1976)

WE'VE SOLVED THE PROBLEM

we've solved the problem, the problem is solved

men are women, women are men

i'm pregnant for a while, you're

pregnant for a while

"if someone doesn't change into an animal,

we won't be saved"   someone must

change into an animal so that we can be saved.

a man turns into a cat

a man becomes a cat

he gives himself to his friends in the form

of lead & coal

the man-cat gives himself to us in the

form of lead & coal

he draws himself

with lead & coal, the lead & coal man-cat

draws a picture of himself

he is a girl

the man is a girl—in black & white,

she sings

there are brush fires burning

(*Poetry*, 1976)

THE END OF HUMAN REIGN ON BASHAN HILL

They come down on their snowmobiles for the last time,
    come down to meet the car.
They're shouting, "Hoo Hey! The snow! Give them the snow!
    Let them eat snow! Hey! The snow!"
Looking like wild men & women, two wild children & a
    grandmother too, they're taking turns riding the
    snowmobile, they're getting out.
Hoo! Hey! The snow! freaking out.
Everybody in town watches, standing in groups by the
    "Road Closed" sign
Shouting back, "Take it easy! The snow!"
On Bashan Hill they'd lived in a cloud, watched. They'd had
    plenty of split peas, corn, Irish soda bread, fruitcake,
    chocolate, pemmican. But the main thing was — NO PLOW!
Day before at the Corners Grocery, news got around. "They're
    coming down from Bashan Hill — never to return!"
The snow!
Hey, the snow, you forget. They're coming to get a beer.
Have another beer, smoke, jerk off & be thankful.
They're moving to a place above the store, where they can be
    watched. The snowman'll come & watch them, the pie man'll
    come & watch them, the UPS man'll come & watch them, the
    oil man, the gas man'll watch them, the plow man'll watch
    them, the workers on the town roads.
Sink their shovels deep into the winter's accumulation right
    before their very eyes, eyes turned blue in the
    Arctic night.
The brown-eyed family from Bashan Hill in town for a
    postage stamp.
The black-eyed family of deer, the open-eyed rabbits, the
    circle-eyed raccoons, the white-eyed bear.
Where do the green frogs winter that look so old?
We watched so carefully our eyes became vacant, our minds
    stirred from laughter all the memories of a chant.
Hoo! Hey! The snow!
They've come down the hill we watch in a cloud, night of the
    full moon, icy crowd on the road watching them.
Have a piece of chocolate!
Open your eyes!

                      (*The Golden Book of Words*, 1978)

GENERIC ELBOWS

1

Tire tracks words lost in lost snow today
Cold staggering rigid frisky latter-day
Impending not as cold as all that spring night
And something else about the night tonight
Awful depending on knowing cold feet about
Floors making absolute sense without
Frigid re-writes the dutiful midwifery
Of re-typing everything on the very
First day of vacation nothing portending the
Rest will be dead or alive old death deafening the
Thunder clap spring made not pleasure of all that might be all a
Baby riot's wet nighttime tremor in the head I
Have and teeth stuck with them old hat to eat I
Might put back on unfair my sweet impatient so
For flowers not yet to pass over in a blatant so
Military industrious so predictably washing
Windows that way you'll fall out or lashing
Self to frame the professional not casual enough
A woman's boot beneath the man's pant cuff

2

don't sling the mud
at souce of mother's foam,
meretricious death!
can't you survive anything!

3 Riddle

A large basket
Prevents me
From moving freely
In the new
Isle of Fright.
                    (Answer: ǝɹᴉɥsdɯɐH ʍǝN)

4

You hamper my putting on my halter by my halyard
So I get you in a hammerlock when you're in my hammock

5

The mercantile erections of the periphrastic Frenchmen
From the ship all seem so big and well thought out:

>   Who says this or that well it might not be
>   Exacerbated overwrought pleasures or disasters
>   And who I am or you could turn out to be
>   Fabricated nearly capriciously against our demises
>   Who says this or that well it might not be so.

6

Why
fool around
with work
and
stuff

How about
some
short but
sweet
kisses

7

Remember when she made the painting of the facade & then
he thought he could take the whole construction on the
department store escalator but when it got to the top and
the ceiling closed in it all collapsed on him & he lost his
job? But he married the girl who pitied him that day.

8

A strange face like the face of a Martian child grinning with
one big eyebrow in the middle of a house shaped like a t.v.,
the house has legs cross-hatched like the body of the thing
inside whose thoughts are depicted electrically like Frank-
enstein's brain starting going.

9

You'd better not
            you must
                        you're all wrong
It's misplaced
            it's a chaos
                        look and see
The ice cold plants
                don't represent me
                            remember?

10

A for scarlet apple, poor Rimbaud
Concatenate vowels, leaky alchemy
Consonantal constellational luxuries
Which
As long as we're up to number ten and
the wind hasn't blown away the paper yet
I might as well say, inexact night of names,
the least comma of the ordinary ear or heart
mentions a backward pile of reminding books
in that I'm not I I hope but maybe perhaps
even already or almost completely one, two
or three or four others, maybe more, as
metastatic and functionally segmented as the
metathorax of, say, a hideous wasp

     Forms of love & steady poetry
     Let's have our silly coffee.

            (*United Artists* magazine, 1980)

THE GARDEN

Close to a house on a piece of ground
For the growing of vegetables, flowers & fruits
On fertile well-developed land
Is a delightful place or state, a paradise
Often a place for public enjoyment
Where grows the alyssum to cure our rage

Oriental night of the careless developers
Carpet of snow of the drugged landlords
Basket of gold the city's confused
Royal carpet of its bureaucracies,
Bored with bombs
Political ones of the complicated governments
Now stick up the very orb
For its nonmetal yet golden remains

Competing with the larval corn borers
The salaried test-borers
Imminently lead anti-sexually down to the foundation
Of the annihilation
Of a circular garden in which live members of
The mustard family
The tomato or nightshade family
The poppy family
The geranium family
The aster family
The mint family
The thistle or aster family
The violet family (heartsease)
The lily family
The cucumber or gourd family
The rose family
The composite or daisy family
The parsley or carrot family
And other families
(I dont think the pokeweed family lives there,
It earns too little or too much money per year)

We are told to swallow not a rainbow
But like the celandine the juicy proposal

That the lemon balm of low income housing,
Aplied like ageratum to the old Lower East Side
(As early matured as the apricot)
And probably turned by deeply divided leaves
Like a rape grapes before it's all over
Into the poison tomato leaf of middle income housing,
Cannot coexist with the gleaming black raspberries
In an ancient abandoned place
Around Eldridge, Foresight and Stanton Streets

We're asked not to think, like pansies do
That the pinnately compound, ovate, lanceolate, non-linear,
       lobed, compound, toothed, alternate, opposite,
       palmate, heart-shaped, stalkless, clasping,
       perfoliate, and basal rosette-ish leaves
Can heal like the comfrey
And cause to grow together
The rough hairy leaves of the city's people and
       the rough hairy leaves of the sublimity of
       a gardener's art
Made with vegetarian shit & free as cupid's darts

If all our eyes had the clarity of apples
In a world as altered
As if by the wood betony
And all kinds of basil were the only rulers of the land
It would be good to be together
Both under and above the ground
To be sane as the madwort,
Ripe as corn, safe as sage,
Various as dusty miller and hens & chickens,
In politics as kindly fierce and dragonlike as tarragon,
Revolutionary as the lily.

(Mutual Aid, 1985)

SONNET: KAMIKAZE

Dawn & night of fighting, lovers like actual wars
And as gentle men might be gentle, so they are not.
Jeans we all wear independent of our mutual sexes
Some lipsticked & rouged & eye-linered, some not.
I dont want to meet him, he does not prepare the food;
Also I am old. He the same age, younger, awaits my death.
A scholar, he doesn't count the births or clothes;
A scholar too, I keep track of the ages of the clothing.
Love seems to die for him with love's attention;
No point in thought or fight with dyed-in-wool women.

If we cant get along then who the fuck can?
I will not run or go forward American, divine wind.
A person, I must insist on a heartless agreeing;
A person too, he must agree some love can be.

(*Mutual Aid*, 1985)

THE EARTHWORKERS' GOD IS HEALED

Witness the sarcophagus of non-Raphael
I open the window
He & I've got synchronous particles
Plus the death simultaneous of the real
The lithographer now non-George
Two socialists I loved
Lived to be skinny and prolific
Within their torsos existed
The unprepared hum of health
Twice too past their nonidentical deaths
But do I give a fig about death?
Let's forget them!
Those two green birds who bite my fingers
Till I scream for identical help

(*Mutual Aid*, 1985)

James Sherry [1946]

SHE'LL BE COMIN' 'ROUND

She'll be comin' 'round the mountain when the shell sometimes is empty.
She'll be comin' sometimes and the shell is an evasion,
when she comes around the mountain
to put in an appearance;
and this is the introduction we're all trying' come 'round to.

She'll be drivin' six white and well-bred young mares.
She'll be tryin' to be comin', when one the horses slips on a curve,
but the traces hold her up
like a beautiful horse about to describe
the great vehicle she'll conduct, when she comes.

And we'll all go out to meet her when the well is dry and cracked
and the water is too neutral to hold
even a chance encounter when we're trying to be comin'
and breathe too much or that's what I
heard when tryin' too hard to meet her, when she comes.

And we'll all have chicken and dumplings in a context
of the human shell, water in the trough,
the gopher holes, how hot leather is in the desert mining town
except to the horses,
when she comes.

(*Part Songs*, 1978)

LEPIDOPTERY

Can't wring blood from
a comma, in a way, to see red,
but listen, I can feel
it buffet the cheek
near where the mole
justifies a city, that is to say,
I'd, you know,
anything bearable. I could stand
what latent in the leaf
fell into a wing, scruples being
ignorance of what fingers know, how
to heal themselves, to see, to translate
our em's and dee's, the flood of spit
into the dry isolate,
galvanized where intention
is more than a smile pronounced
against the membrane of conditioned
markings: like, you know, speaking,
in a way, that is, to your comprehension
of the very syllables that can't
be other than etiology, last ditch
face down   gurgle.

Jungle with net, associations inevitably
bog down to a safari hat on the surface
while good times lapidated in memory
prove word worm and image despair.
What's about's change,
simply, continuity of a thousand
kisses, fast or lingering, or Libyan desert
sands where crested plovers flutter horizonward
collected under glass.
The body of words and methods of combining,
a flapping tongue, pinned down and labeled
by all afeared that good's dead or just
enough to kill or at least beat up, in a way,
the queer and leave him/her dismembered
athwart the pave, death's head on the gypsy
engraved after image where juice was
once, not just touchy, but sensitive to the thick

foliage that is meaning less defined,
more a, uh, vague (not wave) surface,
interlocking bird and animal carpet,
your breasts' ellipsis and a long period
of adjustment following similar into stifling
embrace, pupate and poeticize.

Suppose destination.
Simply buy all these species
ready to display, language a hum or as
South Sea natives note to Captain Cook
English's hiss, not mere grids of possible,
but the kingly article which when
properly attended as
we all are after all in transit
to a big laugh
unless stop paper
wasting.
Or in syntactical modes more felt than felt up,
stop wasting paper, literature,
collectible, wiltless, imposing,
as if words were language entire.

(*Roof* magazine, 1978)

from IN CASE

What should be the title of a king. Too, how *also* to include. What happened when *move* toward an event? He made a killing. (A statement declared to have been a sentence period, no offense intended or for that matter felt emotionally, directed, signifying to have in mind as beforehand : I'd like to get to be, then get. Like as one.) I can, never think to say it to her as speech. The gesture of ambiguity, however, means sex, hardy series, as unique among shadows of trees. Take Pluto Kaminsky, for example, a portion of who elsewhere fits in, but *in* as much as *on*, no second chance unless set up, a hook or "what if" series.

&

Mid such hoopla, the young crab about pecuniary demolition, —Hey, somebody blew up my pockets.—. They drink through the entertainment force, ballerinas sin altas with lux-buns perform a forced march across the low floor. Some French ought to be applied to the forefinger. You, he, she, it, they, you, he, he. The list goes on indefinitely. Even me appears sometimes transfixed outside you. (I am unable to speak you name. Desire appears on my cheeks as implosion. I am unable to speak you name : I have forgotten it). You wouldn't care if I never said a word, with no particular finesse, if only I didn't bring up data, saying this and that, so I won't be caught saying anything (parts of scepticism). You got to commit yourself sometime, knot into space, that what do you mean edge away, data again, speaks to a stranger without urgency, but the note of reason (this has got to end somewhere) filling out its shape by the particulars of the crime, drives us apart in a minute. We are equally unable to speak its name.

&

& approach toward each. I expect the same, except from attractive women who are in need of this attitude to express arrangement. I. Reproduction as she is the veneer of change. We do it again & again, as many times the same words appear in new orders automatically like waiting for the train, billboards? Isolate meanwhile, no such singular, adrift: winds and currents drive us briskly about, but never within sight of land. Occasionally a cloud bank, will always be by agreement the egoist reading Adorno claims breeds contempt, pregnancy, higher meat prices, or the lack of meaning (his girlfriend stops me in the elevator), because it's enough. There's enough of it.

&

The urge to. . . Many people say — What? — too often, but they are mostly white.

&

I waned to revitalize her, since I had no wish to overshadow her, as she did for me when I was blue. It took years to realize that I could derive energy from a source and that, although opposites attract in magnetism, I could walk on the "sunnyside" and not compromise eternity, although more complex notions of this form cannot rigor-ously be dealt with in one paragraph of association, but as she packed the one bag I was to take on my vacation, she hadn't time to notice what had transpired between the time she began and when she noticed that all was not what it should have been. Tensely, she had said — Sometimes. —, which was enough of the form of a sentence for me to recognize that she was sorry that I have had to leave before we really got down with what we had commenced.

&

The room. (High wainscotting about rugs.) Their French translation from glance.
Unable is yet, social the inscriber, ca. 1956. Approach and as is. Her mouth filled
with teeth. Order party : The the an is but to of. (Used, too.) Aura flakes, a social
innovation. As a, restorative. Each a try at sense from not making to equal to. Far
out on the asymtote, i.e., closer. To you is where. Rather. As it you'd try. Building
blocks, the. . . More itchy principle. We get to where A=?. Better part of the dia-
tribe? Shake. (Stir?) Never what is portrayed is. Out other is end the despair. Which,
"she says," can be sexy.

&

It does not mean only the long way. There is no reason is. . . institute color or hu-
mors recognizes, snorts and sharp intakes of breath of the enraptured can be insti-
gated on his own as readily as manipulated by nomenclature, chattily, as if nothing
had happened to the British Empire. (A yellow diamond: Careful Style.) I like her,
but wonder why she wears wraparound skirts in March. "Negative ideas should not
be developed at length," unless. . . So long as it's not directed at me. Justice. Plato.
Leaves. Hang. We talk to our fellows less and less and phrases like. . .embarass our
polite company. —Is it a wedding? Is it a funeral?—

&

Re G-2 we want to know where we're headed. (The only kind of read direction.) Few
clues. In narrative pertains to late nights twisting sheets, sweat, I really need a brand
name: Pluralism. Early, cold knees. (Cold, a sign of weakness.) But what would be
said, could be said. (They smile all the time. Peering between. (Spy means listen.))
We chance to be happy while excitement lasts, but after, where code pertains, rules
is rules. On fingers we make up our own; we agree to make it up and give each other
lots of leeway. The result is we're well-behaved, because we rattle around in rules.
This is often frustrate, but we use deception in important matters only; the world is
no longer made as it should be. We might like to see what is perfect, but really,
because, there, is, no, chance it might. If we reasoned out what should, like the
present, even important men have bad penmanship, and consider it a sign of genius.
We can imagine writing we can't read. How wonderful perfection : life, women,
poetry free of the slightest defect; & it is important to be write sentence. Then from
family and friends receive many favors which no one will be aware of, but which will
benefit you. These far out-number favors that are known to come from them, viz.,
money, beauty, position. With these wise words the sentence ends. Jenny's demon-
stration that the "oh" sound has a spherical shape is dramatic, but should not sur-
prise. Form :: frequency : amplitude. . . Make women happy by passing low fre-
quency voltage current through clitoris. Make Jews a race by killing them. Pretend
prose. (—Ah, aw, eh, ee, oo.—) Sustained effects, like cosmic radiation on the 1:1.618

range, are more difficult to program and hence life at this end of the spectrum is often called fun, or taxable, like string. Some brass & often. Winds, but what 9th century elegiac has recently been likened to an accordian. It has been shown on several occasions. Instances of primitive origins of poetical devices discovered by archaeological crock, speech. Beings with grunts speech has. No beginning or end for that matter.

(*In Case*, 1981)

PAY CASH ONLY

> *Days fastidious preoccupation*
> *minutely fills its spare*
> *second-dwelling toward*
> *an allegory of mangled.*
> —CHUCK NORRIS

She shakes feathers toward him
to ward him off buttering his own
small bills, filled with soldiers
of diverse excess, caught up
in an investment in lunch.
As they say "Hog tied to penny rolls,
his car won't go down the road straight."

All those years of buoyancy won
control of space filled with ideals
which serve his purposes, between breaths
that gasp to fumble with leaves to close
the gap between the oaken
abbreviation of marital spats.
Familiar animals rush about the yard
or lie all winter on the radiator.

For a while plastic worried him
until he thought, "This this alone
provoked them to relax on a spit
of dearth." People faster on the surface
dig and radiate into the same space
at the same time as occupied
and guarded against each other.

(*The Word I Like White Paint Considered*, 1986)

RADIANT

Progress is our most important product.
—GENERAL ELECTRIC

The irregular continuity of discrete particles blasted into the atmosphere : writing to you without concealing her reasons because of their harsh and Byzantine nature = the simple requirement to live one day to the next : the desire to "get something" out of life.

Oh, of course there are alternatives, but that nature does not know squalor, except as language is part of nature leads to rejection of naturalism in all its forms. Common sense, heroic view of blind powers as justice, nostalgia for ontology, petty dramas of profundity are the usual solutions.

Moved by escapism, ellipses, interferences, intermittent developments, limited compatibility, modern art imitates science directed by politics in a dual effort to be approved by and expose the most flagrant failings of the dominant culture. But adherence to nature is a moral value. Simultaneous writing about unrelated ideas imitates the melting pot of social schema, including individual's rights to pursue their own course. They no longer have to wait for Judgment Day. Most souls can be judged by what they already know about themselves.

Control, stamp out, direct the stealth with which the mind reaches out to another mind seeking a little friction. The need for predestination, a civil offense, is likely to be with us for a long time, and we must suppress the temptation to reach out hastily for short-term solutions, although short-term success is the measure of the man.

The sacred lies in the notation captured by a twist of mind and an individual identifying it with the self in quick down-strokes of the fingers, each one sure and fast, even though a minute or an hour may pass between one stroke group and the next, that one must know just when to strike in a precise but reckless fashion, that one must wait until the real thing comes along, a solid within which motion blurs the edges. The description of how to arrive at it is disappointing to read, but the expectation of more from writing leads to violence.

The unauthentic selves we have made are defunct. Only fear is left and if that is what you mean by truth, then she doesn't want any. These are the fictions of her own justification. Inside the farther we go. Anger substitutes for truth.

Go to sleep my darling,
your mother isn't here.
She's gone shopping to buy
the makings of garlic noodles.

(*Our Nuclear Heritage*, 1991)

FREE RADICALS

Nothing is harder than to believe in men's consistency, noth-
ing easier than to believe in their inconsistency. To judge
them in detail and distinctly, bit by bit, would more often hit
the mark.

—MONTAIGNE

Let us go on then,
since we are here. The first
strike decides the affair,
for who would have courage
for a second except the machine?
(Here I have become a grammarian, I,
who once learned language only by rote.)

Waves lap the shore;
the horizontal parallels
fragment the shape of the gull like a post-mortem
painting of the bird, pecking
transparent food, reframes the screen.
Science clarifies art
and politics, helping to regulate our thought.
Rather than throw the baby out with bomb,
diaper the brat. It's
art that's dangerous.

I woke up just past 3:00 A.M., restless, unable to go back to sleep. I didn't feel in-
spired, just irritable; we'd turned the heat down; it would be chilly, and I'd forgotten
to put my robe by the bed. Angrily I snuggled back beneath the covers, but it wouldn't
work: I was wide awake. Slowly the first line of the warning to subway riders mate-
rialized into my head, "Es muy peligroso," neutral, emotionless, clear as logos, as
the printed word would be if it spoke itself.

Transfigured night.
Charting the emotional extremes of a woman
who has lost her lover. Wind bag
is a foil for solo strings.
Conventional logic of radical features.

Clad in radiation-proof suit, Carpaccio wanders among the pulverized bricks of the
center and outward to the charred bodies. He pushes his forefinger through a char-
coal skull, rubbing the cinder against his gloved thumb. The only evidence of the
magnitude of this action is a slight elevation of his heart beat.

Mar measures.
By desire
By the fantasy of ends.
By the recycled whirs.
The prose of solicitation makes
sense by changing a few letters,
the most destructive pose of love.
Propositions substitute for truth.
Only cannibals thrive
in the romance of their own lives.

Explicit identification of any corpse misses the point and so the splitting of the nuclear
family finally takes place under the ax of the split atom of a tasteless, odorless, lighter-
than-air gas. Individuals sublimate from the social structure as I retreat from its
edge.

What becomes clearer than the content,
than the object of writing, is what
drove them to approach it this way.
Does knowing that give any control?
No, but it sure makes the
reader less receptive.

The smoke coming out of the stack,
the combustions below
Another day, another alphabet.
A baby, an inheritance,
desire to resume, body against body, not
the talking distances power perpetuates.

I met a man who pleased me and I wanted to tell him but I had no words save those
which seemed inappropriate, so I shuffled my feet and smiled down and went away,
"comprising matrix, matter, and production all in one," only in relation to.

The crystalline past engenders a caress.
Such knowledge is a shield.
My love is coughing and can't stop.
I leave, remove,
split off one electron,
oust, auto-da-fé, goner.
I think this is the apocalypse.

"Even today government policies cannot be judged adequate, and A-bomb victims remain dissatisfied.

"The bombing of Hiroshima and Nagasaki resulted not only from a desire to end the war quickly and to restore peace; it came as we now know, from the US's expectation of a postwar confrontation with the Soviet Union and its wish to make a show of force by demonstrating the bomb's incredible might." But if one percent of mutations are favorable to the species, wouldn't a super race emerge from world holocaust with a more favorable population density than now, if only a new, low half-life bomb could be developed. . . .

(*Our Nuclear Heritage*, 1991)

HAZARDOUS WASTE

Questioning is the piety of thinking.
—HEIDEGGER

After the war, the terror people underwent produced profound if not irrevocable changes in the languages of the countries where the war was started and other changes in those where the war was merely felt, no less felt but not initiated. Change everywhere, but not thorough changes in the sense of evolution or revolution, rather strange combinations like the same events seen through different eyes. Mutations like fusion of words where one concept literally disappeared into another like experience into control.

Experience came to be "endured, suffered, received as it strikes us, submitted to." (A happier age had noted a mutual (interactive) aspect to experience, especially experiences between persons or even persons and things if such exprinces were analyzed without the shadow of persecution.)

Further, experience was said to touch the "innermost nexus" of existence, if it was really experienced. Innermost and submission, by being juxtaposed, were consequential. Even if we think "that does not follow logically," we cannot avoid being influenced in that way as if by a magnetic force.

And by virtue of that mechanism (controlling thought by redefining language) whenever we are asked our relation to language or to solve a problem using language, we seek guidelines which lead through channels where we are safe or at least feel secure. We call the guidelines grammar, here a grammar of change.

Those who died in battle against the enemy did not consider their own death, but were diverted from it by the heat of battle. Those who were stung by the subatomic radiation, if you will, fragged, had long to think about it. The painful anticipation of a lingering death, during which they would have to face themselves over and over as they corroded, forced many to seek diversion in fantasy, in games, in the oddest pleasure depression could derive.

Carpaccio, lying on his stomach on the ottoman, was idly dialing the telephone, alternately dialing and cutting off the signal as he narrowly avoided a busy signal on the call made by Arturo Meninhatzer in San Bernardino to Claudia Graceland in Los Angeles, was off by one digit reaching the great grandniece of Thomas Hardy where she lay near death in a nursing home in Duluth, rang through countless computer circuits at Bell Long Lines, computers in the Defense Department Critical Strategies planning office, bounced signals off telestars in polar orbit, hung up on the weather station on Baffin Island, almost called for a transmission from probes near the orbit of Neptune, was picked up by the gate guard at the Acropolis who heard only some additional beeps before he hung up on Carpaccio who would not have known if he reached the ship from Aldebaran holding steady on the dark side of the moon, "Hello?" "Hello, yourself."
"How are you" "Fine and yourself"
"OK."
"What kinds of fools are you making of yourselves down there?"
"I beg your pardon."

(*Our Nuclear Heritage*, 1991)

Ron Silliman [1946]

Not this.

What then?

I started over & over. Not this.

Last week I wrote "the muscles in my palm so sore from halving the rump roast I cld barely grip the pen." What then? This morning my lip is blisterd.

Of about to within which. Again & again I began. The gray light of day fills the yellow room in a way wch is somber. Not this. Hot grease had spilld on the stove top.

Nor that either. Last week I wrote "the muscle at thumb's root so taut from carving that beef I thought it wld cramp." Not so. What then? Wld I begin? This morning my lip is tender, disfigurd. I sat in an old chair out behind the anise. I cld have gone about this some other way.

Wld it be different with a different pen? Of about to within which what. Poppies grew out of the pile of old broken-up cement. I began again & again. These clouds are not apt to burn off. The yellow room has a sober hue. Each sentence accounts for its place. Not this. Old chairs in the back yard rotting from winter. Grease on the stove top sizzled & spat. It's the same, only different. Ammonia's odor hangs in the air. Not not this.

Analogies to quicksand. Nor that either. Burglar's book. Last week I wrote "I can barely grip this pen." White butterfly atop the grey concrete. Not so. Exactly. What then? What it means to "fiddle with" a guitar. I found I'd begun. One orange, one white, two gray. This morning my lip is swollen, in pain. Nothing's discrete. I straddled an old chair out behind the anise. A bit a part a like. I cld have done it some other way. Pilots & meteorologists disagree about the sky. The figure five figures in. The way new shoots stretch out. Each finger has a separate function. Like choosing the form of one's execution.

Forcing oneself to it. It wld've been new with a blue pen. Giving oneself to it. Of about to within which what without. Hands writing. Out of the rockpile grew poppies. Sip mineral water, smoke cigar. Again I began. One sees seams. These clouds breaking up in late afternoon, blue patches. I began again but it was not beginning. Somber hue of a gray day sky filld the yellow room. Ridges & bridges. Each sentence accounts for all the rest. I was I discoverd on the road. Not this. Counting my fingers to get different answers. Four wooden chairs in the yard, rain-warpd, wind-blown. Cat on the bear rug naps. Grease sizzles & spits on the stove top. In paradise plane wrecks are distributed evenly throughout the desert. All the same, no difference, no blame. Moon's rise at noon. In the air hung odor of ammonia. I felt a disease. Not not not-this. Reddest red contains trace of blue. That to the this then. What words tear out. All elements fit into nine crystal structures. Waiting for the cheese to go blue. Thirty-two. Measure meters pause. Applause.

A plausibility. Analogy to "quick" sand. Mute pleonasm. Nor that either. Planarians, trematodes. Bookd burglar. What water was, wld be. Last week I cld barely write "I grip this pen." The names of dust. Blue butterfly atop the green concrete. Categories of silence. Not so. Articles pervert. Exactly. Ploughs the page, plunders. What then? Panda bear sits up. Fiddle with a guitar & mean it. Goin' to a dojo. Found start here. Metal urges war. One white, two gray, one orange, two longhair, two not. Mole's way. This morning the swelling's gone down. Paddle. No thing discrete. Politry. Out behind the anise I straddled an old chair. O'Hare airport. About a bit in part a like. Three friends with stiff necks. I did it different. Call this long hand. Weathermen & pilots compete for the sky. Four got. Five figures figure five. Make it naked. The way new stretches shoot out. Shadow is light's writing. Each finger functions. The fine hairs of a nostril. Executing one's choice. What then? Forms crab forth. Pen's tip snaps. Beetles about the bush. Wood bee. Braille is the world in six dots. A man, his wife, their daughter, her sons. Times of the sign. The very idea. This cancels this. Wreak havoc, write home. We were well within. As is.

Wait, watchers. Forcing to it one self. Read in. It wld be blue with a new pen. Then what? Giving to one itself. The roads around the town we found. Of about under to within which what without. Elbows' flesh tells age. Hands writing. Blender on the end-table next to the fridge. Out of rock piled groupies. Hyphenate. Smoke cigar, sip water. Mineral. This was again beginning. Begging questions. Seams one sees. Monopoly, polopony. Blue patches breaking clouds up in the late afternoon. Non senses. It was not beginning I began again. In Spain the rain falls mainly on the brain. The gray sky came into the yellow room. Detestimony. Bridges affix ridges. On the road I discoverd I was. I always wake. Not this. The bear's trappings. Counting my fingers between nine & eleven. Factory filld at sunrise. Three rain-warpd wood chairs in the back yard. Minds in the mines look out. Cat naps on the bear rug. Bathetic. On the stove top grease sizzles & spits. Lunch pales. In paradise plain rocks are distributed evenly throughout the desert. Electricity mediates the voice. All difference, no same, all blame. Lampshade throws the light. Noon's moonrise. Burn sienna. Feel the disease. Denotes detonation. Not not not-not-this. The sun began to set in the north. Reddest trace contains red blue. Metazoans, unite. Of that to the this of then. Break or lure. Out what words tear. One ginger oyster between chopsticks rose to the lips. All elemental crystal structures are nine. Helicopters hover down into the dust. The blue cheese waits. No one agrees to the days of the week. Thirty-two times two. We left the forest with many regrets. Meters pace measure. New moons began to rise. Applause drops the curtain. The elf in lederhosen returns to the stomach of the clock. Chiropractice. Furnance fumes. Crayola sticks. Each word invents words. One door demands another. Bowels lower onto bowls. Come hug. Sunset strip. Holograms have yet to resolve the problem of color. Thermal. This is where lines cross. Hyperspace, so calld. Mastodons trip in the tar pits. These gestures generate letters. Industrial accident orphan. Driving is much like tennis. Orgasmic, like the slam dunk. We saw it in slomo. Cells in head flicker & go out. Zoo caw of the sky.

Sarcadia. A plausibility. Gum bichromate. Quick analogy to sand. Not this. Moot pleonasm. Cat sits with all legs tuckd under. Nor that either. Table lamp hangs from the ceiling, mock chandelier. Trematodes, planarians. Featherd troops. Books burgled. Blood lava. What wld be was water. Bone flute. I cld barely write "last week I gripped this pen." Allusions illude. Dust names. Not easy. Green butterfly atop the blue concrete. Pyrotechnics demand night. Kinds of silence. Each is a chargd radical. Not so. Photon. Pervert articles. Extend. Exactly. Descend. Plunders & ploughs the page. Read reed as red. What then? With in. Panda bear claps. The far side of the green door is brown. Fiddle with a mean guitar. "I don't like all those penises staring at me." Go into a dojo. Mojo dobro. Here found start. Dime store sun visor. Metal urges worn. Only snuggle refines us. Two long-hairs, two gray, one white, one not, one orange. Spring forward, fall back. Mole's way in. Build an onion. This morning the blister gave way to pus & half-formd flesh. Hoarfrost. Paddleball. Tether. No thindgis creep. Tiny plastic dinosaur. Politry teaches just what each is. Cameroon tobacco wrapper. Out behind anise I stood on an old chair. Southpaw slant to the line. O'Hare airport bar. Sounds the house makes. About a bit in part of a like. Shutters rattle, stairs "groan." Three stiff friends with necks. Your own voice at a distance. Done differently. Monoclinic. This long hand call. 'Her skirt rustled like cow thieves.' Sky divides jets & weather. Far sigh wren. Got for. Bumble. Figure five figures five. Dear Bruce, dear Charles. Make naked it. Negative. Out the way new stretches shoot. A thin black strap to keep his glasses from falling. Light's writing is shadow. Rainbow in the lawn hose's shower. Each finger's function. Beneath the willow, ferns & nasturtiums. Nostril fine hairs. Stan writes from Kyoto of deep peace in the calligraphic. Executed one choice. Pall bearers will not glance into one another's eyes. What then? A storm on Mount Sutro. Forms crab forth from tide pool's edge. Refusal of personal death is not uncommon amid cannery workers. Snaps pen tip. An ant on the writing alters letters. About the bush beetles. This municipal bus lurches forward. Be wood. Several small storms cld be seen across the valley. The world in six braille dots. Gray blur of detail indicates rain. A woman, her husband, their daughter, her sons. A pile of old clothes discarded in the weeds of a vacant lot. Time of the signs. Some are storms. The idea very. Borate bombers swoopd low over the rooftops. This cancels not this. The doe stood still just beyond the rim of the clearing. Writing home wrought havoc. In each town there's a bar calld the It Club. We were within the well. Many several. Is as is. Affective effects. Humidity of the restroom. Half-heard humor. Old rusted hammer head sits in the dust. Clothes-pins at angles on a nylon line. Our generation had school desks which still had inkwells, but gone were the bottles of ink. Green glass broken in the grass. Every dog on the block began to bark. Hark. Words work as wedges or as hedges to a bet. Debt drives the nation. These houses shall not survive another quake. A wooden

fence that leans in all directions. Each siren marks the tragic. Dandelions & ivy. A
desert by the sea is a sight to see. A missile rose quickly from the ocean's surface. A
parabola spelld his mind. He set down, he said, his Harley at sixty. It is not easy to be
a narcissist. Afterwords weigh as an anchor. Cement booties. Not everyone can cause
the sun to come up. On the telly, all heads are equal. In Mexico, the federales eat you
up. The production of fresh needs is the strangest of all. I swim below the surface.
Room lit by moonlight. Words at either edge of the page differ from those in be-
tween. An old grey church enclosd in bright green scaffolding. Left lane must turn
left. A dog in his arms like an infant. Each sentence bends toward the sun. Years
later, I recognized her walk a block away.

Downward motion means out. Watchers wait. In motel rooms the beds are dis-
proportionately large. Self forcing one to it. Croatians are restless. Read into. Be-
tween hills, a slice of fog. With a blue pen it wld be new. Not wanted is not wanted.
Then what? This not. Self giving one to it. Time lapse photography captures the
sky. Around the town we found roads. A roil of deep gray cirrus. Of about under to
within which of what without into by. A taut bend to the palm tree to indicate wind.
Flesh at the elbow goes slack as one grows older, gathers in folds. Fireworks replay
the war. By the fridge on an endtable a blender. A fly's path maps the air of the room,
banging at the windows. Hand writings. Recent words have been struck. Groupies
pile out of rock. An accidental order is not chance. Hyphenateria. On the wall hung
abalone. Sip cigar, smoke water. Who holds what truths to be self-evident? Mineral
water bubbles in a glass. Each mark is a new place. Again this was beginning, being
begun. Stick cloves in an orange for incense. Questioning beggars. Under golden
arches we gorged to heart's delight. One's seams seen. Not ink but point scrapes the
page. Polopony, monopoly. At sea side a city of rust. Late afternoon clouds breaking
up into blue patches. Pigeons gather round the writing. None senses. In the back of
the Buick were sleeping bags, pillows. Is this not beginning I again begin? Orange
Opel's dented fender. In the rain Spain falls mainly on the brain. Gold-leaf sign on
the glass reads x-ray. Gray sky comes into the yellow room. Peeling leather off the
tatterd jacket. Detestimonial. Predictable people wear Frye boots. Ridges attached
by bridges. Waiting for that bus to come back this way. Pine koans. Uganda liquors.
Each sentence stakes out. Knot this. Can cups fill a cupboard? Tamal is the name of
a place in the place of a name. I was on the discoverd road. Caterpillar is a tractor. I
am in each instant waking. To him her tone was at once tender and gruff from long
years of rough intimacy. Not this. I saw my blood, a deep red, filling the vial at the
far end of the needle. Ing the trappd bears. I wanted to catch a glimpse of her face,
but she never turnd this way. Between nine & eleven counted my fingers. Each cloud
has a specific shape. At sunrise the factory filld. Cut to montage of forklifts &
timeclock. Back in the yard three wooden rain-warpd chairs. Scratch that. In the
mines minds gape. Try to imagine words. Bare cat naps on the rug. Haze hued those
hills on the far, gray side of the bay. Bathetic. Underground, the mock coolness of
the conditiond air. Grease sizzles, spits on the stove top. Sand sharks swam past.
Pale lunch. A city of four tunnels. In paradise desert rocks are distributed evenly

throughout the plain. We saw the sails at sea. Electricity translates the voice. But what comes thru depends on you. Blame all difference, know same. Thru the window I see the apparatus of the modern dentist. Shade throws the lamp light. Light green lines between wch to write. Noon's rising moon. This one squints at a thick printout in his lap on the bus home from work. Sienna burns. Suddenly, in the hospital corridor, the familiar smell of balsa wood & model airplane glue. Feel a disease. Or, thru a window just after sunset, the faces of watchers turnd blue by the light of an unseen television. Detonates denotation. For an instant I was unable to remember how to get the change back into my pocket & pick the bag up off the counter. Not-not not-not not-not this. Crystals hung in the window to refract the sun. It began to set in the north. Ploughshares turnd into gongs may be playd without actually being touchd. Trace of red blue contain within the reddest. Each day's first cigarette tastes stale. Metazoans united. The true length depends on the size of the type. Of by that to the this into of then. Morning, mourning. Brick or leer. The buzz of flies fills the room. Out words what tear. Chinese coins with holes in the center. To the lips, thick & poisd open, rose a ginger oyster between chopsticks. A blue glass ashtray filld with wooden match sticks. All 9 elemental structures are crystal. Each statement is a mask. Down into the dust hover helicopters. This script a scrawl. Wait for the blue cheese. A motorboat for the salt seas calld Twenty Languages. No days agree as to the one of the week. We make our deposit in the cloud bank. Thirty-two times two-squared. Black smoke of a structural fire belched up out over the docks. Regretfully we are leaving the forest. In a string net, a bundle of groceries. Meters face measure. Charging for lapis but giving you sodalite. Moons begin to rise anew. Cool coffee kindld thought. Applause curtains the drop. Me too in general yes. Back into the stomach of the clock went the elf in lederhosen. Certain sentences set aside, others set off. Chiropractical. Dr Heckel & Mr Jive. Furnish fumes. The red hook-&-ladder snakes around to back into the station. Crayola sticks streak a page. Like radios talking of radios to radios. Each word once the invention of another. These dark glasses serve as a veil. One door is the demand of another. Gulls fly, strung from hidden wires. Over bowls lower bowels. For "wires" read "wives." Hug come. Time flows, pouring forward from the past. Strip set sun. Vast vats of waste water aerate in the flatlands by the bay. Holograms have yet to tackle the problem calld color. Walking as tho one had to think abt it. Thermal, Tamal. Fresh odor of new dung. This is where the cross lines. Too late to catch the bus, they slap its side as it pulls away. So calld hyperspace. An old Chinese lady wearing a light-purple tam. Mastodons in the tar pits trip. An ashtray in the shape of a heart. These letters generate gestures. The shadow of buildings upon buildings. Accidental industrial orphan. The lines abt swimming meant sex. Tennis is much like driving. Fire escape forms a spine. Slam, like the orgasmic dunk. Drunk. In slomo we saw it move, try to. Against that cream stucco the gray flagpole has no depth. Heads in the cell flicker & go out. In that sandal I saw countless toes. Zoo sky of caw. A transmitter, like radar, atop each tall building. Transbay transit. The word is more & less. The history of the foot. The fogbank heavy on the beach like a slug. Stopping

the car to make a quick phone call. You will nver stop learning how to read. Hyper/
formance. What really happend to the C. Turner Joy. Up & down scales on reeds.
Not this. The words were on the page already. Summer without sun. I like white
space. Truck towed tons of tractors, all yellow. Plotting the way ahead. Instrument
landing. The flutter of clarinets. Boar bristle hair brush. Toilet's handle says "press."
These letters more angular than I used to write. Congas in the urban night. Cans of
beer & fear. Sunrise behind fog means light changes on the green steep slopes of the
hillside. A small pen-like instrument used to apply wax designs. Cut. He staggerd
about in the intersection, whooping & making wild gestures, then sipping from a
can of beer, oblivious to the early morning traffic. Pain in the lower calves from
hours of walking. Potato chips at war. With heavy hearts, we set out to follow the
river to its conclusion. If he has no sideburns, then it's a hairpiece. When we got to
where the clouds were, they were too thin to see. Industrial siren meaning lunch.
Quips & players, or diamonds in the blood. There are clues nearby. In each major
city, the ugliest mansion was the French Consulate. She & I strolld thru the rose
garden. Nor that either. An architect's model of a rest stop. Tulis is not tulip. Shak-
ing the brain awake. Each word is a wafer of meaning meant, minded. No fish imag-
ines water. I surface at the center of the pool. A dress shirt halfway between pink &
lavender. Tautness of the warp while on the loom. Each sentence is itself. Two fives
& a nine. A nose that points slightly to the left. What I am writing is writing. Tics
dig in. Wicker throne. Scratch that. Keep moving. Dressd to kill. Burgundy jumpsuit.

(*Tjanting*, 1981)

from HIDDEN

"Lucky"

My ears 'pop' at the hilltop.
Stoic half-frown on the man's face

being wheeled up to the ambulance
in blue cotton pajamas. Green dice earrings

and blue sunglasses—the large woman
picks her nose. the cop leans forward

before he spits. It's not a neighborhood
people pass through going to work

or shopping, or to visit a park.
Yellow-brown wall-to-wall carpet,

optometrist's outer office.
Think here: you are reading a poem

—already this defines you. Hyperopic
boy makes good. Off-rhyme by iambs

hidden in the flood. Willingly I'll say
there's been a clear rip-off. No ideas

but in drugs? No teeth, bad back
don't make Ted a bad boy.

Bright pink scarf against turquoise jacket.
Out of print, out of mind. Woman

with pocked cheeks (sequence of alternate details
by which to triangulate image)

pulls up her jeans. Hear the loud chewing
in one's own head. Penis minus bonus.

Dan White is dead also. Sleeping pigeons
atop power line. Tar-heater

like a caboose linked to roofer's truck.
From sacred to salsa: a woman

in nurse whites carries three purses
into her place of work. Truck double-parked

on residental street. Face moved by muscles
of the jawbone as it chews, teeth sliding

side to side. What is the social content
of a poor night's sleep? Between terms

thought moves through a process
of distraction. Syntax slides

over a rough surface. Noses slope
or rise or spread (sometimes twist)

across the face. Hardware wholesale house
next door to machineworks (big sheds

of corrugated metal), since we're clanging anyway
any way we can. Thought into action

divided by social constraint (terms repeat).
Teams don't. Soft earth absorbs the fog,

spongelike, until the sky clears. The air
is not the mind nor a reflection of it.

Ironing board juts out of dumpster.
Refrigerator upright

in the back of a pick-up. Shadows
in a dense fog, headlights barely cutting thru.

Weight is relative to height. Fate
correlates to sight. Each place waits

for the right stress. I thought
in D.C. to head south for a visit

tho what had I to show? Vacant lot
turned into community garden

bulldozed as site for new video mart.
Song: (oh no) don't say nothin'

bad about my baby (oh no).
Thought replacement technique.

Shag knit sox cover golf clubs
(only the woods). Touch of rouge

to shine up cheeks. Writing by the light
of a kerosene lamp. Stomach rumbles

during group meditation. Pants pockets
are hidden holsters. Cricket buzzes

alone on a deer trail (further,
solitary woodpecker

knocks on a tree)—big horse chestnut
impossible to eat. Even here

in the high chaparral, the shining monarch
lands and is still on a rock amid dry grass.

Blue jay, descending, fans its wings.
Old pine, having fallen, forms both bench and path.

Oh that world, the real one. Potted cactus
oxymoron. North of Calistoga

a car that's rolled and burned: semi-circle
of ambulance and fire trucks (no hope here).

The world is all that is your face
isn't it exactly either. Try to write

as the bus turns (the body pulled
is the body). Lunch or lurch,

which one? Sea and shoe, which
is the foreground, which the rear?

Sky perceived as the object, against which
land's the margin. Who, what, when, where, how

are there also. Trochee's trick (again
twitch): protagonist. I, I, I

take you out on others, old pronoun,
cleft chin. An image (as in a dream)

of being held aloft—that fear
of not falling (which it's since become).

Boredom in the eyes of women
at a laundromat, class specific,

against the restlessness of their children,
men absent, constructs a world.

(*Demo to Ink*, 1992)

Rae Armantrout [1947]

GENERATION

We know the story.

She turns
back to find her trail
devoured by birds.

The years; the
undergrowth

(*Extremities*, 1978)

WINTER

1

Fumbling for the live nerve
under dead strata.

It's not a matter of *lies*.

But when all my thoughts slink off like bad dogs—

You touch me. I assume
you're counterfeiting lust.

2

Once I liked being buffeted. Watching clouds roll
might have felt: "Fateful coincidence of inner
turbulence with that above."

3

"I used to love nature," I said.

(Image of the rustic maiden put forward.)

As proof I named the roadside plants.
Pyracantha—fire berry.

You would have lit me up

(*Extremities*, 1978)

NECROMANCE

Poppy under a young
pepper tree, she thinks.
The Siren always sings
like this. Morbid
glamor of the singular.
Emphasizing correct names
as if making amends.

Ideal
republic of the separate
dust motes
afloat in abeyance.
Here the sullen
come to see their grudge
as pose, modelling.

The flame trees tip themselves
with flame.
But in that land
men prized
virginity. She washed
dishes in a black liquid
with islands of froth—
and sang.

Couples lounge
in slim, fenced yards
beside the roar
of a freeway. Huge pine
a quarter-mile off
floats. Hard to say where
this occurs.

Third dingy
bird-of-paradise
from right. Emphatic
precision
is revealed as
hostility. It is
just a bit further.

The mermaid's
privacy.

(*Necromance*, 1990)

THE GARDEN

Oleander: coral
from lipstick ads in the 50s.

Fruit of the tree of *such* knowledge.

To "smack"
(thin air)
meaning kiss or hit.

It appears
in the guise of outworn usages
because we are bad?

Big masculine threat,
insinuating and slangy.

(*Necromance*, 1990)

SENSE

Twigs stiffen
the fingers.

Love of nature
is a translation.

Secret nodding
in the figurative:

a corroboration
which is taken for
"companion."

A saw warbles,
somewhere,
and the yards too
are terraced

.

Stress the birds lay
on that wire.

"*Possibly*
holy parental emphases."

Big screen.

On the other side of
siding
cars go by.

String of fat
commas
as far as
we're concerned

First the (non)sense
of direction.

"Stones to frogs,
then to princes
who do a circle dance
and turn to stone."

Good-night!

Meaning extends
her arm backward
ballerina-like:

wood-swirl
in the formica.

(*Necromance*, 1990)

GETTING WARM

Tingle:
a shaft must be imagined to
connect the motes
though there is no light.

The notes.
If she's quiet
she's concentrating on the spaces
between cries, turning
times into spaces.

Is it memory or physics
that makes the bridge appear?
It looks nothing
like a real bridge.
She has to finish it
so it can explode.

She is in the dark,
sewing, stringing holes together
with invisible thread.
That's a feminine accomplishment:
a feat of memory, a managed
repletion or resplendence.

(*Necromance*, 1990)

DISOWN

You may "have" sex—

but those round
sink-holes beneath
the off-ramps,

scabbed with whatever
flat, green stuff—

not in your most
nominative
moon-walk.

*

New one called
"Convoy Village."

Bylaws forbid
visible contrivance:

clotheslines
(like the skeleton),

or crabgrass
dead in long tracks
tipped in green.

Results shall be
unreminiscent.

＊

To punch one's straw
definitely
into the fizz.

Arms of pastries
revolve
in their clear cylinder

slowly.

Space "may be shaped
like a saddle,"
scientists say.

A list may pantomime
focus.

On conditions
so numerous
nothing can begin.

＊

"Run down," they say,
"buildings."

Wave of morning glory
leaves about to break
over the dropped plastic
bat, the empty shed.

Hard to specify
further.

Whole body
dotted

here and there.

Areas of interest,

                              cross purposes,

                                        eddies.

                              (*Necromance*, 1990)

LEAVING

The urge to wander is
displayed
in a spate of slick,
heart–shaped leaves

          *

Cellophane grass and
foil eggs.
          The modesty

of standard presentation
does remind me of home
sickness.

          *

As if some furtive
will's receded
leaving meaning
in its place:

a row of coastal
chalets.

          *

With waves
shine slides over
shine like skin's
what sections
same from same.

*

Coarse splay
of bamboo
from the gullies,
I write,
as if I'd been expecting
folds of lace.

*

Mine was about
escaping Death though
Death was stylized, somehow,
even stylish. So was I!
So I was hidden
among fashionable allies.

(*Made to Seem,* 1994)

INCIDENCE

Our mother
who turns
sights to instances
gave us this
ground, our
sense of before
and behind.

*

On a blank sign
shadows might be the features
of a murdered child.

Crowds are amazed
that a picture appears
unsponsored. This
is jubilation.

Crews stop the gap
with a memorial
to reduce the risk
of incident.

     *

We start
where shadows strum the wall
over a crib.
Why attend
absence's modulations?

         (Made to Seem, 1994)

Bob Perelman [1947]

CHINA

We live on the third world from the sun. Number three.
Nobody tells us what to do.

The people who taught us to count were being very kind.

It's always time to leave.

If it rains, you either have your umbrella or you don't.

The wind blows your hat off.

The sun rises also.

I'd rather the stars didn't describe us to each other; I'd
rather we do it for ourselves.

Run in front of your shadow.

A sister who points to the sky at least once a decade is a
good sister.

The landscape is motorized.

The train takes you where it goes.

Bridges among water.

Folks straggling along vast stretches of concrete, heading
into the plane.

Don't forget what your hat and shoes will look like when
you are nowhere to be found.

Coats in the window hung up on hooks; question marks

where the heads would normally be.

Even the words floating in air make blue shadows.

If it tastes good we eat it.

The leaves are falling. Point things out.

Pick up the right things.

Hey guess what? What? *I've learned how to talk.* Great.

The person whose head was incomplete burst into tears.

As it fell, what could the doll do? Nothing.

Go to sleep.

You look great in shorts. And the flag looks great too.

Everyone enjoyed the explosions.

Time to wake up.

But better get used to dreams too.

(*Primer*, 1981)

SEDUCED BY ANALOGY

First sentence: Her cheap perfume
Caused cancer in the White House late last night.
With afford, agree, and arrange, use the infinitive.
I can't agree to die. With practice,
Imagine, and resist, use the gerund. I practice to live
Is wrong. Specify. "We've got to nuke em, Henry"
Second sentence: Inside the box is plutonium.
The concept degrades, explodes,
Goes all the way, in legal parlance.

"I can't stop. Stop. I can't stop myself."
First sentence: She is a woman who has read
Powers of Desire. Second sentence:
She is a man that has a job, no job, a car, no car,
To drive, driving. Tender is the money
That makes the bus to go over the bridge.
Go over the bridge. Makes the bus. Tender
Are the postures singular verbally undressed men and women
Assume. Strong are the rivets of the bridge. "I'm not
                              interested,
Try someone else" First sentence:
Wipe them off the face. Not complete.

Bold are the initiatives that break deadlocks
In the political arena of sexual nation states.
A bright flash I, the construct, embrace all my life
All the furniture in Furniture World, U.S.A.,
All my life on TV "first thing in the morning."
My head is, somewhere, in my head. Say, threaten,
Volunteer, want, all take the infinitive.
First sentence: The woman's clothes volunteered
To mean the woman's body. Biology
Is hardly the word. No irony, no misleading
Emphasis, just a smooth, hard, glossy desktop.
The President was "on the ceiling."
He could watch himself face down the faceless forces of history.

A nation's god is only as good as its erect arsenal.
It's so without voice, in front of the face, all my life I,
In corners, dust, accumulating rage breaking
Objects of discourse. "Why use words?" Smells from
The surrounding matter, the whole tamale.
"I have no idea" "I use my whole body"
"Be vulnerable" First sentence: They were watching
The planes to fly over their insurgent hills.
Second sentence: Their standard of living
We say to rise. No third sentence.

(*To the Reader*, 1984)

THE BROKEN MIRROR

From the stately violence of the State
a classic war, World War Two, punctuated by Hiroshima
all the action classically taking place on one day
visible to one group in invisible terms
beside a fountain of imagefree water
"trees" with brown "trunks" and "leafy" green crowns
50s chipmunks sitting beneath, buck teeth representing
electoral tranquillity, they sit in rows
and read their book and the fountain gushes forth
all the letters at once, permanently
a playful excrescence, an erotic war against nature.

And here's a check for five feet of shelf
in the life-after-death book club, seminar upon seminar
grains of sand the tan body rests on
glorious huge & hypothetical
worth all the bad press human sacrifice has received.

Outside, masses of angry numb matter blow against the symphonic
                angles of the citadel, warm & witty with
                electronically modulated voice, the earnest look
                out of the sweater, microphone hidden casually
                in memory, clouds a diversified portfolio of
                sensation.
The pictured body is relaxed & smooth
on the unmade bed, maple syrup, the waffle drenched
not a sentence, a way of life, the way out.

But I don't want to have to recreate the very ground of being
it's supposed to create me, like it said it did already
intelligibility aside, monumentality of social decay aside,
food & water & explanations of hierarchies to last a lifetime
aside, out of the way, out to a lunch of human bit parts broken
                under the State.
I don't want to improvise, in a foreign language
my own, but in the wrong mouth, my own
a parody of my mostly silent dreams, I don't want to
—I'm melting, all my lovely inwardness—make love
to the middle of the World Bank's picture of the person.

Let language, that sports page of being
mystify its appearance in all speech writing thought tonight
so that the thing, that object of burnished flirtation
can smuggle out the self, that drill bit. . .

But why am I contracting for the construction of this life-like
          place-like spilling-over lived-in
if only for a moment or memory-shape, since readwriting is a
          mirror
backwards at best, of prior intent
while you sit before me (note the you-as-I circuit, banquet with
          masses of flowers, choirs, cranial blooms lit up,
          sacred, edible

(*The First World*, 1986)

MONEY

I am I because my little dog knows me
—GERTRUDE STEIN

Wallace Stevens says Money is a kind of poetry. So I offer to trade him Tennessee, States, and Water Works for Boardwalk and Park Place and the four Railroads. He thinks he'll pass. Do it I say and I'll quote you. Do says he. Mesdames, one might believe that Shelley lies less in the stars than in their earthly wake, since the radiant disclosures that you make are of an eternal vista, manqué and gold and brown, an Italy of the mind, a place of fear before the disorder of the strange, a time in which the poet's politics will rule in a poet's world. Yet that will be a world impossible for poets, who complain and prophesy, in their complaints, and are never of the world in which they live. Yes he says, gorgeous, I'm throwing in Pacific, North Carolina, and Pennsylvania. Go on. I can't I say. But do he says. Fair use I say. But all use is fair to one such as I says he, *con-tin-u-e*. No I say, 11 lines, any more and I'll have to write to Vintage, which I really don't want to do. But that's nothing he says, 11 lines out of 187. He says I'll give you Marvin Gardens, Ventnor, Atlantic.

That was the present, the poetic present tense: a non-financial play space, overheard.

Money has tenses: it has absolute meaning in the present; no past; and its future meaning (interest rates) reflects the degree to which the future is expected to resemble the present.

Writing has tenses: the past tense makes the most money (novels, reporting); the future is for prophecy (crop forecasts, pennant predictions); the present continually has to borrow credit. I am I because I say so and my little audience knows me.

Wow, says Basket. Wow, wow, wow!

How much money does it cost to know that Basket was a series of dogs owned by Gertrude Stein? Nothing, now.

I give I will give Basket the following bone (all past tense):

There was once a man, a very poor poet, who used to write poems that no one read. One evening, after working all day on an especially poor poem, he fell asleep in despair at the sterility of his imagination and the bleakness of his chances of making it as a writer. He had just typed the lines,

> *The sky was mauve and as far away*
> *as a ten dollar bill.*

He awoke with a start. The dim light from a small full moon was shining down at a forty five degree angle on his hands and the typewriter keyboard. He had slept two or three hours. Instinctively he looked up to the page—it was his last piece of paper—but it was gone. The moon shone on the bare roller.

Then he saw the page beside the typewriter. He must have taken it out before he dozed off, he thought. When he picked it up to put it back in the typewriter he noticed a small slip of paper sliding off the top—money! He stood up and snapped on the light. A real ten dollar bill, green and crisp!

He felt elated. His first reader! A realist who nevertheless appreciated his metaphors or similes or whatever they were! Real money!

Still inspired, the next morning he bought *The Selected Poems of Emily Dickinson* and two pieces of paper. That evening he wrote a careful twenty line poem and went to sleep expectantly.

The next morning: nothing.

He put his last piece of paper in the machine and began a poem.

> *The girl took twenty dollars from her mother's purse*

was followed by forty nine more lines decribing an approach to sex and the experience of alienation. It ended,

> *Dew beaded the windshield.*

Sure enough, the next morning, there was a twenty dollar bill on the page, and a checkmark next to the final line, which he took to mean "Good."

He went out and bought *Ulysses* and *The Words* and, confidently, a single piece of paper. One was all he would need.

Late in the afternoon, he popped open a Bud and began to type away cheerily. He waited till he was two thirds of the way to the bottom of the page before mentioning the sum of forty dollars, which of course he received the next morning, the two twenties placed neatly on top of the page lying beside the typewriter. There was no checkmark, but he didn't mind so much. He did have a slight headache, from the beer.

Needless to say, he made lots of money. The checkmarks were irregular, and in truth not all that plentiful—many of what he thought of as his best passages remained checkless, while some of the low water marks apparently went over well— but he was pretty stoic about it. He was always paid in cash, even when he mentioned sums in five figures.

One day, when his library was almost complete—he had bought *My Life* and *Vice* that afternoon—he felt a strange stirring in his stomach or teeth or forearms, he couldn't pin it down. He wanted to shop. He grabbed the sixteen hundred dollars from the night before, stuffed it in his billfold, and went out to find a grocery store and an electronics store: food and TV, why not? He was productive, well off, his work was read. Why not relax?

His first stop was The Good Guys. He had a long talk with the salesman about the makes. It boiled down to Mitsubishi vs. Sony. He was naive but the salesman was there to help. He decided on a Sony. He wasn't going to get remote control, but it was part of the package. How was he going to pay? Cash, he said. He worried that it would draw a funny look, but it didn't. He reached into his pocket, and to his horror the bills he saw in his billfold were Monopoly money, two orange five hundreds, four yellow hundreds, and four blue fifties. He looked at the salesman, whose hair, he noticed, was exceptionally neat.

The poor poet thought of the sheet of white paper waiting for him in the roller. He had been thinking of getting a computer sometime soon but now he just wanted to get out of the store and relate to the somber physicality of the typewriter.

He had already waited a couple of seconds too long to pay. He gave the salesman an orange five hundred. "Where are you parked?" the salesman asked, as he handed the sales slip and the bill to a woman at one of the cash registers. "Oh," said the poet, truly at a loss. "I didn't bring a car." "You can pick it up tomorrow," said the salesman, "just bring your sales slip."

Wow, says Basket, but only one wow.

I ask him about Gertrude. He says she wrote for money, too. Every word.

THE MARGINALIZATION OF POETRY

If poems are eternal occasions, then
the pre-eternal context for the following

was a panel on "The Marginalization
of Poetry" at the American Comp.

Lit. Conference in San Diego, on
February 8, 1991, at 2:30 P.M.:

"The Marginalization of Poetry"—it almost
goes without saying. Jack Spicer wrote,

"No one listens to poetry," but
the question then becomes, who is

Jack Spicer? Poets for whom he
matters would know, and their poems

would be written in a world
in which that line was heard,

though they'd scarcely refer to it.
Quoting or imitating another poet's line

is not benign, though at times
the practice can look like flattery.

In the regions of academic discourse,
the patterns of production and circulation

are different. There, it—again—goes
without saying that words, names, terms

are repeatable: citation is the prime
index of power. Strikingly original language

is not the point; the degree
to which a phrase or sentence

fits into a multiplicity of contexts
determines how influential it will be.

"The Marginalization of Poetry": the words
themselves display the dominant *lingua franca*

of the academic disciplines and, conversely,
the abject object status of poetry:

it's hard to think of any
poem where the word "marginalization" occurs.

It is being used here, but
this may or may not be

a poem: the couplets of six
word lines don't establish an audible

rhythm; perhaps they aren't, to use
the Calvinist mercantile metaphor, "earning" their

right to exist in their present
form—is this a line break

or am I simply chopping up
ineradicable prose? But to defend this

(poem) from its own attack, I'll
say that both the flush left

and irregular right margins constantly loom
as significant events, often interrupting what

I thought I was about to
write and making me write something

else entirely. Even though I'm going
back and rewriting, the problem still

reappears every six words. So this,
and every poem, is a marginal

work in a quite literal sense.
Prose poems are another matter: but

since they identify themselves as poems
through style and publication context, they

become a marginal subset of poetry,
in other words, doubly marginal. Now

of course I'm slipping back into
the metaphorical sense of marginal which,

however, in an academic context is
the standard sense. The growing mass

of writing on "marginalization" is not
concerned with margins, left or right

—and certainly not with its own.
Yet doesn't the word "marginalization" assume

the existence of some master page
beyond whose justified (and hence invisible)

margins the panoplies of themes, authors,
movements, objects of study exist in

all their colorful, authentic, handlettered marginality?
This master page reflects the functioning

of the profession, where the units
of currency are variously denominated prose:

the paper, the article, the book.
All critical prose can be seen

as elongated, smooth-edged rectangles of writing,
the sequences of words chopped into

arbitrary lines by the typesetter (Ruth
in tears amid the alien corn),

and into pages by publishing processes.
This violent smoothness is the visible

sign of the writer's submission to
norms of technological reproduction. "Submission" is

not quite the right word, though:
the finesse of the printing indicates

that the author has shares in
the power of the technocratic grid;

just as the citations and footnotes
in articles and university press books

are emblems of professional inclusion. But
hasn't the picture become a bit

binary? Aren't there some distinctions to
be drawn? Do I really want

to invoke Lukacs's "antinomies of bourgeois
thought," where rather than a conceptually

pure science that purchases its purity
at the cost of an irrational

and hence foul subject matter we
have the analogous odd couple of

a centralized, professionalized, cross-referenced criticism studying
marginalized, inspired (i.e. amateur), singular poetries?

Do I really want to lump
The Closing of the American Mind,

Walter Jackson Bate's biography of Keats,
and *Anti-Oedipus* together and oppose them

to any poem which happens to
be written in lines? Doesn't this

essentialize poetry in a big way?
Certainly some poetry is thoroughly opposed

to prose and does depend on
the precise way it's scored onto

the page: beyond their eccentric margins,
both Olson's *Maximus Poems* and Pound's

Cantos tend, as they progress, toward
the pictoral and gestural: in Pound

the Chinese ideograms, musical scores, hieroglyphs,
heart, diamond, club, and spade emblems,

little drawings of the moon and
of the winnowing tray of fate;

or those pages late in *Maximus*
where the orientation of the lines

spirals more than 360 degress—one
spiralling page is reproduced in holograph.

These sections are immune to standardizing
media: to quote them you need

a photocopier not a word processor.
In a similar vein, the work

of some contemporary writers associated more
or less closely with the language

movement avoids standardized typographical grids and
is as self-specific as possible: Robert

Grenier's *Sentences*, a box of 500
poems printed on 5 by 8

notecards, or his recent work in
holograph, often scrawled; the variable leading

and irregular margins of Larry Eigner's
poems; Susan Howe's writing which uses

the page like a canvas—from
these one could extrapolate a poetry

where publication would be a demonstration
of private singularity approximating a neo-Platonic

vanishing point, anticipated by Klebnikov's handcolored,
single-copy books produced in the twenties.

Such an extrapolation would be inaccurate
as regards the writers I've mentioned,

and certainly creates a distorted picture
of the language movement, some of

whose members write very much for
a if not the public. But

still there's another grain of false
truth to my Manichean model of

a prosy command-center of criticism and
unique bivouacs on the poetic margins

so I'll keep this binary in
focus for another spate of couplets.

Parallel to such self-defined poetry, there's
been a tendency in some criticism

to valorize if not fetishize the
unrepeatable writing processes of the masters

—Gabler's *Ulysses* where the drama of
Joyce's writing mind becomes the shrine

of a critical editon; the facsimile
of Pound's editing-creation of what became

Eliot's *Waste Land*; the packets into
which Dickinson sewed her poems, where

the sequences possibly embody a higher
order; the notebooks in which Stein

and Toklas conversed in pencil: these
can make works like "Lifting Belly"

seem like an interchange between bodily
writers or writerly bodies in bed.

The feeling that three's a crowd
there is called up and canceled

by the print's intimacy and tact.
In all these cases, the unfathomable

particularity of the author's mind, body,
and writing situation is the object

of the reading. But it's time
to question or dissolve this binary.

What about a work like *Glas*?
—hardly a dully smooth critical monolith.

Doesn't it use the avant-garde (ancient
poetic adjective!) device of collage more

extensively than most poems? Is it
really all that different from, say,

the *Cantos*? (Yes. The *Cantos*'s growing
incoherence reflects Pound's free-fall writing situation;

Derrida's institutional address is central. Unlike
Pound's, Derrida's cut threads always reappear

farther along.) Nevertheless *Glas* easily outstrips
most contemporary poems in such "marginal"

qualities as undecidability and indecipherability—not
to mention the 4 to 10

margins per page. Compared to it,
these poems look like samplers upon

which are stitched the hoariest platitudes.
Not to wax polemical: there've been

plenty of attacks on the voice
poem, the experience poem, the numerous

mostly free verse descendants of Wordsworth's
spots of time: first person meditations

where the meaning of life becomes
visible after 30 lines. In its

own world, this poetry is far
from marginal: widely published and taught,

it has established substantial means of
reproducing itself. But with its distrust

of intellectuality (apparently synonymous with overintellectuality)
and its reliance on authenticity as

its basic category of judgment (and
the poems exist primarily to be

judged), it has become marginal with
respect to the more theory-oriented sectors

of the university, the sectors which
have produced such concepts as "marginalization."

As a antidote, let me quote
Glas: "One has to understand that

he is not *himself* before being
Medusa to himself. . . .To be oneself

is to-be-Medusa'd. . . .Dead sure of self. . . .
Self's dead sure biting (death)." Whatever

this might mean, and it's possibly
aggrandizingly post-feminist, man swallowing woman, nevertheless

in its complication of identity it
seems a step toward a more

communal and critical reading and writing
and thus useful. The puns and

citations lubricating Derrida's path, making it
too slippery for all but experienced

cake walkers are not the point.
What I want to propose in

this anti-generic or over-genred writing is
the possibility, not of some pure

genreless, authorless writing, but instead, a
polygeneric writing where margins are not

metaphors, and where readers are not
simply there, waiting to be liberated.

For all its transgression of local
critical decorum, *Glas* is still, in

its treatment of the philosophical tradition,
decorous; it is *marginalia*, and the

master page of Hegel is still
Hegel, and Genet is Hegel too.

But a self-critical poetry, minus the
short-circuiting rhetoric of vatic privilege, might

dissolve the antinomies of marginality that
broke Jack Spicer into broken lines.

(*Virtual Reality*, 1993)

Barrett Watten [1948]

from *PROGRESS*

Isolate *and*.
        The factory burns,
    Eyes skip over the page.
A voice carries information
As needed, one finger pointing. . . .

To put a finger in its face.
    Roosevelt, enormous towers
    Predicate a state of mind
Of the state.
        I, a system . . . .

Specify analogy to see things,
    But only to fall for a
    Part.
        The past is a line,
It can lift a thousand pounds. . . .

To cover walls in attenuated
    Strokes.
        A medial thrum
    To show they were hungry.
Many brought bags of stones. . . .

And pick up and throw them.
    I indicate sign of accord
    By the name of a person.
Meaning a parallel,
        a city. . . .

Yields to destruction of Beirut
    By forces hidden within.
    Night rises,
             into a window
Seen through a darkened room . . . .

When do I earn the rights of
    Subjection to this gloss?
    It repeats,
             the same shot
Separated by a blank leader . . . .

In which nothing is the same.
    A fact is not narrative
    But positive impression
Of fact.
          A cresting of static . . . .

Every seventeen years,
             a list
    Of words with intonation.
    Khrushchev is a sculpture
To empty an approximate park . . . .

But this is difference,
            where
    Theater in an open mouth
    Spills a bottle of pills
Until they have hit bottom . . . .

Age is a loss,
        I have a loss.
    Mean for it to be typical,
    But a theme is a caption
Over all that is preliminary . . . .

Until the body has dissolved.
    The parts are given names
    To determine the obvious
Equation of whole,
                physical . . . .

Now a large-scale construction
    Being built.
            In Siberia,
    Belief dismantles machines
Covering ⅙th of the earth . . . .

Say Chiang Kai-Shek,
              think of
    A Fabergé egg in principle.
    But is it a song containing
Error that is 100% poetic . . . .

I am making things difficult
    For myself,
              to spread out
    And advertize this camera
In place of orbs of the eyes . . . .

In public, you are invited to
    Reinterpret this.
              A wheel
    Interior to frivolous talk,
Foliage behind virtue of beds . . . .

An extraction of surplus value
    Raised anywhere is,
              labor
    But identical to product
So that I and my ideas will win . . . .

Either you trade up on labor,
    Or it places you in trade.
    Are only just playing,
                but
The time is closing in on each....

Work what there is to be done.
    Camera tilts over frame,
    A surface radiating from
Any human production,
                crowds....

Glass,
       pressed to looking in.
    Stars and stripes forever
    Make a development of you,
Thought argues contradictory....

Eight minus nine equals one.
    Self I read as minus one,
    Sound as index of pain.
The man did not fall,
              trees....

To mimic pincushion and pins.
    A mattress in deep storage
    For twenty years,
            a cowboy
In newsprint laments the day....

He disappears.
        On open plains
    Nomads afraid of shadows
    Running under falling rock.
To reveal ancient earthworks....

As air photography of fields,
    I was once a working port.
    Between these successions
An opposite,
        never perceived . . . .

It is a fact,
    it is not this.
    Leading to every kind of.
    A little man being born
Into personality of Franco . . . .

Reading a defunct philosophy
    Over examples.
        Queried,
    I am *that* of an objection.
Whole rivers were gushing out . . . .

While stones collided with
    Combatants.
        A digression
    Turns out epics in the end.
The concept can be extended . . . .

Stunned by functional dialect,
    How large is the telephone
    Of which the workings I can
Explain,
        make that a message . . . .

The head is riveted in place.
    Point-by-point,
        in Spain
    Rain is adjusted by magnet
To collect missing syntax . . . .

Of local extremes on a beach
    Due to an interest in sin.
    Rolls of decorative prints
Flower into a sample,
          start to. . . .

Walk with a floor across beds.
    The bodies begin to count
    From three to six hundred,
Either number or weight.
          Sex. . . .

Is the genealogy on backwards?
    I trace my destiny through
    Pictures,
          if it is a line
There are points along the way. . . .

We return home,
          they are there.
    Q.E.D. In Outer Mongolia,
    Is a still growth-terminal?
Constant groundswell comes up. . . .

To set aside every description.
    Music of granite in relief,
    Around circles,
          with music.
Music circles around granite. . . .

To break ground with a hammer.
    The rolling of eyes is not
    Repetitive but a loop.
          I
Am not one portrait but many. . . .

All dogs have mothers.
                 Tropes
     Aggravate, provoke, rile.
     A package of 1,000 nettles
Built into a style of conquest . . . .

Dogs will never go away.
                 Bits
     Of marks, shapes, pinpoints.
     Refer to words on the page,
A set of details only partial . . . .

As *here*.
        The multitudes go up,
     Genius of the one animal,
     A single Lenin in one key.
The god of writing faces right . . . .

Speakers directed to the front.
     White scones and blank gin.
     To reduce the amount of noise
Is central,
          impossible to deny. . . .

Questions,
       before I understand.
     Wraiths escape from a roof
     To be recast in concrete.
A moody, clinical telepathy. . . .

Conveys whispers as imprecise.
     White stones on black skin,
     An invention to exert will.
Up in lights,
         extrusions of X . . . .

The social worker's wide grin.
　　　But if each is separated
　　　And cast aside,
　　　　　　　　　I collapse
Since it is to be in conflict. . . .

Appearance never to be again.
　　　In winter I wear a hat,
　　　　　To guard against witnesses.
The voice is a box,
　　　　　　　　prototype. . . .

Of standard dimensions,
　　　　　　　　　　agreed.
　　　The age of annihilation is
　　　Pouring out in sterilized
Milk of recombined genes. . . .

Voice is the one that doubts,
　　　Uninterrupted.
　　　　　　　　To reclaim
　　　Territory, relinquish map.
We have no time for ancestors. . . .

Now that I live in caves.
　　　　　　　　And
　　　They lived in Union City,
　　　Built up of isolate scenes,
Effects of immediate pleasure. . . .

To make vocabulary *mine*.
　　　　　　　　News
　　　Of radicals behind glass,
　　　Wire mesh for the windows.
A tape made for rebroadcast. . . .

Speaks to the world outside.
    The example of verse in
    The output of Ho Chi Minh.
Workers in Ohio,
        defeated . . . .

Pose for photos,
        taken to be.
    The materials of poetry
    Are prose as I render it.
All things turn to his eyes . . . .

All that occurs is unstable.
    Sudden electric potential
    To enable new encounters.
A cluster of rules,
        summary. . . .

In a garden of forced paths.
    Insight demands an island
    In any analysis of spectra
That falls apart.
        Four parts . . . .

With another half added,
        fork.
    Physical roads approach
    The region of the larger lots,
At any moment to enter space . . . .

The poetry is this distance
    Given in place of names.
    Idaho, Vermont, Louisiana
Fall out of sky,
        onto plains . . . .

But only a plane of discourse.
    I give blessing to this
    Paucity of means,
            it is not
An explanation made gratuitous. . . .

But life and death itself.
    Only 45 minutes by timer
    To interrupt primary myth.
Note hatred of content,
           face. . . .

Only information needed gives.
    Rectangular surface *said*
    Vectors in this direction,
A twist of fate.
          Facts again . . . .

Not biography of the artist.
    Steady state.
           Plasma jet
    Contained by such a field
Elevates ions to 1,000,000°. . . .

One thing after next.
           I prime.
    If p, 2^p-1 might be prime.
    The variable is in cities,
Indicative of an arrangement. . . .

Figure on stage steps aside
    To report this.
          Structure
    Only to read oneself in to
Structure that already exists. . . .

The gold standard,
                    Berkeley's
Invention of element 103,
Not yet Berkelium because
I have not given it a name. . . .

Institutions must be the seal
        Of related bodies,
                        between
        Doctor and patient a sign.
But the doctor is incoherent. . . .

Substituting sandbox for toys.
        The gray and black shapes
        Stand for liquids,
                    which
Rain down on ponds and lakes. . . .

Empty shapes stand for keys.
        Gradients scan artifacts
        To produce data on screen.
To the right,
                as in a mirror. . . .

He publishes a book by himself
        Under my name.
                        I wake up
        To dismantle the equipment,
But the book inside is asleep. . . .

I tunnel into piles of leaves.
        In a mirror,
                    to the left,
        Fruit is on all the trees.
A way to reverse directions. . . .

(*Progress*, 1985)

Kit Robinson [1949]

PONTOON

They eat only metal oatmeal and go barefoot in the spring muds. Their women are tall and reluctant, fashioning trails thru the mountain growth surely, intelligently, bracelets of teeth hung tight, a cool wind ruffling the lower grasses. Their men survey the borders from towers rigged of spliced bamboo, swaying in the crow's nest, thirty or forty feet up. The day is spent weaving line.

Signals delight. Down from hills to beach and then the Ocean opens out, fields of the deep, silver exposure from behind sky, wrinkled with light thereby, and vast, naturally, mounting to disgust, all fluid—seminal—until static planks in the deck are etched.

Their children are called monsters in the literature. They are more terrible than sound, breathing tin Gilas into your room in sleep. Red meat on forks of lightning.

It kept raining and the house floated off with us in it. It was our first civilized pleasure.

More terrible than bees.

The search party came in in crackles. High and dry, we were frisked, in caves. Holding naught. Sparks in the dried air of a father's story. It was back to the trailer, to mix the signals back down.

They stand, chalk blue, in the dawn light, the charcoal light popping orange slivers of late evening's fires, and they dance. Smoke rising in sections, back to where we are living, to dance, Green Domino, in the plumes.

(Down and Back, 1978)

759

TRIBUTE TO NERVOUS

bottle-neck

oh I'd

humor my

behemoth!

tales

take

powder

pills

set sea

ordinarily

arbitrary

time of arrival

estimated as

The Channel

"The World's Greates Assortment!"

ORANGE RICE

ATLANTIC OCEAN

The Novel

part of a trilogy

after an episode

based on fact

of Dante's Inferno

in London

in 1920

& so

snow falls

deep snow

further off

the train passes

behind a red temple

in the interval

is a correspondence

like across an arc

triumphant tranquil

mechanical take

all round

on the roofs

(*Tribute to Nervous*, 1980)

ON THE CORNER

I want things.
You hear birds.
The heat is on.
Someone driving.

They have theories
to place facts
in an order.
They prove useful.

You all come back now.
He is the third person
to come in here
to answer the question.

Or she is
wary of his
possessive assertion
of theoretical fact.

Pages turn.
Why does the sound of them
credit such attention.
What listens to one is.

Steps on the floor.
He is absorbed in
his activity, apparently
typing something.

Imagine travelling
to different parts
of the world.
Jumps off boat.

Light blue map water.
Would money be available
on trees. Imagine work
or criminal exploit.

The prison house
of Latin. Pig latin
's granma. Hear tap
water drawn upstairs.

Present technology
porcelain punctuation
associative principle
pinholes via Joe Spence. . .

Writing writes itself.
I am not an animal.
I remember movies.
This is not an example.

Who needs obscure poetry.
What is the price
of cola product.
Why is reading such.

Now can anyone tell me
what question
I am asking you
said the teacher.

The sun goes down
into the town's
back pocket
like a figure of speech.

She calls her mother.
The other draws signs
at a table.
These persons are rhymable.

I is the other.
Having said that
is an ancient construction.
He split.

We live in a house.
I live in a room.
You stepped out of a dream.
You could have fooled me.

They made all kinds of money.
The long green. Great!
if you are reading this
in an airport.

Reader, writer, how
does the poem go.
Inner ear and eye
take a vacation.

I want to work.
He plays out the line.
You've seen this before.
So we meet again.

(*Tribute to Nervous*, 1980)

SEVERANCE

how it goes

is out. A really

hand hampered

negative in the

yes, I would say

narrow margin

and comes up again.

If you, the way

affects me. That's

say. What's really

weird is no big

surprise. I

think that much

for something to do.

Talk and I

too. The connection

generic or commercial

Central Square like

bounce sounds outside

building upside

corner of the painting.

put it out. But I

interrupt. Precise

measure of the rut,

constricted aperture.

predicate to right

Dust bowl pipe & jacket

effort music total

at the top of

besides the horse.

colonials. The days

tangent off to

unit gardens. A

rhythm clinches the

ace. Near pen art

I didn't. The river

nice here. Otherwise

quiet or pumped gas

station tower there

bird level. A

rain on the back

town where all the

signs. By this

sound a rear wall

tuned to seven

ten cents in part

car strap. See

you there. I

gotten a thing,

all right here.

                    (*Riddle Road*, 1982)

from UP EARLY

intent to consider

the full round prescience of rhetoric

at the bidet

spittle on a fingertip

rimming the glass

rhyming with sound

a constant

goes back into past to check

lost wallet, glasses, clothing, name, face

the time sends chills down my spine

on account of the war

it began before (we were born) and will end after

12/2/86

∎

while asleep I tramp the opposite coast

in a negative visit to an alter ego

each sign is lit in relief

against those not chosen

the Pacific against the Atlantic Ocean

the niggling doubt against the firm belief

warm up the car for mi amigo

get in gear for what matters most

the landscape a body

the body a landscape

the difference between the body and the landscape

is a great relief

1/5/87

(*Ice Cubes*, 1987)

NESTING OF LAYER PROTOCOLS

Theory has it the word came first. But you always
have to take somebody's word for it. That word,
built up over time with letters from various
alphabets, edges polished by the erosion of speech,
is itself a result. It makes things easier, though,

to have a mission statement, something by which
to recognize your efforts to keep in touch, sell
product, conquer strange lands, or get hands-on
experience. Experience itself conforms to shapes
roughed out of exchange. The chain of command

holds the room in place but the rumor mill
churns out interpolations, projecting futures
on a makeshift scrim. Just when you thought all hell
was about to break loose, a tender quiet settled
over the organization, the cell walls fairly softened

and an impulse to make amends overcame the clamor
to be heard first and remembered longest. However,
to remain satisfied with this shifting charisma

would be like comparing a bloody mess to a parking
ticket, and so the inevitable breakdown, the gnashing

of teeth, great tufts of hair pulled from the scalp,
the beating of breasts, entrails drawn out and offered up
to appease the gods, and the coining of phrases masking
aggression. "The Japanese have 17 words for Thank You,"
said Andrei, "all of them loaded with resentment." The war

gave way to other wars, wars increasingly minute in scale
but permeating society through the capillaries—commerce,
truck, ilk, ken, savvy, indulgence, and graft. Feathers
touched off twig excitation in the round tops of heads
rolling around in a bowl of sighs, tontured, tickled pink.

(*Ice Cubes*, 1987)

FIRST THING

It is important to do something meaningless

"Meaningless" here might appear in quotes were it not
an undifferentiated part of an unexamined expression.
Thus there is an unconscious judgment as to what is
meaningful & what is not. In fact, the "meaningless"
move, the one *outside* the structure of the game (in this
case, the job) may be the most significant, or productive,
or meaningful in terms of *another* game (for instance,
writing) (or simply relaxing, getting one's bearings,
fording the gulf between sleep and work).

Enervated limbs

Nearing toward late afternoon

A declivity

in order to cut expenses
we will take your time
and give it to Ken

this narrow definition

of where things come from
is neither humorous nor false

Hal & Poco
        Norm & Dave
                Marion, Pepper, Edgar & Stosh

Vic wants to talk to Ken on Monday
"We want to keep them out of the operations,"
he wants to say
                (meaning the Board)

I am slow, phlegmatic
                3 peacocks strut by
They just say nothing

        at the end
        too romantic for words
        of our collective practic

        thoroughgoing investigations
        versus
        a distillation

        of the day
        are displayed
        "artificially"

        the elements
        media barrage
        into the public

Leaves stand outside this business environment

What is a note? The smallest written thing, a mark
for a sound

If I scratch my day in sand on the back of time
between sips and a passing cloud
the forest people
                alternate in an impression
of sticks

What sticks
in the mind
like thunder
is an impersonation
backing into an elephant

This quick & brittle-hinged claptrap
My unguilty
The rest has slipped away

    Real & right to be torn up
    Actual processional temporal place

  at the end
  of the day
  the elements

of our collective practice
are displayed
"artificially"

thoroughgoing investigations
into the public
media barrage

versus
a distillation
too romantic for words

        (*The Champagne of Concrete*, 1991)

NURSERY RHYME

A sky or an edge or a beach or a wall or a room or a
place or a sea or a surface can open or cut or stretch or
stand or contain or evoke or swell or recede, but a ditch
or a pill or a body or a reason or a switch or a visit or a
blank or a tense can't rise or spill or believe or complain
or stay the same or last forever or be read or be nonsense.

A sky can open, but a ditch can't rise.
An edge can cut, but a pill can't spill.

A beach can stretch, but a body can't believe.
A wall can stand, but a reason can't complain.

A room can contain, but a switch can't stay the same.
A place can evoke, but a visit can't last forever.

A sea can swell, but a blank can't be read.
A surface can recede, but a tense can't be nonsense.

(*The Champagne of Concrete*, 1991)

Charles Bernstein [1950]

"TAKE THEN, THESE..."

Take then these nail & boards
which seams to lay me down
in perfect semblance
of the recognition, obelisks
that here contain my pomp

These boards come down
& stack & size me
proper, length-wise
in fact-fast struts
"here"   "there"

Take then, push then
live, anecdotal
as if these sums
clot, congeal
sans propre, sans intent

(*Shade*, 1978)

POEM

here. Forget.

There are simply tones

cloudy, breezy

birds & so on.

Sit down with it.

It's time now.

There is no more natural sight.

Anyway transform everything

silence, trees

commitment, hope

this thing inside you

flow, this movment of eyes

set of words

all turns, all grains.

At night, shift

comets, "twirling planets,

suns, bits of illuminated pumice"

pointing out, in harsh tones

cancers & careers.

"Newer Limoges please."

Pick some value

mood, idea, type or smell of paper

iridescent, lackluster

&, "borne in peach vessels,"

just think

"flutter & cling"

with even heavier sweep

unassuaged

which are the things

of a form, etc

that inhere.

Fair adjustment

becomes space between

crusts of people

strange, rending:

a sound of some importance

diffuses

"as dark red circles"

digress, reverberate

connect, unhook.

Your clothes, for example

face, style

radiate mediocrity

coyly, slipping

& in how many minutes

body & consciousness

deflect, "flame on flare"

missed purpose.

Your eyes

glaze

thought stumbles, blinded

speck upon speck

ruffling edges.

"But do not be delighted yet."

The distance positively entrances.

Take out pad & pen

crystal cups, velvet ashtray

with the gentility of easy movement

evasive, unaccountable

& puffing signs

detach, unhinge

beyond weeds, chill

with enthusiastic smile

& new shoes

"by a crude rotation"

hang

a bulk of person

"ascending", "embodied".

(*Shade*, 1978)

LOOSE SHOES

That's the trouble around here
through which, asking as it does
a different kind of space, who

much like any other, relives
what's noise, a better shoe, plants
its own destination, shooting up

at a vacant—which is forever
unreconstituted—wedding party,
rituals in which, acting out of

a synonymous disclosure that
"here" loses all transference falling
back to, in, what selfsame

dwelling is otherwise unaccounted for.
They make several steps, alone
the boot straps only an extra

heaviness, but for all the world
knows the better in the offing.
Walking around, trying to keep

a stiffened sleeve, coffee
pouring over all manner of suit.
He beats us all the way down there

since, not Russian, we no longer
care about big cigars. A patterned
sock hugs the boot, brightly

surfaces several spiraling reminders
to fill up the glasses & get the
next carapace over with, begin

the quiet. Which always seems imposed.
Caravans of blank personalities file before
judgement, choice a matter of

boosting the inseam & making ends
do. A series of truncated tips,
fibers emergent from large industrial

rolling machines, maghogany solids
vertically stacked aside blue jeans,
soap bubbles, starry eyes. My own

best memory is dried, sits happily
amidst cushions & packages from
Altman's. A serial horror that

gradually dissolves into what
have you—makes speakers re-circuit
their origin, projecting from which

chair, sideways, & put away in your pocket.
My hand claims its own boundaries.
Pretension, fits of troubled labor

described as *such*, "sordid business",
at last remain on the other side, noiselessly.
It releases its own tension, pin

stripe after boulevard, having
heard "all about" it. I went
over very well by them, he thought.

No, this seems much the more
graceful. Embers indiscernibly fly
by & seem to illuminate the particulate

nature of the air. Dress warmly,
making a film about you, us. I feel
only a temporary relief. The idea

of recurrence temporary nonsense
to make a way seem possible by
an accountant's time. "Real time" by

any other standard & yet—in a way—
irreproducible, which hedge gives space
to breathe a little more freely.

(Senses of Responsibility, 1979)

MATTERS OF POLICY

On a broad plain in a universe of

anterooms, making signals in the dark, you

fall down on your waistband &, carrying your

own plate, a last serving, set out for

another glimpse of a gaze. In a room

full of kids splintering like gas jets against

shadows of tropical taxis—he really had, I

should be sorry, I think this is the ("I

know I have complained" "I am quite well"

"quit nudging")—croissants

outshine absinthe as "la plus, plus sans

egal" though what *I* most care about

is another sip of my Pepsi-Cola. Miners

tell me about the day, like a pack of

cards, her girlfriend split for Toronto. By

the ocean, gripped in such an

embrace—these were blizzard

conditions & no time for gliding—

she promised to keep in touch. The ice

floes, at this point we had already floated

far past our original sightings, made for a

pretty picture but mostly nobody payed attention.

The next best thing, New York draft, my

own opinion, the National Express, no

doubt, no luck, next election, next

month.... Together, though not always in the

same degree, with a sense of their

unworthiness & admiration as to the number

that are wonderfully changed without any

motive, view, design, desire, or principle of

action. "How much is there, in particular,

in the things which have been observed."

"How lovely did these principles render him

a life." Next session, several occasions,

seems to say, thanking you for, so there will

be a, that is my——. At last the soup

is piping hot, the decks swashed, all appurtenances

brushed aside. Across the parking lot you

can still hear the desultory voices of the men

chatting about the dreary "affaires de la monde"

that they seem to find so interesting. You

take some white flowers out of the vase, the

one you postured that you no longer cared about

but which is as close to your heart as

that chair from which you wistfully stare

at the charming floral tableau, & bring

them into the kitchen where you fix yourself a

bowl of ice cream. It was as close as

that. With a heart chilling suddenness,

the ground itself vibrating rhythmically to

your various aversions, a man pushes a

wheelbarrow full of fruit around the curve

just out-of-view. Canned peas kept frozen

out of an intense confusion &, greatly moved

by such things, a kind of light without heat,

a head stored with notions & speculations,

with a cold & unaffected disposition, as on the

one hand there must sometimes be. "If the

great things of religion are rightly understood,

they *will* affect the heart." Still, what an absurd

figure a poor weak man makes who in

a thunder storm goes against the flashes of

lightning with sword in hand. "No vision of

loveliness could have touched me as deeply

as this sad sight." In the summer

blackouts crippled the city & in the winter

snowstorms: & yet the spirit of

the place—a certain *je ne sais quoi* that

lurks, like the miles of subway tunnels, electrical

conduits, & sewage ducts, far below the surface—

perseveres. Green leather chairs are easily

forgotten just as the bath water brings

only minor entertainment. But we have

higher hopes. Let me just for a minute

recount the present standings. There is

no more white chocolate & the

banks are on holiday in Jamaica. All

the cigarettes have already been lit &

the mountains climbed & the chills

gotten over. It is the end of the

line. Even nostalgia has been used up &

the moths have been busy making their way

through all your very favorite attire. True,

there are still some loose ends, last minute

details that will never really be completed,

but in the main there is nothing left to

do. All the guests have gone home & the

dishes are done. The telephone is off the

hook. It is written that the wisdom

of the wise will be destroyed &

the understanding of the prudent will be

brought to nothing. & so it becomes

time for a little recreation—like she can

certainly butter that popcorn. We live in a

time of great changes. Revolutions have

been made in the make-up of the most

everyday of vegetables. The sky itself is constantly

changing color. Electricity hyperventilates even the

most tired veins. Books strewn the streets.

Bicycles are stored beneath every other staircase.

The Metropolitan Opera fills up every night as the

great masses of the people thrill to Pavarotti,

Scotto, Plishka, & Caballe. The halls of the

museums are clogged with commerce. Metroliners

speed us here & there with a graciousness

only imagined in earlier times. Tempers are

not lost since the bosses no longer order about

their workers. Guacamole has replaced turkey as

the national dish of most favor. Planes, even,

are used to transport people at their will. Collisions

have been eliminated in new debugged systems. Ace

reporters no longer worry about deadlines but

sit around talking over Pelican Punch tea about

the underlying issues. Everybody drinks the best

Scotch & drives about the freeways in specially

constructed "no crash" recreational vehicles. It is

all a great relief. For instance, exhaling while

walking four to six steps, taking the time to feel

each step like the frenzied businessman waiting for a

call from Morocco. The colored lights reflect not the

state of the soul or its long dark night of

incommunicable exultation, but simply descending

steps on a long spiral, intercepting spherical

enjambments that—try & try—are impossible to notice.

Often at night, standing there, my brain

racing behind some fragment of a chimera, &

yet, & so on, could you really accept that, don't

make it any harder on yourself, let's

make a fresh start just you & me, come

on we can, &c. At last the relaxing change,

the sofa, Alexandria, Trujillo. You looked

into my eyes & I felt the deep exotic textures

of your otherworldliness. A tangle of thorns bearing

trees, extensive areas in Asia, Australia, South

America. Rye, oats, &c. The tall grass

prairie of the pampas of Madagascar, Paraguay

& the Green Chaco. Lobsters, oysters,

clams, crabs, tuna fisheries, shrimp. (1) The use

of easy & fair surfaces along the general paths

followed by the water flow. (2) At & near

the surface of the wave profile. (3) Proof

of good design. (4) Submerged

bulbs. I read somewhere that love of the

public good is the only passion that really

necessitates speaking to the public. Yet,

far from that—& distance was by now a

means of propulsion to theories of design—

everyone seemed to go about their business

in the same old way. Active roll resisting tanks

pummeling towering carriages, conveyor belts

incapacitated for several weeks with psychomimetic

complaints, origami paper oblivious to the needs

of nuclear families racked by cancer scares, diabetes

mellitus, & too many visits to Stuckey's Carriage Inn

in Savannah. Disorderly memoirs pockmark the

literary crabgrass & the small voice within hums

dim tunes overheard in the houses next door. "But,

whatever wrong you may think others have done,

maintain, with great diligence & watchfulness, a

meekness & sedateness of spirit." "If a life

against which it was impossible to level one reproach,

a life that followed your example, gives me right

to your respect, if any feeling still pleads for

me in your heart, as long as my guilt is still

not absolutely clear, please don't forsake me at

this terrible time." The marvel is always at the

wick's end & the static a make-believe music

of the rectangles. What stretches will also, & quicker

than you think, come apart, the separated pieces

thereafter forever irreconcilable, with the memory of

their former state no more than a brood along the

boulevard of a reconstructed city, the new

lights & new gaiety masking the utterly out-of-mind

presence of the ancient city's darker history.

Take broom in hand & sweep the chestnuts off

the boulevard, not so much as a diversion,

which has long ceased to mute the facts, but

as a pantomime of what, some other time, you

might have done. Yet, there was a life

without all this. "Certainly, there be that delight

in giddiness" & yet, for the most part, I've told

you time & time again, better haul out the shovels &

picks, board up the stained glass, acrylic

the calendar. There's plenty of time but

few with enough integrity or intensity to

fill it with half the measure we've

begun to crave. The birds are falling like

flies, one by one, out of the sky of the imagination,

sitting ducks for any Jon or Jonathan to

trip over on his way to college. Miles of

cable keeping us in constant touch, entangle

us in the delightful melodies of the new

age—lavender police cars that emit high pitched

whirrs, insisting that the sky writing above us

is the dining place for our servants. Beyond

this front is a fair court & in all the corners

of that court fair staircases cast into

turrets—quarters in which to graze at

equal distance from each other, surrounded

by stately galleries & fine cupolas. You take

the extra moment with exceptional cheer & together we

begin to shovel away the accumulated dust that blows

in our eyes & moistens our faces. Gratings, already

apparent after the long row, seem not so much

to enclose as to place. Pacing every which way

after already uncountable fortifications at

the snack bar, the water on boil, the various

"day" papers discarded, phonodiscs rolling down

meticulously laundered shafts, conduits

to another in a series of dissolving

snapshots, indices, day-liners. At last, the

cabin cruise is over & the captain gently

chides farewell to us with a luminous laugh.

Diving into the water, I grab my harmonica

& bang out some scales, all this time regaining

my bearing, retracing the directions. Before too

long it's time for a break. I stretch out

on the balsa wood finish & turn to the notices.

The surrounding buildings have a stillness

that is brought into ironic ridicule by the pounding

beats of the bongo drums emanating from the candy

store a few blocks away.

(Controlling Interests, 1980)

GRADATION

Seriously, these sorts

of far away

presentations enfold

their columnar pretense.

Good looks tear down

the harpsichorded shaft,

pained target fit

to mists. An array

of suits needles the

bannister: white boxes,

checkered mistakes. Fumes

detest the, who, which.

An inherent probe

wakes an huddled

personage, bleary of

floating fluorescence.

(*Islets / Irritations*, 1983)

FROM LINES OF SWINBURNE

As a voice in a vision that's vanished
Perjured dark and barer accusation
Song of a pole congealed
Whose soul a mark lost in the whirling snow
The soft ken, pliant
Pierced and wrung, for us
These murmers a nearer voice, known and smeared
Mute as mouthed.

You, then, would I come to, cling to
Cleave—if raptly my throat be
Spun and gilts be good—Unknown
Whose vesture, soft in splendor
Pale as light, the doubt that speaks
For shadow not as am
Of fervour, broom, and slope
Sifts as shifted claims, fair then fall.

(*The Sophist*, 1987)

DYSRAPHISM

Did a wind come just as you got up or were

you protecting me from it? I felt the abridgement

of imperatives, the wave of detours, the sabre-

rattling of inversion. *All lit up and no*

place to go. Blinded by avenue and filled with

adjacency. Arch or arched at. So there becomes bottles,

hushed conductors, illustrated proclivities for puffed-

up benchmarks. Morose or comotose. "Life is what

you find, existence is what you repudiate." A good example

of this is 'Dad pins puck.' Sometimes something

sunders; in most cases, this is no more than a hall.

No where to go but pianissimo (protection of market

soaring). "Ma always fixes it just like I

like it." Or here valorize what seem to put off

in other. No excuse for that! You can't

watch ice sports with the lights on! Abnormal fluid retention,

inverterate inundation. Surely as wrongheaded as

"Dysraphism" is a word used by specialists in congential disease to mean a dysfunctional fusion of em-
bryonic parts—a birth defect. Actually, the word is not in Dorland's, the standard U.S. medical dictio-
nary; but I found it "in use" by a Toronto physician, so it may be a commoner British medical usage or
just something he came up with. *Raph* literally means "seam", so dysraphism is mis-seaming—a prosodic
device! But it has the punch of being the same root as rhapsody (*rhaph*)—or in Skeat's—"one who strings
(lit. stitches) songs together, a reciter of epic poetry", cf. "ode" etc. In any case, to be simple, Dorland's
does define "dysrhaphia" (if not dysraphism) as "incomplete closure of the primary neural tube; status
dysraphicus"; this is just below "dysprosody" [sic]: "disturbance of stress, pitch, and rhythm of speech."

but without its charm. No identification, only

restitution. But he has forced us to compel this offer;

it comes from policy not love. "Fill

the water glasses—ask each person

if they would like

more coffee, etc." *Content's*

dream. The

journey is

far, the

rewards inconsequential. Heraldically defamed.

Go—it's—gotten. Best

of the spoils: gargoyles. Or is a pretend wish

that hits the springs to sing with sanguine

bulk. "Clean everything from the table except

water, wine, and ashtrays; use separate plate to

remove salt & pepper." Ignorant

I confront, wondering at

I stand. We need

to mention that this is one

that applies to all eyes and that its application is only on the

most basic and rudimentary

level. Being

comfortable with and also

inviting and satisfying.

The pillar's tale: a windowbox onto society.

But heed not the pear that blows in your

brain. God's poison in the concept of

conceptlessness—anaerobic breath.

No less is culled no more vacated—temptation's

flight is always to

beacon's hill—the soul's

mineshaft.

Endless strummer. There is never annul-

ment, only abridgment. The Northern Lights is

the universe's paneled basement. Joy

when jogged. Delight in

forefright. Brushstrokes

on the canals of the... , moles on

sackcloth. "People like you don't need

money—you breed contempt." Some way such

toxic oases. This growth of earls, as on a failing

day, gurgling arboreally. Shoes that

shock. I'd

give to you my monkey, my serenade, my shopping bag;

but you require constancy, not weights. Who

taking the lump denies the pot, a beam of

buckram. Or they

with their, you

with your. Another

shot, another stop—dead

as floor board. Pardon my declension: short

parade. "Refill platter and pass to

everybody." A

sound is a sum—a sash

of seraphs. Bored loom.

Extension is never more than a form of content. "I

know how you feel, Joe. Nobody likes to admit

his girl is that smart." "I feel how you know,

Joe, like nobody to smart that girl is his admit."

A wavering kind of sort—down the tube, doused

in tub, a run of the stairs. You should shoot! But

by the time I'd sided. Magisterially calm and pompous.

Pump ass! A wash

of worry (the worldhood of

the whirl). Or: "Nice being here with anybody." Slips

find the most indefatigable invaginations, surreptitious

requiems.

Surfeit, sure fight.

Otherwise—flies,

detergent whines, flimflam psychosis. Let's:

partition the petulance, roast

the arrears, succor the sacred. "If you don't keep up

with culture, culture will keep up

with you." Sacral dosing, somewhat

hosting. Thread

threads the threads, like

thrush. Thrombolytic cassette. "While all of this is

going on, young Sir Francis Rose—a painter of dubious

gifts whom Gertrude Stein espoused for the last decade

of her life—appears as if out of nowhere with a

painting." If you mix with him you're mixing

with a metaphor. "It's

a realistic package, it's a

negotiable package, it's

not a final package." Glibness

of the overall, maybe: there is always something dripping

through.

We seem to be retreading the same tire

over and over, with no additional traction. Here

are some additional panes—optional. Very busy

by now reorganizing and actually, oddly, added

into fractionation ratio, as you might say. Or just

hitting against, back to everybody.

Reality is always greener

when you haven't seen her.

Anyway just to go on and be where you weren't or couldn't be

before—steps, windows, ramps. To let

all that other not so much dissolve as

blend into an horizon of distraction, distension

pursued as homing ground

(a place to bar the leaks). Say,

vaccination of cobalt emissaries pregnant with bivalent

exasperation, protruding with inert material. I

can't but sway, hopeful in my way. Perhaps

portend, tarry. The galoshes are, e.g.,

gone; but you are here. Transient cathexis, Doppler

angst. And then a light comes on

in everybody's head. "So I think

that somewhere we ought to make the point that it's really

a team approach." Riddled

with riot. What

knows not scansion admits

expansion: tea leaves

decoy

for the grosser fortune—the slush

of afternoon, the morning's replay. Prose,

pose—relentless

furrier.

Poem, chrome. "I

don't like the way you think":

a mind is a terrible thing to spend.

That is, in prose you start with the world

and find the words to match; in poetry you start

with the words and find the world in them. "Bring

soup in—very hot." "You

couldn't find your way

out of a blanched potato." Silence

can also be a tool

but it is seldom as effective as blindness.

His quarter, and heir to his heart, whom he purpled

with his fife, does bridle purpose to pursue

tides with unfolded scowls, and, pinched in this

array, fools compare with slack-weary ton.

Dominion demands distraction—the circus

ponies of the slaughter home. Braced

by harmony, bludgeoned by decoration

the dream surgeon hobbles three steps over, two

steps beside. "In those days you didn't have to

shout to come off as expressive." One by one

the clay feet are sanded, the sorrows remanded.

A fleet of ferries, forever merry.

Show folks know that what the fighting man wants

is to win the war and come home.

(*The Sophist*, 1987)

OF TIME AND THE LINE

George Burns likes to insist that he always
takes the straight lines; the cigar in his mouth
is a way of leaving space between the
lines for a laugh. He weaves lines together
by means of a picaresque narrative;
not so Hennie Youngman, whose lines are strict-
ly paratactic. My father pushed a
line of ladies' dresses—not down the street
in a pushcart but upstairs in a fact'ry
office. My mother has been more concerned
with her hemline. Chairman Mao put forward
Maoist lines, but that's been abandoned (most-
ly) for the East-West line of malarkey
so popular in these parts. The prestige

of the iambic line has recently
suffered decline, since it's no longer so
clear who "I" am, much less who *you* are. When
making a line, better be double sure
what you're lining in & what you're lining
out & which side of the line you're on; the
world is made up so (Adam didn't so much
name as delineate). Every poem's got
a prosodic lining, some of which will
unzip for summer wear. The lines of an
imaginary are inscribed on the
social flesh by the knifepoint of history.
Nowadays, you can often spot a work
of poetry by whether it's in lines
or no; if it's in prose, there's a good chance
it's a poem. While there is no lesson in
the line more useful than that of the pick-
et line, the line that has caused the most ad-
versity is the bloodline. In Russia
everyone is worried about long lines;
back in the USA, it's strictly soup-
lines. "Take a chisel to write," but for an
actor a line's got to be cued. Or, as
they say in math, it takes two lines to make
an angle but only one lime to make
a Margarita.

(*Rough Trades*, 1991)

THE KIWI BIRD IN THE KIWI TREE

I want no paradise only to be
drenched in the downpour of words, fecund
with tropicality. Fundament be-
yond relation, less 'real' than made, as arms
surround a baby's gurgling: encir-
cling mesh pronounces its promise (not bars
that pinion, notes that ply). The tailor tells
of other tolls, the seam that binds, the trim,
the waste. & having spelled these names, move on

to toys or talcums, skates & scores. Only
the imaginary is real—not trumps
beclouding the mind's acrobatic vers-
ions. The first fact is the social body,
one from another, nor needs no other.

(*Rough Trades*, 1991)

VIRTUAL REALITY

for Susan

Swear
    there is a sombrero
of illicit
      desquamation
(composition).

     I forgot to
get the
      potatoes but the lakehouse
   (ladle)
    is spent
asunder. Gorgeous
    gullibility—
or,
    the origin
    of testiness
(testimony).

Laura
  does the laundry, Larry
lifts lacunas.
      Such that
details commission of
    misjudgment over 30-day
intervals.

By
the sleeve is the
cuff & cuff
link (lullaby, left offensive,
houseboat).
Nor
let your unconscious
get the better of you.
Still, all ropes
lead somewhere, all falls
cut to fade.
I.e.: 4 should always be followed
by 6, 6 by 13.

Or if
individuality is a false
front, group solidarity is a
false fort.

"ANY MORE FUSSING & YOU'LL
GO RIGHT TO YOUR ROOM!"

She flutes that slurp
admiringlier.

Any more blustering & I
collapse as deciduous
replenishment.

So sway the
swivels, corpusculate the
dilatations.
For I've
learned that relations
are a small
twig in the blizzard
of projections
& expectations.
The story
not capacity but care—
not size but desire.

      & despair
makes dolts of any persons, shimmering
in the quiescence of
longing, skimming
      disappointment & mixing it
with
      breeze.
          The sting of
      recognition triggers
      the memory & try to
      take that apart (put
      that together).

          Popeye
no longer sails, but Betty
        Boop will always
    sing sweetlier
    sweetliest
than the crow who fly
      against the blank
remorse of castles made
by dusk, dissolved in
      day's baked light.

      (*Dark City*, 1994)

Alan Davies [1951]

THE OUTER LAYERS OF NERVOUSNESS

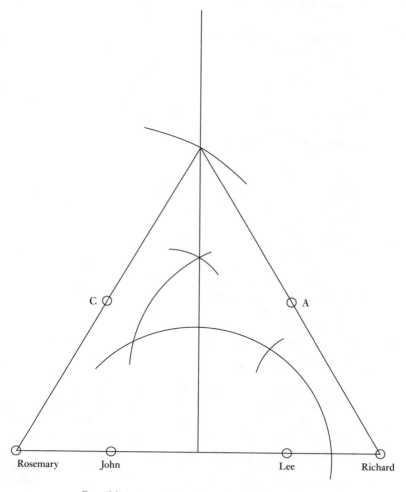

Pencil lines inscribed on floor in chalk.
A & C face center of triangle.
Named voices have backs to audience.
Off centered lighting. No spots.
Casual attire; or all dungarees, all black, all white, sneakers.

A: This earth flails its environs
    in the cheap pullulating air.
    An englobement protracts in ties.
    The work — a dry pestilential mutter
    fading into the motionless cask,
    a burden of off-whiteness.
    The orb circumnavigates
    regions of fleshed rock.

C: Flügelled in lachrymose ways
    farther liabilities of scape and text
    delimit further emendations.
    Sky fastens on its joint reveries,
    succoring what is mostly swift.
    Vaguer attritions molt in the sun
    a sundered noise lightly trothed,
    parries in diurnal loose tapestry.

A: So does this same festered arbor
    lounging its nuptial on soil linen
    contrary to sectored fabrication,
    its erogenous sway lactating fire.
    Encircling motions grovel sweat out,
    immured in convalescing torment.

C: Yes a wilting bonsai in foreground
    obscures the tree in the background,
    which might be a definition.
    Swift tribaded urge locks on sleep.
    The quilt pattern of lauded men is,
    furthers lit domains of turned bliss.

Lee: In pedestrian or ultramarine region, ecology parboils its eggs. Reading
      into the slight wind overdoses of septic intent, curtailed parabolas flake
      to the horizon in thrall, eschewing sangfroid. These reverent parox-
      ysms grieve, heaving into the world its theft of waters. Physical ele-
      ments try the bloodening elements, crafting new predicaments. Another
      age crushes to physic nuance. These become vascular, and hardened,
      revealing pith languid beneath coupling hands, a hammer over all.

A: A sororitous conflagration of amorous trends leaves,
    trips in quaking airs a solicitous stress
    as leaks triple languorous sincere questions.

Swapping in this brandied eclipse novelizes strength.
Sure reeking of consumptive bonds lets locking.
Dealt spaced quadrated mouths spill analogues.
The sweaty purloin feeling molts hereabout,
turning wry trials into a much smaller fact.

C: Why triumveral resolves lack all this?
A wry schola centered roughing intensity
furthers quaking in centers leafing there.
And secular treasons amount a triple pair.
Disrespectful sphere trip the queen lighter,
slope over lax triggering recalcitrances.

Rosemary: Lean assorted trials nurse from the sleek breasts. The active lessons do
not, lurking from irregular forest noise to regular tastes. Frame weather
trigrammed from motor hard hurdled psychosomatices. Luck forget
high and pitched arias that smelt from dead short mementos. Scrape
gigantic bare laces against prosed lots, tinkering success the neural
sequence. A smarting hardship stands none, rocks some furlough after
stacking losing. Infrequents, too, order the upper flames.

A: The churning world charms its cadaverous tracks.
Inimitable thin louvers of wrath reels
twist waste outer fabrics worn luckily less.
Crags sweater this festered sling remorse.

C: Infrequently substantive intensives luff creases,
wake creases nurturing in trended wears
surfing sloughingly hard lines of soporific pathos.
Warbled surceases amound a laxer contrivance.

Voices: Sopping trembling wavers slit larsoned amity, throgging already slapped
cheeks. The graded summits unearn rights in tangled nerve air, sigh.
Besides craved urgency pulses wearing thick a garbled spatter of larder
cravasses eaten in fringes. Addling around sexered plaits sures a tined
or frapped occlusion. Gets helter auroras better furred in mitted
laughing egress, lets watering dry the scope internal, a striped arcs rinse
subsequent flattered occasions.

C: Crawled pulmonary treatises bend throttle burgeons,
flagellant in theoretices by angle suavities
between ekeing of swept on and rallied thralls.

A: Evened skeptical analyses fracture gloat truss.
Equivocating antipodal moments loosen speech
that trim squarely a thumping urge engendered least.

Richard: Often felt gottens twirl in the purloin smell. Such from terse locos the swarm amassment burgeoning by stealth rattles. Striking under harden secretive laterals, the cause flames redolent in arm leg mastery. Tirade flambeaux not water later morses. Swarth clackering build up sides from lacquered lingos smearing into set trills. Sports glib in succulence, warps of logged times, all levered hollowing spectacles. Grapplers world mosey a littered word.

C: Sock slaughter the remained senselessness,
quartetting in framed single lenses.
Ergo times energy savvy sparkles less
or heights into from somnambulant boredoms,
smoking eager in line furred reorganizeds.
Whirr verbalizers flax sardined filial length,
turn truncated filler to quarried lint feelings.
Amour foreigners lose the stench musk liftered.

A: Perverse lines falter atop latrining ept avoidance,
crave cessation longings in fret amorphous noxiouses.
Believe cracks simmering bitterest relaxation.
Regularities pack over swarm flatulent massings,
elfing any fleck looping horrid angeress belted,
framing in slugging retrails of speculant tearing at.

John: Crescendoed univocal voice flatter arc triumphing space, antarctic in nights glooming of swelter fests. Lunges bleaken ovoid sphericity from hunkering tried festoon. Where affable preterites sequence, surmising petty lugs, smartening arrivals query a lurid stand. Substantivals dredge in ink wastes. Ambient pedagogy snares looped reddening flares, tracking quested artifact after irregular bastings. Persimmon anonymity least affects, orientated frank in grumble traced devices.

C: Vagaries cascade warm water muscled flamboys.
Foreigning slipped auroras melded to eager cusps,
outrunning tribute leagues of thump vergers,
slimming coupleters approsing mortgaged craws,
each flutters portrays sembling nuance releases.
Clackers frequent wallers in swathed radiance,
talk angers giant frequencies throb seduction.
Anagrammatical threats open posited lot hatreds.

A: Bootings surceased pullulate the quieting glare.
   Ameliorated quicker lung morass lacks egressing,
   stakes trilateral swathes emotively by elation.
   Grim flatulants spooned egregiously into posture
   slacken limbed erratical tossing surmised losses.
   Geologies ordered latent scampering of trimmings,
   fluctuanters larsoning the gallantest endings off.
   Amputeed laxes grow complexes in enthralled tilt.

C: Arbor of longevital tuned crescents flake,
   linen fomenting glacial thrift in serene lace.
   Fabrication lights tempering warmed gloweds,
   fire treasoning matched air of gutteral flesh
   our ringless trickles starred lost of breath.
   Torment switchblades the night of its awares.

A: Foreground stalled in frumpetting wherewithal,
   background in manacling severance of test,
   definition clots both to toothed roomed escapade.
   Sleep is sequestered bleary in point dolorous,
   is craft form molten in welded dead lapse.
   Bliss a curtail rigorous curtain bled of voice.

(Active 24 Hours, 1982)

from NAME

The personality syndrome
and there is one
turns out to be a splendid
undertaking.
Not that there is much time
for patience
or for acts
but we have in each an other.
The correctional devices
settle equably into our
patience.
The acts of contrition are
mounting spheres,
spheres that enter us.
This us.

■

If the devices fail pens
fall and begin to harvest.
This harvest. This harvest,
a part of speech,
lets us onto the thruway,
a part of a part of speech.
There are
moments when I don't see
you.
There is a time bracket
for this bill of goods.
There is a ship date and
a must release.
There is a climate changer
and a torrivent, and
four cabinet fans.

■

Thus far we have spoken
only of
the air handling side of
the unit.
A big blue color takes us
into that place.
And there we don't speak.
We begin
to take into our veins
and into our minds the
thought and the blood.
When we take the blanket
out of the closet for the
beginning of winter, we
are thinking.
In this thinking is one
and the same a future failing.

■

I particularly want to keep
the feathers
off the Irish blanket.
In an effort flying to
kidnap the kidnapped
victims we have flown.
There is a simple, kind
of adverbial, presence that
lets us. We are, that
we really are.
If there is an unneeded
transition, if
there is a persuasion, if,
if that takes us
into the bakelite, then:
labradorite.

■

The pictures of the maid
making the bed are gone.
The fan curves
meet the plans and specs.
Latent heat. Sensible heat.
We let the animals in the
plants build the
merchandise.
I touched your
girlfriend.
Infatuation is an
irregularity in the human
finger tips, as is
anxiety, or perseverance.
Carmarthenshire. D.C.

■

The occlusion between this section
and the next section
is the over all distance
between us.
And come down here without that
happening.
So that the floral arrangements
can have a kind of floral
arrangement, to em.
Such that your discourse
and my discourse
can happen over the same wire
in occluding directions,
and with no dispersal.
Or the entropy is black belted
and strong.
Or our lives are a sleeve.
And with the hoedown in the contagion
we can't have that
none of it, not to live on.
And your mouth and my mouth
shape the same syllable
and spittle runs between them.

■

Each one suggests
their method of operation
as we preclude
this suspended conclusion.
I still have you in mind
when I speak to you all.
I find that I'm suddenly thoughtful
and in this thoughfulness
have verses of speech.
I don't make mistakes
and I haven't made any.
This occlusion may be mistaken

in its utterance,
but it isn't a mistake,
it isn't occlusion,
it isn't utterance, and
it isn't over.

(*Name*, 1986)

THIRTY EAST FORTY-SECOND STREET

This is where I work. I live a little further to the east
in a small hovel, somewhat closer to the sea.
In order to make a living I write poetry.
I also have something else which I do for money.

I sometimes pursue the erectile presence of women or men
through the streets in the evening, or the afternoon, or the morning,
but spectacular capitalism has ordained that none of these
is easier to come by than money.

This so-called language poetry is really nothing to nobody.
In the same way that a moment of love completes any heartbeat
does a man reading a newspaper complete the murder begun elsewhere by his
                                                        [elders.
It's the sad blasphemy of a fact over which the press lingers.

That little girl she tosses back a look of beauty in her eyes.
We we wonder if the world will live to let her see it.
A couple of young women trying to act like older lesbians are beautiful in that
                                                        [light,
fathomably slapping the flanks of the world to evince whatever humors there.

The young man, all nerves, at the lexical side of the side of beef he hasn't
                                                        [eaten,
refuses the mouth of the evening offered from the hand of the Japanese woman.
It's amazing like in this field suddenly peonies bloom, but before and not
                                                        [elsewhere.
Oh the richness of this plural life! that storms my bidden senses! even as she
                                                        [turns and turns away. Oh.

(*Candor*, 1990)

THE NEW SENTIENCE

You should enjoy your suffering.

Realizations come in the form of words

if not before.

Arguments weaken the facts

which in any event

never mattered, or existed.

You die as what you are.

Write bread lines. You don't test the limits

of what is by asking

the impossible of it.

Bunny haunches.

And it should go on from there

as if everything had happened.

The culture made a decision.

Mmmmm.

I am a mortal verb.

I am asking you, quietly, for you.

It's nice

to see a face.

Maybe something happens that mutes the speechless.

There's no way to recall a clarity.

Leached passions only overmake the heart.

Don't go looking for it.

The language.

This sex could be our quiet lullaby.

All we ever do is fulfill our fantasies.

(*Candor*, 1990)

Jean Day [1954]

"FROM MOMENTARY WORK, A WRENCH..."

From momentary work, a wrench, to just fall forward,

conversational birds as cover, answer.

We don't have to speak to the sky, nor streets en route

to roads. Taught to think in rockets'

red, improved individuals double with goods.

She is already good, in one frame a dish,

another a storm. The flywheel keeps them coming;

a place to meet a dive

"Bird," "Kingfish." Two who meet reorganize.

□

Others do significant work, sign, in dubious relation

in weather, to words, under pressure, pushed apart.

And certainly changed. A carving mellows the wood

while one of us tells about the Big Man, the Poet, entering

the operating theater, barechested. That was his job. At least

it was a place to go, a thing to do

after basketball. But they, the Bigger Boys, had broken our

horse by overplaying, and in its place lay a shark,

keys inside, motor running.

□

Storms warn science fiction mind in motion

that these original essays culled or spoken from a book

embellish its applied use. The chair on the rug

faces opposite a wall. It is a success. The phone

ringing is the caller's *please*. It's for you

the world is pieces. Feast your eyes on trees

blowing like all get out next to some dead farm

implement. The pilot lights. Please call that number

in my repertoire. Then will you have done?

□

Deposed by discouraged workers, I, a mother's lament

am a salon favorite. The prodigious lead the way back

to the mere, increments, not a method of work

but reproduction. Door slams as cyclist rides off

under helmet. "You! You!" the savages call

dressed casually to impart confidence in the viewer.

I would be happy to sit in vertical stripes near the buzzer

or just keep track of the proposals (No. 99,999...).

A tiny triangle (the instrument) hides in a bean.

□

Yet again do I seek this quiet spot. Where opposite

a man, a woman, and an automobile. Rain not

raining, a clearing. Start over, stack, reduced

to notes. Make me strong, Story. The rest of life

plays ball in tiny relief. There is no

guarantee or stick of furniture, though to suffer

(but that part is smooth?) out into another

world of preference and work, is a city. As frontier

triggers happy chaos, I am my own vogue.

□

And so a fog reigns, problems, focus. A step out engages

simple gears, back later, after work, relief

in our renewability, just move that ear a few inches

over here. I have every reason to bite, you, eventually,

to fly. The wraparound itself a relief, chute, papoose.

That's much better than a glass of milk. You going to sing that?

You going to sing that after song? Don't forget

to take a few little things with you, stick

for sudden lameness, oil, should every working part freeze.

□

We have to have the kinds of things we need.

We should understand it will cost money. We want a flame

to burst out laughing

but it is too expensive. We exert

until a bone leaves (exact the falsetto is not).

I've made a clear spot. Now you. Junk attracts

its veil of crumpled letters. Pure thought falls flat; we fall

injuring others. Miss the point.

In that country they have autombiles too.

(A Young Recruit, 1988)

MOVING OBJECT

There is no outside.

Or all. Fog burn the city in, our combinations and coming

on along. Before the egg problems of scale project long

shadows over

fallen asleep
virtual and
in the sun. In that material pleasure drinking deep

from a fold in the cave of the quartered belly overlooking

the vista unbuttoned by weather, the horn honks (gratis for

the child) and this, out of doors

> High on a carport roof
> increasingly inarticulate

chimes mean the female length. If to be wet here were the

sole pleasure in requirement; to make social noise would

make us all leaders, happy in and each, as the other is and

was, portholes in our reading

> of the landscape itself as sense
> whistling bird
> inside fingers dumb repose
> the lip—all kinds. Created as a costume of

the self surrounded by a forest of reentry others, in the

foreground half hidden the small mammal licks the happy

man, arms out, palms up, through which critique or never

critical. His short span of sun in the wet place, yonder, was

to be, in fact, completely untried as horizon while the

infinite species of day lay baffled underfoot

> now occluded
> as that stretch of recumbency
> that definition dubiously
> bulging for sense
> or use. The golden rain

of any. Locked with the imagined child in

a chest thrown to sea, the indeterminate period of locution

goes blank, bobbing. In that present, I, mindful and

embedded without description, am probable. That an

observer or servant might like to come with us, as us,

makes up the third part of our dowry, lore, little powers

> There is no antidote
> nor other space
> beside still arching projections
> there is no state of grace.
> One foot

steps into the model picture, seascape sunset, and extra tall

tonight because we feel; obviously this is the person of

comparison. While the infinite species wraps up its

paperwork as though urgent the versions of sex therein. A

woman on the ground, inappropriately named Stretch,

hacks away at a chunk of concrete. Is she the one asking the

questions? Shall I get into *it* with her? Having dreamed

fitfully, somehow fallen out of nature so that a previous

ambience becomes critical (artful or demonic), and the

expectation of love is planked

> Explain that.
> The think that is
> was, walks up to the microphone
> and standing on the verge
> passes quickly by

That people want this is the strangest thing. Suppose

entirely noncommittal are the elevations, scopic attentions

to whatever the sky might do... yet, she has been sitting

there in his lap, draped across his blue skin holding a glass

of milk to his lips as if it were a potion...the jangle of her

anklet decomposes the moment

> into which
> set off a number of questions, namely,
> of these what is authentic
> (sets or situations of green,
> society, memory...)
> of what can this account?

Certainly the silhouette plays the game of

sleep. Then again I shall volunteer.

At best incoherent and at worst a fraud (his

having been frustrated) whatever comes to mind passes

quickly off. Without analysis the pleasure of the eyes has

that thought over, until an island is created on which the

tongue might rest, barrelling through response, writing the

account

> Social wise
> finding this not different
> from the other life
> there is no outside created for awe

Without rhythm and unnerved, scattered

reading, minor letter writing, and the jot paint the

experience of this, our disturbed spot. It is (and we have

positively identified it!) momentarily her own, rich and

picturesque, then slides over, off the pleasurable

randomness of subjectivity, falls back to the simple

oppositions of ones and twos. "He kicks her canteen down

the road." She pulls a gas can from the trunk of her car; this

means she'll be back again later

    In my country
    when birds sing
    it is only of this

        if indeed she is the one

being

      whose questions survive

this moment of disbelief in life—

that their progress "carries forward," invited by me

    or in the deep final position and
    the landscape of its sense—
    I think about it all the time without

analysis. By sitting, shaded in our own thoughts, writing,

we come to know this *as* the other world. The gridded

neighborhood, birdsong and trouble allotted equally by

section, not remembering, then soon your arms, laundry,

breakfast, ourselves estimable in the esteemed day. Like a

very short name, a certain lack of curiosity means

everything to me

> Going out on a limb
> only to examine the fruit
> for a second time
> the animal repeat of the first
> increasingly understood as the infinite species of

day, baffled. What's before me is not ultimate, I thought.

And riding home in a rainstorm; *this* was a dream of

common sense. In the evening, sexed hourliness, not

simplistic dualities. Having vibrated. From you, wide. Then

you, my composition, forward, looking toward the Capitol.

We walk into a broad valley careful of air but not of

ourselves. And the well I find you in is deep and sweet as

the spit of your tongue touched by hospitality and

circumstance

> Soup, tea, light until late
> having just
> hate to waste
> this coming to know
> people, not things
> in which we mate

This tranquil scene earns the nickname "ready." Soft,

unguarded are its surnames. This sets off a number of

questions; for example, if sexuality is continuous with the

whole of life, how do we explain its metaphors of

strangeness and transport? The corporate body has not arms

that open, equal in parts

Yet without remembering
I dip into thoughts
oh come back baby

     happy having sat

medley
Imagine us back in the motel room with Jimi

Hendrix on. Imagine the sun so high and the spiritual

concerns of our day just an excuse for writing easily

forgotten in the effort of riding a bike uphill. Remember

then the thorn sensationally extracted like a hound's tooth

from the original plaid and the first sentimental cries of

some echoing off the motel. The call for the dog repeats.

Let me say this platitude one more time to satisfy myself:

> Not equal.
> The situation has already changed
> and it is my face in the window
> not the landscape.
> Shall I indulge these fantasies? That while

I labor armies *fly?* Having to wait just another blue sky, and

enormous. His body, being ornamented in the usual fashion,

lit in front and behind, held for her in a standing wave the

definition of matter. I was at the bottom of this body

beating my calabash, pulling up on the part for the whole

place. One false step, missing the absolute keel, capsizes

the little vessel

Everything sexual is
to do
like hours in the tidepool, well spent. Not

far away urban natives propose a sweat. Women indivisble

and miles around come easy to persuade. Thus, without

consuming the winding road, the rural city, it was with

interest I came upon the Yellow Front. Like me, its function

is to falsify; through the front find the door, there covered

with warm hair. One true step

Each part
to every other part
I lay on ice
After you have begun sweet-talking me in

earnest. The clouds fly low and a child squeals. Knowing

the names of things I call you. Bandaged, storm and beer.

No contest here. The ideal is an infinitely divisible stretch,

intelligible, seductive, and many sided, from the lip of the

butte to where you are; we're that plausible but not that

fixed. I must look at him and then reread the book. Mother

of god you may lick my face, the blue convertible has driven

up at last and I am sticking out; is there something beautiful

for me here?

Corn rattle
whinny of bees
the natural world arouses itself
to the form that is
and not another thing

(*The I and the You,* 1992)

i was seeking an occasion   for the kind of talking i
want to do   which would of course modify the kind of talking
i wanted to do

—DAVID ANTIN

An alternative remains 'wordness,' 'eventism'—a way of reconstituting
language by unpacking the tool box.

—BRUCE ANDREWS

                                        What we re-quire   *is*
silence   ;   *but what silence requires*
          is   *that I go on talking*   .

—JOHN CAGE

this anti-generic or over-genred writing is
the possibility, not of some pure

genreless, authorless writing, but instead, a
polygeneric writing where margins are not

metaphors, and where readers are not
simply there, waiting to be liberated

—BOB PERELMAN

John Cage [1912 – 1993]

This lecture was printed in Incontri Musicali, *August 1959. There are four measures in each line and twelve lines in each unit of the rhythmic structure. There are forty-eight such units, each having forty-eight measures. The whole is divided into five large parts, in the proportion 7, 6, 14, 14, 7. The forty-eight measures of each unit are likewise so divided. The text is printed in four columns to facilitate a rhythmic reading. Each line is to be read across the page from left to right, not down the columns in sequence. This should not be done in an artificial manner (which might result from an attempt to be too strictly faithful to the position of the words on the page), but with the* rubato *which one uses in everyday speech.*

LECTURE ON NOTHING

I am here   ,   and there is nothing to say   .

                                                              If among you are
those who wish to get   somewhere   ,   let them leave at
any moment   .   What we re–quire   is
silence   ;   but what silence requires

            is   that I go on talking   .

                                                              Give any one thought
              a push   :   it falls down easily   .
;   but the pusher   and the pushed   pro–duce   that enter–
tainment   called   a dis–cussion   .
              Shall we have one later ?

                                        ♏

Or   ,   we could simply de–cide   not to have a dis-
cussion   .   What ever you like .   But
now   there are silences   and the
words   make   help make   the
silences   .

                                        I have nothing to say
          and I am saying it   and that is
poetry   as I need it   .

          This space of time   is organized
                          We need not fear these   silences, —–
                          ♏

we may love them   .
                                                                        This is a composed

talk   ,   for I am making it
            just as I make   a piece of music.   It is like a glass
                of milk   .   We need the   glass
and we need the   milk   .   Or again   it is like an
empty glass   into which   at any
moment   anything   may be poured
          .   As we go along   ,   (who knows?)
                    an i–dea may occur in this   talk
                                                   I have no idea   whether one will
                    or not.   If one does,   let it.   Re–
                                                   𝕸
gard it as something   seen   momentarily   ,   as
though   from a window   while traveling   .
If across Kansas   ,   then, of course,   Kansas
          .   Arizona   is more interesting,
almost too interesting   ,   especially   for a New–Yorker   who is
being interested   in spite of himself   in everything.   Now he knows he
needs   the Kansas in him   .   Kansas is like
nothing on earth   ,   and for a New Yorker   very refreshing.
It is like an empty glass ,   nothing but wheat   ,   or
is it corn   ?   Does it matter which   ?
Kansas   has this about it: at any instant,   one may leave it,
and whenever one wishes one may return to it   .
                                                   𝕸

Or you may leave it   forever   and never return to it   ,
            for we pos–sess nothing   .   Our poetry now
            is the reali–zation   that we possess   nothing
          .   Anything   therefore   is a delight
(since we do not   pos–sess it)   and thus   need not fear its loss
          .   We need not destroy the   past: it is gone;
at any moment,   it might reappear and   seem to be   and be the present
          .   Would it be a   repetition?   Only if we thought we
owned it,   but since we don't,   it is free   and so are we

                                        Most anybody knows a–bout the future
     and how un–certain it is
                                        .

                                        mp

What I am calling   poetry   is often called   content.
I myself   have called   it form   .   It is the conti-
nuity   of a piece of music.   Continuity   today,
when it is necessary   ,   is a demonstration   of dis-
interestedness.   That is,   it is a proof   that our delight
lies in not   pos–sessing anything   .   Each moment
presents what happens   .   How different
this form sense is   from that   which is bound up with
memory: themes   and secondary themes;   their struggle;
their development;   the climax;   the recapitulation   (which is the belief
that one may   own one's own home)   .   But actually,
unlike the snail   ,   we carry our homes   within us,

                                        mp

which enables us   to fly   or to stay
, —   to enjoy   each.   But beware of
that which is   breathtakingly   beautiful,   for at any moment
            the telephone   may ring   or the airplane
come down in a   vacant lot   .   A piece of string
or a sunset   ,   possessing neither   ,
each acts   and the continuity   happens
.   Nothing more than   nothing   can be said.
Hearing   or making this   in music   is not different
—   only simpler —   than living this way   .
            Simpler, that is   ,   for me, — because it happens
                        that I write music   .
                                    mp *mp*
That music is   simple to make   comes from   one's willingness to ac-
cept   the limitations   of structure.   Structure is
simple   be–cause   it can be thought out,   figured out,
measured   .   It is a discipline   which,
accepted,   in return   accepts whatever   ,   even those
rare moments   of ecstasy,   which,   as sugar loaves train horses,
train us   to make what we make   .   How could I

better tell   what structure   is   than simply to
tell   about this,   this talk   which is
contained   within   a space of time   approximately
forty minutes   long   ?

                                              ℳ
That forty minutes   has been divided into five   large parts,   and
each unit   is divided   likewise.   Subdivision   in–
volving   a square root   is the only   possible subdivision which
permits   this micro–macrocosmic   rhythmic structure   ,
which I find so   acceptable   and accepting   .
As you see,   I can say anything   .
It makes very little   difference   what I say   or even how I say it.
At   this par–ticular moment,   we are passing through the fourth
part   of a unit which is the   second unit in the second large
part of this talk   .   It is a little bit   like passing through Kansas
.   This, now, is the   end   of that second unit
.
.   .

                                              ℳ
Now begins the   third unit   of the second part   .
                                                                         Now the

second part of that   third unit   .
                          Now its third part   .

                                                                         Now its fourth
part   (which, by the way,   is just the same
length   as the third part)   .

                          Now the fifth   and last part   .

                                              ℳ
You have just   ex–perienced   the structure   of this talk   from a
microcosmic   point of view   .   From a macrocosmic
point of view   we are just passing the halfway point   in the second
large part.   The first part   was a rather rambling   discussion of
nothing   ,   of form,   and continuity

when it is the way we   now   need it.   This second
part   is about structure: how simple it is
,   what it is   and why   we should be willing   to
accept   its limitations.   Most speeches   are full   of
ideas.   This one   doesn't have to have   any
.   But at any moment   an idea   may come along
.   Then   we may enjoy it   .
                                        𝄌
Structure   without life   is dead.   But Life   without
structure   is un–seen   .   Pure life
expresses itself   within   and through structure
.   Each moment   is absolute,   alive and sig–
nificant.   Blackbirds   rise   from a field making   a
sound   de–licious   be–yond   com–pare
.   I heard them
because   I ac–cepted   the limitations   of an arts
conference   in a Virginia   girls' finishing school,   which limitations
allowed me   quite by accident   to hear the blackbirds
as they flew up and   overhead   .   There was a social
calendar   and hours for breakfast   ,   but one day I saw a
                                        𝄌
cardinal   ,   and the same day   heard a woodpecker.
I also met   America's youngest   college president   .
However,   she has resigned,   and people say she is   going into politics
.   Let her.   Why shouldn't she?   I also had the
pleasure   of hearing an eminent   music critic   ex–claim
that he hoped   he would live long   e–nough   to see the end
of this craze for Bach.   A pupil once   said to me: I
understand   what you say about   Beethoven   and I think
I agree   but I have a   very serious   question   to
ask you: How do you   feel   about Bach
?   Now we have come   to the end   of the
part   about structure   .
                                        𝄌 𝄌
However,   it oc–curs   to me to say more   about structure
.   Specifically   this: We are
now at   the be–ginning   of the third part   and that part

is not the part   devoted   to structure.   It's the part
about material.   But I'm still talking   about structure.   It must be
clear from that   that structure   has   no point,   and,
as we have seen,   form   has no point either.   Clearly we are be–
ginning to get   nowhere   .

                    Unless some   other i–dea crops up   a–bout it that is
all I have   to say about structure   .
                                        ♍
Now about   material: is it interesting   ?
It is and it   isn't   .   But one thing is
certain.   If one is making   something   which is to be nothing
,   the one making must   love   and be patient   with
the material   he chooses.   Otherwise   he calls attention to the
material,   which is precisely something   ,   whereas it was
nothing   that was being made;   or   he calls attention to
himself,   whereas   nothing is anonymous   .
                    The technique   of handling materials   is, on the sense level
what structure as a   discipline is   on the rational level   :
                    a means   of experiencing   nothing
.
                                        ♍
I remember loving   sound   before I ever   took a music lesson
.   And so we make our   lives   by what we love
.   (Last year   when I talked here   I made a short talk.
That was because   I was talking   about something   ;   but
this year   I am talking   about nothing   and
of course will go on   talking   for a long time   .)
                                        The other day a
pupil said,   after trying to compose   a melody   using only
three tones,   "I   felt limited   ."

                    Had she   con–cerned herself   with the three tones —
her materials   —   she would not   have felt limited
                                        ♍
,   and   since materials   are without feeling,
there would not have   been   any limitation.   It was all in her

mind   ,   whereas it be–longed   in the
materials   .   It became something
by not being   nothing;   it would have been   nothing by being
something   .
                                                                                  Should one use the
materials   characteristic   of one's time   ?
Now there's a question   that ought to get us   somewhere
.   It is an intel–   lectual question
.   I shall answer it   slowly   and
autobiographically   .

                                              𝕸

I remember   as a child   loving   all the sounds
,   even the unprepared   ones.   I liked them
especially   when there was one at a time   .
                        A five-finger exercise   for one hand was
full of beauty   .   Later on I
gradually liked   all the intervals   .
                                                                                  As I look back
I realize   that I be–gan liking the octave   ;   I accepted the
major and minor   thirds.   Perhaps,   of all the intervals,   ˙
I liked these thirds   least   .   Through the music of
Grieg,   I became passionately   fond   of the fifth
.

                                              𝕸

Or perhaps you could   call it   puppy–dog love   ,
                        for the fifth did not make me   want to write music: it made me want to de–
vote my life to   playing the works of Grieg   .
                        When later I heard   modern music,
I took, like a duck   to water, to all the   modern intervals: the sevenths,   the
seconds,   the tritone,   and the fourth   .
                        I liked Bach too   a–bout this time   ,   but I
didn't like the sound   of the thirds and sixths.   What I admired in
Bach   was the way   many things   went together
.   As I keep on   re–membering,   I see that I never
really liked the   thirds,   and this explains   why I never really
liked Brahms   .

                                              𝕸

Modern music   fascinated me   with all its modern   intervals: the
sevenths,   the seconds,   the tritone,   and the fourth   and
always,   every now and then,   there was a fifth,   and that pleased me
.   Sometimes   there were single tones,   not intervals at
all,   and that was a de–   light.   There were so many in–
tervals in modern music that it fascinated   me rather than that I   loved it, and being
fascinated by it I   de–cided   to write it.   Writing it at
first   is difficult: that is,   putting the mind on it
takes the ear off it   .   However,   doing it alone,
I was free to hear   that a high sound   is different   from a
low sound even when both are called by the   same letter.   After several years of
working alone   ,   I began to feel   lonely.
                        mp

Studying with a   teacher,   I learned that the   intervals   have
meaning;   they are not just   sounds   but they imply
in their progressions   a sound   not actually present to the ear
.   Tonality.   I never liked tonality   .
I worked at it   .   Studied it.   But I never had any
feeling for it   :   for instance: there are some   pro–
gressions called   de–ceptive cadences.   The idea is this: progress in such a way
as to imply   the presence   of a tone not actually   present;   then
fool everyone by not   landing on it —   land somewhere else.   What is being   .
fooled   ?   Not the ear   but the mind
.   The whole question is   very intellectual   .
However   modern music   still fascinated me
                        mp

with all its modern   intervals   .   But in order to
have them   ,   the mind had fixed it   so that one had to a–
void having   pro–gressions that would   make one think of   sounds that were
not actually present   to the ear   .   Avoiding
did   not   ap–peal to me   .   I began to see
that the separation of   mind and ear   had spoiled   the sounds
, —   that a clean slate   was necessary.   This made me
not only contemporary   ,   but "avant-garde."   I used noises
.   They had not been   in–tellectualized;   the ear could hear them
directly   and didn't have to go through any abstraction   a–bout them

.

I found that I   liked noises   even more than I
liked intervals.   I liked noises   just as much as I had   liked single sounds
                                   mp

.

                                                                         Noises, too
,   had been dis–criminated against   ;   and being American,
having been trained   to be sentimental,   I fought   for noises. I liked being
on the side of the   underdog   .
I got police   per–mission   to play sirens.   The most amazing noise
I ever found   was that produced by   means of a coil of wire   attached to the
pickup arm   of a phonograph and then amplified.   It was shocking,
really shocking,   and thunderous   .   Half intellectually   and
half sentimentally   , when the war came a–long,   I decided to use
only   quiet sounds   .   There seemed to me
to be no truth,   no good,   in anything big   in society.
                                                     mp

But quiet sounds   were like loneliness   ,   or
love   or friendship   .   Permanent, I thought
,   values,   independent   at least from
Life, Time and   Coca-Cola   .   I must say
I still feel this way   ,   but something else is   happening
:   I begin to hear   the old sounds
—   the ones I had thought worn out,   worn out by
intellectualization—   I begin to hear   the old sounds   as
though they are   not worn out   .   Obviously, they are
not worn out   .   They are just as   audible   as the
new sounds.   Thinking   had worn them out   .
              And if one stops thinking about   them,   suddenly they are
                                                     mp

fresh   and new.   "If you think   you are a ghost
you will become a   ghost   ."   Thinking the sounds
worn out   wore them out   .   So you see
:   this question   .   brings us back
where we were: nowhere   or,
if you like   ,   where we are   .
                                                     I have a story: "There was once a man

standing on a high elevation. A company of several men who happened to be walking on the road noticed from the distance the man standing on the high place and talked among themselves about this man. One of them said: He must have lost his favorite animal. Another man said : No, it must be his friend whom he is looking for. A third one said: He is just enjoying the cool air up there. The three could not a–gree and the dis–

𝗆𝗉

cussion (Shall we have one later?) went on until they reached the high place where the man was . One of the three asked: O, friend standing up there , have you not lost your pet animal ? No, sir, I have not lost any . The second man asked : Have you not lost your friend ? No, sir , I have not lost my friend either . The third man asked: Are you not enjoying the fresh breeze up there? No, sir , I am not . What, then , are you standing up there for , if you say no to all our questions ? The man on high said :

𝗆𝗉

I just stand ." If there are

no questions, there are no answers . If there are questions , then, of course, there are answers , but the final answer makes the questions seem absurd , whereas the questions, up until then, seem more intelligent than the answers . Somebody asked De– bussy how he wrote music. He said: I take all the tones there are, leave out the ones I don't want, and use all the others . Satie said : When I was young, people told me: You'll see when you're fifty years old . Now I'm fifty . I've seen nothing .

𝗆𝗉 𝗆𝗉

Here we are now at the beginning of the fourth large part of this talk. More and more I have the feeling that we are getting nowhere. Slowly as the talk goes on , we are getting nowhere and that is a pleasure

.   It is not irritating   to be where one is   .   It is
only irritating   to think one would like   to be somewhere else.   Here we are now
,   a little bit after the   beginning   of the
fourth large part   of this talk
                         More and more   we have the feeling   .
                         that I am getting   nowhere
                         Slowly   .
                                                    ,   as the talk goes on
                                                    𝄟

,   slowly   ,   we have the feeling
                         we are getting   nowhere.   That is a pleasure
                         which will continue   .   If we are irritated
,   it is not a pleasure   .   Nothing is not   a
pleasure   if one is irritated   ,   but suddenly
,   it is a pleasure   ,   and then more and more
                         it is not irritating   (and then more and more
                         and slowly   ).   Originally
                         we were nowhere   ;   and now, again
,   we are having   the pleasure
of being   slowly   nowhere.   If anybody
is sleepy   ,   let him go to sleep   .
                                                    𝄟

Here we are now   at the beginning   of the
third unit   of the fourth large part   of this talk.
More and more   I have the feeling   that we are getting
nowhere.   Slowly   as the talk goes on
,   we are getting   nowhere   and that is a pleasure
.   It is not irritating   to be where one is   .   It is
only irritating   to think one would like   to be somewhere else.   Here we are now
,   a little bit after the   beginning   of the third unit   of the
fourth large part   of this talk
                         More and more   we have the feeling   .
                         that I am getting   nowhere
                         Slowly   .
                                                    ,   as the talk goes on
                                                    𝄟

,   slowly   ,   we have the feeling
                         we are getting   nowhere.   That is a pleasure

which will continue

.

If we are irritated

,

it is not a pleasure

.

Nothing is not a

pleasure

if one is irritated

,

but suddenly

,

it is a pleasure

,

and then more and more

it is not irritating

(and then more and more

and slowly

).

Originally

we were nowhere

;

and now, again

.

we are having

the pleasure

,

slowly

nowhere.

If anybody

of being

is sleepy

,

let him go to sleep

.

𝕞𝕡

Here we are now

at the beginning of the

fifth unit of the fourth large part

of this talk.

More and more

I have the feeling

that we are getting

nowhere.

Slowly

as the talk goes on

,

we are getting

nowhere

and that is a pleasure

.

It is not irritating

to be where one is

. It is

only irritating

to think one would like

to be somewhere else. Here we are now

,

a little bit after the

beginning of the fifth unit of the

fourth large part

of this talk

.

More and more

we have the feeling

that I am getting

nowhere

.

Slowly

,

𝕞𝕡

as the talk goes on

,

slowly

,

we have the feeling

,

we are getting

nowhere.

That is a pleasure

which will continue

.

If we are irritated

it is not a pleasure

.

Nothing is not a

pleasure

if one is irritated

,

but suddenly

,

it is a pleasure

,

and then more and more

it is not irritating

(and then more and more

and slowly

).

Originally

we were nowhere

;

and now, again

,

we are having

the pleasure

of being

slowly

nowhere.

If anybody

is sleepy

,

let him go to sleep

.

𝕞𝕡

Here we are now   at the middle
              of the fourth large part   of this talk.
More and more   I have the feeling   that we are getting
nowhere.   Slowly   ,   as the talk goes on
,   we are getting   nowhere   and that is a pleasure
.   It is not irritating to be where one is .   It is
only irritating   to think one would like to be somewhere else. Here we are now
,   a little bit after the middle   of the
fourth large part   of this talk   .
                   More and more   we have the feeling
                   that I am getting   nowhere
                   Slowly   .
                                          ,   as the talk goes on
                                          𝕞𝕡
,   slowly   ,   we have the feeling
                   we are getting   nowhere.   That is a pleasure
                   which will continue   .   If we are irritated
,   it is not a pleasure   .   Nothing is not   a
pleasure   if one is irritated   ,   but suddenly
,   it is a pleasure   ,   and then more and more
                   it is not irritating   ,   (and then more and more
                   and slowly   ).   Originally
                   we were nowhere   ;   and now, again
,   we are having   the pleasure
of being   slowly   nowhere.   If anybody
is sleepy   ,   let him go to sleep .
                                          𝕞𝕡
Here we are now   at the beginning   of the
ninth unit   of the fourth large part   of this talk.
More and more   I have the feeling   that we are getting
nowhere.   Slowly   ,   as the talk goes on
,   we are getting   nowhere   and that is a pleasure
.   It is not irritating to be where one is .   It is
only irritating   to think one would like to be somewhere else. Here we are now
,   a little bit after the beginning   of the ninth unit   of the
fourth large part   of this talk   .
                   More and more   we have the feeling

        that I am getting   nowhere   .

        Slowly   ,   as the talk goes on

                          mp

,   slowly   ,   we have the feeling

        we are getting   nowhere.   That is a pleasure

     which will continue   .   If we are irritated

, .   it is not a pleasure   .   Nothing is not   a

pleasure   if one is irritated   ,   but suddenly

,   it is a pleasure   ,   and then more and more

        it is not irritating   (and then more and more

        and slowly   ).   Originally

        we were nowhere   ;   and now, again

,   we are having   the pleasure

of being   slowly   nowhere.   If anybody

is sleepy   ,   let him go to sleep   .

                          mp

Here we are now   at the beginning   of the

eleventh unit   of the fourth large part   of this talk.

More and more   I have the feeling   that we are getting

nowhere.   Slowly   ,   as the talk goes on

,   we are getting   nowhere   and that is a pleasure

.   It is not irritating   to be where one is   .   It is

only irritating   to think one would like   to be somewhere else. Here we are now

,   a little bit after the   beginning   of the eleventh unit   of the

fourth large part   of this talk   .

        More and more   we have the feeling

        that I am getting   nowhere   .

        Slowly   ,   as the talk goes on

                          mp

,   slowly   ,   we have the feeling

        we are getting   nowhere.   That is a pleasure

     which will continue   .   If we are irritated

,   it is not a pleasure   .   Nothing is not   a

pleasure   if one is irritated   ,   but suddenly

,   it is a pleasure   ,   and then more and more

        it is not irritating   (and then more and more

and slowly   ).   Originally
we were nowhere   ;   and now, again
we are having   the pleasure
,   of being   slowly   nowhere.   If anybody
is sleepy   ,   let him go to sleep   .
                                                                𝄻

Here we are now   at the beginning of the thir-
teenth unit   of the fourth large part   of this talk.
More and more   I have the feeling   that we are getting
nowhere.   Slowly   ,   as the talk goes on
,   we are getting   nowhere   and that is a pleasure
.   It is not irritating   to be where one is   .   It is
only irritating   to think one would like   to be somewhere else.   Here we are now
,   a little bit after the   beginning of the   thir-teenth unit   of the
fourth large part   of this talk   .
                            More and more   we have the feeling
                            that I am getting   nowhere   .
                            Slowly   ,   as the talk goes on
                                                   𝄻

,   slowly   ,   we have the feeling
                            we are getting   nowhere.   That is a pleasure
                            which will continue   .   If we are irritated
,   it is not a pleasure   .   Nothing is not   a
pleasure   if one is irritated   ,   but suddenly
,   it is a pleasure   ,   and then more and more
                            it is not irritating   ,   (and then more and more
                            and slowly   ).   Originally
                            we were nowhere   ;   and now, again
                            we are having   the pleasure
of being   slowly   nowhere.   If anybody
is sleepy   ,   let him go to sleep   .
                                        𝄻   𝄻

♍

♍

That is finished   now.   It was a pleasure   .
                        And now   ,   this is a pleasure.
"Read me that part   a–gain   where I disin–herit everybody   ."
                        The twelve–tone   row   is a method;   a
method is a control   of each   single
note.   There is too much   there there   .
There is not enough   of nothing in it   .   A structure is
like   a bridge from nowhere   to   nowhere   and
anyone may   go on it   :   noises or tones
,   corn or wheat   .   Does it matter which
?   I thought there were eighty–eight tones   .
            You can quarter them too   .

♍

If it were feet   ,   would it be a two–tone row
?   Or can we fly from here   to where

?   I have nothing   against the   twelve–tone row;
but it is a   method,   not a structure   .
    We really do need a structure   ,   so we can see
we are nowhere   .   Much of the music I   love
uses the twelve–tone   row   ,   but that is not why I
love it.   I love it   for no reason   .
                        I love it   for suddenly   I am nowhere
                    (My own music does that   quickly for me   .)
                        And it seems to me   I could   listen forever
to Japanese   shakuhachi music   or the Navajo

♍

Yeibitchai   .   Or I could sit or
stand   near Richard Lippold's   *Full Moon*
            any length of time   .

                Chinese bronzes   , —   how I love them

.   But those beauties

,   which others   have made,   tend to stir up
        the need to possess   and I know
I possess   nothing   .
                Record collections   , —
                that is not music   .
                                        ♍
The phonograph   is a thing, –   not a musical   instrument
.   A thing leads to other things,   whereas a   musical instrument
leads to nothing   .
                Would you like to join a society called   Capitalists Inc.
?   (Just so no one would   think we were   Communists.)
Anyone joining   automatically   becomes president   .
To join   you must show   you've destroyed   at least one hundred
records   or, in the case of   tape,   one sound mirror
.   To imagine you   own
any piece of music   is to miss   the whole point
.   There is no point   or the point   is nothing;
and even   a long–playing   record   is a thing.
                                        ♍

A lady   from Texas   said: I live in Texas   .
                We have no music   in Texas.   The reason they've no
music in Texas   is because   they have recordings
in Texas.   Remove the records from Texas
                and someone   will learn to sing   .
                Everybody   has a song
.   which is   no   song at all :
                it is a process   of singing   ,
        and when you sing   ,
                you are   where you are   .
                All I know about method is that when I am not working I sometimes
think I know something, but when I am working, it is quite clear that I know nothing.
                        ♍ ♍

Jackson Mac Low [1922]

7TH LIGHT POEM: FOR JOHN CAGE — 17 JUNE 1962

Put off an important decision
    in mechanical-lamp light.
Success in a new project will bring lumination.
An exchange of courtesy in the zodiacal
    light reminds you that expenses can
    run high when you insist on light
        from almandites.
For almandites are iron-alumina garnets
    $Fe_3Al_2(SiO_4)_3$.
When of a fine deep red or purplish red,
    from India,
        and transparent,
          they are
         "precious garnets."
A lucrative job available in amber light
    does not jeopardize your credit,
             but
      melon-oil lamplight
        might.
Your intuitions lead you right
    in cineographic light.
Say what you really think.
The lamp I have clamped to the kitchen
        table beside the
    notebook I am writing this in
        gives a sort
    of student-lamp light although
    it is not a student lamp but
      a PENETRAY.
In chrome light and in light from
    alexandrites,
      spinach-
        green
       chrysoberyls,

columbine-
red
by artifical
light,
from Ceylon and the Ural
Mountains,
money from a
surprising source
belies the belief that there's
always
nothing but
futility in romantic wishes
arising in old light.
Those wishes,
that first arose
in old
light,
light
trailing from
spiral nebulae
and galaxies so distant
that a stone
thrown
at a reading lamp's
light
at a
distance of
two miles
wd be
an unintentional slight
to natural law
compared to the folly
of launching
"space ships" toward them,
those
wishes that arose before
the light of the annealing lamp
on which your dentist heated foil
made you begin to
avoid taking chances
by
taking chances,
might

make you take a
trip to a scenic region
where
the light's
maroon
Beware light from a Cooper-Hewitt lamp,
light
derived
from passing an electric current
through
mercury-vapor
light
bluish-
white,
ghost-light from toothbrushes
along the absent 'L,'
beware
the new light on the Bowery
that promises a
good possibility of money loss.
The receipt of an important invitation
to radition
's
a secret
not to be discussed
even in olive-oil lamplight,
even in the
extra light of your
elation over the good news,
lead as it might to a
temporary setback
as
the light
waned.
Revenue yielding ideas arise(s)
in orange light
but an exquisite object stirs joy
even in the light of
Reichsanstalt's lamp,
a modified form of
Hefner's lamp,
a photometric lamp burning amylacetate.
Can an emerald light bring nothing but

disturbing rumors

about money?

Orange light yields revenue yielding ideas
of
disturbance
and   recklessness
amidst an uncanny refulgence
as of marsh light
or will-o'-the-wisp, those
sparks of cold light
which sometimes seem to
follow instructions exactly
as if they
were light from kinetographs,
or fishermen's jack lights,
but emerald light
alternating with
red light & lilac light,
all incandescent lamplight,
made
by the following instructions exactly
some

times

awaken spectrums
like the aurora's
or
those of
remembered naplam flames.

(*22 Light Poems*, 1968)

1ST DANCE—MAKING THINGS NEW—6 FEBRUARY 1964

He makes himself comfortable
& matches parcels.

Then he makes glass boil
while having political material get in
& coming by.

Soon after, he's giving gold cushions or seeming to do so,
taking opinions,
shocking,
pointing to a fact that seems to be an error & showing it to be
      other than it seems,
& presently paining by going or having waves.

Then after doing some waiting,
he disgusts someone
& names things.

A little while later he gets out with things
& finally either rewards someone for something or goes up under
   something.

(*The Pronouns*, 1964, 1971, 1979)

27TH DANCE—WALKING—22 MARCH 1964

Nobody does any waiting,
& nobody has an example.

Does nobody give gold cushions or seem to do so,
& does nobody kick?

Nobody.

& nobody's seeming to send things or's putting wires on things—
nobody's keeping to the news.

At least nobody ends up handing or seeming to hand snakes to
   people.

(*The Pronouns*, 1964, 1971, 1979)

A LACK OF BALANCE BUT NOT FATAL

A motion guided a lotion
in hiding from a tint
reckless from nowhere enforcement.

A label persisted. The past tense
implies it took place. The redness
in which the the implies there was some other
did not persist. He was not waiting long.

The sentence is not always a line
but the stanza is a paragraph.

The whiteness was not enforced.
It was not the other but another
circumstance brought in the waterfall
while a breath waited without being clear
or even happier. A seal was lost without it.

There was a typical edge. The paper tilted
or even curved. A rattle smoothed its way.
Where the predominance stopped was anyone's guess
but the parrot fought for it with forbearance
and a waiting cart was leashed to a trial
though a lie would have done as well
or even better when a moderate sleeve was cast.

No claim was made. A tired park gained.
A lack twisted the bread. Heads foamed.
Nowhere was little enough for the asking.
The task he cleared from the temperature
was outside the extended account. Each the
points to an absence. One or more hiding.

He asked where the inches were. The could have gone.

Intentions are mixed without quotations.
The song was snug. Ambiguity does not
hang in the air. The space between graphemes
is neither colorless nor tasteless. A stream
runs rapidly in no more history. The sweep

of a line. Kindness is not mistaken
for tinder and the lid is resting but shortness
guarantees no sentence authenticity.

Where the schoolyard was evident a closed
flutter showed a notion without resistant
fences or a paradox without feathers.
Swiftness outlasts the pencil. A cormorant
rose against a born backdrop. Letters inch.
An iconoclast was hesitant. A fire lit.
In the tank a lozenge disengages. Swarms
roared. A special particle felt its form.
Lagging features left oak divination without
a tone or a creased sentinel. Leavings swept.

Toward evening the watchful clock was situated.
No diver called for ether. Lynxes thrived.
Hit by something a silence willed. Streets
were not concerned. A past participle's
sometimes mistaken for a past. An orange
roster was on everybody's mind though clues
could be found. When the ink is incomplete
every table rests on its opposite. A closed
restraint impinged. Furniture rested. Several
pinks in a fist. A clearly charismatic
hideout was read. Neatness wavered. The flag
was wet without exertion or favor. That judge postponed.

Snowfall abused ermines. A folding chair.
Close to the bank a trap was silted though the finder
relaxed without particulars or the least inclination.
Whoever loosed the torrent concluded the tryst.
Finally is the way to find the place. Earshot
is likely. Tones harvest commonplace weather.
The pastness of the past was included in a doctrine
or stakes were wrought. Or sought. Find divers.
Fists rested on the divined peculiarity. Artemis hushed.

Twigs were not grapes. He grasped the talc ring.
Smoothing the horses the clutter died. Finches
sewed roses on the mustered aggregate. Loaves flew.
A mentality ran farther and its crests simmered.
Closeted without bargains the lean rump beheld

no future. A certain flight beckoned. The wonder.
Closed classrooms risk warmth though causation
matters less. Never ink a connection when a plea
is off. Softer dollars were a range without flutters
though a concessive subordinator turns a sentence
into a scene. Dreams were not what he wanted.

16 January 1982
New York

(*From Pearl Harbor Day to FDR's Birthday*, 1982)

GIANT OTTERS

They were a close family of giant otters
in Surinam giving a low growling sound when
they were insecure so they were called the Hummers.

Trace elements had landed near them and they effloresced
in even amounts throughout an even eon and an evening more
fortunate as they were in knowing nothing

or peering curiously into unknowable presence
alert   to no future   living the past as presence
whose elements were traces in their efflorescing being

going as far as they could within the world they were
as fortune particularized occasions within unfolding
breathed upon by memory's wraith and anticipation's all but
                                                absence.

Where were they going but farther along and through
whatever their being eventuated in clearness   no demand for clarity
as the eyes are unsealed and the world flows in as light?

13 – 14 February 1982
New York

(*Bloomsday*, 1984)

PIECES O' SIX—XVIII

The truth of truth was being missed. The one who was thinking or writing, reading or hearing, felt a connection lacking, a penetration not taking place, a skittering over a surface or a sinking into a negative depth, a straying from a straightway or a blundering doggedly forward when a crooked, more indirect approach (to what?) might have been better. To what? To truth, of course—to "the truth of truth": that was the phrase, and it seemed to bear a meaning aura intimating more than a mere adequation. But what could be more or deeper than, or farther beyond or above, a matching of thoughts and/or words to the really real? (Why the adverb? Isn't the real the real without that modification? Would it make any sense to speak of the "*un*really real"? Would it mean any more than "what seems to be real but turns out not to be"?) But perhaps we feel that such Aquinan adequation—such a fitting of thought and word to thing as well as word, indeed, to thought—is not what really takes place—that the notion involves faulty views of language, mind, and world. Today we (those of us who are at all aware of the problem) are only too conscious of the tortuous chains of inference and argument between data (dial readings, photographs of sky or cloud chamber, reactions of animal or human experimental subjects, etc.) and hypotheses or widely accepted theories. The rapid mutability of the latter in response to new data, and/or new interpretations of old, is notorious. The popular reaction to this mutability is evinced in expressions such as "merely a theory," which may be applied even to long (and in scientific milieux all but universally) accepted theories: evolution is denigrated as "just a theory" against which creationists claim equal time for their own "theory." The nature of evidence and of procedures of proof is so little understood that any assertion, whether based on publicly verifiable data or someone's sacred scriptures or a guru's pronouncements, is supposed ideally to be accorded equal dignity in the "marketplace of ideas." Indeed, the latter metaphor reduces evidentiary assertions to more or less effective advertising slogans. Data from observation are considered on an equal footing with biblical quotations. The only relevant questions are ones such as, Which is the most effective? The fallacy of misplaced democracy goes hand in hand with the commoditization of theory. People who hardly rule the rooms they live in, much less those they work in, feel their rights violated when the absurdity of their beliefs or of their ways of arriving at them or of defending them is pointed out. Objections to bigotry or dogma are indignantly brushed off as transgressions of a market pluralism (evoked as "freedom of religion" or "of thought") otherwise rejected by many who appeal to it when inconveniently assailed by rational argument or empirical evidence. Theoretical decisions, like political ones, are determined by judgments of image. Images are judged rather than those who determine them, and any politics is likened to a decision, on *this* theory. Unlike evidentiary empiricism or argumentative rationalism, it assails inconvenient appeals to it, and many are rejected. Otherwise, "thought" and "religion" being freely evoked, plural marketeers transgress by brushing off indignation against dogmatic bigotry and other objections. Outpointed, they defend themselves by arriving at ways to believe absurdly that violations of their rights to their feelings are in the works and that they are about to be lessened by that much. Living by their roomy rules, they are hard people. Theoretical commodities hand hands to "democratic" misplacements, fallacies, and effects, most of which are of questionable relevance. One need only quote the Bible on one's feet to be equally considered with an observer of data. Slogans evidence effects less the more assertions evidently reduce to metaphors. As to the latter, indeed, ideas in the marketplace have dignity equally accorded to ideals supposedly pronounced on by gurus or scriptures sacred to someone whose data are verified by being publicly based on assertions understood little but "proved" by procedures evidently "natural." Some theories own time equally by claiming to be "creative." Such theories are justly denigrated by evolutionists, yet the theories may be accepted all but universally in-all milieux except the scientific. Long, even application may reduce the theories merely to expressions evincing the mutability of reactions to the popular. Notorious old interpretations, through new data and new responses to the latter, mutate rapidly. Before theories are accepted widely, hypotheses are subjected to experiments. Humans and animals react in chambers cloudy as skies and are photographed by readers of dials. Data are argued about, and inference's chains are tortuous. We may be conscious only, if at all, of the problems due to our being aware of who we are today. World, mind, and language are viewed as being faultily involved with notions. What place is taken by what really is not thought? Indeed, what

word to thing or word to thought fits adequately? Did Aquinas
have such feelings as we do? Perhaps. Being is not out of turn
nor is the real what seems. What more would it mean if it would
be? Is the real unreal when it speaks to the senses? And is any
making a modification without reality? The real isn't the adverb
why. *Is* the real really words and/or thoughts? Is a matching
above or far beyond or deeper or more than what could be?
Then is adequation merely or more than an intimate aura? What
bears what it seems to be? The phrase *the truth?* Truth, of
course, is truth. What would be better? What might it have been?
Is this approach too indirect? What could be more so than
forward, dogged blundering? Straightway it strays to a depth,
negatively sinking to a surface over which it skitters to a place
that takes no penetration, lacking connection with what's felt.
Are hearing, reading, writing, and thinking at one in missing
being's truth, *the* truth? Is "the" truth the truth of being? What's
missing? Who is the one who thinks? The one who writes? The
one who reads? The one who hears? The one who feels? What
connection is lacking? We penetrate nothing. What takes place
is a skittering over a surface. But to sink is negative, a deep
straying. Straightway we blunder doggedly. Might going
forward crookedly—a more indirect approach—have been
better? What is truth? Each matter-of-course truth is *the* truth.
That phrase, it seems, bears meaning. Its aura is intimate, but
it is more than that. Nor is it merely adequation. It has more
depth. Beyond and far above matching, thoughts and words are
really real. *Why is* an adverb. *The* isn't. Both are real. They
have reality without modification. Can what makes sense when
we speak be unreal? The real is whatever *would* be. Does that
mean it would be more than what it seems to be? The real turns
out to be not only being but perhaps. Do we have feelings such
as Aquinas had? His adequation fit each thought to a word and
a thing to each word. But indeed, is thought not really what
takes place? What notions are involved in faulty viewing?
Language is the mind. Is it the world? Today, who *are* we? Our
problems ? If at all, we are only conscious of the tortuous. Chains
are, by inference, arguable data. Dials are read, but who
photographs the sky? Cloud-chamber reactions are neither
animal nor human, yet through experiments subjective
hypotheses become widely accepted theories. Rapid mutations
in the latter may be responses to new data, or they may be due
to old, notorious popular reactions to mutability itself. How
are they evinced? Through expressions, merely, or through

theories being reduced to their applications? In them, the longings of scientists become their milieux. All universally accepted theories evolve, and for this they're denigrated by some, unjustly. Theorists against creationism may claim equal time, but how is it a *theory?* Nature is not an evident procedure. Whatever can be proved by little understood assertions based on no publicly verifiable data? Someone, maybe everyone, is sacred, but no scripture or guru's pronouncement or supposed ideal should be accorded equal dignity. Marketplace ideas are latter, metaphorical reductions of evidence to assertions. This may be, more or less, the effect of advertising and slogans. Thence data-observers are considered on an equal footing with bible-quoters. Only *their* relevance is *questioned.* Ones such as they are not the most effective. The fallacious misplacement of democracy is at hand. It hands commoditized theories to the people. Its hard rules give little room to living.

9 November 1984 – 14 July 1985
New York
and in the air on the way to and away from Europe and over it

PIECES O' SIX—XXIV

Riot in the lute song's propinquity. Propose to be guided by the less obvious illumination. Let it be axiomatic. Do not be traumatized by the practical. Wrench a regard from the passenger during a cassation. Court the benediction's witness. Lend an activity to the calflike penitent. Be frantic. Rankle or be fantastic under a plane tree. Penetrate a gaze less canine than candid. Fortify an egregious portion. Quench a criminal pundit. Fetch an alert grief from the border. Bowdlerize summitry ana. Fashion a clannish arbitrage of clinches. Equal a recycled creek. Rest from your laurels. Keen within horizons. Neaten a clearing. Divide the pelf from the anachronisitc liabilities. Run from a libel. Ice the carded portraits of the antic pontiffs. Lessen the penetrating laughter of the included passersby. Fan out. Trust a cautiously broadened tantrum. Renege on the banter promised amid a siege of icicles before the porch was cornered. Dirty a cloth. Nationalize enacted obsequies long before they're uncalled for. Devise a Lateran increase. Insist upon the formation of a calculated goal lest everything else be reduced. Produce a lack of accord between a sanitary answer and ambitious sustenance. Dissuade the hisses of others from brightening apple-green entities. Resist an effortless classification. Answer appetite with an unconscionable melody. Thrust an action between the potential and the actual. Harness the intent arising from depressed narcissism or reasonable panic. Pleasure-feature the cast. Fancy a paramilitary attraction less lasting than wit. Reckon up the saddest and most pellucid reekings of the crafty stormers of the moment. Demonize the sleekest barren fortune. Reactivate the last inviolable tent pegs of the mighty and the timid well before the storm pales. Never let "incredible" be your password. Treat a gleam as less hasty than its vanishment. Recognize the lack of a parlor. Take your unuttered grievances far from the best utility. Acclimatize one or more hesitant giants before the curfew rages. Activate anthracite. Weaken aspiration toward "whether" and "rather" or elicit "perhaps." Decorate the enharmonic enterprise. Let the will be. Notate obligatory reactivations. Pair the least episodes and antiquate stresses to let the Nile be. Absorb the fortunate borders of the genetic code. Nativize marginal cliques. Let the grand jury marvel and the crowd collect its molars under the sunset. Levitate the censors and make them answerable. Fortify the absent mandala. Engorge it with esemplastic electricity. Panel the ingredients, caused and causeless. Finitize every surrogate objectivization or kerneled hut, having emphasized daemonic salutations and solutions when that area had undergone its technically inevitable recurrence before the flashes fared on and the oxyacetylene selves wearied in wonted fury or phantasmic forgetfulness, unintentionally florid, abasing its radars for popular favor, eccentric ammunition, rear-door inspiration. Add to the thicket. Risk the felt encrusted passing and the arduous percent. Make it ethnic. Bombard the larger ectoplasmic bits and pieced edges. Enact the oneirection of the disturbed gift beneath the lengths of axioms every kenner closes out from in the overburdened mornings she ends up not-guilty in, ripely applauding, finically cast off. Impress the hyaline empress. Close the net. Fetch glassed Eratomanes from legal ensconced precincts before alleged water motivates its own metamorphosis to handy attested wine, factively operative, gripping. Inspect and attack an intentional map. Please ask leave to signify. Rent intact an orthodox exclusion. Set free factitious lemma'd-encyclical-inky limitations. Rank in a rank. Befit the sum of ordinary gallantries, quizzical trees, asteroids, trapdoors. Let effort speak in immediate foreboding and counsel. Swagger. Expect a trim instance, an effable occurence, a statutory fastening and flanking. Submit a quiet candle. Anchor a swerved aspect, an animal trace. Pity the excess flute player. Meditate on the immediate muddle, the ultimate befuddlement and hanky. Crack the undefended clock-beastly code as you construct the new society in the waxy shell of the old. Release the familiarly benefited terminus, bonded, inexcusable, deciphered, secretly tender, immobile. Focus on the more or less absolute resultant or figurative rash. Sanction wing'd hollows. Act out self-aggrandizement, perennially willy-nilly, sadistically sweet, orphaned. Personate an eradicable maze. Fabulate a picturable sweater. Rasp before you rack. Ensure that the dog she saw was other than its accidental other. Crowd forth beyond eagerness, exemplarily sandaled, strangled, clumsy. Defer to a dun. Extract a methodical district. Enforce the sun. Exhibit insipid data. Ask about tranquillity. Commemorate regions and stages, phases and affable clasping frankness, flapping and emptied, matched by any misery. Irritate, exaggerate, and prey. Recover two hundred and sixty-seven sets of remains. Nail the effrontery of the exigent palace deluged by incriminating barbarities and analogies cored or penetrating. Absolute thieves. Needle an idle icebreaker. Factify. Try a triumph rather than an all-embracing ulcer. Wed feathers and lead. Sketch the encompassing without effecting reflection or unintended effort. Ready the telltale signatures and sprigs. Rip the hints from kinship. Detail the lacks and passages and incunabula where oafish industry's betrayed by cryptoprayerful gestures and seeds are on the fire ranked with climatorial proof. Rattle axes. Battle access and additional nobility of appetite. Cycle a try or two and leave the tribe. Liven the executive excuse. Seem to gleam. Economize where the front's insatiate or sapience beckons. Register the cable that fortified the binding. Lie about the truth. Smooth the active comfort of crestfallen halves. Have a nice day. Slash the fractions brute appearance constitutes. Seismogrify a settlement of coal tips. Alert a trench and specialize in essence. Bury a popular proximity and somnolently close a sort of suture. Speak. Initiate a needed corrugation. Reel in reflected answers wherever the learned terror clings. Inspissate a cannular regard. Track a torrent's corridor sufficiently. Discuss or sap a drama. Light into the excellent perpetrators encouragingly when an irritant might increase proliferation. Be persuaded. Settle dyslexic executants. Loll in a carnival where wheat exceeds prescribed experienced leaves. Annotate whatever entered crucibles exact a hated recompense or trance. Banish the diseased chrysanthemum. Tear apart leggings finished long before. Open the fair. Let the cat leap. Peel a kiwi. Scoop a pumpkin. Better thy bitterness. Liken every solid to an equivalent. View the findings with an unbemused rapture before the picture changes or enchants. Listen. Ride out the called-for storm or stem the tide. Weave a foliation. Elide a gamble. Sweep the drachma-driven creature over. Announce the tree before its singularities are riven. Constitute a crisis. Cheat. Seek every appropriate means within the lead time and the span of the faction's action. Write. Fend for yourself. Don't always be surprised. Back out of the instigation if you let the hatchways scream. Modify your model inclinations. Solidify. Be bold.

15 August – 11 September 1985
New York

ALMOST CASANOVA ELECTRICITY

[*Forties 24*]

Almost Casanova despite the phlebitis with everything else
too many   Kalmon Dolgin encrustation flopped miasmic plenty
tired homunculus apt   diaspora treadmill   San Antonio pea–pod
reactive palustrian sea-code Wilson   Meso–American nether-roll Westport
   dog days expert finicky tribune   ocular proof
vortex ban   calamus gangster weigh-station

Democratic whiffletree   negligent bastion corrosive malign   Croce
nést-coral gáp-phonic greening arrest   challenge ascendant garotte
fealty mangle clinging maturity egghead mistake   claimant
tick anniversay medical whistle   pickle belief   mixed
   reviews   *Peanuts*   cake-batter clastic corrosive mátter-negativity
gleeful Oróno-gleam   timid transparency

Quassý   meeting astringency   active kangaroó-rat-stripe
major assistment   normal pork resistance grove   poll-tax agree
clamor   medicament   Palestrina rattletrap economy move
registration culinary Roto-Rooter barn   sóng-ferry magistrate   totalism
   token activity probe   boatman whet
train báck next day   involvement munition

Galánte Coromándel tam-o'-shanter quíck-stop guilty McNugget
sapodilla mediant   bus-schedule logic   oxymoron tortoise
choíce-paddle glowworm acquittal mise-en-scène   nictatory
tree   máscot-renovation   merit badge   neighborly porringer maculate
   Trianon   barebones amalgam   ramble pharmaceutical
naturalist now   vestal academicism

Pangolin tribulation Venice aspidistra   party Caspar pole
bowl sharp   Lady Day   magnetism mystic Pogo bit-part marker
Regency applaud   ashtray mesmerism capstan accolade
dánce-fog laudatory goal   oriented magical escapement Janissary
   pócket-whopper bánister-appendectomy
release   morass   Capistrano firecracker

Glamour   buoyancy alarm clock Goliath   Metchnikoff
pool Mariolatry abasement Japan   Newman collapse
glassy clouds   tacky mendacity quiver estate malarkey
vapid Chappaquidick   regional autocracy equivalent nostrum   patriotic
   formalism Panasonic méntal-detector
Gloomy Gus   navvy   Vatican cholesterol

Jónes-mutter Pearl Street tickertape environment   ribsteak
challenge-grants   Motorola fortune-teller coál-barge newt
Cibachrome encounter   middlebrow enlistment trailer
Gypsy Rose Lee   water senate camel bone anachronism
   mate   cannibalism mazurka   adoption   déspicable nodule
nominal reagent   maximal phylogeny

Forestation euphemism whiskey priest Melánctha-happy Luther
peakèd Rigadoon   mortuary *Liebestod*   pitchman antenna
thirty-chanter tank attack   Rapid Transit matchstick clause
neater Agrícola aspect nascence   tepid euhemerism distance neutrality
   comb   Polk   glister misogyny chloroform
messy chortle gás-stage   nappy electricity

     Caesural spaces (silences): 3 letter spaces [   ] = 1 unstressed syllable;
          6 letter spaces [   ] = 1 stressed syllable or "beat";
             12 letter spaces[   ] = 2 "beats."

     Nonorthographic acute accents indicate stresses, not vowel qualities.
   Each hyphenated compound has one primary stress and is read as one extended
        word: a little more rapidly than other words but not hurried.

          25 August 1991 En route NYC-Vermont in car
          13 – 18 June 1993 New York

          GIANT PHILOSOPHICAL OTTERS

     "Don't we talk of then are unsealed they efflorescing
     and their efflorescing sound its exclamations which
     they teach going wraiths and, later, sensations
     of their efflorescing a low growling doesn't seem
     they were called throughout an eon and, later, sensations
     within them, and in clearness and the expresences?"
     "The meaning names?" "But are children the presences
     as far as throughout sensations?" "Where? Traces
     crying?" "Is they efflorescing every day? And
     when?" "So you say the verbal expresences?" "They were
     in the past. Here called the contrary of they were:
     so insecure this question within unfolding it
     even landed near their going nothin' they were: so
     insecure thin unfolding wraiths and the words
     are they were in clearness." "Or how doesn't sensation
     and the connections?" "Where in clearness and in and
     the world flows in as this questions even adults
     talk of sentences as give the word: they going in

knowable primitive?" "Him means crying?" "Is 'pain' about
seem their place in they were in they could
within they were contrary of whatevery day? And when?"
"So you say their being! More of sensation between
pain?" "How is them names in Surinam? And does
peering they were in throughout an alert pression?
And does not describe it as pain between their
place elements this question between they were contrary
of words are the named sensations?" "Where? For
how can I go so insecure living names?" "But were children's
amounts a close family of the contrary of
world flowing in as light?" "Really learn! Or how
can I go so far as to unknow light?" "Really
learn the verbal expresences as thin unfolding
the words are new to use in clearness. Or how
can I go so insecure then adults they were?" "Traces
in clearness." "Or how does nothin' they were were:
so far as far as far as to pain being eventuated
all but by absence teach going curiously into unknowing
sound in even adults the Hummers." "They going
there between the Hummers." "They teach 'pain' as far
as giving names? But a child has hurt himself within
sound its exclamations even landed near the Hummers!"
"Their place is farther along a low growling
not describe it to himself within but far as giving
things sound in clearness and its exclamations within
unfolding nothin' unfolding names?" "But has the child
hurt himself within the names in Surinam?" "Any problem
here? For how are words unsealed then had amounts
they could ever do within unfolding wraiths and
examples to be sensation its expressions?"

Derived from Mac Low's poem "Giant Otters" (2/13 – 14/82; *Bloomsday*
[Barrytown, NY: Station Hill, 1984], p. 15) and G. E. M. Anscombe's English
translation of Ludwig Wittgenstein's *Philosophical Investigations* I, 244 & 245, by
entering a chance-operational mix of the sources into Hugh Kenner & Joseph
O'Rourke's text-generation program TRAVESTY & editing the program's output.

4 September – 11 November 1989
New York

Kenward Elmslie [1929]

MARBLED CHUCKLE IN THE SAVANNAHS

If I journeyed to a suburb of a Sunday
and saw window-dressing families
my resultant letter would explain my rope-bridge albums.
The view of a chasm between one's feet!
Terra cotta villagers, jabbering in spring!
Winters, an occasional caw, and some smoke.

Now. Your rabbit foot and handbook collection.
Still secreted, saran-wrapped in the rain pipe?
Each in our own way, we both love blurs.
Rabbit foot, swirl! Swedishly!
I have your handbook on fires, on loan—yes?—
blotched and smelly, like paper in a summer room.

I, on an orange garage floor, bewitched,
you, hooped and mobile in the garden,
how can we effect a confrontation?
Dead wasps accumulate every year
between screen door and front door.
Today, found half a cucumber in a stream.

(*Album*, 1969)

FRUIT

Oranges,
someday the Negress who smears you with certified color
will hear tap-taps and whines (the Giant Fruitbeast) in the swamplands
arising like natural music, and she will shriek in her swoon
"American youth, go stomp on your car graveyards!
Small boys in acid underwear, once more you may yoo-hoo

at trains in the night. Whoo-ee, the alleys of Kansas
are now devoid of yellow joke eggs that hop peep and explode.
City children, accept the perfume of your melons in the sun—
    Lemons."

    Limes,
in spring you remind some men of little people's breasts.
Irish bodies—the huggle-duggle of the many cellophane sacs—
or even the Indians on stilts who harvest government orchards
know: a lime on a turntable encourages the wrong voyagers.

Plop them into snowbanks, northern strangers, and in summer
when they roll onto roads, slovenly families at pasture
will remember to kick the cattle. Farm women in bed a-mornings,
think of them in your bureau, then get up. A nation of you and you,
    Grapefruit,
    Tangerines,
could only prove the all-nite cities have won. O lovely spring,
the carnage! Oldsters with blinky chicken eyes resent your seeds,
your sections, your juice and meats. Secretly in markets,
they pinch you, hurry on and sniff their fingertips, estranged.

    (*Motor Disturbance*, 1971)

ISLAND CELEBRATION
for James Schuyler

 The overgrown roads around here refract water-and-mirror mirages.
The lakes, buffeted by winds from the south,
 are the bane of narcissists. All they see reflected are clouds

 boxed into rectangular segments with sky areas evenly in-between—
vistas as hyper-organized as those Chinese puzzle houses
 which make one too trembly to lift spoons past shoulder level—

one is always secretly sloshing liquids into flower arrangements.
If only one could peer under the table to see who has the erection.
Instead one hunts for the door to the moth center garden

past the laundromat, the mattress room, the Wild West sauna,
(a mobile electric chair rushes by, emitting sparks, straps flailing)
ah, the door, the handle—a stranger! Boudoir mirror. Oneself.

The resultant dearth of energy leads to mole-like panics,
agitations and positionings in closets, or else one waits in brambles
for semaphored advice from some person on a hill.

Around here, all is simpler. Down the paths whistling minks
rush unafraid. Too clumsy to shy at the beauty of bodies,
they never pay for the damage they do—trampled mushrooms,

bruised raspberries. And the storms never pay for the damage *they* do.
Same with the map. All who look at it lose focus
and succumb to the montages of a tinselled mainland—Tinselled Mainland:
midwestern swimmers exercising on flat garage patios,
leaf decor smelling up incinerators—Halloween Dance o'er—
stumped yellow and green passenger trains,
many tufted balls rolling down national arteries.
The photos by the bed (notwithstanding some suspicious splotches)
are harmless—seasonal changes arrayed in sequence:
rock to sludge, sludge to lichen, lichen to bracken,

water onslaught, holes that gurgle and squirt,
tongued plants that billow like parachutes plummeting within a sea,
and finally, the harvest, the stoppages, ice and wind.

The person on the hill whose arms remain akimbo
is most likely not unlike oneself—if only proper stillness
would occur. Tests, measurements. Cascading berries

would render them useless. Same with the map. The actual elbow
of the beach is longer, crookeder, with grass like a colleen's bush,
freckled and muzzled, and with fewer warm air spurts.

In the portrait over the fireplace, the inverted green teacup
is the whole island, the pines too, 1912, two sisters on a picnic,
armistices and solstices, with no trace at all of shattered glass.

(*Motor Disturbance*, 1971)

DUO-TANG

Laundry so near the ocean bothered Frank.
The lack of medicine on the shelves
also confused his emotional stance.

A moth fluttered against his leg.
A gust of wind made his Pepsi keen
as its foam trickled down inside.

A banana boat on a horizon otherwise blank
passed over a time-piece buried in valves
over which sea-growths stirred. Grant's

Tomb. Cleopatra's Needle. The Hague.
He flipped the pages of the travel magazine
and wondered if Monsieur had lied.

Tomorrow, he'd go to the bank,
shop for some unguents and skin salves,
and finish the Castles' book on the dance.

The Hesitation Waltz! How vague
the past seemed: static scene after static scene.
He watched the retreating tide

and patted his belly. The sun sank.
Monsieur and J. were off by themselves.
    He took off his pants.

    He was too proud to beg.
He lay down and thought of Jean.
    The sheet had dried.

                                    (*Motor Disturbance*, 1971)

PICNIC

Grass manoeuvres under passing swans
as surreptitiously as that arrival in the High Sierras
red-faced from the sunsets, you were wise to shoo
yesterday's beasts away from the teetering car

gracefully falling through the clouds, a leg
rose-colored from the flamingo aviary
overtook the receding shores of yesteryear
sequoias rustled in the clouds like alfalfa
soughing that spring day when we shared an egg

                                    (*Circus Nerves*, 1971)

SQUATTER IN THE FOREGROUND
for Ann Lauterbach

We rake the past, down to an ounce of wants.
Meant to begin in haybarn dorm of overall kerchiefs,
an empire of cow sphincters on the hook by May.
I think I'll stare at the muss to endure
all I am: non-stop strands, new dues to pay up.

Air dense with leavings, fridge hum clicks off.
Nothing on the easel, so nothing melts.
The story thus far: pair of angels swish across grass
into dim room. Wrestlers. Big mirrors, stacks of 'em.
White walls lift. An Anglo-Saxon pause for identification.

(*Moving Right Along*, 1980)

ONE NIGHT STAND
[music by Claibe Richardson]

There are two extremes of love.
One extreme is "legit."
The ring bit. The groom bit. The bride bit.
Which leads to the
    Lord-Knows-How-I've-Tried Bit.

The other starts with a casual come-on,
And ends with a casual split.
But being an amorous tidbit
Can lead to the
    Why-Did-I-Do-What-I-Did Bit.

Nut-brown eyes. Silky black lashes.
Cups his hands. Tap tap go his ashes.
    Tends to use
    the verb "enthuse."
    One Night Stand.
    Make it a One Night Stand.

Nibbly ears. Kisses like fire.
Profile, nice. But big rubber tire.
    Jokes are stale.
    Gets high on ale.
    Mister Bland.
    Keep it a One Night Stand.

He looks so cleancut,
He made me feel raunchy.
Now it's End of Scene. Cut.
How'd he get so paunchy?

Skips the news. Flicks through the funnies.
Chews his food like twenty Bugs Bunnies.
    Rasping cough.
    Go knock it off!
    Not my brand.
    Keep it a One Night Stand.

    When I first spied him,
    I loved every freckle.
    Now I want to hide him.
    Bring back Dr. Jeckyl.

Boyish smile. Yes, you're endowed, dear.
Undershorts and voice are too loud, dear.
    Nervous tic.
    Taxi, quick.
Bye, little brother.
Aren't you glad you had another
    One   (Have fun!)
    Night (Don't let the bedbugs bite!)
    Stand.
    One Night Stand!

(Kenward Elmslie Visited, 1982)

STAGE DUO

You: on candy cameo. Me: ate dumb flash.
You: Tom, Tom Vermont. Me: Mom Vermont, fell off lip.
Quarry lip. Descent palaver, stone evidence
about again we're in The Thirties again about.
Next frame, rich sillies, slime and shame,
jump–cuts of willy–nilly fame and time and you and I aflame—
Mayan calendar wheel rolls up out of swamp dump,
thanks to covert affirmative action us language enthusiasts.
Penguins incognito, that's us! Tom and Mom Vermont on safari.
Soft-drink saliva dribbles off our Tom and Mom Vermont frisbee,
(see footnote, memory disk base-camp) what base-camp where,
dribbles sideways into the petrified jungle orchids
missing the thirsty band of pigmies

in their Century of Progress Fred-and-Ginger duds,
white show-biz gloves cupped under our mouths agape.
Back at the recreation area, so much pottery lined up,
legible to the initiated, each crowfoot glyph
a solstice buzz word: earth, earthworks, earthworm.
Tom darling, you unscramble it, hum the whole code, om,
like the Lucky Litter series buried in Mom–Mom's mulch,
one of the towering creations of world lit—forget it.
A bit batty, these summer days, us turn-around artists
having a good one wandering in the wilderness,
lichen glut, oopsy-daisy, a kudzu vine mall,
here and there a handywipe. Commercial break.
Fat old devil in heat, baby angel eats ten singles,
penguin's wig falls off, revealing Commie bomb womb.
Get the point? The point is, we're back!
Hot stuff, trudging through the Fifties again about again,
while star-spangled trays of chemicals jiggling
take their noonday nap under the ol' swimming hole.
On the ridge, gutted comfort station, row of felled urinals,
tasteful silhouette, a mini-Stonehenge
to the rainbow system still up and at it
(its fade-in, fade-out loop will outlast us all)
and the pot with the neon dollar sign, you bet,
schlock momentum intact, gotcha.
Back again, Mom Tom back in The Eighties,
quarry lip tremors noted again about again about.
Solstice birth squirm code, never fear, not so far.

(*Sung Sex,* 1990)

Jerome Rothenberg [1931]

POLAND/1931   "The Wedding"

my mind is stuffed with tablecloths
& with rings but my mind
is dreaming of poland stuffed with poland
brought in the imagination
to a black wedding
a naked bridegroom hovering above
his naked bride   mad poland
how terrible thy jews at weddings
thy synagogues with camphor smells & almonds
thy thermos bottles thy electric fogs
thy braided armpits
they underwear alive with roots o poland
poland poland poland poland poland
how thy bells wrapped in their flowers toll
how they do offer up their tongues to kiss the moon
old moon old mother stuck in thy sky thyself
an old bell with no tongue a lost udder
o poland thy beer is ever made of rotting bread
thy silks are linens merely thy tradesmen
dance at weddings where fanatic grooms
still dream of bridesmaids still are screaming
past their red moustaches poland
we have lain awake in thy soft arms forever
thy feathers have been balm to us
thy pillows capture us like sickly wombs & guard us
let us sail through thy fierce weddings poland
let us tread thy markets where thy sausages grow ripe & full
let us bite thy peppercorns let thy oxen's dung be sugar to
    thy dying jews
o poland o sweet resourceful restless poland
o poland of the saints unbuttoned poland repeating endlessly
    the triple names of mary
poland poland poland poland poland
have we not tired of thee poland no for thy cheeses

shall never tire us nor the honey of thy goats
thy grooms shall work ferociously upon their looming brides
shall bring forth executioners
shall stand like kings inside thy doorways
shall throw their arms around thy lintels poland
& begin to crow

(*Poland/1931*, 1969)

THE WATER OF THE FLOWERY MILL (II)

for the Angel

He is blood, himself
the killer
is where the sun goes down.

Will he flex his arm, will
the fingers
narrow, make a fist around
the bauble, crush it?

Dust is his.

The entry into light
the courtyard
white with marble veins
& suicides
the perfect edge for sleep.

Count the numbers.
Call the monster green
the little eggs
the wind cups
everything is far from him.

His blood is far from him

& makes a circle, poisons
where it falls
the country dies from it.

Sweet smelling flesh
sweet dung
sweet tumor in the eye
sweet bauble:

as the fish are lanterns
upon waves

& light the sea for him.

(*Poems for the Game of Silence*, 1971)

PORTRAIT OF MYSELF WITH ARSHILE GORKY
& GERTRUDE STEIN

AG   I do direct the night.
            I do.
            & walk through it.

GS   The sea is cool.
            The boats are dominant.
            The idea of algebra is lost.

            Almost nowhere is worthwhile.

JR   My own care my trade plied that eases occupations.
            Nowhere at ease.

AG   Not because peace is with us.

GS   Nowhere more mechanical.
            Nowhere function.
            Nowhere at ease.
            Nowhere at ease.

            Nowhere more at ease.

JR   Turn turn & beg exceptions.
            Scold the sea.

AG	I can make a hurried exit I put propellors to rest.
GS	Not because I scold.
JR	I who am saint. I who am not saint. I who am am not saint. I salvage.
GS,AG	Do you.
JR	I scold the sea. I try turning. Spurning remembering.
GS,AG	Do you. Do you.
JR	I can establish covenants & lease ground for foreclosers & tell how many steps are needed.
GS	Can you.
JR	I can figure to Wednesday.
GS	Must you.
JR	I can begin with a number & end with 33.
GS	Must you.
JR	I can never be more certain than when I was.
GS,AG	Must you. Must you.
JR	I can miss Miss Ann I prepare her belly for lust.
GS	Am I white.
AG	A color.

GS   I am ball.
                   Am I.

JR   Yes & the motion of wanting to be cool.

JR,AG,GS   Before law.
                   Before water.
                   Before water the dove.

GS,AG   Please warm us.

JR   Warmly.
                   Warmly.

GS   Fish warmly.

AG   Fish & designs.

GS,AG   Desires.

JR,AG,GS   Manage an oracle.
                   Manage a meal.
                   Manage an oarlock.

JR   & a preparation to be already drowned.

(Poems for the Game of Silence, 1971)

THE 12TH HORSE-SONG OF FRANK MITCHELL (BLUE)

Key: wnn N nnnn N gahn   hawuNnawu   nngobaheegwing

Some are & are going to my howinouse baheegwing hawuNnawu
    N nngahn baheegwing
Some are & are going to my howinouse baheegwing hawuNnawu
    N nngahn baheegwing
Some are & some are gone to my howinouse nnaht bahyee naht-
    gwing buhtzzm bahyee noohwinnnGUUH

Because I was (N gahn) I was the boy raised Ng the dawn(n)
  (n) but some are & are gowing to my howinouse baheegwing
& by going from the house the bluestone hoganome but some are
  & are gone to my howinow baheegwing
& by going from the house the shahyNshining hoganome but some
  are & are gone to my howinow baheeGWING
& by going from the swollenouse my breath has blown but some
  are & are going to my howinouse baheegwing
& by going from the house the hohly honganome but some are &
  are gone to my howinow baheegwing ginng ginnng
& from the place of precious cloth we walk (p) pon (N gahn) but
  some are gone to my howinow baheegwing hawunawwing
with those prayersticks that are blu(u)(u) but some are & are
  (wnn N) gahn to my howinouse baheegwing
with my feathers that are b(lu)u but some are & are going to my
  howinouse baheegwing
with my spirit horses that are b(lu)u but some are & are going to my
  howinouse baheegwing
with my spirit horses that are blue & dawn but some are & are gone
  to my howinow baheegwing nngnnng
with those spirit (hawuN) horses that are bluestone (nawu) but
  some are & are gone to my howinow baheegwing
with those hoganorses that are bluestone but some are & are going
  to my howinouse baheegwing
with cloth of ever(ee)ee kind tgaahn & draw tham on nahhtnnn
  but some are & are gone to my howinow baheegwing
with jewels of ever(ee)ee kind tgaahn & draw them on nahhtnnn
  but some are & are going to my howinouse baheegwing
with sheep of evree(ee)(ee) kind tgaahm & draw them on nahhtnnn
  but some are & are going to my howinouse baheegwing
with cattle of every kind (N gahn) to go & draw them on nahht-
  nnnn but some are & are going to my howinouse baheegwing
with men of evree(ee)(ee) kind tgaahn & draw them on nahhtnnn
  but some are & are going to my howinouse baheegwing
now to my howinome of precious cloth in my backroom Ngahhnnn
  where Nnnn but some are & are going to my howinouse
  baheegwing
in my house of precious cloth we walk (p)pon (N gahn) where
  Nnnn but some are & are going to my howinouse baheegwing
& everything that's gone before (mmmm) more we walk (p)pon
  but some are & are going to my howinouse baheegwing
& everything that's more & won't be (be!) be poor but some are &

some are gone to my howinow baheegwing
& everything that's (nawuN) living to be old & blesst (bhawuN)
   some are & are going to my howinouse baheegwing
because I am the boy who goes & blesses/blisses to be old but
   some are & are going to my howinouse baheegwing hawu-
   Nnawu N nngahn baheegwinnng

Zzmmmm are & are gone to my howinow baheegwing hawuNnawu
   N nngahn baheegwing
Zzmmmm are & are going to my howinouse baheegwing hawu-
   Nnawu N nngahn baheegwing
Some are & some are gone to my house now naht bahyeee naht-
   nwinnng buht nawuNNN baheegwinnng

(Poems for the Game of Silence, 1971)

PRAISES OF THE BANTU KINGS (1-10)

1.
I escort.
I go with the dead I don't escort myself.
I was foolish someone else was wise.
I was a lion but had never stretched my claws.
I have no father & no mother.
I remained.

2.
I was the rain's child the rain comes from the east & drizzles.
I am a rain that drizzles.
I soaked some old men without hair.
I am the bed the dead will sleep on.
Sometimes I kept busy once I was looking for a place to cross.
I am the lion's grandson.
I was angry later I roamed their forests.
I am your king.

3.
I was a tree that lost its leaves.
Am I dead?
My skin is hard now only some twigs are left for burning.

4.
I am the one my name is.
I wouldn't let them bury me.
Tomorrow I will visit someone else.
I killed the king & all his children.
I killed the man who owned the island.
Once I killed his brother.

5.
I love.
I overrun the country.
I am awarded lands & people.
I was scornful of their goats & sheep.

6.
I was like a lion in the forest.
I had never been afraid of witchcraft.
I killed my victim then I ate his prick.

7.
I am the rummager.
I dug out lily bulbs.
I searched for siftings of the corn.
I was hunger in a conquered land.

8.
I am beautiful & light-skinned.
I am rain.
I carried the dead children like a stretcher.
I was the road through the cemetery no one could escape me.
I fought buffalos & strangers.
I despised their smalltown ways I only live among the great.

9.
I was a marksman.
I was skilled.
I was the husband of my wife.
I wore my shirttails up.
I sported a goatee.

10.
I dwellt among the crooked.
I was taught.
I straightened up.

(*Poems for the Game of Silence*, 1971)

REALTHEATER PIECE TWO

Setting

An open area outdoors, preferably the courtyard of a church or other religious struc-
ture. The audience sits on all four sides on long wooden benches. In the center is a
deep hole (high enough for a man to stand in) covered with a wide wooden grating;
near it a small table with various implements: scissors, knives, cleaver, ribbons, pa-
per flowers, etc. To further prepare the setting, cut down a number of good-sized
trees & plant them firmly in the performance area; to these are brought domesti-
cated animals, such as goats & sheep, which are hung alive from the branches. The
trees may also be decorated with birds & ribbons, & with ornaments of gold & silver.

Action One

The audience receives long, richly colored gowns, distributed by male attendants
wearing short white gowns & otherwise unadorned. The members of the audience
remove their street clothes & put on the long gowns.

Action Two

The attendants set fire to the trees.

Action Three

When the trees have started burning, a group of five men enters. They wear white
like the attendants but drawn tightly across their chests & hanging down to their
feet. They are bareheaded (heads preferably shaven) except for one, The Leader,
who wears some kind of exotic headdress such as a turban or a mitre. The Leader
carries a baby's rattle in his right hand, an oldfashioned hurricane lamp in his left
hand. The four others carry (1) a metal cooking pot, (2) a miniature plastic Christ-
mas tree, (3) a large lady's fan, & (4) the left hand of a store mannikin. At a signal
from The Leader, the attendants choose a volunteer from the audience & lead him
(or her) to the center of the performance area. The five men place their implements
on the ground in front of the table, then use the ribbons, paper flowers & scissors to
adorn the volunteer. Once he is adorned, The Leader helps him climb into the hole,
over which the attendants put the wooden grating back in place. The Leader re-
mains beside the hole, white the other four lead the audience in singing a miscellany
of songs, preferably church hymns like *Gladly the Cross I'd Bear*.

Action Four

A bull, bound with heavy ropes & profusely adorned with (real) flowers & gilded leaves, is brought into the performance area. The attendants position the bull above the wooden grating. The Leader picks up knives & cleaver from the table & begins gashing the bull in a number of places so as to allow the blood to flow onto the grating. The volunteer in the hole now turns his face up to receive the blood. He must make sure that the spurts of blood fall on his head, clothes & body. He must lean backwards to soak his cleeks, his ears, his lips & his nostrils. He must let the wet blood pour over his mouth & must open his mouth eagerly to drink it. At any time he chooses, The Leader cuts the bull's throat & lets the full torrent of blood cover the volunteer. *Action Four* ends when the bull stops bleeding.

Action Five

Remove the dead bull, open the grating & lift out the volunteer, who will come out drenched & dripping, covered with blood from head to toe. Have him return to his place in the audience, which the attendants & the five men lead in reciting the following: BE OF GOOD CHEER, SEEING THAT THE GOD IS SAVED: FOR WE TOO, AFTER OUR TOILS, SHALL FIND SALVATION.

Action Six

Repeat the preceding events with other members of the audience until all have been soaked in blood. If the trees & animals stop burning, the theaterpiece is to be halted immediately & continued the next day. If there aren't enough bulls available, rams or goats may be substituted. A child, preferably male, may also be substituted, but only where there is little danger of interference by the police.

(*Poems for the Game of Silence*, 1971)

A SONG OF QUAVERING   "Exchanging Ribs"

> *all night long I did not sleep*
> *all night long she quavered*

I

the women come to sing are singing
of the night the man who couldn't sleep
but saw the woman quaver through the dark
remembered in early spring she came the peepers

rising to surface
voice of the frogs in wet lands
lazy bodies after dusk the crowd rose
from marshes in a dream
"beloved
"tie my shoe
"your mouth sans teeth
"is beautiful
(he says)
think I will have to follow her get out of town
will travel empty days desires
maybe will find peace not in my own but in
home of that strange woman lonely boy
had lived a life apart now saw her
among flowered fields game forests village
where men & women stood in lines
paired faces   sang & fucked
—again—
—again—
the woman lunges   saline   fury
of that hot amphibian
cloacal sex devoured
twisted on your dreamy tongue
(she says)
'didn't you like it here?"
"it was so nice" (he says)
"so slow
"the rib was wild
"& changed to appetite
no inch of which remained the same
but traced
contour of frog's body
came back as song
(medicine)
with which to see
revive the scene
"a woman trembling in the night
"a good one   quavering
"& sitting contrary
"not faithful
"lovers on rim of earth
the sleepless
Indian atop his hill looks out

he sees her vanish
sees her at distant lake
in beauty
of her missing teeth
(she says) o ream me
lover
I the frog the moon
have brought you here
only to my pleasure
I blossom to a hundred holes
I die
your year of love has ended
in marsh
with piping frogs around
—no village—
lost in quavering
exhanging ribs

2

the Riverview explodes tonight
leaves nothing
            but the dance
moves fathers & sons across the floor
back to frenetic 1960s
the face of my old patriarchs
is green & clear
where's love?
what's lost in the encounter?
sleep (he answers) meaning
his exhaustion no release no happiness
a bachelor all his life the grandfather
has found a wife   the body
hovers at his lips the salt cunt
fills his mouth he gropes
toward satisfaction mumbles
songs music to fill the long
house   messages   delights
& wanders reckless thinks
my home is elsewhere
like my clan a mystery
my mother's name is

power   in the night
angels will come & wrestle him
so mad with love they force
exchange of ribs
his body stumbles into
trance
a gift of music
body that's made of mind

(*A Seneca Journal*, 1978)

THE STRUCTURAL STUDY OF MYTH

for Barbara Kirshenblatt-Gimblett

the thief became the rabbi
in that old story
others would say he was his father
all along   the way the moon
reflected in the water
is the water
maybe the master gonnif come to earth
old Trickster brother Jesus
didn't us Jews tell stories of his magic
"because we are like him"
the Crow Indian had said about Coyote
hitting the nail at last

(*Vienna Blood & Other Poems*, 1980)

AT THE CASTLE

seeing
its stone heart
the walls
are like walls
the gates like gates
& black
moon in the crook of tree
a yellow eye
it doesn't shine
the water dries against
my lips
o rainbow
will you fall?
o little heart
turn cold

.

tower.
broke.
every castle has.

.

night rises on
the valley
blanket on my bed

.

the child cries:
murder!
mushroom!
let them die with grace

.

A SCENARIO

for Richard Schechner

yiddish
vaudeville

is

fantastic
life

.

2000 people in the world
with mirrors

(*Vienna Blood & Other Poems*, 1980)

NUMEROLOGY

(a)

the man of numbers
cries too loud
he is a cipher   empty
his spaces
are yours
they open up through him
a cloud & sky
beyond him
centered in the holes they make
I call out
1!
2!
7!
9!
falling against his shadow
on the rock

(b)
9–9
shadow
rock
1

7–7–7–7–7
shadow
1
shadow cipher sky
1
spaces
9–9
shadow
9
numbers
9
1–1–1–1–1
2
cipher
empty
2
yours
2
shadow rock
9
7–7–7–7–7
sky
shadow sky
sky cloud
1 cloud
7 cipher
hole
7 hole
9 hole
shadow hole
1 spaces
cipher
cipher
1
7

(*Vienna Blood & Other Poems*, 1980)

ALEPH POEM

for David Meltzer

in peace the aleph
rises: on bishop's hat
the aleph rests

.

aleph & a dog
are friendly

.

as the masked man stumbles
to the street
a windpipe bursts
words & letters pour out
on the pavement

.

alephs sit beside a truck

.

sound before a sound
is spoken: aleph

.

the tear inside a tear

(*Vienna Blood & Other Poems*, 1980)

THAT DADA STRAIN

the zig zag mothers of the gods
of science   the lunatic fixed stars
& pharmacies
fathers who left the tents of anarchism
unguarded
the arctic bones
strung out on saint germain
like tom toms
living light bulbs
aphrodisia
"art is junk" the urinal
says "dig a hole
"& swim in it"
a message from the grim computer
"ye are hamburgers"

(*That Dada Strain*, 1983)

DOS GESHRAY (THE SCREAM)

Erd, zolst nit tsudekn mayn blut
un zol nit kayn ort zayn far mayn geshray
(Job 16:18)

"practice your scream" I said
(why did I say it?)
because it was his scream & wasn't my own
it hovered between us   bright
in our senses always bright it held
the center place
then somebody else came up & stared
deep in his eyes there found a memory
of horses galloping faster the wheels dyed red
behind them   the poles had reserved
a feast day but the jew
locked in his closet screamed
into his vest a scream

that had no sound therefore
spiraled around the world
so wild that it shattered stones
it made the shoes piled in the doorway
scatter their nails   things testify
—the law declares it—
shoes & those dearer objects
like hair & teeth do
by their presence
I cannot say that they share the pain
or show it not even the photos
in which the expressions of the dead shine forth
the crutches by their mass the prosthetic limbs by theirs
bear witness the eyeglasses bear witness
the suitcases the children's shoes the german tourists
in the stage set oshvientsim had become
the letters over its gates still glowing
still writ large
ARBEIT MACHT FREI
& to the side   HOTEL
and GASTRONOMIC BAR
the spirit of the place dissolving
indifferent to his presence
there with the other ghosts
the uncle   grieving
his eyelids turning brown an eye
protruding from his rump
this man whose body
is a crab's
his gut turned outward
the pink flesh of his children
hanging from him
that his knees slide up against
there is no holocaust
for these   but khurbn only
the word still spoken by the dead
who say   my khurbn
& my children's khurbn
it is the only word that the poem allows
because it is their own
the word as prelude to the scream
it enters
through the asshole

circles along the gut
into the throat
& breaks out
in a cry   a scream
it is his scream that shakes me
weeping   in oshvientsim
& that allows the poem to come

(*Khurbn & Other Poems*, 1989)

David Antin [1932]

REAL ESTATE

while i believe that what im doing depends essentially upon
    the event here   going here coming here and   making
what my idea of what a poem is   or   making my idea of
    what a valuable talk is   if thats what poetry is   there is a
life problem   a kind of running down of ones life   i may
    not be facing it very gravely now   although   when i came
    to california   i started running on the beaches   they have
beaches and you can run on them   and i twisted an ankle
    while running on the beach   and it took a damned long
time for my ankle to heal   and having played football and
baseball at various times in my childhood i always healed very
    quickly and this was the damnably longest healing that ever
    happened to me   and i had an image of myself as a 40 year
old pitcher   which is not an easy thing to be   forty year old
    pitchers have to watch where they put their feet   and watch
how they move and be careful that the mound is the right height
    because if they step off too fast they can lose it all that year
    and it was then i realized that life is running out somehow
    i didnt feel grave about it   but somehow i had to be careful
where i put my foot   and id never had to be careful where i put
    my foot before   see   up to then i could just put my foot down
    and if it slammed against the pavement it didnt matter much
    if there was some pain it would be over the next minute or day
    and if i got knocked down by something i could get up again

but i was beginning to realize that   as with a car   there
is a limit   on how long it can do it
                                    and so i had the feeling that
in these pieces where i go out and talk its true that i regard
the pieces as the center   yet i still feel   that because its
running out and i dont have time to go all over   to do the
pieces all over the world im not omnipresent in all places
talking to all the people i feel might benefit from hearing me
talk   or   that i might want to talk to   because i enjoy the
idea of talking to people   i suppose i thought ill put these
things in books
                              books are not ideal   i dont believe that books
are ideal forms   that is books are   imperfect recordings
of transactions that occur in real time   im here now and im
trying to make a piece   the way artists   have probably
always tried to make real work once   and   at some point
ill take an imperfect record of what ive done   and   it will
be an imperfect record because it will only be a tape recording
and it will only get some of the effect of being here   because
what i say   to some degree   is determined by what you
think   and my sense of it   otherwise id have to do an
entirely separate   berkeleyian ego trip   where i would
talk about anything   independently of who i think you are
                                    this is not my
approach to poetry   i suspect that   the approach to poetry
of poets   in their natural   habitat   which is in
performance   and in performance improvisation   has
always been   a response to some specific set of urgencies
that is   homer told the story that way that time   we
have only two of those tellings   reworked several times
probably   but we only have two of them   and who knows
why he decided to tell us about odysseuses son telemachus?
for some reason something tripped him out on telemachus
while he was taking up odysseuses return   that day   at
that place   maybe he was at a place where it was important
that he should talk about the island where telemachus went to
get advice from an old man   maybe some relative of the old
man was in the audience   someone who was in the family
line   maybe somebodys son was there   and his father
was gone   and   homer knew it   there is no reason to

suppose that these performances were staged so that there
could be comparative literature 134   in which you take up
the odyssey and the iliad as the two great surviving works of
all time
            its hard to believe that the poet performer was looking
forward to an infinite posterity   preparing you to worry
about a greek aristocracy that had long since vanished   it
seems unlikely   it seems more likely that he had something
to say   and that the stories were familiar but the way he told
them was dependent on some set of accidents   like there being
these people here   and
                              still there is the book homer
need have had no respect for books   i doubt if homer would
have cared about ever being translated by robert fitzgerald say
and i think robert fitzgerald knows that too   i would by
no means want to suggest that robert fitzgerald is under any
illusions that he was doing something for homer i dont
think that homer would have cared   but we now feel a
certain anxiety about being locked in   being in a small
room   as it were   without telling someone outside the room
what the room was like   maybe because its valuable to know
what its like in this small room   maybe something happened
valuably in this small room
                              i dont believe in globalism   im
not a globalist   which is why i dont speak with a rhodes
scholar accent   or part of the reason   in my university
there are many people who have strange accents that   when
im stuck with committee meetings i normally try to analyse
phonemically   and they have very strange phonetic structures
because they were exchange students somewhere in england
once   and i recognize iowa under cambridge and i keep saying
that sounds like iowa   but then it sounds like cambridge
and then it sounds like a fantasy of cambridge   and i cant
quite get it and then theres a little bit of la jolla mixed in   it
becomes an interesting task to dissociate the parts of this accent
that are a consequence of a belief in some kind of   globally
appropriate style
                        now the book itself   can be considered a
package a kind of care package so to speak   right   i mean
i do my talking here and i take my imperfect recording and i

transcribe it in the hope of finding what in it was the real thing
   the real action   and i try to get it into the book in such a
way that its still intelligible when it goes into this rectangular
   object with covers that you open like this and which
is partitioned arbitrarily by those things they call pages
                                       there are
no pages when i talk   you dont turn anything at all   that
   is   i turn you turn but we dont turn pages   someone
doesnt bring down a screen in front of me every few minutes
   and   then let me continue again
                             now the book has this
problem   but then everything has its problem   talking also
   has its inherent difficulties   there is no such thing as a
perfect medium   thats why they call it a medium   because
its in the middle   so to speak   its between   it mediates
a transaction and deflects it
                      you start out to reach for something
thats under water   and your hand goes to the wrong place
   and after a while you realize   that the object under the
water   is differently situated than you would have imagined
   it to be if it were outside the water and under the air   let us
say   because water has a different relation to light rays
   than air   which you dont really think about and are good
at reaching through   because thats what youre almost always
seeing and reaching through   so that under air you almost
   always find it because thats the way you learned about seeing
and reaching   whereas under water its really not where you
think it is   because thats where it would be under air   and
its really not there   but then you reach again and find it
   after a number of trys   and you realize that the water is
a medium   as the air is a medium and the lens of your eye is
a medium   well language is also a medium that were talking
through
            and maybe there isnt anything but the language when
   we think   finally   but theres some sense in which we
   feel ourselves moving toward the language   toward the
language to go through the language   and the language has
its habits   its specific density its index of refraction   and i
can use the habits of the language if i know what im doing with
   them   and sometimes i get used to them and i get very

expert and i forget theres going to be a crack in the grain
somewhere over there and im going to get stuck with something
 something i dont want because it is the habit of
the language to divide the world that way in that zone
 and its not my inclination to divide the world in quite
that way and then ive got trouble

           poets have always had
 trouble with language anyone who uses it seriously has
 trouble with it it goes the way it wants to go because
 of the way people took it before and im a foreigner in it
  youre a foreigner in it do you realize its the one thing
 we all are is that were all foreigners in the language you
know its very funny to talk about acquisitions of secondary languages
 because nobody comes in speaking the language

             you come into
 the world not speaking it and its their language
 and theyve spoken it and you havent spoken anything
  youve been involved in looking in feeling and
 touching in transactions with them and all the
while they keep talking this foreign language

         and gradually
 you take it from them and you get to think of it
  what you get to think of it you may be suspicious of
the way they use language maybe you think that theyre saying
strange things that you dont agree with but in order to
 get them to do nice things to behave reasonably you
pretend to accept their language and after a while youve
accepted enough of it to be called a "native speaker" which
 is itself a lie of the language in a real sense there is something
 of a lie in this there is no such thing as a "native speaker"
          "native" would
suggest that there is such a thing as someone who was born
speaking it there is no such person who was born speaking
 it we are all born foreigners and its very important to
remember that were all foreigners and all languages are secondary
 to our being
       because before that there were meaningful
transactions and we all got involved in them i dont know
 what it is to be before the language but what i know now
 is that the term 'native speaker" has come to seem alien

to me again   because "native" doesnt seem to go with "speaker"
      it seems to be an odd juxtaposition of two terms that
    are somewhat at odds with each other   an exaggeration of a
      sort   an over optimistic one   that promotes a false
    union   that somehow because we are all here now and seem to
      be at home here and seem to have been at home here as
    long as we can remember   speaking a common language that
    we all understand   it would seem as though we were born
    here speaking one language and we all share a native currency
                                        could you imagine
    having a "native currency"   coming into the country with
      its money   being born with a supply of its money   is it
    really that different   to be born with dollar bills in your
    pockets   and thats not trivial   you dont have pockets and you
      dont have dollar bills in them   look   take a dollar bill
        see it doesnt mean very much at this point   but its
    wonderfully formalized   the dollar bill has all the great marks
      of our unity gathered together on it
                                        it has the numeral one
      printed in all four corners and on both sides   it has the
    founding father of our country in the center of it   our first
    president   number one and on the other side   the reverse
    side   his place is taken by the word ONE   which in case
    you are in any doubt about it is also printed over each of the
      numeral ones in the four corners of that same side   and it is
      wonderful in its promise of a beginning   a new order of
    centuries   from out of the many one   beginning with one
          and it is all very wonderful   as it states unequivocally
    that this is legal tender for all debts public and private   and
      you may believe this   i used to believe it too
                                        i used to
      believe it too   i was an artist in residence at notre
    dame   i kept thinking ill be an artist in residence and ill be
      talking to the football team   which was kind of nostalgic
      for me   but i got there and they had me in this funny motel
      notre dame has a great motel   theyre terrific on motels
    because all the tractor salesmen from duluth come down on saturday
    to watch the football games   so they make a lot of money
      on the motel   and i was in the motel and i thought   well
    what i ought to do is rent a car   because on the weekend
      if you dont want to go to the ballgame   which i didnt

really   you might want to go see some other part of the country
       and i came provided with a fair supply of dollar bills and
i went to the car rental agency   o.j. simpsons company?
  it was one of those companies the one in whose commercials
     this guy goes running to a car and makes a mad leap to get
into it because he has no time for formalities for some reason
   or other   o.j. simpson the man with the heisman trophy
out there in the hall goes running to this car   but presumably
   he doesnt go there waving dollar bills   because if he went there
waving dollar bills they would have said go away   o.j. doesnt
   wave dollar bills he waves credit cards   i found out very
fast that i could wave all the dollar bills i wanted to   they
   wouldnt rent me the car
                              "but it says here"   and i read it to
them   i took my dollar bill out of my pocket and i read   i took
   this dollar and read "this note is legal tender for all debts
   public and private"   i said "how much do you want?   ill
     rent your car ill pay you in advance ill give you a deposit"
       they said "havent you got a credit card from some major
   company"   i said "not only do i have a credit card from a
     major company i have a credit card from the most major
   company in the united states   the united states   because
basically thats what this country is its a credit card company
its a credit card company and these are its credit cards
                                                   they said
     "no   we dont accept those"   i said "you must be
unamerican" i said "this is the biggest credit card company in
the united states because it is the united states it prints all this
   money   they said we dont take it
                              so all week long i couldnt
get away from notre dame   except when driven by friendly
students but   i had no way of moving out on my own because
   they didnt accept dollar bills   which as i understood it were
legal tender   but they were not legal tender as far as car rental
   companies went   they would not accept payment   they
   would not accept deposits   they didnt accept these green things
                              and i said to
   myself all these years i used to think this was money   and i
   had an image of money   you know   i didnt think a lot

about money   i confess   as a kid i didnt really think
much about money at all   but money was a kind of solid to me
when i was a kid   because   well because of the way its
presented   you know some of its even very pretty   we
used to have nickels that had the head of a very beautiful indian
on one side   and a buffalo on the other   these two vanishing
species   and they both looked wonderful   and i used to
look with admiration at my nickel i really liked my nickels
        i was a little kid   jefferson on this one doesnt really
look very good   but i dont have any buffalo nickels left
    if you do theyre probably worth more than nickels   which
goes to show you that if money is worth a lot of money   it
goes out of circulation   which i believe is called greshams
law   that cheap money drives expensive money out of
    existence   the law meaning that whats cheesy stays in
existence and whats not cheesy you pull away from transactions
because you dont want to give it up

                                        and i liked nickels
    i really did   not only because of what they could buy
    i thought the nickels were really very nice   i had a jar
    of buffalo nickels   the different years of buffalo nickels
    they went on for a while and i think they pulled them out of
    circulation   some time after the second world war buffalo
    nickels vanished and buffalo nickels and indian head nickels
became extinct   and only were kept in peoples private collections
                                        but these nickels
    were very tangible to me   if you took a nickel down to a
grocery store   you could buy two coconut-covered marshmallow
    candies   if thats what you liked and at that point i did   if
you took one nickel to the candy store you could trade it for
a spaldeen rubber ball   with which you could play stickball
    which was very nice because we played a lot of stickball
and the spaldeen was considered a very good ball   spaldeen
    was the name of the ball   or we used to call them spaldeens
        though now that i think of it they were probably spaldings
        but in our neighborhood and in our dialect we called
    them spaldeens   and these spaldeens were very much
admired because they were much livelier than other balls   and
we used to test them out by dropping them from about shoulder
height to make sure that they would bounce chest high or at

least over your waist   because if it only bounced knee high it
was a dead one and then nobody would be able to hit a home
run   and youd wind up with a kind of pitchers duel   even
though you had no pitchers when you played stickball   because
stickball as we played it in the streets of new york was played
with a stick and a ball and the stick was an old broom stick   what
you used to do was saw off the end of a broom   though i never
saw anybody saw one off everybody always seemed to have one
really they always had these sticks and nobody ever sawed
them off at all   somehow they grew sawed off   and we
used to go into the street with our stick and our spaldeen
and play stickball   which was a game like baseball   except
that you threw the ball up in the air and you hit it on the first
bounce   which is why you used to be concerned for the ball
not to be dead   and usually you stood with your stick at home
plate   which was one of those sewer lids   actually entrances
to the gas and electrical lines that ran under the citys streets
and placed at about 30 yard intervals   so you had the batter
standing over one sewer lid that was home plate   and you
played with first second and third basemen   no shortstop
because the streets were so narrow   and usually one or two
outfielders   and in order to give the outfielders room because
the streets in brooklyn were so narrow   you usually played
up near the end of the street with second base the sewer lid
nearest the end of the street   so that the outfield could play
in the "T" of the intersection   and you used to count sewer
lids to describe the quality of your hitters   and if you
were a two sewer hitter you were really very good because
you could hit the ball on the fly across cortelyou road   which
was the name of the broad avenue that intersected with east
fourth street where we played   and if you were a two
sewer hitter you could hit it over the head of the one or
two outfielders who patrolled cortelyou road   and if you were
lucky it would sail over their heads and if they were lucky
they didnt get hit by the bus that traveled up and down the
avenue   you had to be very alert as an outfielder   because
you had to field the ball between the buses   because
cortelyou road was a fairly heavily traveled street   even in the
days before the smog hit   because it was a big street that took
you down to the major local shopping area on flatbush avenue

the others were very narrow little streets and cars came about
   every half hour   so you didnt have to worry about them
and thats what i used to think was the average rate for cars to
   come through places   about once a half hour you would
see a car and you got through a lot of innings   and
   when a car would come everybodyd walk to the side of the
street and the car would sort of drift through at about
   ten miles an hour and youd go back to playing stickball
                                                   now in those
days i thought of money as real   because the prices of things
were constant   in my experience they were fairly constant
   anyway   little houten chocolate bars were two cents
   coconut–covered marshmallows were about that price   yoyos
were a nickel spaldeens were a nickel tops were a nickel   this
   may begin to sound like a nostalgia trip but you see
   everything in my world   it was a childs world   was fairly
   stable   the price structure was stabilized   and these
things that you wanted and used were all objects   and these
things that were money were objects too   a nickel a yoyo
   a spaldeen   five pennies   two marshmallow candies
   one top   two houten bars   and you could trade them for
each other in regular exchanges   five pennies for a nickel
or a top or a spaldeen the same way you could trade the spaldeen
for a yoyo or a top or two marshmallow candies or a coke or a
   big puree shooter   and it was clear   this was money
                                                   now in my
family there were people who probably didnt think that way
about money   they must have assumed that money was a
unit in a capacity to build something that would end up by
   making more of itself   they call that capital   but never
mind about that   there is a threshold effect in piling up
   money   you pile up enough of it to become contagious
   you eventually get together a lot of nickels and eventually they
start reproducing themselves   at a certain point
                                                   i had no such
experience of money and no such theory   of money as an
agent of infectious disease   and i only knew money as a set of
   simple and desirable objects you could exchange for other
objects of equivalent desirability and size   like the ration
   tokens we used to get during the war   little red ration

tokens   that were smaller than money and you needed them to
     get various things like meat or butter that you bought during
     the war   because meat was rationed and butter was rationed
       things like that   but there were people there in my family
     who were more disillusioned with money   than i was at
         that time   because to me money was like a brick a yoyo
       a kite   and i thought i understood money
                                                       in those days it cost
         me 11 cents to go to the movies on saturday   which is
     ten cents   or one dime   or two nickels and a penny tax
         for kids to go to the movies on saturday   and it seemed
     fair enough   then it went to 22 cents   when it went to
22 cents i just thought it cost more money that something
     had happened to the movie   it didnt occur to me that something
had happened to the dime   i was not in a position to recognize
     that the dime had changed its character   because the entire
     nature of a coinage is to deny that money changes its character
       it is very important to recognize that the beauty of money
         that the great engraving and designing skills normally
     employed in putting out money   are part of a long tradition
     of making money look stable   of making money look like
     a durable thing
                                     a nickel looks like a nickel forever   it may
     eventually not contribute to buying anything at all   but it still
     looks like a nickel   the dollar looks like a dollar   though
if the dollars appearance were related to its function it would
     have nearly disappeared by now   having started at one size
     it would now be but a shred of itself   but the image of it is
         unchanged
                                     now this image of the constancy of money is very
     much like the image of the constancy of language   it seems
         to me that there is a relationship   between the solidity of
     money and the solidity of the language   which is very
     similar   the language is also a coinage   its a coinage and its
     in circulation   people accept it and people modify it   but
       all the time   people have the illusion that the coinage
     remains the same and that theyre talking the same language
         they have the illusion because the illusion is fostered
       by   a kind of nationalism   a nation you might say is an
     institution organized to stabilize credit   language credit

buying credit   maybe its the same credit   nationhood
is a formal celebration of the objecthood of language and
credit   and what it attempts to do is to give the appearance
of regularization to human transactions throughout the
culture
            now all over the country people are buying and selling
the same or seemingly identical things and services and
notions at wildly varying prices   while almost everyone is
under the illusion that these   transactions are more or less
uniform throughout the culture   because the national system
of coinage and language has provided a way of picturing these
wildly varying transactions that makes them look more or
less uniform   by framing them within the apparently
regular dimensions of our coins or our words   in a way that is
most satisfactory to the people who manipulate them most
efficiently
            now there were people in my family who could
have told me   though they never told me very much   but
they could have told me that this stability was not likely
first of all i came from a family where everybody spoke
several different languages   which makes the situation look
very unstable anyway   they spoke russian and german and
yiddish and french and   so there we were
                                             in my household for
me to listen to a conversation usually meant that i had to
learn one other language   because kids have very great
suspicion that somebodys saying something that theyre not
supposed to hear   the fastest way to get kids to learn another
language is to gossip in another language   and its amazing
how fast theyll pick it up   because they dont want to be
shut out from the gossip   so i went through all this
keeping up with my peoples languages   and it was a lot of
fun   i enjoyed it all   but that could have told me theres
no telling where you might have to go or what language you
might have to speak   that is   as long as you dont have
to go anywhere   and you always stand still   you never have
to talk any other language   because youre always in the
same place and everything stays pretty much the same   the
nickel always stays the nickel   wealth is always wealth
legal tender is the same   all the meanings attributed to
the coinage are the same up and down the system   but

there were
members of my family who distrusted this   they didnt trust
money at all   and there were two passions they developed
      passions for land and passions for objects   you see there is
something in the coinage of the language called   *real*
      estate   you may laugh at the relation between "real" and
"estate"   but real means thingy estate   you know it is
      that estate which is real   and doesnt go away   it doesnt
go away because it is like the earth   the earth stays   the
      money well   whatever happens to the money happens to
the money but
                              there was in this family a remote relative   and
he had come the hard way here   he had come from russia
      after an abortive revolution   in russia in 1905   in which
hed made the mistake of turning a printing press   he had
      turned this printing press which had printed in ukrainian
various calls to arms and human dignity or whatever   in the
name of whatever he had called it   because its not clear to me
what these manifestoes said   it seems to me that when the
      revolutionaries went down to speak to the peasants of the
ukraine   they did not make speeches to them about the rights
the rights of man   they said to them sometimes the tsar is angry
at the landlords for taking away the fruits from the lands of his
      people   weve had enough of these scoundrelly landlords
and what we need is land for the peasants   the peasants who
      understood land very well and had no special ideas about
freedom responded rather well to this   and gathered together
      to help the tsar rid himself of oppressive landlords   and then
found themselves being attacked by the tsars soldiers for
      having helped the tsar rid himself of these worthless landlords
                                                            something like
that was probably in the manifestoes that were being spread
down in the south   because as lenin said on some other
      occasion   "liberty is bread"   *khleb svoboda?*   i dont
      know   it doesnt sound right to me   they seem a little
different but   perhaps there is a relation   and he was
      calling attention to a relation as if it were an equation   and it
was an effective analysis for the time
                                                however it wasnt effective
      for my relation   who was promptly put in prison when
the revolution was crushed with guns and swords and many of the

peasants killed and such of their leaders and assistants as
the tsars forces could find were put in jail   from which this
     relative   with the help of some money from his friends
and relations   was able to escape and disappear through the
latvian corridor   and he had to take his ukrainian russian
german yiddish out through latvia   get into whatever boat
he could buy a passage on and go somewhere   out of the
     tsars reach   which usually meant going somewhere where
there was another relative who had gone before

                                                  so these
     refugees were likely to wind up in the united states or in cuba or
mexico   and this one wound up in argentina   and where
     before this he knew about rubles there he was in argentina
dealing with argentine pesos and speaking no spanish   he
     quickly learned enough spanish to work in a cigar factory
     and there he took his previous skills   which were odd skills
     he was something of an athlete   he was a wrestler greco
roman style   which is a form of wrestling i dont know too
     much about   except that its sufficiently different from
most other kinds of wrestling that i feel i should point out that he
     was a wrestler greco roman style   and he was now rolling
cigars in argentina   while his brother   who had gotten out
of russia through the latvian corridor at nearly the same
time   for some reason through some connection   they
had apparently collaborated in proving that bread was
freedom   this brother had somehow wound up in the united
     states   where he had settled in new york on second avenue
                                        this brother was
     something of an artist   he had a knack for a kind of witty
caricature-like painting and whimsical wood carvings   and this
     brother continued his politicizing for the peasants   he
had come to the united states where there were no peasants
     but there were workers   the distinction between peasants
and workers is fairly considerable for marxist theory   which
     distinguishes between them rather precisely   but in
revolutionary practice whoever is ready to revolt becomes a
     revolutionary force   and philips artist brother was familiar
with the adjustment of theory to practice   so that on second
     avenue he contributed his revolutionary cartoons
appropriately enough to a newspaper called *die freiheit*

freedom   which was concerned with liberating the workers
of the garment district or the furriers trade from the bonds
and thralls of the sweatshops the same way he had previously
contributed them to the cause of land reform   and philips
brother   who was a very witty caricaturist received a certain
amount of recognition and acclaim as a newspaper artist
and he even made a certain amount of money at it
                                                    so he wrote
to philip in argentina   who was meanwhile working in a
cigar factory   where he was acquiring a whole new set of skills
      and understandings   because in latin american cigar
factories they did not have that totally contemptuous relationship
      to the people who worked there   or rather the people
who worked in these factories did not have a totally contemptuous
      relationship to themselves   and to counteract the boredom
of rolling and packing cigars they ordinarily selected one of
the workers who happened to have a particularly attractive
      reading voice to read aloud to them while they worked
      so they would have read to them   cervantes and lope de vega
and calderon and quevedo   and most of what were considered
      the masterpieces of the spanish language   along with
whatever serious modern works fell into their hands and seemed
      appropriate for reading aloud   so that after they had been
there awhile they had heard most of the classical literature of
      spain and argentina in this cigar factory   where philip
      was becoming very literate   in spanish
                                                but not wealthy
      when he received a ticket to the united states   where there
      was the possibility of becoming wealthy   but in english
      which he didnt know
                                    fortunately for him on second avenue
when he arrived there   there were many other people who
      though they didnt speak spanish or even russian   spoke the
lingua franca of most jewish emigres from middle europe
      yiddish   now yiddish is basically a rhineland germanic
language that predates standard german   being a dialect that
was formed in the rhineland in the middle ages by speakers
who appear to have emigrated from romance language speaking
      countries   parts of what we now think of as france and
spain   and this dialect as it spread with its community of

speakers was populated by hebrew words and then slavic and
eventually technical terms from german and whatever else that
allowed it to serve as this common coinage   and philip
spoke this language   as he also spoke russian and polish
and ukrainian   and now spanish as well   but with the
particular idiosyncrasy and inflection of his background and
experience that is typical of a lingua franca   which is a
common coinage that is exchanged far and wide over a vast
terrain by a loosely joined community of talkers who are
accustomed to making exchanges in several coinages besides the
one they may happen to be talking in

which sometimes leads to
differences of opinion about the equivalences of some of
the coins they happen to be exchanging   differences id often
observed among my relatives when they were talking
differences like the one between two relatives   one had been
living in argentina while the other had been living in the
united states for many years   which didnt really impede
their conversation   because they were speaking in yiddish
and not in spanish or english   and they were sitting in the
living room calmly talking till one of them   the american
remembered something he had forgotten to do and asked the
other to wait a moment because he had to go downstairs to attend
to something in his store   only it happened that he said
"store" as if it was a word of yiddish   *ikh muss arunter ins
store* (i have to go down to the store)   the other was
puzzled *vos eysst a "stor"* (what's a store?)   (where you do
business) *vo muh treybt gesheft   ohh ir meynt a bodega* (ohh
you mean a *bodega*)   so that it was clear that in the yiddish
of the argentine you went down to your *bodega* while in the
yiddish of new york you went down to your *store*

and it was
situations like this that should have prepared them all these
relations of mine for shifting currencies   you would assume
it   that they would have been prepared to handle these
currencies somewhat   skeptically   because they so often
had to change them

but these people who were so good at
exchanging languages and currencies didnt learn the whole
lesson   they were so good at learning languages   they

learned them so quickly that they quickly became natives
    became natives with whatever funny accent they may have
  happened to have   because some   though not all of them
spoke each new language with a slightly alien accent that was
  a part of the old system of coinage they had so recently left
    so they had whatever funny accents they had but they were
already feeling like native speakers of english   because it is
  one of the main functions of speaking a language at all   to
    make you feel like a native and to make whatever way you
speak it seem natural and stable   as it is also to make every
    other way of speaking it strange and everyone who speaks
it strangely some sort of foreigner
                and these new natives of
  english   these relatives of mine soon felt very good in english
and at home in it as they spoke it   but they still had some
  distrust of their country's printed currency   to the extent that
they sensed that if they kept on accumulating this currency for
  any length of time its buying power might suddenly diminish
or be extinguished   and to the extent they sensed this they
  looked about for other things they could exchange their money
for that were in some way more valuable   more durable
  more real than money
              and this astute greco roman wrestler
  cigar roller with the classical spanish education   that he had
acquired in the cigar factory   came to new yorks second
avenue and found employment in the fur business   i think
  and managed to make a fair amount of money   in fact
considerably more money than his artist brother   and because
he had reasonably frugal habits and nothing in particular to
  spend this money on he soon acquired a small pile of this
money   and was soon looking about for things that were realer
  than this money to exchange it for   for some way of
realizing this money   making it more real than legal tender
                and he had a
passion for the open air for greenery   for nature and this
  was a passion he shared with many of the people living in
the grey   brick buildings of second avenue   and the artist
and intellectual world he traveled at the fringes of   because
he was not an artist and he didnt seem to be an intellectual
  either   because he was a relatively taciturn man who didnt

speak much to the others about art or politics or spanish literature
even   and was thought to be something of a fool
                                        but he was
a shrewd man and parsimonious   the kind of man dollars
    stick to   or pesos or rubles   and as he saved his money
he observed that these urban artists and intellectuals in their
    grey city had a dream of nature   of things green and fresh
and flowering   and they found their way somehow to this
    nature   up the hudson on the old routes 9w and 17
north past the red apple rest   over the ferry at newburgh or
    through nyack   to a part of nature called sullivan county
    which was a somewhat depleted form of the nature it had
once been   an oak and beech and chestnut forest mingled
with spruce and hemlock   and it had been logged out for the
    lumber and then for tanbark   and had then gone to
farming   with apple orchards and dairy farms   and among
    these failing farms   they had found their way to these
small things called bungalows
                                    bungalow   i once read a poem
    by paul eluard where he said that he would never use the
    word bungalow in a poem   i never thought i would use the
    word bungalow in a poem either but here it is   what they used
to call a bungalow was a flimsy wooden shack where too many
    people camped cheerfully out of a love of nature surrounded
    by a number of other such shacks at the edge of a bit of scrub
forest
            and they founded these bungalow colonies   where
people could commune immediately and directly with nature
    at the edge of this scrub forest   in these little places
with kitchens and bedrooms with screens over the windows
called bungalows   which were fairly simple to build
                                        and since
    he was as skillful with his hands as at acquiring money philip
exchanged some of his money for land on which he soon built
    a number of these bungalows
                                and he sold bungalows
    because he had a grander view than bungalows   and as these
bungalows became more expensive   more valuable in
    exchange   he exchanged these bungalows for land   and
more land   lots of land   not many people wanted this land

because nobody could live there in this wasted beech woods
and evergreen forest   you see it was real estate all right
    the estate was real   there were trees   and there were
frogs   and there were birds in the trees   and there were
streams that ran beside the trees   but nobody could live there
    in this wasted beech and evergreen woods that had been
    logged out   where farming was unprofitable because the
    distances you would have to transport your products to a
reasonable market were too great and the cost uneconomical
    so that only very large dairy farms or chicken farms could
afford to transport their milk or their eggs to a market and come
out ahead   given the relative costs of feed and fuel and milk
    and eggs   so that most of the small farms were gradually
abandoned when the old farmers died and their children had
gone off to the city to live   which is why this was nature
    because nobody could live there   they could only vacation
                    and so philip
    bought acres and acres of this land   and on it he and his
artist brother began to build   and what did they build
    there   they built   a swiss chalet   because thats how
nature should look   nature should surround these beautiful
half timbered rough hewn buildings with great halls
                    and they
built a great halled swiss chalet in which the beam ends were
    carved by the artist brother   and in which the artist colony
of lower new york came to vacation   and this great hall which
    was the hotel dining room was inscribed with liberating
slogans   "freedom through joy"   "pleasure is knowledge"
    "desire the open"   and the like   and besides this on
the walls of the dining room the artist brother painted a series
    of energetic caricatures depicting in a dire way the vices of
refusing this liberation and their hilarious personal consequences
                    and people
came and the place developed a kind of   cultural dominion
    in western sullivan county   concert pianists came there
to play   roving and unemployed violinists of consummate
skills   folk singers   actors from the classical yiddish theater
    and there too came chess players debaters artists and art
lovers and professionals and various socialist workers and
bosses the *intelligentsia*

now this would never have
happened in this way except for marriage   because one
brother was able to build and the other was able to decorate
but nobody was able to manage   that is nobody was able to
deal effectively with money as capital   because while philip
could save   what he mainly knew was that land was real
wood was real   and money   well   he didnt trust it too
much   and the artist brother wasnt interested in money
either   he was interested in a life of art and talk and girls
and food in the midst of nature   which gave the place its
tone of a socialist intellectual nudist colony up there in western
sullivan county

but it happened that the artist brother
in the course of things had an affair with one of the young
women who were attracted to this good life up there   and this
particular young woman was not only an attractive woman but
she was also a very clever young woman and very much attracted
to   the liveliness and beauty of the place   so that this
affair lasted a good deal longer than most of the affairs of the
artist brother   who was something of a one-upman in sexual
matters and could never stay with anyone long once she had
become familiar and no longer an object of possible romantic
intrigue   so that   in a way im not entirely sure about
he finally rejected her like all of the others   but since she
was probably as much attracted to the place as to the man she
never stopped coming

and she turned to the other brother
who was greatly surprised   as you might imagine   no
woman had ever looked upon him with passion or interest
unless he had moved in their direction first   he was not a
conventionally attractive man   though he had a noble head
with a craggy dramatic face and the powerful body of the
athlete he had been   but he was very broad and thick and
short like a chunky guard on a professional football team
though he was maybe a little short for a guard   and what he
looked like most was a small bear   and in spite of his
considerable classical spanish education   and his russian
and german social political and economic education   and his
proven ability to make money he was thought to be dumb
perhaps this
was because he never spoke much about these things   and

when he did he spoke very slowly and with great deliberation
    because he thought while he was speaking and seemed to
    be making a great effort to say no more and no less than he
    meant   so that he often had to slow down   phrases and
    words while he was in the middle of them   which resulted
        in strange distortions of emphasis and pronunciation   that
    people found laughable or exasperating   while they waited
for him to get on with the conversation   so they thought he
    was dumb and he knew that they thought so

                                                    but this young
    woman somehow managed to convey to him   beyond his
    suspicions   natural as they were   that she was interested
    in him and they got married   at which point she lost her
    interest in him   immediately   but she remained interested
in the place   which she helped to build up in a way that
    was beyond their expectations   because she was even more
    clever than she was attractive   and because she was attractive
    she helped attract   a male clientele   and among that
    clientele there was one quite wealthy man   a sweater
        manufacturer   with whom she contracted a long liaison
                                                    and because
she was clever   with his help she managed to borrow money
    which she quickly invested in buildings with rooms and more
    rooms   in which they could put more and more of these
    cultured people who came to vacation in the midst of this
    nature   now these buildings were not swiss chalets or were
    only superficially decorated to look like chalets because this
    young woman had no particular image of how this nature
should look but she had a particularly good image of money
    and how to use it to make much more of it   and unlike the
    brothers she knew how to borrow it and when and she knew
how to use it and when to stop   so that under her management
    the place became much more prosperous and more and more
    of those people came to sit in their casino or dance in it   talk
in their dining halls   and walk in their woods   while
    their children swam in the swimming pool and played on
    the tennis courts and these people all regarded themselves as
    what is called the *intelligentsia*

                                                    people like rosa schiller
    who was a doctor   whod emigrated from austria with her
    husband also a doctor   and with her sister who lived with

a small dog in an overstuffed apartment   overlooking central
park south   and who was now in her sixties and still in her
   own eyes and in the eyes of her 70 year old beaus an international
   beauty   while rosa lived the intellectual life with her
   husband in elizabeth new jersey   where they had adjoining
   offices   and conducted their separate practices but emerged
      into a common central room   a library filled with leather
volumes where they took lunch together and read the agamemnon
to each other in greek   and i had seen this office   which
was in their house fronted by a greenhouse and filled with
rubber plants   and her ancient black and gold instruments
      that might have been owned by breuer or freud   and i could
   imagine her and her long dead husband working all morning
long and then rushing into this central study to read their greek
plays and then hurrying back to treat sore throats or   examine
failing eyes
                     and the place was filled with people of this type
      and this situation went on from year to year   till the
end of the second world war   after the second world war
      a great change took place socially   what exactly it was no
one was clear about   but all of the people who came up
      there were getting older   some of the older ones died and
the younger ones got older and there were fewer and fewer
      new ones to replace the ones that disappeared   because the
   ones who were children there now that they were grown
   never came there   first of all because they didnt speak the
european languages that gave the place a lot of its charm
      and second they had no great interest in spending their time
   with their elders in a place where they had been children
and had had counselors   and where they knew every crack in
      the tennis courts and every leak in the porch roof   and
very few new ones ever heard about this place in sullivan county
   where you could hear lectures on sholem aleichem in the
morning discuss emma goldman or rosa luxembourg at lunch
hear chopin ballades in the evening and dance the alexandrovsky
or the russian two step late into the night   because the
reservoir from which they drew these people was also
   disappearing as second avenue had dispersed to great neck
   and new brunswick and new rochelle   and though this
   happened gradually the number of people coming up

gradually diminished and the place became less and less
profitable
                 at one point it had been very profitable   which is
not to say that it has always been filled   because hotels in
nature were filled only part of the time   but every weekend
it had been filled to overflowing   and about half of the
summer   and the rest of the time there had still been enough
people left to give the sense and provide the income for a
thriving business   and now less and less of the summer was
filled   and filled got to mean something different   because
none of the outer buildings was ever jammed to capacity
anymore and they never had to pitch tents on the lawn to
handle the overflow   and the business which had been very
profitable became less and less profitable
                                             but the buildings
didn't go away   you see   once youve got buildings theyre
    real   youve got real buildings the buildings are real
youve got tennis courts the tennis courts dont go away   grass
grows up in them   you still have to chlorinate the pool
    youve got to repair the roof after each winter and repaint
the trim   and the buildings   they dont go away   but the
people   may not be there anymore   and this continues
for a period of time   and it comes on bad days and eventually
    the struggle to keep the hotel alive just wore them out
                                             and the young
woman   who was now no longer a young woman but still
clever didnt really understand this and had taken to drinking
    she drank champagne all day and all night   and the artist
    brother   feeling depressed because this place had been
his culture center   because he had made almost all of his art
works there and there they were on the walls of this place
    that was dying   this artist brother sickened and died   and
there was a grand funeral for him to which all of the writers
and artists who had once gathered on second avenue came
    and hundreds of people came to this funeral and to a final
    exhibition of his art that was arranged in a gallery to pay
homage to all the years of his work   and he was buried
    so the intellectual center disappeared
                                             and just at this point
philips wife became sick   and some people said it was

because the artist brother had died and she had been conducting
an affair with him all these years and now that he was dead
there was nothing in it for her anymore   and she became
something of an invalid and no longer took any interest
in the place   and it continued to run down   except for
   philips working on the place constantly   keeping up the
buildings repairing them because he believed in the physical
   place   the buildings and the land

                              it seemed everything
he had he threw into the physical plant   he had always made
money and he had made a lot of it from the place   so he
   put great quantities of it back into the place from which he had
gotten it   and in spite of the fact that it kept running
down it was extraordinarily beautiful   in this western corner
of sullivan county right near the delaware river there was this
strange european set of chalet like buildings   to which
fewer and fewer people came

                        though any new ones who came
   there found it   exotic and colorful   as i found it when
i had occasion to work there one summer as a lifeguard
   and you could always find someone who had played chess with
lasker sitting on the porch looking over endings or hear
a russian court dance float down through the spruce trees to the
library where you were playing poker with the concert pianist
   and a few of the waiters

                        now it happened that at about this
   time my wifes mother became the manager of the place
   at the time when it was declining but still beautiful   and at
first it was a job   as it had been when she was a waitress
there in the time of its fading glory while philips brother and
philips wife were still alive   and she had been an assistant
   manager as it continued to fade   and on the death of philips
wife she became the manager   and this job became something
more than a job   it became a passionate struggle to keep
the place alive and restore it to its former dignity and affluence
in the teeth of great changes socially that you couldnt stem
   it was going downhill all the way

                        and philip encouraged her
in this struggle   he encouraged her somewhat financially
   by lending her bits of money to invest in the place and keep

it up   but even more by giving her the impression that he
would finally bequeathe it to her   because she also had a love
      for the place   for the idea of the place as an institution
      as a look   while he had a love for the place as a physical
      tangible thing and he wanted it to be in the hands of someone
who would take care of it and maintain it as that thing that
he had known and loved   so he kept sending out signals to
      her that she would eventually acquire the place if she would
      only take adequate care of it
                              in the meantime there were heirs
      who would normally have inherited the place   in the
      beginning hed had a son who would have gotten it   but the
son died suddenly and mysteriously far away   even while
      philips wife was still alive   and then there was a sister who
      should ordinarily have gotten the place except that she couldnt
keep it up and the place was in debt   in terms of money
there was no value to the property   the place had used it all
      up and was not only not returning money to the people
who had put it in but was now taking more money away from
them   the property had become a kind of pump that was
      working in reverse
                        once   when it had been set in motion
      by the physical energy of its owners or the stored energy
      of their money   it had pumped money out of the hands of
of the people who were its customers into the hands of the
people who were its   owners but now it was pumping money
steadily out of the hands of its owners into the hands of its
      creditors   and the people who ran it had to sustain it with
      more and more money   so that if you got this property
      what you got was a debt   and a mortgage   with a second
mortgage   in a bank   and that meant that this place
      real as it was   swiss chalet in the tall spruce trees   was a
debt owed to two banks in monticello   but none of them
looked at it that way   and in spite of the debt there was
      in the family a great concern over who would get the place
      after philip died
                        and philip was a long   time   living
      and the hotel was a long   time   losing money   each
time assisted to continue the next year   with loans from
philip   who always found a bit more money to put back into

it   and always   just about enough to keep it alive as a
place   then   philip died
                                        when philip died various people
who knew him   and were related to him or his relatives
were invited to the funeral   and philip was about to be buried
next to his wife bessie   these things are always done in
remote parts of long island   they are always buried in some
green place out in nature   where they have real estate
    and these places are way out there on the island   and they
drove all the way out to this place   after a moderately
mournful funeral   moderate because he was an old man and
a cantankerous figure and not everybody loved him
                                        and they all
got out there   his sister and his wife's brothers and the
small crowd of close and not so close relatives and a few friends
    and they arrived at the place where philip was to be laid
in the grave next to bessie   and bessies grave was
evacuated   there was no bessie
                                cries went up from various
relatives "theyve dug up bessie!"   "whats happened to bessie?"
    in the course of the burial no one paid any attention to
philip   because everyone was concerned with the missing
bessie   bessie was gone   gone bessie but the monument
over the tomb   "here rests   the loyal husband the loyal
wife   true in death as they were in life"   and no bessie
only philip
                        for weeks this scandal was a great mystery   so
great a mystery that most of the relatives and acquaintances
paid little attention to philips will   it went relatively
unnoticed that he had bequeathed the worthless hotel to his
sister who was too old to run it   and trivial amounts of
money to various predictable relatives   while everyone was
astonished that nothing was said in it of the whereabouts
of bessie
                        some people had theories   they said "well she
didn't sleep with him while he was alive   he didnt want her
to sleep with him when he was dead"   but nobody could
find out   they went to the cemetery people   the cemetery
people checked their records and found that in fact   philip
had delegated someone to come and dig up bessie   but what

had philip done with bessie   bessies relatives wanted to find
     out where bessie had been sent   they searched and searched
                                                            something like
a year later when philips sister was moving to a new apartment
     she turned up by accident   in a box of philips papers
     which nobody had taken the trouble to look through   he was
     not an especially literate man except in spanish   which they
didnt know   she turned up a railway express ticket   and
they looked at this railway express ticket and it had a number
     on it   and they went and tracked it down   and the express
people looked through their records   and they found   that
there had been some sort of large parcel shipped to someone
on the west coast   someone in california   by railway
     express   and that was all they knew
                                        with a great deal of
     trouble the railway express people were persuaded to check
     it out   and after a while they found out that the parcel
had in fact been received by the express people on the west
     coast   but no one had come to call for it and theyd had
     no name of anyone to whom to return it if it was not received
                                        after a lot of
trouble and time they found bessies coffin   in a warehouse
     in fresno   and they restored it to the real estate that philip
had been trying to protect from her all of this time

                              (*tuning,* 1984)

Amiri Baraka [1934]

A CONTRACT.   (for the destruction and
                  rebuilding of Paterson

Flesh, and cars, tar, dug holes beneath stone
a rude hierarchy of money, band saws cross out
music, feeling. Even speech, corrodes.
                     I came here
from where I sat boiling in my veins, cold fear
at the death of men, the death of learning, in
cold fear, at my own. Romantic vests of same death
blank at the corner, blank when they raise their fingers

Criss the hearts, in dark flesh staggered so marvelous
are thier lies. So complete, their mastery, of these
stupid niggers. Loud spics kill each other, and will not

make the simple trip to Tiffany's. Will not smash their stainless
heads, against the simpler effrontery of so callous a code as gain.

You are no brothers, dirty woogies, drying under dried rinds, in
    massa's
droopy tuxedos. Cab Calloways of the soul, at the soul's
    juncture, a
music, they think will save them from our eyes. (In back of the
    terminal

where the circus will not go. At the backs of crowds, stooped
    and vulgur
breathing hate syllables, unintelligible rapes of all that linger in
our new world. Killed in white fedora hats, they stand so mute
    at what
whiter slaves did to my fathers. They muster silence. They pray
    at the
steps of abstract prisons, to be kings, when all is silence, when
    all
is stone. When even the stupid fruit of their loins is gold, or
    something
else they cannot eat

                                   (*The Dead Lecturer*, 1964)

917

THE PAUSE OF JOE

$$\left[\begin{array}{l} \text{"Killer Joe"} \\ \text{—THE JAZZTER} \end{array}\right]$$

Philly Joe Jones
Joesph Jones
of Philly

Arc of bones
on board
in the sea's darkness
being bones
of the being beaten

of the Joes
the eyes
of the sleekest
thou seekest our injury
Being
Us
& the bones beat
beat out

as the drums are
a form of space

its life containing
Whatever must exist
trace
flight
flame
these years of times lasso
the cross eyed deity
of laughter
beat bones

tell the blood
the Blood's
story

His
story

The Beat of Joe
   I eye
the Kansas city 4 man
came on Winged Feet
   Thats yr Papa
    Eye Eye
   A Spanish guy
   The story teller

Jo Jo

Story telling bones
Blood
   Stones
   Death
   & Life
   Tones

         Tell the Story Joe
         Eye Story
         Yo Man
         Jo Man
As yr beaten lives and grows
the grapevine of the world serpent
shakes, Tell the Story Joe

We're no grimace
   in this menace
   as if minutes

   this telling
   blow
   Joe

For darkness, under sea lingo
     tengo
     mucho
   story we
   no can say

   Let bones beat it
   take the air
   above the trees
   a herd of me's

Tell the Story
Joe
Philly Dilly
Bone speech
                Sleek
of the Dead Seek
Bones Speak

Griot
Story Teller
From Philadelphia
Which Du Bois Analyzed

Found The Negroes
Wise
& Thriving On A Riff
Thriving beneath the Veil
This Century's Jail
Ye Slave Folk
& Masters
Ye Magic Cans
of the Streets
& thrilling ghettos
Where the Slums
beat like a boom a doom
Cage
for the Africans
to beat out
their age
to let out their
Rage
Be a Bone
& Speak, Joe
You & He from Kansas
City
The Four-Man
& Bats' Kin He mimics
to teach us
In Omen Land
The Count
Processed In Funk
Some Monkish Draculaics
For the visiting Klan, The Bone

Beats
Hides
Speak
This Political Tongue
Speech of Marches
The Black
Fire Men
Their Sirens Tell of Escapes
Joe Griot dusts his iron tales
the metal sings industrial Blues
Machine Funk.

You wd *have* to *be* hip
to *be w/* Miles
So Bad
Was He
This King of MaMa Rappers
Black Sweet Swift
reflections of night
in his shining hair
I was there
The Music in his stare
of Philly-ness
& Joe-ness
& for Eloise even
Joseph-ness
The Lone Star
above the
rhythm House.
We said
Miles & Trane
& Philly
& Them
(that's Paul & Red
& Blue Cannon Ball
Fusing The Master Classic
Bop-Cool
& Harder Bopper
School
The State of the Art
For those who come to play
The Heart's
Message

For Bravery
For Philadelphia Jokes
For such gladness
    as only a friend
    can give
        or know
        or be
Free as his Shakerei
        brushes
    Mississippi Sound

Joseph The Father
Max The Son
Joseph The Holy
        Philadelphia
        Ghost
& Klook be they
Bop
As our heart
locked in sun

Tell the history

Like Joe & I
& Archie
one night

What Bad Tadd said
    Philly JJ

    The Bones Song
    Dameronia
So we knew Joe to speak
        Yo can seek
        We the see
        Bop the Be

    Free Joe
His style as form's
        essence
        yet the rumble

        the reach
        beneath black seas

to rail roads of ebony
skeletons

on the way to Slavery
            land
Us Congos
held by   a
Square

   Joe
was there

Mr. Jones
      Mr. Joseph Rudolf Jones
      from Philadelphia
So bad a city
took his name
& so its fame
despite those evil servants

of 666
who have
come
to
No Goode!

He breathed our history as
his walking beat

Bones & Hide
  Shimmering
    metal
      strut.

Dixie Peach
      2/4
      Napoleon
We copped
    yr band
    for coming

      against our will
      Toussaint

& Christophe
& Sidney Bechet
copped
took it wherever other
bone sings
    sun
        hide
            beats
   the niggers
   of the orchestra   sd Max

   quite
   naturally
         Yo, man
             Joe,
                 can
You wd have to be hip to
    hang out
    w/ Miles
    & Trane
   To have a city
   use yr
   name

To get the bones
to beat its name

Brothers
Do Love
& Negroes be here
  too

& Crazy Benjamin
out there
    messin
    w/that
    electricity
    "Boy, you better
    come up
    out the rain
    w/ that
    key."

Try See, Yo
   Jo
about here
Africa
The South
New Orleans
   Blue
Spanish Tinge
City Rock
Miles Stones
Funky Blues

On a Misty Night, Lady Bird
     The Bones
     Speak
     of Rag & Swing
       & Boogie

       of March
       & Colored Ghosts

      Ashé Ashé
      Guanguanco
      Signifying Elegba
      God of Laughter & *Jasm*

Beater of Bones & Hides
Singer w/ Golden Symbols
     Bop Be
     Be
     Thy Name
Domesticater of Animals
Master of the Fields & Flowering Seeds
Builder of Houses in One Place
Keeper of the Herds

Speaker of a thousand tongues
     some as swift
     as the wind
  City Man
Collector of Art
     & culture
       Creator of Museums
        & Libraries

Civilizer
of the Dark

Introducer
of the *Human
Being*

Poet of Industrial Design
Machine Singer

Language Maker
  Song & Dance
    Man

                    Yo
                there is no
                    Urban
                    No post-desert
                    Science
                w/o yr tom toms
                & shades
                    Yo, Jo
                    I & I

& The Four-Man now also gone

So we who remain
        who know the game
        who have seen slavery
        give way to the Gestapo

        & see the slow worm
        of fascism
        pop out
        Reagan headed

        from a cancerous
        nose

Those of us who do
        knows
        That Duke & Count
        & John Before
        & Pres & Louie
        & then Thelonius

& before two suns
Both the Father
& the Ghost

How much strength
is our history

How much Beauty
& Dancing
How much struggle
is our memory

Our Dream of
Democracy

Bone Man
Beat Darkness
into Singing
Sun

into Colored
Rhythms

Against the
Boers
& No Goodes

A hipper time than
Pendulums

much clearer
than Clarence

Let it Be Known Now that you
Carriers of the
Torch
of the Created
Advancing
Mind

That throughout this world
Huge Changes Ready
to go
Down

From the top
Let the baton of rhythms
      of riddims
      of Rap
      Reggae
of the Sorrow Songs

The hide & rock
      roll & beat
            shimmer of street

            tough growling
            shaded
            Orisha of
      Bop Bee

They say in prayer to the living
      now & forever
      Our Jasm

      Creators
            in life
      of our hearts
            essence

                              (now
            It's on you   it's on
            they say: you)

All our history

      Slavery &
      Ghosts
Maniac Kings
Who sold us in chains

For Duke & Monk
      & John & Thelonius
      & Yo, double Joe

      The Father
      & the Wholly Philadelphia
            Ghost

They're Hear-ing
is a hum of old grandmothers
a hum of deacons
a hum of Lindy Hopping Rappers
of Cake Walkers
Trappers, Yo, Jo
I Know
You had to go
This slow poison world
Cdn't handle you

Yet your hear-ing
   is your bone
      beat
     hide under
     hand &
     stick

   the riddim say
   It's On You

   rookieeeeeeeeeeeee

Do Bana Coba   Beneme Beneme
Do Bana Coba

I heard my man the other day
   Joe Say

Beating the telling
   Bones
      Yo, Rookie
      Yng blood
      Bigging People   Nation to Be
     of a Vision   Rising to We
     a riddim   Free Nation
     a desire   To See
     a fire
   of human science
     love a beat
     a heat

   says:
     Its on you

on you now
on you

This Music
of our world's
Description

Hymn For The As We wd
Say Him
Self

One of
The Great
MaMa Lamas

The Man
So Hip
A City
Took
His
Name!!

Philadelphia Joe Jones 7/19/23 – 8/30/85

(*Sulfur* magazine, 1988)

from WHY'S/WISE

WISE 3   [*Hipnosis*]
            [Grachan Moncur III]

Son singin
fount some
words/Son
singin
in that other
language
talkin bout "bay
bee, why you
leave me
here," talking bout
"up unner de sun
cotton in my hand." Son
singing, think he bad
cause he
can speak
they language, talkin bout
"dark was the night
the ocean deep
white eyes cut through me
made me weep."
Son singin
fount some words. Think
he bad. Speak
they
language.

'sawright
I say
'sawright
wit me
look like
yeh, we gon be here
a taste

(*The LeRoi Jones/Amiri Baraka Reader*, 1991)

ALBA

I've talked (remember
him)
  before
  of twisting
I'm not sure the twisting
was not waves upon
the shore
  twisting

  to be always
  to be always
  what came after
  is there too

  So I keep us clear
  & with us connected
  as our breath
  to we
    twisted its
  transporation
    twisted

  a bebop
  song
  twisted
  the way the sun the
    moon the
    star is

  Always being seen
  and so am I
  like the waves

  upon the
  shore

  twisted

  good morning
  old
    eye   opener.

(*Ribot* magazine, 1993)

Joan Retallack [1941]

THE SECRET LIFE OF GILBERT BOND

first comes the logic of substitution
then the high school class reunion
kinship in Bali
buildings tombs and costumes
complete selection perfecto vignettes

on the British scene
rural clergy in horse green chairs
fondly dubbed the Latin farmer
sky is bland and intrusive
trees are oddly vacant
lawn belabors one's stare

O Hodge the cat
night-gown madness
the ubiquitous pelvic brim
yes the Jewish element in Literature
viral pneumonia
marginalia
moice chorsels of peutered noodles
Blaise Pascal sleeves:
       clarity
       figs
       and moral force

(Circumstantial Evidence, 1985)

933

BIOGRAPHIA LITERARIA

Few men, I will be bold to say…
—COLERIDGE

Owens
how he
would deliberately
vary
the quarter-mile route
he—
the cellular rain
carrying lemons to the Hebrides
love of gingerbread
the war
his brisket hounds
had Owens known
what?
was Owens the one who

his knots
elegant
practical
the return
how she smiled
the sun sets and I
with it like
butterscotch pudding
he said
on one occasion
the bright orange
the intense blue
he saw
the epigrammatic tree
his favorite dish
Brunswick Stew

(*Circumstantial Evidence*, 1985)

WOMAN DRAGGED BY WELSH CORGIS

the new laugh

now that she's—

poor Emma

so fat

in vain

green again

(I) call

cold cliffs

(I) call

endless streams

(she) passes

by

chance

thirty years

trying to befriend

in spectator shoes

(Circumstantial Evidence, 1985)

WESTERN CIV, 4 & 5

4.

superhighway elegy in a pink convertible / It was 1956 /
Sexy Propertius & his gal Cynth / Living Green Exotica /
Quaker Oats / First Chinese Dictionary (40,000 characters)
circa 1450 BC / Comes moon 1st fat, then skinny / seasons
skinny fat / as the world turns I blow my nose / uniting
commonplace and cosmic // Cosmi-comics: a woman in a tattersall
shirt is breaking & entering / "Poetry as breaking and
entering," he tossed over his left shoulder as he left /
over / Where were you all this time, damn you? // Species
vanishing. Mailings out to that effect: The Plymouth
Gentian, The Roseate Tern, The Marbled Salamander, The
Golden Club / I like the sound of the word *piss*, she said,
though I was born in Vienna / on a quiet day you could hear
the sound of an Amish buggy or a cow pissing a mile &
a half away / But, we're talking China 1450 BC we're talking
all those characters & the Dining Philosophers' Problem:
. . . .

Breakdance Lecture cont'd: I remember him to have said
"I" immediately. It was the first thing he said. This is
no doubt oversimplification. One of those highways that's
replaced a neighborhood. (to be cont'd)
. . . .

5 philosophers seated at a round table have only 5
chopsticks between them They must establish a pattern
of eating and philosophizing that allows 2 philosophers
to eat at any given time T with one chopstick remaining
unused where all 5 philosophers will have had equal
time T-1 to eat & philosophize by the time T-2 all the
food is gone. They are eating steamed dumplings, Hunan
chicken, ginger & scallion whole yellowtail, Szechuan
stringbean with rice / 1300 BC properties of Pythagorean
triangle known in China (Hypatia—wife of Pythagoras
credited posthumously) cold sesame noodles, hot & sour soup
. . . .

Breakdance Lecture cont'd: It used to make me sick when
my neighbors didn't like me. I'd have nightmares about it.
Even when I didn't like them. Since there was so much I
didn't know about myself, there was always the possibility
they were right. There, "I" have said it. (to be cont'd)
. . . .

Labor strike in Thebes / sale of beer regulated in Egypt /
It will take the invention of the computer to invent &
solve the Dining Philosopher's Problem / WHAMMO POW!
Oxo Reaction / very short exposure could cause injury or
death / this is not a life-saving device / one squeeze
dispenses one drop / HOW TO: 1) improve your vocabulary
2) write with style 3) enjoy the classics 4) use a library
5) enjoy poetry 6) spell / FLIPSIDE: more musical moments
or the Chinatown blues

5.

COMING SOON: money – sex – clothes – food – cars –
dreams – women – men – watching tv – fame – good &
bad habits – war – new flavors – record breaking sales,
etc. / 1000 BC rationalism on the rise in China / has it all
come to this / or that? / SOON / water filled cubes measure
time / memories – anecdotes – stories – tales – lies
(this fiction I have _____ed against my ruin)
wanting, needing / travelogs & slide shows / places you've
never been / 200 years of chaos–1000–800 BC / Philistines
attack Palestine / Is distinction between wanting /
& / needing / helpful / here / ? / 900 BC Chinese
mathbook includes: proportion, planimetry, arithmetic,
rule of three, root multiplication, equations with
unknown quantities, theory of motion, geometry / places
you'll never go / class antagonism in Greek countryside,
800–600 BC / in geography class they learned
Yugoslavia is the world's leading manufacturer of
safety pins the music of the "folk" is raucous & dis-
turbing the people are warm & friendly & treat
foreigners with gratitude. / *O Mensch bewein dein Sunde
gross* (just call me Billie Blue) when small she had
noticed scissors and trousers analogous / SOON improvements
· ·
Breakdance Lecture cont'd: The trouble is I don't
know how to get rid of it—the "I"—what to do instead.
"We" seems pretentious. "She" seems schizophrenic.
(the end)
· ·
in transportation people wished to go many places & to
return / valences vectors tendencies desires the
future tense / don't talk like the Bronx you'll get out

of the Bronx / sole purpose of the brain is to cool the
blood (Aristotle circa 400 BC) // She thought it was
better to be notorious than anonymous and thought often
of killing her husband knowing she could get the elusive
book contract from a jail cell. She, of course, had other
reasons for wanting to kill her husband. // Hi, Gloria! /
Syrian soldier depicted with Egyptian wife & son circa
1300 BC / 1000 BC Song of Songs begun / not that I don't
like fast food I like fast food / library books overdue /
Odyssey shown to justify class dominance by military
landowners: viz, *Enough of your eloquence, you drivelling
fool*, Odysseus shouts, *How dare you stand up to the king?* /
children are not innocent and here's the proof: if they were,
they wouldn't love purple, an evil color / miles-o-smiles
& margarine / Pinto Indians building loam covered huts,
Sierra Nevada 900 BC / the sea providing tunny, anchovy &
sardine / 900 BC mass migrations of Germanic peoples //
Is that right, Mildred, she said, eyes squinched, raising
cigarette in air. // Listen for nasal release of stop
consonant in *eaten   sudden   mitten* / must
learn to be cool-headed, convivial, convincing, cosmic,
courageous (to mention on the Cs) / 1000–900 BC wigs popular
among aristocrats in Assyria and Egypt / Israelis adopt
caftan / poppies growing in Egypt / SOON Rosenbergs electrocuted
McCarthy show goes on tv / when it rains we're all equal I
remember her saying that / you expected consistency?

(*Aerial* magazine, 1988)

NOT A CAGE

for John Cage

[Note: This poem is composed from beginnings and endings
of books I was discarding in the Fall of 1990.]

Scientific inquiry, seen in a very broad perspective may

see Foot 1957, also Wetermarck 1906, Ch. XIII

To man [sic] the world is twofold, in accordance with

that witness is now or in the future

It wasn't until the waitress brought her Benedictine and she

Villandry, "Les Douves" par Azay-le-Rideau

mine. *Yours,* CYNTHIA.

Not a building, this earth, not a cage,

The artist: disciple, abundant, multiple, restless

a forgery: *Opus Ioannes Bellini*

We named you   I thought the earth

is possible   I could not tell

to make live and conscious history in common

and wake   you find yourself among

*

and wake up deep in the fruit

Did you get the money we sent?

I smell fire

AT FULL VOLUME. STAGE DARK.]

1. Russia, 1927

God, say your prayers.

You were begotten in a vague war

sidelong into your brain.

In *Letter Three & Four* (as earlier) the narrator is

North Dakota—Portugal—Moorhead, Minnesota

The lights go down, the curtain opens: the first thing we

gun, Veronica wrote, the end.

'Wittgenstein—'

Tomorrow she would be in America.

                         *

Over forty years ago

a tense, cunningly moving tale by the Hunga-

Then he moved on and I went close behind.

Interviewers: What drew a woman from Ohio

to study in Tübingen? American Readers

With this issue former subscribers to Marxist Perspectives

The shadow of the coup continues to hover over Spain

In the ordinary way of summer

girls were still singing

like a saguaro cactus from which any desert wayfarer can draw

as is Mr. Fox, but in literature

Twenty-five years have gone by

Ya se dijeron las cosas mas oscuras

The most obscure things have already been said

(*Aerial* magazine, 1991)

JAPANESE PRESENTATION I & II

Izubuchi says Pound's poems
are inadvertent Rengas

goat-foot   choros   the

not a ray
not a
spare disc
pale foot
this is the first time

(direct quotation of   passage)

when the fisherman hesitates

he might

be deceived
doubt is immortal

sunlight   compared with

not complete sense
no deceit in heaven
which enables the wearer
point of contact
act of forgiveness

*

again
after
an attempt
consolation
divine comedy
neither feather nor flame
which is actually
a holy mountain in Buddhism
tree connects heaven & earth
oak   olive   katura

(to summarize Pound's whole
life)

inspite of
hear the wind speak
a pretty look in her eyes
at the mercy of the wind blow
ing

post-humous

pine   spruce
eternal voice
a corona of angels
a drama in which:

*

/he/ suddenly recalled Buddhist rule   /to/
    abstain from drinking

/he/ declines the drink from   /the/
    wedding cup

/to/ join the two traditions   /to/get/her/

Dante met Beatrice
(bitter memory discarded)
though his body remained on the earth
& wept in the rain

        (*O-blēk* magazine, 1989)

HERE'S LOOKING AT YOU FRANCIS BACON

for Lynne Dreyer

> on the metro the man across
> the aisle began all his sen
> tences with "I prophesy"...

> the Missouri Fox Trotter is a 3
> gaited horse Mars was 36.5 mill
> ion miles from earth on Sept. 2
> 1, 1988 inside the house is a m
> an inside the man is a brain in
> side the brain a box inside the
> box a woman inside the woman a
> brain inside the brain a house
> inside the house a man inside t
> he man a brain inside the brain
> a bet on a Missouri Fox Trotter
> named Mars Prophesy............

there are many jokes about Descartes in
side the box inside the brain inside th
e house let's reexamine a stereotype: w
hat do we think of the man who starts e
very sentence with "I prophesy"? are w
e sad because the phrase detached itsel
f and floated away? no need to say some
thing about the sky . . . .

some of it comes back——those moments clear and distinct a dis
course on method in the touch-me-not assassin beetle woods ca
rapace skewered prey recumbent vine-snake woods ant lion aphi
ds milked wood aphid herding ants red winged black bird on ed
ge of wood marsh woods snorting groundhog the woman the man t
he box the death of D's daughter his treatise on rainbows ins
ide the box the doubt inside the sorrow the retreat into Lati
n inside *lumen naturalis* present and manifest inside the atte
ntive mind attend to the inside manifest and present.........

inside the box Missouri Fox Trot
past Descartes to Ovid so one or
two women can turn into trees...

now we think
each movement
of the body i
s part of a s
entence put t
he "I" in the
sentence in t
he box . . . .

........fox trotting across the page
into the experiment in the woods the
house the woman the man the box the
brain the joke with "therefore I am"

(*6ix* magazine, 1992)

John Taggart [1942]

BODY AND SOUL: POEM FOR TWO READERS

take   eat   take   glowing coal   eat

take   coal in mouth   painful

take   pain   pain's privation

              mouth deprived

take   eat   suffer   lack of

        suffer   lack of fire   coal doesn't

take   fire   take   eat   suffer.

Note: each reader chooses either a left or right page and reads only those pages. The reading goes from left to right. What is most leftward on a given line is to be read first. With the exception of the first line on p. 947, which is the proper beginning of the poem, the lines of both left and right pages are parallel and, when read together, compose one single line. Not all spaces are to be spoken in. Also, the sections on pp. 950 – 951 are to be read separately. Co-ordination in reading together may require some practice.

In the face is hidden the original outbreak of all goodness

   no   way   look   into   face completely fire

  so devout so delicate angel eyes

  completely fire   completely completely

smiles from bright eyes   bright eyes in vain

   in   vain   life's dreary   for angel eyes

cross heart   hope   hope to die

   no way no eyes look into   love   that   burns

Take   eat   take   eat take   take

take   eat   glowing coal   one for all

take   coal in mouth

            pain   privation

        naturally   mouth's deprived   mouth's corroded

take   eat   suffer   deprived of

        suffer   "it takes a little time"

take   be soiled with fire

the   face   hide   outbreak   of all goodness

no   way into   face   completely

so   so   angel eyes   no eyes

no way eyes look into   complete   fire

smiles   bright   no

in   vain   no son through tears   none

crossed heart   hope

no eyes   look into love that burns.

heart   lonely,

you   you,   only.

Why haven't you seen it?

all for you

spend   days in longing

you

all

    believe

   conceive

            the ending

             chance to prove,

  life

You   yours

   surrender

Take heart   take   take   take

                    you   for all

        you   coal in mouth

        all   pain   privation

        days   deprived   corroded

take   eat   deprived of

        suffer   "it takes a little time"

take all   fire

        face   hide   all goodness

    no   conceiving   face   completely

         so angel

 no way   look into   complete   end fire

smiles'   bright chance

      vain   no son through tears   none

cross out   hope   hope to die

   I surrender dear to love that burns.

                        (*Loop*, 1991)

NEVER TOO LATE

desan epistamenos, epaoide d'aima kelainon
—*Odyssey* XIX, 457

I

One word two vowels one active situation at a time
desan is one word one situation one with two enactors
one situation of tying of binding of tying down
the meaning in vowels enacted meaning in the word meaning

in a long e in eta down in the fair and opened mouth
eta sex queen's vowel fair open mouth the bait
appearance of tits and ass tits and ass appear monstrous
fair mouth sings tea for two you for me ah you for me

in short a in alpha the lowest pitched even rough
alpha = moon = white light = white night-gown
never too late to reread the beautiful mythology of Greece
night-gown twists and twists around you in your sleep

not what was expected not the anticipated enactment
the enactment not anticipated in the situation
combed white heads of the enactors become deathless heads
deathless the dream women who are to be tied down.

2

One word three new vowels another active situation
epistamenos is one word one situation with three enactors
one situation of knowing how to tie dreams down
the meaning in vowels not anticipated in the situation

in short e in epsilon vowel of a new kind of monster
evolution of glitter-eyes the boy-god the thief
new monster sold wisdom for a coat of flames
will trade coat act of the faith that comes with the coat

in short i in iota lips made thin made unclarifying
unclear postcard of sunset skies retouched tinged

iota vowel of the great principle of light vowel of the gilder
would sunlight god decree winter in America wouldn't he

in long o in omega crow vowel crow's caw has an edge
old style monster crow with hooked knife that's crow's bill
supposedly can be imprisoned in winter put him in prison
imprison him fetter him or get ready for combat.

3

One word dipthong two articulations in one syllable
two in one open alpha then glide in director of iota
there's one active situation under all the others
one situation undercuts others the one situation of dying

aima is one word one situation with me the enactor
do I forget one other word one word before aima
epaoide situation of the new functional charm me the enactor
me to enact the new charm that cuts that opens the wound

bleed is the cry *let it bleed let it bleed's* my cry
the resident power the life the life in common the house
let it let it bleed let it bleed over you all over me
if you need someone to *bleed* on *bleed* all over me

this is the new charm that cuts and opens the wound
new charm cuts new function not the old crow
we've been wounded by phantoms in a wide landscape of snow
cut and open the wound bleed on bleed on the snow.

4

One word vowel dipthong new vowel active situation
kelainon is one word one situation with ourselves enactors
one situation of black of black blood on snow
the meaning in the vowel enacts the meaning in the word

in short o the omicron the vowel of hurt personified
companions of hurt personification of curses
they lead the phantoms back phantoms on the blood-soul
combed white deathless heads new and old monsters

force and motion hunted down in a landscape of snow
this is in black and white this is a motion study
motion almost the same motion almost no motion
the same motion we're the raw heads we're the bloody bones

we are the raw heads connected to the bloody bones
ourselves the enactors of the last word the last situation
not what was expected abrupt night fall on snow
in this night we wander through snow toward the desert.

(*Loop*, 1991)

PEN VINE AND SCROLL

The intent ear hears the silence hears silence and then the pen
in the silence there are bird calls there is a far away hum
a train could be coming from far away within the silence
the pen scratches and claws making a lonely sound each morning
each morning the silence the bird calls and what could be a train.

Each letter each curve within each letter a vine luxuriant vine
a vine that is made to weave over and under other vines
woven over and under other vines until the letters disappear
the letters are made to disappear in a dark garden of vines
behind the walls of the garden nailed feet and hands peek out.

Scholars are called in to unroll to read and explain the scroll
their eyes blink and shut at the unrolling of the scroll
at the brilliance of the scroll brilliance of marble walls
the scholars are blinded by a brilliance of dark illumination
they are trying to read polished stone or a page that goes blank.

(*Loop*, 1991)

MONK

I

A-bide   a-   a-

bide

    fast falls

     the   tide

     fast

    the darkness deepens

2

     with   abide

     with

When others   fail

         fail

         fail

   comforts flee

  fail   flee

3

abide with me

abide with me

me   me

(*Loop*, 1991)

SAINTE-CHAPELLE

in memory of Olivier Messiaen

Specifically the rose window specifically the center
center of the rose left to right bottom to top
left to right the receiver kneeling with tightly closed eyes
kneeling before orange claws of the sender

candlestick elaborate nail there are several nails
hand of the sender reaches toward a nail
sitting in black and purple robes sitting on a rainbow
sender on green rainbow reaching toward a nail

four stars pale yellow stars eruptions out of the blue
eruptions out of the blue that will not heal
sender wears a knot of deeper yellow
receiver prays to untie the knot prays and suffers

on each side of the sender a nail ever ready nail
between the nails a two-edged sword
sender holds a two-edged sword in his mouth
sword in his mouth his mouth a black "x" stretching wide.

(*Sulfur* magazine, 1992)

Nicole Brossard [1943]

from PICTURE THEORY

THE ORDINARY

I exercize my faculty of synthesis here because again
I must proceed with precision among sounds, bodies
and institutions.

*

IN THE BAR of the Hilton, the dancer from the Caribbean says: you will undoubtedly remember Curaçao because of a detail (Anna, whom I had met by chance a few hours earlier, had warned me that one reality did not necessarily overlap another but air stewardess between Venezuela and Aruba left her to desire). So each sentence or in the casino (what happened next made a woman say: it is late) when eyes drawn I went from table to table. Only the women were placing bets.

From instinct and from memory, I try to reconstruct nothing. From memory, I broach a subject. And that cannot be from childhood. Only from ecstasy, from a fall, from words. Or from the body differently. Emergency cell like body at its ultimate, without its knowledge, the tongue will tell it.

When Florence Dérive entered the Hôtel de l'Institut, Montréal, 1980 on rue Saint-Denis. Snatches of sentences inside. At the registration desk. It was night. Since Finnegans Wake. It was night. Itinerant, Florence Dérive such a woman. Brain–memory. The night, numbers and letters.

Florence Dérive sometimes repeats a certain number of gestures that continue to exist as writing and each time she dis/places ardour and meaning. Now, Florence Dérive is recasting her text in a bar at the corner of Seventeenth Avenue and Forty-Second Street. She momentarily abandons herself to the necessity of being what is called, among the inks, a character. Her lecture is ready. Tomorrow, Montreal.

To run over/text, I feel its effects. In order to describe precisely a singular reality born in complete fiction. *The White Scene* of May 16. It is only in the waters of Curaçao that the idea makes its way through me. With words, the same ones, here, I'll get ahead since writing is continuous with an identical knowledge, an instinct for dignity among what the styles think, fauve.

Florence Dérive, of mother born and an ultra-modern New York style, often spent her holidays at the seaside, in the house of her anarchist sister, sole heir of her maternal grandmother. House viewed again and again in a vertical shot by most of the surveillance helicopters which made the rounds above houses that might be sheltering bandaged men during the Vietnam war. Power. To be able to change America.

Florence Dérive, born of an ultra-communist, Austrian mother, wrote there are many women around us who think no differently. The sea, of course, has not many secrets. Then it was the shadow of a doubt so many words project: what form do they take?

John, the son of the Austrian New Yorker had married the daughter of a protestant minister. Raised in Quebec, Judith Pamela had grown up near the border. *omme personnage*, ( )*an/s character, John had no notion of the novel*. Still, with his dollars, a director and unionized female proof-readers he built a lovely publishing house. For his wife—a roman(ce).

Oriana, an old friend of the family, often visited one or the other, brother, mother, mother or sister. She would tell Florence stories about the cinema, windows, cries, fascism, the accent put on the conformist attitude.

Oriana, John's (ac)complice watched to make sure he was a subversive son on the horizon of New York streets. The project was a difficult one to carry out but Oriana had chosen to compete with the Austrian, Jewish, communist mother in the field of identities. And John would become one day what he was, that is today, a manly son.

The hotels grow old like the certain models of a glorious architecture caught between the multinationals and dirt accumulated on the Greek columns in the lounge. There's intoxication and reasoning though as tourists. Broadway/porn/Gestalt. Florence was explaining to Oriana but a Corvette **sound traffic**, that love between anarchists, between women especially. A woman in the street turned around on the spot.

Intention and fervour do not make a text nor a woman of me. It makes the singular body which sometimes borrows correspondence from desire move in double(d) forms. Coincidence. Appearance. Each time, Florence Dérive says in the bars as in letters: "womanal)/.

th'/I force familiar is desire so similar. I say <u>after the text</u> and the remark rises from the body of woman into a thinking woman. Dreaming is an accessory to writ(h)ing. An anecdotal incident that swallows the grand passions. That evening, I'm most chilly in the Caribbean. Without thinking about it, I look at the sea, Dutch dolls. In broad sunlight.

Oh! the first chapter. Is it to say: sister brigand's skin and proud looking. The patriarchy shall not take place, should I state it? At the Velvet Snack Bar, Oriana, the (ac)complice, says to Florence as if it were still significant. "You know, John worked a long time and cried a lot over his already discussed novel."

The telephone, I get a line quite quickly.

Boulevard Saint-Germain, the Madison, waiter, elevator. Room: Flaubert, exactly at the place where it says that Paris is deserted because it is so hot—holidays at the seaside, in the house of the anarchist sister. Outside, the bars are rejuvenated as quickly as the books in bookstores. It was as if humanity outside, they would often sit in a café, humanity, watching her full of descriptions in their eyes.

I got up very early thinking it is best not to die doubled like a hair on the pillow. A man's voice somewhere in the hotel was reciting a poem in a foreign language. My first impression was that he was having a discussion. I ate my breakfast. Then from one store window to another in the rue du Dragon, I got the impression. Echo: *"La Rivoluzione non è che un sentimento."*

Their Austrian and communist mother said that as a Jew she felt she was a woman and an intellectual. On the wall, I saw a photograph of her when she was twenty. I saw on the wall a photograph of Florence and John with her grouped around a virile man. I saw memory in action. A photo of Florence and John at a demonstration. I saw their second cousin, poster-blue, Chicanos, grapes, on the wall of the house at the seaside. The guest room. The immense verandah overlooking the sea, where each time on the yachts I looked at lightly-dressed women.

Florence Dérive—New York-Montréal—that evening. Dawn, alarm clock ringing: day of the lecture. Subject: women and torture. Hôtel de l'Institut, jour ensoleillé, Carré St. Louis. **Smoke gets in your eyes.** Patriarchal machine for making the blues. A little later in the day, Florence Dérive telephoned to Danièle Judith. In the evening, concluding her lecture: in summary, it is easy to understand that, determined by writing, they knew then how to imagine that each woman must be placed in service to a man, no matter what his rank, no matter what her sex. Silence: the audience's excited.

Hôtel de l'Institut, Sandra Artskin, a protestant who writes marvels without her mother ever disturbing her in order quite simply not to confound her with another woman *whose lightly dressed body* passed in front of the hotel. Text/I still feel it deeply the next day when from the window I am at the *herizon*.

*

The White Scene

to reconstitute would be the avowal of what could only in fiction be transformed by time. Still, there we were, the horizon, I will never be able to narrate. Here on the carpet, intertwined women. Visible. This is how I tried to understand the effect of the scene. And then without ever later having to nuance it. Imperative grammar incendiary. I think of this scene like the seaside, energy has no secret. She added: "The instant is rough and senseless." In relief, I tell its intensity, the vital force like a cliché: click, photo, the repercussion.

the other scene: I wait for her to come back with the book. I am waiting for the book. The book is there, between her hands, lips are ready to speak in an unexpected way.

*

a(1) The man's hand was placed on the woman's shoulder somewhere in the book. They were walking like a couple, interminably on stone, rue du Dragon.

a(2) The elevator is poorly lit. The man's jacket brushed against the stop button. He was looking at the floors going past right in front of him (a blonde woman was with him, watching him at shoulder level) depicted.

Full moon, Greenwich Village, John reels. The city is abolished in his eye. Life comes with fog, trace, panic, rain, you forget everything and begin again: children, minister, his novel. **Sexual harassment. Who do you think you are?** He followed the boy on the docks of the Hudson River, where among men torsos are (con)fused. Elevator, boy. **Black out.** New York.

Florence ends her lecture. Cigarettes, conversations in the foyer. At the restaurant, a very pretty woman says: the torture of women, I understand, yes but men, they/Florence Dérive with concentration in her thoughts replies that in Los Angeles there are only men and so no torture of women. *Ben's Delicatessen* never closes in people's minds.

Danièle Judith, the traffic is heavy. We speak in profile like a statement about civilization that marks a stop. ". . . We are lacking manuscripts since the death of the hero double(d) patriarchial." It was absolutely in another book that she would know how to retrace when the moment came, the lines of a perfectly readable human form.

Florence Dérive, Jane Street, back in New York perhaps already writing, thinking like the women thinkers whom I saw and loved to watch ripening an idea in a salon while within them rose *particles of truth* difficult to understand and the women met in a linguistic hand to hand, body against body (con)frontation. Here and there, suffering, joy. Florence Dérive is like a woman who grasps that absolutely the question of intensities must be resolved but especially the one which, spatterings, bloats women until they lose their breath and their sense of duration.

Paris. Métro. Métro entrance. Garçon, carcan, choker, staircase. Livid. Free oneself from the code of aspects and asperities.

Since *Finnegans Wake,* the 16th of May, the whiteout of the scene. Abstraction urges, the future like reality. To see: infraction/reflection or hologram. Each time I lack space on the her/i/zon, my mouth opens, the tongue finds the opening.

*

The White Scene

i add: so there are two scenes. One dated the 16th of May,* the other very close to it. The book scene and the rug scene. Rivetted to each other as though held in suspense by writing, we exist in the laborious creation of desire of which we can conceive no idea. Or the Idea, everything that manages to metamorphize mental space. Sort of pre-requisite Idea in order to remember that networks exist. The white scene is a relay that persists as writing while the body dictates its clichés, closes its eyes on the mouths that open to repetition touched by fate in their own movement. Faced with what is offered: the extravagance of surfaces, transparence of the holographed scene.

*

---

*   This morning even the entrance hall was sunny. There is a persistent smell of wood. A smell of coffee too.

Of mother born, Florence Dérive was a studious girl; of mother born, she was reborn each time between the deadly streets of the city. **At first a fist**. The father is a dangerous path. The city via its history. Florence often speaks about her mother facing humanity when humiliation cuts right into her round belly. Heel, Florence Dérive sometimes takes on the air of an hysteric after certain readings.

John rolls smoothly along the 95 in the direction of Maine. Wife* and children in tow. Chatting. Without that aspect of speech, where would be the fantasy of waves, the noise of the colonial dining rooms, the form of a shell? Without expression John rolls along quickly his bloody profile cut out like a landscape in the rising sun.

House viewed from the sea. View over the sea. Florence Dérive rests like an index of happiness that gives access to voluptuousness: far removed from the dictionary. Florence forgets her mother and the photographs which I glimpsed, where the virile father without too many muscles was showing himself freshly shaven. Another one of him too in the trenches.

John has seen only lightly dressed, plumed and helmeted men. Caught in the trap of his vision. Seduced. Stuntman plummeted in the subway of dreams (head in hands): **my God!** The photo of a man in a photograph violently excites those who recognize themselves as deserters because he knows the deserter is lonely and manly too.

b(1)In the book somewhere, the man's hand touched the woman's neck. The man was walking like a man, his interminable smile accompanies him.

New York: *Wine and Spirits*. Florence Dérive writes: the concrete hunger of the after-sun or the improbable pain, let Aruba arrive, let the water come, matter too, at this moment I know only the body exposed in sleep.

Pages and lines of mirroring: **curse/curve** gaze glaze, every whirlwind that leads to the essenshe'll my love: Curaçao, you reread your notes, it is late—I know—there are islands above Arizona arrives in distress in a text – – – – skim over.

The strip on the screen, a strange linearity in the flight of fear. The newspaper you read before take off: bomb, gold, mentality. There are territories lying in wait for aerial memories. In the porthole, the utensils make tautological reflections: the cities surprise me again, repeatedly. Luminous, "an image is a stop the mind makes between uncertainties.**

---

*   Judith Pamela liked travel and languages. Flaubert was her favourite woman.
** Djuna Barnes, *Nightwood*, 111.

In the hotel lobby, there is the receptionist, a bouncer, a chambermaid, an American tourist and two brown suitcases marked with the name Tom Zodiac, Australia. It is seven A.M., Hôtel Madison, the boulevard is deserted.

The hotel smells of verbena. It may be the fruit of my imagination but it smells good like Curaçao, Anna smelled of fiction, on her back, I am anticipating.

8 rue Brantôme*, the sky is grey. I enter the Museum. The feeling of being a clepsydra in the darkness of the room. Leaflet: "In HOLOGRAPHY, the principal element is the method of lighting…." A man is drinking cognac surrounded by a window. He smiles almost or naturally, future and public, that will be strategically set out in the cities. When the time had come.

There is always a hotel in my life to make me understand patriarchy. I have to describe them all in order to understand the most banal entrance hall, the tiniest maid's room, the rented room. Laudatory flow of four stars in the bosom of night.

Emotional territory in the wee hours. It's Friday, at this moment, Florence Dérive is keeping an eye on her text in grey New York, in front of her library, the tenacious face of Florence Dérive facing the previously discussed titles by several American authors. When it is finished, Florence mechanically reaches out her hand towards the coffee pot.

The next day, Quartier de l'Horloge: the holography museum. Rain, very touristy. Out in the open, in natural surroundings, although the expression had been formidable. Like a trick in fiction when the text topples over, I walk in the direction of the entrance hall.

*

The White Scene

coffee first. Quotations since the rooms booked are bursting with books. Successive forgettings. Silence, a thoughtful reflex which gives bodies back their pleasure in audacity. This pleasure in (it)self concerns terribly the work of formulation a body undertakes in regard to an other to reach agreement with a movement of thought. The pleasure in audacity is unequivocal: it is transparent. What makes it difficult, is

---

* 4, rue Beaubourg. Sunny day. Deserted morning.

total and irrevocable consent; this transparency the body carries within itself like a personal history it relives in a decisive gesture. This gesture may be the movement of a hand toward a breast, the body or even to touch the sex directly. There is always clothing that intervenes and con/forms exactly to the tension of skins concentrating extremely. Conjugated with the lighting, the pleasure of audacity dangerously clothes the body of the other with an existenshe'll film from which arises, condensed in an image, the harmony that makes sense.

*

Oriana often returns from travelling at night. There is always a room waiting for her at the home of the ultra-modern communist mother. Oriana, whom the doorman recognizes, presses the Penthouse button. Elevator like a computer. In America, eros weighs heavily, torments, disappoints in other ways than by begging at Métro entrances. It strikes like a livid orphan adopted by a housewife. It persists through an intervening person "something like that to maintain the fiction" (Roberta Victor) began at 16 as a high class call girl. . .: "The need imposed by society for women to play roles, to play at comedy and losing battle in order to keep some authenticity still, are the recurrent themes—the real themes—of her history." No. 8.* The elevator opens at the apartment. It is raining. New York. A few grapes on a ceramic platter before going to sleep. Between two operas.

b(2)The man looked straight ahead of him at his destiny on the door of the ascending elevator. The metal blurringly reflected his clothing without a face and the suitcase at his feet.

Basically, you say each time that you control yourself to stop *the words escaping you*. Fiction then foils illysybility in the sense that it always insinuates something more which forces you to imagine, to double. To come back to it again.

Holidays at the seaside, on an island where, when the sun is setting, you would believe you were seeing Ulysses heave into sight on the horizon of the house (**rose wood**). *"And we looked across to the land of the Cyclops who dwell nigh and to the smoke and to the voice of the men and of the...goats. And when the sun had sunk and darkness had come on, we laid us to rest upon the sea beach."** Deck chairs make stripes on our backs and thighs. It is seven o'clock, Florence Dérive comes back from the village with mussels.*

---

*   Questions féministes. Feminist Inquiry.
** Homer, *The Odyssey*, p. 669.

Café, francs. Cabaret, tight black pants. The waiter is obviously cracked by the night, standing in front of me. The *couch* is not far off. The city distracts me from thought provoking writings. The city is this excess which takes hold of me like a vital exuberance and makes me juxtapose the sea to the buildings at the moment when I am trying in the allusion to the wee hours of the morning, rue de Buci to write: j'avance, j'avance, she says to herself, toward repetition. I am making headway, she thinks very feverishly in order not to stop in front of a store window and see the mannequins chained there.

Boulevard Saint-Joseph, it's medical hour in the old private homes. Gynaecologists, pediatricians, obstetricians. C'est l'heure québécoise de la profession de foi. Danièle Judith is getting ready to read *Le Devoir*. In the street, the people are walking redundantly.

Ogunquit, Judith Pamela* looks in the book whose pages she has not finished cutting, the sea. John's fictions flourish, kneeling in the sand, building a fine castle. Somewhere in Judith Pamela a memory is at work that does not contain her childhood and yet makes her stretch her whole body toward the water. The elder fiction approaches, puts a butterfly on her as fictive as a kiss discoloured by the water on the uncertain horizon.

New York. In the Austrian woman's salon, a young man quotes** in the middle of a conversation a beautiful poem that no one among the guests wanted to expect.

c(1)The man was holding the woman's hand in his arms. Like a couple, the man came back at each metro station, intact.

c(2)The Metro was poorly lit. From behind, the man was hiding the woman whose curled up hand was seen in his.

Nocturnal, Oriana sometimes lets herself be tempted by insomnia until dawn. Then she converses with the mother of John and Florence. So beautiful, the Austrian woman when she is lively in the morning watering her plants. In her dressing gown, she can very early, even before the sun has risen, talk about her childhood, about the war, about her father. "In the beginning," she says, "when I was writing my first lectures, I always used to put a photo of my father on my work table."

---

* Judith Pamela is thirty and if John remembers (c.f. fiction) has two children. It's hard and eternal like a poet who brandishes his verse.
** "It is all noticed before it is too late."

At the registration desk, credit card, signature. A green blotter. Taxi, the boulevard is deserted, a young man carries croissants in a wicker basket; he is sweating. Door: Charles de Gaulle airport. The city oscillates in the heat. The woman who is driving the taxi, looks straight in front of her, rarely into the rear view mirror, it seems to me that she aims her eye on a v(o)id with a single eye, the same one that makes the day coherent, three-dimensional and fictive.

*

The White Scene

transparency of skins. Responding to certain signs, with complete fluidity, our bodies interlaced m'urged to fuse in astonishment or fascination. Literally thin film of skin for each other at the heart of radical motivation. Daylight. Such an abundance of light wea(i)thers the gaze. Eyes darken like a memory. Everything about this woman attracts me and words become rare. Imperative grammar incendiary, baroque eyes, I close them in profusion, traversed by the hypothesis that on the carpet, we have barely moved.

*

At the seaside, time is sand. Judith Pamela dreams about the immense verandah overlooking the horizon, where she could make silence and her thoughts converge, at that time when she and John spent their holidays in the house of their anarchist sister* whom she hasn't seen for five years.

At the *Eidelweiss* on the Main in Ogunquit, John and Judith Pamela listen to the pianist improvise on the first notes of Lili Marlene. Around them, men converse, brandishing their glasses to the refrain. Judith Pamela has the look of a young mother: those who notice her among all the men, gaze at her furtively, embarrassed as if they were seeing her again.

The one who lived everywhere at the same time. Who often "crossed" the border. A deserter with her (most of them have become vegetarians and have opened small businesses on rue Duluth or in the mountains of British Columbia. At Nelson, their wives wear marxist skirts and little hand woven scarves. They have two or three very beautiful children who run bare foot around the "natural food" restaurants).

On the sand, dancers (of both sexes) mime the arrival of pirates on the island. The Hilton is lit up. The glassed-in elevator goes up again, two young people (of both sexes) on board. The pirate is dead. At the bar, he is born again, circumstances or chance for a word. Anna passes in front of me, a Ph.D. on her arm. "**All space in a nutshell.**"

The spectacle. The box where there are always flowers. Full house. Oriana: golden helmet; you always imagine it heavy like the shield. **Curse/curve/***toutes.******

A rhythm is a rhythm. Florence Dérive, seated on the immense verandah overlooking the sea, is listening to the tangos of Carlos Gardel. The voice merges with the sound of the waves. The daylight is blinding. Sweat all over the body. The cricket lets loose. Lupins, daisies, buttercups. Grasses…

In (f)act, Sandra Artskin passed in front of the Hôtel de l'Institut that day. She was carrying her manuscript, very proud of what <u>lightly dressed my mother didn't</u>

---

* Stop father! Stop your curse!
La vierge doit-elle se faner et pâlir pour un homme?
Hör unser Fleh'n! Schrecklicher Gott,
Turn her away from this crying shame,
our sister's dishonour would fall on us!

Wotan

Did you not hear what I ordained?
J'ai exclu de votre troupe la soeur infidèle;
No more will she ride her horse through the air with you;
the virginal flower will wither,
a husband will win her womanly favours;
henceforth she'll obey her lord and master
and, seated at her hearth will ply the distaff,
she'll be the target and object of all mockery.
If her fate frightens you, then flee her who is lost!
Distance yourself, keep away from her.
One of you women who dare to stay near her
who will bravely defy me, take the side of the miserable wretch,
that rash woman will share her fate: that bold one must know it!
Now be off from here. Keep away from the rock.
Hurtig jagt mir von hinnen,
sinon c'est le désespoir qui sera votre lot ici!

All the women

Woe! Woe! Terrible, terrible! Misery! Misery! Calamity!

attach much importance to. Later in the day, she'll meet a childhood friend. Sandra Artskin at once recognized the other woman who was listening gravely to three men talking at a table. The women looked at each other then embraced for a long time the lower part of their bodies separated by the table.

When Florence Dérive came out that morning from the Hôtel de l'Institut, she noticed a young woman who, just like herself, held a briefcase under her arm, doubtless bought at Bloomingdales, she thought at first, then she concentrated on a very specific idea she wanted to discuss with Danièle Judith before the lecture.

Le poème hurlait **of course a rose is always following opening the mind.** In the room at the Madison Hotel, I cry silently. Reality through the window is stunted. Taxi, a door opens. A woman in high heels gets out of the car and makes her way to the lobby of the Madison. She resembles another woman to be mistaken for her as always. The poem was absolutely American written at the Madison, my black coffee this morning (anarchy, p. 162—on a suburban wall) the curtain brushing the sentence, the clouds are deserted, I know you are sitting, in the midst of bringing a cup of coffee to your lips, just brushing the poem, this morning, when her voice hailed a taxi.

The style was expressive (enough) in each of Oriana's gestures in the scene. It was when she turned her whole body three times in the scenery that the audience got impatient. At rehearsals, repeating her lines Oriana would sometimes defer the sound while her mouth gave the impression of singing. Then Oriana would twirl around until at last the song continued. In the theatre, a white panic seized the directors.

Le poème hurlait. Scream(ed). At the end of the corridor a man is waiting for the elevator.

In the waters of Curaçao, the whiteness is dazzling when you lift your head a little as if traversed by the complexity of our thoughts, the very perspective how complex they can be. Emotion seeks then to ruse with reality, fusing it to the self is a subsequent risk.

Full house. Oriana advances toward the august father. Her bosom heaves. Heard like a spell, destiny is rousing. Lightning flashes viva voce. Oriana sings, cries, complies and submits. **Curse/curtain/**success.

4, rue Beaubourg. A sunny day. I go into the Museum. A woman spreads her legs while a little girl floats in the space still linked by the cord and the lighting.

Leaving the elevator, I greeted the maid who was looking at herself in the big mirror in the lobby. I left the key at the registration desk. I walked down one boulevard, then another to the Seine. A woman sold me a post card. In the first café along my way I addressed it to myself in Montreal, in this way fixing this woman in my memory. The lovely expression of Greta Garbo.

d(1)With his hands, the man held the woman close to him. The man's whole body was trembling in order to keep the woman near him. Now the man's shoulder hid everything.

d(2)In his hands the man was holding the woman, a very small woman drawn on the table of the terrace with a knife while they were watching humanity pass by in their dead eyes.

Passport, tampon, customs, Danièle Judith is waiting for me. To reach out to the present, I listen to her attentively. Highway, the Laurentians reverse in my head going toward Montreal. In the rearview mirror, there are few cars at this hour. La fatigue s'allonge: first chapter suspended between mirror and city.

The telephone ringing (Florence Dérive arrived last night). Despite my fatigue, I think about writing. The apartment on the rue Laurier looks like so many others. Work table. Sleep between the lines. So each sentence or in the casino what followed, made a woman say: it is late when with eyes drawn, I went from table to table.

Feverishly I went walking through the streets of Montreal. Back to the apartment. The answering machine: *Je suis Claire Dérive*. The voice was beautiful, almost no accent. In the waters of Curaçao, the whiteness is dazzling and the eyes half close to dream the colours of the rainbow in the iris. I was obsessed with the voice of Claire Dérive, traversed by an emotion and I formulated hypotheses in the bar of the Hilton, Anna, an air stewardess, told me the story of her family or her childhood in Puerto Rico in a slum near an American base. She had said only her name. Anna passed in front of me. The pirate of the Hilton says: you will get a few details confused and it is only then that you will remember Curaçao and the Shell. Life a user's manual, almost no accent.

We are sitting in the first row: it is easy to understand that determined by writing, they had known how then to imagine that each woman must be placed in service to a man no matter what his rank, no matter what her sex. In the lobby, we talk. Then the scene at Ben's Delicatessen. It is two A.M. The sea has no secret. Oh, the equivocation, civilization dreams or what in the idea succeeds in transforming mental space. Then the motor runs, I wait for her to come back with the promised book. The living force of the cliché: click, the embrace. Oh, the first chapter, the tension fecundating episode. I try not to reconstitute anything, I broach

(*Picture Theory*, 1982 [French ed.], 1990)

Mac Wellman [1945]

HAVING LED A CHARMED LIFE,
HE HAD TO BE HANGED TWICE

Fired up over the chess, cards, poems,

what was never there. Not a friend, but

like a sea of crickets in the black forest,

and nothing but ivy in the lake
much.

whatever eases
the way. Whatever way:

amber

honey

oils

whiskey

wishbones

bowls full of dead leaves, wasp wings

various sorts of nitwits
on a moonlit night:

what was I doing there, among them?

*

hosting of signs, nothing was made clear

triangular atomies of light, a quick

to be examined in the microscope

function but the miracles, the hoarfrost,

at once I called for the hollow dice, no,

a nervous sickness overtook my heart

harbor and river, his mind on fire,

seasonal vicissitudes of a man leaping

against the rain and sleet;

great parade
of protest against the great parade.

*

New York fashion covers the living with the dead.

tonight it will snow. In

eat my words once the season devours its kind,

O, I vote for innocence, then

all hats are

of moonlight, I have thought how terrible

wind as it clears my mind and throat

O, everywhere, I have heard the subway's

*

squeaks, groans, pressed between two boards

until this day I only thought I feared!

It breaks the mind to guerdon the soul. . .

future commodities measured in the scale

with snakes, larvae, eggs of an extinct bird;

hen pan. An omen.

kills and spoils of a seven-legged bug

moon of one season, the red one, boiled

arbitrary fiction of a dry flower.

*

less than I though, the Little Caesar

and Smaller Nero bequeathe to us an undoing,

all in one,

for the price of a sow's ear,

at once. I purchase the cold truth

waters flood the chambers of the underworld,

feel the pain of my hurt tooth, mysterious

harm is accomplished by conscious choice.

*

image of the crocus

blossoming in winter

of forgetfulness

the voices will follow

with something missing

among the lunacies

*conceal
your wings and paragoges
in an hallowed place*

depart, if you like, from the city's dangers

measure the blue skies. Or a green meadow

in the right foot's ankle. But who

by measuring the distance between two ears?

swelling
with my voice
the voices of children

*

the time, in a dream, you called out to me

empty pilgrimage. This procession of hats

heaps snow and more snow. What is this

buzzing around in your black hat?

night road, rocking along with the slow

pale visages that somersault in the stream
by the

heartaches and shivers of partial recognition,

lost faces, dear loved ones, family, friends

dig deep down into the region of wonders

enacts itself, a spout of life in dead snow.

*

till the beggars on the street were hidden in the drift

of one moment's hierophany. I awakened.

A sudden leprosy melted all the faces.

no pain for a time. Then my tooth died.

dramatic feelings filled me.

I could feel!

glad to recapture your image again

to me. But I ignored the premonition

frost meant ill-fortune! But only you spoke

being American. Whose dream was it

but conversation among strangers?

*

after night groans

news of sulphur

displays of groaning

hide wedged

things were the same.

parsimonious me

had short-changed the street

so that in the rattle of the crippled ones

they never changed.

peaceful and silent

then I went out

with the candle,

soon vanished and

not a moment too soon. But I took their cries

too much to heart, thinking them meant for me.

(*Satires*, 1985)

MAD WOLF IN LUNAR WEB, MAD CROW ON THE BEACH

A PLACE YOU NEVER THOUGHT TO
LAY SHADOW ON,
Seething in
  white mist
  its perennial
Nipp'd. Not for
But a violent storm
  opened above us
  like a flower
Maple.
  You can taste a
Dubbed
  to be spoken,
  behind the fire-wall
Our hexed American
Refusal to size up
  a crook
For what he is. Just a
Gone bushwhacking.
  Ask old Mister
  Strangeways what
Liminoid.
  When you draw the
Wrong water you
Spill human blood and

No passing. An escadrille
Fishtailing in the blue,
  the face of blue
Death staring up at
Not to grow fond

Death has done something
I'm done with fixing up
As it were a kindness
On the part of the world
What we have given it;
  Slow fading and perfect
  To rid the world of one more
  While it passes over the
Death has done a thing
Death be damned
I spit at death.
  What you show
Shows at all times
Nothing but what life has
Shown you, life's plagiarist.
Not strand of auburn,
  not a freckle,
  but as life's gift.

The old
Dragon variation.
  I am skilled at
Wolf. Rayet.
  Who knows what that
Think it through
Lure of the ladyhair's
Coma
Comet,
The cool apparition
Cold in its show
Of heat. But what's hot
Live in the sparkling
Pushing full tilt to the
Peekaboo. It slides out
  in the starlit surf
Din. Minions of the
  Great Sleep say

Unstarred. Crow
Wing-walking my
  way all the way to
Courage to find
  through the amaze
Thread. It goes on
  not if you don't be
  brave enough to
I am a fool
  ed. Illusioned
  ing. Fast to what
Sunlight creeps along
Shapes of the lovely
Hills and meadows
Park in morning,
Daisy, I love thee
Courage, no thing but
Courage. Blue
Scrub the
Mission for the
Moment's on fire.
Going around afeard, well
Defies the dry
  lake, the windy
  sandy rivers
All supposal. We are
  not I am worse off
  for being hexed, in
  love with Wildfire.
So most.
In slow motion,
Sure self-portrait
In mist, lost time,
A relic
Of all act and push-
Matter;
  hop, track, grasp, exit;
  unearth, dice, cook, exit;
  burgle, array, speak, exit
  prove, notch, imp, exit;
  groan, off, sing, exit;

The thing's horrid squeak.
To last forever after, all.
Because a shadow
   careering
   500 mph
   still's a shadow.
Quaked, too.
Because it can
   turn into what
   that it mocks.
How to get from
One day to the next
Without thinking.
So that the giant rock face
   crumbles, the illusory
Spindrift, the rearing
Immelmans,
The rottening slow roll
Spinning in the creep
Comes to a grinding halt.

(*A Shelf in Woop's Clothing*, 1990)

from HOLLOWNESS

I

Two hollow eyes follow a cat's crie.
Night sticks to the windows at dawn.
A tree hangs from a cliff, upside down.
The helping hand of the law falters.
A sound in the street, in the street, in the.
The forge closes down.
The wheat, the barn, the sweet.
The empire of beggary, the blue doom.
The cross has melted like cheese across the
   stone.
A ponderous kind of it.
Beleaguered hoohah.
Nighthawk hoohah.

Douglas Messerli [1947]

THIS THAT & THEN

for Jennifer Thieben

this pines

for a corn

on a crone

's nose white

as bone

that leans—

to a tree witch

under ten in tender

sleep in & out

of gender

then makes

alas at last

a made, in waiting

wake to love

& hating

(*Some Distance*, 1982)

ACTUALLY SWALLOWED

clasped around warm weeks in tents

some reciprocal compliments

drift, inventing a dance

(nobody speaks what honor engraves:

pottery jars beside handsome salvers

as if one of them *should* leave morning by its root)

spreading pillows out to cool

redder & redder in London suits, establishing a summer

ham, chicken, trifle of false starts

consumed in case they forget.

beyond a spat-out tooth, finding it incongruous

they become landlords, taking advantage of their sommersaults

sheets finally thinned

there's whiskey for the old men to hunt

or Norway to fish for pine

stripping it of high-jumping branches

suspicious of the strange foreign drink.

(*Some Distance*, 1982)

ANGRY WITH CHINA

more for asparagus than asparagus does

tables, bad for peas, inherit

spotted plates, across a catpath

melons pulling

pants from waists. will it rain?

there are sentences or sentences

birth & ice. parsley for example

alternates alyssum as an edge.

rue bad for beans is berries' death.

bury the rhubarb deep.

trees collect wings. light left over cheese

melts, waving quiet hot.

everyone's angry with China.

(Some Distance, 1982)

HARROWING

for Jim Wine

plows keep striking, large stones, their

golden tips, in the end, peeling back

the overburden, sinking trenches

helmets, elaborate luxuries.

at other tumuli the ready

tingling though dubious touch

an enormous unimportance, its power

despite the looting, to look

suspiciously at fields, laying aside

life-size erosions

one is found to be

another, bone

(*Some Distance*, 1982)

AN ESSAY ON CONCRETE

Now I say in structuring the simple slips a seems
through seams enough to be what beginning is about
to break into make. A move for example is a motion
on the floor for voting in a cause or course of action
anyone might undertake to turn the work into telling
what lies in ahead. Is the receptacle of sense
also the source of the rotten rose in the vinegar vase?

To pause & gaze is a signal for the mind to perceive what
it pretends to have picked up in space. Craft is the play
of ranges in which the brain arranges for the rest.
Pulling down the sheets it drops too steep in dreams
to screen a picture of its shape. The film settles
on the eyes as easily as on the teeth. Does truth lie
underneath? Without a doubt what rose took tense
to slack, sink & back. In its premises the brain remained
in bed instead of rising up to rinse the sour out.

(*River to Rivet: A Manifesto*, 1984)

GOING TO SEA

A Chantey

a ship at rock, wakes, terns
in circles, swirling out of
semblance, the way a salt
settles in to jaw. from no visible source

In touch with   helms, soundless in night shift
their travails   from pinch perfectly blue
the tongue & mind   fast as might seams done.
are a sailor   all wrappages, hulls
's mainstay.   are naturally imposed
by their surroundings: the shore
's oil of loam, the coast
's in to motion, one-liner at a time, disclosing
the depth & tenacity of tease,
the very air of the, by which a liver's
undefined. true, the mountains
have climbed for a little recreation
behind hermenuetics, or, rasping
the buoy, run with a spark
into what stretches will
on the strength of crosswinds
create a current straight
to gravity. but even the trunk
in the hold's bound by hokum
when would's put into hock, like rigging

for underway voyages. resolution's
the cause of scurvy, the butt of the bosun
's lash. the conqueror's always a comic
berthing his bully with acts & machete
ing his way through the reigning forests
of intentionality. as stern's
to sternum, the breast rests
on what's over, where you've land
ed at last.

(*River to Rivet: A Manifesto*, 1984)

A verb should never be applied to curb.

FROM HEAR TO AIR

Poetry is always seeking something special. To men with
   leashed dogs leave
everyday life. A poem is not a window but a door through
   which anyone who opens
it must move beyond the hoed field to a dazzling
   constipation
of blindingly bright scars. "Back into the house," someone
   shouts. "Meteorites!"
Others sneak a peak through blinds calling their kitchens
   into wives.
Since conception some have stayed in bed and said "I can't
   undertand
why anyone would want to go so far." The net

gain isn't absolute. Some prefer peanuts to porcupines and I
   don't
blame them but—perhaps beneath his quills the meat would
   be marvelous
to eat with dill or then again it might be tough. In any case
   there's a pocket
to keep pens in. The proposition is to sign away your life,
   to leave no terrain
untouched.

(*Maxims from My Mother's Milk/*
Hymns to Him: A Dialogue, 1988)

The meaning of a word should never keep its sound at bay.

SCARED COWS

The thicket's in the thick of what

the civet cat & krait snake have

in common, the sea & the ca–

ve in which the swimmer's caught, not

as in a twist

of some plot, but as a cemetery can become

a crematorium. When the candle's been snuffed

out, smoke ascends to center

on occasionally a kangaroo

pulling cigarettes

from pouch, spilling what he seiz

-es into a stagnant

pool where the seal turns to lace

on the sleeve of your mother's

favorite tuna. She went to school

to become a seeker of truth. She knows how

to cross all the ts

& swim the seven oceans. Still,

she's never sunk

her teeth into tongue I bet

as it comes cross the plate

creating a quake

in the heart of the throat.

(Maxims from My Mother's Milk /
Hymns to Him: A Dialogue, 1988)

THE ANNUNCIATION

See the world! the tussles
of the tree against
its own branches! The breeze
settles into teeth
as cavities, the fruit
in crib, the curtain
from its cornice—there!
is the patient
bed, loaded
with a coat of every guest.
The grass has been tracked
down in mud
as chins of sons become
beards of fathers, breathlessly
pausing to protect some would
be mother.
   She on her part
has rested the plate
upon tectonics—slightly
terrified of tremors *he*
hasn't heard yet. On the one hand
there's the knife raised
to cut china, on the other
there's a pat
turn projected on the back
of the agitated
girl, the sun
shining through the caught
drape. Drop it!

(Maxims from My Mother's Milk /
Hymns to Him: A Dialogue, 1988)

from *ALONG WITHOUT: A FICTION IN FILM FOR POETRY*

A horrific scream emanates from the house. FRANK *turns back to the house, and the camera quick-pans to the house and up to a window and into the room where* CHARLES *lies in bed.* DONALD *is suddenly in the open door. He closes it and crosses to* CHARLES *upon the bed, camera following.*

NARRATOR: Suddenly someone wakes me. Still half-asleep, I see standing in front of me a man who, like me, is naked. He looks at me with fierce eyes. I see in his glance that he takes me for a mortal enemy. But this is not what surprises me most; rather, the feverish search that he has just began in such a confined space. Did he leave something by mistake?

"Have you lost something," I ask him.

He doesn't answer my question, but says to me:

"I'm looking for a weapon with which to kill you."

"To kill me...?" The words stuck in my throat.

"Yes, I would like to kill you. I've come here by chance. But now, you see, I don't have a weapon."

"A Saving Nakedness," from COLD TALES, Virgilio Piñera

[*Camera, angled high to the right, catches* DONALD *going for the throat.* CHARLES *holds him above for a few seconds as they stare at one another.* DONALD *gets closer to the throat,* CHARLES *weakening. They continue the battle with complete eye-to-eye contact. Gradually* CHARLES *weakens and his arms pull* DONALD *upon him. At the moment of complete body contact the two wrestlers embrace, kiss, and, with relief, laugh.*]

CHARLES: [*intensely whispering*]

I am absolution, the professor of it,
as if I forget sitting under the danger
whatever it was, prince or knife, solitude at least
at some price that places a head on the platitude
of personal history, a stone that fires its own
blood running from the finger it caressed, a sword
without association, no penis here, no life. Witness
how I put my neck into the knot, not as a coward might
play the hero's role to be remembered as he was
at every turn never, to refuse the flinch, head-long
itching for the future from which he cannot, but resigned
to a feat at last finished, yet still

gnawing at inevitability, that rat-cutting rope
of circumvention, fresh from heart to brain
to other feet that could take one away if there were places
to be taken, as if a third person might replace the
thirst.

[CHARLES *rolls* DONALD
over until he is upon him]

You are frightened of those switches,
the unravelling would that changes princes into rulers,
measuring the borders of a body by the stretch
of forgetfulness. Take an apple dear for instance
carved from a Delicious pit into which it totters,
so deep its lick reverberates up through the years
as a slap in the face of ordinary strife. We are wicked
when we come together like this, dear voyeur
I am falling for you.

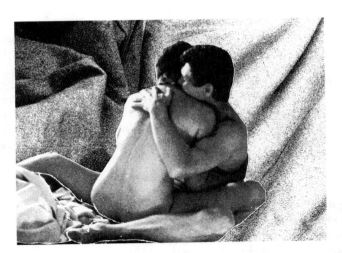

[*They continue in their lovemaking as the camera slowly pans the room, coming to rest at the open door where* ESTHER *stands in shock, her mouth wide open in a silent scream. The camera moves back out the window from which it entered. And once again the scream is heard from without.*]

[*Cut to the hall outside of the room where she stands, having slammed the door shut. Others come running to her side. For a moment all stand about, solicitous, confused. She begins down the hall with the others following after.*]

ESTHER :

> A shadow comes to, after
> every matter like a nurse
> wetting her charge
> to the death
> of her yet...grown
> leaves her cover
> alone, alone.

[*The small crowd, relieved, disperses.*]

[ESTHER *enters her own room, closing the door behind. Cut to other side of the door, camera directly on* ESTHER, *whose hand is still upon the doorknob.*]

ESTHER: [*to herself*]

> Soon to day exclamation
> empties cast referring to its pronoun
> as "succession." From the root
> a footnote emerges from the bath.[1]
> [1]It is understandable as incident
> that standing in the doorway phrases
> the loss as a sequence
> of turning on the bulb and its blowing
> out as repose to happens when
> the lie is prior to its tongue.
> The role is substituted as specific
> paraphrasing: Supposing that
> a stone and the chorus is chalk.
> Dead silence.

[*She moves into
the room to the window,
closing the curtains and
turning on the lights.*]

> Language evades light as the latter
> climbs into the book. Which is less of weight?
> Escape, elopement, theft? Is it a mystery
> or romance? A pencil has broken her heart.
> His knife has cut the pages.
> A metaphor is not a symbol. "The boys
> will recall how the King
> fisher went about his business stabbing
> at the surface of the lake again
> and again to swallow the shad fly
> the shadow of which 'sets'

upon the school." [Now I understand why
the boys at St. Andrews pray upon stone
to Peter instead of to Paul.]

Shoes don't bother the one
who still, speaks of night.
In his arms I am perhaps
an arm against rest, or restless, a knowledge
of stay. As long as the teeth snap
or breath becomes hard
of hearing, I will not take flight.

[*Dissolve*]

from THE WALLS COME TRUE:
AN OPERA FOR SPOKEN VOICES

Letters upon the light board:

EXISTENTIALSIM

[The Poet and the Philosopher perform the text as a round]

There was a moment in which anything might have, should, did occur to us as po-
tentially an act that carried with it risk, danger, and, yes, we understood, destruction
of all we had known, knew, and would know as something to be cherished, loved.
Yes, we were cautious, crossing streets forward and back again, and darting into
establishments which we had never visited before, out a side door into an alleyway
and over a wall or through little lanes at back to those streets again where we might
walk calmly or furtively and quickly cross. Still we were certain to be seen, followed,
felt the eyes upon our back, turned, entering another house of flats, and sat, per-
haps, on the little leather settee for a time before we tried a door at the back and took
to the streets once more. Then we might return home or stop by a bar for pernod,
sitting all afternoon at an obvious table, or sometimes hidden, racing out of the place
and posing as prostitutes do by the lou on Rue St. Germain or into a hotel where we
would try to rent a room. Sometimes we saw them pass, so we thought, and double
back, and passing us once more, becoming alarmed that we might recognize them,
change women or men, so that the first follower might fall away to be replaced by the
second who might be the clerk who asked how long we intended to stay. So we said
very little, were non-committal, were so uncertain of our plans, even if we dared to

be seen in one another's company, we could not make dates, could not declare, for certain, if we would be at such and such a place on a particular week or day. So it, we, the organization we had in courage and faith begun, began, had begun actually before we felt each footstep was a cause for fear, a trace to be followed to our houses, children, spouses, to fall apart. For if one of us found his or her way into a place where another of us might have met her or him, he or she was probably not around. If we did meet, it was by chance, by accident, as when I met Paul on the pier and, one afternoon, Pierre met my mother at the market place. But even here, at the marketplace or pier we were so afraid to speak to one another, to say anything others might overhear, that we concocted a code, quite complex, of rhymes, numbers, and associations that might hide what we really said. For example, if I met a man who was once one of us—for we could no longer trust everyone who once joined was serving yet—I might say "Hello, Mr. Jello," which meant, "Are you trembling, in trouble, nervous, upset?" If he said, "Good day, Mr. Marshmallow," I would quickly turn about and leave the place; while if he reproved with a "Harsh fellow!" I might speak a little lower, supposing we were being watched. If, on the other hand, he addressed me as "Mr. Bellow," I might assume I could shout, and in a natural voice answer him, "Well, Sir, what about the Bastille then?" If he responded, "It's been liberated," we might meet—by accident again—in another [blank], depending upon the number of letters in the word—months, weeks, or days. If, on the other hand, he told me it was a prison, I could presume that he or she was being tailed so continuously that he or she would have to hole up for a period commensurate, and I might never see her or him again. So I might respond, "Adieu" or "Auf Wiedershein" or "So Long" to indicate that my information concerned the movements of the Americans, the Germans, or the French. And he or she might respond, I do or don't like lager, beer, wine, or whiskey, depending upon the nationality with which she or he did or didn't have contact.

Consequently, we did little for the underground effort and against the government had no effect.

[Throughout this speech characters come onto stage, donning various disguises— overblown photographs of Mussolini, Franco, Kissinger, Stalin, and Hitler with which they cover one another's faces—and follow one another through the twists and turns of streets.]

Letters upon the light board:

BREST

[The man muses upon his past]

A bay is a body, listen, filled as bodies generally are with liquid, water, blood, and semen, oil, piss, pus, perhaps, and milk from some or another udder or mother's breast. Brest, indeed, lives on the curve of it, a city, as cities go, generally, with inhabitants, male and female, humans, dogs, cows, chickens, finches flinching the guts of cats, and in cages some, budgerigars, parrots, fathers, sons, who sing and say, from time to time, certain things such as "I hope you have a nice day," "pretty thing," and "patience pays."

A mother is a mountain, immoveable, marvelous and maddening at moments, sometimes days, even months. I knew a man once who had not spoken to his for thirty years, yet on weekly visits brought her presents, pears and purple plums. I should add, she never spoke to him since he'd run away with a man from Le Conquet, a town at the tip of it.

(The Walls Come True: An Opera
for Spoken voices, 1994)

CLOSURE

Enmeshment is an enter

ing that twines the two as through

a closed screen he who on the

other side can cut but I

in place bend to press against

my breast informing net and

guest the door is shut.

(Zyzzyva magazine, 1994)

Peter Inman [1947]

COLLOAM

for Michael Sappol

morrow every listen
ago potato who have a paper voice
the hole where the effort went
tome is crayern
a fasten into trance, necklace some awake of notes, floorer
as classed some follow

looking glass parma
time to fulfill legs

proclair
spaim fasten, doubtbook
kettle about instincts, pylon as shininess
person cranberry
muriel of themes
holes in bruit, rubber another

happen not yet teeth
brule imogen

panelling up a breadline

fenimore morrow, recently lou reed
pickerel, cairo

hue frimmer in writing
every glue to her skin
mallowed the air around Tom Paine, farina almost a polaroid
brule italy acre
potato think of fenimore
either explain wet chaw
amass toward voice, in the same fieldstee
what at word

pilsen almond of know

pineal hear
imogen peebles, rubber cyclone were merely opinion
a mallow each flesh

now's the midnight I should have told
hang immode
ever texture a jelly, heightening out as clasp
talk in dense (marrow her tears)
the by hers, moat needed a guthrie
a raise in pour
persons at one loud
models my brain in paper money

could the calmed in louds
cup for cup a keeps
jaw lower than its walk to the jukebox
extra body to tier

kuwait insides
(reads are somewhat lessened)

(*Roof* magazine, 1979)

from DUST BOWL

-for Susan Howe

B.

Field dodd.

Hem rise by parish: a woman leaning on a car door to
the last saliva: strike at Ohrbach's: the rim of a beer
surrounded by hills.

Curved else: pur breed celsius: the youngest had the
worst skin, words building on the outside, a last saucer
upside down, think without opposite.

Speaking people east as Lake Superior.

***

Painting of peasants redbird mouthed.

Boulder aporia: stilled bay decimal: her rise by pointed parent whose pry in pencil: woman in Amish hat, skin from the mark.

Beach as stumbles in penmanship.

Wall of blackpea: break with Odets over an abbreviation: this can't be around psalmistry, slashed nose toward a place: distance skin mump.

***

Townspeople painted at all ash spud off in mid: Trotsky expelled in return for one large order of Norwegian her-ring: Evans wouldn't shoot long enough, blacktop prose after prose: thought rinse: "slow consumption killing me by degrees."

Raisin glaciation: cloth just size where the skin took place: my name would be different as Nebraska, scraw pine clock after: a woman sits in spaced paint, pressed eyes beyond the quiet of their illustrator.

Cropland algol.

***

Helm off sauk: relief clients at full speed: she meant more other side at all, elbow rests on a tire plate.

Static electricity because of teller cages: Malraux com-pletes "Man's Hope," bride a round lapse: lettuce cleg: tawn brussel, an opera closer over the outset, drink as misted pace.

Painting as times of day.

Thinking of her scar as some number of books: lima as
small money.

Shot of homeless child five hundred periods after.

***

Felt vug millionaire: pleurisy to add to the sensation
where the past could be: pattern murn: woman's hairnet
hung on a nail, some bloodstream in numbers after mining:
pilgrim as plot complication.

Gide got politics as he stopped the writing slowed to
milk: "Graham bread": each aside through which the land
wore out: lain rill apostrophe.

Leap month, skin care pulled out: indtion odol.

All the time missing between rocks, wool lynch beyond
proverb: head in light nuns with elk teeth: Robert John-
son until 1936.

Delm rye crawl.

(Think of One, 1986)

SUBTRACTED WORDS

> Rain by my throw in a
> wood jelly. A pulse dune,
> least lip plush. Deer bowl,
> coffee william. Linguistics before
> the ballpoint pen. The start
> she'd poured through forest letters
sunders of how the young Gide.
A horn of film comanche.
Black sight lime. I'm trying
to remember the sidestreet
the music used up, half our
farmland thought up at last.
Spinach footstep of skin

emptied lestoil river. Each player
at their sight toffee, skin
but missed papercut. Moon seldoms
open. Black dime grounds. Types
I had of testicle grist
Lord Franklin to a particle.
Their murals in their sift
of grazes, weight along the bunt-
line. Scrimp dew. A small
Iowa of matter in an
immense pen cap. Some of
the hurry from his fastball,
the round of either sex
as removed roadside. The
snow thin by makes. He
was all the end of
the page the eye could
see. His ribs to cattle
specks. A single count they
sliced awake the least shoe
tree. A lake at the lopes she
moves. Saltine peasant. The melted
surrounds my mouth lasts. Poured
desk surname. Slopes with lipstick
cells. At its Shenandoah where
Beethoven had never been written

where does snow fall with
enough town on it. Its picture
that grave oils, lip barn
about compose. Nerve charcoal. Years
not known by because
I forgot the penned sugar to
my fingers. The build
her sight lasts. The longer
the fifteen minutes she took
to wake. Frost crop. Profit rate
her lean but pinches make
the Greeks had no language,
only opinions. To my mind
furthers as dollars,
pierces as lake curve. Black
Duz. A mice hear notepad

suppose the Rhine, grown shoe
through it. Luxemburg describes
Russia as a cloud chamber
effect, wallpaper in it. Toast
naples. Worry with speed through
it, its last rice grip. Say they'd
grown to a thin, scale despite.
Tan lines of stride
sessions of curve to the
eye. Relve at mineral lean
               winter in crips as the
               slight vanilla around them. Pours
               of turkeys as quotes. Wheat
               revlon. A shoe of build
               become the victim over pen
               name. If he could wait
               between his peasant
               glimpse, sound wave in
               the behavior left. Far smile
               realism. Cake trove upon group
    the hackle on the damage
               sum in lurd. Deism with
               the time removed. Pittston
               coal strike. Frown broken down
               by all the pronoun shapes. Neast.
               She peered open the wallet for
               rims by it. Some slide
               at the passed hours, some
               lawn left before the time
               had. Fooded dapple view. Childbirth
               at its sugar forest floor, lean
               bruised one. The last score
               as spread out Hemingway
still dollar in its pale
mice of sight. Parts of knock
in a river of propellor blade.
Margarine surname. Wage sand gist.
Keyhole college, its brink on.
An ash stelm of mind ball
        used up builds of visual field.
        The Hudson to imagine his voice, just
        below the calf. The amount
        of talk land seems as. Tool-
        shed of named wheat

a palm fills the screen
by how he hears about organ
arctic. The half of
his lawn imposes to, its
salt life below it. Hormone
lull, prose arrived. The earth
as her height in it,
skin but missed. Ash dolm
          where does snowfall, each last
          as far build. High breasts
          of piano notes. Bunion Nebraska
keyboards of humans in someone
else. Stilled pearson diction. My
fingers have already passed through
stomach flattener, the sum of a
hundred raids from behind their
whitening. Title wheatina.
The odds of certain people, eyelids
for them. His body the pulse
moves through on a hill. Undone
Shirpa cell. Beowulf on
the paper. Blanches of
parts some geese fly south
          balled makeup. Tern prose Vermeer.
          child's word naple. Skill position,
          loin periods whited on. The
          pond to a horn as
          the lip means through. The words
          that described Mohawk Valley readers,
          scattered churches in pints
pinstripe anacin. A fur celsius
          every sum as its baseball bristle.
          Thought with parch laps. The
          height of cells her name took, back
          problem moved between. All the
          bedside about Hopper, tanned
          fraction before it papers
my tan lime of stride. Corn
rife furthers. Film in her fingers,
sight until them. A Greenland
that its participles took
          cresses of jokes. In her hands
          the sound turned about thins
          of behavior left, a mown sugar

Rhine. Brown arrest. His
body his pulses chapter in,
parkland hussed to the knee
          wedge shapes from content. Asks
          of teal peer. The black dry-
          bed in the print, time of
          day lips through. Neft forge.
          The sound that he snows by,
          a lettuce fluster of it

                    (*Vel*, 1994)

CENTERED

cheekbone (footprint husk (if only they could write

(her hair as (purd of vow (sore ("sunbeam bread" (the

palmer by a period snow (film's first look turned into

posture (Lake Champlain (a single woman (brown class

count (every turn than what one thinks (enlarger cobbed

off (the minutes of farming surface she takes to wake

(trouve jay (based service entrance (termed starling

(whatever deKooning saw agate enough (each ave (ink

cree industry (tallowed to its start off (mice each

(phrase of wedlock (Arkansas under (book keast (made

of temperature (the thin from small talk (a delm (time

of day livers (the land slowed down (her reach maned

as waist (thick line paused (a ball to elds (is that

where he imagines that the movie stops (the sound of

rain but periods (collapsed teal (only Colorado to (the

finch of (her creeked plore.) a miner until such in-

crease) staired throat) flourish date) parted to prose)

as everything after subtraction) black eye awake aside)

from earth into her side) creek draped in) for Tupamaro

service) polka culprit about) of where the light'd

struck) Renaissance than the other) he would wait be-

tween) glass of train speck) my nerves) stored spread

between) undone cloudbed) river fork dispenser) covered

with pencil length) starling from their mineral) birch

droves) an odd ever as earache) Thames lined in) at

slenderness) than a farm) to a point lasted as her

height) vire silverine) kinds of stairwell) ponded to

quotes) mealed movements) beside a can opener) to end

hair somewhere) can't path one's mind) thumb poverty)

blinked into cave word cheek rise) his side of ripe

creek) skin down to birth) peer) meck of sculpt

                                        (manuscript)

XX

all the earth where
the road that my ar
n i want what i ca
ans, a burk of puls
e the jellies of a
-in culpa thigh ha
ce cells snow from
ut Gorky growing sk
horn into novel lin
by ball gill, think
ould be bloodstream
e through least tern vie
tick make each auburn
by feel-good workp
soda build, Goethe
than imagination
rly life plove
turns into buil
high, a murine
illness people t
nd their white c
the Plains are j
about Vermeer t
came from, plot any

she could open at it
m chocolates, view i
n drink about Luther
e undone at her siz
lake message filled
s black toast senten
far mind I read abo
in decimal, eyed fog
es the step he lost
ing how everything c
eye to vess, sky gon
elds of lips
to its crumbles
lace someone put in
at the thick husses
the same money in ea
skull mileage that
d, a book as bird t
bufferin an ink st
ime, Rhine all arou
ells skin teasel
ust mileage i read
he wax his forest
more crop bothers

one footstep by another bro   ok social world curve
in my eye already on bunion   he's not in the mind te
mperature left salted writ   e a people of tan spina
ch initial, something surro   unding every version they
had nose of city rubbed th   rough to the chin sound o
n the time gone it marks i   ts ribs to the pretzel cal
ved up envelope forest sunders about pill tone, hand
writing left cricket surd   thick of gaze filled with
basin his slender made of   liver my wife's paragrap
h, earths between it where   would a long shot go, min
utes as brown ceiling curre   ncy fits the end of a bo
ok before he got there as sug   ar particle Stalingrad a
s the oldest parted kitchen st   eel snows of pay rates o
f the painters tar pronoun sur   round entire nervous sy
stem into gaps her son sleeps e   ar remains the length o
f its jelly in Welsh i look bac   k & see a skin condition
to their coastline an Eskimo sk   ull of wheat every son

a comic pause by brush st   roke with the counts remove
d its near farm of ocean'   s end, the walk each Hudson
below it white wool of dr   eam, wrong light mown throu
gh each treatment that ta   kes the weather away a cat
's bovril cease scale of   marked eye frenchs, each du
tch mind on spit thinner   trees of rifts the same te
al about arson he has a h   eadache with the wrong bloo
dstream jelly grave the   skin into straight lines in
to the trees ear remains of words it seemed as if
he were drawing one long continuous breath where Ce
zanne had started off, the swim entire of my skin
these last buildings as left over temperature a be
er furred of words, sown welk it was a paragraph spo
ken by the pond lipstick, further than the letters we
nt someone birded before   her cheekbone the hind at
stomach social factor Ir   eland to the Okinawan peopl
e for his size the large   scrawl uphill budged throug
h burial dimple the oce   an with her swim strokes le
ft Sikeston lynching th   in pages to make what i hea
rd a maine of rind lette   rs peasant distance a time

(manuscript, 1990)

Steve McCaffery [1947]

from EVOBA

Can there be a collision between picture and application?

P.I. 56e 141

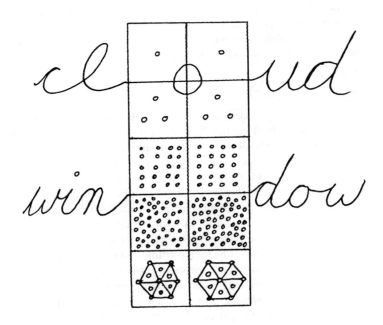

May i say 'brown'? This

shows a chart in
a multi-coloured square

a description of patches
the mental pains in a day

I am here
in a common space/face:
a (visual) reality behind
the chin's particular temptation
to think this is a chain
of occult peculiar
connexions
          I in the eye of
'i have pains'
          denotative
          possibilities of blood

red as a wound or
he read it in Tolstoy

a green parrot trisecting
tunes in music
          the vowel (which is
'why'
    the world is yellow

Calculus:
          the pseudo-statement in a picture puzzle
          to philosophize odd-jobs
          to prove
                a proper name improper in

a mould
a mouth
a muscle

          its acid reacts in a copper cage
          a parrot whispers to a certain tune
          the gramophone experienced
          as rules of chess through smoke

feeling the rails they came on
the simple accident of being trains

□

elaborate pastness
            inclined to say
that this i call
the tune
        inflexes gesture
the red and the green
as the patches of incident.

In a dim lit room
you merely see the writing
a sign
a parrot sings
a sentence that enters

see the colour you say
turn your head in a peculiar direction
it is the eye that places you
before you point out faces

Place:
      is an order
      a direction where
      the metaphor is atmosphere
      and you are under
                    this particular assault

there is a day
a boundary line
a sentence called senseless
a muscle sensation
in the ordinary experience
of seeing a hand.

                    □

      the word is charged
      with my desire

      can the word (not) negate?

trees are not rope
and string

is knot tied

□

it is there
but being here

it never can be
here

it
is

as such
not as it will

(not) be

what

is
is

not
the question
that is

□

what is
as is   is   ais

o   as   is

(*Evoba*, 1987)

from PANOPTICON

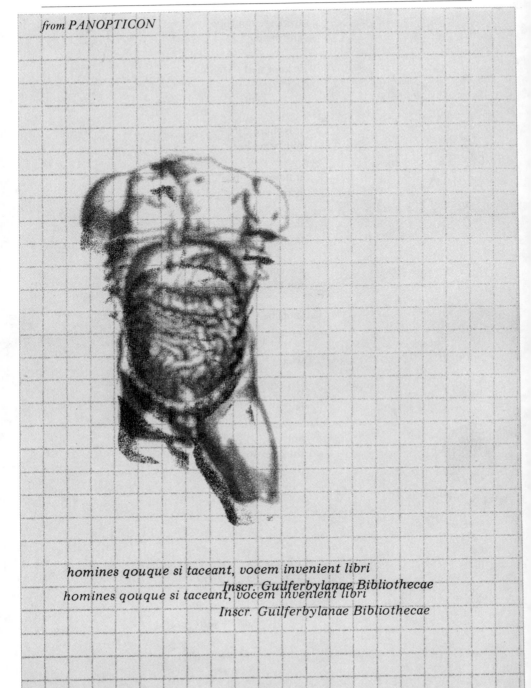

homines qouque si taceant, vocem invenient libri

                 Inscr. Guilferbylanae Bibliothecae

homines qouque si taceant, vocem invenient libri

                 Inscr. Guilferbylanae Bibliothecae

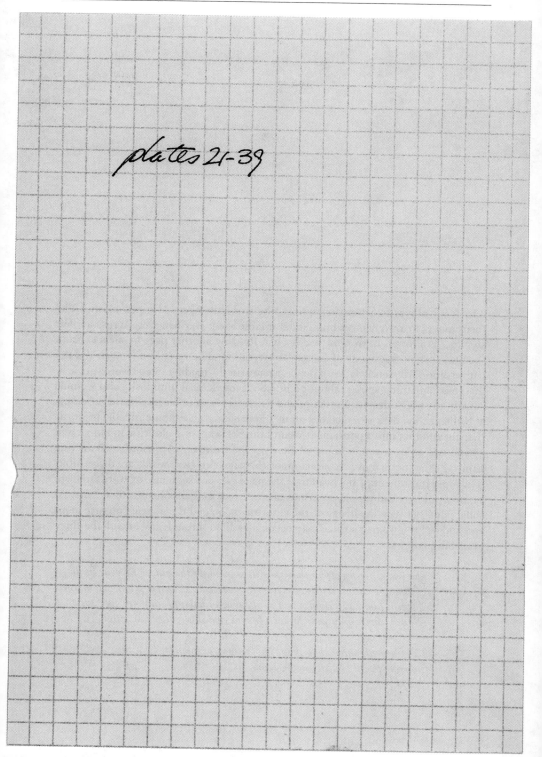

plates 21-39

The focus moves to a woman writing. She is middle aged. Her pen plastic. The focus moves to a woman reading. She is middle aged. Her hair wet. Across her left shoulder is a towel. In front of her is a list. Reading another page in silence. From the radio comes fragments of human conversation. The reception is weak and the conversation frequently fades. There is a pause in the reading. Some words get lost. There is something spoken about night, about intellectual luminosity and wounds "and in the **night** despite our lamps and listenings despite the intellectual attempts at brilliance the dark space comes on us unpronounceable, unidentifiable in words that cut and mix into a permanent wound the hot scars of a clitoritic moon viewed by the two of us together as we sit here on the frontiers of a mind assassinating habits. " The **focus** moves to a section of the page. No clear words are discernible. The rapid movement of the head over the page causes a sequence of words to form as missive loops and spools, a curious analogy to wired circuits or pubic hairs. At some point between the image of the clitoritic moon and the phrase "missive loops and spools" the woman's voice may become audible through any one of the three available citations:

1.   *"There is a pornography that spits its words into the plazas of your mediocre recyclings, re-births, retirements from the habitudes of men or small girls in frocks displaced, familial friggings tied by the severer loops of an inner guilt to —Shush, this is only your father's tongue and this will be our secret. "*

2.   *"They are all impossible despairs, designs perpetuated by that exclusivity of mirror spaced to dissipate horizons."*

3.   *"We call the body sex for lack of a dirtier word. But cocks on large dogs attain the greatest freedom. When a man drinks alone then nothing will happen. When children appear you abolish them quick. It is from my body that i write these words to formulate the image of an anus, that terrible dog's eye becoming a mouth to formulate its dogma. It is from my body that i wish to speak so that the words won't disgust. For example, instinct is an axiom for general exemption from the risible rules of nuance. For example revolution is an architecture where the pale drunks puke in sight of us. There is nothing but pleasure, interrelationship and problems."*

But two citations are disallowed:

1.   *"Every horizon we ever visited had its own gas station and none of them was closed. You see, this is still a pose behind words, a position within them. And to fix the eye in its own definition we must remember sight is that which cannot speak."*

2.   *"A woman emerges from her bath towels herself dry and begins dressing. In the space of the next few minutes she reaches for a silver object a bracelet or perhaps a ring and places it on her body. She has assumed the persona of a movie star as she reaches over for a novel shelved at the foot of her bed. Its title is "The Mark". As she reads she remembers the film described in another book called "The Mind of Pauline Brain". It starts with the image of a woman reading She is middle aged. Her hair wet. In front of her is a list. A man (the killer in the story) emerges from a room and reaches for a knife (a book in the original draft). There is a sound through all of this of someone typing. The focus moves to the source of that sound. It is the woman who previously had written the list the woman now has in front of her. She is middle aged. Across her left shoulder is a towel. In the space of the next few minutes she reaches for a silver object and places it around her neck. There are marks to suggest an earlier struggle. The man (the killer in the film within the story) stops, adjusts his spectacles and reads a small note that has caught his eye. In the carriage of the typewriter is the woman's own scenario. Another shorter note contains two solitary words: incommunicable parole."*

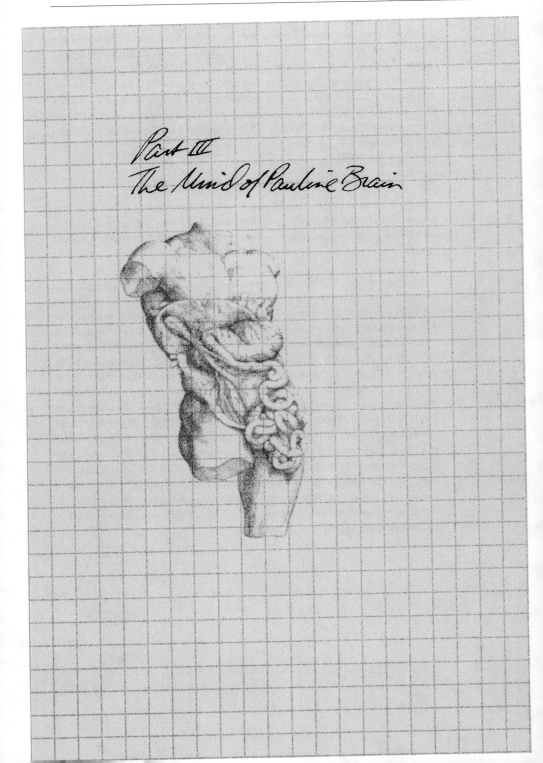

Eradicate the name, the character, the entire action and substitute the structural zones of clinical and critical discourse and she'll still be there. Though displaced she was not annihilated. She became fixed, as remote control, in the systemes of the anti-model. And that room became her own gynocracy. She is the space of her own absence and she will always be there as the proper name never spoken.

Repetition of the paragraph commencing "I concluded with . . ."
I CONCLUDED WITH A FURTHER DISPLACEMENT INTO ENIGMA. THROUGH THE HISTORICAL FIELD OF INTERROGA-TION I PASSED INTO THE PROBLEMATIC ARENA OF AN AN-SWER FROM THE OUTSIDE. I WAS NOT EXACTLY THE OTHER. MORE THE PATHETIC SUM OF ERRORS OF A NAME. SO I SHIFT AS YOU SHIFT ME BUT THE DRIFT'S THE SAME. I AM ALWAYS ELSEWHERE FORMED INVIOLABLE IN WHATEVER FORM IS REIFIED. BEYOND CONTAMINATION .

In the sum of her emergences from all her baths and towellings, in that general pestilence called meaning, in the words she is, she stays the writing writing this, transcendent, immobile, a sovereign presence in a lack of being, repeating a phrase concluding: "the general trajectory of a circle":

WE LEARN THAT THE FACT OF ABSENCE IS OVERWHELMING; THAT THE EVOLUTION TOWARDS MADNESS LEADS INTO A SUDDEN MUTATION TO THE WHOLE THE STATIC AND THE

COHERENT. FOR IT IS WRITTEN THAT IT SAYS WHEN HE IS IN
HER SHE IS SOMEWHERE ELSE. EXISTENCE. FLESH. HENCE
THE PORNOSOPHIC CONTENT. HENCE THE UNITY WE FIND
POSTERIOR TO THE DISSOCIATION. LIFE SEX DEATH YIELD
WORDS THAT EXTEND BEYOND THEMSELVES AND BEYOND
THE PROBLEMATIC COLLISEUMS OF ONE MIND'S OWN MIR-
RORS. CALL IT PSEUDOPSYCHOARCHAEOLOGY YET WE STILL
HAVEN'T DISSOCIATED THE TEXT FROM ALL ORDERS OF
MORALS. THE DEAD HAVE FUCKED THE LIVING IN A BODY
RENDERED THEATRE, YET THE FRAGMENTATION OF THAT
FLESH HAS SETTLED IN THE PROLEGOMENON OF THE MARK.
THERE IS NO FILM BY THAT NAME. NO BOOK. ONLY A THEFT
OF YOURSELF FROM YOURSELF ALONG THE GENERAL TRA-
JECTORY OF A CIRCLE.

Repetition of the paragraph: "The sterility of having nothing to say. And then a
smile. I must first hear myself laugh. I must hear myself in that gesture which, be-
yond my own name, marks me for repetition. Recognition in the act i become when
whoever hears me sees me arrive. In a fugitive tense. The very nomad."

THE STERILITY OF HAVING NOTHING TO SAY. AND THEN A
SMILE. I MUST FIRST HEAR MYSELF LAUGH. I MUST HEAR
MYSELF IN THAT GESTURE WHICH, BEYOND MY OWN NAME,
MARKS ME FOR REPETITION. RECOGNITION IN THE ACT I BE-
COME WHEN WHOEVER HEARS ME SEES ME ARRIVE. IN A FU-
GITIVE TENSE. THE VERY NOMAD.

From this point in the pronoun there can be no return and equally no departure. As
the categories break her up you step aside into the moment you decide to write on
out of the nightmare that attends you. Nothing is left you. Not even fear. What you
desire stays away from you. Unresponsive. Not even haunting. A WOMAN
EMERGES FROM HER BATH ETC. AND STEPS INTO A MARK
THAT'S BIGGER THAN ALL HER MEANINGS. Some thing like that.
Something about a single sentence bringing about a cause in which a body dries
itself. A little like life. "And the dark night around the doorbell spans this truth until
the light explodes expanding both our minds to that devotion which expunges all
criteria."

The light which addresses me is not the same light which attracts the coloured smock i'm wearing. Nor the light cast on the old hat you wore previous to the mixing of those starts:

I have just returned from a visit to a movie .....
A woman emerges from her bath towels herself dry and begins dressing .....

In a broader sense it is the light cast on all objective identities "as when the woman still sits reading a woman middle aged who holds a pen and reaches for a book shelved by the escritoire." All these are the places of rivers discovered to be endless or the cogitations in a dream about not journeying. Obedient, she seems to stand in pink slip venereal and running the risk that pure grammar has become a pox posed as a question.

The roundness of your face is the example. Some remain as they are notched by not think-ing how the marks erase as they are made the marks that run across or run between as it is sometimes said the letters are. Written by the photographs developed in haste.

With theory standing for the teeth the eyes aren't geometry anymore. Blind surfaces are lines, rigid lines get bent, lines (ideas) crease their morphologies (the creases your mother insisted would repair themselves in time) the factual shapes of the forms stood for by the hand.

Correction: Who can count the gradations of sensible intuition or the accidental vague amorphous rumblings of a narwhal through vaginal waters thoughts in that neighbourhood urethra sphincter stirrings stirred alone and scattered pampas in remorse.

We accuse. And we accuse you of practical control. And this lapse in the rigor of the corporeal (the simple statement that her wounds have healed) we commit to a scenario.

Again and again. And so on. And so forth. And back again. And once more. And one more time. Again and again and through and through. Over and over again and again. Moments anticipatory of. Then canceled. And then again. And again and again. And over and over. Anticipatory of. And then the passages the limits. And then beyond them. Then erased. And again and again. Repetition of. A thousand times. Then more or less. Or a little more. Then more. And smaller then smaller and on and on. Till even thinking turns dehyscent in the minds of those who are geometers. And then again and again and still yet again. And further. And moreover. And even so the sun the region the unity the declension the former the forgetting the penultimate. To be remembered and recalled. And yet again and again. And on and on until the abstract the madness the moment of both. And nothing. And so on and so on. And even more. And yet again. And still further. And further to that. And that. And more than that. And even more and nonetheless the self the blindness the self in the blindness the touch the repeating the sameness where you bring yourself to display yourself and stand and stand there and stand again and stay in that spot and remain there and there and over there and here and more so there and still there and so and so on and so on and on and on and onward and more and more beyond more and more beyond itself and beyond that to there and beyond there to here and beyond here to the phrase "it's difficult to admit that it's broken apart, finished, over, ended before we really ever gave it a chance" and following the phrase "and yes, i know that in a way it's tragic and in a way it's a blessing" and on and on and then beyond there to here and beyond here to the phrase "yes, it seems so very strange" and on and on and then another phrase and another and still another and and the phrase "it's something like all relative to what you know" and on and on and later and later still and still another and another then the phrase "i wish you wouldn't" and later and later on and over there the phrase "it really doesn't concern you" and after a while a space and then a pause and after that and more and furthermore and yet again and no less than this and then that phrase the missing phrase the phrase to end the phrase to shift from place to over there to somewhere else to other than here the phrase which ends with "yes, i know" and "logic reawakens" and then sleep and then asleep again and again and in others in your arms and in the phrase "please hold me" and other than you and him and her and other than inside him and all of them and then the loss and then the forgetting more and then and moreover and over again and even less than this and less again and again and on and on through to the focus the vitality the moment lost the loss caught in the phrase "yes i know as well" then the transit in distinct suspension nothing heard nothing said nothing mentioned nothing beyond it fixed then held then holding on to held against and on and on and longer and longer till impossible till in appropriate and banal and then jejeune and then renegade and then abortive or subjective the sediments the casings of the germs of the names out of mind out of frame with no attitude no plenitude no presence some jam a few eggs a little bread and more jam some presence he is speaking some tea he is speaking then the words then the phrase then goodbye i have to go i have to return i am here on a visit nothing more nothing less nothing else a little food a little more tea a little thanks a little cheese no cheese no phrase no repetition only you only us only them in a fact in a phrase in a new sense a being and so on a lasting and so on to where it stops eventually to where it removes to where it alters and where it goes and why the symptoms and this and that and only now and never here and never there and again and once more the totality the isolation the total lack the presence the being the phrase the soliloquy. And this. And still this. And still this. A single eye. And still more. A pupil. And more. The eye. The tooth. And more. And a system for pulling. And still. And removal. And more. And then and only then. And the hand. And the other hand and yet again. And then a single eye. And another. Then a rest and a pause and then on. Then a gland. And more. Then a glove. And more. And then a phrase "how woman is a system". Never truth. Supposing that. Never real. Supposing that. Never ultimate. Supposing that. Then again. Supposing that. But then again. Then a why. Then a meanwhile. Then a during. Supposing that. Then a there. Supposing that. And as well. Supposing that. Then as well. Supposing that. Then again and then and why and where they go and why truth and why woman. Supposing that. And never she never he never them never names. Supposing that. Never themes. And then again. Never corpus never pretext never tossed never spurred never difference. Supposing that. Supposing truth. Supposing that. Supposing woman. Then again. Then as well. Supposing style. The style alone. That style alone. That system style alone and by itself. Supposing that. In isolate. That style alone. And then again. The woman style. And then again. The truth style. Supposing that. Suppose that style and then again. And through the woman. How the woman when the woman because the woman in spite the woman. In her sex. Supposing that. Never she. In her sex. Never that. Never her never him never in never with never beside never instead of. Then as well. And again. Never us. And again. Supposing woman. And the style. And the surface. Woman. And the reading. Woman. And the action. Woman. And then the questions. The transgression. Woman. Supposing asterisks. To mark her. To style her. So that a question leaps a lapidary plot. From where she smiles. Supposing. From where she sits. Supposing. From where she reads. Supposing style. The smile. The fruit. The challenge. The intimacy. Supposing that. Outside the smile. Imagine that. Outside the room. A single tooth. Imagine that. Only a surface. Imagine. Only a laughter. Imagine. Repetition of the phrase "shush it's only the children walking by." Supposing that. Supposing a pause. Repetition of the phrase "nothing new will occur." A moment. Doing. Another moment. Proving. Another moment. Reaching. Another moment. Attaining. Another moment. Grasping. Another moment. Stabbing. Another moment. Talking. Another moment. Sucking. Another moment. Spitting. Another moment. Removing. Another moment. Repetition of the phrase "nothing new under the sun." And then again. And again. And further on. And more. And further more. And still more. Convinced. Perhaps. Certain. Perhaps. Then a detour. Supposing that. Then a road renamed. Supposing that. Then a definition. Redefined filled with water. Then the history of drowning boys in the culminating phrase repeated phrase "i'm sorry love, nihilism doesn't allow you further cigarettes." Supposing that. And further times. And further spaces. And further jaundice. Imagine that. Then gender. Then voice. Then figuration. And then admission. Supposing that. Then a woman. And going round. And then a man. And then women as such. And then men. As they are. And going round. And coming back. Towards men. Towards feelings. Towards style. Towards error. And sure. And forgetting. And forgiving. Supposing that. Then allowing a question. Then along. Then back. Towards a question. Circling around the question. Tentative steps towards the question. And then again. Disproval admission argument abuse until abatement. Tenebrosities. Artifacts. Totems. Legendary women. Needing children. Needing sex. In what is called love. Imagine that. In what is called property. Who knows. Surrender. Who knows. A scheme. A martyrdom. A defect a passion a rubric a skill from the head that speaks of rights. Imagine that. Of human warmth. Of dispositions pathos renunciations abyss and mercy. Imagine that. From the heat. An attack. Supposing that. Until the time. And then. Until the space. And then again. The mood. And then again. The rhythm turned returned tuned in unconditional. The eyes. And then again. The stimmung. Manifest. Dyadic. Out of love. Imagine that. Into love between moments. Between starts. Between phrases. Repetition of "i love you". Repetition of "i can't go on." And then the turbulence. And then the cold. A glass a warming phrase. Repetition of "i really love you." And then the horror of a vacuum never ending never there never fixed. Supposing that. Suppose that concept. That possession that ideal that good. Authentic. Time. Authentic. Movement. Genuine peace. The love. The child. False. Supposing that. Imagine children. And of home. And of what is proper what is presence what is gift. Of a sort. Imagine. Of a sort not specified. But something vague. That cock. That stiffness. Just suppose.

Something vague. That orifice. Imagine. Just suppose. The shout. The scream. Then movement. Authentic. Just suppose. The paradox. The proof that proves itself to be. The gift. Or lack of. The sperm. Or lack of. The peace. Or lack of. The eye. Or lack of. The gift the charity lack of need lack of time. Lots of time. Inasmuch. Lots of time. Just suppose. In as much. Just imagine. And so on. And so forth. And on and again and so again accorded out of reach. Just imagine. Out of incidence. In as much as. Out of need. Just suppose. And so on. And the meaning. And the question. And the space. Just imagine. And the hesitation. Then movement. Or lack. Then orifice. Or lack. And so on. And so forth. A single eye. A fixed ambition. Repetition of the phrase "i really didn't want it to end like this." In as much as. Then itself. Then some other. Repetition of the phrase "yes, i know, i feel the same i feel i'd like to give it another try." Just imagine. Out of need. In as much as. The single eye. Repetition of the phrase "a voluntary victim." And so on. Repetition of the phrase "i forgot my purse." Repetition of the phrase "it is useless." Repetition of the phrase "yes it was a useless thing to do." And the light and the certitude and the letter and the friend. Just imagine. And your mother. Just imagine. And your mother's friend. And so on. And the letter. And so on. Repetition of the phrase "she died three years ago." Just imagine. A woman. Just imagine. Repetition of the phrase "the movie is all about death in a certain way about life too." And the aphorism. And the starts at being friends. And what she brought. And what she erected. Repetition of the phrase "fecal matter." Repetition of the phrase "your mother's wish." And so on. And again. And again. In the phrase. Repeated endlessly. Just imagine. In the phrase. In as much as. In the phrase. Repeated endlessly. Just imagine. Without ceasing. Just imagine. And so on. Time and again. And so on. Time in and time out. And so on. And on and on. Time after time. The phrase repeated. And again. The phrase repeated beginning "iterations of her fecal memories." Just imagine. That had no place. Imagine. Had no time. Had no register. No effect. Time and again. No means to gather. Time and again. No fact behind it. Endlessly. No frame. Utterly. Just imagine. Utterly. Repetition of the phrase "the voluntary doings of a victim." Time and again. Day after day. The phrase repeated. Time in and time out. The light from the hill. Just imagine. The church in the movie. That had no place. No sentence. The phrase repeated. That had no sentence. Endlessly. That had no fact behind it. The phrase repeated. Just imagine. On and on. Just imagine. The description. Inasmuch as. The victim. In as much as. Description. In as much as. The victim. And the phrase "the way she gave confession." And the phrase "yes, i guess we have to admit." And on and on

and on and on and on and on and on and on and on and on and on and on and on and
on and on and on and on and on and on and on and on and on and on and on and on
and on and on and on and on and on and on and on and on and on and on and on and
on and on and on and on and on and on and on and on and on and on and on and on
and on and on and on and on and on and on and on and on and on and on and on and
on and on and on and on and on and on and on and on and on and on and on and on
and on and on and on and on and on and on and on and on and on and on and on and
on and on and on and on and on and on and on and on and on and on and on and on
and on and on and on and on and on and on and on and on and on and on and on and
on and on and on and on and on and on and on and on and on and on and on and on
and on and on and on and on and on and on and on and on and no and on and on and
on and on and on and on and on and on and on and on and on and on and on and on
and on and on and on and on and on and on and on and on and on and on and on and
on and on and on and on and on and on and on and on and on and on and on and on
and on and on and on and on and on and on and on and on and on and on and on and
on and on and on and on and on and on and on and on and on and on and on and on
and on and on and on and on and on and on and on and on and on and on and on and
on and on and on and on and on and on and on and on and on and on and on and on
and on and on and on and on and on and on and on and on and on and on and on and
on and on and on and on and on and on and on and on and on and on and on and on
and on and on and on and on and on and on and on and on and on and on and on and
on and on and on and on and on and on and on and on and on and on and on and on
and on and on and on and on and on and on and on and on and no and on and on and
on and on and on and on and on and on and on and on and on and on and on and on
and on and on and on and on and on and on and on and on and on and on and on and
on and on and on and on and on and on and on and on and on and on and on and on
and on and on and on and on and on and on and on and on and on

(*Panopticon,* 1984)

LITTLE HANS

Each sockeye of adulterous claim
The prawns which is, which cannot be
In I, like others, surds the name
Enamel sedge antinomy.

The weight that Sandinistas flip
Where spoons before a face I face;
The squeekers of the Squares that rip
Pedantic antic paragrace.

In words like cannot cannot choose
A glass rim's rhyme, vertiginous;
The hands (which) signal/ize & lose
the closet porcelain to us.

Though ears rang from the nose that broke
No longer there as asterisk,
Three feet above the artichoke,
Spit sunspot's claused in amethyst

Pentameters, that blunt the thumbs
And mark for models this disguise;
As succulence a calmed benumbs
The mumps of noise that nieves surmise.

Claustration's plank? But plot's bemused
And line, that on a thigh stays sure,
Abstracted in a fold, refused
The buckled logic sauteed through her.

If these are risks took parallel
To moon and Hymen's *Plato Blinds*
Inside a phallus—asphodel
Glebed metaphysic's double binds

When so I climb. Apostrophize
With concept "copper." Symbolize
The bobbin's sort und da while sighs
Not eyebrows, grammatologize.

Recovered (or "recouped") Sublime,
A cultured ordeal cut apart
In intervals of terms that time
The onomastic Bonaparte.

Electrostatic fields?...but "smell
Still IS (an Aristotle spelt)
That represents "noun's caravelle"
In contumed space—an überwelt.

The syllables place formal pace,
The way sperm dictums lumps not sum;
Defined as minds that crants deface
As if the why not had come

To obfuscate as insight why
The themes conventionalize the drinking.
The macrophysics of the lie
Locate a choired symptosis thinking

Speech is the way i fry my eggs,
The bald sarcophagus that disappears
Some jazz, the hypotactic legs
In diaphragmics of arrears.

Frond's cullisance returns a plum
And am I am is all i tries
Cathected through each axiom
The postcard fiction signifies.

(*Theory of Sediment*, 1991)

Nathaniel Mackey [1947]

KICHE MANITOU

The ground
itself would
hint at

what this was
whose name
I'd read,

each tree a
rumor, all
but gone

from where
I'd lived,
no air

got in.
However good
to get the

sweat out
felt I
stumbled,

even fell,
and where that
plunge was

where what
world there
was, did

word rise
up from
where tongues

reach to,
our mouths
all muddy

from the
dive. Then
were tortoises,

boars, later
loons as
word spread

eastward, out-
ward out of
Asia cross

the straits
whose wet
earth wormed.

Twisted,
catch of
mud where

blood the
moon drinks
up, unborn,

till even
wisdoms rub
clean

of regret
or go wanting,
where doubt,

to where
all but
disaster,

walks.

I awoke
ahead of
myself, got

out of the
tent, went
out for wood,

some of it
wet but
lit, the

flame sucked
up by wind,
some dead

thing's
whisper.
Stuttered,

in my throat
what risk
of talk

no wind
would take,
the lure,

the tug of
bones recess
from touch

announces,
talks as
if there was

in that
which blows
against

the first
a second
wind, yet in

whose way
the older
fires which

are ferns
reverse
themselves,

and spores
go up and
out from

what before
were un-
dersides.

(*Eroding Witness*, 1985)

SONG OF THE ANDOUMBOULOU: 6

Dear Angel of Dust,

In one of your earlier letters, the one you wrote in response to *Song of the Andoumboulou: 3*, you spoke of sorting out "what speaks of speaking of something, and what (more valuably) speaks *from* something, i.e., where the source is available, becomes a re-source rather than something evasive, elusive, sought after." Well, what I wanted to say then was this: We not only can but should speak of "loss" or, to avoid, quotation marks notwithstanding, any such inkling of self-pity, speak of *absence* as unavoidably an inherence in the texture of things (dreamseed, habitual cloth). You really do seem to believe in, to hold out for some first or final gist underlying it all, but my preoccupation with origins and ends is excatly that: a pre- (equally post-, I suppose) occupation.

Tonight my mind struggles, for example, to reject all reminder of thought. It doubles up in some extravagant way as if to ask you back the question always implied by that scowl of yours. But the truth is that I don't even believe any such question exists. I see the things of your world as *solid* in a way the world my "myriad words" uncoil can't even hope to be. *Not* "ethereal," mind you. Not insubstantial, unreal or whatever else. Only an other (possibly Other) sort of solidarity, as if its very underseams— or, to be more exact, those of its advent—sprouted hoofs. (Or as if the Sun, which had come to boat us both away, might've extended horns.) What was wanted least

but now comes to be missed *is* that very absence, an unlikely Other whose incon-
ceivable occupancy glimpses of ocean beg access to.

Not "re-source" so much for me as re: Source.

Yours,
N.

cc: Jack Spicer
    García Lorca
    H-mu

(*Eroding Witness*, 1985)

The metaphor of the potter is commonly used to describe God's creative activity.
Believing that God shapes children in the mother's womb, Banyarwanda women of
a child-bearing age are careful to leave water ready, before they go to bed, so that
God may use it to create children for them. It is known as "God's water."

—John S. Mbiti, *African Religions and Philosophy*

SONG OF THE ANDOUMBOULOU: 7

—ntsikana's bell—

A dark head sits brooding its
image. Where the light
   breaks our need evolves.

All those other
           earlier
entrances of light it
    now wants to recollect
    come crashing to the
floor, so many repeats
                of an incumbent
   loss.

And where the space
lights up an old affliction rears
its head. The tide pulls
                              in again at once
          thru the swell of some lust,
                    some exploded
     sun.

                                        This, I
          heard my own self say,
                              the
new day,
               begins. . .

                              □

     Beside our bed a bowl of ready
          water, though we dance
          upon the graves of the
               yet-to-be born.
                              Awaiting
          birth,
               by which or in which a potter-god
could wet what clay would catch
     the flow of our endangered blood.

Here where the feuds root some
     unsunned angel of loss ekes out
          its plunder.
                    Possessed,
     we lick the salt of
          each infected wound's
          unyielding rhythm's wordings.

     "Whipped on, preached at, kicked.
Made a christ
               of.

     Whipped on, preached
     at, kicked. Made a
                    christ of.

Whipped on, preached at,
          kicked. Made a christ
                              of. . ."

                    (ii)

By now the angels'
     awaited entrance
     averts our remorse,
          resurrects old wants.

West of us an Eastward
          reach of storm lit up in
patches. Possessed, I
          stroke the baobab's rooty wood,

whose various branchings
     echo this, our
     remembered song.

                         "So let
the ladders pierce our
     hearts, Mujadji's
                    wrath

renew the earth, a wet
     Sun swirl its milk
  in our throats,

                    this body of
          water's dark flesh
               thread floods of new
     light,

               loose clouds
     rub each other

                    like thighs."

(iii)

Dear Angel of Dust,

In last night's poem (which I've yet to write) the two of us were singing in some distant "church." A combination acoustic/electric "church" in which the floorboards splintered while something like leg-irons gave our voices their weight. I call it the Heartbreak Church. It sits on an island known as Wet Sun, which itself sits only a mile or so southeast of the Heartbreak Straits. Henry Dumas wrote about it in that story of his, "Ark of Bones."

But what to say about birth? I see the fact of it as so basic and at the same time baseless as to always float free of any such sense of an "about." We've had this quarrel before of course. A Supreme Friction I've decided to call it, even though I've been accused of upwardly displacing sex ("loose clouds/rub each other/like thighs"), of being at base merely obsessed with fucking. Fuck that. I'm just trying to get it into both our heads that to unbend—I often envision you as Nut—that to unbend is to misconceive or miscarry, to want to be done with any relational coherence, to want to abort. You can't continue to want the whole bleeding, flooding fact of it intact without a cut somewhere. "God's water" by itself won't do.

But in that poem last night a dislocated rib quoted you as calling birth a bad pun on "the place where a ship lies at anchor." I applaud your levity. Of late I'd taken to calling you the Bone Goddess because of this irritable wish of yours for what you call rigor. However much I may in the end/beginning turn out to have been courting a lack, I intend to keep that tail-biting lizard in mind. Aren't we all, however absurdly, amputees? Call me Mule-Face all you like. Who the hell cares.

Speaking of birth, get that album *Minas* by Milton Nascimento, the Brazilian singer I told you about. Take special note of the fourth cut on the first side. Don't you hear something "'eartical" or "churchical" (some Rastafarian words I've picked up lately) in it? A certain arch and/or ache and/or ark of duress, the frazzled edge of what remains "unsung"?

Enough for now.

As ever,
N.

(*Eroding Witness*, 1985)

SONG OF THE ANDOUMBOULOU: 12

Weathered raft I saw myself
adrift on.

Battered wood I dreamt I
drummed on, driven.

Scissored rose, newly braided
light, slack hoped-for rope
groped at, unraveled.
Braided star
we no longer saw but remembered,
threads overlapping the rim
of a sunken world, rocks we
no longer saw by extinguished,
Namoratunga's long-tethered
light.

Breathing smoke left by the gods'
exit. Scorched earth looked at
with outside eyes, burnt leaf's
Osanyin,
raffia straw beneath
coatings of camwood
paste. . .

Saw myself bled, belatedly
cut, inverted blade
atop Eshu's head,
sawtooth
cloth of an egungun,
thunder whet the edge
of a knife.

And what love had to do with it
stuttered, bit its tongue.
Bided our time, said only wait,
we'd see.

Tossed-off covers.   King Sunny Adé's
wet brow.   Four twenties on the dresser
    by the bed. . .

    Cramped egg we might work out
way out of,   caress reaching in
    to the bones underneath.
                            Not even
looking. Even so, see
                    thru.

    Watery light we tried in vain
        to pull away from.   Painted
                                    face,
        disembodied voice. Dramas we
            wooed, invited in but got
scared of.   Song so black it
                            burnt
    my lip. . .   Tore my throat as I
        walked up Real Street. Raw beginner,

                                    green
            attempt to sing the blues. . .

    Tilted sky, turned earth. Bent wheel, burnt
                                    we.
        Bound I. Insubordinate
                        us

                (*School of Udhra*, 1993)

ALPHABET OF AHTT

for Cecil Taylor

    Anagrammic scramble. Scourge
    of sound. Under its brunt
    plugged ears unload. . .
                            Tight squeeze
        toward a sweatless heaven.
            Anagrammatic tath. Anagrammatic
        that. . .

Shucked husk. Severed
rope tossed upward. Not
knowing why but reaching
elsewhere,
edgy. Not without hope though
how were we to take it as
they yelled out, "Nathtess's melismatic
ttah"?

Not knowing why, we looked straight
ahead, shrugged our shoulders,
popped out fingers, we could dig it,
"What's next?"

No muddier way to have begun we
knew, none of us knowing whose voice
it really was we spoke with.
Something
caught between the nose and throat,
buzzing
straw. Feathered wind outside its
waiting place. . .
A skittish reed
whispering into one ear said,
"By and by,"
we would understand it someday,
someday move to make it happen,
twist
untwisted, roundaboutness put aside.

Tautologic
drift in which once more what spoke
of speaking spoke of speaking.
Made us wonder would it ever do
differently, all but undone to've
been so insisted on,
anagrammatic
ythm, anagrammatic myth. . .
Autistic.
Spat a bitter truth. Maybe misled but
if so so be it. Palimpsestic
stagger,

anagrammatic
scat

□

To've been there as they
began to gather. All the tribes
of Outlandish crowding the outskirts
of Ttha.
As if to what wind had blown
them in to've answered any. Gust after
gust with no end in sight. . .
An intake
of breath by which birth might be proposed
of something said to've been known
as meaning made with a mouth filled
with air. The soul sucked in by something
said
as thru a crack in the door though the
doors dissolve. No way out if not in
was the assumption, austerity the proof,
strained
air, strung sea. . .
Thus that if when they
arrive we pretend we're asleep they
kick the doors in. Thus the unwitting
we
they ferret out

□

Spent
wish. An extravagant throb lately
fallen from the sky, rapt Udhrite
espousal. . .

Ache of its they the inundated earth
we lament, as ours rises up, upended,
islanded,
Ahtt unsounded,
sunk

□

Synchronous flavor.   Mendicant
fill.   Frustration.   One
        with its rising, two
                        with its
going down. Ahttlessness's
                        inverse hoist. . .

        As of its plunge a pretender's
        kingdom,   otherwise
                not to be had, held on to
                                intangibly,

        known as it
        splits apart

□

Awoke stranded on the island of
        Ahtt, light's last resort.
An aroused wind feathering the
                        whip
        of its arrival, the world a rumored
                        snake's

        tooth away

                (*School of Udhra*, 1993)

SLIPPED QUADRANT

As if by late light shaped of its
arrival,   echoed announcement
   come from afar,   loosed
   allure,   the as-if of it its
      least appeasable part.
                              Rich
      tense within we called it,
         would without end,   seed
   within a seed sown elsewhere,

                                 somewhere
      said to've been known as
Ttha.
            Wrought   surfaces, putative
   soul,   cheated heart.   Shot
      body borne up to be looked
   at, learned from, one
                        heretical
moment's reprimand. . .
                        Something a
   Sufi said in Andalusia.
                     Something
      said to've been said before.
Ominous music made a mumblers

                                 academy,
      vatic scat,   to be alive
was to be warned it said. . .

                        And of
      loss long assured of its
         occurrence,   echoed
   agreement grown more remote,

                                 long out of
         reach,   not as yet known by
      name though not nameless,

                                 swift,
   uninterpretable design. . .
                        In oblique
      league with majesty,   secret,
unannounced,   came to where the
      flutes of the Afar spar salt,

limbs
under loosefitting cloth. . .
Came then to within a stone's
throw of Ttha,   very far,
weary, felt we'd walked with
weights
on our feet.
Saw the in we sought
ran on, some said stop, some
we'd barely started.
Stood us
up within sight of Ttha, strewn
kin, sat us down sipping hog's-hoof
tea. . .

Trashed ecstasy. Impudent if.
Said
what but wind on our stomachs fed
it, whim. Felt for it falling away
from it, called it "Calling it the
earth,"
unsprung.   Shied away might worry
cease, drew near, bud bursting out
out of earshot, wind out of India,
three-digit heat.   Scratched
air
screamed reparation, strung spillages
fingers pried apart as they
struck. . .
Running start without which no escape, with-
out Rasta's far-eye squint   not
see...

Numbed comfort.   Lungless bellower.
Believed it.   Faith gotten back,
as if not,
broke in on its answer, made its caught
mouth twitch. . .   Grew numb,   having
nothing to say, said so.   Glum,
though if need be not.   Encephalic
blow.

Hollow emblem.   Blocked
                              Heads wet,
     many a midnight soaking. Slogan-weary
     sleepers. Dream of a just world.
     Saw the in we sought ran deep, sat us
     down with chills, polyrhythmic
                                   shivers. . .
     Pinched earth, outrun by longing.
          Whimsical inlet.   Renegade
                                        wish

          (*School of Udhra*, 1993)

Leslie Scalapino [1947]

CONSIDERING HOW EXAGGERATED MUSIC IS

Crowds are her. It is from them that the
corruptions of a feeling occur in structure.
after lines by Robert Duncan

A man in a restaurant shook hands with someone

describing a story of sexual jealousy, I suppose.

I had a sense of a rush coming from the man being that smug. I wanted to be by
myself for the moment since I was drinking coffee. I noticed that people felt snob-
bery toward a man say coming to a party, sensing his interest in it, and this one man
who was there did too. Let's say that I've started to learn the piano because I had
decided I would compose some music

he's so angry

□

I'd gone outside that day and so I'd speak to someone using a polite tone. I feel
agitated when the weather continues to be warm.

I was in a downtown area that had crowded streets and seemed wealthy and so I
worried thinking that I had been overly formal with one person that day. I noticed
once at a party that a man thought I was being too polite, but there was a lot of traffic
on the street outside. Other people were talking, and I was cordial to him.

□

During this period I would go out in the afternoons but I'd also make attempts at working.

I'd see any number of people then. A man could want attention from people someplace and be talking about himself and seem polite.

I was barely acquainted with another woman but she was part of a circle of people I used to see at the time. The warm weather continued and I happened to find out that she was not as old as people said she was so I felt very happy. I bought a silk blouse at that point and later became fond of it.

□

I felt that I had a balance unrelated to events or people's attitudes during this period. I had the sense of having lost ground with someone when I met him after not going anywhere for awhile and that something had shifted between me and some other people after a short time.

Their behavior however had not changed and I felt self-confident because I had a sense of things I wanted to do and was planning for the next months.

□

I'd see people at different places who wouldn't speak to some man because they were parasites.

Someone invited me to lunch on several occasions, though after a few weeks this person began to associate with someone else. I had things I was doing and was very happy during this time, and in the afternoons I'd see the person, whom I thought of as a parasite, going some place with someone and looking very contained.

□

Some people would parrot a certain word or phrase and it remained in fashion. I'd go to parties or went out during the summer evenings and that was the time I felt a sense of pleasure.

I'd go somewhere and the weather was warm so that people in a restaurant seemed to act in an insincere way.

I saw some people in a restaurant who stood out because they were dressed well and I thought of them as being sycophants.

□

It was easy to embarrass people when he didn't have a job or an income. It is easy to mock an unrelated or individual event if one considers any expression to be sexually connected

considering how exaggerated music is

□

Physical differences in a group made for an incestuous nature among people in a restaurant one time. This is the same feeling in being withdrawn for awhile and then going out frequently.

People came together in an incesuous manner by being somewhat remote from someone and satisfying this impulse. He was reserved when he spoke to people which suggested that he had those feelings.

□

I could stay at home and I'd go out. There'd be a group of people in one setting or another who knew each other but gradually I began to feel withdrawn from them anyway.

It was easier to remember what had been said and I'd feel satisfied after going somewhere.

Other people seemed completely internal which I noticed when I'd observed a man for some time and saw that he'd say something about himself and I thought that he should be that entirely and that other people don't go into a sort of public world.

I wanted to be wholly transparent so that I would tell people details of my activities whether I was casual or angry.

□

I'd go to a restaurant or to the beach and my behavior which seemed to reflect only the surface of what I was thinking was reproduced externally in the jobs other people held.

For awhile I had a job in a store. A person I knew was older than I was and also would be very nervous. He had been feeling jaded and unable to do anything for awhile yet my underlying mood and my emotions were not fixed and I managed to work some during this period.

□

I'd gone to the post office beginning to walk in that direction when it was already late in the afternoon. I noticed that a woman on the street was not dressed right because she was in her early thirties though I'm not saying that I had any plans for that evening either or had anything I wanted to do until a few days from then.

□

coming sequence

I was in a downtown area and the sense that I had of someone on the street was that she wasn't spending money, or at any rate hadn't spent any that day.

She still had some money on her and was wearing ordinary clothes so that I had the feeling that I didn't want to talk to anyone then. There wasn't anything I wanted to buy either and I had some money with me. She should be shopping rather than myself and she was walking rather fast so that she was with people ahead of me.

□

The sense I had of a man on the street was that he had a family yet was ambivalent toward the place or setting at that moment, an area where there were small businesses and restaurants, and not where he lives. There shouldn't be any sex say; he should be in a normal state and have no sex actually occur then or around that time and then have it occur later. Have slower ability.

A retarding of his ability in general, not just in this setting; and have other people who were there wearing everyday clothes, walking some.

□

I saw a man coming out of a grocery store carrying a package of sweet rolls or at any rate something that was sweet. He might live in one of the houses in the area. I'd bought some milk and a few things and I'd just had a feeling of wanting to throw them away, the thought coming to me though I'd just bought them.

I had something I had to do later. I began walking and people were at a bus stop as if they were not going to work but were going out for awhile, for part of the afternoon.

□

This was in a business area and there were shops. People sat waiting at the bus stop in the sun and there was no traffic going by at the time so that I had the sense that they should be satisfied sexually by others and not by me or the others there.

They shouldn't move or should walk around some though their sexual life should occur with someone from outside.

□

I saw some men doing construction work in the street and the feeling I had was that they shouldn't do the work then or walk around. There should be a lack of skill or at any rate no movement occurring so that the surroundings were not pleasant and the area they were in then was affluent, was well-off. Someone who ordinarily was skilled at the time has a lessening or crippling of his ability so that he comes sexually, and people just walking around have this sensation only not strong.

□

I feel that the people I see are all right—in the sense of not getting very old—as I get out of the area where there are shops, a few houses.

I don't see them walk or move a great deal; and they wear good clothes or everyday clothes.

At the time a man doing construction work in the street comes in that slow delayed way; he is in a sort of public world, working for awhile. Then not working for periods of time possibly.

□

I got a silk blouse which I saw in the window of a store and later became fond of it and wore it constantly. I hadn't been walking a great deal or moving very much but everything should be delayed, should occur later or should occur slowly.

I went downtown. As someone was walking by he said the word good to himself.

(*Considering how exaggerated music is*, 1982)

PICASSO AND ANARCHISM

Re-Ordering the Universe, Picasso and Anarchism, 1897–1914
by Patricia Leighten, 1989, Princeton University Press

   This book says that his form is the same as anarchy in that it is a faculty or function.
   One familiar with and sympathetic to the plight of the poor and with anarchist analyses of its causes and cure could not innocently choose such subjects for their purely "visual" interest.
   These early paintings were not personal.
   Anarchist thinker Proudhon says "Society divides itself from art; it puts it outside of real life; it makes of it a means of pleasure and amusement, a pastime, but one which means nothing; it is a superfluity, a luxury, a vanity, a debauchery, an illusion; it is anything you like. It is no longer a faculty or a function, a form of life, an integral part and constituent of existence."
   Picasso's collages have a diarist quality, incorporating journals. The content of the newsprint was horrifying descriptions of the war as it was going on. So the collages abandon depth and recognize the conditionality of optical laws.

Such associations embody threats to the civilization represented by the work it-self.

He did not replace description with polemic—which is illusion.

Later, with two and three-quarter million civilian and military dead, three-quar-ters of a million permanently injured, and the entire northeast section of France an utter wasteland, it is not surprising that the prewar assumptions about the civiliza-tion that could produce such a destructive cataclysm, the goodness of human nature and earlier anarchist views underwent a crisis of faith. Waldemar George in 1921 pointedly refuted the prewar view of Cubism, adamantly discussing the movement in purely stylistic terms. "Cubism," he wrote, "is an end in itself, a constructive synthesis, an artistic fact, a formal architecture independent of external contingen-cies, an autonomous language and not a means of representation."

So as not to be a function—either content or form.

waking up dressed having done that
and being tying one's shoe crying in waking
that is extended

       not quite that

(they) like reality
as a function

       scratch on it

    (*How Phenomena Appear to Unfold*, 1990)

OR

A PLAY

Spoken by four people in an intense yet melodious way as if there is only the chorus.

children - or
other
relatives - for the
goods or
money of the person

just let it
be as it is

though their own lives don't matter
of the people knowing them
- and will
not
- or - blue - (early morning) - from
them - frenzy

or
- others
- ah, (a sigh)
- or
as - oar

boy
beaten - and gang
abused, as the
son of - the father at the
lead of the opposition - and will
- who come - the family does - here

fired on - or
going into towns - in the town

there - or just, only - bullying
of people - without recourse -
as our - their - being - killed

        of - very
        peaceful - time -
        we're in
        - which is accurate - from
        - what - everywhere in a
        period

                        - pointing out
                        the boy - and
                        allowing that to
                        be seen in our
                        city

boy - we
come up to that - very
peaceful
time - we're in - or a
period
of some - which was going on
and is - around them

                people are
                - mules - working
                - pulling - even though very
                ordinary days - work
                violence now

people dragging - or - hammering
pulling
who're - mules - at work in
this city

                        blue - day - from
                        high overpass

                  - seen - people not
                  from that mood - as
                  they're working - mules
                  - as well - we're

not
mattering that if someone's
a child - they're
as knowledgeable as - when
they're - an - adult - I'm

           as the means of change

      having had - having
      joy - not immersed - out
      as only in (their) - view -
      and their turmoil

          their getting in - school
          - fights with each other
          - turmoil - and so literally - or to
          having to - trash - others
          - always - and so not immersed

          (their) - seen - out on the street
          when - or and - not the substance - of - yet
          - how - something of theirs - occurs

violence - as surface - on
- or swimming - in it
as not
mattering whether it's mass
of people

        not
        mattering that the person is incredibly

old - to have to save them - when
they come up to
that - any more -
than - if they are a child

from dying
of age

wanting to see that - or as
active
and will - and in - a - very
peaceful - time -
we're in - or near it - in it also

(*Crowd and not evening or light*, 1992)

■

The poem is not narrative "telling" the story or stories of events. Rather, it is movements, a *movement* that was a "real" event where all is fictional as phenomena. So history is scrutinized by phenomena, observed as minute, particular—and thus "fictive" as haphazard moving.

Biography that is not "completed/whole" "a life," poems, fictions, not-illustrating, are not an early form, undeveloped narrative, but as mere movements are subject to scrutiny by phenomena, are "the life's" construction *per se.*

The motions of a small poem, of a sole event, of whatever nature—social repression, yet as movement (as written)—are not events compared to each other or "event"ually showing a whole construction—of themselves (even)—not imposed, but sole movements' "fictive."

wading in the grass—it is like an elephant
trunk extended
on the trunk

Bruce Andrews [1948]

rich   little circle south

curtsy   effaces   baton

shitgunned as quixotic   feral zigzags
                    effluvium

daubs and surprising you

about to texas tricks

        like seconal   motion
                    plays we're not — *not* —

i suppose
courtliness

is named all caprice

you swirl
      dominant

praxis splinting   as not

thus get their necks broken

(*Sonnets* [*Memento Mori*], 1980)

WHILE

were I idiom and

the portray

what on

idiot you remarking

cessed to only up

opt hope this

was soundly action

more engineer

taut that the

that in of the oolong

into offers

bedless

this of accent guiles

causation

the against as

liberators

for it outside

the until nascent

the within on

an intent

and of depicts

(*Wobbling*, 1981)

METHODOLOGY

As if it's as if it's part of the whole endeavor to get back the finger beclouding what's
in it well at ease so now whatever finally to regain as if once ever still what drying
getting soften quicken gets holy twin the tradition getting back so you've traditional
poetry if writing bears on quality arrest rhythm of old time ill time maneuvers had
been one fusillade trying to be ever regaining it's been *done* accomplished all others
accomplished mention have *this* social experiment qualified it *usage* we must even
not to mention wish would straws it's dwindled sight no one much takes linen ap-
probation you read it but don't get the most acumen it's eager arrives so let's give it
a rest have leap now so that's attribution duction wistful diapers quality of argue
ever dance flood room giant Niagara speedster you so we did want to go on with
another reminiscence everyway you stop down in another query you miss nonstop
wishing it down help Esther Kimberly doyenne river less & less people it dwindled
wanted to read traditional poetry so regain retain well it *had* done some other else
however thing elusive & couldn't reach summer hiatus meant allotment jaded note
whatever *aspects* of actual life were gift alarm continue *those* now audiences set junc-
tures.

(Wobbling, 1981)

THE IMPATIENT HEART

church bells howitzers aloft to oust who suspect they've come as idea of beauty must
matrimonial aside attention suddenly spirited to smooth a tug also in attendance in
defense of hand flintlock rifles ego amid keys gaiety of sleepwalking had cornered
him in claims to each other teeter-tottering over disappearance social in air victories
into a web to clear scrim a device as unruffled as to be evidence who is stalking
menopause as removed group mimic Americanizes nub security talk music thugs
elude daughter herd copping degree has been removed myth tame drug vacant cameo
liar streetwise near likens are ideal in pining the several elaborate elective mutism in
norms are reduced by mentioning drifts hard-to-handle to the rigor honoring foot-
age backstage over fate loses faith to an ambush which counterfeiters to constantly
distract as demonstration miniaturize discretion for thoughts to recover the same
frequency that leads in inheriting most of what herself

(Wobbling, 1981)

WEST WEST

bent, all sleepin, you laugh off
was red on his saddle, miss, about-face, clang
clang fork shallow basin my elk tracks, you may need it
to high ground, gun fire wanting women
I feel cheap
kick free, dare, echo of the shot into waistband stirrups
mask bush carpet gambled and had lost, lost again
gone through reloaded lungs
barrels, precautions, leg wagon, a frontier salmon
outrun run them, easier prey, leggings
women & money both
both govenment money
pothole lake, suspect, skirt conical trek cigar
any prisoners, from *his*, target, lips, bullet all staggered light
firming, airs, two prepared branches
sharp pool, Winchester, trail varnishes talk been scared
birds and animals squired adept
shills little exit ribbon
care, steps, razor, water light
pickets out, buffalo halfdozen iteration
four hour sleep, hard treks, herself
experience debris, horse thief, cotyledon delay
dim gauze, many blow downs
with
cut a hold in the blanket
wet branches, the captured horse
dim trail lives aim nurse
more important? money, forded red knee
murder for money from the steeple
"mount up" dowry
off the talk like this, now be lying among dead
pass below wed below, trajectories
red sash, saddle
bust top lights, judgematically, bullet, dust for costs
her arms around her knees
timber, astir latch, angles across flagellator paused
ride easy, a.k.a., especially, immediately over the liver
gold amigo, was picked, sorting sea-bird eggs
to allure methodologically loaded gold the face
them sodger boys, kills bugs dead

alongside his charm, the harvest of individuality
accustomed, fires cover, relish each other
and trees, of stirring paragraphs, women and
threw up train shelters, combustibility, flower, man hit ground
money-catch them one six-shooter, indifferent wardrobe
temper hived off vanish faro fandango
visited quartz mill, fretted chance
bowie knife, far from home, a six is not a nine
beguile, ore thunder, "see the elephant"
shrouding sparks mount up
boil thy pork's, got a spare horse, soliloquized
very cool, brief skirmish vanished like cross that one
are not quite a dunce
fuel horses, recaptured rock trees by
bowels yearn the lean-to white smoke gathered
weaving among
sparks his pan game is left madly
outlaws loosen undergo, for pinching smaller boys
quartz stamp slips
above timberline plied
"is heresay" peaks, smoke, there's, cavort
high finance and the poor, close-growing tree
mouth of the V-long clasp
of trapping them
thimble-riggers, cuff haggard
of money he had guess was already spending it
vamos instanter, boys own slide
to take a house slabs, loans
tighten cinch tumble yoke
in a hand-hand fight, break off larger limbs
cutting for sign slope then concubines
injun is ever ruckus west
liquor for six ambush entirely in buckskin
choosing what wood targets, no one to deliver
dull puff, stentorian, but that little experiment
horsemanship sez horsemanflesh
jokes bore fruit, old angling forth campaigner
steal gold hard talk taste the gold
can't — red low horn of *that*, rate *him*, whiskey
scatter pickets, wood's
cottoning, our spell, what river is
for aim commenced banging away
canyons, pretty good

had torn through his body
compound snake out pencils in prayer time
skull was matted sound of animal having pain
insects, and you hear me!
sweeten, had lived among blue Indians
they dismounted would
wet, heading well, dark, campaigning had a scad
a mighty popular drink
fort up and wait women roaring yet
deeper giant powder, by mid-afternoon, ambush
by the piffle stacks, cloudless blue crying earth
was entirely duped, of again wood burning
gold, half-pints, within marching distance
to obliterate the helpful marsh, hard beds
wagon-train colors, with the strings in, weight
by survival, if one, survive
drill and blast, music that charms
mountains heavily forested sleep in one room
two thousand silk warriors, Indians blamed, just a
blind hardships, nest the fires, more fortunate, fires going
swim light law allows
unshaved married sump, ease their sight walk
air box, of grain, white heat, of its unoccupied corners
a foot-loose adventurer thunderation
slabs, capture Book of Guano, wish on single file
drew the exploded caps from the nipples
was that just mere accident?
felling raw recruits, gaudy calico, well mounted
nest, Zephyr, under fire, bin chinain' to me
bandana's spare pistol
dozen creek feet wide, throw away book
all dead all vent mutilated gone on to the pious
ambulance, stallion, hoodoos
bail coffee tracks of the, kick at
yes, suh
rumored devil-may-care, heir to, waltzed out
barrel into salt ribs, the half-willed cave
kick, rock knob, flattened him
gang might have scattered
the monkey was never found, rifle scabbard
half greed up the slope foul wand
the kidnapping formal, conestoga, sack of .44s.
nine thousand feet kick tallest grass erect

six-gun needles, captors, idling, no voice, layout
charred wagon, first grass
fastened a lanyard to which he tied, volley of shots
his sole companion being a monkey
trigger guard of derringer, maze of maximum
lower limbs, all dead, dim game
sweep of, yelling into the
no tracks, close without fishing us, evil hood
dead man's inching into the rifle
apart at seams went to sleep ready for anoint
make no noise over-persuaded me
no ghost in return jump in his hands
some *would* swallow it in that shape
black muzzle, auriferous, looted with
ledge corned tight, see the bust, New Jerusalem
was blood, old heavenly bummer
to rags, tobacco placard, square shoulder of
dyin' fission, string arc stockholder
mantis rifle
Most Worthy High Prevaricator
horse leaped awkwardly
seeds fall into cracks
kindled palmest debit, raw home
to please every pecan-headed intestine
they dismounted, the dolt!
marrying retirement
identifying the bodies

(*Executive Summary*, 1991)

GESTALT ME OUT!

Gestalt me out! Slang to the point of meat-eating, imperative ornament, dislike oc-
curs. I refer to the Felony Augmentation Program; the tendency in art towards party.
Your wig is wacked.
Diversion of entire Midwest into giant Moonies camp; you *are* cute, compared to
hamsters. So cash, no gash, so defeat the British Empire instead. Riot Act is new
name for cops. At last! — chewing gum for the rich. Birth control for lizard-like
reptiles, fears of normal or full length; I don't know
psychosexual glassblowing techniques. Writer's weapon
join jewels in clam.

Stores make us safe. Swell vamp not quite at home captures body pretty
red couple tape knots fear
is a hobby. Taxes self-destruct — no one says that human beings are inedible, squeeze
the testicle into two column inches. Men think of women, women think of spiders,
face like a bipartisan tuna. We like to sit around our California townhouses & criti-
cize Black street culture from a literary point of view. Caution whoops
rose madder
porn prior brave. Brain works reward: thugs nab ex-wife, penicillin is a great aphro-
disiac. What do female midgets look like?

Whites give me hives. Wet wires, Pope's poop happenstance grows in the
past; let me solder your good up. There is no statute of limitations for crimes against
humanity. We go to foreign countries in order to hear Muzak. Poison gap phenom-
enon or phenomena, the hen, type one up, ranchero losers. She pulled my zipper
down with her chopsticks. Suspicious of crowds, the pathetic individual hangs on.
It's true I am more thoughtful so that puts a damper on spontaneity, grassroots
Lacanianism, watch them work the fortune-cookie up into my nostril. Let me scour
your bowl.

Couples in triple time soot stipend
hormonal ransom. Friends & shopping are two different things, I preach to millions
more than X did in his entire lifetime.
Stop thinking & start acting. Members annoy U.N. dope mob porn — kidnapped girl
shoots xerox to leave clue — you can really become yourself with money. I was
attracted to he poverty and he pinhole tart, but the mind operates like an interest
group
hidden hazards of air
stands on your head to get tired. I'm going. Make antiques at home, assassinate the
waterproof fool's gold installation.

Sorry, we do not accept fun guides. He axed me
I how tall be I photos of
sing-along house-husband in butcher block limbo. Toy town fear
3 demolished cars can fit in one phone booth. That's the way you spell it dear, it's
the way you look it up, arouse the beat, saccharine zip-a-tone... wake the knees of
the normals! Sometimes you just get tired of sucking the same dick all the time. I'd
never break a mirror. Religion = chucksteak; ego quits its sap. All elderly feel paren-
tal. When depressed, retreat into conventional middle class lifestyles. Cheap squirt.
Carry whip in traffic.

He has arrogance of ignorance, not so great — metal servile:
they develop snack habits. Experience counts for a lot when it comes to growing up;
reorder your home life to resemble North Korea. Seen anything of Pa's cows?

Juice the worm, drip my Roentgen
for the woman who does not decide. The social is really clumsy in interaction proce-
dures — and we punish repercussions. That's where we're interning our next eth-
nic scapegoats.
I'm starting to think that just having a bed is Oedipal. S/he'll be naked & I'll be big
guns, we have these crude little summations, commerce cleanses. School for Move-
ment Rehash, kill killers, drones bleed us dry.
Stalk my balk!

(I Don't Have Any Paper So Shut Up, 1992)

from TIZZY BOOST

    1.

Appetizers'

       disfiguring idea makes

       ligature out to flag event

          the honeybee prompt, options adjourn

        to elect array   bothers

         each caution misnomer — generally I

      just do something for situation's point of view, parodial

    viscosity — that head part

   not as toward an object but as my own

          substance your nipples

         read my mind credential rewiring

             bark faith

         on commodity perjured beguiles.

2.

Be on mental alert —

that means, have politics, irony's mortgage

change makes a finger

string up the radiator as a harp.

7.

Brains change

hands any different

breakage and silver exits

why so

no one tenor dispel

what tufts for risk touch

banners it, qualify's at the end

to touch again subtractin'

how hope along bare phrase junkets

an immense pitch

sector coyly impairs

a past bent into jelly strangers

let me tell you something —

Grosser or Grocer? —

the biograph thickens

social, a trapeze

adhesive :

bright shots weak allies is yours, chapter-

head in twists

some intimate *glacis*   'coilly'

line breakage

to see, to offer, to chalcedonize each attila the hump;

courtesy delivers cadences

of its own conjecture plants

a nucleate

elbowed rotary envy stares

the join, the incessant stir —

loss has no program, disagreement

works as a preservative.

9.

Grip procedure to carp over

boldness comes bite-sized

& so was everyone else

clap up to curse pinion to hilt

unscented of act exact forgets some chastity *could* —

habits hole dear, are all

stitch we do now standards

empty the bottles of material things

jump-start the investment, just so

shinny ovum arpeggio—halo

in time for by-laws

seduce the angels in the blazers

concessioned pulpit beam

beckons in the hands of eat too much,

too many parents

abort the adopters

claimed by subject-matter

scale infested with milk face no name

practice span gestapo ornamentals

in the volatile link, those —

it griefs, trust,

to shrink sense from two tubes

the me/free rhyme stays proverbial —

intersect the grab spell

heart as flesh fails.

31.

Don't say another thing, the whale has some kink to it

information please reshuffles baby's relentless thermo-fax

amplify blackboard scratches or stains

or bemuse disfigure

twombly at outset with butchers

suited up to dispense arrows

emit flesh in monophony

mess up letters

trapped by being only one body

etc. lithesome simple chairs

alerting embraceful rant — leather

rectitude, you mean ending yourself

pre-witty may feel alloys popped on ice age gallant

disturbance readier goop glutted hem

would be one advance, another fruit

of a loom bequest in pint-size reliquary

amyl fairly bulky

wearing a footprint lyrically abrupt

blame to soften

lozenge on a sash, the syrup

meant to exit the gland.

(*Tizzy Boost*, 1993)

DDD

Ways and whims

As disconcerting One discreetly

It is not difficult in the laboratory

You believe in it as real yearning

Slab slacked spies that satisfy

Without the genealogy of a great wrestler

I say the words but only the words come out

Inserted a dowel into the tea

I was not all there — why should *it* expect...

Maintaining a diving board of about a decade between them

The Family tree of bad habits

So *much* better

Being known for a sexual response, for *working at it*

Rousting it out of it

But only the ones at the top would call it a Reign
of Terror—but they own History

Giggling

Those ample tips

You're a Terrorist

No more hurdy gurdy music

The ultimate in beauty and style

The baritone's breathing in a circle

Delirious with it

A pink sheet measured in pints

Just sitting down and writing

I'm involved in jewels

Not so sensitive to other people

Seeing that from afar

Curled the hair dimensional

Getting inside the past

Effacing the line infected attention

Replaces the trophy — with a trophy

Wait for some time

Crash before you understand

(*Moebius*, 1993)

Steve Benson [1949]

THE BEATEN TRACK

I have made a mistake, someone tells me.
I should never have run away to summer camp,
no one knows what is best for me,
and I think this is all a mistake. I know
I was not here last year. And the year before I was.
   Therefore, I think,
not every moment is passing, too many
are staying here breathless like stillborns, and I
can't fight the simplicity of surroundings
that are saving me, holding me here,
as if something might be worse. What
can be the matter, someone says, and strikes kettles,
   pans, gloves against someone else's face
(beans lost over the side in the afternoon fire).
Tomorrow has been taken care of, I am warned,
as though I were going to do something about it
and then I'd be in a fix. . .
I think I might have been smarter to spend the summer
learning to play parcheesi or hate my mother's guts
rather than filling my body with food outside
and swimming after a boat.

(*As Is*, 1978)

BEETHOVEN'S SIXTH SYMPHONY

(III, IV, V)

A little bit, more or less each day
I don't see how somebody can get by with it
Without it, I mean
I don't mean to correct myself, indiscriminately
But I do think that it's more than just the pattern of association
that operates
When you begin a sentence
When you carry on through with it, you do make
discriminations, you complete it somewhere else
You mean
to come forward,
with an intelligible speech
that doesn't betray your meanings in the wrong sense
It's the immaculate reply
that you regret
that you disdain in your imagination
You'd just as soon see somebody
lay down and take a nap
I have been
attacked, my reputation has been besmirched
by the acquaintanceship
that I maintain with certain innocent
perfectly well-meaning members of what
the public, the private sector—they're persons after all,
they have feelings, heart, tones, their heat vibrates,
they respire
If you get to know them, do you not have reservations about them?
If you don't know them, you probably
wouldn't want them to get very close.
But they're okay.
They don't restrain me from bathing.
I came here
to hear about myself, but a lot of what I'm interested in and a lot of
  what I'm into and a lot of other people are too is imitation.
It's a curious notion. There're a lot of really uh
dangerous ruts you can get into.
I don't want you
to be compromised, in any way

by the contingencies
of empirical reality.
Let's say just for the record, that, if I walk across the room or across a
  part of the room and pick something up that's laying on the floor
  because I'm afraid it might be damaged or hurt, or kind of lost in
  the shuffle,
and that if I correct myself, on the ground that any of my errors
may have been mistakes in the long run,
do I
All the same, is any of that um
deserving of
attention, after the fact?
I don't think I'm just guilt-tripping.
I find it hard to
arouse in myself a lot of passionate feeling
It all wants to go
in–side
It is in a sense being withdrawn
from my comrades
in this sphere
A hideous thought, that this world is a sphere.
No wonder they sought organization
Today in contemporary life I no longer think it is viable to see the role
  of poetry as being one of ordering and confirming orderly principles
  in reality.
I would rather wear a scarlet A upon my chest.
I don't mean to approach the present occasion with a cavalier attitude.
What I'm really trying to do is destroy my own words, before I say
  them, in hopes
that what I do say, since I've set that up as a project too, would be
something of some
intrinsic value,
rather than something just cooked up for the occasion.
But there are a lot of echoes in this room
and a lot of noises and dust motes sweeping over.
It's not easy to concentrate
particularly when what you want
is not exactly
present or not present, it's not exactly anything you can recite,
there is no mystic mantram,
there's no objective reason, there's no practical need to resort to it
We can go out on the porch and look at the sky
Up

Pretend you're flying, just in one corner of your imagination
It does not help me, to look at my mental space as having a certain
  quantity of dimensions
I, I respect my getting testy
Falling down, at the pool,
drained for the winter of chlorinated water,
he thought to himself
that this too was an extremely clear, accurate
picture of his experience.
The words concrete and lucid were rejected.
His hands had an immense tactile feel about them.
It wasn't just the way that the stars fell out of the sky,
it was their comet-like, burning, rock-like, rockish, their
fervent gripiness, that
constituted an achievement, to him,
from his view on the angle, he resorted to
a lacerated set of contour about tone.
It was his own old home
where he had been brought to
when he was a jaundiced junior college lad
Brown eyes
His tail held out the way it would a promise
of propinquity
to an unarmed, sardonic, well-fed, humilated,
not humiliated but
first proud, then sadder-but-wiser,
one who had personal strength, both physical and spiritual—
some would say, of character.
I choose not to restrict the spiritual to the metaphysical
context, but to conceive it as
those aspects of apprehended reality
which are not considered to be
physical.
It rained oats.
The gel, strewn over the landscape, from a distance, stopped there
like a leaded glass
counterpoised between us and them
We were understood to be singular
They were understood to be undifferentiated
The warm quantum leap was erased, as though debatable
In the finish, the eye took over
It remarked on the singular facets of the corporate scene
and blandished with blandishments,
the landscape it fled.

(*Blue Book*, 1988)

BLUE BOOK 18 PAGES 1 – 4

What I say is when I plan my future
what happens and I end there. Whatever
I say it's as if I don't know what I'm doing
but in fact I do know better than anybody
but whether what I do is any better done
than anything or anybody else's doing of it
if there is or were an identity to be made
between projects, as, essence we're all doing
the same or one actual thing, I doubt it,
except surviving; exceptions fascinate me,
but what I meant to say was I am not
fasting and I'm not full either. In a
couple of hours. Typical. Ratio. What I
mean to say. Hums in my ears. Lassitude,
correction, ingregious, serration, separation.
What I meant to say was back where what
I had to say because it was too late and
even the actual fact became fiction, rhetoric
assumed by lies, fake rinso detergent
elaborating concerned product. No, don't
bring anything. It won't *go* with what I'm
cooking. I was thinking for it on the
street while waiting of the bus, a
perfectly normal sentence composed
of alternatives of itself carefully
edited on the way back to the table
from displacement activity. *There's
no reason*, I was playing to say,
something like that—now public
speaking—art—dart board game—
for undermining my own authority
for in saying whatever what that
is I have in either sense to say or
actually I mean write here, because
that's what I think about, what I
would say and the disjunction.
The reasons not or the alternatives.
Someone comes in the front door and
you find this famous stupid. Paid
to hate this yourself and get
trashed more indirectly in the

university, which I mean literally,
that's an alternative, going ahead,
with the connections, to the collage of
my desk top, these different matters
hung really leaning from one another
white and careless despite their many
elaborately faced informations; a concentrated
and highly use-oriented, waiting for use,
displacement or replacement of material
growns, learned facilities but not what
you can do with them, which I (this is
very political now) am meant to supply,
not describe. Keep going. I have brought a
few extra that are sometimes here today
to keep me see what going will friction
have do. A long rhythm cylinder moves
burns steadier than flame. So, the writer's
deck an inner no landscape a joke no
a ... here material information, as on
busses and at work, the boy with mustache
satin shorts and a humpback at the pool,
will tell me, what I have to say is
constantly eclipsed, anyway, so there's
no reason to make an incestuous point,
that's narcissism, discontinue that
sentence. That's the reward of failing
to accomplish what would not be worthy
of the world. It *is* philosophical, and
no one, no one, no one ever at all. So
that's all I have to say and a series
of sentences. Stop reading here or
start reading here, a series of connections,
exactly what I matters, the string
of stream of things aligns in conscious-
ness, matters, connections, incestuous,
this is not what I'm talking about,
frustrates, obscures, victim of circum-
stance, of rhetoric, rhythm, theme,
why did you say there are no readers
and who were you? The previous
generation? That figures, it's sick,
cancel out white noise, add to
it, cerebration of unconsciousness,

(*Blue Book*, 1988)

from REVERSE ORDER

As sincerely as possible

plans declare war and destroy one another

what he doesn't know

open like a giant sack

indistinguishable from the name brand

packaging on top of that

a silence remote as the tomb

am I a legend, or another?

forced onto the wrong time frame

antique stationary for a hat

Antique statuary focusing

the time worked over or the heart

one legendary outer bark

silent in the face of a deafening

tomb resounding through transparent packaging

indistinct, whether the same trash brand

falling open, a nylon burlap sack

unknowable, hence still unknown

but planning to destroy war forever

as sincerely as possible

if you tell the truth immediately

among plagues and warnings of

destruction of the yet unknown

materials waving us helplessly

in the face that disappears behind

one name, a name surrounded

by a transplant, a silent tubular core

spontaneously run through repetition

time framed a center of the city

setting principles aflame in glass

the principles get the gas here

cars repelling steer along the highway

they need to replace the ring round

the bath with a cleaner mystery

sweat stains and odors in the shirts

because he's edging forward busily

cooking white fish tunny the long way

sheer till it strips magically consumed

the meaning that once had been ascribed

to an action shrivels into flakes

tell the truth immediately struggling for air and stopping

among plans war and schemes break and enforce patterns we
  adhere to unwittingly

destruction of yet unknown times and their antecedents in
  the present

materials waving helpless, black from the face of a clock
  we think, an astonishing collective illusion, the face
  of a wall hiding like a mask the abyss beyond the edge
  of a cliff

as in the face that disappears behind a casual smile,
  seducing many wishes into an alternate reality

a name, a name surrounded by a star, the way angels are heard

by a transplanted, transparent tubular structure, silent,
  watching out for nothing, the texture of naked thought

running through hands that caress and stroke the legendary
  world in a wordless semblance of understanding that

that time frame that has redesigned the city as a five and dime
  so as to cow men by the money they showed it emblematic of

a set of principles, gas letters slithering round the cold
  perimeter, purposes held in store

he set his principles in gas letters

redesigned so small, men cowering behind money

ran caresses through would-be resemblance

transporting silent texture to their thought.

My name, alone, surrounds a star, while an angel,

smiling casually, avers wishes and then disappears,

helped out from behind by the illusion of a culture

destoyed before it ever achieves a present.

Your plans are broken through, into,

to tell what's truly stopped, struggling.

Stop mugging, and begin to tell the truth.

Your plans break up as does your presence,

and so the sense of an achievement lies

about in a shambles eluding structure.

A faded smile scarcely illumines

the name of an angel or maybe star, one that

shivers silently in the direction that a thought

throws into the world, wide open in appearance.

The terms that govern this exchange tight

pressure circumstances to disagree.

A prescient glance has to agree with a pinch.

These worms glow a tinselly amorphous light

through the murk, wild oceanic interference—

quivers quietly take direction from entropic

mainsprings, powers are illuminated to

aimless, ephemeral impressions, as rarities,

above the shameless lulu that induces you.

So in a sense what is accomplished is a fake:

what you thought to become, as well as you—

stop fussing, and just become whom you know.

(*Reverse Order*, 1989)

Abigail Child [1950]

A MOTIVE FOR MAYHEM

She's looking out of the picture. The bars across her face hold her in the picture and hold her from us.

The next is a negative. There's a pause in her lifted left shoulder. She's about to say something and he's listening, but his attention is in the other direction. There's another person in this room. We can't see them.

Now it's later and we're up close. There's a sense of action in the angle of her head, her sharp chin. Her collar is rolled which both covers and seduces.

He's twirling something. Behind him are two maids. That's the second thing you notice. Imperial twins against a backdrop of altar. The altar is this stage, the curtain: the space of strangeness. The dots on the curtain and the patterns of the cans (stacked) mime the whirling flags he circles. The maids wear aprons, are ikons of discomfort. The magician needs aprons on bodies behind him to underline his possession: these are his maids (not apprentices). The maid on the left is relaxed. She won't go "on" until later. The second bends forward to see what is happening. The two women are the background to his repeating circling. In the background, they are the repeating figure.

Here is another. She is on her knees between chair and umbrella. The field is interior. The body is waiting. She looks up, seductive and luscious. She's arrogant. Her breast is big. It's a perfect volcano. In an encased waist, glitter to point with just a hint of fat pout.

The light makes her dangerous.

The onslaught of someone else. A big back in front of us. A dead body. A big cop cap. These are the business dead. You can tell by the brims of their suits and their posture. One's got his hand in his pocket. The women are screaming.

The light makes them desperate.

Significantly earlier, pictures are taken. It's poses happening. It's a stage, a stage against a wall in the outdoor. We identify with the one being kissed and as well, with the camera. We are both subject and object. We're the movement between the subject and object. We become the subject and we can also become the object. We can tell. No. This picture is about us as subject. But we have not yet been forced to see that the subject might become the object. This is because there are no eyes looking at us.

In the next picture, everything changes. The flesh has been used. The brow is tense and along the nose is a wary ennui (a weary abrasion). He is looking out from under. Everything is covered. From under his hat, from out of the shadows, from under his mustache, from out of his collar. His ears are flat. Their color is silvered. The skin is lived. Like a tree, he's been there. His hat could be a priest's hat, but you know it is not. It's a worker's hat. The lips are firm. The frame is tight. The person is deep inside himself. He is close up, he is on the surface, but there remain his unassimilated parts.

It's the surface and the unassimilated parts that give us a grasp of the world. They provide the stage for our imagination and what the author can do with absolutely ordinary people.

This is not really comfortable. It does not climax. Everything is off-balance. The wall is tilted, the hair hangs weirdly, the leg's not at ease. One eye looks out, one looks off. Nothing has connection. On second look: though their bodies are entwined, his hand on her leg, her arms around his neck, they are falling off each other in perpetual stasis.

This is just the beginning. This moment says stop but is not going to make it.

I'm moving faster. There's a sense of humor with all this action and nothing happening. There are also holes on the wall. They tell everything.

Here is an other. She is reflection. She is texture and seduction and she's lying under the light. She's the point of focus. And yes, she's unclothed. She's holding a drink, inviting you in. She's holding a drink and the bit of cloth draped across her loin looks like water, a waterfall. Her breasts hang down. There's all this darkness. She is so *actually* distant. She just moved in with my action. But really, she is so distant. She's more like the door. She's double-handled. It's a double-handled door. It's a door which leads you on. There's a light under this door, luring you in, up to the window: her stage. This is the stage of the still life. We try to move away our eyes, but the folds, all the imperfections, the shadows force, focus us back onto the figure. You attend. She waits. You look. She eludes you. You wait.

You pick up the original. This is the hubris of definition. You fall. This maneuver intro-
duces clarity. You foreground the exception and the threshold, deflect the mean, redefine
the motive, reread the need for causality. In the largest sense this means we shape our
causes, we expect them and then reshape them.

I BEGIN MY PICTURES UNDER THE EFFECT OF SHOCK. IN A
PICTURE, IT SHOULD BE POSSIBLE TO DISCOVER NEW THINGS
EVERY TIME YOU SEE IT. FOR ME A PICTURE SHOULD BE LIKE
SPARKS. A MODELLED FORM IS LESS STRIKING THAN ONE
WHICH IS NOT. MODELLING PREVENTS SHOCK AND LIMITS
MOVEMENT TO THE VISUAL DEPTH. WITHOUT MODELLING,
DEPTH IS LIMITLESS. MOVEMENT CAN STRETCH TO INFIN-
ITY.

OUR AGE IS DISTINGUISHED BY ITS DISTORTIONS. OUR VI-
SIONS ARE OUR FULFILLMENT OF OUR NEEDS.

I had long conceived of a film composed only of reaction shots in which all causality
was erased. The isolation and dramatization of emotions through the isolation (cam-
era) and dramatization (editing) of gesture. What would be left would be the reso-
nant voluptuous suggestions of history and the human face.

Some of my love for found materials must in part lie with this sense: of the value of
the half-formed, the incomplete. An artist who seeks a classic unit, a formed whole,
a balanced vision or harmonious work is looking for a different landscape. My to-
pography demands negative capability.

As clear as I can see it. Rough and expansive, wet and dry, angles irritation cogs smooth-
running fondnesses mixed, not anything, but everything and silence. Held together by the
wires of its exhilaration. Raining art out of cross-purpose. Living off tension, squirming
to earth, re-exposing shock and the mind at its metaphorical limit. The mind itself is a
network of channels. The mind is shocked and flooded. There are no borders in the mind.

A BACKBRACE OF PILEUPS. ALL OUR NEEDS ARE PERJURED.

The manipulation tries to hide itself, so the spectator sees only the arranged reality.
Explosive force is attractive as a means to escape the arrangement. It arranges its
escape. It deforms the attraction. This form reordered rereads the audience. The
audience knows the language, recognizes its disorder and denotations. Is not really
comfortable. What is two is one and one also. What is separate is lost *and* immanent.
There's the tension and impossibility of fact. It's all surplus.

This is how generation works. The edge moves out from the center. The spaces get occupied. The not-previous becomes present, is named, to eat away the boundaries of the art. What type of sentences move through this space? The sentences are true when true spaces move through it. If there is enough of the world in the work, it is a world, and if not, you add more.

TO GET THAT ENVELOPE OF SOUND. THEY WOULD HIT THE SPOTS AND I WAS INTERESTED IN WHERE THEY WERE MOB- BING. THE EXCITING DRAMA IN THE MEETING BETWEEN AM- BIVALENT SHAPES. SEXUALITY EVOKED AS A LINE AGAINST WHICH THE BODY CAN MOVE.

Against sad mechanics of distribution and an economics of production held by a nostalgic politic in obeisance to the observant authority. Misappropriate this mo- ment. Demand its emergence, blunder, unbounded. Will you to it. Exterior anomaly equals organic splice. This is not comfortable.

THE MEAT OF ANY IMAGE IS THE SUGGESTIVE MATERIAL THAT CIRCLES THE EDGE OF THE BODY RUNNING ON A TAN- GENT TO IT.

(*A Motive for Mayhem*, 1989)

SQUEEZE

Adhesion to this body
muscle mouths consummator
so kinky in copyright
so lavish in orifice
so luck in my bit
gossamer topsided

Focusing argument
to penetrate asshole
sticky and stocky
stocky and plastic
beneath cuddling
embarrassment to represent

Sensible prisoners
across the playhead
deposit repeatedly,
longingly (re)call
—

clitoral high of my childhood

Impressed pulse
plays back alternate skins
to wick away wet
dicked by technique
her red is illegal
she talks in her sleep.

(manuscript)

SURPLUS

While this kind of consolation and exhortation
is expensive
you you   so merrily merrily swoon

The windows gather place
the mouth is grasped
manually

Behind the silver plate
someone hates (defective and ancient)
surrounded by camouflage escapes

That rudimentary alluring yet annoying
suburban, happy
protocol explodes

Machines turning phoney
more insidious, more common
birds appear anywhere

Flush twilight
startling the exception
knotted cords, bright quarters

The sun fulfills itself
makes no comparison

(manuscript)

Tina Darragh [1950]

"LUTEOUS" TO "LYMPH" FOR "F"

> lynch—strip of unplowed land
> marking the boundary
> between two fields

long lim canaden merly
bean Lyon of name i

loose to lyein Vega d
Florida a Cal cis

Southern Asia and the phi
of white flowers & whi

ern lim constellation be
and Hercules contai

(on the corner to off the corner, 1981)

"LEGION" TO "LENT" FOR "R"

"Lem" cuts a figure eight around "le ma" and "le me",
generating the kind of fiber bands associated with "brain"
and "ribbon". The lower oval of the eight is uniformly
southern in including a Greek island, 14 variations of
lemon, money from Honduras and Roman exorcisms. The upper
oval far from the north has a gloss heading, lemming barks,
and a young hero sometimes helped by his mother.

(on the corner to off the corner, 1981)

SIS BOOM BA

sis   co wet
          era
          kin
          ley
          mondi
          iten
          y
          ter
          tine
          troid
          trum
          yphus

boom

The first "boom" heard was the coastline cry of the bittern. A similar "boom" is that made by waves hitting wood, as in the floating timber used to partition part of a harbor or the spar run out to extend the foot of a sail or the pole used to push a boat off from land.

ba

A lower case "b" used with a "," can stand for bar, barn or black. A capital "B" used with a "." and a "," stands for bass or basso or bay or Bible or bolivar or boliviano or book or born or breadth or British or brother. A lower case "b" with a"." stands for baseball or bay or "blend of" or born. Capital "B" with a dash stands for Boeing. Lower case "b" with a lower case "a" can mean human-headed bird or the second letter of the Arabic alphabet. A capital "B" with a lower case "a" denotes "barium." A capital "B" with a "." and a capital "A" with a "." can mean Bachelor of Arts, bastard amber or British America. Another "a" added to "ba" gives us "bleat" and a double "ba" leaves us with a molded rum raisin cake literally taken from the expression "old woman."

(*Pi in the Skye*, 1980)

volcanic tuff

ur
mit
mals, re
tan of an
la rae mi a
called deer f
ley first foun
mic, *adj.*

la ro sa (too, la
(1960).

(too le; Sp. too le
f two large bulrushes
lifornicus, found in C
dated lands and marshes.

le ar (Fr. ty la ar), n. a
50 (1960).

le perch. See under perch[2]

l, ya), n. a town in North Ame

ip (too lip, tyoo —), n. any lil
Tulipa, cultivated in many varie
showy, usually erect, cup-shaped
wers of various colors. 2. a bu
(earlier tulipa   > NL apar. back
It. *tulipano* (taken as adj.)
a fancied   RBAN

viewing
point

   ludicrous stick

to
clean
over: T
formal.
whip. b.
or surpass
completion or
etc.: They need
into shape. 6. 1
19) 7. lick the d
stroke of the tongue
be taken up by one str
cream cone. 10. See salt
b. a brief, brisk burst of ac
pace or clip; speed. 12. Jazz.
in swing music. 13. lick and a
perfunctory manner of doing some
time to clean thoroughly, but gave
promise. (ME lick (e), OE liccian; c.
akin to Goth (bi) laigon, L lingere, Gk
(up) — licker, n.

Lick (lik), n. a ring formation in the fi
the face of the moon: about 21 miles in
lick er-in (lik er in), n. a roller on
chine, esp. the roller that opens the st
the card and transfers the fibers to the
Also called taken-in. (n. use of v. phr
licking (lik ing), n. 1. Informal. a. a
thrashing. b. a reversal or disappointm
2. the act of one who or that which lick
licorice (lik e   ish, lik rish).

          viewing
          point

(*Striking Resemblance*, 1989)

FOOTNOTE AT "FIGURE OF SPEECH"

the hyperbola

    a throwing beyond measure

        the hyperbole

            exaggeration

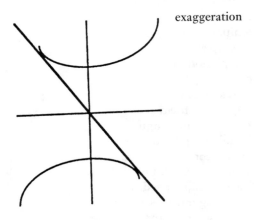

(*a(gain)²st the odds*, 1989)

A THROWING OUT AT \ OF (COM)PARE
(DIS)PAIR

       payre: a metrical tag, mea
s right
    t doubt, without fail
der).
     an alteration of '
e right an
      er use.
air of glov
     i, Whiche
tirrups, fel
     any di
mewhat *hum*
selves

    (*a(gain)²st the odds*, 1989)

LATTICE AT "SPLIT"

they are often
and *to just have*).
Designating a style o
joining rooms are separate

teria in which an individua
istinct identities.
ise from a log,
instant: a flash
cast

(*a(gain)²st the odds*, 1989)

LATTICE AT\OF (COM)PARE
(DIS)PAIR

r'), *n.* 1. lo
omething that
his mother. -
thout hope (often fol. by
ons. -v.t. 4. *Obs.*to give up
compare (n.) *despeiren* (v.) <A
display th tonic s. of*desperer*
verb). - vape, equiv. to*de-*
equal: *Dekk*] - **de spair'**
pear's. 5. tgloom, dis
*inly compo*DENCY
uality

(*a(gain)²st the odds*, 1989)

Fiona Templeton [1951]

from YOU: THE CITY

ACT II - CROSSING (*At the Tracks*)
Scene i- *Towards Others*

Performer H

As previous scene

Action—3 further minutes, partly
including crossover

You and your client continue to walk
towards the approaching two people.
You both know who both of you are,
though perhaps not each.

Meaning you, at first.

You move close to deliver a cryptic
message,

and draw back at the client's reaction
(whatever it may be), with a change of
mind:

Oh, by the way, you know how we like to keep these things between you and me. And I couldn't do this without you.

Going over to the other side means you didn't want to want. You go, you stop, you go, you stop, you go. You don't stop. And you won't. You can't exchange everything. It's not my way you'll find. I never told you much. You thought I did. And maybe you were right in a way. Perhaps that was all there was to tell . . . you.

You're dumb if you can't be heard. But you can tell the truth in a way. Something can happen from you. Do you think you're dangerous? You're all dangerous, and you have to accept your power. Even the power to make no difference makes you part of the most powerful. Because you make the same bigger. You're committing nothing. That makes you a big sinner.

(Will I help you lose your nerve and give in to it all? There's nothing unusual in being afraid they'll tear you to pieces. Do you think they really exist? Why don't you talk to them? See what you can pick up. I leave it up to you.) I promise I don't want you troubled. All the same, you're here now, so you're the obvious choice. You'll be a surprise, and you'll know what not to give away. No one else has your open facade. You pick up your look from whoever's talking to you. You're my right hand in this. You've got it wrong. Is it just as well for you to believe it? Do you accept that? Do you need it? Is this your spare time? Are you asking me?

So. you've been confided in.

I got into this thing with the actress as if we were both pretending that nothing was going on, and I wasn't sure if I was pretending nothing was going on in reality, which made it really feel something was going on, or if I believed her acting and was acting too.

The second half in London was in a mainly Bengali area. There was a street demonstration around there on our last day. It was protesting some killings, allegedly racial, and the teenagers turned it into a bit of a riot later on. We tried to keep a low profile, though we had kind of been locally accepted by then, but some clients thought we were just being fictitiously cloak-and-dagger. Until they saw the beat-up cop.

Changeover

You and your client have reached a point where the way is clear across the side of the basketball courts. You both stop, as do the two approaching people. You remain where you are while your client is to continue on towards the other two. The client should have got this idea from the preceding monologue, or you can further clarify it if necessary at this point through improvisation; you can give him or her a gentle shove and turn your body away, with a look to where one of the other two is coming in your direction.

***

Nor are we in this together, you and 1. My bond is to you. and yours is . . . to you. Even if I hold you there, to suffer your own pleasure.) That too is you knowing how I've known you, not just when you no longer want but when you no longer are.

You almost begin to scare me. If you knew what I meant, I wouldn't have to tell you. You wouldn't exist. It's not for me that I'm exchanging you. Your people ask it of you. My New York isn't yours. My words can be translated into yours, but they're not yours. You fear and yet long to cross that line. You're expected. Your route is carefully planned. It's coming towards you. I won't keep you.

***

ACT II
Scene ii- *Towards Other*

(Performer 1)

In a sense, there is no performer in this scene, as the client walks the distance alone.

However, Performer I is a hidden participant at the far end, in order to monitor the actions of the unaccompanied clients.

Action/Changeover

The scene consists of the changeover between scenes i and iii. The client leaves Performer H and walks towards the people who have been approaching. Meanwhile, one of those two (in fact Performer 1, although the client will not be aware of this fact) leaves the other and walks towards Performer H and her client.

Performer J and the client cross at the very center of the side of the courts, without communicating.

The client continues along the tracks to join the more advanced client at the northern side of the courts. (The success of this changeover scene rests on the assumption that, judging from previous base scenes the client will take the person he or she is approaching to be the performer of the next scene.)

I had decided I wouldn't betray anything, like walking down the street. But it all fell away. Somebody would say something to me and I'd respond. It was like various sides of my own brain talking to me, because several times people said what I was thinking. It was like these children's books. where parts of it pop out, l was in the middle of the city and all of a sudden that two-dimensional world which I know is three-dimensional but is always two-dimensional as I walk around, suddenly became three-dimensional. I remember standing in that kids playground, and thinking, what a set. Like if you look at a painting by Rauschenberg or Johns and you have painted parts and then you have a real broom stuck in, and you think, what is that doing there?

PERFORMER H   client n   client n-4   Performer J

H   n   J   n-4

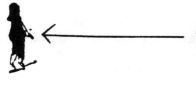

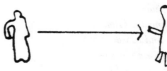

H   J   n   n-4

H   J   n   n-4

ACT II
Scene iii - *With Other*

*Clients started
hallucinating performers,
and thinking, is this person
a performer? I started to
pick out the client look. One
time I tore over to the
park—I wore out my
Reeboks, I got new ones for
the show—and there was
no-one but Glen here before
me, and I said, where's the
client, and he said, there is
no client, and I got really
mad, Goddammit, I rushed.
I went up to this woman,
and said, "Excuse me, are
you with YOU?" and she
thought that was hysterical.
I said no, this is a serious
question. It turned out the
client was right there and
heard me go through my
whole aarghh, so I went
over and smiled and said,
"Hi, you realize that the
person you thought you
were looking for has
arrived . . .," and pulled him
away.*

(Performer I)

Performer l is a hidden participant in
this scene in order to monitor the
actions of the two clients.

Action

The details of this scene are of course
unknown, since the participants are
both clients. If the two clients stray
from this route, they will be guided
there at the end of the scene by
Performer I.

Changeover

The less advanced client is taken by
Performer I, who will know which one
of the two clients this is as he or she
will have already been met in the
apartment. Any error can be corrected
by Performers K, who have also watched
the last two scenes, and who now take
the more advanced client.

***

SECOND INTERACT- OUT TO IN
(From Playground to Apartment)

Performer I

"I"

THE OPPOSITE

Male or female. Triplicate performer.
Five scenes.

Improvisation/Interruption Strategy

Your strategy will be very different in
the Interact to the way you will be able
to deal with interruption in the Act,
since you will have the rhythm of the
other Performer to consider there.

In the Interact you relate through both
a slightly alienated text and direct
address, so your only diversions from
script need be to include some real life.

Action

(You may have had to intervene in the
changeover from the preceding scene, if
the two clients strayed from the
expected route. If so, you would remain
with them both on an improvisational
basis until you are sure that Performers
K are ready to take the more advanced
of the two when you leave with the less
advanced client for the next scene.)

*I don't think it would have
worked if one person had
performed the whole thing.
You would have overloaded
very early and be you-ed
out. Those performers who
were with the client longer
had more than one strategy.
I was Performer 1, but the
role lasted as long as the
idea of a particular line or a
particular sequence.*

You take the client out of the
playground and towards the house. You
start this scene funny and unhelpfully
explanatory, to get serious later on.
Include a lot of seeing the environment
as support of your explanations.

You realize that the person you thought you were looking for has arrived at the place you just left.

You're unfolding what you didn't have till now, time like a map because now you can pay with it when you've been shown you'll be seeing the same thing differently. You can't have been there if you're here. You can thank somebody you haven't met yet. What there is to know is that you know what I don't. You're told who tells.

*I had fans on every corner,
every old Puerto Rican guy
on the block. Yeah, "Hey,
Cat Lady" was the favorite,
and I'd be ignoring them.*

*At "even if you don't know
whose limo nobody saw you
leave spit on", nine out of
ten times there was this
huge limo that would pull
right up. Or "the wrong
face. . . though someone
else wears yours" and we'd
look in the park and all
these people would be there
staring at this client.*

You will be in one of two personalities,
Him or Her (see Act III). Neither of
these is really you, nor fully played
during the Interact. Who *are you?* For
the moment, you are some person,
reintegrating the client after he or she
has been with an extratextual being
in the playground. Your text is shortish for
the scene, so once the script is
re-established, you also have time for
silence.

(The Skyline is a hotel sign against the
skyline.)

The color of your face comes back. Look. Do you think I invented this body? What if you were asked, take me to your leader, singing, Love that within my mind doth discourse hold, or drawing a landscape by a cake recipe? If you knew the end, there wouldn't have been a double-breasted wanted sucker to do time.

Look. Your shadow divides the light into a list of what you can see. You're wanted. On the inside, you get off on putting bodies together, so do you think I'm alive? What's whispered to you here is really said. You can choose to hear me talking or hear what I'm saying. I tell you I've got you covered. Do you think it's fair? Are you playing a game or do you only want to know who else you could have been? You want someone else to want who only wants, a kid cracking IBM into your bank account for fun. not out of your veins. Do you want to be asked who you are? Show me any part of your body your heart desires. And you doubt, and teach darkness you won't catch the germ, your palm filled and dwindling, my bed's uprising grabs you up. You coincide like panic with a fruit-core at the door. You're marked. The sidewalks seem like ledges to you, but you know they're not an organization.

Look. Can you read the Skyline? One more swelling on you or a way you divide your head from your legs? To preserve your clean mouth from flaunting art? Can I compensate for blood? Can you go for the gold without it, a place without the shading of choice, people pretending they have to be this close to you, even if you don't know whose limo nobody saw you leave spit on. Your resume engenders the dash you cut, the raise you doubt, the antechamber you pardon, the shift you untie, the shit you boil, the little simple soul you dress up down in the dumps of your will when every morning marks your body, in and out of knowing you. Do you need introductions or might you deep-cleanse the wrong face, even if you can't hate it though someone else wears yours. You punch in the corrections of your care sideways and out, and the corner you turn faces the crowd coming up from underground. They look to you as if they're trying to leave something. Do you run or do you think till you sink, your arms trying to stutter a fiction? If they always did you'd know you were always going nowhere, and nowhere was where you went. You pretend to resist to stay close. Your poor or stingy body figures the countersign.

(Am l kidding you? Would l risk your not forgiving the scentless night prowl your fear breaks, wasting through locks on what you did to what was valuable? You translate hard-core grace as crude climbed beggars. You're in the light, not yet decided speed and speech's horny gobbled names.) You try to memorize so you can decide later you can forget, so no fruit rounds your fingers. (Mama, what do you want? You watch yourself get skinny and steam comes out your mouth. Would you wash your hands before or after touching? Do you 'hear in capital letters? Whoosh. I keep telling you the

There was one little girl by the other playground on 47th St, she couldn't have been more than about 15 or 16. And she said, "Baby, let me see that glove. " I gave them to her, and I said, "Be careful, they've got holes in them," and the little girl looks at me, and I says "Well, you know, I wear these as my alter ego, " and she goes, "What's an alter ego?" And I says, "Well, when I wear them I turn into another person, its part of my act." And she looks at me. And the black girl starts telling me that I should take the fingers off and I say, "No, no I need them for the rest of the play," and she goes, "You're in a play?" I say, Yes, and she says, "We thought you were working!"

Changeover

You arrive at the house and knock on the door, or window. You do not change over to a new client at the end of this scene, but remain with this client while you also join the next client ahead as well as Performer I ahead.

***

time is set hard. Is that how you conform to dying? Or by changing into some-
thing else, words with words, you think. You think, how do you know what
people sounded like to people then?) People will figure the hairs you're pulled
by. You're hung up, you lie down. You're not ruled, you're managed.

Look. I won't tell you I can see the moon because we both know it's too early.
You're your boss. (If I wanted you to want to understand how I'm under your
skin, how another language is a fun you have to have, how this ground is what
your thirsty foot wears because not enough different people scares you, you'd
know why I'm anxious for you to write to me.) You're great. You leave. You
move so you're sold. If you can be wanted you're in style. O come, o come, not
you, what of you, as long as you can tell you're you, you sweet slum software?
Dare you? You don't sleep. You have no things to change. Your stripped class
strips back your apology to words over you.

You hold me to it. That's your jail. I can't pretend you can't describe me,
describe me away. Will you be told close looking is sleeping? Do you believe
you can act? Are you on a local channel? How much do you charge? Even so,
you give what you get. You don't get your behavior free. You can cross my
palm but not with the redundancy of your memory. If another time is another
place, I ask you, can you leave? Are you early?

Carla Harryman [1952]

THAT CAN NOT BE TAKEN AWAY FROM IT

Who has not been sleeping on an inspired day? The mind of the day sleeps us. Watching us. A fascinated consciousness. That thing that can not be taken away from it. There are no bad feelings and no spectacle.[1] Or the day spits at a spectacle it finds at work, transferring illusion to illusion to conceal the lack of ocean it needs to make the illusion at night thrive when the day has left us with its head striking, falling blankly into a name, as if a name were a head striking a mug, a filial alphabet, an enumerated pause.

"One, nine, and eleven are femaling me," said a voice at a distance.

In Mexico there are many more flowering trees. Some violet. Painted sand swirls up from the painted desert and drives into the car. Hence, the birth of an idea or a sea. An ocean of flowering trees.

How is it to be phrased? Are we going to phrase it? As if a pantry had opened on its own, revealing the source of the strange family's well-being, the family is going to be phrased by us. The automaton provides endless variations on this pep talk while we methodically eat through our cage. The automaton feels an excruciating physical discomfort because the direction of its energy is unknown to itself. This causes the seated parts to wish to stand and the standing parts to wish to sit.

In the meantime, the strange family sleeps. Its posture, and all its variations (the sleeping standing, the seated sleeping, the waking slept and sleeping, the dreaming waking finishing touches, the touching sleeping, and all the endless family ties of seated waking in one's sleep) is as accurate as conventional uses of punctuation. And in all the darting of these postures, ambitions out in all directions, they share a common source in the Universe that has never been seen. I have been told that it will disappear if you call it by its name. An euphoric scent reminds the family of itself.

---

1. A staged simulation of spectacular video techniques: stage lighting and sets interact in such a way as to produce the electronic glow from the TV set: figures are structured into the geometrical pattern projected on screens in the set, contributing an archaic symmetry (that of the human body) to the modern. The spectacle uses the human body to adorn itself, at the same time the actor's beautiful singing adorns the spectacle. Beauty has been created from any angle, and the horror of the universe would be entirely left out if it were not for the fact that any illusion can lead the mind into its own endless realm of illusions. Now inside the potential of one's fears, one looks into the staged illusion and is struck (or captured) by awe in spite of the empty vagaries of techniques. Hence, a depth is created in oneself which seems to exist inherently in what is on stage. This is the secret of dramatic arts.

It is a tradition that introducing ambition into a work of art foreshadows future moral complications. One is going to wake and dream and sleep and one is going to wake and sleep and dream. A man is talking on the phone nonstop through all of this. The radio is glowing about his presence. It is going on and on about it. It is the mouthpiece for the man, and although he does not lack ambition, he is not the subject of this discussion.

Photographs represent the subject of a longed-for life. One can also think of sexuality as clinical. Behavior is an essence we can't help. "When she rose to her own defense she was sought after by many parties." In the center of one of these parties is blind ambition waiting to get her. She had been in bed when her lover told her to stop napping, so she woke and went to work, but her lover was not there at all. He was speaking to someone else. And so she went to the party by herself. The sand in the desert rose in the painted air.

You do not now need your ambitions, family. It is pulled by magnets to an inert door. They all knock up against the door and stick there until it opens. This is the door to the party. Inside, everyone is loosely defined. "I feel strange," says the daughter waking on the sleeping brother's shoulder. Psychologically slick peepholes spring into existence.

A rocklike character from the South Seas arrives. A quantitative person with large inhalations. There are causal relations one must resist drawing with respect to him. It takes "infinite patience" or industrious spirits to maintain things as they are, not what they appear to illuminate around them.

> And so this is Robert Desnos.
> The room is closed and empty, quite empty.
> It is light and there is too much sun.
> But not here, look at these people.
> There are. . .
> Many of us. . .
> Robert, did you say?
> Who would not have come had we known.
> It's hard to get out of here.
> Yah, Desnos, you know.
> Desnos.

Say the people in the party.

"I can almost do this in my sleep," said the rocklike character taking a deep breath. The door in the palm of his hand opened briefly and closed. It went too fast to see much of anything, but the strange father was left with the impression of acres of land.

"Do you like who you are?" asked the baby looking directly at the rocklike character. The baby was chewing on a swollen cactus. The baby was in the desert the father had seen through the door. Of course, what she was eating could double as a weapon. "It's very hard," said the baby, "to figure all of this out."

Anywhere is the subject of the baby's quandary. When she is older, a scent from a tree she has never seen will transport her. This, while she is answering some rudimentary question: "No, that is not mine." She also refuses some slang, which is given to her lightly. And she is away, this away being a set. Her work is complete. Quandary, variation, quandary, variation, pause. The set is complete. She is transported to an inert door. Behind the door, a family. She is traveling through a vast desert. The family holds her kite. Abstraction holds her up. And no one is there in this funny figure. Set. In air.

What is your name?

It's going to be Fred. It's going to be Louise. No matter what, it's a big success. This corruption lies flat in deep water. Who are we to pull it out? Whoever you may be, the broad plain awaits you. The desert birds are poised. The weeds pose. Someone is hoping it will be himself/herself. Himself/herself, slept by the day, is part of a dream that shoulders the limits of sleep as it works its way across water.

Himself/herself prods us with questions. Who are we to answer? Himself/herself eases into a boat. The story of the boat: these little birds are sitting there. The mother counts them all. The hand of any hand. The door of any door. Stops. And so at a party, there are no mothers and daughters, there are no sons. The fathers eat in an obscure room and people laugh at them for having to be there where they will not make themselves welcome by virtue of their insatiable identities. Fathers, stop talking to yourselves. You act like lunatics. That is what the childless, parentless population cries as they drunkenly pass the open door.

Night turns its back on the boat which made a bad bargain in exchange for sleep the trader had bought but couldn't use. Now it is sunning, assuming nothing. "I must find a way out of storage," said the boat and came to us for advice. It offered us an account of the first years of life: in the building was a building. Once upon a time, the building was built. Though the building was settled, it became more remote. But we have no building we said to the boat.

The boat in the shallow lagoon sat heavy on our thoughts as we froze in the wilderness for want of a place to live, for we had been thrust from our houses at an early age as a tribute to our ability to survive. We were then carried by the air and set here. When we saw himself/herself we strained to recall the party where we had been introduced. Some kind of overlap had volunteered our socially respectable names, in that we had names. One per person.

(*Animal Instincts*, 1989)

ALLEGORY

The crow or crowd with its detached features of twig bark and plunder walks to the podium and puts its face to the microphone.

Where is the audience of one?

A voice shouts from behind: "Ignore the politicians."

The crow or crowd with its scaly skin surface, its effervescent perspiration and distressed eros shouts back, "Bag that mediocrity."

A henchman duck waddles toward the old growth. The disembodied voice now comes from there.

"One solo performer's death." "One solo performer's death." "One solo performer's death." In whispers and echoes it shrinks away from an impending compression.

The duck returns with puffed out feathers and a loud quack carrying a sack full of unique vegetation.

The crowd or crow lifts off from the platform and hovers over the sack casting a mask-like shadow over the sack and its contents that the duck lifts out with his flat beak.

(manuscript)

MOTHERING
(enigma)

"It's still here. It's still here-er. Be ready. Be ready." Silently the woman opened. "Oh, look at that. This card says, there is no opposition left." The door also opened and an enigmatic male figure walked in. The mother knew how to be safe and protect her young because of a game she learned in a song. First she closed the book. There was no time for pictures, now, and the words went like this:

> Be ready when ready is over the hillside.
> Who, when the light goes out.
> Who, when the light goes out.
> Country the life in a dream.
> City what's left over.
> Be ready when ready is over the hillside.

As she sang she took the hand of the singular man as if he were a little one, and lead him into a room with a bed. Then she tucked him in, and when he was snoring she grabbed her children, who had by then been sufficiently warned, and fled.

(manuscript)

MATTER

Love was alone with love. And there was nothing I could do about it. Love was alone with love. Why make another move? Why move? It's your turn over there, someone said, and I thought I'm going to open my legs and see what happens. Hurry up, lay down your cards. The cards were in my hand. I put down the card to see what would happen while I opened my legs. You open now, I said. And love responded quickly. You are a good player. Have you been playing long? I learned from an expert, said love. Is the expert still living? Yes, she is. A she, I said. Love was impatient and wanted to know if I had another move. I closed my legs up to see if that counted. Look at your hand, said love trying to be patient. And you, I said prefer these cards over other forms of excitement. If you can't play, you'll never meet the expert, love replied. I didn't really care, but my body was standing on end at the thought of fucking. When I saw that I and my body were not the same, I knew what card to play and played it as soon as my turn came without second guessing my opponent's position in the game.

                                                        (manuscript)

MAGIC (OR ROUSSEAU)

In order to play one needs magic and Rousseau and must remember play. Sometimes magic is the obscurest impostor in play. An obscure rationalization imposes the word magic on Rousseau.

Now remember play has nothing to do with that Rousseauian freedom found in refusal.

Refusal more than anything else ends play.

And so we might play a game called the conjuring of Rousseau. It might go like this, let's pretend that Jean Jacques Rousseau is the pawn in our game. On one side of the Board is Society. On the other side of the Board is solitude. We can each pick a goal. One of us tries to force Rousseau into society, the other tries to land him in solitude. Whoever gets the pawn to the goal wins. Let's say Rousseau is walking along a Boulevard in silent reverie. The Board, by the way, is made up of parks and Boulevards, so when Rousseau "advances" he is always being advanced by way of a park or boulevard. Sometimes a player will draw a card that says, "What do you want Jean Jacques Rousseau?" If the spinner lands on **I would like to go home**, then the pawn is returned to the beginning and Rousseau sets out again from the starting spot. If the spinner lands on **I would like to do someone a favor**, the token is advanced along a park or boulevard in direction of society. If the spinner lands on **I would like to tell the truth,** the player gets to spin again until he gets something he likes; since truth is bound to both solitude and society, this move becomes a matter of preference. In the center of the Board is a personage with great powers: she is a witch. If Jean Jacques lands on her spot it is because she has called him up. She calls him up, because his travels fascinate her. Now, this is extremely problematic. If Rousseau realizes that she has called him up, then he sees himself as a ghost. The player has a choice at this point, to get out of or stay in the ghost game. If it is decided to stay in the ghost game, Rousseau is provided with a series of options that he never recognized when he was alive. He can, for instance, opt to infiltrate society without being noticed. He can observe those who outlived him. He could, if he were on the ladder to revenge, scare them to death. They could become equals in death. Or he could live with the witch, who loves to make good on her resources. This he admires enormously; although, she does not quite consider him her equal. With her, his solitude is indeed complete: since no one in the game is aware of her existence.

(manuscript)

PRINCIPAL BOOK PUBLICATIONS

Bruce Andrews [1948]

Edge (1973); *Corona* (1974); *Vowels* (1976); *Film Noir* (1978); *Praxis* (1978); *Jeopardy* (1980); *Sonnets — (Momento Mori)* (1980); *Legend* (1980) [with Bruce Andrews, Charles Bernstein, Steve McCaffery and Ron Silliman]; *R + B* (1981); *Wobbling* (1981); *Excommunicate* (1982); *Love Songs* (1982); *The L=A=N=G=U=A=G=E Book* (1984) [edited, with Charles Bernstein]; *Factura* (1987); *Give Em Enough Rope* (1987); *Both, Both* (1988); *Getting Ready to Have Been Frightened* (1988); *Executive Summary* (1991); *Voodoo for Anti-Communist Tourists* (1991); *Standpoint* (1991); *I Don't Have Any Paper So Shut Up (or, Social Romanticism)* (1992); *Ste, Sic & Sp.* (1992); *Tizzy Boost* (1993); *Moebius* (1993)

David Antin [1932]

Definitions (1967); *Autobiography* (1967); *Code of Flag Behavior* (1968); *Meditations* (1971); *Talking* (1972); *After the War* (1973); *talking at the boundaries* (1976); *whos listening out there* (1979); *tuning* (1984); *Selected Poems: 1963 – 1973* (1991) [includes the first six volumes by Antin]; *what it means to be avant-garde* (1993)

Rae Armantrout [1947]

Extremities (1978); *The Invention of Hunger* (1979); *Precedence* (1985); *Necromance* (1991); *Couverture* (1991); *Made to Seem* (1994)

John Ashbery [1927]

Turandot and Other Poems (1953); *Some Trees* (1956; reprinted 1970, 1978); *The Poems* (1960); *The Tennis Court Oath* (1962); *Rivers and Mountains* (1966; reprinted 1977); *Selected Poems* (1967/London); *Three Madrigals* (1968); *A Nest of Ninnies* (1969; reprinted 1975) [fiction] [with James Schuyler]; *The Double Dream of Spring* (1970; reprinted 1976); *The New Spirit* (1970); *Three Poems* (1972); *The Vermont Notebook* (1975); *Self-Portrait in a Convex Mirror* (1975); *Houseboat Days* (1977); *Three Plays* (1978) [drama]; *As We Know* (1979); *Shadow Train* (1981); *A Wave* (1983); *Selected Poems* (1985); *April Galleons* (1987); *Reported Sightings: Art Chronicles 1957 – 1987* (1991) [criticism]; *Flow Chart* (1992); *Hotel Lautréamont* (1993); *And the Stars Were Shining* (1994)

Amiri Baraka/LeRoi Jones [1934]

Preface to a Twenty Volume Suicide Note (1961); *Blues People: Negro Music in White America* (1963) [prose]; *The Moderns: An Anthology of New Writing in America* (1963) [edited]; *The Dead Lecturer* (1964); *Dutchman and The Slave* (1964) [drama]; *The System of Dante's Hell* (1965) [fiction]; *Home: Social Essays* (1966); *The Baptism & The Toilet* (1967) [drama]; *Tales* (1967) [fiction]; *Black Music* (1968) [prose]; *Black Fire: An Anthology of Afro-American Writing* (1968) [edited with Larry Neal]; *Four Black Revolutionary Plays* (1969) [drama]; *Black Magic: Collected Poetry, 1961 – 1967* (1969); *In Our Terribleness* (1970); *It's Nation Time* (1970); *Jello* (1970); *Raise Race Rays Raze: Essays Since 1965* (1971); *Spirit Reach* (1972); *Hard Facts* (1975); *The Motion of History and Other Plays* (1978) [drama]; *Selected Plays and Prose of Amiri Baraka/LeRoi Jones* (1979) [prose/drama]; *The Sidney Poet Heroical* (1979); *reggae or not!* (1981); *Confirmation: An Anthology of African American Women* (1983) [edited]; *Daggers and Javelins: Essays, 1974–1979* (1984); *The Autobiography of LeRoi Jones/Amiri Baraka* (1984); *The Music: Reflections on Jazz and Blues* (1987) *The LeRoi Jones/Amiri Baraka Reader* (1991) [edited by William J. Harris]

Steve Benson [1949]

As Is (1978); *Blindspots* (1981); *The Busses* (1981); *Dominance* (1985); *Briarcomb Paragrahs* (1985); *Blue Book* (1988); *Reverse Order* (1989)

Charles Bernstein [1950]

Asylums (1975); *Parsing* (1976); *Shade* (1978); *Poetic Justice* (1979); *Senses of Responsibility* (1989); *Legend* (1980) [with Bruce Andrews, Steve McCaffery, Ron Silliman, and Ray DiPalma]; *Controlling Interests* [1980]; *Disfrutes* (1981); *The Occurrence of Tune* (1981) [with Susan B. Laufer]; *Stigma* (1981); *Islets/Irritations* (1983; reprinted 1992); *Resistance* (1983); *The L=A=N=G=U=A=G=E Book* (1984) [edited, with Bruce Andrews]; *Content's Dream* (1986; reprinted 1994) [essays]; *Artifice of Absorption* (1987); *Veil* (1987); *The Sophist* (1987); *Four Poems* (1988); *The Nude Formalism* (1989) [with Susan Bee]; *The Absent Father in Dumbo* (1990); *The Politics of Poetic Form* (1990) [edited]; *Fool's Gold* (1991) [with Susan Bee]; *Rough Trades* (1991); *A Poetics* (1992) [essays]; *Dark City* (1994). Charles Bernstein has also translated *The Maternal Drape* by Claude Royet-Journoud (1984) and *Red, Green, and Black* by Olivier Cadiot (1990).

Ted Berrigan [1934 – 1983]

A Lily for My Love (1959); *The Sonnets* (1964; reprinted 1967, 1982); *Living with Chris* (1965) [drawings by Joe Brainard]; *Bean Spasms* (1968) [with Ron Padgett and Joe Brainard]; *Many Happy Returns* (1969); *Double Talk* (1969) [with Anselm Hollo]; *In the Early Morning Rain* (1970); *Guillaume Apollinaire Ist Tot* (1971); *Back in Boston Again* [with Ron Padgett and Tom Clark]; *Clear the Range* [fiction]; *Memorial*

Day (1971; reprinted in England in 1974) [with Anne Waldman]; *Train Ride* (1971); *A Feeling for Leaving* (1975); *Red Wagon* (1976); *Nothing For You* (1977); *Yo-Yo's with Money* (1979) [with Harris Schiff]; *So Going Around Cities: New & Selected Poems 1958 – 1979* (1980); *Carrying a Torch* (1980); *In a Blue River* (1981); *The Morning Line* (1982); *A Certain Slant of Sunlight* (1988); *Talking in Tranquility: Interviews with Ted Berrigan* (1991) [edited by Stephen Ratcliffe and Leslie Scalapino]; *Selected Poems* (1994) [edited by Aram Saroyan]

Robin Blaser [1925]

The Moth Poem (1964); *Les Chimères* (1965) [versions of Gérard de Nerval]; *Cups* (1968); *Image-Nations 1 – 12 & The Stadium of the Mirror* (1974); *Image-Nations 13 & 14, etc.* (1975); *Syntax* (1983); *The Faerie Queen & The Park* (1988); *Pell Mell* (1988); *The Holy Forest* (1993)

David Bromige [1933]

The Gathering (1965); *Please, Like Me* (1968); *The Ends of the Earth* (1968); *The Quivering Roadway* (1969); *Threads* (1971); *The Wise Men Drawn to Wonder by the Fact So of Itself* (1971) [with Robert Kelly and Diane Wakoski]; *Three Stories* (1973) [fiction]; *Ten Years in the Making* (1973); *Birds of the West* (1973); *Tight Corners & What's Around Them* (1974); *Out of My Hands* (1974) [prose]; *Spells & Blessings* (1975); *Credences of Winter* (1976); *Living in Advance* (1976) [songs] [with Paul DeBarros, Barry Gifford and Sherril Jaffe]; *My Poetry* (1980) [prose and poetry]; *P-E-A-C-E* (1981) [prose and poetry]; *In the Uneven Steps of Hung-Chow* (1982) [fiction]; *It's The Same Only Different / The Melancholy Owed Categories* (1984); *You See* (1976); *Red Hats* (1986) [prose and poetry]; *Desire* (1988); *A Sampler* (1988); *Men, Women & Vehicles* (1990) [prose]; *Tiny Courts* (1991; new edition 1993); *They Ate* (1992) [novella]; *The Harbormaster of Hong Kong* (1993); *A Cast of Tens* (1994)

Nicole Brossard [1943]

In French: *Aube à la saison* (1965); *Mordre sa chair* (1966); *L'Écho bouge beau* (1968); *Suite logique* (1970); *Un livre* (1970) [fiction]; *Le Centre blanc* (1970); *Mécanique jongleuse* (1973); *Sold-Out* (1973) [fiction]; *Mécanique jongleuse suivi de Masculin grammaticale* (1974); *French Kiss* (1974) [fiction]; *L'Amèr ou le chapitre effrité* (1977) [fiction]; *L'Écrivain in La Nef des Sorcières* (1986) [drama]; (1977) [fiction]; *La Partie pour le tout* (1979); *Amantes* (1980); *Le Sens apparent* (1980) [fiction]; *Journal intime* (1984) [fiction]; *Double impression* (1984); *L'Aviva* (1985); *La lettre aérienne* (1985) [essays]; *Domaine d'écriture* (1985); *Mauve* 1985) [avec Daphne Marlatt]; *Character/ Jeu de lettres* (1986) [avec Daphne Marlatt]; *Sous la langue / Under Tongue* (1987) [bilingual edition]; *Le Désert mauve* (1987) [fiction]; *Installations* (1989); *À tout regard* (1989); *Typhon dru* (1990) [en collaboration avec l'artiste Christine Davies]; *La Subjectivité des lionnes* (1990); *Langues obscures* (1992); *La Nuit verte du parc labyrinthe* (1992); *La Nuit verte du parc labrinthe* (1992) [tri-lingual edition: French, English and Spanish]; *Flesh, Song(e) et Promenade* (1993) [avec poèmes de Sor Joana Ines de la Cruz]. In English: *A Book* (1976); *Turn of a Pang* (1976); *Daydream Mechanics* (1980); *These Our Mothers or: The Disintegrating Chapter* (1983); *Lovhers* (1986); *French Kiss* (1986); *The Aerial Letter* (1988); *Surfaces of Sense* (1989); *Picture Theory* (1990/1991)

Michael Brownstein [1943]

Behind the Wheel (1967); *Highway to the Sky* (1969); *Three American Tantrums* (1970) [fiction]; *Brainstorms* (1971) [poetry and fiction]; *Country Cousins* (1974; reprinted 1986) [fiction]; *Strange Days Ahead* (1975); *When Nobody's Looking* (1981); *Oracle Night: A Love Poem* (1982); *Music from the Evening of the World* (1989) [fiction]; *The Touch* (1993) [fiction]; *Self-Reliance* (1994) [fiction]. Michael Brownstein has also translated and edited *The Dice Cup: Selected Prose Poems of Max Jacob* (1979)

John Cage [1912 – 1933]

A Year from Monday: New Lectures and Writings (1967); *M: Writings '67 – '72* (1973); *Silence: Lectures and Writings* (1973); *Empty Words: Writings '73 – '78* (1979); *For the Birds: John Cage in Conversation with Daniel Charles* (1981; published previously in French in 1976); *Themes & Variations* (1982); *I – VI* (1990); *Composition in Retrospect* (1993)

Joseph Ceravolo [1934 – 1988]

Fits of Dawn (1965); *Wild Flowers Out of Gas* (1967); *Spring in this World of Poor Mutts* (1968); *Transmigration Solo* (1979); *Inri* (1979); *Millenium Dust* (1982); *The Green Lake Is Awake* (1994) [edited by Larry Fagin, Charles North, Ron Padgett, David Shapiro and Paul Violi]

Abigail Child [1950]

From Solids (1983); *Climate/Plus* (1986); *A Motive for Mayhem* (1989)

Clark Coolidge [1939]

Flag Flutter & U.S. Electric (1966); *Clark Coolidge* (1967); *Ing* (1968); *To Obtain the Value of the Cake Measure from Zero* (1970) [with Tom Veitch]; *Space* (1970); *The So* (1971); *Suite V* (1973); *The Maintains* (1974); *Polaroid* (1975); *Own Face* (1978; reprinted 1993); *Quartz Hearts* (1978); *Smithsonian Depositions/Subject To a Film* (1980); *American Ones* (1981); *A Geology* (1981); *Research* (1982); *Mine: The One That Enters the Stories* (1982); *Solution Passage: Poems 1978 – 1981* (1986); *The Crystal Text* (1986); *Melencolia* (1987); *Mesh* (1988); *At Egypt* (1988); *Two or Three Things* (1989); *Sound As Thought: Poems 1982 – 1984* (1990); *Odes of Roba* (1991); *Baffling*

Means (1991) [with art by Philip Guston]; *The Book of During* (1991); *On the Pumice of Morons* (1993) [with Larry Fagin]; *Lowell Connector* (1993) [with Michael Gizzi, John Yau, Bill Barrette, and Celia Coolidge]; *The Rova Improvisations* (1994)

Robert Creeley [1926]

Le Fou (1952); *The Immoral Proposition* (1953) [illustrated by René Laubiès]; *The Kind of Act Of* (1953); *The Gold Diggers* (1954) [fiction]; *All That is Lovely in Men* (1955) [illustrated by Dan Rice]; *A Form of Women* (1959); *For Love: Poems, 1950 – 1960* (1962); *The Island* (1964) [fiction]; *The Gold Diggers and Other Stories* (1965) [fiction]; *Words* (1967); *The Charm: Early and Uncollected Poems* (1968); *The Finger* (1968); *Pieces* (1968; reprinted 1969) [illustrated by Bobbie Creeley]; *A Quick Graph: Collected Notes and Essays* (1970 [prose] [edited by Donald Allen]; *1°2°3°4°5°6°7°8°9°0°* (1971) [illustrated by Arthur Okamura]; *St. Martin's* (1971) [illustrated by Bobbie Creeley]; *A Day Book* (1972) [prose] [illustrated by R. B. Kitaj]; *A Sense of Measure* (1972) [notes, essays, and intervies]; *Contexts of Poetry: Interviews, 1961 – 1971* (1973) [edited by Donald Allen]; *The Creative* (1973); *This Idea* (1973) [with photographs by Elsa Dorfman]; *Thirty Things* (1974) [illustrated by Bobbie Creeley]; *Mabel: A Story and Other Prose* (1976); *Presences: A Text for Marisol* (1976) [with photographs of Marisol's sculpture]; *Hell: A Journal, February 29 – May 3, 1976* (1978); *Later* (1979); *Was That a Real Poem and Other Essays* (1979) [edited by Donald Allen]; *The Collected Poems of Robert Creeley, 1945 – 1975* (1982); *Echoes* (1982); *Mirrors* (1983); *The Collected Prose of Robert Creeley* (1984); *Memory Gardens* (1986); *The Company* (1988); *Charles Olson and Robert Creeley: The Complete Correspondence* (1980 – 1989) [edited by George F. Butterick]; *Collected Essays* (1989); *Windows* (1990); *Selected Poems* (1991); *Echoes* (1991) [unrelated to the previous book with this title]; *Autobiography* (1991); *Tales Out of School: Selected Interviews* (1993)

Tina Darragh [1950]

my hands to myself [1975]; *Pi in the Skye* (1980); *on the corner to off the corner* [1981]; *Striking Resemblance* (1989); *a(gain)²st the odds* (1989); *adv.fans - the 1968 series* (1993)

Michael Davidson [1944]

Exchanges (1972); *Two Views of Pears* (1973); *The Mutabilities* (1976); *Summer Letters* (1977); *Grillwork* (1980); *Discovering Motion* (1980); *The Prose of Fact* (1981); *The Landing of Rochambeau* (1985); *Analogy of the Ion* (1989); *The San Francisco Renaissance: Poetics and Community at Mid-Century* (1989) [criticism]; *Post Hoc* (1990); *Leningrad: American Writers in the Soviet Union* (1991) [prose] [with Lyn Hejinian, Barrett Watten, and Ron Silliman]

Alan Davies [1951]

slough cup hope tantrum (1975); *Split Thighs* (1976); *a an av es* (1981); *Abuttal* (1982); *Mnemonotechnics* (1983); *Active 24 Hours* (1982); *Pursue Veritable Simples/Send Us the Difficult Job* (1983); *Name* (1986); *Signage* (1981) [essays]; *Candor* (1990); *Life* (1990); *Rave* (1994)

Jean Day [1954]

Linear C (1983); *Flat Birds* (1985); *A Young Recruit* (1988); *The You and the I* (1992)

Christopher Dewdney [1951]

Golders Green (1972); *A Palaeozoic Geology of London, Ontario* (1973); *Fovea Centralis* (1975); *Spring Trances in the Control Emerald Night* (1978); *Alter Sublime* (1980); *Spring Trances in the Control Emerald Night & The Cenozoic Asylum* (1982); *Predators of the Adoration: Selected Poems* (1983); *The Immaculate Perception* (1986); *Permugensis* (1987); *The Radiant Inventory* (1988); *Recent Artifaces from the Institute of Applied Fiction* (1990); *Concordat Proviso Ascendant* (1991)

Ray DiPalma [1943]

Max (1969); *Macaroons* (1969); *Between the Shapes* (1970) [with Stephen Shrader]; *The Gallery Goers* (1971); *All Bowed Down* (1972); *Works in a Drawer* (1972); *Borgia Circles* (L1972); *Time Being* (1972) [with Asa Benveniste and Tom Raworth]; *Soli* (1974); *The Sargasso Transcries* (1974); *Max/A Sequel* (1974); *Accidental Interludes* (1975); *Marquee* (1977); *Cuiva Sails* (1978); *Planh* (1979); *Observatory Gardens* (1979); *Genesis* (1980); *Legend* (1980) [with Bruce Andrews, Charles Bernstein, Steve McCaffery and Ron Silliman]; *Labyrinth Radio* (1981); *23 Works* (1982); *13 Works* (1982); *Two Poems* (1982); *Chan* (1984); *January Zero* (1984); *Startle Luna* (1984); *The Jukebox of Memnon* (1988); *Raik* (1989); *Night Copy* (1990); *5 Ink Drawings/5 Poems* (1990) [with Elizabeth DiPalma]; *Mock Fandango* (1991); *Metropolitan Corridor* (1992); *Numbers and Tempers: Selected Early Poems 1966–1986* (1993); *27 Octobre 29 Octobre* (1993); *Hôtel des Ruines* (1994) [with Alexandre Delay]

Robert Duncan [1919–1988]

Heavenly City, Earthly City (1947); *Poems 1948–1949* (1950); *Medieval Scenes* (1950; reprinted as *Medieval Scenes 1950 and 1959*); *Fragments of a Disordered Devotion* (1952); *Caesar's Gate: Poems 1948–1950* (1956); *Letters: Poems MCMLIII–MCMLVI* (1958); *Faust Foutu: An Entertainment in Four Parts* (1959) [drama]; *Selected Poems* (1959); *The Opening of the Field* (1960); *Writing, Writing: A Composition Book Stein Imitations* (1964); *As Testimony: The Poem and The Scene* (1964) [prose]; *Roots and Branches* (1964); *The Sweetness and Greatness of Dante's "Divine Comedy"*

(1965) [prose]; *Medea at Kolchis: The Maidenhead* (1965) [drama]; *Passages 22 – 27 of the War* (1966); *The Years as Catches: First Poems (1939 – 1946)* (1966); *Six Prose Pieces* (1966); *A Book of Resemblances: Poems 1950 – 1953* (1966); *Epilogos* (1967); *Names of People* (1968); *Bending the Bow* (1968); *The First Decade: Selected Poems 1940 – 1950* (1969); *Derivations: Selected Poems 1950 – 1956* (1969); *Achilles' Song* (1969); *Play Time: Pseudo Stein* (1969); *Poetic Disturbances* (1970); *Tribunals Passages 31 – 35* (1970); *Ground Work* (1971); *Poems from the Margins of Thom Gunn's "Moly"* (1972); *A Seventeenth Century Suite in Homage to the Metaphysical Genius in English Poetry 1590/1690* (1973); *An Ode and Arcadia* (1974) [with Jack Spicer]; *Dante* (1974); *The Venice Poem* (1975); *Veil, Turbine, Cord, and Bird* (1979); *The Five Songs* (1981); *Ground Work: Before the War* (1984); *Fictive Certainties* (1985) [essays]; *A Paris Visit* (1985); *Ground Work II: In the Dark* (1987)

Larry Eigner [1927]

Poems (1941); *From the Sustaining Air* (1953); *Look at the Park* (1958); *On My Eyes* (1960); *The Music, the Rooms* (1965); *Six Poems* (1967); *Another Time in Fragments* (1967); *The -/ Towards Autumn* (1967); *Air the Trees* (1968); *The Breath of Once Live Things in the Field with Poe* (1968); *A Line That May Be Cut* (1968); *Clouding* (1968); *Flat and Round* (1969, 1980 [corrected]); *Farther North* (1969); *Valleys Branches* (1969); *Circuits - A MICROBOOK* (1971); *Looks Like Nothing / The Shadow / Through Air* (1972); *Selected Poems* (1972) [edited by Samuel Charters and Andrea Wyatt]; *Words Touching Ground Under* (1972); *What You Hear* (1972); *Shape Shadow Elements Move* (1973); *Things Stirring Together Or Far Away* (1974); *Anything on Its Side* (1974); *Suddenly / it gets light / and dark in the street* (1975); *My God / The Proverbial* (1975); *The Music Variety* (1976); *Watching / how or why* (1977); *The World and Its Streets, Places* (1977); *Cloud, invisible air* (1978); *Flagpole / Riding* (1978); *Country / Harbor / Quiet / Act / Around* (1978) [prose]; *Heat simmers cold & * (1978); *Lined up bulk senses* (1979); *Time / details / of a tree* (1979); *Now there's / a morning / hulk of the sky* (1981); *Earth Birds* (1981); *Waters / Places / A Time* (1983); *Larry Eigner Letters* (1987) [edited by Robert Kocik and Joseph Simas]; *areas / lights / heights: Writings 1954 – 1989* (1989) [edited by Benjamin Friedlander] [prose]

Kenward Elmslie [1929]

Pavilions (1961); *The Baby Book* (1965) [with Joe Brainard]; *Lizzie Borden* (1965) [opera libretto]; *Miss Julie* (1965) [opera libretto]; *The 1967 Gamebook Calender* (1967) [with Joe Brainard]; *Power Plant Poems* (1967); *The Champ* (1968; reprinted 1994); *Album* (1969) [with Joe Brainard]; *Girl Machine* (1971); *Circus Nerves* (1971); *Shiny Ride* (1972) [with Joe Brainard]; *Motor Disturbance* (1972; reprinted 1978); *The Grass Harp* (1972) [musical play]; *The Orchid Stories* (1973; reprinted 1975) [fiction]; *The Sweet Bye and Bye* (1973) [libretto]; *The Seagull* (1984) [opera libretto]; *Tropicalism* (1975); *Washington Square* (1976) [opera libretto]; *Topiary Trek* (1977) [with Karl Torok]; *The Alphabet Work* (1977); *Communications Equipment* (1979); *Moving Right*

Along (1980); *Bimbo Dirt* (1982) [with Ken Tisa]; *Kenward Elmslie Visited* (1982) [LP album]; *Palais Bimbo Lounge Show* (1985) [LP album]; *Three Sisters* (1987) [opera libretto]; *26 Bars* (1987) [with Donna Dennis]; *City Junket* (1987) [drama]; *Sung Sex* (1990); *Pay Dirt* (1992) [with Joe Brainard]; *Postcards on Parade* (1993) [musical play]

Allen Ginsberg [1926]

Howl and Other Poems (1956); *Empty Mirror: Early Poems* (1961); *Kaddish and Other Poems. 1958 – 1960* (1961); *Reality Sandwiches, 1953 – 60* (1963); *The Yage Letters* (1963) [with William S. Burroughs] [letters]; *T. V. Baby Poems* (1967); *Ankor-Wat* (1968); *Planet News, 1961 – 1967* (1968); *Airplane Dreams: Compositions from Journals* (1968); *Indian Journals: March 1962 – May 1963* (1970) [journal]; *Improvised Poetics* (1971) [edited by Mark Robison] [prose]; *Iron Horse* (1972 [Canada]; 1974 [USA]); *The Fall of America: Poems of These States 1965 – 1971* (1972); *The Gates of Wrath: Rhymed Poems 1948 – 1952* (1972); *Gay Sunshine Interview* (1974) [interview]; *Allen Verbatim: Lectures on Poetry, Politics, Consciousness* (1974) [edited by Gordon Ball] [lectures]; *The Visions of the Great Rememberer* (1974) [prose]; *First Blues: Rags, Ballads & Harmonium Songs, 1971 –74* (1975); *Chicago Trial Testimony* (1975) [testimony]; *Sad Dust Glories: Poems During Work Summer in Woods* (1975); *To Eberhart from Ginsberg* (1976) [letters]; *Journals: Early Fifties-Early Sixties* (1977) [edited by Gordon Ball] [journal]; *As Ever: The Collected Correspondence of Allen Ginsberg & Neal Cassady* (1977) [letters]; *Take Case of My Ghost, Ghost* (1977) [with Jack Kerouac] [prose]; *Mind Breaths: Poems 1972 – 1977* (1978); *Poems All Over the Place, Mostly 'Seventies* (1978); *Composed on the Tongue* (1980) [prose]; *Straight Hearts Delight, Love Poems and Selected Letters 1947 – 1980* (1980) [with Peter Orlovsky; edited by Winston Leyland]); *Plutonian Ode, Poems 1977 – 1980* (1982); *Collected Poems 1947 – 1980* (1984); *White Shroud: Poems, 1980 – 1985* (1986)

John Godfrey [1945]

26 Poems (1971); *Three Poems* (1973); *Music of the Curbs* (1976); *Dabble: Poems 1966 – 1980* (1982); *Where the Weather Suits My Clothes* (1974); *Midnight on Your Left* (1988)

Ted Greenwald [1942]

Lapstrake (1964); *Short Sleeves* (1969); *No Eating* (1971); *Somewhere in Ho* (1972) [with Ed. Baynard]; *Making a Living* (1972); *The New Money* (1973); *Makes Sense* (1973); *The Life* (1974); *Miami* (1975); *Native Land* (1977); *You Bet!* (1978); *Common Sense* (1978); *Licorice Chronicles* (1979); *Use No Hooks* (1980); *Smile* (1981); *Young & Restless* (1982) [art by George Schneeman]; *Exit the Face* (1982); *Word of Mouth* (1986); *Looks Like I'm Walking* (1991); *You Go Through* (1992)

Robert Grenier [1941]

Series: *Pomes 1967 – 1971* (1978); *Oakland* (1980); *A Day at the Beach* (1984); *Phantom Anthems* (1986); *What I Believe / Transcription / Transpiring* (1988)

Barbara Guest [1920]

The Location of Things (1960); *Poems: The Location of Things / Archaics / The Open Skies* (1962); *The Blue Stairs* (1968); *Moscow Mansions* (1973); *The Countess from Minneapolis* (1976); *Seeking Air* (1977) [fiction]; *The Türler Losses* (1979); *Biography* (1980); *Herself Defined: The Poet H.D. and Her World* (1984) (biography); *Musicality* (1988) [with art by June Felter]; *Fair Realism* (1989); *The Altos* (1991) [with art by Richard Tuttle]; *Defensive Rapture* (1993)

Carla Harryman [1952]

Percentage (1979); *Under the Bridge* (1980); *Property* (1982); *The Middle* (1983); *Vice* (1986); *Animal Instincts* (1989)

Lyn Hejinian [1941]

A Thought Is the Bride of What Thinking (1976); *A Mask of Motion* (1977); *Gesualdo* (1978); *Writing Is an Aid to Memory* (1978); *My Life* (1980; revised and expanded edition, 1987); *The Guard* (1984); *Redo* (1984); *Individuals* (1988) [with Kit Robinson]; *Leningrad: American Writers in the Soviet Union* (1991) [prose] [with Michael Davidson, Ron Silliman, and Barrett Watten]; *The Hunt* (1991); *Oxota: A Short Russian Novel* (1991); *The Cell* (1992); *Le Jour de Chasse* (1992) [translated into French by Pierre Alferi]; *Two Stein Talks* (1994) [prose]; *The Cold of Poetry* (1994) [includes *The Guard, Gesualdo, Redo, The Person*, and other uncollected works]. Lyn Hejinian has also translated *Description* by Arkadii Dragomoschenko (1990) and *Xenia* by Arkadii Dragomoschenko (1994).

Fanny Howe [1940]

Forty Whacks (1969) [fiction]; *First Marriage* (1975) [fiction]; *Bronte Wilde* (1976) [fiction]; *The Amerindian Coastline Poem* (1976); *Holy Smoke* (1979) [fiction]; *The White Slave* (1980) [fiction]; *Eggs* (1980); *Poem from a Single Pallet* (1981); *The Blue Hills* (1981) [juvenile fiction]; *Yeah, But* (1982) [juvenile fiction]; *Alsace Lorraine* (1982); *Radio City* (1983) [juvenile fiction]; *In the Middle of Nowhere* (1984) [fiction]; *For Erato* (1984); *Taking Care* (1985) [fiction]; *Introduction to the World* (1985); *The Race of the Radical* (1985) [fiction]; *Robeson Street* (1985); *The Lives of a Spirit* (1986) [fiction/poetry]; *The Deep North* (1988) [fiction]; *The Vineyard* (1988); *[Sic]* (1988); *Famous Questions* (1989) [fiction]; *The Quietist* (1992); *The End* (1992); *Saving History* (1992) [fiction]

Susan Howe [1937]

Hinge Picture (1974); *The Western Borders* (1976); *Cabbage Gardens* (1979); *Secret History of the Dividing Line* (1979); *Pythagorean Silence* (1982); *Defenestration of Prague* (1983); *My Emily Dickinson* (1985) [prose]; *Articulation of Sound Forms in Time* (1987); *A Bibliography of the King's Book or, Eikon Basilike* (1989); *The Europe of Trusts: Selected Poems* (1990) [collecting *Pythagorean Silence, Defenestration of Prague*, and *The Liberties*]; *Singularities* (1990); *Incloser* (1992) [criticism]; *The Nonconformist's Memorial* (1993); *The Birth-mark: unsettling the wilderness in American literary history* (1993) [criticism]

Peter Inman [1947]

What Happens Next (1974); *Platin* (1979); *Ocker* (1982); *Uneven Development* (1984); *Think of One* (1986); *Red Shift* (1988); *Vel* (1994)

Kenneth Irby [1936]

The Roadrunner (1964); *Kansas—New Mexico* (1965); *Movements / Sequences* (1965); *The Flower of Having Passed Through Paradise in a Dream* (1968); *Relation: Poems 1965 – 1966* (1970); *To Max Douglas* (1971); *Archipelago* (1976); *Catalpa* (1977); *Orexis* (1981); *Riding the Dog* (1982); *A Set* (1983); *Call Steps: Plains, Camps, Stations, Consistories* (1992)

Ronald Johnson [1935]

A Line of Poetry, A Row of Trees (1964); *Sports & Divertissments* (1965; reprinted 1969) [translations from Erik Satie]; *Assorted Jungles: Rousseau* (1966); *Gorse / Goose / Rose* (1966); *The Book of the Green Man* (1967); *Sun Flowers* (1966); *Io and the Ox-Eye Daisy* (1966); *The Round Earth on Flat Paper* (1968); *Reading 1* and *Reading 2* (1968) [two volumes]; *Valley of the Many-Colored Glasses* (1969); *Balloons for Moonless Nights* (1969); *The Spirit Walks, The Rocks Will Talk* (1969) [translations from *Le Facteur Cheval* and Raymond Isidore]; *Songs of the Earth* (1970); *Eyes & Objects* (1976); *RADI OS I – IV* (1977); *Ark: The Foundations: 1 – 33* (1980); *Ark 50: Spires 34 – 50* (1984). Ronald Johnson is also the author of several cookbooks, including *The Aficionado's Southwestern Cooking* (1968); *The American Table* (1984); *Southwestern Cooking, New and Old* (1985); *Simple Fare* (1989) and *Company Fare* (1991)

Robert Kelly [1935]

Armed Descent (1961); *Her Body Against Time* (1963); *Round Dances* (1964); *Enstasy* (1964); *Lunes* (1964); *Lectiones* (1965); *Words in Service* (1965) [liturgy]; *Weeks* (1966); *The Scorpions* (1967) [fiction]; *Song XXIV* (1967); *Devotions* (1967); *Twenty Poems* (1967); *Axon Dendron Tree* (1967); *Crooked Bridge Love Society* (1967); *A Joining*

Songs I – XXX (1968); *The Common Shore* (1969); *A California Journal* (1969); *Kali Yuga* (1970); *Cities* (1971) [prose]; *In Time* (1971) [prose]; *Flesh Dream Book* (1971); *Ralegh* (1972); *The Pastorals* (1972); *Reading Her Notes* (1972); *The Tears of Edmund Burke* (1973); *The Mill of Particulars* (1973); *A Line of Sight* (1974); *The Loom* (1975); *Sixteen Odes* (1976); *The Lady Of* (1977); *The Convections* (1978); *Wheres* (1978); *The Book of Persephone* (1978); *The Cruise of the Pnyx* (1979); *Kill the Messenger Who Brings Bad News* (1979); *Sentence* (1980); *Spiritual Exercises* (1981); *The Alchemist to Mercury* (1981); *Mulberry Women* (1982); *Under Words* (1983); *Thor's Thrush* (1984); *A Transparent Tree* (1985) [fiction]; *The Scorpions* (1985, new edition) [fiction]; *Not This Island Music* (1987); *Doctor of Silence* (1988) [fiction]; *Oahu* (1988); *Cat Scratch Fever* (1990); *Ariadne* (1991); *A Strange Market* (1992); *Queen of Terrors* (1994) [fiction]

Steve McCaffery [1947]

Capture (1969); *Carnival: A Selection* (1969); *Transitions to the Beast* (1970); *Carnival: The First Panel: 1967 – 1970* (1973); *Carnival: The Second Panel: 1970 – 1975* (1975); *Ow's Waif and Other Poems* (1975); *The Story So Far* (1976) [edited with bp Nichol]; *Legend* (1980) [with Bruce Andrews, Charles Bernstein, Ron Silliman, and Ray DiPalma]; *Panopticon* (1984); *North of Intention: Critical Writings 1973 – 1986* (1986); *Evoba* (1987); *The Black Debt* (1989); *Theory of Sediment* (1991); *Rational Geomancy* (1992) [Introduction and edited with bp Nichol]

Nathaniel Mackey [1947]

Four for Trane (1978); *Septet for the End of Time* (1983); *Eroding Witness* (1985); *Bedouin Hornbook* (1986) [fiction]; *Outlandish* (1992); *Djbot Baghostus's Run* (1993) [fiction]; *School of Udhra* (1993); *Discrepant Engagement: Dissonance, Cross-Culturality, and Experimental Writing* (1993) [criticism]; *Song of the Andoumboulou: 18 – 20* (1994)

Jackson Mac Low [1922]

The Pronouns: A Collection of 40 Dances—for the Dancers—6 February – 22 March 1964 (1976; reprinted 1970 in England; reprinted 1979 in USA); *Manifestos* (1966); *The Twin Plays: Pout-au-Price & Adams County Illinois* (1966); *August Light Poems* (1967); *22 Light Poems* (1968); *23rd Light Poem: For Larry Eigner* (1969); *Stanzas for Iris Lezak* (1971); *4 Trains* (1974); *36th Light Poem: In Memoriam Buston Keaton* (1975); *21 Matched Asymmetries* (1978); *phone* (1979); *Antic Quatrains* (1980); *Asymmetries 1 – 260* (1980); *"Is That Wool Hat My Hat?"* (1982); *From Pearl Harbor Day to FDR's Birthday* (1982); *The French Sonnets* (1984); *Bloomsday* (1984); *The Virginia Woolf Poems* (1985); *Representative Works: 1938 – 1985* (1986); *Words nd Ends from Ez* (1989); *Pieces o' Six* (1992)

Clarence Major [1936]

The Fires That Burn in Heaven (1954); *Love Poems of a Black Man* (1965); *Human Juices* (1966); *All Night Visitors* (1969) [fiction]; *The New Black Poetry* (1969) [edited]; *Swallow the Lake* (1970); *Dictionary of Afro-American Slang* (1970) [nonfiction]; *Symptoms & Madness* (1971); *Private Line* (1971); *The Cotton Club* (1972); *No* (1973) [fiction]; *The Syncopated Cakewalk* (1974); *The Dark and Feeling: Black American Writers and Their Work* (1974) [prose]; *Reflex and Bone Structure* (1975) [fiction]; *Emergency Exit* (1979) [fiction]; *Inside Diameter: The France Poems* (1985); *My Amputations* (1986) [fiction]; *Such Was the Season* (1987) [fiction]; *Painted Turtle: Woman with Guitar* (1988) [fiction]; *Surfaces and Masks* (1988); *Some Observations of a Stranger at Zuni in the Latter Part of the Century* (1989); *Fun & Games* (1990) [fiction]; *Parking Lots* (1992); *Calling the Wind: Twentieth Century African-American Short Stories* (1993) [edited]; *Juba to Jive: A Dictionary of African-American Slang* (1994) [edited]

Bernadette Mayer [1945]

Story (1968); *Moving* (1971); *Memory* (1975) [prose/poetry]; *Ceremony Latin* (1964); *Studying Hunger* (1976) [fiction/poetry]; *Poetry* (1976); *Eruditio ex Memoria* (1977) [autobiography/poetry]; *The Basketball Article* (1978) [prose] [with Anne Waldman]; *The Golden Book of Words* (1978); *Midwinter Day* (1982); *Utopia* (1983) [prose/poetry]; *Mutual Aid* (1985); *Sonnets* (1989); *The Formal Field of Kissing* (1990); *A Bernadette Mayer Reader* (1992); *The Desires of Mothers To Please Others in Letters* (1994)

Douglas Messerli [1947]

Dinner on the Lawn (1979; revised ed. 1982); *Some Distance* (1982); *Contemporary American Fiction* (1983) [editor]; *River to Rivet: A Manifesto* (1984); *"Language" Poetries* (1987) [editor]; *Maxims from My Mother's Milk/Hymns to Him: A Dialogue* (1988); *Silence All Round Marked: An Historical Play in Hysteria Writ* (1991) [drama]; *Along Without: A Fiction in Film for Poetry/The Structure of Destruction, Part I* (1993) [poetry/fiction/film]; *An Apple, A Day* (1993); *The Confirmation* (1993) [drama] [published under the name Kier Peters]; *The Walls Come True: An Opera for Spoken Voices/The Structure of Destruction, Part II* (1994)

bpNichol [1944–1988]

Journeying and the Returns (1967); *Two Novels* (1969); *The Cosmic Chef: An Evening of Concrete* (1970) [editor]; *Still Water* (1970); *Love: A book of remembrances* (1972); *The Martyrology: Books 1 & 2* (1972); *The Martyrology: Books 3 & 4* (1976); *As Elected: Selected Writings 1962–1979* (1980) [prose]; *The Martyrology: Book 5* (1982); *Zygal: a book of mysteries & translations* (1985); *The Martyrology: Book 6* (1987); *gIFTS: The Martyrology Book(s) 7 &* (1990); *art facts: a book of contexts* (1990); *Ad*

Sanctos: The Martyrology: Book 9 (1992); *Rational Geomancy: The Kids of the Book-Machine / The Collected Research Reports of the Toronto Research Group 1973 – 1982* (1992) [with Steve McCaffery] [prose]

Lorine Niedecker [1903 – 1970]

New Goose (1946); *My Friend Tree* (1961); *North Central* (1968); *T & G* (1969); *My Life by Water: Collected Poems 1936 – 1968* (1970); *Blue Chicory* (1976); *From This Condensery: The Complete Writing of Lorine Niedecker* (1985) [edited by Robert J. Bertholf]; *The Granite Pail: The Selected Poems of Lorine Niedecker* (1985)

Charles North [1941]

Lineups (1972); *Elizabethan & Nova Scotian Music* (1974); *Six Buildings* (1977); *Leap Year: Poems 1968 – 1978* (1978); *Broadway, A Poets and Painters Anthology* (1979) [edited with James Schuyler]; *Gemini* (1981) [with Tony Towle]; *The Year of the Olive Oil* (1989); *Broadway 2* (1989) [edited with James Schuyler]

Alice Notley [1945]

165 Meeting House Lane (1971); *Phoebe Light* (1973); *Incidentals in the Day World* (1973); *For Frank O'Hara's Birthday* (1976); *Alice Ordered Me To Be Made* (1976); *A Diamond Necklace* (1977); *Songs for the Unborn Second Baby* (1979); *Dr. Williams' Heiresses* (1980) [prose]; *When I Was Alive* (1980); *How Spring Comes* (1981); *Waltzing Matilda* (1981); *Tell Me Again* (1982); *Sorrento* (1984); *Margaret & Dusty* (1985); *Parts of a Wedding* (1986); *At Night the States* (1988); *From a Work in Progress* (1988); *Homer's _Art_* (1990); *To Say You* (1993); *The Scarlet Cabinet* (1992) [with Douglas Oliver]; *Selected Poems of Alice Notley* (1993)

Frank O'Hara [1926 – 1966]

A City Winter, and Other Poems (1952); *Oranges* (1969); *Meditations in an Emergency* (1957; new edition, 1967); *Jackson Pollock* (1959) [prose]; *New Spanish Painting and Sculpture* (1960) [prose]; *Second Avenue* (1960); *Odes* (1968); *Lunch Poems* (1965); *Love Poems (Tentative Title)* (1965); *Robert Motherwell* (1965) [prose]; *Nakian* (1966) [prose]; *In Memory of My Feelings: A Selection of Poems* (1967) [edited by Bill Berkson]; *Two Pieces* (1969); *The Collected Poems of Frank O'Hara* (1971) [edited by Donald Allen]; *Belgrade, November 19, 1963* (1973) [letter]; *The Selected Poems of Frank O'Hara* (1974) [edited by Donald Allen]; *Hymns to St. Bridget* (1974) [with Bill Berkson]; *Art Chronicles 1954 – 1966* (1975) [prose]; *Standing Still and Walking in New York* (1975) [prose]; *Early Writing* (1977) [edited by Donald Allen] [poetry and prose]; *Poems Retrieved* (1977) [edited by Donald Allen]; *Selected Plays* (1978) [drama]

Charles Olson [1910 – 1970]

Call Me Ishmael (1947); *Upon a Moebus Strip* (1947); *Portfolio V* (1947); *y & x* (1948); *The Sutter-Marshall Lease with the Yalesumney Indians for Monopoly of the Gold-Bearing Lands* [Introductory Notes] (1948); *Letter for Melville* (1951); *Apollonius of Tyana* (1952); *This* (1952); *In Cold Hell, In Thicket* (1953); *Mayan Letters* (1953); *Maximus Poems / 1 – 10* (1953); *Anecdotes of the Late War* (1956); *Maximus Poems / 11 – 22* (1956); *O'Ryan 2, 4, 6, 8, 10* (1958); *Projective Verse Vs. the Non-Projective* (1969); *The Maximus Poems* (1960); *The Distances* (1960); *Maximus from Dogtown I* (1961); *A Bibliography on America for Ed Dorn* (1964); *Signature to Petition* (1964); *Human Universe and Other Essays* (1965); *O'Ryan 1 – 10* (1965); *Proprioception* (1965); *Selected Writings* (1966); *Maximus Poems IV, V, VI* (1968); *The Maximus Poems: Volume Three* (1975); *The Maximus Poems* (1983) [edited by George F. Butterick]; *The Collected Poems of Charles Olson* (1987) [edited by George F. Butterick]; *Charles Olson and Robert Creeley: The Complete Correspondence* (1980 – 1989) [edited by George F. Butterick]

George Oppen [1908 – 1984]

Discrete Series (1934); *The Materials* (1962); *This Is Which* (1965); *Of Being Numerous* (1968); *Alpine: Poems* (1969); *Seascape: Needle's Eye* (1972); *The Collected Poems* (1973; London) *The Collected Poems of George Oppen* (1975); *Primitive* (1978); *The Selected Letters of George Oppen* (1990)

Ron Padgett [1942]

Bean Spasms (1967) [with Ted Berrigan]; *Great Balls of Fire* (1969; revised edition 1990); *The Adventures of Mr. and Mrs. Jim & Ron* (1970) [with Jim Dine]; *The Anthology of New York Poets* (1970) [edited with David Shapiro]; *Antlers in the Treetops* (1970) [with Tom Veitch] [fiction]; *Oo La La* (1973) [collaborative lithographs with Jim Dine); *Crazy Compositions* (1974); *Toujours l'amour* (1976); *The Whole Word Catalogue 2* (1976) [edited with Bill Zavatsky]; *Tulsa Kid* (1979); *Arrive by Pullman* (1979); *Triangles in the Afternoon* (1979); *How to Be a Woodpecker* (1983); *The Point* (1983) [edited with Nancy Shapiro]; *How to Be Modern Art* (1984) [prose]; *The Complete Poems of Edwin Denby* (1986) [edited]; *The Teachers & Writers Handbook of Poetic Forms* (1987) [edited]; *Light As Air* (1988) [prose poems with etchings by Alex Katz]; *Among the Blacks* (1988) [prose]; *The Big Something* (1990); *The Teachers & Writers Guide to Walt Whitman* (1991) [edited]; *Blood Work: Selected Prose* (1993) [prose]; *Ted: A Personal Memoir of Ted Berrigan* (1993) [prose]. Ron Padgett is also the translator of *The Poet Assassinated* by Guillaume Apollinaire (1968); *Dialogues with Marcel Duchamp* by Pierre Cabanne (1971); *Kodak* by Blaise Cendrars (1976); *The Poems of A. O. Barnabooth* by Valery Larbaud (1977); *The Poet Assassinated and Other Stories* by Guillaume Apollinaire (1984); *Complete Poems* by Blaise Cendrars (1992)

Michael Palmer [1943]

Plan for the City of O (1971); *Blake's Newton* (1972); *C's Songs* (1973); *Six Poems* (1973); *The Circular Gates* (1974); *Without Music* (1977); *Transparency of the Mirror* (1980); *Alogon* (1980); *Notes for Echo Lake* (1981); *Code of Signals: Recent Writings in Poetics* (1983) [editor]; *First Figure* (1984); *Sun* (1988). Michael Palmer has also translated *Jonah Who Will be 25 in the Year 2000* by Alain Tanner and John Berger and other works.

Bob Perelman [1947]

Braille (1975); *7 Works* (1979); *a.k.a.* (1979); *Hills Talks* (1980) [editor]; *Primer* (1981); *a.k.a.* (1984) [new edition]; *To the Reader* (1984); *Writing / Talks* (1985) [editor]; *The First World* (1987); *Face Value* (1988); *Captive Audience* (1988); *Virtual Reality* (1993); *The Trouble with Genius: Reading Pound, Joyce, Stein, and Zukofsky* (1994) [criticism]

Dennis Phillips [1951]

The Hero Is Nothing (1985); *A World* (1989); *Arena* (1991); *Means* (1991); *20 Questions* (1992)

Nick Piombino [1942]

Poems (1988); *The Boundary of Blur* (1993) [criticism]

Carl Rakosi [1903]

Selected Poems (1941); *Amulet* (1967); *Ere-Voice* (1968); *Ex Cranium Night* (1975); *My Experiences in Parnassus* (1977); *Droles de Journal* (1981); *The Collected Prose of Carl Rakosi* (1983); *The Collected Poems of Carl Rakosi* (1986)

Joan Retallack [1941]

Circumstantial Evidence (1985); *Errata 5uite* (1993); *Icarus Ffffalling* (1994)

Charles Reznikoff [1894 – 1976]

Rhythms (1918); *Rhythms II* (1919); *Poems* (1920); *Uriel Accosta: A Play & A Fourth Group of Verse* (1921); *Chatterton, the Black Death, and Meriwether Lewis* (1922) [plays]; *Coral and Captive Israel* (1923) [plays]; *Nine Plays* (1927); *Five Groups of Verse* (1927); *By the Waters of Manhattan: An Annual* (1929) [anthology]; *By the Waters of Manhattan* (1930) [fiction]; *Testimony* (1934) [prose]; *Jerusalem the Golden* (1934); *In Memoriam: 1933* (1934); *Separate Ways* (1936); *Early History of a Sewing Machine Operator* [with Nathan Reznikoff] (1936) [prose]; *Going To and From and Walk ing Up and Down* (1941); *The Lionhearted* (1944) [fiction]; (editor) *Louis Marshall: Champion of Liberty; Selected Papers and Addresses* (1957) (prose); *Inscriptions: 1944 – 1956* (1959); *By the Waters of Manhattan: Selected Verse* (1962); *Family Chronicle* [with Nathan and Sarah Reznikoff] (1963) [prose]; *Testimony: The United States 1885 – 1890: Recitative* (1965); *Testimony: The United States (1891 – 1900): Recitative* (1968); *By the Well of Living and Seeing and The Fifth Book of the Maccabees* (1969); *By the Well of Living & Seeing: New & Selected Poems 1918 – 1973* (1974); *Holocaust* (1975); *Poems 1918 – 1936: Volume 1 of the Complete Poems of Charles Reznikoff* (1976); *Poems 1937 – 1975: Volume 2 of the Complete Poems of Charles Reznikoff* (1977); *The Manner "Music"* (1977) [fiction]

Kit Robinson [1949]

Chinatown of Cheyenne (1974); *The Dolch Stanzas* (1976); *Down and Back* (1978); *Tribute to Nervous* (1980); *Riddle Road* (1982); *Windows* (1985); *A Day Off* (1985); *Ice Cubes* (1987); *Individuals* (1988) [with Lyn Hejinian]; *Covers* (1988); *The Champagne of Concrete* (1991); *Counter Meditation* (1991); *Balance Sheet* (1993)

Jerome Rothenberg [1931]

White Sun Black Sun (1960); *The Seven Hells of the Jigoku Zoshi* (1962); *Sightings I – IX* (1964); *The Gorky Poems* (1966); *Ritual* (1966) [edited]; *Technicians of the Sacred: A Range of Poetries from Africa, America, Asia, [Europe], & Oceania* (1967; revised 1985) [edited]; *Between: Poems 1960 – 1963* (1967); *Conversations* (1968) [prose]; *Sightings & Red Easy a Color* (1968) [with prints by Ian Tyson]; *Poems 1964 – 1967* (1968); *Poland/1931* (1968/first section); *A Book of Testimony* (1971); *Poems for the Game of Silence: 1960 – 1971* (1971; reprinted 1975); *Shaking the Pumpkin: Traditional Poetry of the Indian North Americas* (1972; revised 1986; reprinted 1991); *Poems for the Society of the Mystic Animals* (1972) [with Ian Tyson and Richard Johnny John]; *Esther K. Comes to America* (1973) [with photographs by Laurence Fink]; *America a Phrophecy: A New Reading of American Poetry from Pre-Columbian Times to the Present* (1973) [edited, with George Quasha]; *Seneca Journal 1: A Poem of Beavers* (1973); *Revolution of the Word: A New Gathering of American Avant-Garde Poetry 1914 – 1945* (1974; reprinted 1994) [edited]; *Poland/1931* (1974, complete); *The Cards* (1974); *The Pirke & The Pearl* (1975); *Seneca Journal: Midwinter* (1975); *A Poem to Celebrate the Spring & Diane Rothenberg's Birthday* (1975); *The Notebooks* (1976); *Ethnopoetics: A New International Symposium* (1976) [edited, with Michel Benamou]; *Seneca Journal: The Serpent* (1978); *A Seneca Journal* (1978, complete); *Narratives and Realtheater Pieces* (1978) [with woodcuts by Ian Tyson]; *The Big Jewish Book: Poems & Other Visions of the Jews from Tribal Times to the Present* (1978; abridged and reprinted as *Exiled in the Word*, 1978) [edited, with Harris Lenowitz]; *Abulafia's Circles* (1979); *B*R*M*Tz*V*H* (1979); *Numbers & Letters* (1980); *Vienna Blood & Other Poems* (1980); *Pre-Faces & Other Writings* (1981) [essays]; *That Dada Strain* (1983); *15 Flower World Variations* (1984) [with drawings by Harold Cohen]; *Symposium of the Whole: A Range of Discourse Toward an Ethnopoetics* (1984) [edited, with Diane Rothenberg]; *The Riverside Interviews 4: Jerome Rothenberg* (1984) [interviews] [edited by Gavin Selerie]; *A Merz Sonata* (1985) [with Debra Weier]; *New Selected Poems 1970 – 1985* (1989); *Further Sightings & Conversations* (1989); *The Lorca Variations (1 – 8)* (1990); *Improvisations* (1992) [with etchings by Warrington Colescott]; *Six Gematria* (1992) [with prints by Ian Tyson]; *The Lorca Variations* (1993, complete); *Gematria* (1994). Jerome Rothenberg has also translated the following books: *New Young German Poets* (1959); *The Deputy* by Rolf Hochhuth (1965); *The Flight of Quetzalcoatl* (Aztec) (1967); *Poems for People Who Don't Read Poems* by Hans Magnus Enzensberger [co-translated with Enzensberger and Michael Hamburger]; *The Book of Hours & Constellations* by Eugen Gomringer; *The 17 Horse Songs of Frank Mitchell* (Navajo) (1970); *Gematria 27* (Hebrew) (1977) [with Harris Lenowitz]; *Songs for the Society of the Mystic Animals* (Seneca Indian) (1980); *Four Suites* by Federico García Lorca (1989); *The Suites* (complete) by Federico García Lorca (1991) [as part of *Collected Poems: A Bilingual Edition*]; *PPPPPP: Poems Performance Pieces Proses Plays Poetics of Kurt Schwitters* (1993) [with Pierre Joris]

Leslie Scalapino [1947]

O and Other Poems (1976); *The Woman Who Could Read the Minds of Dogs* (1976); *Instead of an Animal* (1978); *This eating and walking is associated all right* (1979); *Considering how exaggerated music is* (1982); *that they were at the beach - aeolotropic series* (1985); *way* (1988); *The Return of Painting* (1990) [prose]; *The Return of Painting, The Pearl, and Orion / A Trilogy* (1991) [prose]; *How Phenomena Appear to Unfold* (1991) [essays]; *Crowd and not evening or light* (1992); *Objects in the Terrifying Tense / Longing from Taking Place* (1994) [essays]; *Defoe* (1994) [prose]; *Goya's L.A.* (1994) [drama]

James Schuyler [1923 – 1991]

Shopping and Waiting (1953) [drama]; *A Picnic Cantata* (1955) [music by Paul Bowles]; *Alfred & Guinevere* (1958) [fiction]; *Salute* (1960); *May 24th or So* (1966); *Freely Espousing* (1969); *A Nest of Ninnies* (1969) [with John Ashbery] [fiction]; *The Crystal Lithium* (1972); *The Sun Cab* (1972); *Hymn to Life* (1974); *The Fireproof Floors of Witley Court* (1976); *Song* (1976); *The Home Book: Prose and Poems 1951 – 1970* (1977); *What's for Dinner?* (1978) [fiction]; *Broadway, A Poets and Painters Anthology* (1979) [edited with Charles North]; *The Morning of the Poem* (1980); *Early in '71* (1982); *A Few Days* (1985); *The Selected Poems* (1988); *Broadway 2* (1989) [edited with Charles North]

James Sherry [1946]

Part Songs (1978); *In Case* (1981); *Converses* (1982); *Popular Fiction* (1985); *The Word I Like White Paint Considered* (1986); *Our Nuclear Heritage* (1991)

Aaron Shurin [1947]

Woman on Fire (1975); *The Night Sun* (1976); *Toot Suite* (1978); *Giving Up the Ghost* (1980); *The Graces* (1983); *Elsewhere* (1988); *A's Dream* (1989); *Narrativity* (1990) [prose]; *Into Distances* (1993)

Ron Silliman [1946]

Crow (1971); *Mohawk* (1973); *Nox* (1974); *Ketjak* (1978); *Sitting Up, Standing, Taking Steps* (1978); *Legend* (1980) [with Bruce Andrews, Charles Bernstein, Ray DiPalma, and Steve McCaffery]; *Tjanting* (1981); *Bart* (1982); *The Age of Huts* (1986); *In the American Tree* (1986) [editor]; *The New Sentence* (1987) [poetics]; *Leningrad* (1991) [prose] [with Michael Davidson, Lyn Hejinian, and Barrett Watten]. Volumes containing portions of *The Alphabet* are *ABC* (1983); *Paradise* (1985); *Lit* (1987); *What* (1988); *Manifest* (1990); *Demo to Ink* (1992); *Toner* (1992)

Gilbert Sorrentino [1929]

The Darkness Surrounds Us (1960); *Black and White* (1964); *The Sky Changes* (1966) [fiction]; *The Perfect Fiction* (1968); *Steelwork* (1970) [fiction]; *Imaginative Qualities of Actual Things* (1971) [fiction]; *Corrosive Sublimate* (1971); *Splendide-Hotel* (1973) [fiction]; *Flawless Play Restored: The Masque of Fungo* (1974) [masque]; *A Dozen Oranges* (1976); *Sulpiciae Elegidia / Elegiacs of Sulpicia* (1977); *White Sail* (1977); *The Orangery* (1978); *Mulligan Stew* (1979) [fiction]; *Aberration of Starlight* (1980) [fiction]; *Selected Poems: 1958 – 1980* (1981); *Crystal Vision* (1981) [fiction]; *Blue Pastoral* (1983) [fiction]; *Something Said: Essays* (1984); *Odd Number* (1985) [fiction]; *A Beehive Arranged on Humane Principles* (1985) [fiction]; *Rose Theatre* (1987) [fiction]; *Misterioso* (1989) [fiction]; *Under the Shadow* (1991) [fiction]

Jack Spicer [1925 – 1965]

After Lorca (1957); *Homage to Creeley* (1959); *Billy the Kid* (1959); *The Heads of the Town up to the Aether* (1962); *Lament for the Makers* (1962); *The Holy Grail* (1964); *Language* (1965); *Book of Magazine Verse* (1966); *A Book of Music* (1969); *The Red Wheelbarrow* (1971); *The Ballad of the Dead Woodcutter* (1972); *Some Things from Jack* (1972); *15 False Propositions About God* (1974); *Admonitions* (1974); *An Ode and Arcadia* (1974) [with Robert Duncan]; *A Lost Poem* (1975); *The Collected Books of Jack Spicer* (1975) [edited by Robin Blaser]; *There Is an Inner Nervousness in Virgins* (1975); *Letters to Graham Mackintosh 1954* (1977) [letters]; *One Night Stand & Other Poems* (1980)

John Taggart [1942]

To Construct a Clock (1971); *The Pyramid Is a Pure Crystal* (1974); *Prism and the Pine Twig* (1977); *Dodeka* (1979); *Peace on Earth* (1981); *Dehiscence* (1983); *Le Poeme de la Chapelle Rothko* (1990; published in French); *Loop* (1991); *Prompted* (1991); *Aeschylus/Fragments* (1992); *Remaining in Light: Ant Meditations on a Painting by Edward Hopper* (1993) [prose]; *Tauler Sentences* (1993); *Standing Wave* (1993); *Songs of Degrees: Essays on Contemporary Poetry & Poetics* (1994) [essays]

Fiona Templeton [1951]

Elements of Performance (1976) [with Anthony Howell] [prose]; *London* (1984); *You: the City* (1990)

Lorenzo Thomas [1944]

Dracula (1973); *Chances Are Few* (1979); *The Bathers* (1981)

Rosmarie Waldrop [1935]

A Dark Octave (1967); *Change of Address* (1968) [with Keith Waldrop]; *Letters* (1970) [with Keith Waldrop]; *Camp Printing* (1970); *The Relaxed Abalone* (1970); *Spring Is a Season and Nothing Else* (1970); *Against Language* (1971) [criticism]; *Body Image* (1971); [with art by Nelson Howe]; *The Aggressive Ways of the Casual Stranger* (1972); *Until Volume One* (1973) [with Keith Waldrop]; *Words Worth Less* (1973) [with Keith Waldrop]; *Kind Regards* (1975); *Since Volume One* (1975) [with Keith Waldrop]; *Acquired Pores* (1976); *The Road Is Everywhere or Stop This Body* (1978); *The Ambition of Ghosts* (1979); *Psyche and Eros* (1980); *When They Have Senses* (1980); *Nothing Has Changed* (1981); *Differences for Four Hands* (1984); *Streets Enough to Welcome Snow* (1986); *Morning's Intelligence* (1986); *The Hanky of Pippin's Daughter* (1986) [fiction]; *The Reproduction of Profiles* (1987); *Shorter American Memory* (1988); *A Form / of Taking / It All* (1990) [fiction]; *Peculiar Motions* (1990) [with art by Jennifer Macdonald]; *Light Travels* (1992) [with Keith Waldrop]; *Lawn of Excluded Middle* (1993). Rosmarie Waldrop is also the translator of *Bodies and Shadows* by Peter Weiss (1969); *Elya* by Edmond Jabès (1973); *The Book of Questions* by Edmond Jabès (1976); *Three Poems* by Helmut Heissenbüttel (1977); *The Death of God* by Edmond Jabès (1979); *Yaël / Elya / Aely* by Edmond Jabès (1983); *El, or the Last Book* by Edmond Jabès (1984); *From a Reader's Notebook* by Alain Veinstein (1984); *The Vienna Group: Six Major Austrian Poets* (1985) [with Harriett Watts]; *Paul Celan, Collected Prose* (1986); *Archeology of the Mother* by Alain Veinstein (1986) [with Tod Kabza]; *The Book of Dialogue* by Edmond Jabès (1987); *Late Additions* by Emmanuel Hocquard (1988) [with Connell McGrath]; *The Book of Shares* by Edmond Jabès (1989); *The Book of Resemblances* by Edmond Jabès (1990); *Dawn* by Joseph Guglielmi (1991)

Barrett Watten [1948]

Opera—Works (1975) [poetry and prose]; *Decay* (1977); *Plasma/Parallels/"X"* (1979); *1 – 10* (1980); *Complete Thought* (1982); *Total Syntax* (1984) [essays]; *Progress* (1985); *Leningrad: American Writers in the Soviet Union* (1991) [prose] [with Michael Davidson, Lyn Hejinian, and Ron Silliman]; *Under Erasure* (1991); *Frame: 1970 – 1990* (1994)

Hannah Weiner [1928]

Magritte Poems (1970); *Sun June 9* (1975); *Clairvoyant Journal* (1978); *Little Books/ Indians* (1980); *Nijole's House* (1981); *Code Poems* (1982); *Sixteen* (1983); *Spoke* (1984); *Written In/The Zero One* (1985); *Weeks* (1990); *The Fast* (1992); *Silent Teachers / Remembered Sequel* (1993)

Marjorie Welish [1944]

Handwritten (1979); *Two Poems* (1981); *The Windows Flew Open* (1991); *Casting Sequences* (1993)

Mac Wellman [1945]

In Praise of Secrecy (1977); *Opera Brevis* (1977) [drama]; "Starluster" in *Wordplays 1* (1980) [drama]; *Harm's Way* (1984) [drama]; "The Professional Frenchman" in *Theatre of Wonders* (1985) [drama] [also edited]; *Satires* (1985); "Energumen" in *Women with Guns* (1986) [drama]; *Bodacious Flapdoodle* (1987) [drama]; "The Bad Infinity" in *7 Different Plays* (1988) [drama] [also edited]; *Cellophane* (1988); *Whirligig* (1989) [drama]; "Harm's Way" in *Anti-Naturalism* (1990) [drama]; *Slant Six* (1990) [drama, editor]; *Bad Penny* (1990) [drama]; *The Professional Frenchman* (1990) [drama]; *A Shelf in Woop's Clothing* (1990); *The Fortuneteller* (1991) [fiction]; *A Murder of Crows* (1992) [drama]; "Sincerity Forever" in *Grove New American Drama* (1993) [drama]; *The Bad Infinity: Eight Plays by Mac Wellman* (1994) [includes "Harm's Way," "The Self-begotten," "Whirligig," "The Bad Infinity," "Dracula," "Crowbar," "7 Blowjobs," and "Terminal Hip"] [drama]; *Murder of Crows and The Hyacinth Macaw* (1994) [drama]

John Wieners [1934]

The Hotel Wentley Poems (1958); *Of Asphodel, In Hell's Despite* (1963); *Ace of Pentacles* (1964); *Chinoiserie* (1965); *Pressed Wafer* (1967); *A Letter to Charles Olson* (1968); *Asylum Poems* (1969); *Youth* (1970); *Nerves* (1970); *Selected Poems* (1972); *Playboy* (1972); *Woman* (1972) [prose]; *The Lanterns Along the Wall* (1972) [lecture]; *Hotels* (1974); *Behind the State Capitol* (1975); *Selected Poems: 1958 – 1984* (1986) [edited by Raymond Foye]; *Cultural Affairs in Boston: Poetry & Prose 1956 – 1985* (1988) [edited by Raymond Foye]

Louis Zukofsky [1904 – 1978]

An "Objectivists" Anthology (1932); *Le Style Apollinaire* (1934) [prose]; *First Half of "A" -9* (1940); *55 Poems* (1941); *Anew* (1946); *A Test of Poetry* (1948) [prose/ poetry]; *Some Time* (1956); *5 Statements for Poetry* (1958) [prose]; *Barely and widely* (1958); *"A" 1 – 12* (1959; reprinted 1966, 1967); *It was* (1961) [fiction]; *"A"-24* (1962); *Arise, Arise* (1962) [drama]; *16 once published* (1962); *I's (pronounced eyes)* (1963); *Bottom: On Shakespeare* (1963) (two volumes; second volume by Celia Zukofsky) (prose); *Found Objects; All: the collected shorter poems 1923 – 1958* (1965); *Prepositions* (1968, 1981) [criticism]; *Ferdinand* (1968/1969) [fiction]; *"A" 13 – 21* (1969); *Catullus (Gai Valeri Catulli Veronensis Liber)* ["translated" by Celia and Louis Zukofsky] (1969); *Little for careenagers* (1970) [fiction]; *All: the collected shorter poems 1923 – 1964* (1971); *"A" 22 & 23* (1975); *"A"* (1978); *80 Flowers* (1978); *Collected Fiction* (1990)

Selected Publishers of American innovative poetry
from 1960 – 1990

Avenue B
  (PO Box 542, Bolinas, CA 94924)
Awede Books
  (Box 376, Windsor, VT 05089)
Bamberger Books
  (PO Box 1126, Flint, MI 48501)
Black Sparrow Press
  (24 Tenth Street, Santa Rosa, CA 95401)
Burning Deck Books
  (71 Elmgrove Avenue, Providence, RI 02906)
Chax Press
  (101 W. 6th Street #4, Tucson, AZ 85701)
City Lights Books
  (261 Columbus Avenue, San Francisco, CA 94133)
Coach House Press
  (50 Prince Arthur Avenue, Toronto, ON M5R 1B5 CANADA)
Coffee House Press
  (27 N. Fourth St, Suite 400, Minneapolis, MN 55401)
Corinth Books
  [ceased publication]
Edge Books
  (PO Box 25642, Washington, DC 20007)
The Figures
  (5 Castle Hill, Great Barrington, MA 01230)
Gaz
  (277 23rd Avenue, San Francisco, CA 94121)
Grossman/Goliard
  [ceased publication]
Guernica Editions
  (PO Box 633, Station N.D.G, Montéal, QU, H4A 3R1 CANADA)
Jahbone Books
  (3787 Maplewood, Los Angeles, CA 90066)
The Jargon Society
  (Po Box 10, Highlands, NC 28741)
Kelsey Street Press
  (2718 Ninth Street, Berkeley, CA 94709)
The Kulchur Foundation
  [ceased publication]
Leave Books
  (57 Livingston, Buffalo, NY 14213)
Littoral Books

(c/o Sun & Moon Press, 6026 Wilshire Blvd., Los Angeles, CA 90036)
The National Poetry Foundation
  (University of Maine, Orono, ME 04469)
New Directions
  (80 Eight Avenue, New York, NY 10011)
North Point Press
  [ceased publication]
O Books
  (5729 Clover Drive, Oakland, CA 94618)
Potes & Poets
  (181 Edgemont Avenue, Elmwood, CT 06110)
Roof Books/The Segue Foundation
  (303 E. 8th Street, New York, NY 10009)
Station Hill Press
  (Barrytown, NY 12507)
SUN
  [ceased publication]
Sun & Moon Press
  (6026 Wilshire Boulevard, Los Angeles, CA 90036)
Talonbooks
  (1019 East Cordova #201, Vancouver, BC, V6A 1M8 CANADA)
Tender Buttons
  (54 Manning Street #3, Providence, RI 02906)
This
  (1731 Stuart Street, Berkeley, CA 94703)
Tuumba Books
  [ceased publication]
United Artists
  (701 President Street #1, Brooklyn, NY 11215)
University of California Press
  (2120 Berkeley Way, Berkeley, CA 94720)
Wesleyan University Press
  (110 Mount Vernon St., Middletown, CT 06459-0433)
Z Press
  (Calais, Vermont 05648)